MW01054207

רבנו בחיי/כד הקמח

Encyclopedia of Torah Thoughts

רבנו בחיי/כד הקמח

Encyclopedia of Torah Thoughts

Translated and Annotated by

Rabbi Dr. Charles B. Chavel

Ph.B., M.A., LL.B., D.H.L., D.D.

Shilo Publishing House, Inc.
New York, N.Y. 10002

© Copyright 1980

by Shilo Publishing House, Inc.

Library of Congress Catalog Card No. 80-65234

ISBN
0-88328-016-7 (cloth binding)
0-88328-017-5 (paperback)

1990 Printing

Contents

Note that Rabbeinu Bachya did not arrange his themes in strictly alphabetical order. See Preface, Note 14, for further explanation. The English translation appears in the same order as the original Hebrew text. — A comprehensive Table of Contents, arranged alphabetically according to the English titles, will be found on page 715.

Translator's Preface

Rabbeinu Bachya ben Asher, the author of Kad Hakemach[1] lived in the second half of the thirteenth century. He attested to this fact himself in his Commentary on the Torah, where he wrote, "The sixth day of Creation alludes to the sixth millennium, of which we are now in the fifty-first year."[2] Since the sixth millennium of the Hebrew calendar began in the year 1240 Common Era, "the fifty-first year" was 1291, the year in which Rabbeinu Bachya was engaged in writing his first major work.

---

(1) Literally, Kad Hakemach means "The Jar of Meal." The origin of this title goes back to an event in the life of Elijah the prophet. Opposing King Ahab's and Queen Jezebel's introduction of the worship of Baal into the Kingdom of Israel, Elijah vowed that *there would be neither rain, nor dew in these years.* Fleeing the wrath of the king and the queen, he was directed by G-d to go to Zarephath, where a widow would support him. Upon his arrival in Zarephath, Elijah found the widow gathering sticks in a field. *Fetch me a morsel of bread,* he directed. The widow replied that she had nothing in her house besides *a handful of meal in the jar, and a little oil in the cruse* . . . (I Kings 17:12). The prophet then said to her, *Fear not, go and do as thou hast said, but make me thereof a little cake first, and bring it forth unto me, and afterwards make for thee and for thy son. For thus saith the Eternal, the G-d of Israel: The jar of meal shall not be spent* . . . *And she went and did according to the saying of Elijah; and she and he and her house did eat many days. The jar of meal was not spent* (ibid., Verses 13-16). Clearly, Rabbeinu Bachya used this episode in a double sense. It alludes to the spiritual famine which prevailed in his generation as a result of the oppressive conditions in the exile (see Introductory Verses). Moreover, Rabbeinu Bachya's "Jar of Meal" contains the thoughts and teachings of the Sages which sustain the people of Israel in their hour of need. (2) Commentary on Genesis 2:3. In my Hebrew edition, p. 55, Note 86. See also my introduction there, p. 8.

We know that Rashba (Rabbeinu Shlomo ben Adereth),[3] Rabbeinu Bachya's mentor and the foremost personality of his generation, passed away about the year 1310.[4] Thus, from Rabbeinu Bachya's statement above, we may conclude that he was already active at the height of Rashba's activity.

The era in which Rabbeinu Bachya flourished was a stormy one, for the Jewish community was beset by problems from within and without. The Church was utilizing every means possible — from ordinary missionary work to elaborate public disputations[5] — in order to achieve the apostasy of the Jews or failing that, to make their lives miserable. Within the Jewish community itself, there was a struggle raging between the pro-Maimonists and the anti-Maimonists.[6] This controversy later culminated in 1305 in Rashba's proclamation of a ban against the study of philosophy by anyone under twenty-five years of age. Moreover, the Spanish government fell more and more under the influence of the Church, which gradually began to turn the Golden Era of Spanish Jewry into a remembrance of the past. In this period of storm and stress, Rabbeinu Bachya first made his voice heard as a

(3) The name of Rashba does not appear in Kad Hakemach, but is mentioned several times in Rabbeinu Bachya's Commentary on the Torah, e.g., "I so heard from the mouth of my master Harav Rabbi Shlomo, may his life continue" (Vol. III, p. 382). Such references are also found in his Commentary on Aboth, pp. 558-9 (see Note 11 below). See also Index to Kithvei Rabbeinu Bachya, p. 674, "The great Rabbi, my master Rabbi Shlomo." Rashba, who was born in 1235 C.E., was the best known disciple of Ramban. He is especially famous for the thousands of responsa covering every aspect of Jewish law, which he sent to inquiring communities throughout the world.   (4) The year of Rashba's death is not mentioned in early sources. However, we know that in 1305, he signed the ban against the study of philosophy by persons younger than twenty-five years of age, and that shortly afterwards he welcomed Rabbeinu Asher (known as Rosh) and his sons who had come from Germany seeking refuge in Spain. It is reasonable to assume that Rashba lived a few more years after these events. Thus, we have given 1310 as the approximate year of his demise.   (5) The most famous example is the Barcelona Disputation, participation of which was forced upon Ramban. See the latter's Writings and Discourses, Vol. II, pp. 653-696.   (6) On the broader aspects and significance of this struggle, see *op. cit.*, Vol. II, pp. 357-417.

preacher in the synagogues of Saragossa[7] and perhaps those of Barcelona, in the Kingdom of Aragonia, as well.

That he was a preacher can be unmistakenly inferred from many bits of information. For example, at the beginning of his Introductory Verses, he stated, "My lips' offering will I bring to G-d the Creator." Again in the ten themes on *Reshuth* (Deference to the Congregation), Rabbeinu Bachya elaborated on the required reverence a speaker must have of the audience he is about to address. The remarks in those discourses reflect undoubtedly the author's own feeling upon ascending the pulpit. How touching are his words:

". . . to speak before a large assembly. The latter constitutes
G-d's camp, which is equal in importance and significance to
the ministering angels themselves! However, we shall rely upon
the protection of the merits of the assembly when I speak a few
words of Torah. Although the speaker is most insignificant ..."[8]

Preaching was not the only activity of Rabbeinu Bachya, for in addition to Kad Hakemach, he wrote three other major works which live on through the generations: the great Commentary on the Torah,[9]

---

(7) Saragossa was a bastion of support for the pro-Maimonists, but Rabbeinu Bachya remained neutral in the controversy. Throughout his writings, he freely utilized philosophic ideas although he did express his opposition to the study of philosophy *per se,* unless it was within the framework of Torah. See his theme on Passover, Part I, p. 499. (8) *Reshuth* (Deference to the Congregation),   pp. 581-2. The particular introduction of which I have quoted a small segment here seems to have been used by Rabbeinu Bachya on the Day of Atonement. This is evident from the text of Leviticus 16:3, which he used for his central theme.   (9) His Commentary on the Torah has been printed in many editions. See Introduction to my edition (Mosad Harav Kook), Vol. I, p. 7. — The great popularity of Rabbeinu Bachya's Commentary on the Torah may be gathered from the fact that Yaakov ben Yitzchak Ashkenazi drew largely from this commentary for his own Tz'enah U'renah, originally a German — Yiddish text on the Pentateuch for the use of women. Consequently, Rabbeinu Bachya's name, ideas and thoughts became known to countless audiences throughout the generations.

Shulchan shel Arba (The Table of Four),[10] and his Commentary on
Tractate Aboth.[11] It is most enlightening to observe that in all four of
his major works, Rabbeinu Bachya tended to stress the ethical and
philosophic aspects of his themes,[12] again revealing his understanding
of the audience.

Kad Hakemach, written after the completion of his Commentary on
the Torah,[13] contains sixty discourses on various topics arranged
according to the Hebrew alphabet.[14] Each discourse begins with a verse
which forms the theme of the subject and is followed by a pertinent
discussion based upon various Midrashim, and teachings of the
Talmud. The opening verse thus assumes a richer meaning and brings
a clear and vital message to the audience. It should be noted that never
is the sight of the central theme of any of the subjects lost.[15]

(10) A discussion from four perspectives of every phase of man's sustenance and the
laws pertaining thereto. It is found in my edition of Kithvei Rabbeinu Bachya, pp.
455-514. (11) In my edition, *ibid,* pp. 517-642. (12) Rabbeinu Bachya's proficien-
cy in the legal aspects of the Torah can be seen most noticeably in the Shulchan Shel
Arba, where he delves profoundly into the many laws affecting the washing of hands,
the blessings over food and the saying of Grace after meals. He is also quoted by Rabbi
Yoseif Karo as the final authority in legal matters. See my edition of Kithvei Rabbeinu
Bachya, p. 456, Note 5. (13) This is obvious from certain references in Kad
Hakemach, e.g., "I have already explained this in the section of the
Torah." (14) The subjects were arranged alphabetically only insofar as the first
initial of the Hebrew title is concerned. With each letter group, however, alphabetical
order was not observed. Thus, at the very outset of the work, Rabbeinu Bachya commenced with *Emunah* (Faith), although *Eivel* (Mourning) should have been first.
Eivel, in fact, was placed last among the subjects in this letter group. Undoubtedly,
this was because the subject of Faith is more fundamental than the other topics in its
group. Similarly, under the letter *samach,* the opening theme is *Simchah* (Joy), which
is not spelled with a *samach* but with a *sin,* having the same sound. Yet even granting
the interchangeability of *samach* and *sin,* if the alphabetical sequence were being
strictly observed according to the second letters of each title, *Succah* should have been
first. Instead, *Succah* is the second theme in this letter group. It is obvious that the
author gave precedence to the title of *Simchah* (Joy) because he felt it to be a more appropriate opening theme. (15) The translation of this work is based upon my
Hebrew edition (Mosad Harav Kook, Jerusalem, 5730), with notes and commentary.
Consideration of the smooth flow of the central thought in each theme necessitated
certain omissions of the Hebrew text.

These discourses were written in pure classical Hebrew. Seldom did the author venture into philosophic terminology, as he often did in his Commentary on the Torah, nor for that matter did he use any Cabalistic concepts.[16] The speaker's awareness of the level of the audience he was addressing was undoubtedly responsible for this characteristic feature of Kad Hakemach,

Throughout the Kad Hakemach, Rabbeinu Bachya utilized some ideas and material of the works of:

Ramban's[17] Commentary on the Torah, Commentary on the Book of Job, The Gate of Reward; also Emunah U'bitachon, and Commentary on the Book of Song of Songs,[18] which are attributed to Ramban.

Rabbeinu Yonah's[19] Commentary on the Book of Proverbs, and Gate of Repentance.

Rabbi David Kimchi's (R'dak) commentaries.[20]

Abraham ben Chiya's Higayon Hanefesh.[21]

Rabbeinu Bachya ibn Pekuda's Chovoth Halevavoth.[22]

---

(16) As expressed in his theme on The Sabbath (p.615): "From here we have clear proof that one should not reveal and 'expound mystical matters in public." (17) Rabbeinu Bachya's high esteem of Ramban may be gathered from the following words in his introduction to his Commentary on the Torah: "The man Moshe, the wonder of the generation, whose sweet words emanate from the sweetness of the manna. This is the great Ramban, who has taught us the way to ascend on high, who has guided us in the path of truth . . . . " (18) The influence of this work is felt very strongly in the enumeration of the positive and negative commandments in the theme on Shavuoth. (19) Our author was greatly influenced by Rabbeinu Yonah's works. In the introduction to his Commentary on the Torah, he calls Rabbeinu Yonah "the man of G-d, a pillar of strength and foundation of the Torah." (20) In many places our author cites R'dak's interpretations, without quoting the source. (21) In Kippurim (Atonement), Part I, our author cites the Commentary on the Book of Jonah, taken from Higayon Hanefesh. See my commentary in the Hebrew edition of Kad Hakemach, p. 213. (22) Quoted in *Yichud Hasheim* (Unity of G-d) and in *Parnassah* (Sustenance).

Kad Hakemach occupies a unique place in Hebrew sacred literature, for not only was it the first of its kind, but to this day, nothing like it has been written. Israel al-Nakawa's[23] *Menorath Hama'or* (Lamp of Illumination), an anthology of all dicta of the Sages of the Talmud and Midrashim on individual topics, approaches Kad Hakemach, but it does not contain the urgency of the personal message delivered by Rabbeinu Bachya.

Among the sixty themes in Kad Hakemach the discerning eye will find a golden thesaurus of Jewish thought and ethics. It contains not only discussions for all seasons of the year, but also topics of paramount importance in the life of the individual and of society as a whole. In short, this encyclopedic work is a notable contribution to our understanding of those basic Torah concepts which form the eternal message for the Jew in all walks of life and in all times. Delivered in a Spanish synagogue almost seven centuries ago, these discourses still carry the message of Torah to our homes today.

In closing it is my pleasure to express my thanks and appreciation to Mr. Alan Augenbraun for his invaluable suggestions on reading the manuscript. To Mr. Henry Petzenbaum and Mr. Joseph Salomon of Shilo Publishing House, Inc., I gratefully acknowledge my indebtedness for their vision and determination of bringing the Jewish spiritual glories of former generations into our times. May they be counted among the *matzdikei harabim* (they that turn many to righteousness).

10 Sivan 5739   C.B. Chavel
June 5, 1979
Edgemere, N.Y.

---

(23) Rabbi Israel al-Nakawa lived in Spain in the second half of the fourteenth century. Along with other martyrs, he was killed during the massacres of 1391.

KAD HAKEMACH

BY

RABBEINU

BACHYA BEN ASHER

שיר פתיחה
Introductory Verses

Introductory Verses

I will begin writing *Kad Hakemach*[1]
with the help of G-d
who brings forth his servant *Tzemach.*[2]

I shall call upon every thirsty man
to drink of the waters of the well [of the Torah].
He shall neither hunger nor thirst,
and the shoot [of righteousness][3] shall sprout.

My lips' offering[4] will I bring
to G-d the Creator.
Living waters[5] are its libations,
and there is also *the jar of meal.*[6]

This is the book of *the generations of those
who seek for Him,*[7] the weary ones [of the exile].

---

(1) See Preface, Note 1. (2) See Zechariah 3:8. Literally, *tzemach* means "a shoot," a reference to the Messiah. — The message of the coming redemption, which is one of the main features of this work, is thus introduced by the author in his opening remark. (3) Jeremiah 33:15. This phrase "shoot of righteousness," too, is a reference to Messiah. (4) This alludes to the fact that these compositions are the product of his oral presentations to the public. (5) The Torah is considered a fountainhead of living water. (6) A sacrificial offering required a meal-offering and a libation of wine (see Numbers 15:1-16). Since the author speaks of his work as "an offering" to G-d, he states that he will bring as its libation the living waters of the Torah, and *the jar of meal,* which is, of course, the *Kad Hakemach* as its meal-offering. (7) Psalms 24:6.

3

The generation of those
who are tired of the exile and grief
will find repose in it.

Hearts are closed up,
and discerning ones are decreasing.[8]

Because of their hardships,
[their] thoughts are confused,
their yoke weighs down upon them.

When they stand in the straits,
their heart is distressed
and their mind too impatient
for gradual discernment.

Their foot is trapped in snares,[9]
their defense [of the truth] removed,
and their intellect limited from finding
the ladder upon which to ascend
the mountains of the Talmud,
which is *more to be desired than gold,*
yea, more than much fine gold.[10]

In the explanation of the commandments,
permissible action, and [various] laws,
and in the land of brooks of sermons and homilies,
they will find a stream of thoughts
and *quiet resting places.*[11]

---

(8) Because of the constant persecutions that the Jew had to endure, the learning of Torah decreased, hearts were closed, etc. Hence people's minds about the tenets of faith were confused, and their minds were too impatient for profound study which would lead them to the discernment of truth.   (9) These snares are the secular forces which drive one away from the pursuit of sacred studies, as the author continues.   (10) Psalms 19:11.   (11) Isaiah 32:18. In other words, in this book of *Kad Hakemach* people will find a source of learning and comfort.

How sweet will they find
the homiletical interpretations!
Although only a part of their roots appear,[12]
they will bring forth branches and bear fruit,
old and new [interpretations], for they are most holy.

Their [living] waters [of the Torah] are endless;
everyone's soul yearns for them.

Therefore, I wished to compose this work
to bring forth a sprouting with the rod of sermons.[13]

I devised *Kad Hakemach*[1]
as the name of this book,
since the foundations of the faith
are buttressed by it,
for when people are now asked
about the righteous ordinances,
they do not know enough to answer
"No" or "Yes" correctly.

Therefore, my heart resolved
to cause a sprouting of discourses
to be prepared for these people,
and I called this book *Kad Hakemach*.[1]

From it will be fed all who hunger
to hear the word of G-d.

They will ascend on it[14]
to approach the altar

(12) Although this work admittedly does not contain all the material of these homilies, yet whatever will be cited here will bring forth further branches and bear fruit of good deeds. (13) Reference is to the rod of Aaron which vindicated his priesthood by its budding and bringing forth fruit (see Numbers 17:23). Our author's words express the hope that his "rod of sermons" will also bring a sprouting of return to Torah. (14) By studying this work people will be induced to continue to delve deeper

and the Sanctuary which stands
in its innermost recesses.

There is food in it for all,
as listed in the ode of twenty-two strophes.[15]

Some of the Torah's commandments
are intertwined therein,
and it clutches the branches of ethics.

The rows are replete with precious stones,[16]
sought out by those who desire them.
Its themes are sixty in number.

There are sixty subjects in it
necessary for man's [proper] conduct,
subjects "which declare
the glory of G-d and His holiness."[17]

I will mention therein the law of man,
his worship [of G-d], and his other duties.

I will explain therein G-d's festivals
and some of His commandments.

Students and colleagues
who delight to draw near unto G-d,[18]
will understand and discern thereby
and will not stumble by running.[19]

---

into more advanced works of the Torah.   (15) This twenty-two stanza poem, composed by the author, is found at the end of this work.(16)The breastplate of the High
Priest contained four rows of precious stones (see Exodus 28:17-20). The author is thus
saying that the subjects contained in this work are similarly replete with all precious
things.   (17) The phrase is borrowed from the Morning Service benediction, "Creator
of the Luminaries."   (18) Isaiah 58:2.   (19) The serious student who finds delight in
learning will not run through this book in haste and stumble.

Therein they will see
the dwelling-place of the Eternal G-d,[20]
and they will couch in their paths.[21]

Therein they will see
*the way wherein they must walk
and the work they must do.*[22]

Because [this work] is arranged
along a well trodden path,[23]
the seeker will easily find his goal.

I have endeavored to compose this work of mine
according to the successive letters of the alphabet
so that each commandment and subject
will be found under its designated letter.

When a person will be stirred
and will lift his head, desiring to seek [some topic],
let him look at the strophes
at the end of this book.

They will lead him to the high path,
which is found by all who seek it
and sought by all who care for it.
This is the path ascending to the House of G-d.[24]

In the Rock Who took me out of the womb[25]
will I place my trust.

May He deliver us from errors
and show us the wonders of His Torah.

---

(20) Deuteronomy 33:27.   (21) They will repose in satisfaction of understanding some of the mysteries of the Torah.   (22) Exodus 18:20.   (23) That is, because this book is arranged according to distinct subjects, the seeker will easily find his quest.   (24) See Joshua 16:1.   (25) See Psalms 22:10.

May He grant that our lot
be with those who take delight
in His rivers of pleasure.[26]

May we live by these things[27] in eternal life
with all Israel united in friendship,
as it is written:

O Eternal, by these things men shall live,
and through all of them is the life of my spirit sustained;
therefore do Thou restore me, and make me live again.[28]

---

(26) See *ibid.*, 36:9. The expression is of mystic significance.   (27) "These things"
refer to the sixty subjects the author has endeavored to clarify in this
work.   (28) Isaiah 38:16. Hezekiah is saying: "I know that by G-d's decree, the resurrection will occur, but above all restore me now to my health, and bring me to life
again." (Metzudath David). Such was King Hezekiah's prayer in his sickness, and his
prayer was answered affirmatively when fifteen years were added to his life (Isaiah
38:5).

אמונה

Faith in G-d

Faith is the essence of Torah and the commandments / One must believe in the existence of the Creator, Who is One and Who, in his beneficent providence, watches over His creatures generally and specifically / Through belief in G-d's providential care, one proceeds to believe in prophecy and the Torah / By merit of such faith, we will be worthy of having His Divine Glory dwell among us and we will return to Jerusalem / Incorporated within this faith is the principle that one should love the truth and deal faithfully with his fellow man, since by doing so, one comes closer to his Creator, Whose seal is truth / All of the prophets have exhorted Israel concerning faith / Related to the concept of faith, is the duty of maintaining proper intent of heart when answering Amen / Israel was redeemed from Egypt by merit of faith; in like manner, the future Redemption will occur by virtue of faith.

Faith in G-d

OPEN YE THE GATES, THAT THE RIGHTEOUS NATION
MAY ENTER, THOSE WHO KEEP THE FAITH.[1]

Faith is the essence of the Torah and the commandments.[2] In fact, it would have been better for a person who has no faith not to have been born at all.[3] [The obligation to have faith] is a commandment, the fulfillment of which is dependent upon the heart [and not upon utterance of mere words. It entails] the belief that the universe has a Creator, Whose existence is absolute,[4] Who is One, and Whose providential care extends over this lower world, guarding the human species generally and specifically. Accordingly, [faith] helps to eliminate from the heart the false opinion of the disbelievers, transgressors and rebels against the Holy One, blessed be He, who maintain

---

(1) Isaiah 26:2. Our author opens his work with this verse which in a way expresses the theme of the entire work—an appeal to his audience *to keep the faith* amidst the many pressures of an antagonistic outside world. It is likewise an appeal to the Jew of all times: *Open ye the gates* of your heart and mind *to keep the faith* amidst a world of foreign ideas.   (2) "The Torah and the commandments" is an expression of Biblical origin. See II Chronicles 14:3. The meaning here—as well as throughout this work—is that both the narratives of the Torah and the sections which state the commandments are rooted in our faith in the existence of the One Creator.   (3) Since the purpose of creation is the acknowledgment of the Creator, that man should know of His existence and be thankful to G-d for having created him, whoever reneges on this duty fails to realize the essential purpose of his life. See further on this topic in Ramban's "Writings and Discourses," pp. 35-36.   (4) That is to say, existence has never been a new element or external occurrence in relation to Him. Consequently, His existence has always been absolute. See Guide of the Perplexed I, Chapter 57.

10

that Divine Providence does not extend to anything below the sphere of the moon.[5] This was the [erroneous] opinion of Job when suffering came upon him. [To refute this false doctrine], Eliphaz said to Job, *And thou sayest: What doth G-d know? Can He judge through the dark cloud? Thick clouds are a covering to Him, that He seeth not; and He walketh in the circuit of heaven. Wilt thou keep the old way which wicked men have trodden?*[6]

Thus, the prophets always mention the theme of providence and elaborate on it. Jeremiah, peace be upon him, explained it as follows: *Great in counsel and mighty in work, Whose eyes are open upon all the ways of the sons of men, to give every one according to his ways, and according to the fruit of his doings.*[7] From this verse, we derive the principle that His providential care extends over all mankind generally and specifically, and thus the opinion of the disbelievers is utterly discarded.

King David, peace be upon him, also referred to this principle when he said, *O Eternal, Thou hast searched me, and known me. Thou knowest my downsitting and mine uprising. Thou understandest my thought from afar off.*[8] He further elaborated, *The Eternal looketh from heaven; He beholdeth all the sons of men. From the place of His habitation He looketh intently upon all the inhabitants of the earth.*[9]

---

(5) There are nine spheres, the lowest of which is that of the moon, nearest to us on the earth (*Hilchoth Yesodei Hatorah* 3:1). See Ramban, "Writings and Discourses," p. 31, Note 8.   (6) Job 22:13-15. Thus, while Job contended that G-d was not concerned with events which transpire on the earth, Eliphaz reprimanded him by stating that such was the belief of the ancient sinners, who, as he explained further, were overwhelmed by the torrents of the Flood. — See further in *Hashgachah* (Divine Providence) that there were other three contestants to Job's opinion: Bildad, Zophar and Elihu, and how they circumvented Job's doctrine.   (7) Jeremiah 32:19. *"And mighty in work:* this means that it is beyond man's ability to fully comprehend G-d's work" (R'dak).   (8) Psalms 139:1-2. Although G-d is *afar off* in the uttermost reaches of the heavens He is nevertheless aware even of man's secret thoughts.   (9) *Ibid.*, 33:13-14. By including *all the sons of men*, the verse rightly expresses the thought that G-d, Who is the G-d of Israel, is clearly the Ruler of the entire human race.

This is the thought expressed by our Sages of blessed memory:[10] "Everything is foreseen, yet freedom of choice is given."[11] I will explain this further under the letter *hei,* which covers the subject of *Hashgachah* (Divine Providence). Similarly, [in the Book of Job], we find that Elihu, whose wise words were received from learned men of the [true] faith, explicitly stated, *For His eyes are upon the ways of a man, and He seeth all his goings. There is no darkness, nor shadow of death, where the workers of iniquity may hide themselves.*[12]

From faith in Divine Providence, man proceeds to believe in prophecy and the Torah,[13] and comes to believe that the Creator, exalted be He, has instilled an abundance of Divine inspiration in a

---

(10) Aboth 3:19. Aboth, a collection of the ethical teachings of the Tannaim, the Sages of the Mishnah, covers a period of some five hundred years beginning with the post-Biblical era about the year 300 B.C.E. and ending with the redaction of the Mishnah about 200 C.E. All of the Sages quoted in Aboth lived in the Land of Israel, and their teachings embody the quintessence of Rabbinic wisdom on the ethical and religious problems facing man.   (11) This teaching enunciated by Rabbi Akiba, constitutes a basic principle of Judaism. Affirming the faith in G-d's perfect knowledge of the future, it also upholds with equal fervor the belief in man's freedom of choice and, consequently, his responsibility for his actions. The apparent contradiction between G-d's foreseeing knowledge and man's freedom of action is resolved by Maimonides in *Hilchoth Teshuvah,* Chapter 5, wherein he explains that "G-d does not know from a source external to Himself, like human beings whose knowledge and his self are two separate entities, but He and His knowledge are One." Thus, while man's knowledge comes from an external source and is perforce limited, that of the Creator is not a separate entity. His knowledge is of His real Essence, and is therefore, beyond the comprehension of man. There is, thus, no contradiction between the Creator's foreseeing knowledge and man's freedom of choice.   (12) Job 34:21-22. With his imperfect knowledge, man is capable of only superficial judgment, but G-d, from Whom nothing can be hidden, is the true Judge; His verdict represents the ultimate truth. See further in *Hashgachah* (Divine Providence) that Elihu represents the school of true wisdom in the painstaking problem of the righteousness that pervades the world.   (13) The simplicity of this serves to heighten the solemnity of its message: G-d's providential care of everything on the earth manifests itself not only in His providing for the physical existence of His creatures, but also in His desire for them to lead a certain kind of life for the welfare of their existence. This Divine wish is expressed through the Torah and its commandments. Thus, belief in prophecy and the Torah is

certain individual to the extent that he begins to make prophetic utterances, and the Torah [or the word of G-d] can be transmitted through him. The Torah is man's guide to his spiritual success; it provides him *with an everlasting salvation.*[14] It instructs him how to conduct himself in an upright manner, affords him the knowledge to keep his body and soul pure in all circumstances of life, and teaches him how to improve himself and his character. *And this is the Torah which Moses set before the children of Israel,*[15] which we have been charged not to forget, as it is written, *Only take heed to thyself, and guard thy soul diligently, lest thou forget the things which thine eyes saw.*[16] The purport of this verse is that we should not forget any of the principles of the Torah and the commandments that were given to us, and it further teaches us that our forgetfulness would constitute a very grave sin which would be detrimental to our souls. This is why He cautions, *and guard thy soul diligently.*

And how could this fellow reconcile himself unto his Master[17] and be saved from forgetfulness? [Forgetfulness can be avoided] only by constantly uttering the words of Torah and meditating on them by day

a consequence of the belief in Divine Providence. — It should be noted that the author mentions "prophecy and Torah," because the belief that G-d communicates His Will to man is really the ideological basis of Torah. Hence, "prophecy" is correctly mentioned first and "Torah" second. This order is also followed in the *Yigdal* prayer which summarizes the teachings of Maimonides on the thirteen basic beliefs of Judaism: "He has bestowed an abundance of prophecies to His chosen and glorious men. Yet, never like Moses did a prophet arise who beheld His similitude." (14) Isaiah 45:17 *Everlasting* means that its beneficence is in this world as well as in the World to Come. (15) Deuteronomy 4:44. His Torah, in other words, is right before us, and it is our duty to observe it. (16) *Ibid.,* Verse 9. The life of Israel as a nation is dependent upon its observance of the Torah. Therefore, *guard thy soul diligently* and protect the nation's life by observing the Torah and not forgetting any part of it and its commandments. (17) I Samuel 29:4. This question was posed by the Philistine princes to their king when they requested that David not be permitted to join their forces in the coming battle against the army of Israel under King Saul. Rabbeinu Bachya borrows their words to phrase his rhetorical question here, which asks how anyone can assure himself of not forgetting the Torah.

and by night. This is the only way that they will be preserved in the [in-
dividual's] heart, as Solomon mentioned, *Let them not depart from
thine eyes; keep them in the midst of thy heart.* [18] This verse stresses
that even if you are involved in certain affairs or matters which per-
sistently agitate your mind, let them not deter you from always keeping
the commandment [of G-d] in your memory.

It is a fact that Israel is *a holy seed.* [19] *For all that, when they are* in
exile *in the land of their enemies,* [20] [the people of Israel] do not forget
the principles of the Torah and the commandment [of G-d], but
instead they stand firmly on guard [against transgression] and remain
steadfast in their belief. In each and every generation, there are nations that urge [or attempt to coerce] them to change their religion and
to replace their faith with another, but they refuse to heed them.

This is just as the Sages of blessed memory interpreted[21] the verse,
*Return, return, O Shulamith; return, return, that we may look upon
thee.* [22] The word *return* appears four times in this verse, corresponding
to the four kingdoms,[23] each of which called upon us to turn to their

---

(18) Proverbs 4:21. Forgetfulness of the commandments may be due to two factors:
temporary heedlessness, and permanent oblivion. He is, therefore, saying, *Let them
not depart from thine eyes* so that you do not forget them even for a moment, and *keep
them in the midst of thy heart* so that they be not obliterated from you permanently
(Rabbeinu Yonah, and quoted by Rabbeinu Bachya at the beginning of *Eikev,* —see
my edition, pp. 290-291).   (19) Isaiah 6:13. The phrase signifies that Israel is a nation
which "abides by His holiness" (Rashi). This means that the people of Israel will remain loyal to Him regardless of the persecutions they will have to endure for their
fidelity to G-d. This idea is clearly presented in the text which follows.   (20) Leviticus
26:44.   (21) Shir Hashirim Rabbah 7:1.   (22) Song of Songs 7:1. This book depicts
the mutual love between G-d and Israel through the generations and how their fidelity
to one another has remained unshaken through all the successive tragedies and
traumas of Jewish history.   (23) The four kingdoms, which Daniel saw in a vision, are
the world powers which were destined in their respective times, to rule over the entire
civilized world. They are: Babylon, Persia, Greece, and Rome. When they came into
contact with the Israelites, these powers attempted to make them forsake their belief in
the One G-d and adopt their own form of religion. The word Shulamith is thus a name
for Israel, being enticed by the nations to turn from the historic path of dedication to

faith and promised to reward us, in return, with high position and power. This is the purport of the expression, *that we may 'look upon' thee,*[22] which is related in its phraseology to the verse, *And thou [Moses] shall 'look upon' all the people, for men of ability.*[24] Israel, however, answers, *"What will ye see in the Shulamith?*[22] What position and power can you give us? Can you give us anything like the distinction we attained at Mount Sinai?" This is the intent of the next phrase in the verse, *as it were a dance of two companies.*[22] That is to say, "Does your deity have the ability to create for us anything like that *dance of two companies,* the [company of] six hundred thousand people who stood at Mount Sinai and the company of ministering angels, as it is written, *The chariots of G-d* [that were present at the time of the Revelation on Sinai] *were myriads, even thousands upon thousands?"*[25] By merit of Israel's steadfast faith in the Holy One, blessed be He, He will cause His Divine Presence to rest among us and will return us to Jerusalem as at the beginning, and the children who were exiled from their Father's Table[26] will return as of old.

It is with this thought in mind that Isaiah states here, *Open ye the gates, that the righteous nation may enter, those who keep the faith.*[1] Since he had mentioned the walls of Jerusalem in the preceding verse—*[We have a strong city]; walls and bulwarks doth He appoint for salvation*[27] — he therefore concluded by saying, *Open ye the gates,*[1] meaning the gates of Jerusalem, which have been locked until now, and let Israel enter, [for Israel is] *the righteous nation* that has kept faith in the Holy One, blessed be He, throughout the exile. Such indeed is [the power of] faith: the Israelite sees the Land being ravaged by foreigners, rebels, and transgressors, and *they that regard lying*

---

the Unity of G-d, and join them.   (24) Exodus 18:21. Moses was to *look upon* or search for certain men of quality fit and capable for the office of judgeship. Thus, the expression *look upon* connotes an offering of power and distinction.   (25) Psalms 68:16.   (26) Berachoth 3a. This refers to the Sanctuary, which marks the earthly habitation of the Divine Glory.   (27) Isaiah 26:1.

vanities[28] dwelling therein, while he himself is evicted from his home and is subjugated by the nations, nevertheless, he continues to be loyal to his faith.

David referred to this thought when he said, *Thou hast ascended on high, Thou hast carried away captives; Thou hast received gifts among men, yea, among the rebellious also, that the Eternal G-d might dwell there.*[29] The Midrash[30] explains: "*Thou hast ascended on high:* When His Glory ascended on high [at the time of the destruction of the Sanctuary], He exiled Israel, for as long as the Divine Glory resided in the Sanctuary, Israel did not suffer banishment. *Thou hast received gifts among men:* You have taken back from them the gifts which You had [originally] given them so that Your Glory would dwell among them, and then *the rebellious* ones came and dwelled where the Divine Glory had rested."

To inform us that faith is the essence of the entire Torah and that all commandments are founded upon it, the Sages of blessed memory commented:[31] "Habakkuk came and expressed all [of the *taryag*[32] commandments] in one principle, as it is said, *And the righteous shall live by his faith.*"[33] Solomon, too, said, *A faithful man shall be richly blessed.*[34]

It is important to understand why the Sages ascribed this matter to Habakkuk rather than to David. They might just as well have said, "David came and expressed all [of the *taryag* commandments] in one

---

(28) Jonah 2:9. See more on this topic in Ramban's "Prayer at the Ruins of Jerusalem," Writings and Discourses, pp. 699-725. (29) Psalms 68:19. (30) I have found this text, not in any Midrash, but in R'dak's commentary on the Book of Psalms, *ibid.* See Introduction about our author's usage of Midrashim. (31) Makkoth 24a. (32) *Taryag* is a composite word of the Hebrew letters *tav-reish-yod-gimmel,* the numerical values of which equal 613, the total number of the commandments of the Torah. (33) Habakkuk 2:4. *By his faith* in the One Whom we have heard proclaiming at Sinai, *I am the Eternal thy G-d* etc. This commandment is of course the heart of all *taryag* commandments (Maharsha, Makkoth 24a). (34) Proverbs 28:20.

principle, as it is said, *All Thy commandments are* [based on] *faith.*"³⁵
The explanation is that because of Habakkuk's additional phrase, *shall
live* — which clearly implies that if a person has faith, he will deserve
life in the World to Come — the Sages ascribed this principle to him
rather than to David, who did not mention the subject of reward [in his
verse]. *The righteous shall live* means that he will be rewarded with the
everlasting true life and not merely with the brief earthly life. The expression is similar to that mentioned in connection with the observance
of the commandments: *which if a man do, he shall live by them.*³⁶ [In
this verse], the main intent of [*shall live*] is life in the World to Come.
Onkelos similarly rendered it: "he shall live by them in eternal life."

The concept of faith entails the obligation to love the truth, to prefer
it [over alternative options of falsehood], and to speak it, as the prophet Zechariah said, *These are the things that ye shall do: Speak ye
every man the truth with his neighbor; execute the judgment of truth
and peace in your gates.*³⁷ Solomon, too, said, *The lip of truth shall be
established forever,*³⁸ thus exhorting us to speak only the truth and to
avoid falsehood under all circumstances. He who possesses *the lip of
truth* will succeed and endure. Knowing his lifelong habit [of speaking
the truth], people will believe all that he says. However, he who has *a
lying tongue*³⁸ will be believed for only a passing moment, for when his
words are subsequently examined and analyzed, people will recognize
them as having been deceitful.

This verse, [*Speak ye every man the truth,* etc.],³⁷ exhorts people to
be pure in their speech and to speak only the truth even in such matters
that affect no one. In their business dealings, people should certainly
act faithfully and stand by their word so that their "yes" or "no" will be

(35) Psalms 119:86.   (36) Leviticus 18:5.   (37) Zechariah 8:16. Quoting this verse
Rabban Shimon ben Gamaliel derived the principle that by three things the world is
preserved: by truth, judgment, and peace (Aboth, end of Chapter 1). See also in
Dinim (The Laws), Note 5.   (38) Proverbs 12:19.

true, just as the Sages commented:[39] *"A just ephah, and a just hin:*[40] let your 'yes' be just and your 'no' be just." Needless to say, if a person utters his "yes" or "no" twice, he is certainly bound by [his statement] since [his repetition] is equivalent to an oath. The Sages of blessed memory declared,[41] "Saying 'no' twice constitutes an oath, as it is said, *Neither shall all flesh be cut off any more by the waters of the flood; nor shall there any more be a flood to destroy the earth.*[42] It is also written, *For this is as the waters of Noah unto Me, for as I have 'sworn' [that the waters of Noah should no more go over the earth, so I have sworn that I would not be wroth with thee].*"[43] Yet, we do not find any Divine oath in the entire chapter on the Flood with the exception of this twofold negation: *[neither shall all flesh,* etc.; *nor shall there any more,* etc.*[42]* We may conclude that] since the repetition of "no" constitutes an oath [as evidenced above], uttering "yes" twice assuredly possesses the same [binding force].

The Sages of blessed memory furthermore said[44] that if one does not abide by his word in his business transactions as well as in all of his affairs, he brings upon himself the malediction, "He Who punished the generation of the Flood and the generation of the Dispersion will punish him who does not stand by his word."[45] Generally, he who does not stand by his word will eventually utter falsehoods, and once he is accustomed to lying, he will ultimately commit even perjury. King Solomon said, *A false witness breatheth out lies.*[46] Thus, he profanes the power of speech, which was given to man for the [lofty] purpose of praising the Creator. This is the purport of the statement, *And ye shall not profane My holy Name.*[47]

---

(39) Baba Metzia 49a. (40) Leviticus 19:36. An *ephah* is a dry measure, a *hin* a liquid measure. Since the word *hin* resembles the word *hein* (yes), the Sages derived from this verse the moral principle of being truthful in speech. (41) Shebuoth 36a. (42) Genesis 9:11. (43) Isaiah 54:9. (44) Baba Metzia 44a. (45) Where no definite contractual obligation exists, the court cannot compel a man to honor his oral commitment. Nevertheless, such a man is subject to punishment from on high for failing to keep his word. — On the generation of the Dispersion, see Genesis 11:1-9. (46) Proverbs 6:19. (47) Leviticus 22:32.

Incorporated within this principle is a lifelong guide to all who heed it: they should be sensitive to the nuances of their speech, for the power of truth is mighty indeed. He who unfalteringly adheres to the truth will merit having his prayers heard, as David said, *The Eternal is nigh unto all that call upon Him, to all that call upon Him in truth.*[48] When one resolves to act always in compliance with the truth, he comes closer to his Creator, blessed be He, Who is the True One. This proximity [to G-d] is the prodigious reward and the immense privilege which is called "life in the World to Come." It is impossible for anyone to attain this status unless he adopts G-d's attributes and walks in His ways, as we have been commanded, *and thou shalt walk in His ways.*[49] Our Rabbis of blessed memory clearly explained this [verse]:[50] "Just as He is the Merciful One, so should you be merciful. Just as He is the Gracious One, so should you be gracious. Just as He clothes the naked,[51] so should you clothe the naked. Just as He visits the sick,[52] so should you visit the sick. Just as He comforts mourners,[53] so should you comfort mourners. Just as He buries the dead,[54] so should you bury the dead." The same could be said with regard to His other attributes: Just as He is the Holy One, so should you be holy, as it is said, *Sanctify yourselves, and be ye holy, for I am holy.*[55] Just as He is the Perfect One—as it is said, *As for G-d, His way is perfect*[56]—so should you strive to be

(48) Psalms 145:18. If they call upon G-d in truth, that is, if they are sincere in the prayer they utter, then *the Eternal is nigh* to them. This would not be the case if the worshippers' hearts were not in their prayers.   (49) Deuteronomy 28:9.   (50) The original text of this passage is in Sotah 14a, but the language here follows Maimonides' version in *Hilchoth Dei'oth* 1:6.   (51) Genesis 3:21. This refers to the clothes G-d made for Adam and Eve.   (52) *Ibid.*, 18:1. When Abraham was sick, "the Holy One, blessed be He, came and enquired about the state of his health" (Rashi).   (53) *Ibid.*, 25:11. After Abraham's death, "G-d comforted Isaac with consolatory words" (Rashi).   (54) Deuteronomy 34:6. Since no mortal was present at Moses' demise, G-d Himself performed his burial.   (55) Leviticus 11:44. This verse, which is stated at the end of the chapter dealing with the forbidden foods, perforce means that the spiritual purpose of these dietary laws is to facilitate the individual's attainment of sanctity. He will then be worthy of partaking of G-d's Divine Nature.   (56) II Samuel 22:31.

perfect, as it is said, *Thou shalt be wholehearted with the Eternal thy G-d.*[57] It is further written, *Walk before Me, and be thou wholehearted,*[58] for it is known that he who is wholehearted, whose inner personality is in harmony with his external appearances and actions, has the principles of faith firmly planted in his heart and deeply engraved in his mind.

To achieve this status is a great accomplishment for man, and [it serves as] a mighty fountainhead for all the other precious qualities of character. It was a trait possessed by the patriarchs of the world, the prophets and the righteous, and it is included among the virtues by merit of which man will sojourn in the Tent of G-d and dwell upon His holy mountain, as David said, *O Eternal, who shall sojourn in Thy Tabernacle? Who shall dwell upon Thy holy mountain? He that walketh in wholeheartedness, and worketh righteousness.*[59] He further said, *I will give heed unto the way of the wholehearted.*[60] Solomon, his son, also stated, *He that walketh in wholeheartedness walketh securely.*[61] David previously informed us in another verse that the reward for wholeheartedness is eternal existence in the presence of G-d, blessed be He, as it is said, *And as for me, Thou upholdest me because of mine integrity, and settest me before Thy face forever.*[62]

It is known that there is no nation so inclined to follow the truth like Israel, for the Torah, the true Law, was given only to the Israelites, as it is written, *He declareth His words unto Jacob, His statutes and His ordinances unto Israel. He hath not dealt so with any nation.*[63] Similarly, the Sages said in Midrash Bereshith Rabbah:[64] *"And if a man will*

---

(57) Deuteronomy 18:13.   (58) Genesis 17:1.   (59) Psalms 15:1-2.   (60) *Ibid.,* 101:2. This means: I will deliberately choose the way of integrity to walk in as the king of my people.   (61) Proverbs 10:9.   (62) Psalms 41:13.   (63) *Ibid.,* 147:19-20. Israel's great privilege is thus, having been given the knowledge of His words, statutes, and ordinances. It is for this special right with which we have been invested that we should be grateful to Him.   (64) The Rome manuscript of Kad Hakemach identifies the source of this quotation only generally as Midrash Rabbah. This is correct. The

sell his daughter to be a maidservant, she shall not go out as the men-
servants do.[65] [This passage may be explained as follows]: *And if a man*
will sell: This refers to the Holy One, blessed be He, as it is said, *The*
Eternal is a man of war.[66] . . . *His daughter to be a maidservant:* This
alludes to the Torah which He 'sold' to Israel and which is taken from
the Ark wherein it is guarded. . . . *She shall not go out as the men-*
servants do: This warns [Israel] not to treat the Torah in a con-
temptuous manner or to take liberties with her. *If she please not her*
master:[67] If Israel does not observe the Torah, *then he*—meaning her
father [who in this interpretation is] the Holy One, blessed be
He—*shall redeem her,*[67] for *unto a foreign people he* [her master] *shall*
not sell her.[68] The Almighty has given over the Torah to no nation and
ethnic group other than Israel, *even when Israel hath dealt deceitfully*
with her.''[68]

It is also known that the Torah is called Truth, as it is said, *Acquire*
the truth, and sell it not.[69] It is further stated, *My mouth shall utter*
truth.[70] You will find that *emeth*, [the Hebrew word for truth], is composed of the first, middle, and last letters of the Hebrew alphabet.[71]

---

text here is found in Shemoth Rabbah 30:4, not in Bereshith Rabbah.   (65) Exodus
21:7. Literally, the verse states that unlike a Hebrew male servant, a Hebrew maidservant does not gain her freedom if her master causes the loss of her tooth or eye. Instead, as the following verses explain, her period of servitude terminates either after six
years or at the Jubilee, or, if she was sold as a minor, her servitude ends when she
reaches puberty, if that event precedes any of the conditions above. The Midrash
however, enlarges the scope of the verse to include the relationship between G-d, the
Torah, and Israel.   (66) Exodus 15:3.   (67) *Ibid.,* 21:8. "That is to say, He will
remove His Divine Presence from them." So clearly explained by our author in his
Commentary on the Torah, *ibid.,* (p. 218, in my edition).   (68) *Ibid.,* The implication is obvious. Even when Israel has sinned and the Sanctuary has been destroyed, yet
will He not transfer the Torah to any other people or race. In other words, G-d will not
exchange Israel, under any circumstances, for another nation.   (69) Proverbs 23:23.
Sell it not, but teach it to others free even though you acquired it at a
price.   (70) *Ibid.,* 8:7.   (71) The word *emeth* is spelled with these three letters:
aleph, the first letter of the Hebrew alphabet, *mem,* which occurs in the middle of the
alphabet, and *thav,* the final letter. This spelling, which is no mere coincidence, intimates that the Torah is the all-inclusive source of truth.

This alludes to the fact that the Torah is founded upon truth, for letters are to the Torah as a foundation is to a building. Our Rabbis of
blessed memory expounded,[72] "Truth is the seal of the Holy One,
blessed be He, as it is said, *And the Eternal G-d is the true G-d.*"[73]
Therefore, [when we recite the *Sh'ma*], we are obligated[74] to adjoin the
passage of Fringes, which concludes with the words, *I am the Eternal
your G-d,*[75] to the word "True,"[76] [with which the following prayer
commences]. We are to do so [in our recitals of the *Sh'ma*] in the morning and at night. [The prayers adjoining the passage of Fringes are]
"True and firm" in the morning and "True and faithful" at night. If
one does not say [his prayers] in this manner, he has not fulfilled his
obligation.[77]

Faith stems from truth, the source of which is the Holy One, blessed
be He. Therefore, all who desire *to draw near unto G-d*[78] must conduct
their business affairs faithfully, as it is said, *Dwell in the land, and feed
in faith.*[79] This means that when you live in the land and have business
associations with people, act faithfully and do not covet anything
which is rightfully theirs. This aspect of faith is rational, for man can
reasonably be expected to understand that his needs will be satisfied by
his own possessions and that consequently he has nothing to gain from
whatever belongs to another person. We have already heard of
countries which have no Torah at all, but based only on their
understanding, they manifest great faith in their business dealings.
Thus, merchants come with their wares and leave them unguarded in
certain places, and they return on the next day and find money lying
upon their merchandise. If the amount of money is satisfactory to

(72) Shabbath 55a.   (73) Jeremiah 10:10. I have been unable to find any material
in Rabbinic literature which indicates that this verse supports the statement, "Truth is
the seal of the Holy One, blessed be He."   (74) Berachoth 14 a-b.   (75) Numbers
15:41.   (76) We thus proclaim the validity of all G-d's words that we have recited in
the three Scriptural passages of the *Sh'ma* by concluding with the word *emeth* (true).
Hence, truth is indeed G-d's seal.   (77) Berachoth 12a.   (78) Isaiah 58:2.
(79) Psalms 37:3.

them, they take it and leave the merchandise; if not, they leave the money and take back their belongings. They do this because of their faith [in one another] and not out of fear of the authorities.

All of the prophets unanimously exhorted Israel concerning faith. In one chapter, Jeremiah began speaking about the offerings and concluded with [the subject of] faith. He wanted to inform the people thereby that if they were lacking faith, their offerings would be unacceptable [to G-d]. Thus, he stated at the beginning of that section, *Add your burnt-offerings unto your sacrifices, and eat ye flesh,*[80] by which he meant they shall add these whole burnt-offerings, [which were unacceptable to G-d], to their usual peace-offerings, which they themselves could eat. Thus, they would at least [accomplish] eating an abundance of meat. [Jeremiah] explained that this rebuke was due to their lack of faith, as it is said at the close of this section, *Faithfulness is perished, and is cut off from their mouth.*[81]

The prophet Isaiah likewise censured Israel regarding the matter of faith, as he said, *None sueth in righteousness, and none pleadeth in truth; they trust in vanity, and speak lies, they conceive mischief, and bring forth iniquity.*[82] It is subsequently written, *They hatch vipers' eggs, and weave the spider's web; he that eateth of their eggs dieth, and that which is cleft breaketh out into a viper.*[83] Thus, as soon as the prophet mentioned, *None sueth in righteousness,* which indicates a lack of faith, he exposed for us how they are led astray in thought and in deed. He compared their thoughts to the vipers' eggs, from which, when cleft, come forth venomous vipers and serpents. Similarly, from the thoughts of the faithless, only evil and bitter fruits issue forth. He also compared their deeds to the insignificant spider's web, the sole

(80) Jeremiah 7:21. In other words, since G-d found no delight in the offerings of the people because of their sins, Jeremiah sarcastically suggests that instead of wasting the effort of bringing a whole burnt-offering, they should rather designate it as a peace-offering so that they could eat the meat of the offering and so derive at least some benefit from it.   (81) *Ibid.,* Verse 28.   (82) Isaiah 59:4.   (83) *Ibid.,* Verse 5.

function of which is to trap the fly for the spider so that the latter may feed upon it. So, too, the goal of the activities of the wicked in this world is only [that they] may eat, drink, and celebrate. Such activity is likewise meaningless, for only those necessities without which man could not live are important. Isaiah continues, *Their webs shall not become garments, neither shall men cover themselves with their works,*[84] for just as the web spun by the spider cannot serve as a permanent garment, so the deeds of the wicked can never come to full fruition or permanence. The prophet Isaiah himself previously mentioned that the entire Torah is founded upon faith, as he said, *O Eternal, Thou art my G-d, I will exalt Thee, I will praise Thy Name, for Thou hast done wonderful things, even counsels of old, in faithfulness and truth.*[85] *Counsels of old* alludes to the Torah, which stems from [G-d], the Hidden Source Who is farthermost from us and yet nearest to us. Nevertheless, the verse explains that [the Torah] is founded upon *faithfulness and truth,* the faithfulness originating from the Perfect One Who is the Truth.

Many miracles were performed for Israel which were founded upon faith. The descent of the manna was due to faith, as it is said, *Behold, I will cause to rain bread from heaven for you; and the people shall go out and gather a day's portion every day, that I may prove them, whether they will walk in My law, or not.*[86] The test was whether they would have faith [in Him and follow all the injunctions connected with this miraculous food]. Similarly, David said, *And they tried G-d in their heart by asking food for their craving.*[87] Regarding those who lacked faith [and retained some of the manna for the following day], Scripture says, *and it bred worms, and rotted.*[88] A similar instance concerned the waters of Marah,[89] which were originally sweet but were [temporarily] turned bitter only to test whether the people would remain firm in their faith. This is the intent of the expression, *and there He proved them.*[90] In like manner, when the people desired water in

(84) *Ibid.,* Verse 6. (85) *Ibid.,* 25:1. (86) Exodus 16:4. (87) Psalms 78:18. (88) Exodus 16:20. (89) *Ibid.,* 15:23. (90) *Ibid.,* Verse 25.

Rephidim, Moses said to them, *Why strive ye with me? Why do you try the Eternal?*[91] Concerning Moses, the man who was perfect in faith, Scripture states, *and his hands were 'emunah' (faithful* or *steadfast in faith).*[92]

The Sages said in the Midrash:[93] "*Open ye the gates, that the righteous nation may enter, those who keep 'emunim' (the faith).*[1] Read the word, not as *emunim,* but rather as *amanim* [from the root *amen*], which refers to [the people of] Israel, who respond Amen." In like manner, the Sages expounded in Tractate Shabbath:[94] "Rabbi Shimon[95] said that anyone who answers Amen with all his might has the gates of the Garden of Eden opened for him, as it is said, *Open ye the gates, that the righteous nation may enter, those who keep 'emunim' (the faith).*[1] Read the word, not as *emunim,* [but rather as *amanim*], which refers to those who respond Amen." According to this Midrash, then, Israel is called *the righteous nation* because it responds Amen.

At public prayers and benedictions, therefore, it is important that one take heed to answer Amen, a word which stems from the [grammatical] root of *emunah* (faith). All people whose ancestors stood at Mount Sinai and accepted the Torah, which is called *emunah,*[96] and who are descendants of our patriarch Abraham, the founder of belief, as it is written, *And he believed in the Eternal,*[97] are obliged to maintain [proper] intent of heart and mind when answering Amen. When the reader recites the benedictions [during public prayer], the people should not be *as a deaf man* who does not hear *and as a dumb man*

---

(91) *Ibid.*, 17:2.   (92) *Ibid.*, Verse 12.   (93) I have not found the precise wording of this text in any Midrash.   (94) Shabbath 119b.   (95) The text in our Gemara ascribes this exposition to Reish Lakish. It is likely that "Rabbi Shimon" in our text here does not refer to the Tanna Rabbi Shimon ben Yochai, as one might think, but rather to the Palestinian Amora Rabbi Shimon ben Lakish, who was also known as Reish Lakish. Thus there is no conflict between the passage in the text and the Gemara.   (96) I know of no source where *emunah* is a synonym for Torah.   (97) Genesis 15:6.

that openeth not his mouth,[98] nor should any man converse with his
friend as if he were in the streets of the city, which practice is prevalent
among some of our people. Such conduct is sinful and requires retribution, for when a servant hears someone blessing his master, it is
reasonable to expect him to answer Amen. [Certainly then], when one
blesses G-d, *in Whose hand is the soul of every living thing,*[99] those who
hear it are all the more obligated to answer Amen. This is certainly so,
since He Himself, blessed be He, has established a commandment
obliging us to bless Him, as it is said, *and thou shalt bless the Eternal
thy G-d.*[100] The same applies to answering Amen, an expression which
affirms the blessing. Our Sages of blessed memory said in Tractate
Berachoth:[101] "Rabbi Yosei says, 'When one answers Amen, [his
reward] exceeds that of him who pronounces the benediction [itself].'
Rabbi Nehoraie said to him. 'By Heaven, it is so! The common soldiers
start the battle, but the veterans, the experienced soldiers [their allied
companions] wind up with victory.' " That is, the veterans are being
rewarded over the common soldiers, [for having achieved the
victory].[102] The reason for this [dictum of Rabbi Yosei] is that the one
who answers Amen draws forth the [specific] Divine Power mentioned
by the reciter of the benediction from the Source of all Divine
Powers.[103] Hence, the strength [of him who answers Amen] is greater.

Consider the following: When a mortal king is welcomed by the
public and is blessed by them, an individual who does not participate
in answering Amen is considered to be spurning the king and
denigrating his honor. Furthermore, when a mortal king is blessed, it is
deemed virtuous to respond Amen because he is the cause of peace in
the land, as it is written, *The king by justice establisheth the land,*[104]

---

(98) Psalms 38:14.   (99) Job 12:10.   (100) Deuteronomy 8:10.   (101) Berachoth
53b.   (102) Nazir 66b (see Tosafoth).   (103) In other words, the reciter of the blessing just states the fact that a certain power stems from the Source of all powers, while
the one who answers Amen actually draws it forth and brings it nearer to the congregation. In that sense the reward of whoever answers Amen is greater than that of the
reciter of the blessing.   (104) Proverbs 29:4.

and our Rabbis of blessed memory said,[105] "If not for the fear [of government], men would swallow each other alive." Therefore, by the syllogism of *kal vachomer*,[106] one may conclude that [it is so much more important to respond Amen] in the case of the Supreme King in Whose hand lies the heart of the mortal king, as it is written, *The king's heart is in the hand of the Eternal as the watercourses*,[107] and Who is the source of [the mortal ruler's] kingdom and dominion and the beginning of all things! When the Sanctuary existed, the reader would utter the Tetragrammaton [during public prayer] and all the people would respond, "Blessed be the Name of His glorious Kingdom forever and ever."[108] However, now that we are in exile, we use [*Adonoy*], a substitute for the Divine Name, and our answer of Amen is equivalent to the [ancient response], "Blessed be, etc."

Some scholars explained[109] the Rabbis' statement[101] that "when one answers Amen, [his reward] exceeds that of the one who pronounces the benediction [itself]" in the following manner: When one pronounces a benediction, he is testifying that G-d is the source of all blessings. However, the testimony of only one witness is not considered to have legal force. When one answers Amen [to the blessing of the first], he serves as the second witness. Since the testimony is validated through his participation, his reward is therefore greater.

Come and see how great is the power of faith, for Israel was redeemed from Egypt only as a reward for faith, as it is said, *and the people believed*.[110] In the future, too, Israel will be redeemed as a reward for their faith, as it is said, *Open ye the gates, that the righteous nation may enter, those who keep the faith.*[1]

---

(105) Aboth 3:2.   (106) Literally: "a minor and major." This is a form of reasoning by which a certain stricture applying to a minor matter is established as applying all the more to a major matter. Conversely, if a certain leniency applies to a major matter, it must apply all the more to the minor matter. It is one of the thirteen rules by which the Torah is interpreted.   (107) Proverbs 21:1.   (108) Yoma 66a.   (109) This explanation is also cited by the author in his commentary on Exodus 14:31 (p. 122 in my edition).   (110) Exodus 4:31.

אהבה

Love of G-d

It is our duty to contemplate the manifold aspects of the Divine
Commandments and attain thereby a conception of G-d so
that we will be able to attract others to love Him / The complete worship of G-d is possible only by loving G-d, not by fearing Him, for love entails fear, but fear does not include love /
From the first moment of life until our very last breath, we are
obligated to love G-d whether He governs us with the attribute
of justice or compassion / Our duty to love G-d is augmented
by His having been the first to love Israel and His refusal to exchange us for another nation / G-d's love for Israel is evinced
by the fact that all of the exhortations of the prophets and their
messages of retribution always conclude with words of consolation / Desiring G-d is superior than loving Him. The Song of
Songs is based on the theme of desiring G-d, and Moses himself
attained that high distinction as evidenced by his death with a
Divine Kiss.

Love of G-d

AND THOU SHALT LOVE THE ETERNAL THY G-D WITH
ALL THY HEART, AND WITH ALL THY SOUL, AND WITH
ALL THY MIGHT.[1]

The love of G-d is an obligatory commandment[2] constituting a principal cornerstone for the fulfillment of the Torah. This love requires that a person should contemplate the bases and principles of the commandments so that he may attain a conception of G-d, blessed be He. He will then derive the utmost delight from this conception to the extent that he will attract many to the righteous life and will bring the love of G-d into their hearts. Thus, in the Sifre, our Rabbis expounded:[3] "*And thou shalt love the Eternal thy G-d.*[1] However, you do not know how mortal man can love G-d. Therefore, Scripture states, *And*

---

(1) Deuteronomy 6:5. The verse expresses the highest requirement of Judaism, which is the love of G-d in all its inferences. It is a logical follow-up to the preceding theme of *Emunah* (Faith), suggesting that genuine faith is founded upon love. (2) Among the *taryag* (613) commandments — see *Emunah* (Faith), Note 32 — there are certain duties which are not obligatory in the sense that they need be performed under all circumstances. Such for example, are the commandments concerning vows or divorce. There is no obligation to make a vow or to divorce one's wife. The commandments in question prescribe the manner of conduct in case one has made a vow, or the procedure required if one is determined to divorce his wife. On the other hand, there are commandments which are absolutely obligatory on every man, at all times, in all places, and under all circumstances. Maimonides lists sixty of these positive commandments, which he calls the Unconditional Commandments. (See "The Commandments," Vol. I, pp. 257-260.) It is in this sense that Rabbeinu Bachya calls the love of G-d "an obligatory commandment." (3) Sifre, *Vaethchanan,* 33.

these words, [which I command thee this day, shall be upon thy heart].[4] Through them you will come to recognize the One Who created the world by His word." The Rabbis also stated:[5] *"And thou shalt love the Eternal thy G-d.*[1] Make Him beloved by mankind as your patriarch Abraham did, as it is said, *and the souls they had gotten in Haran."*[6] Scripture also testifies concerning him [when it states], *Abraham My friend.*[7] Just as Abraham summoned mankind to believe in G-d out of his own great love for Him, you too must love Him so as to summon people unto Him and bring them to His service.

It is known that although the fear of G-d is one of the great principles in worshipping Him, such homage cannot be complete unless it stems from love, for while love entails fear, fear does not include love. It is generally recognized that one who loves his friend is also fearful of transgressing his friend's will, but if he merely fears him, it is quite possible that he does not love him at all. Thus, the main element in the worship of G-d is love. Accordingly, the Rabbis of blessed memory expounded:[8] "A person should not say, 'I will study Torah so that I will be called a wise man or a rabbi, or so that I will become honored or rich,' but he should rather study Torah out of love." They also stated[9] that the reward of one who fears G-d extends to a thousand generations, while the reward of one who loves G-d extends for thousands of generations.

Scripture mentioned the two Divine attributes, mercy and justice,[10] in connection with this love in order to explain that one is obligated to love Him, blessed be He, under all circumstances, regardless if G-d

(4) Deuteronomy 6:6. The study of Torah thus brings about a love of G-d. (5) Sifre, *Vaethchanan*, 32. (6) Genesis 12:5. This is interpreted to mean "the souls which he had brought under the sheltering wings of the Divine Presence" (Rashi). See "The Commandments," Vol. I, pp. 3-5. (7) Isaiah 41:8. (8) Nedarim 62a. (9) Sotah 31a. (10) In the commandment, *And thou shalt love the Eternal thy G-d*, Scripture used two Divine Names, each of which signifies a distinct attribute with which G-d governs the world: *the Eternal* indicates the attribute of mercy or compassion, and *thy G-d* signifies the attribute of strict justice.

judges him by the attribute of mercy or justice. Scripture states *With all thy heart*[1] [to teach you] that your love should not be divided between Him and any of those higher powers referred to as "lovers," as it says, *I will go after my lovers, that give me my bread and my water.*[11] Rather, all the powers of your heart should be exclusively devoted to the love of G-d alone, praised be He. The expression *with all thy heart* also includes the charge that you are to love Him [throughout your life] until the last moment before death. Scientists know that in the formation of the embryo, the heart is the first organ to develop, and in the blood of the heart lies the source of the body's natural heat, although there are some scholars who attribute this heat to the liver and the brain. The heart, of all the parts of the body, is also the last to die. Therefore, the Torah, which includes all wisdoms, commanded that a person shall love the Holy One, blessed be He, [with all of his heart] from the beginning of his existence to the moment of his death.

It is known that the heart is the seat of the rational soul [and is not disposed towards the expression of love, an emotion]. Nevertheless, when G-d stated *and with 'all' thy heart* He meant to include that part of the soul which is lustful, for the latter is the force which naturally motivates man to trample upon [and disregard] the love of G-d, praised be He. It is the antithesis of what David [referred to when he] said, *O Lord, all my desire is 'negd'cha' (before Thee),*[12] by which he explained that all [of his heart's] desires were directed towards G-d.

[In the phrase], *and with all 'm'odecha' (thy might),*[1] the word *'m'od* [which is translated here as "might" but literally means "much" or "abundance"] signifies that you are to love Him exceedingly. That is to

---

(11) Hosea 2:7. The "lovers" are but a surname for those powers which séem to control man's supply of food, such as the sun, the wind, and the rain. Man's dependence upon them for his subsistence was in fact responsible for worshipping them. (12) Psalms 38:10. *Negd'cha* (before Thee) is understood by certain commentators: "to be before Thee." David is thus saying, that justification for his own existence is "the desire 'to be before Him' constantly." Our author's explanation is near to this interpretation.

say, your property should not be dearer to you than [the fulfillment of] the commandments. [For example], if you can only find an *ethrog*[13] for a thousand *zuzim* [a *zuz* was a silver coin equal in value to one fourth of a *shekel*] you are obligated to buy it as Rabban Gamaliel once did.[14] Our Rabbis of blessed memory said:[15] "The expense [to which one should go] in adorning a religious duty [e.g., buying an *ethrog* of better quality or a finer copy of the Law] extends to one third [of the original cost one intended to spend]."

From this verse,[1] the Sages further derived the principle that one is obligated to praise G-d for the evil [which befalls him] just as he blesses Him for his good fortune, as they taught in Tractate Berachoth:[16] "One is obligated to bless [G-d] for the evil [which occurs to him] even as he blesses Him for his good fortune, for it is written, *And thou shalt love the Eternal thy G-d with all 'l'vavcha' (thy heart)*,[1] meaning with both your good inclination and your evil inclination." This is derived from the double use of the letter *beth* [in *l'vavcha*], for He could have stated "with all *'libcha'* (thy heart)." This thought is expressed in the psalm, *I will give thanks unto the Eternal with my 'whole heart,'*[17] that is, with both inclinations, the good and the evil.

"[The expression] *and with all thy soul*[1] [teaches that you must love G-d] even if He takes away your soul."[16] Similarly, the Sages said in the Midrash:[18] "The villainous [Roman] government once decreed apostasy upon [the people of] Israel, forbidding them to study the

(13) The *ethrog* is one of the Four Species used during the Festival of Tabernacles.   (14) Succah 41b. "Rabban" is the title of the *Nasi* (Prince of the Sanhedrin).   (15) Baba Kamma 9b.   (16) Berachoth 54a and 60b. The thought suggested is that there is no extra word or even a single letter in the Torah which is not intended for instruction, as expounded in the text.   (17) Psalms 111:1. *Whole heart.* Even so that man's natural desire is to accept the reward and reject punishment, the verse bids us to accept the retribution joyously as well as we welcome the reward.   (18) Tanchuma, *Ki Thavo*, 2. — Papus ben Yehudah was a Jew who gave in to the Roman decree and advised others to do likewise.

Torah. Rabbi Akiba, however, defied [the Romans] and continued to
study the Torah. Papus ben Yehudah found him and asked him, 'Why
do you endanger yourself by violating the emperor's decree?' Rabbi
Akiba replied: 'I will relate a parable to you. Walking by a river bank,
a fox saw some fish hiding in the water. He asked them why they were
hiding, and they told him that they feared the various nets and traps
that people set for them. The fox said to them, Come to me and I will
hide you in the cracks of the rocks so that you will have no fear of people. They responded, You are supposedly the wisest of the beasts, yet
you are very foolish! We can only exist in the element of water, and yet
you tell us to come ashore! So it is with us. Our entire existence is possible only through the Torah, as it is said, *Keep her, for she is thy life.*[19]
[Thus, by obeying the decree of the Romans and not studying the
Torah], it is you who exposes himself to danger, [not I].' Subsequently,
[Papus and Rabbi Akiba], were [arrested by the Romans and] placed
in the same prison. Papus remarked to Rabbi Akiba, 'Happy are you
who were arrested for studying the Torah, and woe to Papus ben
Yehudah who was arrested for absurdities.' [Some time later], Rabbi
Akiba was led to his execution just at the time of reciting the *Sh'ma.* As
[the Roman executioners] tore his flesh, Rabbi Akiba devotedly recited
the *Sh'ma.* His disciples cried out to him 'Our master, up to this
point!'[20] He said to them, 'All my life I worried about how I could
fulfill the verse *and with all thy soul,* [which means] even when He
takes your soul. Now that the opportunity has finally come, should I
not fulfill it?' While he was saying the word *Echad* (One) [of the
Sh'ma], his soul departed. A Heavenly Voice then came forth and said,

(19) Proverbs 4:13. (20) There are three negative commandments—idolatry, immorality and bloodshed—which must never be violated, and one must even surrender
his life, if necessary, in order to observe them. "But," ask Rabbi Akiba's disciples, "is
one obligated to suffer up to this point of self-sacrifice for any of the other commandments [such as studying Torah]?" Rabbi Akiba answered, "All my life, etc." In other
words, it was his express desire to be more stringent with himself even in case of all the
other commandments (Berachoth 61b, Maharsha).

'Happy are you Rabbi Akiba whose soul departed with the word *Echad* [on your lips]."

[The Gemara expounds]:[16] *"and with all 'm'odecha' (thy might)*[1] means your wealth.[21] Another lesson to be learned [from *m'odecha*] is that regardless of the *midah*[22] (measure) He metes out to you, you should be grateful to Him. Accept it all joyfully,[23] as it is said, *I will sing of mercy and justice,*[24] which means that if He deals with me in a merciful manner I will sing, and if [He deals with me strictly] in justice I will also sing. It further states, *In G-d, I will praise His word, in the Eternal, I will praise His word."*[25] Isaiah likewise referred to this [theme] when he said, *I will greatly rejoice in the Eternal, my soul shall be joyful in my G-d.*[26] [That is, "I will rejoice] regardless if the measure He metes out to me is of mercy or of justice," for the righteous will rejoice even when dealt with by the measure of justice. Since it is man's nature to rejoice more when treated with mercy, Isaiah therefore stressed the term for "rejoicing" by repetition: *sos asis,* [which is translated, *I will greatly rejoice*].

One is duty-bound to contemplate and to be ever mindful of his great obligation to love the Holy One, blessed be He. This is all the more true because He was the first to love Israel with a great love.

---

(21) Being that the word *m'odecha* is etymologically a difficult expression, the Mishnah explains it on the basis of the word *m'od* (muchness, abundance), a synonym for wealth, since a person ever desires to have more of it. Accordingly, the verse is bidding us that our love of G-d should supersede our desire for money. Hence, a person is obligated to spend his wealth in order to avoid violating a prohibition of the Torah (Tosafoth Anshei Sheim, Berachoth 9:5, and Orach Chayim 656).   (22) Additionally, the Mishnah explains the word *m'odecha* as being based upon the word *midah* (measure), meaning to say: "Love G-d for whichever measure He bestows upon you, whether by the attribute of justice or of mercy."   (23) In the language of Maimonides: "In the abounding love of G-d enjoined upon us, we are obligated that even in ill fortune we are to thank and praise Him with joy" (Mishneh Torah, *Hilchoth Berachoth* 10:3).   (24) Psalms 101:1.   (25) *Ibid.*, 56:11. The two Divine Names indicate the Divine attributes of justice and mercy respectively. See Note 10 above.   (26) Isaiah 61:10.

Thus, Scripture metaphorically speaks of His love for Israel in terms of the love of a man and his wife, as it is written, *And I will betroth thee unto Me forever.*[27] It is further stated, *For thy Maker is thy husband.*[28]

Because of His abundant love for us, we do not find any [mention of] punishment or chastisement of Israel throughout all of the books of the prophets without an accompanying consolation. Even in the passages of chastisement themselves, we find that the very language [of rebuke] includes consolation. An example of this is found in the words of Hosea, where it is written, *Call her name 'Lo-ruchamah' (She that hath not obtained compassion), for I will no more have compassion upon the House of Israel, that 'naso esa' (I should in any wise pardon) them.*[29] The words *naso esa* convey a sense of "uprooting" and "cutting off," as in the verse, *Pharaoh 'yisa' (will lift up) thy head from off thee.*[30] Yet, in the words *naso esa,* there is a hint of consolation, for the words are also an expression of forgiveness. Thus, Yonathan [ben Uziel] rendered it, "But if they will repent, I will pardon them."

Because of His abundant love for Israel, He confined His Glory to the space between the two cherubim [on the Ark of Testimony and He spoke to Moses therefrom]. This is the purport of the interpretation of our Rabbis of blessed memory,[31] "When our love was strong, we found sufficient room to sleep together on the broadside of a sword." Moreover, because of His abundant love for [the people of] Israel, He has never wanted to exchange them for another nation. Thus, the Rabbis expounded:[32] "[When G-d told Hosea that Israel had sinned],

---

(27) Hosea 2:21. (28) Isaiah 54:5. (29) Hosea 1:6. (30) Genesis 40:19. (31) Sanhedrin 7a. — "When our love was strong" is a reference to the Tabernacle in the wilderness, which in spite of its limited space G-d confined His Glory to the space between the two cherubim from where He spoke to Moses (Exodus 25:22). But in the spacious structure of the Sanctuary which Solomon built, we find no such case of G-d speaking to any prophet from between the two cherubim. Instead His Glory filled the entire House, and later on when Israel had sinned the Sanctuary was destroyed (Maharsha). (32) Pesachim 87a.

the prophet said to Him, 'Then exchange them for another nation.'
G-d answered, 'I have already sworn not to do so.' " Thus, it is written,
I have loved you, saith the Eternal,[33] upon which the Rabbis commented,[34] "The nations cannot nullify this love," nor can they quench
it, as it is said, *Many waters cannot quench the love.*[35] The expression
many waters refers to the many nations which cannot quench G-d's
love for Israel. Since G-d's love for us is so strong, we are bound to love
Him. Therefore, Moses our teacher charged us, *And thou shalt love
the Eternal thy G-d.*[1]

Although the quality of loving [G-d] is indeed great, that of desiring
[Him] is even greater. In the case of love, one can occasionally forget
the object of his love when he is preoccupied with other matters, but
this is not so in the case of desire which is all-consuming even when the
individual is asleep, and sees the object of his desire in a dream. In
order to emphasize the merit of desiring [G-d], David compared his
longing for G-d, praised be He, to that of a person, thirsty for water.
Thus, he exclaims, *My soul thirsteth for Thee, my flesh longeth for
Thee, in a dry and weary land, where no water is,*[36] thereby comparing
his desire for G-d to the thirst of one who longs for water in the
wilderness. He states, *my flesh longeth for Thee,* for all of his senses
have been numbed, and he can concentrate only upon his desire for
water. Thus, he referred to *a dry and weary land,* for there in addition
to his weariness, it is [naturally] more difficult to satisfy his thirst. To
further accentuate the superiority of desire over that of love, the
psalmist said, *Because he hath 'chashak' (desired* or *clung affectionate-
ly to) Me, therefore will I deliver him.*[37] He did not say, "Because he
hath loved Me," but rather, *Because he hath 'chashak' Me,* thus
instructing us that one who truly knows His Name, blessed be He, and
clings fast to Him will merit eternal life.

(33) Malachi 1:2. (34) Shir Hashirim Rabbah 8:7. (35) Song of Songs
8:7. (36) Psalms 63:2. (37) *Ibid.,* 91:14.

The Song of Songs is devoted to this theme of desire, as it begins, *Let Him kiss me with the kisses of His mouth.*[38] Our Rabbis said,[39] "All of the writings of Scripture are holy, but the Song of Songs is the holy of holies," for man's desired goal is to thoughtfully cleave to [G-d], the Holy of Holies, which is the theme of this book. This was the achievement attained by Moses our teacher, who expired with a Divine Kiss. The Sages explained,[40] "[The verse], *And Moses the servant of the Eternal died there in the land of Moab by the mouth of the Eternal,*[41] teaches us that he expired with a Divine Kiss." [This means that he died] without experiencing the pang of death or the destructive power of the angel of death. Rabbeinu Hakadosh[42] passed away in a similar manner, which prompted the Rabbis to say in Tractate Kethuboth,[43] "When Rabbi[42] died, sanctity was voided." In other words, even priests, [who are normally required to remain undefiled by a corpse], were able to participate in his burial, for his death was through the Divine Kiss and not through the angel of death. Priests could therefore be engaged in his burial without becoming defiled because only the angel of death can cause a corpse to convey impurity. For this reason, the Gaonim[44] instituted the custom that anyone who enters a room containing a corpse must wash his hands in order to be cleansed of the

(38) Song of Songs 1:2. (39) Yadayim 3:5. (40) Baba Bathra 17a. (41) Deuteronomy 34:5. (42) Rabbeinu Hakadosh, which means "Our Holy Teacher," refers to Rabbi Yehudah Hanasi (Prince of the Sanhedrin) who is often called simply "Rabbi." His immortal contribution to Torah was his redaction of the Mishnah into its present form, which is the basis of the Talmud. (43) Kethuboth 103b. (44) Gaon, which means Excellency, was the title accorded to each of the spiritual leaders of the Torah academies at Sura and Pumbeditha in Babylon. The Gaonic period, which followed the Talmudic era [that ended in the year 500 Common Era] continued for approximately five hundred years, by which time the Jewish communities in northern Africa and western Europe had established centers of Torah study in their own countries. These locals centers, from which came forth authoritative decisions in Torah matters, ultimately supplanted the great Babylonian academies as the focal points of authority in Jewish religious life.

resulting impurity.[45] However, when one expires with a Divine Kiss, his body remains pure and his soul is pure. Happy is he who merits this kind of death and this manner of parting of body and soul. It is the lot of those who are truly worthy and who are satisfied with the goodness of the Holy One, blessed be He, as it is said, *Happy is the man whom Thou choosest, and bringest near, that he may dwell in Thy courts; may we be satisfied with the goodness of Thy house, the holy place of Thy temple.*[46]

(45) It should be noted that the method of purification by washing the hands mentioned here is quite distinct from the procedure requiring the ashes of the Red Heifer. See Numbers 39:1-22. This procedure is unavailable today, since we have none of these ashes. According to our belief, the ashes of the Red Heifer will be revealed to us at the time of the future and complete Redemption, which we pray, will speedily occur.   (46) Psalms 65:5.

אורחים

Hospitality

> *Hospitality springs from the virtue of compassion, which is one of the attributes of G-d / Our patriarch Abraham was the first to adopt and practice this beneficent deed / Whoever cultivates this virtue will merit life in the World to Come, and in this world he will be rewarded with children, as was Abraham / Whoever consistently practices hospitality is praiseworthy / Our Rabbis spoke at length about the great importance of hospitality / The prophet Isaiah urged us to practice this virtue which is highly valued by G-d, and assured us that whoever adheres to it will be amply recompensed in both this world and the World to Come.*

Hospitality

AND HE [ABRAHAM] PLANTED AN "EISHEL" (AN INN) IN
BEER-SHEBA, AND CALLED THERE ON THE NAME OF
THE ETERNAL, THE EVERLASTING G-D.[1]

Hospitality is a mighty virtue. It stems from the characteristic of
compassion, which is one of the attributes of the Holy One, blessed be
He, Who feeds and sustains all of His creatures. Our patriarch
Abraham was the first to consistently practice [hospitality], as it is said,
For I have known him, that he will command his children, etc., *that
they will keep the way of the Eternal, to do 'tz'dakah' (charity,
righteousness) and justice.*[2] Abraham personified compassion, and so
we find in the Yerushalmi:[3] *"And he* [Abraham] *kept My charge.*[4]
What is meant by *My charge?* The Attribute of Compassion said,

---

(1) Genesis 21:33. The duty to love G-d, as explained in the preceding theme, leads
one to the love of man, which besides its many attributes of charity and kindliness expresses itself in welcoming wayfarers to one's home and offering them food and lodging. It was Abraham who first taught the world this virtue, and our author chose the
verse which first mentions it. (2) *Ibid.,* 18:19. As interpreted in the Midrash
(Bereshith Rabbah 49:4) Abraham would begin with charity and end with justice.
How so? After the wayfarer had dined, Abraham would bid him to thank G-d. If he
refused, he demanded to be paid in items that are unavailable in the desert, such as
meat and wine. Being unable to comply, the wayfarer would then declare, "Blessed is
the Eternal G-d of whose bounty we have eaten." Hence Scripture writes here first
tz'dakah (charity) and then justice. (3) This quotation is not found in our editions of
the Talmud Yerushalmi, but in Sefer Habahir, 191 (Margoliuth
edition). (4) Genesis 26:5. The verse is part of a passage in which G-d, speaking to
Isaac, refers to the virtues of his father, whose merits will be remembered by G-d and
ascribed to his descendants.

'While Abraham lived in this world, I did not have to do My work, for Abraham stood in My place and kept *My charge.*"

Our Rabbis of blessed memory taught that Abraham would go in search of wayfarers and bring them into his house. Thus, they said in the Midrash:[5] "Abraham's house had four entrances, one for each of the four directions of the world. Whoever entered one side left through a different side so that he would not suffer embarrassment of those passing on the road. Moreover, Abraham would go searching for the wayfarers and would run to meet them, as it is said, *and when he saw them, he ran to meet them.*[6] Scripture states of Abraham, *There is a man that spends, and yet grows richer.*"[7] For this reason, the verse, [*And he planted an 'eishel,'* etc.],[1] informs us that in Beer-sheba, where he lived, Abraham was heedful of this virtue and sustained wayfarers. The Rabbis of blessed memory interpreted[8] the word *eishel* as an acronym devised from three words: *achilah* (eating), *sh'thiyah* (drinking), and *l'vayah* (escorting). In Midrash Tehillim,[9] the Rabbis expounded: "*Who has roused one from the east, at whose steps righteousness was called forth?*[10] The nations of the world were sluggish in coming under the wings of the Divine Presence, but it was Abraham who roused them, as it says, *Who has roused one from the east.*" However, not only did [Abraham bestir the nations to recognize the existence of G-d], but he also awoke in them the need for charity, which lay dormant until Abraham erected an inn.

The word *eishel* literally denotes a tree, which explains why the Torah says, *and he planted an 'eishel.'* By interpreting the word *eishel* as an acronym [representing eating, drinking, and escorting, as above], the Rabbis intended to suggest that the mighty virtue of hospitality is analogous to a fruit-bearing tree, for by means of

---

(5) Midrash Tehillim, 110. (6) Genesis 18:2. (7) Proverbs 11:24. If one devotes his wealth to charitable causes, he will be bountifully rewarded for his magnanimity. The Midrash properly interprets the verse with reference to Abraham. (8) Midrash Tehillim, 37:1. This interpretation is also found in Rabbeinu Bachya's commentary on Genesis 21:33. (9) Midrash Tehillim, 110. (10) Isaiah 41:2.

[hospitality], Abraham planted a tree for himself in heaven which would produce for him fruits [of reward]. Throughout the entire Torah, the expression *and he planted* occurs in only two instances: *and he planted an 'eishel,'*[1] *and the Eternal G-d planted a garden in Eden.*[11] This intimates that one who consistently practices this virtue will merit *Gan Eden*[12] [in the World to Come]. All of the commandments are like trees which produce various kinds of fruit. The trunk, however, which is the principal part of the tree endures. The commandments too produce fruits of reward in this world, but the principal reward remains reserved for the World to Come.

In my opinion, the verse, *He who keepeth the fig tree shall eat the fruit thereof, and he that waiteth on his master shall be honored,*[13] can be interpreted as follows: Besides his wages, the worker who guards the fig tree has the additional satisfaction of being able to eat its fruits. Similarly, *he that waiteth on his master shall be honored.* There are kings who surround themselves with guards not out of any fear for their personal safety, but out of respect for their royal status, and the guardsmen, besides earning their regular wages for protecting the monarch, enjoy the additional benefit of having other people respect and even fear them because of their close connection to the king. Therefore, Solomon devised this analogy of the commandments of the Torah [and the faithful watchmen], for when one observes the commandments, not only is his principal reward set aside for him in the World to Come, but he enjoys the fruits of [his reward] in this world. We thus learn that in this world, some of the commandments[14] of the

---

(11) Genesis 2:8. (12) *Gan Eden,* which literally means "the Garden of Eden," is the paradise of the hereafter in which the righteous will be rewarded after death for their good deeds in their lifetime. Gehenna serves as the place of punishment for the wicked. (13) Proverbs 27:18. (14) These commandments are: honoring one's father and mother, practicing charity, timely attendance at the house of study in the morning and evening, extending hospitality to wayfarers, visiting the sick, dowering the bride, escorting the dead to the grave, being devoted in prayer, and making peace

Torah entail varying fruits [of reward]. For [the observance of] some commandments, the reward is longevity, for others riches and honor, and for others children.

We find that the reward for hospitality is children, for this was the case with Abraham and similarly with the Shunamite woman, who offered hospitality to Elisha the prophet, as it is written, *Let us make, I pray thee, a little chamber on the roof, and let us set for him there a bed, and a table, and a chair, and a candlestick.*[15] She was a notable and wise woman, as it is written, *and there was a great woman,*[16] meaning [that she was] notable. Her words were uttered in wisdom and premeditation. [In the verse above] she first mentioned *a bed*, for a person who is weary from his travel wishes to lie down and rest more than [he wants] food. She spoke next of the table and chair and [mentioned that] at sundown, they would light the candlestick. [Thus, she arranged for Elisha's needs in the proper sequence of occurrences.] She said to her husband about Elisha, *this is a holy man of G-d that passeth by us 'tamid' (continually).*[17] "Rabbi Yosei the son of Rabbi Chanina commented in the name of Rabbi Eliezer ben Yaakov, 'He who receives a learned scholar as a guest in his home and invites him to partake of his wealth is [considered] as if he brought the *t'midim* (daily whole burnt-offerings) [upon the altar in the Sanctuary].' "[18] Because of this virtue, the Shunamite woman merited a son, who [later] became Habakkuk the prophet. There is an allusion to this in the Scriptural passage.[19]

between man and his fellow. The study of Torah, however, is equal to all of these (based on Peiah 1:1). (15) II Kings 4:10. The Shunamite woman said these words to her husband, suggesting that they offer the hospitality of their home to Elisha. (16) *Ibid.*, Verse 8. (17) *Ibid.*, Verse 9. (18) Berachoth 10b. (19) The allusion is explained in accordance with a text in the Zohar (*Beshalach* 44b-45a), which bases it upon the expression of the prophet when he promised her *thou shalt 'chobeketh' (embrace) a son* (II Kings 4:16). The word *chobeketh*—instead of *chabuk*—suggests the name of Habakkuk, one of the prophets, whose words are recorded in the Twelve Minor Prophets. See further on this point, in my Hebrew edition, pp. 37-38.

One who consistently practices this principle of hospitality and meticulously honors and serves his guests is worthy of praise and merits great reward. In Tractate Baba Metzia,[20] the Rabbis commented with regard to Abraham: "Whatever Abraham himself did for the ministering angels [who appeared in the guise of men], the Holy One Himself, blessed be He, did for his descendants, and whatever Abraham did for the angels through a messenger, G-d did for Abraham's seed through a messenger. Thus, it is written, *And Abraham ran unto the herd,*[21] and of the Holy One, blessed be He, it is said, *And He brought across quails from the sea.*[22] Of Abraham it is written, *And he took curd and milk,*[23] and of G-d it is stated, *Behold, I will cause to rain bread from heaven for you.*[24] Of Abraham it is written, *and he stood by them,*[23] and of G-d it is said, *Behold, I will stand there before thee upon the rock in Horeb.*[25] Of Abraham it is written, *and Abraham went with them to bring them on the way,*[26] and of G-d it is stated, *And the Eternal went before them by day,*[27] [*the Eternal . . .* Himself], not by means of a messenger. It is written that Abraham said, *Let now a little water be brought,*[28] and it is stated that G-d said to Moses, *and thou shalt smite the rock, and there shall come water out of it.*"[25]

Hospitality is indeed great. Our Rabbis commented about it at the end of Tractate Berachoth[29] as follows: "Rabbi Yosei began his speech in honor of hospitality and said, 'It is written, *Thou shalt not abhor an Edomite, for he is thy brother; thou shalt not abhor an Egyptian, because thou wast a stranger in his land.*[30] We deduce *a fortiori:* If the Egyptians were so greatly [rewarded, as the above verse indicates], although they received the Israelites only for their own benefit—as it is said, *And if thou* [Joseph] *knowest any able men among them, then*

---

(20) Baba Metzia 86b.   (21) Genesis 18:7.   (22) Numbers 11:31.   (23) Genesis 18:8.   (24) Exodus 16:4.   (25) *Ibid.,* 17:6.   (26) Genesis 18:16.   (27) Exodus 13:21.   (28) Genesis 18:4.   (29) Berachoth 63b. The occasion was an assembly of the Sages in the academy at Jabneh. While other Sages directed their opening words "in honor of the Torah," Rabbi Yosei and some scholars spoke first "in honor of hospitality."   (30) Deuteronomy 23:8.

make them rulers over my cattle[31] — then how much greater will the reward be for one who [selflessly] receives learned scholars in his home!' Rabbi Nechemyah began his speech in honor of hospitality and said, 'It is written, *And Saul said unto the Kenites: Go, depart, get you down from the Amalekites, lest I destroy you with them.*[32] If Jethro was so greatly [rewarded] although he received Moses only for his own benefit,[33] then how much greater will the reward be for one who [selflessly] receives a learned scholar in his home!' Rabbi Eleazar the son of Rabbi Yosei the Galilean began his speech in honor of hospitality and said, 'It is written, *And the Eternal blessed Obed-edom and all his house.*[34] If Obed-edom was so rewarded although he only swept and sprinkled [the dusty floors] before the Ark of G-d, then how much more will the reward be for one who receives a learned scholar in his home and supports him!' "

The Sages similarly commented in Chapter *Cheilek:*[35] "A little refreshment plays an essential role, for its refusal estranged two families [Ammon and Moab] from Israel, as it is said, *Because they met you not with bread and with water.*[36] Rabbi Yochanan said, 'A little of refreshment alienated relatives and brought near those who were distant.' It alienated relatives as in the case of Ammon and Moab.[37] It

(31) Genesis 47:6. (32) I Samuel 15:6. The Kenites were descendants of Jethro, who offered Moses hospitality when the latter fled from Pharaoh. Moses married Zipporah, one of Jethro's daughters. (33) In other words, Jethro's motive in showing hospitality to Moses was that the latter might marry one of his daughters. (34) II Samuel 6:11. Obed-edom provided hospitality for the Ark of G-d for three months. (35) The chapter in Tractate Sanhedrin begins, "All [of the people of] Israel have a portion in the World to Come." The passage quoted in the text here is on pp. 103b-104a. (36) Deuteronomy 23:5. Because of this lack of hospitality, Scripture prohibited an Ammonite or Moabite proselyte from marrying an Israelite woman. The prohibition does not extend to a female Ammonite or Moabite proselyte, such as Ruth the Moabitess who married Boaz, a member of the Sanhedrin, a forebear of David. Females were excluded from the ban because it was not the way of women to go out and meet the wandering tribes with bread and water. Hence, no blame can be attributed to them in this matter. (37) Ammon and Moab were related to Israel through their ancestor Lot, a nephew of Abraham. See preceding note.

brought near those who were distant as in the case of Jethro, for Rabbi
Yochanan said, 'In reward for Jethro's offer of hospitality to Moses,[38]
Jethro's descendants merited membership in [Israel's highest court,
which convened in] the Chamber of Hewn Stones [in the Holy
Temple].' Moreover, the practice of hospitality by the wicked averts
the punishment [due them for their sins] as in the case of Micah.[39] The
Sages said, 'Why did the Rabbis of the Mishnah not include Micah
among Jeroboam[40] and his companions who have no share in the
World to Come? It is because his bread was accessible to wayfarers.' "
[In Chapter *Cheilek*], the Sages further stated:[41] "When the smoke rising from the pyre [of the Tabernacle at Shiloh] mingled with the
smoke of the incense burned before the idol of Micah, the ministering
angels wanted to thrust Micah down. The Holy One, blessed be He,
said to them, 'Let him go, for his bread is accessible to wayfarers.' "
You can thus see the importance of a small quantity of refreshment,
for it averts the punishment due the wicked.

The prophet Isaiah exhorted us concerning this principle of
hospitality. He stated that it is highly valued by G-d, blessed be He,
and that one who consistently practices it inherits two worlds: this
world and the World to Come. It is said, *Is it not to deal thy bread to
the hungry, and that thou bring the poor that are cast out to thy
house? When thou seest the naked, that thou cover him, and that thou
hide not thyself from thine own flesh?*[42] He specifies *thy bread* [rather

---

(38) See Exodus 2:20.   (39) Micah dwelt in the hills of Ephraim. His house was
always open to wayfarers, a redeeming feature which saved him from punishment for
erecting an idolatrous image. See Judges Chapter 17.   (40) Jeroboam was the first
ruler of the Kingdom of Israel, which was established when most of the nation broke
their allegiance to the House of David. Jeroboam prohibited his subjects from making
the three annual pilgrimages to Jerusalem, which remained the capital of Judah and
the seat of the House of David. He also introduced idolatry into his kingdom. To his
eternal disgrace, he is known as "a sinner who also caused the multitude to
sin."   (41) Sanhedrin 103b.   (42) Isaiah 58:7. The prophet chastises those who
spend their day of fasting just perfunctorily and think that they have done their duty.
"But," asks he, "is this not the true function of the day, *to deal thy bread,*

than " of thy bread," which would indicate that you have an abundance thereof], to teach you that although you have but one piece of bread, you should share it with whoever asks you for it. *And that thou bring the poor that are cast out to thy house* . . . .[42] This teaches that if the poor do not come to your house, you are obligated to seek them and bring them into your home, for this is what Abraham did, as it is written, *and when he saw them, he ran to meet them.*[6] *When thou seest the naked, that thou cover him* . . . .[42] In other words, if among the poor you find one who is naked, you must clothe him, for you are bound to walk in the ways of G-d, blessed be He, as it is said, *and thou shalt walk in His ways.*[43] Just as He clothes the naked—as it is said, *And the Eternal G-d made for Adam and for his wife garments of skins, and clothed them*[44]—so should you clothe them. Job also mentioned this theme: *If I have seen any wanderer in want of clothing, or that the needy had no covering; If his loins have not blessed me, and if he were not warmed with the fleece of my sheep.*[45] . . . *And that thou hide not thyself from thine own flesh?*[42] This teaches that relatives take precedence over other poor. Our Rabbis interpreted it thus:[46] *"The poor with thee.*[47] [If you must choose between supporting] the poor of your city and the poor of another city, the poor of your own city have priority, for it says, *with thee,* meaning those who are physically near you as well as those who are related to you." The Rabbis further explained[48] that paternal relatives take precedence over maternal kin.

If you will observe these practices, *then shalt thou call, and the Eternal will answer.*[49] That is, He will answer immediately and will not avoid helping you just as you did not avoid helping your own kin. *And the Eternal will guide thee continually, and satisfy thy soul in*

etc.?"—This, incidentally, is the Reading from the Prophets on the Day of Atonement. (43) Deuteronomy 28:9. See the text of *Emunah* (Faith) at Note 49 for full elaboration of this theme. (44) Genesis 3:21. (45) Job 31:19-20. In defending the righteousness of his life, Job pointed to his consideration for the needs of the poor. (46) Baba Metzia 71a. (47) Exodus 22:24. (48) Sifre, *R'eih,* 116. (49) Isaiah 58:9.

draught,[50] meaning that the Holy One, blessed be He, will fulfill and gratify your thirsty soul by satisfying it with the clear and splendid Higher Light[51] and will give you *free access among those that stand by*[52] who exist forever. *And He 'yachalitz' (will strengthen) thy bones.*[50] This refers to the tranquil rest of the bones in the grave. Our Rabbis commented:[53] "Rabbi Eliezer ben Yaakov said, 'This is the best of the blessings.' "[54] Another interpretation of the word *yachalitz* is that "He will deliver you from the punishment of Gehenna."[12] When one is saved from that punishment, he can rest and be invigorated, as one is refreshed in *Gan Eden*.[12] This is the meaning of the conclusion of the verse, *And thou shalt be like a watered garden, and like a spring of water, whose waters fail not.*[50]

---

(50) *Ibid.*, Verse 11.   (51) In the World to Come when body and soul will be reunited, the manner of how the body will sustain itself will be provided through this Higher Divine Light. This will be enhanced by the Glory of the Divine Presence and one's lofty perception of G-d (see Ramban, Writings and Discourses, Vol. II, pp. 531-534, for a full discussion of the subject).   (52) Zechariah 3:7. The phrase refers to the ministering angels.   (53) Yebamoth 102b.   (54) This is the best of all the preceding blessings mentioned by the prophet, for they concern conditions outside of the body while this blessing is directed to the inner health and well-being of the body itself (Maharsha *ibid.*).

אבל

Mourning

Part One

Visiting a house of mourning induces humility, one of the chief principles in the worship of G-d, while going to a house of feasting induces pride / If Adam had not sinned, he would have lived forever / An intelligent person must regard worldly activities as essentially vain; the only worthwhile activities are studying Torah, giving charity, and performing good deeds / The Torah commands that one should mourn over his dead, and this constitutes a consummate service of G-d. The obligation to mourn is especially great at the death of a learned person / This world is the scene of trial and tribulation, and death is better for the soul than the day of birth.

Mourning

IT IS BETTER TO GO TO THE HOUSE OF MOURNING,
THAN TO GO TO THE HOUSE OF FEASTING; FOR THAT IS
THE END OF ALL MEN, AND THE LIVING WILL LAY IT TO
HIS HEART.[1]

The principal intent of this verse is to exhort man to regard the affairs of this world as utter vanity. He should not make them his mainstay, but he should instead contemplate his final lot and make his nature yield to the service of G-d. It is known that [visiting] a house of mourning induces humility, one of the chief principles in the worship of G-d. When one sees how the generations pass on and how his friends and acquaintances depart from him, he fearfully derives instruction [from these experiences] and his *uncircumcised heart is then humbled.*[2] This is not so in a house of feasting, which induces pride and causes one to forget what is of primary importance in life. This is akin to the statement, *And thy heart be lifted up, and thou forget the Eternal thy G-d.*[3] With this end in mind, our Rabbis of blessed

(1) Ecclesiastes 7:2. Going to a house of mourning is an act of lovingkindness to the bereaved relatives who find consolation in another person sharing their sorrow, and is a matter of respect for the dead. The subject is thus a logical sequence to that of *Orchim* (Hospitality), previously discussed, which deals with the theme of lovingkindness to the living, while the present discussion deals with the lovingkindness to the living and the dead. The subject of Mourning is broadened by the author to include the function of a eulogy (Part Two), the nature and function of the soul (Part Three), and the national mourning over the destruction of the two Temples (Part Four). (2) Leviticus 26:41. (3) Deuteronomy 8:14.

memory warned man,[4] "Know whence you came and whither you are going."

Death was decreed upon Adam, the first man and progenitor of all mankind, and no one can escape it. Adam died because of his sin, and were it not for that, he would have lived forever. Naturally, if the trunk of the tree suffers loss, the leaves must share therein, [and so, Adam's descendants are subject to the same destiny]. This decree [of universal death] applies not only to the righteous who sin [occasionally], but also to the thoroughly righteous who have never sinned. The Sages commented[5] "Four persons died through the instigation of the serpent." That is, they died not through any sin of their own, but only through the sin of the ancient serpent [which incited Eve to transgress the will of G-d. Eve, in turn, led Adam to sin, and consequently, the punishment of death was decreed upon Adam and his seed. The four persons enumerated by the Sages are]:[5] "Benjamin the son of Jacob, Amram the father of Moses, Jesse the father of David, and Chileab[6] the son of David." Enoch[7] and Elijah[8] were completely spared death so that [by their example], they can attest that were it not for Adam's sin, man would have lived forever as they do, for indeed, they did not sin and they live forever [on high].

Every intelligent person, therefore, should contemplate the day of death. He should be mindful that the earth and all it holds, including his wealth and all his power, are utter vanity. Solomon, who ruled over the entire world and who was superior to all by virtue of the gift of wisdom which was given to him, unqualifiedly declared the absolute

(4) Aboth 3:1. On Aboth, see *Emunah* (Faith), Note 10. (5) Baba Bathra 17a. (6) II Samuel 3:3. Chileab was the son of Abigail, whom David married after the death of her husband Nabal. Chileab's piety was above reproach, and among all of David's attendants, he was renowned for his outstanding scholarship. (Berachoth 4a). (7) Genesis 5:24. Enoch is considered one of the foremost righteous persons of all times. Scripture, *ibid.*, uniquely describes his end in this world: *and he was no more, for G-d took him.* This is understood to mean that he was completely spared death. (8) II Kings 2:11.

vanity of the world. This is expressed in the opening statement of his book [Ecclesiastes]: *Vanity of vanities, saith Koheleth, vanity of vanities, all is vanity.*[9] His father David had also written on the theme that wealth is not the means of obtaining security. He said, *For when he dieth he shall carry nothing away, his wealth shall not descend after him.*[10]

Our Rabbis explained this [idea of the vanity of materialism] by means of the following parable:[11] "A very hungry fox entered an enclosed vineyard through a small opening in its fence and satiated himself with the grapes. When he returned to the same hole in the fence, however, he could not pass through it. [In order to leave], he had to starve himself into the same condition in which he had been when he entered." The same is true of man and [his quest for] the pleasures of this world and the abundance of silver and gold [he wishes to possess]. All of it will remain here [upon his death]; he will carry nothing away with him. The only things that will precede him [after death to intercede on his behalf before the heavenly tribunal] are his adherence to Torah, his good deeds, and the giving of charity. He will then be rewarded commensurately [in the hereafter] according to his own deeds. [In this world], physical death equalizes rich and poor. In the World of Souls, however, [no two are alike, for] reward is granted to each individual in accordance with the measure of his good deeds. This is analogous to a king and his legions who enter a city through the same gate, but the lodgings [of the king and his troops] vary in accordance with each one's station.

In the Chapters of Rabbi Eliezer,[12] the Rabbis interpreted this matter as follows: "A person has three friends in his lifetime: his wife and children, his money, and his good deeds. At the time of his departure

---

(9) Ecclesiastes 1:2.   (10) Psalms 49:18. No person will consent to give up his life in order to have wealth. This shows that the aim in life is not the accumulation of wealth.   (11) Koheleth Rabbah 5:21.   (12) Pirkei d'Rabbi Eliezer, 34.

from this world, he calls his wife and children and members of his household and urges them to save him from the evil decree of death. They answer him, 'Have you not heard that there is *no power over the day of death?*[13] Is it not written, *No man can by any means redeem his brother, nor give to G-d a ransom for him?*[14] He then turns to his money with the same request [for salvation], but the answer comes back, 'Have you not heard that *riches profit not in the day of wrath?*[15] Finally, he turns to his good deeds, and they say to him, 'We will even precede you [to plead on your behalf before the heavenly tribunal], as it is said, *But charity delivereth from death.*[15] It is further written, *And thy charity shall go before thee.'* "[16]

Since the main goal in life is to humble the heart in the service of G-d, Solomon explained, *It is better to go to the house of mourning,* etc.,[1] because [visiting] a house of mourning induces humility. He further stated, *The heart of the wise is in the house of mourning.*[17] He specified, *and the living will lay it to his heart,*[1] rather than "and man will lay it to his heart," for his intent was to state that one who thinks that he will live forever should instead carefully consider the day of death. He should resist his passions and repent completely so that when the day of his death will arrive, he will have been set aright. Thus, the Rabbis said,[18] "Repent one day before your death. But does a man know when he will die? Rather, he should repent each day lest he die on the morrow. Hence, his entire life will be in order." The Rabbis devised a parable on this theme:[19] "A sailor's wife, whose husband was away on a long voyage, used to adorn herself daily. When her neighbors asked her, 'Is not your husband away at sea? Why do you adorn yourself?' She answered, 'Perhaps a favorable wind will quickly bring his ship back, and he will find me adorned.' " Similarly,

(13) Ecclesiastes 8:8. No one, not even the greatest king, has it in his power to postpone the day of death willed by G-d. (14) Psalms 49:8. (15) Proverbs 11:4. (16) Isaiah 58:8. (17) Ecclesiastes 7:4. (18) Shabbath 153a. (19) Koheleth Rabbah 9:6.

Solomon said, *Let thy garments be always white, and let thy head lack no oil.*[20] The "white garments" allude to the purity of soul through repentance, and "the oil" refers to good deeds.

The Torah commands that one should mourn the death of his relative[21] because mourning, significant in itself, affects one's devotion to Divine service. Our Rabbis commented:[22] "Rabbi Yehoshua ben Levi said in the name of Bar Kappara, 'When one sheds tears over the demise of a worthy person, the Holy One, blessed be He, [lovingly] counts those tears and stores them among His treasures, as it is said, *Thou hast counted my wanderings; put Thou my tears into Thy bottle! Are they not in Thy book?*' "[23] This metaphor reflects the favor [with which G-d regards] the tears which are stored away in His treasure house. The expression "a worthy person" signifies a scholar who possesses both erudition and fear of Heaven. Upon his passing, a very great obligation rests [upon the living] to grieve and mourn over him. In their gradations of people, the Sages of blessed memory said,[24] "A scholar takes precedence over a king." They similarly said,[24] "A scholar who has died is irreplaceable, but when a king dies, [his loss is less grievous, for] all Israelites are suited for royalty, [and a replacement can be found]!" This thought is motivated by Scripture's statement, *But wisdom, where shall it be found?*[25] "*For there is a mine for silver, and a place for gold which they refine. Iron is taken out of the dust, and brass is molten out of the stone.*[26] When these metals are lost, there are others to replace them. However, when a scholar dies, who will bring us his replacement? Who will provide us with his equivalent? And who will be his equal?"[27]

---

(20) Ecclesiastes 9:8.   (21) See my translation of Maimonides' "The Commandments," Vol. I, pp. 47-49.   (22) Shabbath 105b.   (23) Psalms 56:9. Since crying [except in prayer] is permissible only for one who is deceased, the verse . . . *put Thou my tears,* etc., can only refer to one who sheds tears of anguish over the passing of a worthy person (Maharsha, Shabbath 105b).   (24) Horayoth 13a.   (25) Job 28:12.   (26) *Ibid.,* Verses 1-2.   (27) Bereshith Rabbah 91:7.

Our Sages further commented:[28] "Who has a share in the World to Come? It is the one who is humble, polite, and meek of spirit, who bends his head when entering and leaving a house, who constantly toils in the study of Torah, and who does not ascribe credit to himself." Note that the Sages mentioned humility first, for it is the superlative virtue. Afterwards, enumerating the manifestations thereof in body and soul, they stated that [the one who has a share in the World to Come] is "polite," which means that he is forbearing in his dealings with other people, and that he is "meek of spirit," which means that he utterly avoids arrogance.

It is well known that the world is the scene of trial and tribulation in which it is determined whether man will walk in the path of the Creator or whether he *will turn* his *step out of the way.*[29] It is therefore incumbent upon each intelligent person to realize that just as he is born crying so does he leave the world crying. It was taught in the name of Rabbi Meir: When a person comes into the world his hands are clenched like fists, as if to say that the entire world is mine, for I will conquer it. But when he leaves the world his hands are opened wide, as if to say I take nothing of the world with me." We further find the following statement in Midrash Shmuel:[30] "A person is known by three names: the name given to him by his father and mother, the name he acquires by his actions, and the name with which he is endowed by the Book [of Creation].[31] Rabbi Yitzchak said we did not know which of these names is the most precious one until Solomon came and explained it by saying, *and the day of death [is better] than the day of one's birth.*[32] This can be understood through the following parable: Two ships were sailing on the ocean: one was entering the harbor and

---

(28) Sanhedrin 88b. (29) Job 31:7. (30) Midrash Shmuel, 30. (31) I.e., he may be endowed with some special natural gift or talent for which he becomes known. For example, he may be an outstanding singer, a prodigious craftsman, etc. In this sense "the Book [of Creation]" is thus a synonym for the creative powers which an individual is endowed with. (32) Ecclesiastes 7:1.

one was just going out to sea. When the one entering the harbor came in, no one was rejoicing over its successful voyage, but as the one going out to sea left, however, many people were rejoicing over its departure. A prudent individual who was there [in the harbor] said, 'The opposite should be the case. The ship entering the harbor should be a source of joy because it safely arrived from the dangers of the sea, but the one departing for the voyage should not be a source of joy because one does not know what may happen to it.' The same is true of a person's life. When he is born, all rejoice, and when he dies, all are in tears. Yet, at his birth, there is no reason to rejoice, for it is not known how his life will fare, and when he dies, his death should be a source of joy to all, for he has left the world in peace. You must therefore concede [the truth of Solomon's declaration that] *the day of death [is better] than the day of one's birth.* "[32] Thus far the Midrash.[30]

Death is the means by which one can acquire life in the World to Come. Therefore, the soul derives greater benefit from the day of death than from the day of birth, for birth may lead [the soul to a lifetime of] impurity and sin, while death facilitates [the soul's] acquisition of the Clear [Divine] Light [in the World of Souls]. All things return to their roots. The body returns to the element of earth from which it was taken, and the soul, which comes from above and is called *the lamp of the Eternal,*[33] returns to its [Divine] root and foundation. Thus, Solomon said, *And the dust returneth to the earth as it was, and the spirit returneth unto G-d Who gave it,*[34] and concerning the soul of the righteous, the prophet said, *and I will give thee access among these that stand by.*[35]

---

(33) Proverbs 20:27.   (34) Ecclesiastes 12:7.   (35) Zechariah 3:7. *These that stand by* refers to the ministering angels, among whom there is never any need for reclining or sitting. The prophet is thus assuring the righteous person that after death, his soul will be among the ministering angels.

Part Two

> *A cursory reading of the Book of Ecclesiastes may convey the impression that it is contrary to certain principles of the faith, but upon contemplation, the reader will find that it actually strengthens the faith / The philosophy of the Torah requires one to ascribe his success to G-d's mercy and his failures to his own shortcomings / The purpose of a eulogy / The world needs righteous people as it does the luminaries in the heavens / Israel's four unique characteristics.*

I TURNED ABOUT, AND SAW UNDER THE SUN, THAT THE RACE IS NOT TO THE SWIFT, NOR THE BATTLE TO THE STRONG, AND ALSO THE WISE HAVE NO BREAD, NOR YET THE MEN OF UNDERSTANDING RICHES, NOR YET MEN OF SKILL FAVOR; BUT TIME AND CHANCE WILL OVERTAKE THEM ALL.[36]

All of Solomon's words are of profound wisdom, the ultimate meaning of which is beyond the grasp of even the erudite. In fact, [scholarly] readers may consider them contrary to the faith, yet, they are the essence of the faith itself. Thus, our Sages said,[37] "The prophets and scholars [who compiled the Sacred Scriptures] wished to conceal Ecclesiastes [from the public]," for due to the profundity of its language, the book was likely to cause misapprehension of certain ideas. However, they did not conceal it because of its ending, which reads, *The end of the matter, all having been heard: fear G-d,* etc.[38] This ending undermines the standing of those who argue that the book is contrary to the faith. If they persist in their argument, [it would become evident that] they can be compared to a weak-eyed person who

(36) Ecclesiastes 9:11.　(37) Shabbath 30b.　(38) Ecclesiastes 12:13.

59

looks at the bright sun and insists that it is dim, failing to realize that his own [visual] shortcoming is the cause [of the erroneous perception].

Among the verses in Ecclesiastes which appear contrary to the faith is the one above.[36] It seems to state that everything is controlled by the stars, as it says, *but time and chance will overtake them all,* which means that everything is determined according to the vicissitudes of time. Nevertheless, the verse expresses the very essence of faith. The intent of its statement is that *the race is not to the swift, nor the battle to the strong,* etc.; the victory is given only to those who merit [success] and are therefore provided with the means of attaining [the desired goal in] these ventures. Thus, in this world, man's [degree of success] striving for the attainment of peace and prosperity is determined according to the merits of the individual.

The philosophy of the Torah requires one to ascribe the peace and prosperity enjoyed by other people to their merits or those of their ancestors, and his own peace and prosperity to the mercy of G-d, blessed be He. [He should] not ascribe his good fortune to the constellations or his own merits, for one should never regard himself as being worthy of being counted among the righteous.

The expression *I turned about*[36] indicates that Solomon originally thought that the race is indeed to the swift and the battle to the strong, for that is the natural law. However, after pondering the matter, he realized that it is not so. His statement, *[I turned about, and saw] under the sun,*[36] expresses the thought that all natural vicissitudes are under the sun [meaning: the earthly scene of man's activities] and not above it, whereas a man's reward for the fulfillment of the Torah and the commandments is stored away for him above the sun [i.e., in eternal life in the World to Come].

For this reason, David mentioned the subjects of Torah and the sun in one psalm.[39] In that psalm, he first mentioned the sun, saying, *In*

(39) Psalm 19.

them [the heavens] *hath He set a tent for the sun.*[40] Afterwards he stated, *The Law of the Eternal is perfect,*[41] in order to explain that the stature of Torah and the commandments and the merit therein are above the sun and exceed its grandeur. Similarly, in the prayers preceding the reading of the *Sh'ma,*[42] we first mention the creation of the luminaries, saying, "Blessed art Thou, O Eternal, Who createst the luminaries." Subsequently, we pray, "O G-d, enlighten our eyes in Thy Torah and make our hearts cleave to Thy commandments."[43]

Therefore, each sincere G-d-fearing person should concern himself with making the service of G-d his only activity. Such service necessitates that he contemplate his death, the date of which is unknown to him. Thus, the Sages said,[44] "Seven things are hidden from man: the day of his death, the day of relief from trouble, the depth of the law,[45] whether a certain project will succeed financially, the inner thoughts of his fellow man, when the Kingdom of the House of David will arise, and when the wicked government [of Rome] will fall." Since it has been established that worldly activities are utter vanity and that a person should devote himself only to Torah, repentance, and good deeds, one should ponder death, which is the ultimate of

(40) *Ibid.*, Verse 5. From the sun's "tent" or sphere of activity in the heavens, its benefits extend to the earth below. (41) *Ibid.*, Verse 8. (42) *Sh'ma (Hear) O Israel: The Eternal our G-d, the Eternal is One* is Israel's affirmation of faith in the morning and evening prayers. The entire reading of the *Sh'ma* consists of the recitation of three Scriptural passages: Deuteronomy 6:4-9 and 11: 13-21, and Numbers 16:37-41. The Sages ordained two benedictions to precede each reading of the *Sh'ma,* one to express our gratitude for G-d's creation of the luminaries and the nocturnal darkness, and one to thank G-d for giving us His Torah. (43) Rabbeinu Bachya's thought here is of wide significance. That the themes of the two prayers preceding the reading of the *Sh'ma* follow the design of Psalm 19 is not unique to this instance alone; the same principle of design applies throughout our prayers. In formulating the daily prayers for Israel, the Sages derived their inspiration from the Sacred Scriptures. Hence, our Prayer Book follows the word and spirit of the Bible. (44) Pesachim 54b. (45) Accordingly, when rendering a legal decision, one should patiently consider its possible implications and be sensitive to all its nuances (Maharsha, *ibid.*).

every man. Furthermore, one should rather go *to the house of mourn-ing, than to go to the house of feasting*[1] and should take heed to honor the living when eulogizing the deceased.[46] He will thereby turn his heart and mind away from the pleasures of this world and will think only of the service of G-d.

The question has been raised in the Gemara Sanhedrin[47] whether the delivery of a eulogy is in honor of the deceased or in honor of the living. [The Gemara asks], "What difference does it make [in either case? The answer is that the distinction between these alternatives becomes clear in situations] where the deceased left a wish that he should not be eulogized and [where it must be decided by the court] whether the heirs [can be forced] to pay the expense of the eulogy."[48] The question was finally resolved [in favor of the opinion] that a eulogy is in honor of the deceased.

The purpose of a eulogy is to recall the kindness of the deceased, his good deeds and noble character, the activities in which he was in-terested in his lifetime, and his family descent. An example [of such a eulogy] is: *Saul and Jonathan, the lovely and the pleasant in their lives, and even in their death they were not divided.*[49] The eulogy should be

(46) Further in the text, the author quotes sources which state that the eulogy is in honor of the deceased. His statement here perforce must be understood as intimating that the function of the eulogy is to make the living realize that the only worthwhile and enduring activity is the worship of G-d. To achieve this goal is "to honor the living." (47) Sanhedrin 46b. (48) If a eulogy is in honor of the deceased, then his wish not to be eulogized must be respected. Furthermore, if a eulogy is in honor of the deceased, the court can force his unwilling heirs to pay for a eulogy provided the deceased never expressed a wish to the contrary. (49) II Samuel 1:23. This was part of the eulogy delivered by David upon the deaths of Saul, King of Israel, and his son Jonathan, who fell together in battle against the Philistines. According to the Targum of Yonathan ben Uziel, the purport of the verse is to state that notwithstanding their having been informed of their tragic end in that battle, Saul and Jonathan still did not separate themselves from the people, but entered into battle with them against the

commensurate with the grief engendered by the loss, as it is said, *I am distressed for thee, my brother Jonathan,* [50] and it should correspond to the occasion, as it is said, *And the king lamented for Abner, and said, Should Abner die as an ignoble man dieth?* [51] The Sages, too, mentioned that the purpose of a eulogy is to recount the nobility of the decedent's character. Such was the case at the demise of Rabbi P'doth: [52] "The eulogist began by saying, 'This is as difficult a day for Israel as the day when the sun will set at noon, as it is said, *And it shall come to pass in that day, saith the Eternal G-d, that I will cause the sun to go down at noon, and I will darken the earth in the clear day.*' " [53]

The intention of the eulogy, then, is to transform the occasion into one of sincere Divine worship, for the deceased was a righteous man who was faithful to the way of G-d. He was imbued with a love for the Torah and good deeds, and in fulfilling the commandments, he served as the instrument of the pure soul. Thus, the Torah has ordained the commandment of mourning, and the Sages have cautioned us against being slothful about eulogizing a righteous person.

It is common knowledge that the righteous shield their generation [from punishment], and they are taken away because of the sins of the generation. Thus, during the forty years of Israel's sojourn in the wilderness, clouds of [Divine] glory were spread over Israel due to the

---

enemy. David eulogized their laudatory action, a worthy feature of their characters. (50) II Samuel 1:26. Jonathan's friendship for David is history's finest example of such a human relationship. Though Jonathan was heir to his father's crown, he forewent his right of accession and supported David because he realized that the latter's qualities were fitting for a king of Israel. When Jonathan died, David specifically mourned the loss of such a devoted friend. (51) II Samuel 3:33. Abner was the supreme commander of Saul's armies. After Saul's death, Abner was treacherously slain by Joab the son of Zeruia, the commander-in-chief of David's military forces. In his eulogy, of which the verse quoted here is part, David expressed his shock and grief over Abner's murder, thus, declaring that he played no part in the slaying of the general of his late rival, Saul. (52) Moed Katan 25b. Our editions of the Talmud identify the eulogist as Rabbi Yitzchak ben Eleazar. (53) Amos 8:9.

merit of Aaron. When Aaron passed away the clouds of glory departed. [The presence of these clouds] explains why the nations were originally afraid to wage war against Israel, but desired to do so [after Aaron's death], for [following his demise], it is written, *And the Canaanite, the King of Arad, who dwelt in the south, heard that Israel came by the way of Atharim, and he fought against Israel.*[54] Based on this verse, the Sages expounded:[55] "*And the Canaanite . . . heard.* What did he hear? He heard that Aaron had died and the clouds of glory, [which previously protected Israel], had departed." Therefore, Scripture adjoined [the passage beginning] *And the Canaanite . . . heard* to [the passage describing] Aaron's death.

Scripture intended to teach you that the death of a righteous person is equal in severity to the burning of the Sanctuary, for Aaron died in Ab[56] the month in which the destruction [of the Temple] occurred [generations later]. Elsewhere,[57] the Sages concluded, "The death of the righteous is as severe as the breaking of the Tablets of the Law," based on Scripture's having adjoined those two subjects.[58] Thus, the world needs the righteous just as it needs the heavenly luminaries. However, the advantages derived from the former outlast those from the latter, for the benefits of the luminaries are only in this world, but the beneficence of the righteous is for this world and the World to Come. When the lights are extinguished, people sit in the darkness. Similarly, when a righteous man dies, darkness descends upon the generation. Therefore, all are obligated to mourn his passing and to bestir themselves regarding the eulogy for his honor, for we have already established that the eulogy constitutes an honor for the departed.

In the World to Come, eulogies will be abrogated, for the evil inclination will have been voided, *and tears will be wiped away from off all faces,*[59] and all Israel will be rewarded with resurrection of the

(54) Numbers 21:1. (55) Taanith 9a. (56) See Numbers 33:38. (57) Yerushalmi Yoma I, 1. (58) Deuteronomy 10:2-6. (59) Isaiah 25:8.

dead, — one of the four unique characteristics which distinguish Israel from the other nations. These characteristics are the Land [of Israel], Torah, prophecy, and resurrection of the dead, and Scripture attests to the truth of each. It states, *And Israel dwelleth in safety, 'the seed of Jacob alone,' in a land of corn and wine.*[60] This makes it clear that the Land was given to Israel alone and not to any other nation. Regarding the Torah, it is stated, *Moses commanded us a Torah, an inheritance of the congregation of Jacob,*[61] which means that the Torah was given only to Jacob and to those who associate with him. In connection with prophecy, Moses said, *The Eternal thy G-d will raise up a prophet unto thee, of thy brethren, like unto me.*[62] To prevent you from misapprehensively including the seed of Edom and Ishmael in the expression *of thy brethren,* Moses therefore specified [Israel] by saying, *like unto me,* that is to say, "of the seed of Jacob as I am." Pertaining to the resurrection of the dead, it is written, *Yea, his heavens drop down dew,*[60] which means that Israel's heavens will drop down that dew with which the Holy One, blessed be He, will revive the dead.[63] Immediately adjoining that verse, it states, *Happy art thou, O Israel, who is like unto thee?*[64] That is, no other nation will merit this gift. Thus, it is written, *And many of them that sleep in the dust of the earth shall awake.*[65] The phrase *many of them* refers to Israel, as it says, *and many from among the peoples of the land became Jews.*[66] This was also expressed by the prophet Isaiah when he said, *Thy dead shall live,*[67] meaning the dead of Israel, for he was addressing them directly. May G-d privilege us to be included among the righteous at that time [of the resurrection] so that we can attain that distinction, for the Sages commented at the end of Tractate Kethuboth,[68] "The righteous will break through [the ground] and rise in Jerusalem, as it says, *and they will blossom out of the city like grass of the earth.*"[69]

---

(60) Deuteronomy 33:28. (61) *Ibid.*, Verse 4. (62) *Ibid.*, 18:15. (63) Chagigah 12b. (64) Deuteronomy 33:29. (65) Daniel 12:2. (66) Esther 8:17. (67) Isaiah 26:19. (68) Kethuboth 111b. (69) Psalms 72:16.

Part Three

> *Man's function in the world is to fulfill the Torah and commandments / A person's soul is G-d's messenger, bestirring him to his duties / The Sages taught us about the great distinction of the soul / Consequently, man is obligated to heed the call of the soul and to engage himself in deeds of lovingkindness / The elements of lovingkindness as explained in Rabbinical sources / One who practices deeds of lovingkindness is humble in spirit and fearful of G-d, and these qualities crown his head in perpetual glory.*

THE SOUL OF MAN IS THE LAMP OF THE ETERNAL, SEARCHING ALL INWARD PARTS.[70]

One who has the fear of Heaven implanted in his heart should concentrate on the thought that in this world he is a messenger of the Holy One, blessed be He, whose mission is to fulfill the Torah and its commandments.[71] He must faithfully fulfill his mission as commanded, and when he does, his *reward is with Him, and* his *recompense before Him.*[72]

Regarding this concept, Solomon said *I have taught thee in the way of wisdom, I have led thee in the path of uprightness.*[73] *That thy trust be in the Eternal, I have made them known to thee this day, even to thee.*[74] *That I might make thee know the certainty of the words of*

(70) Proverbs 20:27. The soul, which emanates from a Divine source, is entrusted to man for his utilization. Its function is to serve as a lighted lamp in surroundings of darkness. Herein lies the source of Judaism's most abiding teachings on the dignity of man and his responsibility for his actions. (71) Regarding "Torah and its commandments," see Note 2 in *Emunah* (Faith). (72) Isaiah 40:10. (73) Proverbs 4:11. (74) *Ibid.*, 22:19.

truth, that thou mightest bring back words of truth to them that send thee.[75] [In other words], he is stating, *I have made them known to thee this day*[74] that you are a messenger in this world. You have been sent to fulfill your mission, which is to know *the certainty of the words of truth*[75] so that you may return and give an accounting of these *words of truth* to Him Who sent you. *The words of truth,* which are the words of Torah, constitute a testimony and proof of G-d's solicitude for mankind, for due to His providence over them, He has commanded and warned them regarding *the words of truth.* The causal agent of His providential care is the soul which illuminates the body [in bestirring it to the observance of the Torah and its commandments]. Thus, Solomon compared the soul to a lamp, saying, *The soul of man is the lamp of the Eternal, searching all the inward parts.*[70]

The simple meaning of *the lamp of the Eternal* is that it refers to the sun, the greatest luminary in the heavens. Because of the sun's immensity, Scripture ascribes it to G-d and informs us thereby that even as the sun illumines the earth and its inhabitants, so does the soul of man illuminate the actions of the body. G-d, Who searches all the inward parts of the body and soul, recompenses the person for his deeds and hidden thoughts.

There is another interpretation for the soul being called *the lamp of the Eternal:* Just as the lamp is kindled from another source of light, so is the higher soul [i.e. the rational soul] of man derived from the First Light.[76] The principal reason for man's existence is only for the sake of the soul. This will clarify the essence and distinction of the soul and its eternal existence. It is thus like the Higher Light[76] itself. In the Biblical account of the first day of Creation, you will find the word "light" men-

(75) *Ibid.,* Verse 21.   (76) The First Light was created on the first day of Creation (Genesis 1:3) and was subsequently hidden [in the heavens] as G-d saw that the wicked were unworthy of using it. At the time of creation of the First Light, the souls of all generations were formed. (Rabbeinu Bachya on Genesis 2:7, and see my notes there). The First Light is to be distinguished from the Higher Light, as explained in *Orchim* (Hospitality), Note 51.

tioned five times.[77] This corresponds to the Sages' statement:[78] "The
soul has five names: *n'shamah* (soul), *yechidah* (the unique one),[79]
ruach (spirit), *nefesh* (the vital one), *chaya* (living being)." This matter
was alluded to by G-d when He answered Job out of the whirlwind, He
cited the subject of the First Light together with that of the creation of
the souls, saying, *Where is the way to the dwelling of light, and as for
darkness, where is the place thereof?*[80] *Thou knowest it, for thou wast
then born, and the number of thy days is great!*[81] This is the explanation of those verses: "Tell me if you know the way of the Light which
was created on the first day, and whether you have surveyed its paths?
If you know it, then you also know that you were born then *and the
number of thy days is great!*" All this was said with regard to the creation of the soul, which is called *a lamp* and is ascribed to G-d [as it says,
The soul of man is the lamp of the Eternal][70] because it is taken from
the [First] Light [created by G-d].

Our Sages said in the Midrash:[82] "The Holy One, blessed be He, said
to man, 'Your lamp is in My hand, and My lamp is in your hand. Your
lamp is in My hand, as it is said, *The soul of man is the lamp of the
Eternal.*[70] My lamp, which is the Torah, is in your hand, as it is said,
For the commandment is a lamp, and the Torah is light.[83] If you will
guard My lamp, I will guard yours.' Rav Chiya said, This is analogous
to two people, each of whom owned one vineyard. One was in Judea,

(77) *Let there be light. And there was light* (Genesis 1:3); *And G-d saw the light
that it was good; and G-d divided the light,* etc., (*ibid.,* Verse 4); *And G-d called the
light Day,* etc., (*ibid.,* Verse 5).   (78) Bereshith Rabbah 14:11.   (79) "As the Eternal is unique in His world, so is the soul unique in the body" (Devarim Rabbah
2:26).   (80) Job 38:19. After Job's friends were unable to answer him satisfactorily on
his complaints regarding the suffering of the righteous and the prosperity of the wicked, G-d answered him *out of the whirlwind,* unfolding before him the Divine
grandeur, and mystery of Creation, until Job was humbled into realizing how futile it is
for him to understand the mysteries of G-d's moral government of the
world.   (81) *Ibid.,* Verse 21.   (82) Midrash Tehillim, 17. A shorter version is also
found in Devarim Rabbah 4:4.   (83) Proverbs 6:23. *The commandment is a lamp* to
illumine a path through darkness, but the study of Torah is "*the light* of the day itself."
The supreme virtue of the study of Torah, which affords us knowledge of the particular commandments, is thus explicitly stated.

and the other was in Galilee. The Judean owned the vineyard in Galilee, and the Galilean owned the one in Judea. At a certain time they met, and one said to the other, 'Watch my vineyard in Galilee, and I will watch yours in Judea. If you will let mine lie fallow, I will do likewise to yours.' Similarly, the Holy One, blessed be He, said to Israel, 'If you will guard My Torah, I will guard your soul,' as it is said, *If 'shamor tishm'run' (ye shall diligently keep) [all this commandment]*:[84] if you will keep [all this commandment], you will be guarded."[85]

The soul undergoes three stages of experience: the formation of the body in the mother's womb, the world after birth, and the World to Come. The first stage is of limited duration. From the time of creation you can recognize and contemplate the wonders of the Creator's deeds, when for a period of nine months the foetus is fed through the mother's food, and upon leaving that world it is under pressure and force. The second stage, this world, is superior to the first, for in it the individual has the opportunity to increase his knowledge of Torah and the commandments and to attain some perception of the Creator. Notwithstanding its superiority, however, this stage, too, is of limited duration. The third stage is infinite in scope, and in it, man is rewarded for his fulfillment of the commandments and his performance of good deeds in this world. Thus, it may be said that with regard to these three stages, man always proceeds to a higher state of beneficence. The first stage, that of formation, is in darkness and has no light; [the second stage], this world, consists of both darkness and light, while [the third stage], the World to Come, is all light and has no darkness at all.

David stated five times, *Bless the Eternal, O my soul,*[86] for which the Sages gave the following reason: "David's five statements correspond

(84) Deuteronomy 11:22.   (85) The interpretation is based upon the use of the Hebrew infinitive *shamor* together with the verb *tishm'run*.   (86) Psalms 103:1,2,22; 104:1,35. The text which follows explains the specific intention of each of these five identical expressions. It will be shown that the soul, which is Divine in origin, has five features which represent the true dignity of a human being.

to G-d's qualities. Just as G-d fills the entire world, so does the soul fill the entire body. Just as G-d sees and is not seen, so does the soul see and is not seen. Just as G-d sustains the entire world, so does the soul nourish the entire body. Just as G-d is pure, so is the soul. Just as G-d is in the remotest recesses, so is the soul. Thus, let the soul, which possesses these five qualities, come and praise Him Who is the source of it all." [87]

The explanation of this passage is as follows: "Just as G-d fills the entire world, etc." Although there are places in the world wherein the might of G-d was made more apparent, e.g. Mount Sinai, Mount Moriah, [88] Beth-el, [89] and the like, He nevertheless fills the entire world. In the same way, although the human soul manifests itself in certain parts of the body—such as the brain, heart, and tongue—more than in others, it nevertheless fills the entire body. Thus, we see that the hands and feet, which perform constructive functions of a durable nature, derive their efficiency from the wisdom of the soul. The capacity to produce work which can survive the test of time is found only among human beings, not among any of the lower creatures. This is the purport of the verse, *Bless the Eternal, O my soul, and all that is within me, bless His holy Name.* [90] Even as His holy Name fills the entire world, so does the soul fill the entire body.

"Just as G-d sees and is not seen, etc." It is impossible for any creature, including the holy angels, to visibly see G-d. Similarly, while the soul perceives, albeit not through the physical senses, it cannot be perceived by the human eye. This is the intent of the verse, *Bless the Eternal, O my soul, and forget not all His benefit,* [91] which refers to the kindness He has bestowed upon the soul in making it like Himself, able to see and unable to be seen.

---

(87) Berachoth 10a. (88) The Sanctuary in Jerusalem, the dwelling place of the Divine Glory, was built upon Mount Moriah (II Chronicles 3:1). (89) It was in Beth-el that Jacob dreamed of *a ladder set up on the earth and the top of it reached to heaven, etc.* (Genesis 28:12-19). (90) Psalms 103:1. (91) *Ibid.,* Verse 2.

"Just as G-d sustains the entire world, etc." [G-d sustains both] the higher and lower spheres, for the latter derive their sustenance from the former, which are directly sustained by the Divine Glory. So too the soul nourishes the entire body, not by food and drink, but by the luster of joy derived from perceiving G-d. Thus, Moses was maintained on Mount Sinai *forty days and forty nights; he did neither eat bread, nor drink water.*[92] We also have the case of Elijah, whose life was sustained by his soul when he traveled for forty days on the little physical food [he had consumed] as it is written, *and he went in the strength of that meal forty days and forty nights.*[93] This feature of the human soul corresponds to the concluding verse[94] of that psalm. The sequence of the last three verses there[95] indicate that it is G-d Who sustains all the worlds and strengthens them by His powers.

"Just as G-d is pure, etc." Although there are obviously some impure places in the world, G-d is nevertheless pure. The following example will clarify this thought. The sun, one of His mighty servants, sheds its pure rays upon a dunghill even as it does upon the clear and shining waters. "So is the soul pure," even though there are limbs in the body which are not pure, the soul nevertheless is pure. No impurity can attach to it but only to the body and the soul is not part thereof. With reference to this quality of the purity of the soul, David stated, *Bless the Eternal, O my soul. O Eternal my G-d, Thou art very great, Thou art clothed with glory and majesty,*[96] for something which is impure has neither glory nor majesty.

---

(92) Exodus 34:28.   (93) I Kings 19:8.   (94) Psalms 103:22.   (95) *Ibid.*, Verses 20-22. David first mentioned the angels (Verse 20: *Bless the Eternal, ye His angels*), then the heavenly hosts (Verse 21: *Bless the Eternal, all ye His hosts*), and finally the creatures of this world (Verse 22: *Bless the Eternal, all ye His works*). The sequence proceeds from the highest sphere to the lowest, respectively, indicating as the text concludes, that "it is G-d Who sustains all the worlds." Thus, in recognition of that sustenance, the psalm ends with the words *Bless the Eternal, O my soul.*   (96) Psalms 104:1.

"Just as G-d is in the remotest recesses, etc." Anyone who desires to know G-d and to attain a conception of Him must enter the chambers of wisdom, each of which is further inward than the preceding one, until he finds Him. "So is the soul," for he who desires to learn its essence must also enter the chambers of wisdom. He must understand that the soul is the carrier of the body, dwelling within it and yet being outside it, and that it is not one of the physical elements, but is a simple rational substance which emanates from the Throne of Glory. This corresponds to the end of that psalm in which David says, *Let sinners cease out of the earth, and let the wicked be no more. Bless the Eternal, O my soul.*[97] This teaches us that sinners will perish, but the soul of the righteous will be preserved near the Throne of Glory.

Since we have learned about the distinction of the rational soul, it is therefore necessary for man to follow its dictates and engage himself in deeds of lovingkindness, which include visiting the sick, clothing the naked, consoling mourners, and burying the dead.[98] "What did Solomon do when he saw how highly G-d considers the attribute of compassion? When he built the Temple, he erected two gates: one for bridegrooms, and one for mourners and excommunicants. [On the Sabbath], people would go and sit between these two gates. They would greet one who entered the bridegrooms' gate by saying to him, 'May the One Who dwells in this House gladden you with sons and daughters.' If one entered the mourners' gate and his upper lip was covered, they knew that he was a mourner and would say to him, 'May the One Who dwells in this House console you.' If his upper lip was not covered, they knew that he was an excommunicant and would say to him, 'May the One Who dwells in this House cause you to listen to the words of your colleagues and cause your colleagues to receive you.' After the destruction of the Temple, the Sages ordained that bridegrooms and mourners should go to synagogues and houses of

---

(97) *Ibid.*, Verse 35.   (98) Pirkei d'Rabbi Eliezer, 17. The entire passage is quoted by Ramban in Torath Ha'adam (Kithvei Haramban, Vol. II, p. 218) and subsequently incorporated in the Tur, Yorei Deiah, 393.

learning and that the people there should rejoice with the bridegroom, and join the mourner in sitting upon the ground. The purpose of all of this was [to give] the entire people of Israel [the opportunity] to fulfill the obligation to engage in deeds of lovingkindness."

Our Sages expounded in Tractate Succah:[99] "*It hath been told thee, O man, what is good, and what the Eternal doth require of thee: only to do justly, and to love mercy, and to walk humbly with thy G-d.*[100] *To do justly* means [to live by] the law. *And to love mercy* refers [to deeds of] lovingkindness. *And to walk humbly* refers to [financially assisting] a bride to get married and [paying the cost of] a funeral escort. Now, is this not an *a fortiori* conclusion? If the Torah tells us *to walk humbly* in matters which are ordinarily done overtly, how much more should we covertly perform matters which are generally done in privacy![101] Rabbi Eleazar said that [the giving of] charity is greater than all the offerings, as it is said, *To do charity and justice is more acceptable to the Eternal than offering.*[102] Rabbi Eleazar further said that lovingkindness is greater than charity, as it is said, *Sow to yourselves according to charity, reap according to kindness.*[103] The Sages taught that lovingkindness is greater than charity in three ways. Charity can be given only with one's wealth, but lovingkindness can be done with both one's body[104] or his wealth. Charity can be given only to the poor,[105] but lovingkindness can be accorded to the poor and the rich. Charity is dispensed only to the living, but lovingkindness can be dispensed to both the living and the dead."

---

(99) Succah 49b.   (100) Micah 6:8.   (101) Charity, for example, should be given to the poor in secrecy so that the poor man should not be embarrassed by anyone knowing about it. In the case of funeral and wedding costs, however, the one who pays the expenses will become known because other people are involved in the affair (Rashi, Succah 49b).   (102) Proverbs 21:3.   (103) Hosea 10:12. The prophet thus classifies the giving of charity as an act of sowing, while he terms deeds of lovingkindness as reaping. As explained further in the text, it is better to reap than to sow (Rashi, Succah 49b).   (104) Rashi, *ibid.*, cites these examples: eulogizing, carrying, and interring the deceased, gladdening a bridegroom, and escorting a friend on the road.   (105) If an undeserving person is the recipient of the charity, then the donor has not fulfilled his obligation to give alms.

A person should stringently observe [practicing] the attribute of kindness, for he thereby walks in the ways of his Creator. Kindness is one of His attributes, and He directs His world with it, as we say in the Morning Prayer, "He guides His world with lovingkindness and His creatures with tender mercies." The world was created with it, as it is said, *I have said, The world was built upon kindness.*[106] One who is strict in the observance of kindness is humble in spirit and fearful of G-d. This quality, to which he adheres in his lifetime, draws his soul to the life in the World to Come and covers his head like a crown. Thus, King David said, *But the mercy of the Eternal is from everlasting to everlasting upon them that fear Him, and His righteousness unto children's children.*[107]

(106) Psalms 89:3.   (107) *Ibid.*, 103:17.

Part Four

Mourning over the Destruction of Jerusalem

Isaiah's prophecy of the destruction of Jerusalem / Had the destruction not been decreed by Heaven, no nation could have captured Jerusalem / The First Temple was destroyed because of idolatry, and the Second Temple because of causeless enmity / The destruction of the Holy Temple was decreed in the wilderness as a result of the affair of the spies / Even the angels mourned the destruction of the Temple / For the mourning on the ninth of Ab, the Sages enacted restrictions as stringent as those on the Day of Atonement / One who mourns and grieves on the ninth of Ab together with the public merits seeing the consolation of the public.

THE BURDEN CONCERNING THE VALLEY OF VISION.
WHAT AILETH THEE NOW, THAT THOU ART WHOLLY
GONE UP TO THE HOUSETOPS,[108] THOU THAT ART FULL
OF UPROAR, A TUMULTUOUS CITY, A JOYOUS TOWN?
THY SLAIN ARE NOT SLAIN WITH THE SWORD, NOR
DEAD IN BATTLE.[109]

With these words, Isaiah prophesied the destruction of Jerusalem. He censured Israel for mustering all their strength to safeguard against the impending enemy assault without preparing to repent and engaging in good deeds. With repentance, the people of Israel would be safe even without implements of war, but armaments without repentance would be to no avail. Therefore, the prophet, foreseeing punishment coming upon them, proclaimed, *The burden concerning the Valley of Vision.* [108]

Although it is known that Jerusalem is higher than all the lands,[110] Isaiah called Jerusalem a *valley*, a term connoting lowliness, in order to teach that she will fall from her height and become lowly. [She will be] thrown "from a high vaulted roof to a deep cavity."

What aileth thee now, that thou art wholly gone up to the housetops?[108] When a city is besieged, people usually gather in their homes or go up to the housetops or towers to be secure from the reach of the enemy. The prophet is thus saying with regard to Jerusalem: "Why are you gathered now in your homes and why have you ascended to the roofs? How has this come about? It is due to your sins. Yesterday, you were *full of uproar, a tumultuous city, a joyous town.*[109] You did not have to go [outside of] the city to war against the enemy, nor did you have to stay in the city and die from famine. Thus, they were *not slain with the sword, nor dead in battle.*[109]

(108) Isaiah 22:1. *The burden* is a synonym for prophecy. The subject matter of this prophecy is fully explained by the author in the text that follows.   (109) *Ibid.,* Verse 2.   (110) Sifre, *Shoftim* 152, Kiddushin 69a-b.

75

In this vein, Isaiah continues the prophecy, finally stating, *And in that day the Eternal, the G-d of hosts, called to weeping, and to lamentation, and to baldness, and to girding with sackcloth.* [111] The expression [*the Eternal*] . . . *called* means "that He decreed," for were it not that Heaven had decreed the destruction of the Temple, the enemy would have been unable to destroy it. Scripture expresses this thought by saying, *From on high hath He sent fire into my bones, and it prevaileth against them.* [112] In Midrash Eichah, the Sages said, [113] "Jerusalem said to her Babylonian conquerors, 'If the fight had not been against me from on high, would you have been able to vanquish me? If fire had not been sent against me from on high, would you have conquered me? You have slain a dead lion, you have razed a burnt city, you have ground milled flour.' " Thus, we have been taught: [114] "On the seventeenth day of Tamuz, [the wall of] the city was breached." That is, it split by itself because it was so decreed on high. Therefore, [the Tanna] used the expression "the city was breached" even as is the Scriptural expression *Then the city was breached.* [115] Isaiah also spoke of Jerusalem in terms of a valley [to indicate the depths to which it fell].

The subject [of the destruction] is also explained in the Book of Deuteronomy, where it is written. *The Eternal will bring a nation against thee from far, from the end of the earth, as the vulture swoopeth down.* [116] This refers to the wicked Turnus Rufus, [a Roman commander in the days of Rabbi Akiba]. The Sages said in Midrash Eichah: [117] "The wife of Turnus Rufus bore him a son on the night of the ninth of Ab when all [of the people of] Israel were in mourning

(111) Isaiah 22:12. (112) Lamentations 1:13. (113) Eichah Rabbah 1:43. (114) Taanith 26b. (115) II Kings 25:4. (116) Deuteronomy 28:49. The commentaries of Ramban and Rabbeinu Bachya on Deuteronomy 28:42 and 29:6, respectively. indicate that the chastisement there refers to the destruction of the Second Temple and the post-Temple era. (117) Eichah Rabbathi 1:8. Our edition of the Midrash ascribes the episodes to Trachinus (Emperor Trajan).

[over the destruction of the Temple]. The child died [later that year] on Chanukah, placing the Jews in a quandary over whether or not to kindle [the Chanukah lights]. They decided to kindle them, saying, 'We will fulfill our obligation, and whatever will befall us will come.' Evilmongers then told the wife of Turnus Rufus, 'When you gave birth to a son, these Jews mourned and now that he has died, they have lit candles.' Thereupon, she sent a message to her husband, saying, 'Instead of conquering barbarians, come and vanquish these Jews who have rebelled against you.' Turnus Rufus immediately boarded a ship for the Holy Land, expecting to arrive in ten days, but a favorable wind brought him [to his destination] in five. Upon his arrival, he found the Jews engaged in studying the verse, *The Eternal will bring a nation against thee from far, from the end of the earth, as the vulture swoopeth down.*[116] He said to them, 'I am that *vulture* who thought to come in ten days and whom the wind brought [here] in five.' His legions then surrounded and killed them. It was over this [tragedy] that Jeremiah mourned, *For these things I weep,* etc."[118]

Which sins caused the destruction of the Temple? Our Sages taught us:[119] "The first Temple was destroyed because of idolatry,"[120] as explained in the Book of Jeremiah and Ezekiel. "However, we know that during the era of the Second Temple, the people were pious and men of good deeds. Why was that [Temple] destroyed? It was destroyed because of causeless enmity."

The Sages commented in Midrash Eichah:[121] "On the night of the ninth of Ab, our patriarch Abraham entered the Holy of Holies. G-d

(118) Lamentations 1:16.   (119) Yoma 9b.   (120) Rabbeinu Bachya was well aware that the text in Yoma mentions two other sins—immorality and bloodshed—for which the First Temple was destroyed. The author, however, singled out idolatry not only because it is the root of the other two sins, but also because missionary activity was so rampant in his times and Jews everywhere were being subjected to it. Thus, Rabbeinu Bachya felt it necessary to emphasize idolatry as the sin responsible for the destruction of the First Temple.   (121) Eichah Rabbathi 1:21.

said to him, *What hath My beloved to do in My house?*[122] Abraham countered, 'Master of the universe, where are my children?' G-d answered, 'They sinned, and I exiled them among the nations.' Abraham asked, 'Were there no righteous ones among them?' G-d replied, *'She hath wrought lewdness'*[122] [That is, they engaged in sinful acts]. Abraham argued, 'You should have looked at the good ones among them.' G-d responded, *'With many.'*[122] That is, they were generally bad. Abraham defended them, 'You should have looked at the sign of circumcision in their flesh.' G-d answered, 'By your life! They denied it, as it is said, *And the hallowed flesh is passed from thee*[122] [that is, they have removed the sign of the covenant of Abraham from their flesh]. Moreover they rejoiced in the failure of one another, as it is said, *When thou doest evil, then thou rejoicest.*[122] It is further written, *And he that is glad at calamity shall not go unpunished.'*"[123]

Thus, the principal sin that precipitated the destruction of the Second Temple[124] was causeless enmity, not idolatry, for [the people of that era] gave their lives for the Sanctification of the Divine Name in order not to worship idols. The Sages told of one woman and her seven children[125] who gave their lives in order not to prostrate themselves

(122) Jeremiah 11:15.   (123) Proverbs 17:5. One who rejoices at another's misfortune will certainly be punished. Hence, this was the principal cause of the destruction of the Second Temple. See the following note.   (124) That the following narrative refers only to the Second Temple may be deduced from G-d's justification of the punishment. No mention is made of idolatry, immorality and bloodshed, which were responsible for the destruction of the First Temple, attested to by the prophets. Furthermore, the verse, *And the hallowed flesh is passed from thee,* which means that they removed the sign of the covenant of Abraham from their flesh, may possibly refer to the actions of the Hellenists during the Grecian period. This is another indication that the narrative points to the period of the Second Temple.   (125) Eichah Rabbathi 1:53. In the Hebrew text, Rabbeinu Bachya quotes the entire lengthy story of the emperor who wanted to entice the seven children to prostrate themselves before his statue. Each child was separately killed as one by one refused. — The mother voluntarily took her life in order not to be coerced to prostrate herself before the statue (Meiri, Gittin 57b, p. 242).

before the emperor's statue. "As the youngest was being killed, his mother cried out to him, My child, go to your patriarch Abraham and tell him, this is what my mother said: 'Do not be overbearing because you built an altar and brought [your son] Isaac as a whole burnt-offering. Our mother built seven altars and offered up seven children in one day. Moreover, you [Abraham] were only being tested, but my experience was real.' At that point, the nations of the world exclaimed, 'What does their G-d do for them that they give their lives for Him at all times!' With regard to these martyrs, it is written, *But for Thy sake are we killed all the day.*[126] The mother then went to the rooftop and threw herself down and died. Thus was fulfilled the statement, *She that hath borne seven languisheth.*[127] A Heavenly Voice came down and said, *a joyful mother of children,*[128] and the Holy Spirit cried out, *For these things I weep.*"[118]

The destruction of the Temple was decreed in the wilderness during the affair of the spies. Israel sinfully believed in the spies' [disheartening] report and wept without justification, as it is written, *And all the congregation lifted up their voices, and cried, and the people wept that night.*[129] This occurred on the eve of the ninth of Ab. "The Holy One, blessed be He, said, 'You have wept without cause. Therefore, I will set aside a cause for you to weep [on this night] for generations.' "[130]

In the Midrash[131] the Sages said, *"The burden concerning the Valley of Vision,*[108] refers to the valley from which all seers prophesied, for

___

(126) Psalms 44:23. (127) Jeremiah 15:9. (128) Psalms 113:9. (129) Numbers 14:1. (130) Taanith 29a. Hence, from the days of the wilderness, the ninth of Ab was to be the date on which the Temple would be destroyed, an event which would be the cause "for you to weep [on this night] for generations." It is obvious of course that had Israel not sinned later during the era of the First Temple, the destruction would never have occurred. But having sinned, Israel lost the Temple on the particular night of the ninth of Ab which was reminiscent of their former sin in the wilderness. (131) P'sichta Eichah Rabbathi, 24.

Rabbi Yochanan said that any prophet whose name and city of origin
have not been specified comes from Jerusalem." It appears to me that
in the opinion of this Midrash, the term *valley* [as applied here to
Jerusalem], connotes the city's praise and distinction. Just as a valley
receives rain water, so is Jerusalem prepared to receive the flow of prophecy, for [Jerusalem] is *the gate of heaven*[132] and prophecy came
therefrom to the seers.[133] Thus, Jonah the son of Amittai fled to Tarshish[134] [outside Israel] to avoid being vested with prophecy in the
Land.

[The Sages[135] continue its exposition]: *"What aileth thee now, that
thou art wholly gone up to the housetops?*[108] This refers to the young
priests who took the Temple keys and ascended to the roof of the burning Sanctuary, declaring before G-d, 'Master of the universe! Since we
have not been worthy of being [Temple] officers before You, we now
hand the keys over to You.' As they threw the keys heavenward, a sort
of hand came forth [from on high] and took them, and the young
priests jumped and fell into the fire [burning below in the Temple]
which the enemy had kindled.

On the ninth day of Ab, towards the eve of the tenth, the enemy lit
the fire, and the Temple burned until the end of the tenth day. Thus,
Rabban Yochanan ben Zaccai[136] said, "If I had lived in that genera-

---

(132) Genesis 28:17. Cf. the statement of Ramban: " . . . the soul of a person who
stands in Jerusalem clothes itself with *Ruach Hakodesh* (the Holy Spirit) and a mission
of prophecy through the Will of G-d, etc." (Gate of Reward — Writings and Discourses,
Vol. II, pp. 515-516).   (133) "Before Jerusalem was chosen [to be the seat of the
Sanctuary], the entire Land of Israel was fit for prophecy. After Jerusalem was chosen,
prophecy was removed from the Land" (Tanchuma, *Bo*, 5).   (134) See Jonah 1:3. See
also, further, *Kippurim* (Atonement, Part One).   (135) Taanith 29a.   (136) In
Taanith *ibid.*, this statement is correctly attributed to Rabbi Yochanan, a Palestinian
Amora who lived several generations after the destruction. On the other hand, our text
here mentions Rabban Yochanan ben Zaccai, who lived during the destruction. It is
difficult to conceive how the latter could have said, "If I had lived during that generation, etc."

tion, I would have designated [the fast] on the tenth of Ab." It was set for the ninth day because the principal [tragedy] is attributed to the commencement of the punishment, [rather than its conclusion]. Regarding this event Scripture states, *Woe unto us! for the day declineth, for the shadows of the evening are stretched out,*[137] and it was for this that Isaiah mourned, saying, *The burden concerning the Valley of Vision. What aileth thee now that thou art wholly gone up to the housetops?*[108]

The ministering angels, too, gathered in groups and formed rows of mourners, saying, *The highways lie waste, the wayfaring man ceaseth; He hath broken the covenant, He hath despised the cities, He regardeth not 'enosh' (man).*[138] "The angels said before the Holy One, blessed be He, 'How desolate have become the highways you built for Jerusalem so that travelers should not cease therefrom! *The wayfaring man ceaseth.* The roads on which Israel traveled [on pilgrimage] for the holidays have ceased [to be used]. *He hath broken the covenant,* the covenant of our patriarch Abraham, who cultivated the world and through whose efforts the world came to recognize that You are *G-d the Most High, Maker of heaven and earth.*[139] That [covenant] has been broken. *He hath despised the cities* of Jerusalem and Zion after He had chosen them. *He regarded not 'enosh' (man).* He did not regard Israel as [the equal of] even the generation of Enosh,[140] the father of idolaters.' " Thus, it is written, *Behold, their angels cry without, the messengers of peace weep bitterly.*[141] The Holy One, blessed be He, Himself joins in the mourning, as it is said, *And in that day did the Eternal, the G-d of hosts, call to weeping, and to lamentation.*[142]

---

(137) Jeremiah 6:4.   (138) Isaiah 33:8.   (139) Genesis 14:19.   (140) See *ibid.*, 4:26, and Mishneh Torah, *Hilchoth Akum* 1:1. In the generation of Enosh, men began to call the profane by the Name of the Eternal.   (141) Isaiah 33:7.   (142) *Ibid.*, 22:12.

Because of the profound degree of mourning which is appropriate for the destruction of the Temple, the Sages enacted stringent restrictions for the ninth of Ab, for on that day, both the First and Second Temples were destroyed. The restrictions so enacted are equal to those on the Day of Atonement. Thus, it is forbidden to put even a finger into water. Whoever mourns and grieves on the ninth of Ab together with the public merits seeing the consolation of the public, as it is said, *Rejoice ye with Jerusalem, and be glad with her, all ye that love her; be very joyful with her, all ye that mourn for her.* [143]

(143) *Ibid.*, 66:10.

בטחון
Trust in G-d

Trust in G-d means that one should rely on G-d to help him fulfill the commandments and to supply him with all of his needs/ One should not rely on G-d's help as a reward for his good deeds, for this attitude will cause his sins to be remembered on high/ One should not be lax in his efforts to earn his sustenance/ One who trusts in G-d also has faith, but one who has faith might not have trust for fear that his sins will prevent the fulfillment of certain Divine promises/ Rabbeinu Yonah explained trust to mean that one should know for a certainty that everything lies in the hands of Heaven. Even in moments of distress, one should believe that salvation is near/ One should attribute his success to G-d's mercy and blame his failure on his own shortcomings/ The attribute of trust entails one's readiness to give his life for the sanctification of G-d's Name/ Trust in G-d is one of the fundamental principles of the Torah.

Trust in G-d

TRUST IN THE ETERNAL, AND DO GOOD; DWELL IN THE
LAND, AND CHERISH FAITH.[1]

[In this verse], King David first mentioned and urged trust [in G-d]
and then spoke of good deeds in order to make known that one should
rely on G-d's help to fulfill His commandments and to supply him with
all the necessary requisites thereto. If David had said, "Do good and
trust in the Eternal," one would have thought that the trust of which
he spoke referred only to the [expected] reward for the good deed, not
to the means required for the performance of the deed. Therefore, he
first stated, *Trust in the Eternal*, that is, trust that G-d will help and
support you and will supply you with those necessities which will enable
you to do the good deed.

If we were to explain the phrase *Trust in the Eternal* to mean a trust
in His reward for our good deed, that [interpretation] would in reality
greatly hinder our trust. Our Sages cautioned us,[2] "Be not like servants
who minister to their master in order to receive a reward"

---

(1) Psalms 37:3. The author chose this verse which mentions *trust* and *faith*, since
trust is intertwined with faith. Whoever has trust also has faith, as the discussion later
on will show. (2) Aboth 1:3. (3) The addition of the word "immediately," is
enlightening. Rabbeinu Bachya's intent is to emphasize that there is nothing spiritually
wrong believing that a good deed will be rewarded. In fact, to think otherwise would
deny the fundamental principle of reward and punishment. However, to do a good
deed "in order to receive a reward 'immediately'" is contrary to the teaching of the
Sages, as stated in the text.

84

immediately.[3] If you do so, you will bring about a recollection of your sins, as the Sages said,[4] "Three things cause the recollection of a person's sins: [walking near] a collapsible wall, expecting an immediate granting of one's prayer, and appealing to Heaven for judgment against one's neighbor."

[The verse under consideration concludes], *Dwell in the land, and cherish faith.*[1] That is to say: "Even though I have cautioned you to trust that G-d, blessed be He, will supply you with those necessities which will enable you to do the good deed, I am not saying that you should completely abandon your work and your means of livelihood to pursue the good deed, for if you do so, how will you support yourself?" Therefore, David said, *Dwell in the land,* meaning, do not be lax in the matter of support and livelihood, for *it is good that thou shouldest take hold of the one; yea, also from the other withdraw not thy hand.*[5] Our Sages have commented,[6] "Where there is no food, there is no Torah," for without [satisfaction of his] material needs, man can neither worship G-d, blessed be He, nor accord the Torah [the devotion] due her.

You are aware that in the Sanctuary, the Candelabrum, which signified wisdom, was placed on the south,[7] and the Table containing the Showbread, through which sustenance and abundance came upon the world, was on the north.[7] Since north and south are in alignment with each other, [the arrangement of the Candelabrum and the Table in the Sanctuary] teach us that wisdom cannot exist in this physical world without sustenance and satisfaction [of material needs]. Therefore, David said, *Dwell in the land,*[1] meaning engage in com-

---

(4) Berachoth 55a. Each of the cases mentioned indicates a sense of self-righteousness, which causes one's records on high to reveal the person's sins (Rashi, *ibid*).   (5) Ecclesiastes 7:18. Trust in Divine Providence should be combined with one's own efforts to earn a livelihood.   (6) Aboth 3:17. Literally: "Where there is no 'flour,' etc.," the Mishnah teaching us incidentally that Torah can be acquired only upon the simple requirements of life, not upon its luxuries (Midrash Shmuel). (7) Exodus 26:35. See Ramban, Commentary on the Torah, Exodus, pp. 450-451.

mercial matters so that you will be able to obtain your sustenance and livelihood. However although you should seek to earn a livelihood, you should not assume that you may do so through both just and unjust means. Hence, David concluded the verse by saying, *and cherish faith.*[1] That is to say, dwell in the land and associate with people, be faithful in your dealings, and do not think to accumulate wealth unjustly. Thus, the prophet declared, *He that getteth riches, and not by right, in the midst of his days he shall leave them, and at his end he shall be a fool.*[8]

The verse begins with *trust* and ends with *faith* in order to explain that faith [in G-d] is included within [the concept of] trusting [in Him], for it is known that one who trusts also has faith. However, one who has faith might not have trust for fear that he may be deprived of Divine help on account of his sins or perhaps because he has already been [amply] rewarded for his good deeds; if not for such fear, it would indicate a lack of his trust in the Divine assurance. Therefore, only for fear of having sinned, will he employ the customary ways of the world to try to save himself from distress or to achieve his desire, as our patriarch Jacob prepared normal defensive measures [against the approach of his brother Esau],[9] for he feared that because of his sins, he might be deprived of G-d's assurance of protection.

One who is motivated by the attribute of trust, however, is certainly inculcated with faith, too, for trust is like the fruit of the tree and faith is like the tree itself. Just as the fruit signifies [the existence of] the tree although the tree is no proof of the existence of the fruit, so does trust signify the presence of faith although faith is no proof of the existence of trust. You will also find this to be true of wisdom and piety. One's piety is a sign of his wisdom, for he could not have attained the stature

(8) Jeremiah 17:11.   (9) See Genesis 32:14-21. Thus, would Jacob not have feared that on account of his sins he might be deprived of G-d's help, he would not have sent Esau that large of a gift, nor the message of almost subservience. But as it was, he went all out to find favor in Esau's eyes.

of piety without wisdom, as the Sages said,[10] "An ignorant person cannot be pious." However, one's wisdom does not betoken his piety, for it is possible to be learned and wicked, as were Menasheh[11] and his colleagues.

The saintly Rabbeinu Yonah of blessed memory[12] explained that the purport of trust is that man should recognize in his heart that everything lies in the hands of Heaven, that it is in G-d's power to alter the laws of nature and change one's fortune, and that *there is no restraint to* Him *to save by many or by few.*[13] Even when distress is close at hand, G-d's help is imminent, for He *can do everything and no plan can be withholden from* Him.[14] Even when the sword is upon one's neck [i.e., when death is imminent], he should not discount the possibility of being saved, for the Book of Job explicitly states, *Though He slay me, yet will I trust in Him.*[15] Thus, [when the prophet Isaiah visited King Hezekiah, who was ill, and said to him, *Set thy house in order, for thou shalt die, and not live].*[16] Hezekiah replied to the prophet, "I have received a tradition from my ancestors that even when the sword lies outstretched upon one's neck, one should not despair of [Divine] mercy,"[17] for the Almighty has many alternatives.

(10) Aboth 2:6. (11) Menasheh, one of the kings of Judah, was the son of the famous Hezekiah. His reign of forty-five years (see II Kings 21:1) was characterized by some of the worst features of idolatry, as described there by Scripture. (12) Rabbeinu Yonah of Gerona, a contemporary of Ramban (Nachmanides), was known for his great scholarship and piety. Among his works are the *Sha'arei Teshuvah* (Gates of Repentance) and a commentary on the Book of Proverbs, a portion of which on Proverbs 3:26 is adapted here. (13) I Samuel 14:6. Jonathan, the son of King Saul, and his armor-bearer, were the only ones that were about to attack an entire Philistine garrison. Said Jonathan to the young man that bore his armor: '*Come and let us go over to the garrison . . . for there is no restraint to the Eternal to save by many or by few.*' And so indeed it happened. (14) Job 42:2. (15) *Ibid.*, 13:15. That is, even if He causes me to be slain, I am not separated from Him in the World to Come. Therefore, I always trust Him to save me from being slain. (16) II Kings 20:1, and discussed in Berachoth 10a. (17) Hezekiah, indeed recovered and reigned another fifteen years (II Kings 20:6).

One of the essentials of trust in G-d is that man should unwaveringly rely upon G-d to choose for him only that which is beneficial. Furthermore, [man must never suppose] that the final choice [in any matter] rests with himself, for occasionally, one considers his decision to be favorable for his welfare, but the opposite is the result. Therefore, in all matters, every person should submit to G-d's superior choice, for it is He Who chooses, not we, and the Creator knows best what will help or harm us. Concerning this thought, David prayed, *Cause me to know the way wherein I should walk.*[18] Even when a mishap befalls him, he should attribute it to G-d's chastisement, *for whom the Eternal loveth, He correcteth.*[19] It is all for his own good: to remove his sin, to bring him closer to G-d, and to augment his portion in the World of Reward.

To trust in G-d is to rely upon Him not only in general, but in every detail of one's activity as well. Thus, he will be conscious of the fear of Heaven every moment. In that way, although he may not succeed in his venture, the reward for trusting in Him will far outweigh the profit he might have had from his activity, and in case of success, his reward is then twofold. Thus, it is written, *In all thy ways acknowledge Him, and He will direct thy paths.*[20] This means that besides [receiving] the great reward from on high for your trust, you will also succeed in that activity in which you were cognizant of His Name, blessed be He. Because this verse, *In all thy ways acknowledge Him,*[20] is the foundation of the attribute of trust, the Sages said,[21] "Bar Kappara expounded, 'Upon which small section [of Scripture] are all of the Torah's essentials dependent? I must conclude it is [the verse], *In all thy ways acknowledge Him.*' "[20]

Fundamental to one's trust in G-d is a complete absence of reliance upon man and the realization that no mortal can benefit him or save him [if such action is] contrary to the Almighty's decree, as it is said,

---

(18) Psalms 143:8. (19) Proverbs 3:12. (20) *Ibid.*, Vese 6. The explanation which follows is adapted from Rabbeinu Yonah's commentary. See Note 12 above. (21) Berachoth 63a.

Cursed is the man that trusteth in man.[22] It is further written, *Blessed is the man that trusteth in the Eternal.*[23] If one bears in mind that any approaching trouble comes from G-d, blessed be He, he will not fear the blow, for *The king's heart is in the hand of the Eternal as the watecourses; He turneth it whithersoever He will.*[24] Similarly, in the affair of Sennacherib,[25] Scripture declares, *Should the axe boast itself against him that heweth therewith.*[26] The prophet here likened man to an axe. Just as the activity of the axe stems not from itself but from the hewer [who wields it], so are the actions of man, whether for good or bad purposes, controlled by G-d. Sennacherib prided himself in the vastness of his forces, but he did not know that the power of the blow is dependent not upon man, but upon Him Who had raised him to rulership. So indeed it was. A plague came upon Sennacherib's armies before dawn, as it is written, *And the angel of the Eternal went forth and smote in the camp of the Assyrians.*[27]

[When the people of Israel go forth to battle], the Torah forbids them to fear the nations,[28] stating, *What man is there that is fearful and fainthearted? let him go and return unto his house.*[29] It is possible that this [fearful] man really believes that everything is in the hands of the Almighty, but because his soul is not adept in the attribute of trust, his heart is consequently weakened and is of humble spirit. Hence, G-d commanded that he return to his home. It is written, *The fear of man bringeth a snare.*[30] This means that one's fear of man is a sin—it constitutes a snare for him and gives his enemy the opportunity to vanquish him—for man should not fear the might of another mortal man.

---

(22) Jeremiah 17:5. (23) *Ibid.*, Verse 7. (24) Proverbs 21:1. (25) Sennacherib, King of Assyria, brought his armies to Jerusalem intending to destroy the holy city. But "Scripture declares etc." (26) Isaiah 10:15. *The axe* is Sennacherib whom G-d has chosen as His instrument and given him power to rule over nations. But he cannot boast himself against the One Who has given him that power. And if he will not acknowledge G-d's superiority, he will be cut down, as indeed it happened. (27) II Kings 19:35. (28) Deuteronomy 20:1. (29) *Ibid.*, Verse 8. (30) Proverbs 29:25.

But whoso putteth his trust in the Eternal shall be set up on high[30] and escape the trouble in reward for his trust, although in reality, the trouble should have befallen him.

An essential point of trust in G-d is that if a person is blessed with wealth, property, tranquility, and honor, he should not attribute them to his good deeds but solely to G-d's bestowal of mercy upon him. If troubles and misfortunes befall him, he should not attribute them to chance or the powers of the stars, for that is the way of the infidel. Instead, he should ascribe them to sins and transgressions which he had committed. If he does ascribe [his misfortunes] to chance, he will be stricken with even more trouble, as it is said. *And if you walk contrary unto Me, I then will walk contrary unto you in fury.*[31]

An additional point concerning trust in G-d is that one should be ever ready to give his life for G-d. If enemies threaten to slay him unless he transgresses the Torah, he should be prepared to accept death rather than violate [the commandments]. Thus, David said, *Unto Thee, O Eternal, do I lift up my soul,*[32] and it is further stated, *O my G-d, in Thee have I trusted, let me not be ashamed.*[33] He similarly stated, *Nay, but for Thy sake we are killed all the day.*[34] Now, a person can be slain only once. [How then could David say that for the sake of G-d, a person's martyrdom occurs *all the day?* David's intent], however, is that for each moment that one is mentally prepared to give his life for G-d, immense reward and abundant recompense are stored away for him [in the World to Come]. That is why David spoke of martyrdom *all the day,* for with respect to the reward and recompense, it is as *if we are killed all the day.*

One of the principles of martyrdom is that one must consider anything which G-d does as good, as the Sages said,[35] "Everything done

---

(31) Leviticus 26:27-28. (32) Psalms 25:1. (33) *Ibid.,* Verse 2. (34) *Ibid.,* 44:23. (35) Berachoth 60b. In our editions of the Gemara: "Whatever the Merciful One does is good." The version quoted in the text here is also found in Ein Yaakov.

by Heaven is good." Whether rich or poor, one should also accept everything out of love, trusting in His Name at all times and under all circumstances. If one is poor, he should trust that the Creator of all things, Who gives food to all flesh, will sustain him and provide him with his livelihood. [On the other hand], if one is rich, he should bear in mind that every moment he enjoys his wealth he is receiving a gift from G-d. Even if he were to ascend to royalty on par with David and Solomon, the wealth associated with such royalty would still be from G-d, for it is written, *Mine is the silver, and mine is the gold, saith the Eternal of hosts.*[36] You know that David, who amassed untold wealth for the construction of the Temple, admitted that he personally had no part of that wealth and referred to himself as poor, as it is written, *Now, behold, in my poverty, I have prepared for the House of the Eternal a hundred thousand talents of gold, and a thousand thousand talents of silver; and of brass and iron without weight.*[37] He then confessed, *But who am I, and what is my people, that we should be able to offer so willingly after this sort? for all things come of Thee, and of Thine own have we given Thee.*[38]

One who trusts in G-d, blessed be He, is encompassed on all sides, by the Divine attribute of mercy, for it is said, *And he that trusteth in the Eternal, mercy compasseth him about.*[39] G-d provides him with sources from which to derive his livelihood, for nothing is restrained from Him. This is known, for example, from the case of Elijah, who was fed by the ravens,[40] and the case of the hundred prophets, who were hidden, fifty to a cave, by Obadiah.[41] Thus, it is written, *O fear the Eternal, yea His holy ones, for there is no lack to them that fear Him.*[42] *The young lions do want, and suffer hunger; but they that seek the Eternal lack not any good thing.*[43] The verse is stating that G-d feeds all the weak, such as the babe in its mother's womb and the chick within the

(36) Haggai 2:8. (37) I Chronicles 22:14. (38) *Ibid.*, 29:14. (39) Psalms 32:10. (40) I Kings 17:6. (41) *Ibid.*, 18:4. (42) Psalms 34:10. (43) *Ibid.*, Verse 11.

egg, and He can withhold the prey from the strength of the mighty lion, *but they that seek the Eternal lack not any good thing.* [43]

The Rabbis commented[44] on the subject of trust, "One who has bread in his basket and asks, 'What shall we eat tomorrow?' is deficient in faith." For this very reason, the manna descended [in amounts of] *a day's portion every day.*[45] The people would thus be dependent upon G-d for their daily food. However, those who kept their portion for the following day were deficient in faith, as Scripture mentions, *and it bred worms, and rotted.*[46]

By virtue of their trust in G-d, Israel was redeemed from Egypt. Thus, the Rabbis said in Midrash Tehillim,[47] *"Unto Thee they cried and were delivered.*[48] Why so? *In Thee did they trust, and were not ashamed.*[48] All of this by virtue of trust." Because the attribute of trust is one of the fundamental principles of the Torah, we find that the Torah itself is called "trust," as it is written, *A wise man scaleth the city of the mighty, and bringeth down the strength in which they trusted.*[49]

---

(44) Sotah 48b. (45) Exodus 16:4. (46) *Ibid.,* Verse 20. (47) Midrash Tehillim 22:6. (48) Psalms 22:6. (49) Proverbs 21:22. The thought is made clear in a Midrash on this verse. *"The city of the mighty* is the heaven which is the seat of the angels. *A wise man scaleth* alludes to Moses, who ascended to heaven. *And bringeth down the strength in which they trusted* refers to the Torah." Thus, the Torah is spoken of as "the trust."

ברכה

Blessings we Recite Daily

Explanation of the term 'Blessing'/ The blessings we utter infuse G-d's powers into the world, for He is the source of all wisdom and infinite blessing, but He is in no way augmented by these blessings/ Whoever strictly observes the laws of blessings indicates his good faith and purity of heart/ One should recite the blessings with devotion of heart before and after the meal and during the Divine Service, for all of these blessings combined comprise the hundred blessings which everyone is obligated to recite daily/ The reason for and the specific enumeration of the hundred daily blessings instituted by the Sages/ The explanation of the Priestly Blessing by the guarding influence of which the world continues to exist.

Blessings we Recite Daily

BLESSED ART THOU, O ETERNAL, TEACH ME THY
STATUTES.[1]

In this verse, King David asked G-d to provide him with an overflowing abundance of knowledge about Him and to show him the wonders
in His Torah. That is why he used the term "blessing," which includes
copious abundance.

The verse contains both a laudation and a prayer. *Blessed art Thou,
O Eternal* is an expression of laudation and praise. [It is as if David
were] saying, "Since You are the fountain of blessing from Whom the
abundance of goodness emanates to all existence, *teach Me Thy
statutes.*" The latter clause constitutes a prayer that G-d transmit to
him an abundance of perception by which he might know *His statutes.*

David used the word *blessed,* a passive verb form, in order to indicate that His powers are infused into the world when the blessing is
uttered, for He is the source of [all] wisdom and infinite blessing, [but
He is in no way augmented by the blessing]. The word *b'rachah* (blessing) is derived from the expression *b'reichath mayim* (a pool of water),
[which flows from a source]. David chose the word *statutes* rather than
"commandments" because the statutes contain secrets of the Torah
and hidden teachings of wisdom, and through them man is able to increase his knowledge of the Creator.

---

(1) Psalms 119:12. The author appropriately chose this verse as the central theme of
his discussion, because it is the only verse in all Scripture that contains the form of the
traditional blessing: *"Blessed art Thou, O Eternal . . . "*

Although G-d is the source of blessing, we nevertheless find that He desires to hear the blessings of His creatures in order to magnify the reward of the righteous [who bless Him] and to heighten the splendor they will enjoy in the World to Come. Furthermore, G-d desires blessings so that this world may be blessed with an abundance of food and an increase of good. Thus, the Torah contains a positive commandment to recite grace after a meal so that the food of the world will be blessed, as it is written, *And thou shalt eat and be satisfied, and thou shalt bless [the Eternal thy G-d].*[2]

There is a simple explanation of this subject. Blessings do not serve the needs of [G-d] on high; they serve the needs of [the world] below. Since He is the source of all blessing, the benedictions of His creatures are valueless to Him, for He is the Creator of all existence. All things depend upon Him, but in no way does He need anything at all. If all of His creatures were to bless Him and recite His praises throughout the day, what would they be giving Him *or what receiveth He* of their hand?[3] [We must conclude], perforce, that we alone derive the benefit of the blessings. By reciting a blessing, one bears witness to Divine Providence [and attests] that G-d provides food for His creatures so that they might live. By the merit of the blessing, He causes the abundance of produce and the increase of fruits. However, one who enjoys G-d's bounty and does not recite a blessing is considered as if he robs G-d of His providence and hands over the care of worldly creatures to the stars and constellations. Thus, the Sages said,[4] "One who enjoys this world's goods without reciting a blessing is considered as if he robs the Holy One, blessed be He, and the congregation of Israel," for he robs Him of His providence and robs Israel by causing a diminution [of the crops] of fruits.

This applies even to an individual, as the Sages said,[5] "Each person should always regard himself as if the entire world depends upon him.

---

(2) Deuteronomy 8:10. (3) Job 35:7. (4) Berachoth 35 b. (5) Kiddushin 40 b.

If he fulfills [just] one commandment, how happy he should be, for he has elevated himself and the entire world towards merit. However, if he commits [just] one sin, woe to him, for he has lowered himself and the entire world towards guilt." Since there is an explicit verse in the Torah in which He has commanded us to recite grace after a meal we may therefore deduce that a great obligation rests upon us to be careful with mandatory blessings [like grace after a meal] and blessings before partaking any food or drink, as well as blessings prescribed for certain occasions. One who strictly observes [the laws of blessings] shows his good faith and purity of heart and attests thereby that his belief [in the Torah] is deeply rooted and that he is pious and fearful of sin.

The Sages formulated the wording of blessings in the second and third person [e.g., "Blessed art 'Thou' . . . Who hast sanctified us by 'His' commandments etc."[6] Their purpose was] to firmly implant in our hearts that G-d is both revealed and hidden, near and far. He is revealed and near by virtue of our intellectual power [that we can conceive His presence] and He is hidden and far by virtue of His essence. Therefore, we say, "Blessed art Thou," which indicates that He is revealed, [and we conclude by saying], "Who hast sanctified us [by His commandments and charged us, etc.,]" which teaches that He is hidden. It is possible to understand this by the analogy of the sun, for our only means of speaking of the Creator is by the analogy of His creatures. A person can physically perceive the roundness of the sun, and he may rationally understand that its light is a boon to the world's existence. However, he cannot conceive its essence and the strength of its light unless he looks at it, and then his eyes will be blinded [by its brilliance, and so it is with G-d: we know His existence, but we cannot know His essence].

I will now enumerate the hundred blessings which one is obligated to recite daily. I shall begin with the eight blessings recited at the meal,

(6) See Ramban's Commentary on the Torah, Exodus, pp. 214-215.

for some people treat these lightly. [As a preface to this enumeration, it should be stressed that] before uttering any blessing one should first contemplate to Whom he is offering it, and only then should he recite it. David said, *I will exalt Thee, my G-d, O King, and I will bless Thy Name forever and ever.*[7] First, *I will exalt Thee* in thought, and then *I will bless Thy Name.*

The eight blessings recited at the table are: one on washing the hands, one over the bread, four in the grace after the meal, and one before and one after the drinking of wine. By pronouncing these blessings one's table becomes *the table that is before the Eternal.*[8] [He will thus avoid a common pitfall, for] food and drink usually lead one to physical rudeness and spiritual arrogance, which in turn cause man to forget G-d. The general rule in this matter is contained in this verse: *And they* [the nobles of the children of Israel] *beheld G-d, and did eat and drink.*[9] This means that they were contemplating the Divine Glory in their hearts [that had appeared at Sinai] while they were eating and drinking. It is known, moreover, that the table corresponds to the altar [in the Sanctuary], as the Sages commented in Tractate Berachoth:[10] *"The altar, three cubits high,* etc., *and he said unto me, This is the table that is before the Eternal.*[8] The verse begins by [describing the measurements of] the altar and ends by calling it *the table.* This teaches you that just as the altar atones [for one's sins], so does the table," for when one gives of his bread to the poor, he is considered to have brought an offering upon the altar.

[We will now turn to] the first blessing on washing the hands [before partaking of bread. For that washing], it is necessary that the water be

---

(7) Psalms 145:1.   (8) Ezekiel 41:22. It should be noted that wine of course is not obligatory as part of a regular meal, but see in our author's Shulchan shel Arba, Gate One, Blessing Three, where he discusses the importance of digesting food, and for this wine is especially helpful. Moreover, the table being *the altar that is before G-d,* it should resemble the bringing of an offering, of which the wine libation is part thereof. On Schulchan shel Arba, see Preface, Note 10. (9) Exodus 24:11. (10) Berachoth 55 a.

poured upon the hands. It is not sufficient to merely wash the hands in water. The reason for this is based on the verse, *And Aaron and his sons shall wash their hands and their feet from it.*[11] [The verse specified that they had to wash] *from it,* not "in it." Because the priest could not wash his hands in the water within the laver. He had to pour water from the laver upon his hands and then perform the Service. The Sages said,[12] "One who neglects the observance of washing the hands will be detached from the world," for he has indicated his readiness to cast off his subservience to the Sages in a matter not involving lust, but by showing the evil feature of his character.

When reciting the second blessing, that over bread, it is best to hold the bread with all ten fingers to signify the ten words in the *Hamotzie,* the blessing [over bread. The ten fingers] also correspond to the ten commandments connected with produce: *Thou shalt not plow with an ox and an ass together,*[13] *Thou shalt not muzzle the ox when he treadeth out the corn,*[14] the heave-offering which is given to the priest, the first tithe which is given to the Levite, the tenth of the tithe which the Levite gives the priest, the second tithe, the poorman's tithe, gleanings, the forgotten sheaf, and [the produce in] the corner of the field which is given to the poor. One should first recite the blessing and then break the bread, for otherwise he indicates that he is more anxious for the bread than for the reciting of the blessing. If one is entertaining guests, he should not recite the benediction over the bread for them unless he eats with them. [If he is not eating with them, he may not

(11) Exodus 30:19. The verse is referring to the laver, from which the priests washed their hands and feet before performing the Service. — The purpose of washing the hands before partaking of bread is of course entirely different from that of the priest washing his hands and feet before performing any of the Divine Services. The verse quoted here teaches us that any kind of religious "washing" cannot be performed inside the vessel containing the water. It must be done by pouring the water from the vessel over the limbs as specified by the law in such instance. (12) Sotah 4 b. (13) Deuteronomy 22:10. (14) *Ibid.,* 25:4.

recite the blessing for them] because there is no special obligation upon him to eat [and one who bears no obligation may not free others of their duty by his action]. However, in a matter which is obligatory, such as the *Hamotzie* over the unleavened bread [on the first two nights of Passover] or the blessing over wine during the *Kiddush* [i.e., the proclamation of the sanctity of the Sabbath or festivals] he may recite the blessing for others even though he has already pronounced the blessing for himself and is now not eating or drinking with them, for all Israel are responsible for one another as far as the commandments are concerned.

There are four blessings in the grace recited after a meal: "Who givest food unto all," "For the Land and for the food," "Who buildest Jerusalem," "Who art kind and dealest kindly." The first three are required by law of the Torah. Moses formulated the first benediction when the manna came from heaven, and Joshua ordained the text of the second benediction when Israel entered the Land. David devised the wording of the third benediction when he captured Jerusalem, and Solomon added to it when he built the Temple. The fourth benediction, "Who art kind and dealest kindly," was decreed by law of the Sages in memory of those slain at Bethar.[15] "[We say], 'Who art kind,' because the bodies of the slain did not decay; [we say], 'and dealest kindly,' because they were permitted to be interred."[16] At the conclusion of the third blessing, we say Amen to differentiate between the first three blessings, which are required by law of the Torah, and the fourth one, which was decreed by the Rabbis. That the source of the

(15) Bethar was the stronghold of Bar Kochba, who led the great rebellion against the Romans about sixty years after the destruction of the Second Temple. When Bethar after three years of Jewish insurgence finally fell, the Romans were so infuriated that they forbade the burial of the defenders slain in the battle. However, the bodies were miraculously preserved until another emperor granted permission for their burial. In commemoration of the miracle the Sages ordained a special blessing.

first three blessings is in the Torah is based upon the Sages' comment:[16] "What is the meaning of the verse, *And thou shalt eat and be satisfied, and thou shalt bless the Eternal thy G-d for the good Land He hath given thee?*[2] *And thou shalt bless* alludes to the blessing 'Who givest food unto all,' *for the Land* alludes to the blessing 'For the Land,' and *the good* refers to the blessing 'Who buildest Jerusalem,' for it is written, *that goodly mountain, and Lebanon.*"[17]

These are the hundred blessings in accordance with the order of the Gaonim,[18] may their soul rest in peace:

a) [In the morning service], the eighteen blessings[19] before *Baruch She'amar* . . . (Blessed be He Who spoke and the world came into existence) plus *Baruch She'amar* itself and *Yishtabach* . . . (May Thy Name be praised), make a total of twenty.

b) The three blessings in connection with the *Sh'ma*[20] in the morning[21] and the four in connection with the *Sh'ma* in the evening[22] bring the total to twenty-seven.

(16) Berachoth 48 b.   (17) Deuteronomy 3:25. This verse is part of Moses' prayer to be permitted to enter the Land of Israel. *That goodly mountain* refers to Jerusalem.   (18) The subject of one hundred blessings is mentioned in the Talmud (Menachoth 43b), as well as in each of the places where their individual contents are specifically discussed. The later Sages, known as the Gaonim, arranged the blessings in their proper place in the Service. Hence, Rabbeinu Bachya refers here to "the order of the Gaonim." — On Gaonim, see Note 44 in *Ahavah* (Love).   (19) These eighteen blessings begin with the blessings over studying the Torah and conclude with "Who sanctifiest Thy Name amongst the many."   (20) See Note 42 in *Eivel* (Mourning).   (21) There are two blessings before the morning *Sh'ma* — "Creator of the luminaries" and "Who hast chosen Thy people Israel in love" — and one blessing "Who hast redeemed Israel," after it.   (22) There are two blessings before the evening *Sh'ma* — "Who bringest in the evening twilight" and "Who lovest Thy people Israel" — and there are two after it: "Who hast redeemed Israel" and "Who guardest Thy people Israel forever."

c) The three *Amidoth*[23] of the day, each of which contains nineteen blessings. Thus there are fifty-seven[24] in all, which brings the total to eighty-four.

d) The eight blessings in each of the two daily meals total sixteen. All together, there are thus one hundred.

The Sages taught us that after the destruction of the Temple, the entire world has continued to exist by merit of the Priestly Blessing.[25] I shall now explain the three verses therein. [First], *The Eternal bless thee, and guard thee.*[26] According to the simple purport of Scripture, this means the augmentation of blessing and the abundance of good. With this blessing will come protection, something which mortal man cannot offer. Man may enrich his fellow, but he cannot guarantee that the riches will remain with him nor can he guard them. The Sages said,[27] "A man in Syria was a good friend of the King of Rome. [Once], the king sent for him and presented him with a certain amount of gold. On his return home, brigands attacked him and took whatever he had. It was impossible for the king to ensure his safety. Thus, it is written, *The Eternal bless thee, and guard thee.*"

[The second verse of the Priestly Blessing is] *the Eternal make His face shine upon thee, and be gracious unto thee.*[28] G-d will be favorably disposed towards you if you deserve it, and if not, *He will be*

---

(23) The *Amidah* (plural: *Amidoth*) literally means "standing." It is that part of the daily prayers [i.e., The *Sh'moneh Esreih* (Eighteen Blessings)], which must be read while standing. Three *Amidoth* are recited every day: at the Evening Service, the Morning Service, and Afternoon Service. — To those Eighteen Blessings there has been added a nineteenth blessing against the secterians. (24) On Sabbaths and festivals, each of the *Amidoth* contains only seven blessings. There are various suggestions for complementing the resulting deficiency in the hundred blessing. The most acceptable method is to answer Amen after the blessings recited by others, e.g., when they are called up to the Torah, etc., for responding Amen is equivalent to reciting the blessing itself (Orach Chayim 46, 3, Beiur Heitev). (25) Midrash Tehillim 7. (26) Numbers 6:24. (27) Tanchuma, *Naso*, 10. (28) Numbers 6:25.

gracious unto thee by giving you a gratuitous gift, as it is written, *G-d be gracious unto us, and bless us.* [29]

[The final verse in the Priestly Blessing is] *the Eternal lift up His countenance upon thee,* [30] [which means that He will] protect you wherever you turn. This is the opposite of the statement, *I will hide My face from you.* [31] Since the person is protected by the Master of providence, he will be blessed with peace, as it is written, *and He will give thee peace.* [30]

The Midrash [offers this exposition of the Priestly Blessing]: [27] "*The Eternal bless thee* [26] with sons, and *He will guard thee* with daughters, since the latter are in need of being guarded. *The Eternal make His face shine upon thee* [28] means that He will raise from you children who are learned in the Torah, as it is said, *For the commandment is a lamp, and Torah is light.* [32] [Furthermore], He will raise from you priests [33] who will kindle the fire upon the altar. [The verse concludes], *and He will be gracious unto thee,* [28] which the great Rabbi Chiya explained as meaning that He will dwell with you. Another interpretation is that He will raise from you gracious ones [i.e., prophets], as it is said, *And I will pour upon the House of David, and upon the inhabitants of Jerusalem, the spirit of grace and of supplication.* [34] [The final verse in the blessing is] *the Eternal lift up His countenance upon thee.* [30] However, is it not written [elsewhere], *Who regarded not persons?* [35] The answer is that if [the sinner] repents before the Divine decree has been issued, *the Eternal will lift up His countenance upon him,* but once the decree has gone forth, He *regarded not persons.*"

---

(29) Psalms 67:2.   (30) Numbers 6:26.   (31) Isaiah 1:15. The verse reads: *And when you spread forth your hands, I will hide Mine eyes from you.* This is generally interpreted to be a reference to the spreading of hands in prayer. But from the context here it may be referring to the spreading of the hands by the priests when they recite the blessing. Hence, our author's statement: "This is the opposite of etc."   (32) Proverbs 6:23. The light of Torah will thus shine upon Israel.   (33) A daughter of an Israelite could marry a priest, and their sons would thus be able "to kindle the fire upon the altar."   (34) Zechariah 12:10.   (35) Deuteronomy 10:17. How then could it be said that He is favorably disposed towards us?

In Bereshith Rabbah,[36] the Sages said: *"And I will bless them that bless thee.*[37] The priests bless Israel, as it is said, *And they shall put My Name upon the children of Israel, and I will bless them.*[38] The Holy One, blessed be He, said, 'I will bless the priests and their entire tribe. In this world, the tribe of Levi blesses you, but in the World to Come, I in My Glory will bless you, as it is said. *The Eternal will bless thee, O habitation of righteousness, O mountain of holiness.*"[39]

(36) This quotation is not found in Bereshith Rabbah, but in Tanchuma, *Lech Lecha,* 4. (37) Genesis 12:3. (38) Numbers 6:27. (39) Jeremiah 31:22.

בית הכנסת
The Synagogue

Before entering a synagogue, one should be heedful of his physical cleanliness as well as his spiritual readiness/ When one attains purity of heart, G-d will more readily hear his prayers/ The power of a synagogue is great, for it is in many respects like the Temple and has therefore been called 'the miniature Sanctuary'/ Praying there is more acceptable because of the public's presence/ Before entering a synagogue, one should purge himself of all evil thought, for such thought defiles the heart and is worse than physical impurity/ One should refrain from engaging in irreverence or idle talk in the synagogue/ The obligation to kindle lights in a synagogue/ The great merit of doing even a small thing for a synagogue/ The severity of the sin of not attending synagogue services, and conversely, the magnitude of the reward for regularly attending morning and evening services.

The Synagogue

GUARD "RAGL'CHA" (THY FOOT) WHEN THOU GOEST TO THE HOUSE OF G-D, AND BE READY TO HEARKEN; IT IS BETTER THAN THE OFFERINGS OF FOOLS, FOR THEY KNOW NOT TO DO EVIL.[1]

This verse teaches people to purify themselves inwardly and outwardly when going to a house of prayer. No person is considered pure until he combines both purity of the body and purity of the heart. Both of these are included in the term *ragl'cha* (thy foot). It applies to the entire body because the foot supports the body and also functions either to lead one to the source of his desire or to avoid harm. It is appropriate to attend to physical purity because the body is the instrument of the higher pure soul [i.e., the rational soul]. Only [when the body is] in a state of purity can the soul function. It will then be possible for the soul to reveal itself in deeds *in a clean vessel in the House of the Eternal,*[2] [and it will be able] *to stand to minister in the Name of the Eternal.*[3]

(1) Ecclesiastes 4:17. While the *House of G-d* mentioned in the verse is traditionally taken to refer to the Sanctuary in Jerusalem (see Targum), Rabbeinu Bachya takes it to refer to a house of prayer or synagogue, and interprets the whole verse accordingly. (2) Isaiah 66:20. *The House of the Eternal* refers to the Sanctuary in Jerusalem. Rabbeinu Bachya uses the expression here metaphorically, explaining that when the body will be purified before coming into the synagogue, then the soul will be able to function properly and reveal itself *in a clean vessel* [i.e., the body] in the House of G-d. (3) Deuteronomy 18:5.

106

The term *ragl'cha* also refers to purity of heart, for *regel* also means "cause,"[4] as in the expression, *'l'regel' (because of) the cattle [that goeth before me].*[5] Among the causes which induce one to follow the path of truth is purity of heart, and so David prayed, *Create me a pure heart.*[6] Similarly, our Sages warned us that one must direct his thoughts in the path of truth and concentrate on uprightness at the time of prayer. G-d will then more readily hear his prayer, and his prayer will be more acceptable than the offering of the fools who do not know how to turn away from doing evil.

The Sages expounded:[7] "What is the meaning of the verse, *Guard thy foot when thou goest to the House of G-d?*[1] Guard yourself so that you do not sin, but if you do sin, bring an offering [of atonement], *and be ready to hearken*[1] to the words of the Sages. If they sin, they bring an offering and repent, unlike the fools who bring an offering without repenting, *for they know not to do evil.*[1] If that is so [if they know not to do evil], then they are righteous! However, the meaning is that the fools sin and bring an offering and do not know whether they bring it for the good they have done or for the evil they have committed, [and therefore they do not bring a sin-offering as an act of repentance, but rather as just any offering]. The Holy One, blessed be He, says, 'They do not distinguish between good and evil, and yet they bring an offering before Me!' " According to this interpretation, the meaning of the expression *for they know not to do evil*[1] is that they do not discern nor understand of having done evil.

The power of a synagogue is great, for it is [in many respects] like the Temple and has therefore been called "the miniature Sanctuary." The Sages commented,[8] *"And I shall be to them as a miniature Sanctuary*

---

(4) This interpretation of the word *regel* is found in Guide of the Perplexed I, Chapter 28. (5) Genesis 33:14. (6) Psalms 51:12. (7) Berachoth 23 a. (8) Megillah 29 a.

in the countries where they are come.[9] This refers to the synagogues and houses of learning." Prayer is more acceptable there than elsewhere because the public assembles there, and "G-d never rejects the prayer of assemblies, as it is said, *Behold, G-d does not despise* [the prayer of] *the many.* "[10]

It is further written, *In the multitude of people is the King's glory.*[11] The Sages commented upon this verse in Midrash Mishlei:[12] "Rabbi Chanina said, 'Come and see the praise and holiness of G-d, blessed be He! Although He has myriads of ministering angels before Him, He nevertheless desires only the praise of Israel, as it is said, *In the multitude of people is the King's glory.*[11] The term *people* refers only to Israel, for it is written, *This people which I formed for Myself, that they might tell of My praise.*[13] This means that I have created them so that they might praise Me to the world. Similarly, Scripture states, *The princes of the people are gathered together, the people of the G-d of Abraham.*[14] Rabbi Simon said, 'G-d is exalted in the world when [the people of] Israel assemble in synagogues and houses of learning and listen to a scholar's homiletical exposition [of some Torah subject]. At that moment, G-d says to the ministering angels, Come and see how the people whom I have formed for Myself praise Me and adorn Me with pride and beauty. Thus it is said, *In the multitude of people is the King's glory.*' "[11]

Just as the Sanctuary was built on the top of the mountain, so are we commanded to raise the height of a synagogue above the other houses [in the area], as it is said, *to raise up the House of our G-d.*[15] Those

----

(9) Ezekiel 11:16. The prophet lived among the exiles in Babylon, and there he assured the people that although they lived far from the Land of Israel, G-d *shall be to them* etc. This verse is the source of sanctity for synagogues and houses of learning throughout the world, wherever Jews assemble for prayer and study.   (10) Job 36:5 and quoted in Berachoth 8 a.   (11) Proverbs 14:28;.   (12) Midrash Mishlei on the verse *ibid.*   (13) Isaiah 43:21.   (14) Psalms 47:10.   (15) Ezra 9:9 and discussed in Shabbath 11 a. "At present, because of the many tall government buildings, we are in no position to comply with this stricture" (Bei'ur Heitev, Orach Chayim 150, 3).

who attend [services in the synagogue] should invest themselves with a sense of awe, for we have been commanded to fear the awesome presence of the Divine Glory, as the Sages said,[16] "When one prays, he must act as if the Divine Glory rests opposite him, for it is said, *I have set the Eternal always before me.*"[17] This statement refers to one who prays anywhere, for the Divine Glory is everywhere, and it certainly applies so much more to places designed for prayer and to service in synagogues and houses of learning.

Before entering a synagogue, one should purge himself of all evil thought, for evil thought defiles the heart. This conclusion is derived *a fortiori* from Jacob's charge to his family when they were about to go to Beth-el, as it is said, *And purify yourselves, and change your garments.*[18] If he called upon them to purify their bodies when coming to the House of G-d, it is all the more true that one should purify his heart [when he enters there to pray]. It is known that impurity of the heart is much harsher for the soul than impurity of the body, as the Sages said,[19] "Sinful thoughts are more injurious than the sin itself." After cleansing his heart of any evil thought, one should discipline himself against unbridled conversation pertaining to secular or personal matters while he is in a synagogue. Instead, his words should be few when he is not engaged in prayer and praising G-d. Certainly, he should not converse during those parts of the service where the Sages prohibited interruptions.

One is obligated to kindle lights in a synagogue, for that place is designated for prayer, one of the functions of the soul, and the soul is likened to a lamp, as Solomon said, *The light of the righteous rejoiceth.*[20] Therefore, the soul greatly rejoices because of that light and

(16) Sanhedrin 22 a.   (17) Psalms 16:8.   (18) Genesis 35:2.   (19) Yoma 29 a. See further in *Taharath Haleiv* (Purity of Heart), where the author elaborates on the meaning and significance of this saying.   (20) Proverbs 13:9. The flame of a burning candle gives the impression that it is rejoicing. So, too, is *the light of the righteous* a symbol of joy (Ibn Ezra). In other words, the teaching and conduct of the righteous lead to the path of a happy and peaceful existence.

exudes joy and happiness, for the light is the soul's identification. Because of its elation, the soul proceeds to worship G-d joyfully which is the perfect form of worship. This is also the plain explanation for the kindling of the Candelabrum in the Tabernacle and Sanctuary. Although the light of the candle is physical and the essence of the soul is a rational light, we nevertheless find that man's soul clothes itself with happiness and gladness because of it and that it enables him to worship in joy. Therefore, our Rabbis charged us to kindle lights in a synagogue, as they commented,[21] *"Therefore glorify ye the Eternal 'ba'urim,'*[22] such as those lanterns,"[23] for a home containing lighted lamps is glorified and honored in the eyes of people more than a home which is dark. This is similar to the Sages' statement,[24] "A palace with guards is not to be compared to a palace with no guards."

It is forbidden to conduct oneself irreverently in a synagogue as do those who, for example, enter during the service and speak loudly as if they were in a public thoroughfare. They go about *in the stubbornness of their evil heart*[25] and are oblivious to the sanctity of the place. Thus, the Sages taught:[26] "Synagogues and houses of learning must not be treated with irreverence. One must neither eat nor drink nor beautify oneself in them. One must not leisurely stroll through them, nor may one use them as a shelter from the sun or the rain. However, they may be used for study and review, as well as for funeral services in cases of public mourning, [i.e., for a distinguished person]. They must be swept and sprinkled. Rabbi Yehudah said, 'These rules apply when they are in a habitable condition, but when they are in a state of desolation, they should be left that way and the weeds should be allowed to grow there because of grief of the soul.'[27] Rav Asi said,

---

(21) P'sikta d'Rav Kahana, 21.   (22) Isaiah 24:15.   (23) In quoting this text of the P'sikta, Ramban adds, " . . . which burn in synagogues" (Commentary on the Torah, Genesis, p. 161).   (24) Sifre Zuta, *Korach*, 18 a.   (25) Jeremiah 7:24.   (26) Megillah 28 a-b.   (27) When people see the desolate condition of the synagogue, they will recall its former glory and will resolve to rebuild it (Rashi, *ibid.*).

'Synagogues in Babylon are built with the proviso [that they may be used for all purposes], yet nothing irreverent, such as accounting, should be done in them, and one must not use [synagogues] for a short-cut,' " for it is disrespectful to utilize them like ordinary houses. If, however, he entered one for the sake of prayer, he is permitted to use it as a shortcut [when his prayer is finished].

When one builds a wall of a synagogue or any part thereof, even if he affixed only one nail that was necessary and essential, it is accounted to him as a great merit, for the matter of a synagogue entails a general commandment which in turn includes many detailed commandments, each one of which constitutes an act of Divine Service. You already know that the same principle applies to all of the 613 commandments, which are general in scope and infinite in detail. Thus, David said, *I have seen an end to every purpose, but Thy commandment is exceedingly broad.*[28]

The Sages expounded in the first chapter of Tractate Berachoth,[29] "One who has a synagogue in his city and does not enter it [for prayer][30] is called an evil neighbor,[31] for it is said, *Thus saith the Eternal: As for all Mine evil neighbors.*[31] Moreover, he brings evil upon his children after him, as it is said, *Behold, I will pluck them up from off their Land.*"[32] [On the other hand], one who attends synagogue services each morning and evening merits ministering to the Holy One, blessed be He, in the World to Come. The Sages commented in Midrash Tehillim,[33] "*He that walketh in a way of integrity, he shall minister unto Me.*[34] That is to say, he who ministers to Me in this world shall minister to Me in the World to Come." Similarly, in this world, he merits longevity, as the Sages related in Tractate Berachoth:[29] "They said to Rabbi Yochanan,[35] 'There are old people in Babylon.' He was

(28) Psalms 119:96.   (29) Berachoth 8 a.   (30) Our text of the Talmud clearly states, "for prayer."   (31) An evil neighbor does not enter his neighbors' homes (Mishneh B'rurah, Orach Chayim 90:37).   (32) Jeremiah 12:14.   (33) Midrash Tehillim, 101.   (34) Psalms 101:6.   (35) A leading Palestinian Amora.

surprised and said, 'It is written, *That your days may be multiplied, and the days of your children, upon the Land.*[36] [The Torah promised long life only *upon the Land*], but not outside the Land!' When they told him that those old people go to a synagogue in the morning and evening, he said, 'That is what aids them [to attain old age], as Rabbi Yehoshua told his children, Go to the synagogue in the morning and evening so that your lives will be prolonged.' " The Sages have proven[29] from Scripture that the reward for this commandment is longevity, as it is said, *Happy is the man that hearkeneth to me, watching daily at my gates, waiting at the posts of my doors.*[37] *For whoso findeth me findeth life and obtaineth favor of the Eternal.*[38]

(36) Deuteronomy 11:21.   (37)   Proverbs 8:34.   The speaker here is Wisdom. (38) *Ibid.*, Verse 35.

גזילה

Robbery

Part One

One who possesses anything acquired through robbery is far removed from 'the mountain of the Eternal' and 'His holy place' / Robbery is a sin against G-d and man / In cases of robbery, restitution is possible, but is most difficult to accomplish. If the victim cannot be located, the sin remains with the robber and any offering he may bring will be of no avail, nor will his repentance achieve any degree of forgiveness / One who robs a poor man is subject to death by hand of Heaven / It is forbidden to take anything illegally from a non-Jew / It is insufficient to have one's heirs make restitution after one's death; the robber himself should make restitution and so clear himself during his lifetime / Justice is the opposite of robbery, and one should always endeavor to pursue justice.

Robbery

IN RIGHTEOUSNESS SHALT THOU BE ESTABLISHED; BE
THOU FAR FROM OPPRESSION, FOR THOU SHALT NOT
FEAR, AND FROM RUIN, FOR IT SHALL NOT COME NEAR
THEE.[1]

In this verse the prophet Isaiah mentioned the subject of robbery.
[He advised] that a person should remove himself from robbery, for it
is an unpardonable sin calling for judgment and its punishment is a
burning fire which consumes the world.

The prohibition [against robbery] constitutes one of the rational
commandments. A person would institute it out of his own understanding even if it were not stated in the Torah. The prohibition
against robbery was included in the seven commandments with which
Adam, the first man, was charged.[2] It is therefore incumbent upon a
person to conduct honest business transactions and to keep his hands
unstained by robbery so that he may be worthy of ascending the holy
mountain of G-d. Thus, David said, *Who shall ascend the mountain of
the Eternal? And who shall stand in His holy place? He that has clean*

---

(1) Isaiah 54:14. The verse thus expresses the author's theme: through
righteousness, and not through robbery and oppression, shall you be established; only
then will you be assured that you will avoid ruin. (2) The seven precepts are: to
establish courts of justice, and to abstain from idolatry, incest, murder, robbery,
blasphemy, and eating flesh cut from live animals. — It should be noted that according
to Maimonides only six commandments have been given to Adam, while the seventh
one was given to Noah after the Flood (Mishneh Torah, *Hilchoth Melachim* 9:1).
These seven commandments are generally referred to as the "Noachide command-

hands, and a pure heart.[3] From here we learn that one who possesses anything dishonestly acquired is removed from *the mountain of the Eternal* and *His holy place.*

The laws of the sacrifices offer a great inspiration on this matter. The Torah banned from the altar the stomach of a fowl, as it is written, *And he shall take away its crop with the feathers, and cast it beside the altar.*[4] [The stomach of a fowl] is an implement of robbery which no amount of washing can cleanse, unlike in the case of cattle, for cattle eat at their master's crib, while fowl feed upon anyone's property. This, then, constitutes an urgent reminder and a wonderful lesson, bestirring the people to the realization that one who possesses anything acquired through robbery will not be permitted to approach the altar of G-d and will not ascend [His mountain] to be accepted by Him. Instead, G-d will utterly detest him and utterly abhor him[5] unless he restores that which he took by robbery. Since charity and robbery are absolute antitheses, one of which maintains the world and the other of which spells its destruction, the prophet therefore mentioned the two together, saying, *In righteousness shalt thou be established; be thou far from oppression,* and continues, *for thou shalt not fear,*[1] thus urging us to strive to approach the good quality, namely, righteousness, and thereby you will avoid the fear of destruction, since fear is only a result of sin. We find that the first man had no fear at all before he sinned, but immediately after he had sinned, it is written, *And I was afraid, because I was naked.*[6]

How strict is the prohibition against robbery! Heaven hastens to hear the cry of the victim, for the Sages expounded in Tractate Baba Metzia:[7] "Rabbi Abahu said, 'There are three wrongs for which the

---

ments" with which all mankind is charged to observe. (3) Psalms 24:3-4. (4) Leviticus 1:16. (5) See Deuteronomy 7:26. (6) Genesis 3:10. Before Adam sinned, he heard the Divine Voice and had no fear (*ibid.*, 2:16), but after he ate of the forbidden fruit, he admitted his fear upon hearing the Divine Voice. — It is with this thought in mind that the prophet here said, *for thou shalt not fear* (Isaiah 54:14). (7) Baba Metziah 59 a.

curtain [of heaven] is never closed:[8] fraud, robbery, and idolatry. Fraud is derived from the verse, *And, behold, the Eternal stood beside a wall made by a plumbline, with a plumbline in His hand.*[9] Robbery is mentioned in the verse, *Violence and spoil are ever before Me.*[10] Idolatry is derived from the verse, *A people that provoke Me to My face continually.' "*[11]

All transgressions in the Torah are divided into two categories. First, there are sins of man against the Creator, in which the person's soul feigns to be a stranger to the mercies of G-d and provokes Him with evil deeds and thoughts. In reality, though, the sinner harms only himself, as Solomon said, *he that doeth it would destroy his own soul.*[12] The second category is comprised of sins of man against his fellow, such as embarrassing him by word or deed. In this case, the sinner wrongs another person. The sin of robbery, however, is [perpetrated] against G-d and man, and this is the purport of the [seemingly] redundant language of the verse, *Then it shall be, if he hath sinned, and is guilty, that he shall restore that which he took by robbery.*[13] This means *if he hath sinned* against the robbed one *and is guilty* before the Creator, as it is stated. *It is a guilt-offering, he is certainly guilty before the Eternal.*[14]

Regarding the sin of robbery, Solomon said, *The getting of treasures by a lying tongue is a vapor driven to and fro; they that seek them seek death.*[15] He is thus saying that wealth accumulated through oppression

---

(8) That is, the outcries over them never go unheeded. "The curtain [of heaven]" is "the partition which separates the place of the Divine Presence" (Rashi, Berachoth 18b).   (9) Amos 7:7. The phrase *with a plumbline in His hand* indicates that it is always "in His hand" and that He uses it to check upon the wrongdoer.   (10) Jeremiah 6:7.   (11) Isaiah 65:3.   (12) Proverbs 6:32. The first half of the verse clearly speaks of adultery. Our author uses the second half of the verse independently, to express the general thought that a sinner harms only himself.   (13) Leviticus 5:23. The phrase *and is guilty* seems redundant, since it already states *if he hath sinned.*   (14) *Ibid.,* Verse 19.   (15) Proverbs 21:6.

and robbery is like *a vapor driven to and fro* and they that gather it are [in reality] seeking death. Similarly, the prophet said, *Woe unto him that buildeth his house by unrighteousness, and his chambers by injustice,*[16] after which it is written, *For the stone shall cry out of the wall, and the beam out of the timber shall answer it.*[17]

The negative commandment [forbidding] robbery is juxtaposed to a positive commandment [charging the robber to restore the object he took] and thus clear himself. Nevertheless, the prohibition should be considered extremely severe, for occasionally, the victim will not be found because he may now live in a distant land or he may have died. Even if the robber does locate him, the victim may not be willing to forgive, or the robber may be destitute and unable to restore [the value of] the robbed object. In case one robs the public, the robber will not even be able to identify the individual victim. As long as the robber keeps the robbed property in his possession, a guilt-offering [he brings] will be of no avail, nor will his repentance atone for his sin, for repentance is not based upon words but on deeds, and in this case the deed is the restitution of the property. Thus the prophet cried out, *Wash yourselves, make yourselves clean, put away the evil of your doings from before Mine eyes, cease to do evil. Learn to do well.*[18] It is further written, *Though your sins be as scarlet, they should be as white as snow.*[19]

The principle of restitution in robbery is that he must return the very thing which he took by force. If the object itself is not available, such as where he has already intermingled it with permissible things, the law requires that he restore its value. The Rabbis stated:[20] "If one robbed a

---

(16) Jeremiah 22:13. (17) Habakkuk 2:11. This is a metaphorical way of saying that the act of robbery is so well known that the structure of robbed stones cries out the injustice that has been perpetrated here, and so also a structure made of robbed timber (R'dak). (18) Isaiah 1:16-17. (19) *Ibid.*, Verse 18. Thus only after having put away the evil of our doings will we attain atonement for our sins. (20) Gittin 55a.

beam and emplaced it in a large structure, he must pull down the entire structure and restore the beam to its owner. These are the words of the scholars of the House of Shammai, but those of the House of Hillel said that the robber need only repay the value of the beam. [Their decision is] based on the decree of [inducing] the penitent."[21] The law has been decided in accordance with the House of Hillel. [Regarding] the repentance of the men of Nineveh, Scripture testifies, *and from the violence that is in their hands,*[22] which the Sages explained as follows:[23] "If one robbed a beam and built it into a structure, he pulled down the entire structure and restored the beam to its owner." Their repentance was beyond the requirements of justice.

All of the above applies to one who robs his fellow who is his equal in wealth. However, if one robs a poor man, he does not satisfy his liability with restitution. Instead, he is liable to death by the hand of Heaven, for Solomon said, *Rob not the weak, because he is weak,*[24] *for the Eternal will plead their cause.*[25]

Do not be misled into thinking that what we have said about the gravity of the sin of robbery applies only to robbing an Israelite but not a non-Israelite. It is not so. Robbing a non-Israelite is also forbidden by law of the Torah. In fact, in our dealings with the non-Jew, we must be more stringent than the law requires in order to sanctify the Name of G-d. Thus, our patriarch Jacob charged his sons to return the money [they had found in their sacks], as it is written, *And the money that was returned in the mouth of your sacks carry back in your hand.*[26] Although the Egyptians were idolators, Jacob commanded [his sons] to

(21) If the robber had to pull down his structure in order to return the beam, he would refuse to repent. Thus, the House of Hillel's more lenient stance serves to induce the robber's repentance. (22) Jonah 3:8. This was the king's proclamation to the people of Nineveh: *Let them turn every one from his evil way, and from the violence . . .* (23) Taanith 16a. (24) Proverbs 22:22. *Because he is weak,* he is therefore unable to resist you (Rashi). (25) *Ibid.,* Verse 23. See my Hebrew introduction to Kad Hakemach p. 13, Note 8, that our author based this thought on Rabbeinu Yonah's teachings in his Sha'arei Teshuvah. (26) Genesis 43:12. Upon their first trip

return the money for the sake of sanctifying G-d's Name. This occurred before the Torah had been given, and nowadays, [after the Revelation at Sinai], one is so much more obligated to do so. Thus, it is written in the Tosephta[27] of Baba Kamma: "One who robs a non-Israelite
is obligated to restore the object to him. Robbing a non-Israelite is
worse than robbing an Israelite because it involves the profanation of
G-d's Name." The reason for this is: when one robs his fellow Jew, the
victim does not consider the outrage injurious to the reputation of his
religion, but when one robs a non-Jew, the victim complains and
strikes against the Jewish faith and reviles the Law of Moses.

Having been made aware of the gravity of this sin, each person who
knows himself to be guilty of robbery should remove [the onus of this
sin] from upon himself, for he will not be cleansed of it until he casts it
completely away. Thus, if one's heirs make restitution of some property
which he had acquired by robbery, it is not perfect restitution. It is
necessary that the offender himself make restitution while he is alive
and not leave it to be done by others. This is like lighting the way with
a candle. [Such lighting] is effective only if he carries it before him, not
if he carries it behind him. It is based upon the thought that Scripture
states, *And thy righteousness shall go before thee, the glory of the Eternal shall be thy rearguard.*[28] This means that if you will vindicate
yourself so that your righteousness will go before you, that is, in your
lifetime, then *the glory of the Eternal shall be thy rearguard* in eternal
life. We have been commanded in the Torah, *Justice, justice shalt*

---

to Egypt to buy food for the family, Joseph had ordered his men to put their money into the sacks of his brothers. When they came home and found the money, they were in
consternation as to how it happened. Later, when they needed food again and were
forced to make another trip to Egypt, Jacob told them, *And the
money* . . .   (27) Literally meaning "Addition," the Tosephta is a collection of Tannaitic teachings compiled by Rabbi Chiya and Rabbi Oshaya after the redaction of the
Mishnah was completed by Rabbi Yehudah Hanasi in the year 200 Common Era. The
Tosephta follows the arrangement of the Mishnah throughout its six large divisions.
The text quoted here is in Baba Kamma 10:15.   (28) Isaiah 58:8.

thou follow.[29] The repetition of *justice, justice* serves many purposes. One is to indicate that we should always follow justice whether in profit or loss, and another is to teach us that we should be just in both speech and deed, the two aspects of man's activity. A third interpretation is that the repetition of the word *justice* teaches us that we should be just to both Jew and non-Jew. As an indication of the high virtue of justice, we find that Jerusalem was praised because of it, as it is said, *Justice lodged in her.*[30] By acting justly, one merits to wait on the Divine Presence, as it is said, *As for me, I shall behold Thy face in justice; I shall be satisfied when I awake with Thy likeness.*[31]

(29) Deuteronomy 16:20.   (30) Isaiah 1:21.   (31) Psalms 17:15.

Part Two

> *The observance of all commandments depends upon faith. If one does not deal faithfully with his fellow man, he is also deficient in his faith in G-d / The explanation of the eleven commandments set forth by David in Psalm 15 by the observance of which one merits entry into the Divine Presence / The opposite of faithfulness is the sin of robbery. It is man's accuser on high and destroys his life. This is all the more true if he possesses things acquired through violence / One must be extremely careful to avoid the sin of robbery.*

ETERNAL, WHO SHALL SOJOURN IN THY TABERNACLE?
WHO SHALL DWELL UPON THY HOLY MOUNTAIN?[32] HE
THAT WALKETH UPRIGHTLY, AND WORKETH
RIGHTEOUSNESS, AND SPEAKETH TRUTH IN HIS
HEART.[33]

Our Sages said,[34] "A person should always begin with a good subject
and conclude with one. 'Good' refers to G-d, for it is said, *O give
thanks unto the Eternal, for He is good.* "[35] The Sages thereby directed
that a person's opening remarks should always be on a matter that is
good, i.e., G-d. Therefore, when the Sages of Israel addressed the
public, they would begin with a verse upon which their entire address
was founded. Thus, we find in the Midrash: "Rabbi Abba commenced
[with a verse] and expounded,"[36] "Rabbi Zeira commenced [with a
verse] and expounded,"[37] "Rabbi Yehudah the son of Rabbi Simon
commenced [with a verse] and expounded."[38] Each of these Sages
began his address with a verse, for each verse in the Torah is inherently
sacred and is called "a good thing," a reference to the Divine Name.
Therefore, it is proper to explain the above verse with which we introduced [our remarks].

In the [fifteenth] psalm, David set forth eleven commandments, including faithfulness [by which one may merit entry into the Divine
Presence]. It is known that the observance of all commandments is
dependent upon faith. If a person does not conduct himself faithfully
in his dealings with his fellow man, regardless of the nature of those
dealings, he lacks faith in G-d. That is why David said that the one who

---

(32) Psalms 15:1.   (33) *Ibid.,* Verse 2.   (34) I have been unable to find the precise
language of the quotation mentioned here, but I did locate the following text in
Yerushalmi Megillah III, 7: "One who rises to read in the Torah should both begin and
conclude with a beneficent theme."   (35) Psalms 106:1. An identical verse appears
elsewhere as well.   (36) Bereshith Rabbah 38:2.   (37) P'sichta Eichah Rabbah
33.   (38) Bereshith Rabbah 1:8.

deserves to sojourn in the Tabernacle of G-d and to be in His Presence
and dwell upon His holy mountain is the One who fulfills these commandments. Thus, David said, *Eternal, who shall sojourn in Thy
Tabernacle?*[32] This refers to the Holy Temple on earth, which is called
a *Tabernacle* while it exists, but *a field* when it has been destroyed, as
it is written, *Zion shall be plowed as a field.*[39] [The next part of David's
statement], *Who shall dwell upon Thy holy mountain?*[32] refers to the
Sanctuary on high. In connection with the *Tabernacle,* David used the
term *sojourn* because a person is but a sojourner in this world.
However, with regard to the Sanctuary on high, he spoke of *yishkon*
(dwell), which is associated with the word *Shechinah* (Divine
Presence). Thus, David is saying that in order to merit both worlds [the
earthly Temple and the Sanctuary on high] one must possess certain
qualities, [which we will now discuss].

First, [he must be one] *that walketh uprightly,*[33] meaning that "his
inside is like his outside."[40] [Second, he must be one who] *worketh
righteousness,*[33] acting properly whether he is rich or poor. If he is rich,
he should strive to do charitable deeds and to distribute part of his
wealth in a noble and dignified manner. If he is poor, he should "work
righteousness" by performing acts of lovingkindness which do not require the expenditure of money.[41] [The third quality is that he must be
one who] *speaketh truth in his heart,*[33] meaning that he does not orally
violate that which he had agreed upon in thought. [Fourth, he must be
one] *that hath no slander upon his tongue,*[42] rejecting any aspersions
and disparaging gossip. [Fifth], *he doeth not evil to his fellow*[42]
although he may have been wronged by him, [and sixth], *nor does he
cover up a reproach against his relation.*[42] If one of his relatives sinned,

---

(39) Micah 3:12.   (40) That is, his outward appearance and mien reflect his inner
feelings. He is not deceitful.   (41) Acts of lovingkindness are greater than charity in
three ways. See above at end of *Eivel* (Mourning), Part III.   (42) Psalms 15:3.

he is first to confront him and not to conceal his transgressions. [Seventh], *A vile person is despised in his eyes.* [43] Even if he has fulfilled many commandments, he considers them to be few, but if he has committed one transgression he magnifies its significance and he is displeased with himself over it. One who has this quality of character will naturally choose rather to be the persecuted than the persecutor, for the persecuted come near to G-d. The Torah declared fit for the altar only those animals that are pursued; beasts of prey are unfit for the altar. Thus, the Sages said, [44] "Be of those who are insulted and not of those who insult; be of those that are persecuted and not of those who persecute. Of those [who are insulted and persecuted], it is said, *But they that love Him shall be as the rising sun in its might,* " [45] for the sun submitted to offense and therefore remained the greater of the two luminaries. [46] Regarding this thought, Solomon said, *That which is hath been long ago, and that which is to be hath already been; and G-d seeketh that which is pursued,* [47] which means that He seeks to reward the persecuted. Note that Solomon said *seeketh* rather than "help" because the word *seeketh* has two connotations: He seeks to reward and to punish. G-d may now seek to punish him for his past activities of persecuting others. This is why the Divine Name *Elokim* (G-d) is mentioned here; it is indicative of the attribute of justice. The

(43) *Ibid.*, Verse 4. Our author explains the verse as applying to one's own self, that one should always minimize his own importance. The verse is thus saying that one should not deem himself as morally perfect. (44) Gittin 36b. (45) Judges 5:31. (46) This refers to the following tradition: When G-d created the luminaries, the sun and moon were both equal in power. It says, *And G-d made the two great lights* (Genesis 1:16), which implies that both were equal. The moon, however, complained to G-d, "How is it possible for two kings to wear the same crown?" G-d answered, "Go then and make yourself smaller." This explains the continuation of the aforementioned verse: *the greater light to rule the day, and the lesser light to rule the night.* Thus, because the sun remained silent, it retained its original strength (Chullin 60b). (47) Ecclesiastes 3:15.

Sages taught,[48] "Because you have drowned others, others have drowned you. Ultimately, those who drowned you shall themselves be drowned."

[Psalm 15 continues with the eighth quality]: *But he honoreth them that fear the Eternal.*[43] One who bestows honor upon G-d-fearing people indicates thereby that he himself possesses that characteristic. [Ninth], *he sweareth to his own hurt, and changeth not*[43] even if his oath causes his own discomfort or loss.[49] [Tenth], *he putteth not out his money on interest.*[50] According to the interpretation of the Sages,[51] this applies even to interest from a non-Jew; there is no commandment [obliging us] to take interest from him. Although Maimonides enumerates [taking interest from a non-Jew] among the commandments because of the verse, *Unto a foreigner 'tashich' (thou shalt lend upon interest),*[52] that is not conclusive. The intent of the verse is to augment the negative commandment against taking interest from a Jew. Thus: *"Unto a foreigner thou shalt lend upon interest,* but not to an Israelite,"[53] as Ramban stated it with definitive proofs.[54] [Finally, David enumerated one who] *taketh not a bribe against the innocent,*[50] for one who accepts a bribe blinds his eyes from seeing the truth. *He that doeth these things shall never be moved.*[50]

(48) Aboth 2:6. The Mishnah thus teaches us the principle of "measure for measure:" in the same way the sinner committed his crime, he will be repaid.   (49) For example, he swore to fast or to deprive himself of certain pleasures, or to give charity. In any case, he does not try to release himself from his self-imposed obligation.   (50) Psalms 15:5.   (51) Makkoth 24a.   (52) Deuteronomy 23:21. Maimonides' view is expressed in his *Sefer Hamitzvoth* (Book of Commandments), 198. See my translation, "The Commandments," Vol. I, p. 213.   (53) Thus by lending money to a Jew on interest, one violates both a positive and a negative commandment. The verse positively specifies that lending on interest is permissible *unto a foreigner,* which negatively implies that this may not be done to an Israelite. When a negative commandment is derived from a positive precept, the negative retains the force of its positive origin. Hence, one who lends on interest to a Jew is in effect also transgressing a positive commandment. The negative commandment on usury from a Jew is *Take thou no interest of him* (Leviticus 25:36).   (54) See Ramban's Critical Comments on Maimonides' Sefer Hamitzvoth, and his Commentary on the Torah, Deuteronomy p. 295.

These eleven commandments which David mentioned in this psalm include the entire Torah. Regarding this theme, the Sages said:[55] "Six hundred and thirteen commandments were declared to Moses on Sinai, as it is said, *Moses commanded us a Torah, an inheritance of the congregation of Jacob.*[56] The numerical value of the word Torah is 611.[57] [The remaining two commandments], *I am the Eternal thy G-d,* etc.,[58] and *Thou shalt have no other gods before Me,*[59] we heard directly from the Almighty Himself. David then reduced [the 613] to eleven, [as mentioned in Psalm 15]. Isaiah came and reduced them to six, as it is said, *He that walketh uprightly, and speaketh uprightly, he that despiseth the gain of oppressions, that shaketh his hands from holding of bribes, that stoppeth his ears from hearing of blood, and shutteth his eyes from looking upon evil.*[60] Micah came and reduced them to three, as it is said, *It hath been told to thee, O man, what is good, and what the Eternal doth require of thee: only to do justly, and to love mercy, and to walk humbly with thy G-d.*[61] Isaiah further reduced them to two, as it is said, *Keep ye justice, and do righteousness.*[62] Finally, Habakkuk came and reduced them to one commandment, as it is said, *And the righteous shall live by his faith.*"[63] We may conclude from all this that the entire body of commandments is included in [the concept of] faith, which is the essential part of the entire Torah.

Since Habakkuk taught us that faith includes the entire Torah and that by virtue of faith one merits eternal life, it follows that the opposite of faith nullifies the entire Torah and causes the loss of eternal life. What is the opposite of faith? It is the sin of robbery, which is man's accuser on high and the destroyer of his life in the World to Come. Of course, this also applies to one who fails to pay his share of

---

(55) Makkoth 23b-24a.   (56) Deuteronomy 33:4.   (57) The word *Torah* is spelled as follows: *tav* (400), *vav* (6), *reish* (200), *hei* (5). Thus the numerical value totals 611.   (58) Exodus 20:2.   (59) *Ibid.,* Verse 3.   (60) Isaiah 33:15.   (61) Micah 6:8.   (62) Isaiah 56:1.   (63) Habakkuk 2:4.

taxes along with the other people of his town. He thereby robs the public[64] and demonstrates that he has no faith and that he does not believe in reward and punishment. How many sins and transgressions are accountable to him who has faltered in this matter! How many homes of the contentedly rich have been destroyed because of this sin! How much wealth has been forfeited because of this violation!

Many sorrows are included in this sin, like robbery of the public, which is an unpardonable sin calling for judgment because the public includes poor, orphans, and widows. It entails the profanation of the Divine Name. Violation of an oath is also involved, for one who swears to pay his taxes faithfully and does not do so is a sinner and disgraces the King, Whose attributes include truth. Moreover, [the robber's actions] testify that he does not acknowledge the Creator, a sin which will certainly be punished, as we find in the case of the wicked Pharaoh. He did not acknowledge the Creator, as it is said, *I know not the Eternal.*[65] The Creator said to him, "Since you do not recognize Me, I will make you do so," as it is said, *In this thou shalt know that I am the Eternal.*[66]

Do not wonder why the sinful robber is not punished immediately as was the company of Korach.[67] G-d is long-suffering and waits [for the sinner to repent], as Solomon said, *If thou seest the oppression of the poor, and the violent perverting of justice and righteousness in the state, marvel not at the matter; for One higher than the high watcheth over them, being the Highest Power.*[68] We learn from this verse that G-d temporarily forgoes even the wickedness of the sinner and transgressor; He does not destroy him immediately. Thus, we find that when the first man sinned and caused death to come upon him and all

---

(64) Taxes in those days were not levied by the government against the individual, but upon the Jewish community as a whole, the leaders of which then apportioned the tax among the individual member of the community. Failure to pay one's fair share meant that others would have to pay additional taxes to compensate for his portion. Thus, the tax evader was in effect robbing his neighbors. (65) Exodus 5:2. (66) *Ibid.*, 7:17, and explained in Midrash Mishlei, 27. (67) Numbers 16:32. Korach and his company challenged the authority of Moses. (68) Ecclesiastes 5:7.

mankind, the mercy of G-d was still with him, as it is said, *And the Eternal G-d made for Adam and for his wife garments of skins, and clothed them.*[69]

If the sinner [who robs the public by giving less than a fair share of the tax] thinks that he can rely on G-d's mercies to forgive him, he should know that there is no atonement for his sin. We have been taught,[70] "If a person said, 'I will sin and repent, I will sin again and repent,' he will not be given an opportunity to repent," for he intentionally committed the sin while relying on forgiveness. Ultimately, G-d's retribution will surely overtake him, for there is no escape from His reach in this world or in the World to Come.

[We have said that robbery involves] the sin of profaning G-d's Name, a sin for which even repentance, the Day of Atonement, and suffering cannot atone. When one is expected to be faithful in paying his tax and does not, he consequently endangers his life because of this sin, and this is all the more true if he held a Scroll of the Torah in his arm and swore to pay the tax fairly and faithfully. If he is then lax therein, there is an additional sorrow of violating an oath. If he is not trustworthy to himself, how can he be relied upon in relation to others, as the Sages said,[71] "How can a person who has no pity for his son and daughter [have any pity for me]?"

Thus, a person must be very careful to guard himself from any form of robbery, especially the evasion of taxes, which is equivalent to robbing the public. We have proven it from Scriptural verses and the words of our Rabbis, of blessed memory. May the Holy One, blessed be He, purify us from sins and from the transgressions of robbery, oath and ban, and may He teach us to do His Will with a perfect heart, as David prayed, *Teach me to do Thy Will, for Thou art my G-d; let Thy good spirit lead me in a straight path.*[72]

---

(69) Genesis 3:21. (70) Yoma 85 b. (71) Taanith 24 a. In the name of Rabbi Yosei bar Avin. (72) Psalms 143:10.

גאוה
Haughtiness

The two types of pride—a high opinion of one's achievement and a sense of satisfaction stemming from one's evil ways—are both despicable / Statements of the Sages on haughtiness of the spirit / An overbearing spirit is recognizable in one's conduct, speech and deed, and all the more in his performance of the Divine Commandments / The Torah has prohibited both the High Priest and the king from indulging in pride or haughtiness / To avoid the pitfalls of the sin of haughtiness, it is not enough to assume the moderate course of mere humility. One must rather tend towards the opposite extreme, which is meekness / The meaning of meekness / The reward of those who are meek in spirit.

Haughtiness

THE FEAR OF THE ETERNAL IS TO HATE EVIL, PRIDE,
AND ARROGANCE; AND THE EVIL WAY, AND PERVERSE
SPEECH DO I HATE.[1]

Solomon related this verse in the name of Wisdom, which dictates
that one who fears G-d will despise an evil person,[2] just as [the verse]
and I am prayer[3] means *"and I am* a man of *prayer."* An evil person is
one of *pride, and arrogance, and the evil way, and perverse speech.*[1]
Solomon mentioned pride first because it is the most objectionable of
all human characteristics. Whoever possesses it is called *an abomination to the Eternal.*[4]

There are two types of pride. A person may pride himself over his
wisdom, his dignified way of life, the good attributes of his character,
and his being more fortunate than the rest of his generation, and a person may pride himself over his evil qualities and all his deeds of *oppression and perverseness.*[5] Of course, the Sages detest one who takes
satisfaction in deeds incited by the evil inclination, but the Sages also
abhor one who entertains a high opinion of his merit because of his
good deeds, as they said in the Midrash,[6] "Israel is likened to a vine, to

---

(1) Proverbs 8:13. The sense of the verse is simply that it is not enough to avoid doing evil, but to have an abhorrence thereof, and of all that can be classified as
evil.   (2) Thus, the expression *to hate evil* means *"to hate* a person, who is *evil."* — The
collective body of Wisdom, personified in Scripture, is here speaking to Solomon dic-
tating to him rightful principles of life.   (3) Psalms 109:4.   (4) Proverbs 16:5: *Every
one that is proud in heart is an abomination to the Eternal.*   (5) Isaiah
30:12.   (6) Midrash Shmuel, 16.

teach us that just as a vine has large and small clusters of grapes, the larger ones hanging lower than the smaller ones, so is Israel," [the greater the person the profounder his meekness].

Solomon mentioned *perverse speech*[1] because pride, which is one of the aspects of the evil way of life, causes a person to speak perversely. Pride forces him to deviate from the way of truth and to speak of things which are unfounded.

Our Sages commented,[7] "Whoever is haughty should be chopped down like an *asheirah* (a tree devoted to idolatry),[8] for here it is written, *and the high ones of stature shall be hewn down,*[9] and there it is said, *and hew down their asheirim.* "[10] The Sages further stated,[7] "The Divine Presence cries over one who is haughty, as it is said, *and the haughty He knoweth from afar.* "[11]

The severity of the prohibition against pride applies to a person's activities in the areas of his speech and the practical affairs between him and his fellow man. His arrogance is discernible if he speaks haughtily, as it is written, *He that exalteth his gate seeketh destruction.*[12] The term *gate* is a metaphor for the mouth, for the mouth is to the body as a gate is to a house. His arrogance is recognized in his deeds if he deals with things that are too great and too wonderful for him, as David said, *Neither did I exercise myself in things too great or too wonderful for me.*[13] Needless to say, it is a sin of great magnitude and of harsh punishment to pride oneself in the performance of the commandments [in matters] between himself and the Creator, and to entertain a high opinion of one's own importance while

---

(7) Sotah 5a.   (8) The thought conveyed by the Sages is that even as we are charged to remove idolatry by utterly uprooting it, so should a person who wishes to rid himself of his presumptuousness be prepared to uproot this evil trait in all its manifestations, for impertinence is a form of self-worship (Maharsha, *ibid.*).   (9) Isaiah 10:33.   (10) Deuteronomy 7:5.   (11) Psalms 138:6. G-d brings the humble near Himself, but not the arrogant. He knows the latter from afar and mourns over them (Maharsha, Sotah 5a).   (12) Proverbs 17:19.   (13) Psalms 131:1.

disrespecting the commandment, as in the case of one who exalts himself when walking to the synagogue while carrying the palm branch, and other similar instances.

The Sages said,[14] "One who parades in a scholar's cloak to which he is not entitled is denied entry into the Divine Presence, for here it is written, *The haughty man abideth not,*[15] and there it is written, *to Thy holy abiding place.*"[16] In Tractate Sanhedrin, we find [the following]:[17] "Jeroboam's haughtiness drove him out of the World [to Come], for it is said, *And Jeroboam said in his heart: 'Now will the kingdom return to the House of David.*[18] *If this people go up to bring offerings in the House of the Eternal at Jerusalem, then will the heart of this people turn back unto their lord, even unto Rehoboam, King of Judah.*[19] By tradition, only the kings of the House of David may sit in the Sanctuary Court. When the people will see Rehoboam sitting and me standing, they will say that Rehoboam is the king, and Jeroboam is his servant. If I sit down, however, they will say that I am rebelling against the Kingdom [of David] and they will kill me.' Thereupon, *The king took counsel, and made two calves of gold, and he said unto them: Ye have gone up long enough to Jerusalem; behold thy gods, O Israel,* etc."[20] [In Tractate Sanhedrin], it is further written:[17] "G-d said to

---

(14) Baba Bathra 98a.   (15) Habakkuk 2:5.   (16) Exodus 15:13. The aforementioned verse, *The haughty man 'abideth' not* is thus explained by the present verse, that he is not privileged to be in His *holy abiding place.* — The reason for the punishment is generally explained as follows: Since he parades in a scholar's cloak to which he is not entitled, he is of course a person who speaks falsehoods, of whom it has been said, *he that speaketh falsehood shall not be established before Mine eyes* (Psalms 101:7.)   (17) Sanhedrin 101b.   (18) I Kings 12:26.   (19) *Ibid.,* Verse 27. This occurred just after Jeroboam had established the Kingdom of Israel by leading ten tribes away from the Kingdom of Judah. Jeroboam feared that if his subjects would make the festival pilgrimage to Jerusalem, Rehoboam, King of Judah would regain their loyalty for the reason explained further in the text. To keep his people away from Jerusalem, Jeroboam introduced idolatry into his realms.   (20) *Ibid.,* Verse 28.

Jeroboam, 'Repent, and I and you and [David] the son of Jesse will walk about in the Garden of Eden.' Jeroboam answered, 'Who will be at the head?' G-d replied, '[David] the son of Jesse will be at the head.' Thereupon, Jeroboam said, 'If so, I do not want it.' "[21]

One who is proud by nature usurps "the garb of the King," as it is said, *The Eternal reigneth, He is clothed in majesty,*[22] for majesty befits G-d alone and not any mortal being. He alone is exalted over all existence, and this is also so in this lower world where He subdues the sinners and rebels, who would otherwise have brought about the destruction and foundering of the world as a punishment for their arrogance. Thus, the verse continues, *Yea, the world is established, that it cannot be moved.*[22] Scripture teaches you thereby that were it not that He is exalted over the presumptuous and brings them low unto the earth and subdues them, the world would have foundered.

Our Sages commented:[23] "One who is haughty denies the essence of religion, as it is said, *Then thy heart be lifted up, and thou forget the Eternal thy G-d.*[24] One who is haughty is considered as if he worshipped idols, for here it is written, *Every one that is proud in heart is an abomination to the Eternal,*[25] and in the case of idolatry it is written, *And thou shalt not bring an abomination into thy house.*[26] The

---

(21) Thus, Jeroboam's haughtiness was his undoing in both worlds. Had he submitted in this one matter and agreed that the king of the House of David should take precedence over himself, he would have gained for himself and his descendants a place of honor in the annals of our people. As it is, however, he is known as "a sinner who caused many to sin" (Aboth 5:20). — It should be noted that the Talmudic text does not mention "David" but merely speaks of *ben Yishai*, literally: "the son of Jesse," who is David. But it may well be translated as "a descendant of Jesse," meaning any king of the House of David. Jeroboam was thus voicing his refusal to be second to Rehoboam. (22) Psalms 93:1. (23) Sotah 4 b. (24) Deuteronomy 8:14. The Torah "deems it unto you as if you had forgotten G-d" (Rashi, Sotah 4 b). (25) Proverbs 16:5. (26) Deuteronomy 7:26. The term *abomination* with which Scripture refers to the haughty man is thus here explained to be a reference to idolatry.

haughty person is also considered to have engaged in the practice of immorality, for there too it is written, *for all these abominations have the men of the land done.*"[27] The Sages further declared[23] that one who is haughty will not be resurrected.

The Torah has prohibited even the High Priest from being proud of his high position in the priesthood. Thus, it commanded that he himself take up the ashes from the altar.[28] Because he was the person designated to perform the Service in the Sanctuary, he was therefore charged to do this lightly regarded act while he was dressed in the four priestly garments.[29] All this served to remind him to shun haughtiness, and to be low and submissive instead.

The Torah also warned the monarch against the evil of haughtiness. Thus, it is written, *that his heart be not lifted up above his brethren, and that he turn not aside from the commandment to the right, or to the left.*[30] The Torah thereby admonished the king against being proud of his realm and the breadth of his dominion. Instead, he should regard himself merely as one of *his brethren* who do not possess such power and authority. Although it is natural for a king to indulge in pride over the standing of his kingdom, the Torah [specifically] cautioned him against being proud. How much more does [this warning] apply to all [common] people, [who do not have any reason for pride and arrogance, as does a king]! Even the Holy One, blessed be He, Whom majesty is befitting and Who is clothed therein,[22] conducts Himself with humility in His relation with His creatures. This is the meaning of the statement, *The Almighty, Whom we cannot find out,*

(27) Leviticus 18:27. The chapter there lists all kinds of illicit intercourse. (28) *Ibid.*, 6:3. On the Day of Atonement the removal of the ashes was done by the High Priest. On any other day of the year it could be done by any common priest. (29) The four garments of the ordinary priest were the tunic, drawers, turban and belt. In addition to these, the High Priest wore the breastplate, the robe, the upper garment, and the frontlet. The reference here to the "four priestly garments" must necessarily apply to a common priest. (30) Deuteronomy 17:20.

is surpassing in strength.[31] That is to say, we have not found that the Almighty, Who is surpassing in strength, should come to us in a forceful and overbearing manner; [He comes] only with humility and integrity. This is why Scripture mentions the Divine Name *Sha-dai* (Almighty) here because it indicates His wondrous power over the higher forces when He makes the stellar constellations submissive to His will. However, the Divine Name *Sha-dai* is not found with regard to the lower creatures [for their strength is insignificant altogether].

It is known that haughtiness is one extreme of human characteristics while meekness is the opposite extreme. The moderate course between these two traits is humility. In all [other] moral problems, it is always proper to choose the course of moderation, and that is the intent of Solomon's words, *Weigh the path of thy feet.*[32] Just as a balance brings two opposing weights into equilibrium, so should you balance your path between the two extremes [of a particular moral issue]. However, with regard to the evil of haughtiness, it is insufficient to merely remove oneself to the moderate position of humility. Rather, we are charged to attain meekness, the antithesis [of haughtiness]. With respect to this principle, the Sages said,[33] "*M'od m'od* (be exceedingly) low in spirit." They used the double expression *m'od m'od* to teach us that in this case, one should bend towards meekness, the opposite extreme. It is written of Moses our teacher, *And the man Moses was very meek.*[34] The word *very* indicates that Moses was not satisfied with just being humble, which is the moderate course, but he was inclined to meekness.

To be meek does not mean that one should disgrace himself in any matter or allow himself to be tread upon by others, for man, who was created *in the image of G-d,*[35] is precious and therefore must care for

(31) Job 37:23. (32) Proverbs 4:26. (33) Aboth 4:4. (34) Numbers 12:3. (35) Genesis 1:27.

his honor and the high stature of his rational soul. Certainly, if he is a scholar, he should protect the honor of his Torah knowledge. To be meek means, instead, that one should be gentle in word and deed to all people, needless to mention his peers and superiors. He should hear himself reviled and remain silent, and he should forbear relating against one who unwittingly sinned against him on some single occasion.

To show that meekness is as beloved by G-d as haughtiness is despised by Him, He chose to give the Torah on Mount Sinai, as it is written, *the mountain which G-d had desired for His abode.*[36] The Sanctuary in Jerusalem, too, which stood in the land of Benjamin, was not located directly on the top of the mountain, all as a means of indicating meekness and humility. Similarly, the phylactery of the head is not placed on the highest point of the head, but a bit lower, "the place on the head where the child's brain pulsates."[37]

Therefore, one should be careful in these two matters: he should shun haughtiness and adopt meekness. Since one is beloved and the other hated by G-d, a person should emulate Him [in this regard]. Whoever is meek in spirit merits honor and the Divine Glory rests upon him. He merits honor, for Solomon said, *And he that is of a low spirit shall attain to honor.*[38] The Divine Glory rests upon him, as it is said, *For thus said the High and Lofty One, that abideth eternity, Whose Name is Holy, I dwell in the high and holy place, with him also that is of a contrite and humble spirit, to revive the spirit of the humble, and to revive the heart of the contrite ones.*[39]

(36) Psalms 68:17. This psalm is devoted to the theme of the Revelation at Sinai. G-d chose to give the Torah on this low mountain rather than on some higher one to indicate that meekness is preferable to haughtiness. (37) Menachoth 37 a. (38) Proverbs 29:23. (39) Isaiah 57:15.

A Stranger, A Proselyte

Any Jew who is exiled from his home town is called a 'geir' (stranger). We are commanded to feed him and to be kind to him / The differences between 'a resident proselyte' and 'a righteous proselyte,' and how proselytes are accepted / The reason that acceptance of proselytes is not beneficial for Israel / We should learn a lesson from Job, a non-Jew, who befriended every stranger. All the more, we who accepted the Torah, are obligated to practice that meritorious deed / In the Messianic era, the nations of the world will voluntarily convert to Judaism.

A Stranger, A Proselyte

THE STRANGER DID NOT LODGE IN THE STREET; MY
DOORS I OPENED TO THE WAYFARER.[1]

The Sages commented,[2] "Rabbi Eliezer the Great says, 'In thirty-six places, the Torah has charged us concerning a proselyte.'" It is common knowledge that any Israelite who is exiled from his home town is called a *geir* (stranger). This term also applies to any non-Jew who converts to the faith of Israel. He is further called "a righteous proselyte" because he has come to take refuge under the wings of the Divine Glory. On the other hand, a non-Jew who obligates himself not to worship idols and comes to settle among us is termed "a resident proselyte."

An Israelite who is exiled from his home town is called *geir*, which stems from the expression *gargir*, (a single berry) which has been separated from its root. We are commanded to provide him with food and drink and to be kind to him. The latter is the most important of all to him. These are Solomon's words, *Ointment and incense rejoice the heart, so doth the sweetness of a man's friend from advice of the soul.*[3] The verse informs us that a person is obligated to gladden the heart of the wanderer by supplying him with food and drink and showing him a

(1) Job 31:32. The verse was uttered by Job, a non-Jew, who recalled his former days, when he was well and prosperous, how he offered hospitality to the wayfarer, and was engaged in many other meritorious deeds to the orphan and widow. (2) Baba Metzia 59 b. (3) Proverbs 27:9. That is, advice given with a genuine desire to be helpful to the stranger.

friendly countenance, for besides *oil and incense* he is still in need of *the sweetness of a man's friend.* The verse states *from the advice of the soul,* meaning that this sweetness and friendly countenance should issue from one's rational soul. [It should come forth] through love and esteem, not through flattery, for sweetness of [genuine] friendship will be more beneficial to the stranger than all [material things] one can give him.

The righteous are also called *geirim* (strangers), for they consider this world insignificant and their dwelling here is only temporary. The word *geir,* which [as explained] stems from the expression *gargir,* (a single berry) which has been separated from its root, applies to the righteous because they are cognizant of their separation from their holy origin. Even as a stranger yearns to return to the land of his birthplace, they too, long to return to their root and origin, the Throne of the Glory, from which the rational soul stems. Therefore, we find that all of the patriarchs were called "strangers." Regarding Abraham, it is written that he said, *A stranger and sojourner I am with you.*[4] In the case of Isaac, G-d said to him, *'Gur' (sojourn) in this land,*[5] and it is written of Jacob that he dwelt *in the land of his father's sojournings.*[6] David called himself a *geir,* as it is said, *I am a stranger in the land.*[7] He compared himself to a stranger, who knows he must move on but does not know when, and therefore he must always keep his traveling outfit ready lest his time of departure come suddenly. What is his traveling outfit? It is the fulfillment of the commandments, as the verse continues, *hide not Thy commandments from me.*[7]

When a non-Jew who obligates himself not to worship idols but still eats forbidden foods comes to dwell among us, he is termed "a resident proselyte" or "a proselyte of the gate."[8] We are commanded to give

---

(4) Genesis 23:4.   (5) *Ibid.,* 26:3. The word *gur* (sojourn) stems for the word *geir* (stranger).   (6) *Ibid.,* 37:1.   (7) Psalms 119:19.   (8) I have not located the expression "a proselyte of the gate" in Talmudic literature, but it is found in Ibn Ezra's commentary on Exodus 12:49 and in Ramban's Commentary on the Torah, Exodus, p. 316.

him the food forbidden to us, as the verse states, *Thou shalt give it un-to the stranger that is in thy gates, that he may eat it.*[9] Similarly, in the case of the Sabbath, it is written, *Thou shalt not do any manner of work, thou, nor thy son, nor thy daughter, nor thy manservant, nor thy maidservant, nor thy cattle, nor thy stranger that is within thy gates.*[10] This means that you should not do work by means of minors, cattle, and the stranger, "the proselyte of the gate" or "the resident proselyte" who wants to dwell among us and has renounced idolatry. He himself has not been commanded to observe the Sabbath, [and therefore he may do work for himself but not for an Israelite]. For this reason, the Torah adds the phrase *that is within thy gates,* for if the [Torah's] intent was to refer to "a righteous proselyte" [as explained further], it would have merely said *nor thy stranger.* We have been commanded concerning this "resident proselyte's" sustenance[9] because he has publicly obligated himself not to worship idols.[11]

A non-Jew who converts to Judaism is called "a righteous proselyte." His conversion requires three things: circumcision, ritual immersion, and a sacrificial offering, for with these three things Israel entered the covenant at the Revelation on Sinai.[12] Similarly, one who wishes to be converted bears these three obligations, as it is said, *As ye are, so shall*

---

(9) Deuteronomy 14:21. This verse refers to *n'veiloth,* a term which means either a clean animal which died of natural causes or had not been properly slaughtered, or the carrion of any unclean animal.   (10) Exodus 20:10.   (11) "He has accepted the prohibition against idolatry together with the rest of the precepts which the Noachides were commanded (see *G'zeilah* (Robbery), Note 2), but he has not undergone circumcision and immersion [in a ritual pool] and he is classed among 'the pious of the nations of the world' " (Mishneh Torah, *Hilchoth Isurei Biah* 14:7). " 'Resident proselytes' are accepted only in the time when the laws of the Jubilee apply" (*ibid.,* 14:8).   (12) On circumcision, see Joshua 5:5: *For all the people that came out* [of Egypt] *were circumcised.* On ritual immersion, see Exodus 19:10: *and let them wash their garments.* The Mechilta comments on this verse: "There is no case in the Torah where washing of the garments is required without a concurring requirement of immersion." On a sacrificial offering, see Exodus 24:8: *And he* (Moses) *sent the young men of the children of Israel, who offered burnt-offerings.*

the stranger be. [13] He must be circumcised and undergo ritual immersion in the presence of a court [of three Rabbis], and [although he cannot do so now], he will have to bring his sacrificial offering when the Temple will be rebuilt.

The Sages commented[14] that "you must first inform him about some of the commandments and the punishments for failure to observe them." We advise him of the punishments to discourage him from converting, for proselytes are not beneficial to Israel. *The mixed multitude*[15] [that left Egypt with Israel] were proselytes and they were the motivating force behind the making of the [golden] calf.[16] They were also responsible for the plague which erupted over the meat which they desired, as it is said, *And the mixed multitude that was among them fell a lusting.*[17] Therefore, the Rabbis clearly stated,[18] "Proselytes are as bad for Israel as a *sapachath* (a sore on the skin), for it is said, *'V'nispechu' (and they shall cleave) to the House of Jacob.*"[19] The reason for this is that they are not versed in the details of ritual laws, and Israelites could learn from their deeds.

There are some scholars[20] who explained that proselytes must be informed of some of the punishments for violating the commandments so

---

(13) Numbers 15:15. "In the manner in which you entered into the covenant, so shall the stranger [enter therein]" (Mishneh Torah, *Hilchoth Isurei Biah* 13:4). (14) Yebamoth 47 a. (15) Exodus 12:38. (16) Tanchuma, *Ki Thisa*, 19. (17) Numbers 11:4. (18) Yebamoth 47 b. (19) Isaiah 14:1. At the beginning of the verse, the prophet states that *the stranger shall join himself with them, 'v'nispechu' (and they shall cleave),* etc. The word *v'nispechu* is etymologically associated with the word *sapachath* (a sore on the skin). The verse thus intimates that proselytes retain their pre-conversion practices, and the Israelites might adopt their ways and customs. (20) This refers to Rabbi Moshe of Coucy, France, who flourished in the first half of the thirteenth century. He was the author of Sefer Mitzvoth Hagadol, also known as *S'mag*, which deals with the commandments. It is divided into two sections: "Negative Commandments" and "Positive Commandments." The text quoted here is found in "Negative Commandments," 116, and Rabbi Joseph Karo quotes it in his commentary on Tur Yoreh Deiah, 268.

that afterwards, they will not be able to claim that if they had known the punishment, they would not have converted, which [assertion would render] the conversion erroneous. Therefore, we must inform prospective proselytes of some of the punishments so that their conversion should be sincere and their acceptance [of our faith] complete.

There are other scholars[21] who explained that the Sages' statement, "Proselytes are as bad for Israel, etc.,"[18] was not intended to slight the proselytes themselves but rather to rebuke Israel. G-d sees that the proselytes have left their families and their native land and have come to cleave to the Divine Glory. [Thus, by their act of devotion], they [further] incriminate the Israelites when the latter fail to worship G-d with perfect hearts. Thus, we find in the Midrash:[22] "Reish Lakish said, 'Nowadays, proselytes are more distinguished than the Israelites who stood at Mount Sinai. The Israelites *beheld the thunderings, and the lightnings, and the voice of the shofar,*[23] and the great and awesome wonders, but the proselytes saw none of these things and still they came, under stress and pain, to take refuge under the wings of the Divine Glory.' "

In the aforementioned verse,[1] Job lauds himself that his home was wide open to all wayfarers, strangers, and sojourners, and that [he ensured that] no one, regardless of his nationality, ever lodged in the street. Job was a decandant of Abraham but not of Israel.[24] Still, he was an extremely pious and thoroughly righteous person. He worshipped G-d by means of the rational commandments, and he was kind to all people as well as to his own countrymen. This should be an inspiration for man to broaden the extent of his compassion, as the Sages

---

(21) Found in *S'mag* (see preceding note).   (22) Tanchuma, *Lech Lecha,* 6. The text quoted here, though, follows the *S'mag's* version.   (23) Exodus 20:15.   (24) This is the explanation of Ramban, found at the beginning of his commentary on Job. It is cited by our author again in the discourse on *Hashgachah* (Divine Providence). — Only Isaac and Jacob (Israel) are considered the seed of Abraham.

said,[25] "One who shows mercy to [G-d's] creatures will be shown mercy [in heaven], as it is said, *And He will give thee compassion, and show compassion unto thee.*"[26] We may conclude *a fortiori* that if Job, who did not know the Torah, practiced this quality [of kindness],the Israelites, who have accepted the Torah, are certainly obligated to practice it in all its aspects.

It is common knowledge that the Torah was given even to proselytes. The Sages commented,[27] "*Moses commanded us a Torah, an inheritance of the congregation of Jacob,*[28] which includes all who congregate unto Jacob." They further commented,[29] "*Which if a man do, he shall live by them.*[30] The verse does not say priest, Levite, or Israelite; it specifies *a man*, thus teaching us that even a non-Jew who occupies himself with the Torah is the equal of a High Priest." By right, [non-Jews who become] proselytes in these times of the exile and subjugation, are entitled to the great reward [destined for Israel] and should be classed among the highly distinguished ones of Israel. [However], there will be no reward for those nations that will convert in the days of the Messiah after they see Israel's preeminence when our people shall have been raised *high above all nations* of the earth, *in praise, and in name, and in glory.*[31] Their conversion will not have been for the sake of G-d, for they failed to convert in the time of [our] distress. Even though they will come voluntarily to be converted, we will not accept them willingly, as the Sages commented,[32] "*Whosoever shall gather with thee, shall settle on account of thee.*[33] *Whosoever*

(25) Shabbath 151 b.   (26) Deuteronomy 13:18. "*And He will give thee compassion* so that you should have mercy upon others, [and then *He will show compassion unto thee*]" (Rashi, Shabbath 151 b).   (27) Tanchuma, *Vayakheil*, 9.   (28) Deuteronomy 33:4.   (29) Baba Kamma 38 a. According to Sanhedrin 59 a, the non-Jew who occupies himself with Torah refers to a non-Jew studying the seven commandments enjoined upon the Noachides.   (30) Leviticus 18:5.   (31) Deuteronomy 26:19.   (32) Yebamoth 24 b.   (33) Isaiah 54:15.

shall gather with thee in your poverty, *shall settle on account of thee* in your success." From this we learn that only those who converted when we were impoverished will dwell among us. Nevertheless, [the people of] all nations are destined to become proselytes in the World to Come. That is, they will voluntarily convert, as it is said, *For then will I turn to the peoples a pure language, that they may all call upon the Name of the Eternal, to serve Him with one consent.* [34]

(34) Zephaniah 3:9.

גאולה

The Future Redemption

Part One

> *Distinguished by its unflinching devotion to G-d, Israel is His people and portion / Even when the people of Israel sinned and were punished with exile and subjugation, they could not be utterly destroyed as a nation / There are two reasons for the exile having been chosen as a form of punishment. The first is that the nations may learn of the existence of the One G-d and His providence over all, and the second is that it may atone for our transgressions / Although we remain in exile, our future Redemption is nevertheless assured, and every individual Jew must strongly believe in G-d and in the words of His prophets / Isaiah's prophecy on the duration of the exile and the future Redemption, which depends upon our repentance, and Moses' assurance to us that everything depends upon repentance / At present, we are principally subjugated by the Kingdom of Rome, the fall of which we have been assured of by Isaiah.*

The Future Redemption

I WAIT FOR THE ETERNAL, MY SOUL DOTH WAIT, AND
FOR HIS WORD DO I HOPE.[1]

It is common knowledge that the people of Israel are distinguished above those of the other nations because they are assigned to the Name of the Holy One, blessed be He, that they are His people and His portion. This is akin to the statement, *For the portion of the Eternal is His people, Jacob the lot of His inheritance,*[2] and [naturally] one who is the king's [personal] servant occupies a more distinguished position than the rest of the monarch's lords and ministers. Thus, Moses mentioned, *and the Eternal thy G-d will set thee on high above all the nations of the earth,*[3] for they are assigned to His Name, and that is their praise and glory.

One may ask: "Why is this nation [of Israel] different from all the other nations? They are subjugated by the nations, and have undergone the exiles of Babylon, Media, Greece, and Edom (Rome)? Do we not find that in ancient times, when a nation was wicked and

---

(1) Psalms 130:5. This great psalm of repentance is the sinner's cry for forgiveness. The psalm is recited during the morning service on the Ten Days of Penitence, which start with the New Year and end with the Day of Atonement. Our author uses this verse as the motto for his theme on Redemption, because of its allusion to repentance, which is our assurance that in spite of all the hardships of the exile we will get to see the fulfillment of G-d's deliverance. (2) Deuteronomy 32:9. (3) *Ibid.*, 28:1.

sinned against G-d, He completely annihilated it from the world, such as the generation of the Flood and their like? Why then was Israel different? Of all other nations, why did He punish only them with dispersion and subjugation?"

The answer is as follows: The duration of the exile is indeed most surprising, and Israel's state of decline is very depressing to a sensitive soul. Nevertheless, it is impossible that He should utterly destroy them, for they constitute the essential foundation of the world and their existence is assured by an everlasting bond which is mighty and strong. Thus, Joshua asked G-d, *And they* [the Canaanites] *will wipe us off the earth, and what wilt Thou do for Thy great Name?*[4] Our Sages also commented in Tractate Berachoth,[5] "Rav Huna raised a question. It is written [that G-d said to David at the time he was planning to build the Temple in Jerusalem, that He will appoint a place for His people, Israel, that they may dwell securely in their own land, *and be disquieted no more*], *neither shall the children of wickedness 'afflict' them anymore,*[6] but in the Book of Chronicles, the same verse is written, *Neither shall the children of wickedness 'destroy' them anymore.*[7] At first, it was intended that the enemies should not afflict Israel, but ultimately it was that they should not destroy them." The purport thereof is that when the Sanctuary was originally built it was intended to be a bulwark of spiritual defense against the enemies ever afflicting Israel, but when Israel subsequently sinned, affliction, but not destruction, was decreed upon them. Thus He said, *For I the Eternal change not, and ye, O sons of Jacob, are not destroyed,*[8] which means that even as G-d's Name is unalterable, so is it impossible for Israel to be utterly destroyed. Hence, when they sinned, He decreed upon them the Dispersion and the subjugating exile among the nations.

(4) Joshua 7:9. See Ramban's Commentary on the Torah, Deuteronomy, p. 364, where he speaks at length about why Israel's existence is necessary for the world. (5) Berachoth 7b. (6) II Samuel 7:10. (7) I Chronicles 17:9. (8) Malachi 3:6.

In my opinion there are two reasons for the exile [being chosen as the mode of punishment]. The first is that the nations may learn thereby of the existence of G-d, blessed be He, and of His providence over the affairs of men, and the second is that we may be cleansed of our sins and thus be saved from the judgment of Gehenna.[9] Accordingly, Abraham our patriach chose exile and subjugation for us, [as will be explained].

In Midrash Tehillim, the Sages expounded:[10] "Rabbi Shimon bar Aba said, 'G-d showed Abraham four things: Torah, the sacrificial offerings, the kingdoms [that will subjugate Israel], and the Gehenna. G-d said to him, The Sanctuary will be destroyed and the offerings suspended. Is it your wish that your children should then be subjugated by the kingdoms and not be subject to Gehenna, or would you rather that they be subject to Gehenna and not subjugated by the kingdoms? When Abraham made no reply, G-d said, they rather be under the dominion of the kingdoms than in Gehenna, for Scripture stated to Israel, *Look unto the rock whence ye were hewn,*[11] *Look unto Abraham your father,*' "[12] [who consented to exile as opposed to Gehenna]. Although [the people of] Israel are in servitude to the kingdoms and are exiled from the Holy Land, they will exist forever. Jeremiah prophesied to that effect in his wondrous utterance which assured us of an awe-inspiring future. Thus in the first section[13] [of his prophecy] he promised us that Israel will exist as long as the heavens, moon and stars will function. In the second section,[14] he assured us that G-d will never cast us off, for that is an impossibility.[15] In the third

---

(9) See above in *Orchim* (Hospitality) Note 12. (10) Midrash Tehillim, 52. (11) Isaiah 51:1. (12) *Ibid.*, Verse 2. The thought conveyed is that as bad as the exile is, it is still preferable to total destruction, for someday, the exile will come to an end, thus assuring Israel's rebirth, as the text continues. — It should be noted that while the text before us has it that Abraham merely consented to exile, there is a difference of opinion on this point in various Midrashim. See Bereshith Rabbah 44:24. In Midrash Tehillim 52 (ed. Buber) it is stated clearly that Abraham chose expressly exile. (13) Jeremiah 31:34-35. (14) *Ibid.*, Verse 36. (15) As stated in the verse (*ibid.*): *If heaven above can be measured, and the foundations of the earth searched out beneath, then will I also cast off all the seed of Israel,* etc.

section,[16] he declared that the Sanctuary will be rebuilt, never again to be demolished or destroyed. Based upon these prophecies, the Sages incorporated the following in the Sh'moneh Esreih (Eighteen Blessings) [as a principal component]: "and may He rebuild it [the Sanctuary] in our days as an everlasting structure which will not be demolished or destroyed."[17] Rabbeinu Shlomo wrote,[18] "Among all the words of the prophets, there are no fortifying consolations which are destined to be fulfilled at the end of the Redemption like those of Jeremiah, which will transpire against the will of the infidels,[19] for that prophecy was not fulfilled during the era of the Second Temple." Because every Israelite is obligated to strongly believe in the assurances of the prophets and fervently hope that G-d will fulfill the words of His prophets. David mentioned, I wait for the Eternal, my soul doth wait, etc.[1] Inspired by the Holy Spirit, David foresaw this long exile and therefore prophetically spoke of it in terms of hope and expectation. He repeated the expression [I wait . . . my soul doth wait] to strengthen the hope for [the fulfillment of] the promise of the Redemption. Whenever Israel will despair thereof, there will be a remembrance of redemption. Thus, the prophet says, Look onto the rock whence ye were hewn, etc.,[11] Look unto Abraham your father, etc.,[12] For the Eternal hath comforted Zion, etc.[20] The prophet adjoined the comfort of Zion to the subject of Abraham and Sarah, for they were blessed [with a child] after despairing [of having offsprings] and after the nations had come to believe that they would have no progeny. The same is true regarding the Redemption. Although all nations say that there is no hope for Israel, we do not despair of the deliverance.

(16) Jeremiah 31:37-39.   (17) Our text in the Sh'moneh Esreih do not contain the words, "which will not be demolished or destroyed."   (18) I have not found this quotation in Rashi's commentary and the reference could not be to Rabbi Shlomo ben Adereth (Rashba), for whenever our author cited Rashba's name, he always precedes it with the epithet "my master." See Introduction.   (19) See Writings and Discourses of Ramban, "Book of Redemption," pp. 595-608, where he devotes the entire Second Gate to this theme, i.e., that prophecies of many prophets have not yet been fulfilled and perforce must be the indications of the future perfect Redemption.   (20) Isaiah 51:3.

In the succeeding verse, David stated, *My soul is for the Eternal,
more than watchmen for the morning.*[21] This means: "Even though I
am in exile, I do not abandon my faith and my Torah, but *My soul is
for the Eternal.*" This is similar to the statement, *One shall say, I am
the Eternal's.*[22] David specified, *'My soul' is for the Eternal,*[21] rather
than " 'I' am for the Eternal," in order to instruct us that "even when
my life is taken from me, my soul will still be thankful to G-d alone.
Hence, *'My soul' is for the Eternal.* Furthermore, I am one of those
who wait incessantly for the time of the Redemption." This explains
the redundant language, *more than watchmen for the morning, yea,
more than watchmen for the morning.*[21] *The morning* refers to the
beginning of the Redemption.

Isaiah also compared the Redemption to the morning, as it is said,
*The burden of Dumah. One calleth unto me out of Seir: Watchman,
what of the night? Watchman, what of the night?*[23] *The watchman
said: The morning cometh, and also the night,* etc.[24] It is possible that
he called the Kingdom of Edom (Rome) by the name *Dumah* (silence
or stillness) because while the end of all other exiles to which Israel was
subjected had been known beforehand, the termination of this exile of
Edom is hidden and sealed. Thus, the prophet is saying: "Israel calls
me out of the distress of the exile of Seir[25] and asks, *Watchman, what
of the night?* What will happen at the end of the night, at the end of
the exile of Edom, which is likened to the night?" This is similar to a
sentinel who stands at his post and people ask him, "How much time of
the night has passed? How long will it still last?" So do they ask the
prophet, "You are the watchman, as it is said, *I will stand upon my
watch, and set me upon the tower, and will look out what He will speak
with me, and what I shall answer when I am reproved.*[26] Tell us, then,

(21) Psalms 130:6.   (22) Isaiah 44:5.   (23) *Ibid.*, 21:11.   (24) *Ibid.*, Verse
12.   (25) Seir is another name of Edom, who is synonymous with Esau. See Genesis
36:8. Edom is also called the Kingdom of Rome.   (26) Habakkuk 2:1.

what the Holy One, blessed be He, has answered you concerning [the exile of] this Kingdom of Rome?" The prophet answers them, *"The morning cometh.*[24] You are asking me how much time of the night has passed. Know that it is already near the morning and that the Redemption is about to occur. *The morning cometh.*[24] The Babylonian exile, which was like the day because it lasted only seventy years, has already passed, and *the night,*[24] which is the exile of Edom, has also already passed. What then is hindering our Redemption? Nothing deters it but [our failure] to repent. *If ye will inquire, inquire ye,*[24] which means that if you wish to be redeemed, plead for mercy before Him, return from the exiles, and come to Jerusalem." Scripture thus teaches us here that the Redemption is dependent upon repentance, and so the Sages commented,[27] "By merit of repentance, Israel will be redeemed, as it is said, *And a redeemer will come to Zion, and unto them that turn from transgression in Jacob.*"[28] This means [that the redeemer will come] by merit of those in [the House of] Jacob who turn from transgression.

Moses, peace be upon him, promised us that repentance is the cause which will bring on the Redemption, as he said, *And thou shalt return and hearken to the voice, of the Eternal.*[29] This is an assurance that Israel will [ultimately] return penitently. Moses also pledged that our distinction at that time will be greater than that of all past periods. Thus, he stated, *And He will do thee good, and make thee prosper above thy fathers,*[30] above the distinction of David and Solomon. He further assured us of avenging our cause from the nations that persecuted us, as it is said, *And the Eternal thy G-d will put all these curses upon thine enemies, and on them that hate thee, that persecuted thee.*[31] [The latter part of this verse refers] to the two nations to whom we are subjugated: Edom (Rome) and Ishmael (the

(27) Yoma 86 b, with some changes. (28) Isaiah 59:20. (29) Deuteronomy 30:8. (30) *Ibid.,* Verse 5. (31) *Ibid.,* Verse 7.

Arab kingdoms). Thus, he mentioned *them that hate thee,*[31] who are the children of Esau, and those *that persecuted thee,* who are the children of Ishmael. Micah likewise prophesied concerning them, *Let Thy hand be lifted up above Thine adversaries, and let all Thine enemies be cut off.*[32]

Although we are now dispersed and subjugated by both [Edom and Ishmael], our principal exile is that of Edom,[33] for Rome exiled us and destroyed our Sanctuary. Even if Israel were now dispersed among the seventy nations, our exile would still be deemed as that of the wicked Kingdom of Rome alone. The Sages said in Midrash Mishlei,[34] " *'Sh'momith' (the spider) thou canst take with the hands, yet is she in the king's palaces.*[35] Sh'momith refers to the Kingdom of Edom. Just as the spider is hated, so is the Kingdom of Edom, as it is said, *But Esau I hated.*[36] [The verse states that] *yet is she in the king's palaces,*[35] for she destroyed the House of the King of kings, the Holy One, blessed be He."

Isaiah the prophet clearly assured us of the ultimate destruction of the Kingdom of Rome.[37] *Then the eyes of the blind* in faith *shall be opened, and the ears of the deaf shall be unstopped.*[38] This is not to be understood literally, i.e., that they will be completely healed. It is rather a parable, as indicated by the following expression in the same verse, *for in the wilderness shall waters break out, and streams in the desert.*[39] This alludes to the abundance of wisdom and extent of con-

---

(32) Micah 5:8.   (33) This is definitely Ramban's theory. See his Commentary on the Torah, Numbers, pp. 288-290, and Writings and Discourses, pp. 623-626. In this regard, Ramban takes issue with Ibn Ezra's explanation, which considers the Islamic kingdoms' subjugation of Israel as a separate exile.   (34) Midrash Mishlei, 30. (35) Proverbs 30:28.   (36) Malachi 1:3.   On various occasions, Edom displays unusual cruelty towards Israel. See Amos 1:11, especially Psalms 137:7, for the role of Edomites in the destruction of Jerusalem. Their barbarity towards Israel, despite their kinship, earned them their due punishment of being the hated ones of G-d.   (37) See Isaiah, Chapter 34, for a detailed description. (38) *Ibid.,* 35:5. (39) *Ibid.,* Verse 6.

ception in the [field of] knowledge of G-d. Concerning this, the prophet states in the following verse, *And the parched land shall become a pool, and the thirsty ground springs of water; in the habitation of jackals herds shall lie down.*[40] This is said of Jerusalem, which had become like a wilderness. *And there shall be* in that wilderness *a highway, and a way, and it shall be called the way of holiness; the unclean shall not pass over it, but it shall be for those*[41] designated ones of [the people of] Israel, who are the holy and pure. *The wayfaring men, yea fools, shall not err therein.*[41] All who walk the way [to Jerusalem], even those who are devoid of understanding, will not err therein. *No lion shall be there.*[42] This refers to the Kingdom of Babylon, which has been compared to a lion, as it is said, *A lion is gone up from his thicket.*[43] *Nor shall any ravenous beast go up thereon,*[42] meaning the swine, the most ravenous of beasts, a reference to the Kingdom of Edom, which is like a ravenous beast. *But the redeemed shall walk there,*[42] that is, they alone shall walk there. Thus, the prophet continues, *And the redeemed of the Eternal shall return, and come with singing unto Zion, and everlasting joy shall be upon their heads; they shall obtain gladness and joy, and sorrow and sighing shall flee away.*[44]

(40) *Ibid.*, Verse 7.   (41) *Ibid.*, Verse 8.   (42) *Ibid.*, Verse 9.   (43) Jeremiah 4:7. This alludes to Nebuchadnezzar, King of Babylon, who destroyed the First Temple.   (44) Isaiah 35:10.

Part Two

> *Israel's mournful condition during the exile and the abuse and revilement it must constantly suffer for refusing to abandon its faith / The delay of the coming Redemption / Our only counsel is to strengthen our belief in the coming Redemption.*

AS THE HART "TA'AROG" (PANTETH) AFTER THE WATER BROOKS, SO PANTETH MY SOUL AFTER THEE, O G-D.[45] MY SOUL THIRSTETH FOR G-D, FOR THE LIVING G-D: WHEN SHALL I COME AND APPEAR BEFORE G-D?[46]

The sons of Korach, [the authors of this psalm],[47] prophesied here concerning the present exile in which Israel cries out and pants *as the hart panteth after the water brooks* because of the painful desire for drink. Their use of the word *ta'arog*, [the feminine conjugation (she panteth)], rather than *ya'arog*, [its masculine counterpart], indicates that they compared Israel to the female hart because Israel is as weak and helpless in the exile as a woman. The sons of Korach, who were prophesying about the people of Israel in general, compared their craving [for the Redemption] to the thirst of the hart, which is a most striking and unsurpassable analogy. They stated, *my soul thirsteth . . . for the living G-d,*[46] which is in contrast to the Kingdom of Edom that worships another deity. *When shall I come and appear before G-d?*[46] This refers to the long duration of the exile. *My tears*

---

(45) Psalms 42:2. (46) *Ibid.,* Verse 3. (47) All psalms are attributed to David even though some were composed by others, as in the case of Psalm 42, which is clearly attributed to the sons of Korach. According to the Sages, "David wrote the Book of Psalms and incorporated within it the works of ten elders, etc." (Baba Bathra 14 b). Thus, Rabbeinu Bachya here ascribes the authorship of this psalm to the sons of Korach, but later (at Note 58) attributes it to David himself.

have been my food day and night, while they say unto me all the day:
Where is thy G-d?[48] The verse is stating: "The Kingdom of Edom
taunts me all day with abuse and revilements as steady as the bread I
eat day and night. They say to me, *Where is thy G-d?* while I know that
our G-d, unlike theirs, is the Living One."

All of the prophets have foretold that our enemies will abuse and
revile us, call us "the unclean ones," and charge us with their own
defects, as the Sages said,[49] "He who tarnishes others is himself tarnish-
ed." Isaiah prophesied concerning this, *Hearken unto Me, ye that*
know righteousness, the people in whose heart is My law; fear ye not
the taunt of men, neither be ye dismayed at their revilings. For the
moth shall eat them up like a garment, and the worm shall eat them
like wool; but My favor shall be forever, and My salvation unto all
generations.[50] The prophet is saying of the people of Israel, *in whose*
heart is My law, that they do not pay mere lip service [to the teachings
of G-d], but they fulfill what they learn [in the Torah]. It is they who
will see the Redemption. [The prophet encourages them], *"Fear ye not*
the taunt of men who abuse you in the exile because you do not believe
in their faith and because of the long duration of the exile. *The moth*
shall eat them up like a garment, etc., *but My favor shall be forever.*
They will be obliterated from upon the earth while you will continue to
exist. To you I will give My salvation."

Concerning this state [of abuse in which Israel finds itself], David
said, *Arise, O G-d, plead Thine own cause, remember Thy reproach*
all the day at the hand of the vile.[51] He called the Kingdom of Edom
the vile, and he referred to it in a preceding verse, *O deliver not the*
soul of Thy turtledove unto the wild beast.[52] This is [Rome, the
metaphorical] fourth beast[53] [in the vision of Daniel]. Moses too mentioned [Edom], saying, *I will provoke them with 'am naval' (a vile na-*
tion),[54] for *naval* is the term used for one who does not remember his
brotherly covenant and repays good with evil. Thus, it is written, *For*

(48) Psalms 42:4.   (49) Kiddushin 70 a.   (50) Isaiah 51:7-8.   (51) Psalms 74:22.
(52) *Ibid.,* Verse 19.   (53) Daniel 7:23-27.   (54) Deuteronomy 32:21.

the violence done to thy brother Jacob shall cover thee [Edom], *and thou shalt be cut off forever.*[55] David also stated, *And render unto our neighbors sevenfold into their bosom,* etc.,[56] and also, *Remember, O Eternal, the taunt of Thy servants, how I do bear in my bosom* [the taunt of] *so many peoples.*[57]

Because of these steady, daily taunts, David said, *Why art thou cast down, O my soul? and why moanest thou within me? Hope thou in G-d; for I shall yet praise Him, the salvation of my countenance, and my G-d.*[58] In the next psalm, he mentioned, *Be Thou my judge, O G-d, and plead my cause against a nation not pious,*[59] thereby informing us that their words are but flattering utterances and pretense of piety, as it is written of Esau, *there was game in his mouth.*[60] That is to say, he ensnared people and his father by his mouth.[61] Therefore, the psalmist calls him *a nation not pious,*[59] meaning that he makes a pretense of being pious, but in reality he is not. Similarly, he appears to be truthful, but he is really *a deceitful and unjust man.*[59] *For Thou art the G-d of my strength; why hast Thou cast me off?*[62] That is to say, "You are the G-d of my strength, and You have the power to save me from his hand." Therefore, *O send out Thy light and Thy truth, let them lead me.*[63] *O send out Thy light:* this is King Messiah; *and Thy truth:* this refers to Elijah, as it is written, *The law of truth was in his mouth.*[64]

It is stated in the Midrash:[65] "*O send out Thy light and Thy truth, let them lead me.*[63] Israel said to G-d, 'Redeem us as You redeemed our ancestors from Egyptian oppression. *Why go I mourning under the oppression of the enemy?*[62] Did You not send our ancestors two redeemers, Moses and Aaron? Send us also two [redeemers] cor-

(55) Obadiah 10. (56) Psalms 79:12. (57) *Ibid.,* 89:51. (58) *Ibid.,* 42:12. (59) *Ibid.,* 43:1. (60) Genesis 25:28. (61) Esau was deceitful in speech. For example, he asked his father how tithes were to be taken of salt and straw, thus leading his father to believe that he was very pious (Bereshith Rabbah 63:15), although he knew that salt and straw do not have to be tithed. (62) Psalms 43:2. (63) *Ibid.,* Verse 3. (64) Malachi 2:6. (65) Midrash Tehillim, 43.

responding to them, as it is said, *O send out Thy light and Thy truth, let them lead me.*[63] One is Elijah, and the other King Messiah.' Just as it says there [in the Song at the Red Sea], *Thou shalt bring them in, and plant them in the mountain of Thine inheritance,*[66] so it says [in the psalm] here, *Let them bring me unto Thy holy mountain.*"[63]

At the end of this second psalm, David mentioned the verse *Why art thou cast down*, etc.? a third time,[67] for then [at the time of Redemption] our thankfulness will be complete, as it says in the verse above, *Then will I go unto the altar of G-d, unto G-d, my exceeding joy, and praise Thee upon the harp, O G-d, my G-d.*[68] Then will prophecy be restored to its former state, *for the earth shall be full of the knowledge of the Eternal, as the waters cover the sea,*[69] and G-d will pour upon Israel a spirit of prophecy even as He pours out the rain upon the earth, as it is said, *For I will pour water upon the thirsty land, and streams upon the dry ground; I will pour My spirit upon thy seed, and My blessing upon thine offspring.*[70] Similarly, the prophet Isaiah assured us that the perception and knowledge [of G-d at the time of the Redemption] will be on a higher level of perfection than at the Revelation at Sinai. There, it was experienced through a cloud, as it is said, *and the glory of the Eternal appeared* in the cloud *unto all the children of Israel,*[71] and as it is clearly written, *inasmuch as Thou Eternal art seen face to face, and Thy cloud standeth over them.*[72] In the future, however, at the time of the Redemption, all Israel will see the glory without the intervening cloud, as it is said, *Hark, thy watchmen! they lift up the voice, together do they sing, for they shall see, eye to eye, the Eternal returning to Zion.*[73]

---

(66) Exodus 15:17. (67) The verse, *Why art thou cast down*, etc., is mentioned three times in Psalms 42:6, 12, and 43:5. The words are the same, but at the end of Psalm 43, they are read with a triumphant note, as if to say, "Why then do I go cast down when the Redemption is a certainty." (68) Psalms 43:4. (69) Isaiah 11:9. (70) *Ibid.*, 44:3. (71) Numbers 14:10. The verse reads *and the glory . . . appeared in the Tent of Meeting.* The phrase "in the cloud" is not mentioned there. (72) *Ibid.*, Verse 14. (73) Isaiah 52:8.

Part Three

The great distinction of Israel / The source of Israel's strength / The Revelation on Mount Sinai / Isaiah's prophecy about the future Redemption.

WHEN THOU DIDST TREMENDOUS THINGS WHICH WE LOOKED NOT FOR—OH THAT THOU WOULDEST COME DOWN, THAT THE MOUNTAINS MIGHT QUAKE AT THY PRESENCE!—[74] AND NEVER HAVE MEN HEARD, NOR PERCEIVED BY THE EAR, NEITHER HATH THE EYE SEEN A G-D BESIDE THEE, WHO WORKETH FOR ONE THAT WAITETH FOR HIM.[75]

The prophet Isaiah informed us here of two things. First, he indicated the great distinction of Israel, for whom were done things that have not been done for any other nation or ethnic group. Therefore, Isaiah mentioned the awe-inspiring deeds, the wonders, and the miracles which He wrought in Egypt, and the subject of the holy Revelation on Mount Sinai. Second, the prophet mentioned the absolute elevation and exaltation of the Holy One, blessed be He. Although He created seventy celestial powers and appointed them over the seventy nations of the earth, none of these celestial powers has done the wonders and miracles for its nation as the G-d of Israel [has done].

It is known that the wonders and miracles were all done by the Almighty Himself for an undeserving people. Israel in Egypt worshipped idols, and thus, all [of the miracles were] an act of mercy on His part. From here it follows that no other nation or ethnic group is as

(74) Isaiah 64:2. (75) *Ibid.*, Verse 3.

obligated to G-d as are the people of Israel for they are His nation and have been designated as His portion. Although every created being is obligated by force of reason to worship his Creator, and all of the world's seventy nations are bound to extol and praise Him because He created them, brought them into existence from nothingness, provides them with food, and holds their life in His hand, nevertheless, their obligation is unlike that of the people of Israel, for they are His nation and have been designated as His portion. Thus, the Sages commented,[76] "*O praise the Eternal, all ye nations, etc.*,[77] and all the more should we His people [praise Him] Whose *mercy* has been *great toward us.* "[78] Isaiah also stated, *I will make mention of the mercies of the Eternal, etc.*[79] That is to say, His praises [can be heard] throughout the entire world, but on *the House of Israel*, He has showered *abundant goodness;*[79] He bestowed His compassions and His mercies upon them more than upon all others. Thus, David said, *So let Israel now say, for His mercies endureth forever,*[80] which means that Israel should testify concerning His mercies, for they bear witness thereto more than the other nations.

The essence of faith is to believe in the existence of G-d, blessed be He. This is a matter which has not been clarified among the nations and has not begun to be known in the world through public miracles, except [for the wonders performed] for Israel in Egypt. The matter [of G-d's existence] was completely verified at the Revelation on Mount Sinai, as it is written there, *Unto thee it was shown, that thou mightest know that the Eternal is G-d.*[81] Therefore, the prophet specified here [in the aforementioned verse][74] the awesome events which occurred in Egypt and the subject of the Revelation, through which G-d's existence was clearly demonstrated. These events were both the inception and the culmination of the proclamation [of the world] concerning the existence of G-d. Thus, the prophet stated, *When Thou didst tremendous things which we looked not for—Oh that Thou wouldest*

---

(76) Pesachim 118 b. (77) Psalms 117:1. (78) *Ibid.*, Verse 2. (79) Isaiah 63:7. (80) Psalms 118:2. (81) Deuteronomy 4:35.

come down, that the mountains might quake at Thy presence![74] The prophet is saying: "When You performed those tremendous feats for us in Egypt, we had not sought them because we were not worthy of them. When You came down upon Mount Sinai, the mountains quaked out of anxiety and fear," similar to the statement, *And the entire mountain quaked greatly.*"[82]

Thus, the people of Israel are highly distinguished, for they have been elevated above the other nations by virtue of the tremendous things done for them in Egypt and the Revelation of the Divine Glory on Mount Sinai. We can also recognize the exalted state of G-d, blessed be He, for no other power can perform such signs and miracles as He alone did wondrously with His people and His nation as the [recognized] Power of Israel. Therefore, it is written, *And never have men heard, nor* have the nations *perceived by the ear, neither hath the eye* of any one nation *seen a god*[75] doing so to his people who wait for him. You, [O Eternal are the sole exception; there are] *none besides Thee.* Thus is the testimony and proof of the elevation of G-d. He is the Power of Israel, *He is the G-d of gods, and the Lord of lords,*[83] and there is no one like Him, as Moses mentioned, *There is none like unto G-d, O Jeshurun.*[84]

It is also possible to explain that in the first verse,[74] the prophet is speaking with G-d, and in the second[75] with Israel. He is thus saying: "The nations have never heard the voice of G-d as you [Israel] have heard it, and no other person has seen G-d except you, for you have seen Him out of the cloud, as it is written, *inasmuch as Thou Eternal art seen face to face, and Thy cloud standeth over them.*[72] Thus will He do to those that wait for Him, and that is the perfect reward."

It is furthermore possible to explain: "Never have the nations heard or perceived such wonders which He did [for Israel] in the past, neither

(82) Exodus 19:18. (83) Deuteronomy 10:17. (84) *Ibid.*, 33:26.

will any eye see what He will yet do in the future for those that wait for him." This alludes to the subject of our future Redemption, concerning which it is written, *Happy is he that waiteth, and cometh to the thousand three hundred and five and thirty days.*[85] It is known to every understanding person that this present exile has been given three terminations, as was the case with the exile in Egypt.[86]

(85) Daniel 12:12.   (86) This subject is explained by the author in his commentary on Exodus 12:40.   (See my edition, Vol. II, pp. 97-98).   With respect to the exile in Egypt three durations were given: Four hundred years (see Genesis 15:13) from the birth of Isaac to the Exodus, 430 years (see Exodus 12:40) beginning with the Covenant Between the Parts until the Exodus, and 210 years from the time of the descent into Egypt by Jacob and his family until the Exodus. With respect to the present exile, there are also three possible durations provided in the Book of Daniel: 1150 (8:14 — half of 2300 is 1150), 1290 (12:11), and 1335 (12:12). Rabbeinu Bachya explains that these three dates represent various stages in the coming Redemption.

דינים
The Rule of Law

The entire Torah is dependent upon the administration of justice, without which the world could not exist / The significance of justice / The duty of settling disputes in a Jewish court of law rather than elsewhere / Justice was one of the three things for which Moses was ready to give his life.

The Rule of Law

HE DECLARETH HIS WORDS UNTO JACOB, HIS STATUTES
AND HIS ORDINANCES UNTO ISRAEL.[1]

It is known that were it not for [the administration of] justice, the order of the world would lapse into chaos and society would be utterly unable to exist. The very creation of the world was founded upon justice, as it is said, *In the beginning 'Elokim' (G-d) created.*[2] The Divine Name *Elokim* is indicative of [the Almighty's role as the Supreme] Judge, as it is said, *For 'Elokim' (G-d) is Judge.*[3] The Sages likewise commented,[4] "The world is preserved by three things: justice, truth, and peace, as it is said, *Judge ye the truth and the judgment of peace in your gates.*"[5] The prophet Isaiah warned Israel concerning justice, as it is said, *Keep ye justice, and do righteousness.*[6] The generation of the Flood was doomed to destruction because they undermined justice and violence was prevalent among them. The final decree of their punishment was sealed because of violence, as it is said, *The end*

---

(1) Psalms 147:19. After describing the creative might of G-d in the material universe, and the bounteous provisions He has made for all creatures to sustain their lives, the psalmist concludes by saying *He declareth His words,* etc., meaning that He has likewise made provision for Israel's spiritual welfare, thereby assuring them a meaningful existence. (2) Genesis 1:1. (3) Psalms 75:8. (4) Aboth 1:18. (5) Zechariah 8:16. The preceding verse speaks of the condition under which Jerusalem and Judah will prosper, and this verse concludes: *Judge ye . . . .* It is thus obvious that the world is preserved by these three things: justice, etc. (6) Isaiah 56:1.

164

of all flesh is come before Me, for the earth is filled with violence
through them.[7]

The entire Torah is dependent upon justice. Therefore, the section
which begins [with the words], *And these are the ordinances,*[8] was
declared to Moses immediately following the Ten Commandments.
The Sages said in the Midrash:[9] "The Torah [given on Sinai] was
preceded by laws and followed by laws. The Torah was preceded by
laws, as it is said, *There He made for them a statute and ordinance,*[10]
and it was followed by laws, as it is said, *And these are the ordinances.*[8]
The Ten Commandments are between [these two sets of laws]. Scripture expresses it thus: *I* [Wisdom] *walk in the way of righteousness, in*
the midst of the paths of justice."[11]

[Our ancestors, by word and deed, taught us the importance of
justice]. Our patriarch Abraham warned us concerning justice, as it is
said, *For I know him* [Abraham], *that he will command his children*
and his household after him, and they shall keep the way of the Eter-
nal, to do righteousness and justice.[12] Judah merited royalty [for his
offspring David] only because of [his devotion to] justice. He had
sentenced his daughter-in-law Tamar to death by burning,[13] but after
she sent him his signet and the cord [as proof that she had conceived
through him], he acknowledged the truth and said, *She is more*
righteous than I.[14] Subsequently, she gave birth to Peretz and
Zerach.[15] It is also written of David, *And David executed justice and*
righteousness unto all his people.[16]

---

(7) Genesis 6:13; Sanhedrin 108 a.   (8) Exodus 21:1.   (9) Shemoth Rabbah
30:3.   (10) Exodus 15:25. The verse refers to the time after the Israelites had crossed
the Red Sea. As they were on their way to Mount Sinai, certain laws of the Torah were
declared to them. See Ramban, Commentary on the Torah, Exodus, pp.
208-210.   (11) Proverbs 8:20. In other words, in the paths of the wisdom of Torah
there is the assurance of righteousness and justice.   (12) Genesis 18:19. G-d's statement that Abraham will charge his children to do justice is thus the greatest assurance
that Abraham will certainly so command them.   (13) *Ibid.*, 38:24.   (14) *Ibid.*, Verse
26.   (15) *Ibid.*, Verses 29-30. Peretz was the ancestor of David, King of Israel (Ruth
4:18-22).   (16) II Samuel 8:15.

Scripture states in praise of Jerusalem, *She that was full of justice.*[17] When justice was undermined, the destruction of Jerusalem became imminent, as it is written, *They deny justice to the fatherless.*[18] Through justice, Jerusalem will eventually be restored, as it is said, *Zion shall be redeemed with justice.*[19] The plain meaning of the verse, however, is that Zion, which has not sinned, *shall be redeemed with justice.* That is to say, she [herself] is rightfully entitled to be redeemed, but *they that return of her,*[19] who have sinned, must plead for compassion. They cannot be redeemed by the Divine attribute of justice, for [their redemption] is possible only by [G-d's] charity, which is the [Divine] attribute of compassion.

Where there is no justice, there is no peace, as it is said, *Judge ye the truth and the judgment of peace in your gates.*[5] Thus, the Sages said,[20] "Pray for the welfare of the government, for if not for the fear thereof, men would swallow each other alive." Peace in a country is possible only through justice, as it is said, *By justice, the king establisheth the land.*[21] Thus, after counseling Moses on the establishment of courts of justice, Jethro said, *Then thou [Moses] shalt be able to endure, and all this people also shall go to their place in peace.*[22]

The power of justice is great, for when there is justice upon the earth, G-d judges mankind with [the attribute of] mercy, but when there is no law and order He judges mankind with the attribute of justice. [Immediately after the verse quoted above],[1] the psalmist stated, *And as for His ordinances, they* [the nations] *have 'bal' (not) known them.*[23] [He uses *bal*] rather than the word *lo* [which also means "no"], to teach us that the entire Torah, from *'Bereshith' (In the beginning) G-d created*[2] to *in sight of all Israel*[24] is dependent upon justice. Therefore, the psalmist utilized the word *bal* [instead of *lo*].

---

(17) Isaiah 1:21. (18) *Ibid.*, Verse 23. (19) *Ibid.*, Verse 27. A reference to those who must first repent for their sins (Rashi). (20) Aboth 3:2. (21) Proverbs 29:4. (22) Exodus 18:23. (23) Psalms 147:20. (24) Deuteronomy 34:12. The word *bal* marks the beginning and end of the Written Torah, for its first letter, *beth* is also the first letter of the first word of the Torah — *Bereshith* — and its last letter, *lam-*

Justice is the foundation of the Throne of Glory, as it is said, *Righteousness and justice are the foundation of Thy Throne.*[25] Therefore, one who establishes justice confirms the Throne of Glory, and one who perverts justice and disrupts it, abuses the Throne of Glory. Likewise, the throne of royalty is founded only on justice, for it is written of King Hezekiah, *And a throne is established through mercy, and there sitteth thereon in truth one that judgeth, and seeketh justice, and is ready in righteousness.*[26]

In the Midrash,[27] we find the following: *"He declareth His word unto Jacob*[1] refers to the Ten Commandments. *His statutes and His ordinances unto Israel*[1] refers to the section beginning, *And these are the ordinances.*[8] *He hath not dealt so with any nation*[23] means that He has given all [His commandments] only to Israel. Adam, the first man, was charged with six commandments.[28] When Noah came, a seventh commandment was added—the prohibition against cutting off a limb from a living animal.[29] An eighth commandment, circumcision, was given to Abraham. When Jacob came, he received the ninth commandment—the prohibition against eating the sinew of the thigh-vein.[30] When Israel came [to Mount Sinai], G-d gave them the Ten Commandments, and thereby He gave them all.[31] *He hath not dealt so with any nation.*[23]

---

ed, is also the final letter of the last word of the Torah— *Yisrael*— as the verses cited indicate. Thus, the word *bal* as used in the psalm, signifies that the entire Torah is dependent upon the administration of the Divine ordinances, a matter which G-d has not revealed to any other nation, since they refused the Torah when offered. (25) Psalms 89:15. (26) Isaiah 16:5. (27) Shemoth Rabbah 30:6. (28) As enumerated by Maimonides in his Mishneh Torah, *Hilchoth Melachim* 9:1, the six commandments concerned idolatry, blasphemy, murder, immorality, robbery, and the establishment of courts of justice to preserve the order. (29) This is also mentioned by Maimonides, *ibid.* (30) See Genesis 32:33. (31) In place of this last sentence, Shemoth Rabbah 30:6 reads, "however, G-d gave all [the commandments] to Israel." The reading cited by our author may be understood in light of the thought, which he develops later in *Shavuoth* that the Ten Commandments are the chief precepts from which all of the 613 commandments are derived.

It is forbidden to litigate under other than Jewish laws. The Torah states, *And these are the ordinances which thou shalt set before them,*[8] upon which the Sages commented,[32] *"Before them,*[8] [the Israelites themselves] and not before non-Israelites." The Sages thus taught that it is forbidden to litigate in a non-Jewish court even if its laws are identical with ours. Rather, one should bring his dispute before the scholars of Israel.

It is important to know that this transgression lends substance to many severe sins. It brings about a profanation of the Divine Name. Woe to the resulting confusion and abashment when people transgress knowingly and sinfully in this matter. [Bringing a litigation in a non-Jewish court] also entails robbery, for one who forsakes the laws of Israel and collects [money due him] through a non-Israelite court is considered an actual robber. However, since the litigant does not consider it so, he will not return the money [so collected], and therefore will never be pardoned for this sin.[33]

One who does not conduct himself according to the ordinances of the Torah and litigates under the laws of the nations is considered as if he removed himself from the sphere of G-d, for the Torah states, *Ye shall have one law,* etc., *for I am the Eternal your G-d.*[34] In my opinion, Scripture is stating: *"Ye shall have one law,* the law of the One [G-d], the law which was given to you on Mount Sinai. [That is the law you shall have] and no other, *for I am the Eternal your G-d.* If you accept that law, then *I am the Eternal your G-d."* From this positive statement: ["If you accept . . . then *I am* etc.,"] we may derive its negative counterpart: ["If you do not accept that law, then I am not your G-d"]. It is common knowledge that the religions and laws of the

---

(32) Gittin 88 b; Tanchuma, *Mishpatim,* 3.   (33) If the debtor, however, is a strong handed person, and the creditor cannot recover his debt from him, he should sue first in a Jewish court of law, and if he refuses to appear, the creditor takes permission from the court and proceeds to a non-Jewish court (Choshen Mishpat, 26:2).   (34) Leviticus 24:22.

various nations are [merely the] "fruits of the Torah,"³⁵ but the civil ordinances of the Torah are among their essential principles. Our
neglecting to be judged by them constitutes an act of profanation of
G-d's Name. Those who can protest [against such practices] and do not
are likewise guilty. They too are instrumental in destroying Jewish
wealth and will be held responsible for their inaction.

*Judge the people with righteous judgment.*³⁶ Scripture terms it
righteous judgment because the judges perform righteousness to both
the innocent victim who recovers that to which he is entitled and the
guilty party who must restore what he had gained by illicit means.
Thus, Scripture states, *Truth springeth out of the earth, and
righteousness looked down from heaven.*³⁷

We find that Moses our teacher risked his life for three things:
Torah, justice, and Israel. He was ready to surrender his life for
Torah, as it is said, *And he [Moses] was there with the Eternal forty
days and forty nights.*³⁸ He risked his life for Israel, as it is said, *Yet
now, if Thou wilt forgive their sin.*³⁹ Finally, he was ready to give his
life for justice, as it is said, *And he saw an Egyptian smiting a Hebrew,
one of his brethren.*⁴⁰ Thus, Moses was the first to risk his life for
justice, and that is why the appointment of judges is ascribed to him, as
it is said, *Judges and officers shalt thou make thee.*⁴¹

(35) A phrase used by Ramban. See Writings and Discourses, p.
34.   (36) Deuteronomy 16:18.   (37) Psalms 85:12. When *truth springeth out of the
earth*, that is, when a righteous judgment is executed upon the earth, the
Righteousness looks down from heaven, and rewards the earth with an abundant
measure of goodness (Tanchuma, *Shoftim*, 6).   (38) Exodus 34:28. The verse continues: . . . *he did neither eat bread, nor drink water.* Thus, he forwent caring for his
physical needs, and with complete abandon engaged in receiving the Torah from
G-d.   (39) Exodus 32:32. The thought is incomplete. Moses, pleading that G-d
forgive Israel's sin with the golden calf, was saying: "*Yet now, if Thou wilt forgive their
sin*, well and good, let me live, too, *and if not, blot me, I pray Thee, out of Thy book
which Thou hast written.*   (40) Exodus 2:11. Moses then killed the Egyptian and consequently had to flee Egypt.   (41) Deuteronomy 16:18. *Thee* refers to Moses, thus
crediting him with the establishment of courts of justice in Israel.

May G-d, blessed be He, restore our judges and counsellors to their original positions, for He has assured us, *And I will restore thy judges as at the first, and thy counsellors as at the beginning.*[42] It is further written, *Zion shall be redeemed with justice, and they that return of her with righteousness.*[19]

(42) Isaiah 1:26.

הכנעה
Submissiveness

Submissiveness is one of the essential principles of the Torah and worship of G-d. Through it, one's heart becomes completely devoted to Him and one is removed from temptation of sin / The meaning of submissiveness which is better than sacrificial offerings / Man's submissiveness is beloved by G-d. The Divine Glory, which usually dwells in the heaven of heavens, rests on earth with the righteous who are submissive / Only through submissiveness does one's prayer enter before Almighty G-d.

Submissiveness

THUS SAITH THE ETERNAL: THE HEAVEN IS MY
THRONE, AND THE EARTH IS MY FOOTSTOOL; WHERE IS
THE HOUSE THAT YE MAY BUILD UNTO ME, AND WHERE
IS THE PLACE THAT MAY BE MY RESTING PLACE?[1]

It is known that submissiveness is one of the essential principles of
the Torah and worship of G-d. Through it, one's heart becomes completely devoted to G-d. Submissiveness entails the rending of the heart,
as the prophet said, *And rend your heart, and not your garments.*[2]
This means that one should make his heart submissive before the
Master of all, and he should be fearful and tremble at His words. By
being submissive, one becomes far removed from sin and all his sins are
forgiven, as Scripture clearly states, *If then perchance their uncircumcised heart be humbled, and they shall then have made amends for
their iniquity.*[3] G-d assured Solomon, too, that with submissiveness,
Israel's prayer would be heard and their sins forgiven. Thus, it is written in the Book of Chronicles, *If I shut up heaven that there be no*

---

(1) Isaiah 66:1. Thus, the Temple which man builds for the Divine Presence cannot
possibly contain Him, as the heaven of heavens cannot suffice for Him. Its purpose,
rather, is to lead man to revere His glory abiding there, and to teach man submissiveness to His will.   (2) Joel 2:13. Commenting on this verse, Ibn Ezra explains
that the heart of the sinful person is impenetrable to the teachings of the better way of
life. Hence the covert of the heart must be rent so that he will be able to understand
the word of G-d.   (3) Leviticus 26:41. The humbling of the heart is the way of making amends for the iniquity committed.

rain, or if I command the locust to devour the Land, or if I send pestilence among My people;[4] if My people, upon whom My Name is called, shall humble themselves, and pray, and seek My face, and turn from their evil ways; then will I hear from heaven, and will forgive their sin, and will heal their Land.[5]

Suffering causes submissiveness, as it is said, *And He humbled their heart with travail.[6]* When one endures suffering without being submissive, it is a very grievous matter, for suffering, when coupled with submissiveness [of heart], atones for sin, as David said, *See mine affliction and my travail, and forgive all my sins.[7] Affliction* refers to submissiveness and *travail* to suffering. Thus, David explained that submissiveness and suffering constitute an altar of forgiveness.

To be submissive is to have a broken heart, as David mentioned in the psalm which he composed on the occasion *when Nathan the prophet came to him.[8]* Therein, David confessed his sins and stated at the end [of the psalm], *The sacrifices of G-d are a broken spirit, a broken heart and a contrite heart, O G-d, Thou wilt not despise.[9]* Thus, he exhorted us concerning submissiveness.

The Sages compared this concept to impure [earthen] vessels which become pure when they are broken.[10] Thus, [the prophet] Micah said, *Wherewith shall I come before the Eternal, and bow myself before G-d on high?[11]* That is, how shall I come before G-d to thank Him for His

---

(4) II Chronicles 7:13.   (5) *Ibid.*, Verse 14.   (6) Psalms 107:12. The verse speaks of those held in captivity, who sit in darkness and the shadow of death, *because they rebelled against the words of G-d* (Verse 11). *Therefore He humbled them*, etc. When they cried unto Him in their trouble, *He saved them out of their distresses* (Verse 13).   (7) Psalms 25:18.   (8) *Ibid.*, 51:2. The occasion was the matter of Bath-sheba, and the prophet Nathan came to chastise David.   (9) *Ibid.*, Verse 19. The broken spirit in man will thus not be rejected even by the attribute of justice which is here indicated by the Divine Name *Elokim* (G-d).   (10) Keilim 2:1. Man, who originates from earth, (Genesis 3:19) is thus likened to an earthen vessel which once it becomes impure cannot regain its purity until it is broken (Leviticus 11:33). The broken spirit similarly regains for man his state of purity.   (11) Micah 6:6.

many mercies? How shall I bow myself and be submissive to G-d on high for the many sins? *Shall I come before Him with burnt-offerings, etc.?*[11] The answer to this question lies in the prophet's statement, *It hath been told thee, O man, what is good, and what the Eternal doth require of thee: only to do justly, and to love mercy, and to walk humbly with thy G-d.*[12] Serve Him humbly, for that is the principal form of submissiveness, about which he had asked, *Wherewith shall I come before the Eternal?*[11] Submissiveness is more acceptable than *the thousands of rams*[13] and all the burnt-offerings he had mentioned.

Man's submissiveness is beloved by G-d. As long as a person subdues his own will and makes it comply with [the requirements of] the service of G-d, then even if he had been as thoroughly wicked as Ahab, [King of Israel, who worshipped idols], he is still assured of some great benefit of his submissiveness. In the case of Ahab, who was counted as one of the [worst] sinners of Israel, it is written, *And there was none like unto Ahab, who did give himself over to do that which was evil in the sight of the Eternal.*[14] Yet, when he humbled his will, it is written that G-d said to Elijah, *Seest thou how Ahab humbleth himself before Me? I will not bring the evil in his days.*[15]

Similarly, we find that Menasheh, [King of Judah], did all things abominable to G-d, but when he was humbled and turned [to G-d] in penitence, his repentance was accepted. It is written, *And when he was in distress, he besought the Eternal his G-d, and humbled himself before the G-d of his fathers.*[16] *And he prayed unto Him, 'vayei'ather' (and He was entreated) of him.*[17] The Sages commented,[18] "Do not

---

(12) *Ibid.*, Verse 8. *To do justly* includes all the duties involved between man and his fellow. *And to love mercy* is a reference to essential acts of lovingkindness, and of doing more than the letter of the law requires. *And to walk humbly with thy G-d* embraces all duties of man towards the Creator (R'dak). (13) *Ibid.*, Verse 7. (14) I Kings 21:25. (15) *Ibid.*, Verse 29. Although Ahab himself died in battle (*ibid.*, 22:35-38) his dynasty continued to rule over the Kingdom of Israel through the reigns of two more kings. (16) II Chronicles 33:12. (17) *Ibid.*, Verse 13. (18) Sanhedrin 103a. See Ramban, Writings and Discourses, pp. 443, 449.

pronounce [the word] *vayei'ather,* but *vayeichather,* [meaning], an opening was made for him in heaven so that his prayer would be accepted."[19] In contrast [to Ahab and Menasheh], Pharaoh, who did not humble himself [before G-d], was punished by drowning, and Nebuchadnezzar, who was conceited and made a deity of himself, was humbled by G-d, Who lowered him to the state of the animals, eating *grass as oxen*[20] for seven years. This punishment was [inflicted] measure for measure, as Solomon said, *Pride goeth before destruction, and a haughty spirit before a fall.*[21]

The Sages explained to us that the humbling of one's will supersedes the Torah's positive commandment of unloading.[22] They stated,[23] "If [one is simultaneously called upon to assist] a friend in unloading an animal that has fallen under its burden and an enemy in loading a burden, he must [first] assist the enemy in order to bend his [own] will."[24] Thus, the principal object of the Torah is that a person should bend his will and humble his heart [to curb his] pursuit of the physical passions and that he should do nothing which is contrary to the word of G-d. One who succeeds in attaining these goals is more commendable than an angel, for while man has an inherent impulse to satisfy his desire, the angels do not. [Accordingly, if he conquers his passions, he

(19) Because the angels protested against acceptance of Menasheh's repentance, "the Holy One, blessed be He, made for him a sort of opening in the heaven in order to accept his repentance (Sanhedrin 103a). (20) Daniel 4:30. In addition to his eating *grass as oxen,* Nebuchadnezzar *was driven from men, and his body was wet with the dew of heaven, till his hair was grown like eagles' feathers, and his nails like birds' claws,* until he came to acknowledge *that the Most High ruleth in the kingdom of men, and giveth it to whosoever He will* (Verse 29). (21) Proverbs 16:18. (22) We are commanded to assist our fellow man in unloading a burden from his beast, or in removing a burden from him himself if he is alone (Exodus 23:5; Maimonides, "The Commandments," Vol. I, pp. 217-218). (23) Baba Metzia 32b. (24) Since animals in general may be used for man's benefit, it is permitted to delay relieving a friend's animal that has fallen under its burden in order to assist one's enemy. By doing so, one will overcome his own enmity for a fellow man and will cultivate the other's friendship (Minchas Chinuch, Commandment 451).

is worthy of great praise.] The Sages therefore said,[25] "The righteous
are greater than the ministering angels." Thus you learn that submissiveness is preferred and accepted by G-d, blessed be He, and it is
the principal aim of all Divine worship. Fasting, prayer, and flagel-
lation [administered by the court] serve only to achieve submissiveness.

We have also been commanded to give charity to the poor in order
to realize that fortune constantly changes. One must therefore be fearful for his own fortune, and consequently, his spirit will be humbled.
Rabbi Akiba stated,[26] "Beloved are pains," but he said it only because
[suffering] causes submissiveness, which in turn makes a person obe-
dient to the will of G-d. Those who persist in the stubbornness of their
hearts and refuse to accept the yoke of submissiveness will be punished
in this world and also in the World to Come. They will be unable to
save themselves from the power of the Almighty. This is the thought
expressed here by Isaiah, *Thus saith the Eternal: The heaven is My
throne, and the earth is My footstool,* etc.[1] *For all these things has My
hand made,* etc.[27] G-d is saying: "All created things in the heavens and
on the earth are Mine. Where is the house that you could build that
would be worthy of Me? *All these things hath My hand made, and so
all these things came to be, saith the Eternal,* yet I look only *upon him
that is poor and of a contrite spirit.*"[27] That is, Divine Providence is
manifested principally in the righteous man who is humble. Even after
he unwittingly sins, he regrets his transgressions and trembles at G-d's
word which he violated. Thus, G-d said, *But upon this man will I look,
even upon him that is poor and of a contrite spirit and who trembleth
at My word,*[27] and the prophet thereupon said, *Hear the word of the
Eternal, Ye that tremble at His word.*[28] Similarly, [at the affair of the
golden calf], Moses our teacher challenged, *Whoso is for the Eternal,*

(25) Sanhedrin 93 a. It should be noted that this statement is indicative of the cardinal position that the Torah attributes to man, who when entitled to being called "a
righteous person" has a more auspicious station in the universe than the ministering
angels on high.   (26) *Ibid.,* 101 a.   (27) Isaiah 66:2.   (28) *Ibid.,* Verse 5.

let him come unto me,[29] which means: "[Let him] who is fearful and who trembles at the word of G-d [come unto me]." Then all the sons of Levi came to Moses for they trembled at the word of G-d they heard at Sinai, *Thou shalt have no other gods before me.*[30] Israel, however, had violated it [by making the golden calf].

The Sages said in Midrash Tanchuma:[31] *"Great is the Eternal, and highly to be praised, and His greatness is unsearchable.*[32] It is further stated, *Yea, My hand hath laid the foundation of the earth, and My right hand hath spread out the heavens.*[33] From G-d's dominion you learn [something] about His greatness, for although these heavens, [which were mentioned in the verse], are spread over the oceans, the inhabited regions, and the deserts, they do not fill His throne. From the hollow of His hand, you learn *Who hath measured the waters,*[34] and from His span you surmise *Who meted out the heaven.*[34] Woe to the mortal who sins before G-d, and happy is the one who is found meritorious before G-d, Who will reward him in the future, as it is said, *Behold, the Eternal G-d will come as a Mighty One, and His arm will rule for Him; behold His reward is with Him, and His recompense before Him."*[35]

Great is the power of submissiveness, for the Divine Glory, which [usually] dwells in the heaven of heavens, also rests on earth with the righteous who are humble. Isaiah attested, *For thus saith the High and Lofty One, that inhabited eternity, whose Name is Holy; I dwell in the high and holy place, with him also that is of a contrite and humble spirit,* etc.[36]

---

(29) Exodus 32:26. (30) *Ibid.,* 20:3. (31) Tanchuma, *Bereshith,* 5. (32) Psalms 145:3. (33) Isaiah 48:13. (34) *Ibid.,* 40:12. G-d's might is thus incomparable. Yet, man, weak in wisdom and faith, dares to violate His will. (35) *Ibid.,* Verse 10. (36) *Ibid.,* 57:15. The expression *with him* [and not "with Me"] clearly indicates that the person who is of the contrite and humble spirit is uniquely honored in that the Divine Glory, so to say, leaves the heavens and comes down to abide with that person.

To attain submissiveness, it is essential that one realize that he is but
a stranger in this world and that he is destined to depart therefrom at
some unspecified time. Even a king should consider himself a stranger,
for we find that King David said, *I am a stranger in the land, hide not
Thy commandments from me.*[37] Since David is but a stranger and does
not know the time of his departure [from this world], he asked G-d not
to hide the commandments from him. Rather, G-d should help and
assist him so that [by fulfilling the commandments], he will have provisions for the journey which could suddenly come upon him. Just as a
stranger [in the land] is alone and relies on G-d's mercies, so is man.
[Upon his death], he will leave his silver and gold behind him, and his
family and friends will leave him alone in his grave and walk away.
Thus, his only source of friendship is G-d. No one will have mercy
upon him except the Merciful G-d, praised be He. Thus, David was
justified in saying, *I am a stranger in the land.*[37] It is therefore proper
that man should contemplate this and return to G-d. He should hope
for G-d's reward and be fearful of His punishment, and he should concern himself with that which is essential in life and abandon the
unessential.

How incongruous it is that man could possibly be so arrogant before
G-d and not be abashed before Him! How can man fail to realize his
lowliness—dust and ashes in life, worms and maggots in death—and
not think of the inestimable greatness of the Master of all, which is
manifest from His majestic and awesome works and deeds! Does man
not see that the earth has been established upon the waters—as the
daily benediction ordained by the Sages declares, "Who spreadest
forth the earth above the waters"—that the waters rest upon the wind,
and that the wind is controlled by the power of G-d? Moses exhorted us
to remember, *And underneath* [all] *are the Everlasting Arms,*[38] which
means that the power of G-d is the cause of all things [in nature]. The
limbs of man have also been created with profound and wondrous

(37) Psalms 119:19.   (38) Deuteronomy 33:27.

wisdom. If one of them were to lose its proper function so that what should be stationary becomes movable or what should be movable becomes stationary, the person would die immediately. Therefore, everyone is obligated to contemplate the wonders of G-d, Who created him with wisdom and formed all his limbs with a mighty providence so that none of them deviates from its assigned task. With all this [in mind], one's heart will be broken and contrite, and he will never leave the service of G-d and the line of Torah and the commandments.

Seafarers are more humble than other people because they endanger their lives when they go to sea. Since only one wooden plank lies between them and death [by drowning], their hearts and eyes are turned to heaven. Certainly, when they occasionally see the fantastically enormous sea creatures, they recognize the inexpressible greatness of the Creator through the immensity of the bodies [of these creatures]. Scripture clearly states: *They that go down to the sea in ships, that do business in great waters, these saw the works of the Eternal.*[39] This is all the more true when the seafarers find themselves in great trouble and see the raging seas and the roar of their waves. At that time, their hearts are truly humbled, as it is written, *They mounted up to the heaven, they went down to the deeps, their souls melted away because of trouble.*[40] Based on this, the Sages said,[41] "The majority of sailors are pious." They recognize that were it not for the mercies of G-d, all of their wisdom and cunning would be of no avail, as it is written, *They reeled to and fro, and staggered like a drunken man, and all their wisdom was swallowed up.*[42] With their own eyes, they see the mighty power of G-d manifested in the stormy waves which seem bent upon flooding the world and yet cannot pass the weak wall of sand [along the coasts]. All this attests to the power of the Master of all, Who observes His covenant[43] that the ocean should not exceed its bounds.

(39) Psalms 107:23-24. (40) *Ibid.*, Verse 26. (41) Kiddushin 82 a. (42) Psalms 107:27. (43) *Or who shut up the sea with doors . . . and prescribed for it My decree . . . and said, 'Thus far shalt thou come, but no further, and here shall thy proud be stayed?'* (Job 38:8-11).

In the case of Jonah the son of Amittai, we find that there was a mighty tempest on the sea. *Then the men feared the Eternal exceedingly, and they offered a sacrifice unto the Eternal.*[44] Their *sacrifice* was the submission of their hearts, for on the boat they did not have the means to bring an actual sacrifice. Because of their submissiveness, G-d saved them from the raging sea, as it states, *And the sea ceased from its raging.*[45] He also saved Jonah from the deeps when He accepted his prayer, *Yet I will look again toward Thy holy Temple.*[46] Jonah further mentioned the miracles at the Red Sea, which brought deliverance to Israel.[47] Jonah's prayer finally came before G-d out of his submissiveness and faintness of spirit, as it is said, *When my soul fainted within me, I remembered the Eternal.*[48]

(44) Jonah 1:16.   (45) *Ibid.*, Verse 15.   (46) *Ibid.*, 2:5.   (47) *Ibid.*, Verse 6.   (48) *Ibid.*, Verse 8.

השגחה

Divine Providence

Providential care pervades the lower world in a general and a particular sense. This has been explained by the psalmist Asaph and the prophet Jeremiah / The Book of Job, which the Sages attributed to Moses our teacher, is specially devoted to this theme / The interpretation of the various theories presented in the Book of Job, as explained by Rabbi Moshe ben Nachman (Ramban).

Divine Providence

THE ETERNAL LOOKETH FROM HEAVEN; HE
BEHOLDETH ALL THE SONS OF MEN.[1] FROM THE PLACE
OF HIS HABITATION HE LOOKETH INTENTLY UPON ALL
THE INHABITANTS OF THE EARTH.[2] HE THAT
FASHIONETH THE HEARTS OF THEM ALL, THAT CON-
SIDERETH ALL THEIR DOINGS.[3]

In these three verses, David mentioned the subject of providence. He explained that in the lower world, providence pervades mankind in general and individuals in particular, for G-d perceives the thought of all men and considers all their doings. Thus, it says, *He that planted the ear, shall He not hear? He that formed the eye, shall He not see?*[4] Scripture is explaining that G-d, Who created the organs of sight and hearing, must certainly be all-seeing and all-hearing, and so Solomon said, *For the ways of man are before the eyes of the Eternal.*[5] Similarly, the Sages said,[6] "Know that above thee are a seeing eye and a hearing ear, and all thy deeds are recorded in a book."

---

(1) Psalms 33:13. (2) *Ibid.*, Verse 14. (3) *Ibid.*, Verse 15. Although the Creator sees their hearts together, yet he considers all their doings individually (Maharsha, Rosh Hashanah 18 a). Thus, the principle of individual providence is here clearly enunciated. (4) Psalms 94:9. The verse mentions the power of hearing first because it is a stronger instrument of understanding spiritual things than that of sight (Hirsch). (5) Proverbs 5:21. (6) Aboth 2:1. "The seeing eye" penetrates one's secret thoughts, "the hearing ear" listens to one's speech, "and all thy deeds etc.," is the registering of one's actions.

The psalmist Asaph broadened the explanation of the subject of providence in Psalm 73. In order to forestall the disbelievers' claim that the higher powers [such as the stars and constellations] bring good or evil upon man and that there is no Divine Providence at all, Asaph therefore said, *Surely G-d is good to Israel, even to such as are pure in heart.*[7] This means that all good proceeds from Him to those who are pure in heart, while evil proceeds from Him to the wicked. Jeremiah also explained that all good and evil come from Him, as it is written, *Who is he that saith and it cometh to pass, when the Eternal commanded it not?*[8] *Out of the mouth of the Most High proceedeth not evil and good?*[9] Certainly, everything comes from Him, the One Source from Whom both good and evil come.

The psalmist proceeds to mention the suffering of the righteous and the prosperity of the wicked. He says, *But as for me, my feet were almost gone, my steps had well nigh slipped. For I was envious of the arrogant, when I saw the prosperity of the wicked.*[10] He is saying that he almost turned aside from the way of truth when he saw the righteous suffering. He expressed this in a personal sense by saying *as for me* and *I was envious.* He was envious of the prosperity of the wicked when he saw the suffering of the righteous.[11] Regarding those wicked men, he says, *For there are no pangs at their death,*[12] meaning they die peacefully, and during their lifetime, *their body is sound.*[12] *In the*

---

(7) Psalms 73:1. Ramban's introduction to his commentary on the Book of Job is the source of the explanation that follows in the text. See Kithvei Haramban, Vol. I, p. 20, and Writings and Discourses, pp. 452-453. (8) Lamentations 3:37. (9) *Ibid.*, Verse 38. It is clear that our author explains the verse as being connected with the preceding one, meaning: "*Who is he that says . . . Out of the mouth of the Most High proceedeth not evil and good?*" Certainly that is not true, as everything comes from Him. (10) Psalms 73:2-3. (11) It is the contradiction between the wicked men triumphing and the righteous men suffering that distresses the psalmist's spirit. Were it not for the sight of the wicked's success, he might have accepted the suffering of the righteous. But it is the success of the wicked at the same time that creates in him the doubt. (12) Psalms 73:4.

trouble of man they are not,[13] *therefore pride is as a chain about their neck.*[14] *They have set their mouth against the heavens, etc.,*[15] *and they say: How doth G-d know? And is there knowledge in the Most High?*[16]

Scripture is thus explaining that these wicked men [are part of the sect which] denies the knowledge [of G-d]. It is known that there are two sects [among the disbelievers], one which denies the knowledge [of G-d] and one which denies providence. The sect which denies providence admits that the Creator does have knowledge of the lower world, for knowledge is an aspect of perfection and G-d is the summation of perfection. However, [that sect maintains that] G-d does not extend His care over the world, for if He did, how could He permit the perversion of justice by the suffering of the righteous and the prosperity of the wicked? Therefore, this sect contends that it is better to deny His providence than to be forced to say that He does bestow His care but punishes and rewards indiscriminately. The other sect believes that the Creator has absolutely no knowledge [of the world]. If He did, He would also bestow His care, and if there were providential care, perverted justice would never come forth in the world. Therefore, that sect concludes, He has absolutely no knowledge [of the lower world], and since there is no [Divine] knowledge, there is also no Divine Providence. With regard to this latter group, Scripture states, *And they say: How doth G-d know? And is there knowledge in the Most High?*[16] The repetition of the expression means *How doth G-d know* in the future, *and is there knowledge in the Most High* about the present?

The psalmist concludes his words by saying that destruction is the end of the wicked, as it is written, *Surely Thou settest them* [the wicked] *in slippery places, Thou hurlest them down to utter ruin.*[17] *How they have become a desolation in a moment, they are wholly consumed*

(13) *Ibid.*, Verse 5. The normal vicissitudes of life leave them untouched, as if they were never plagued by any evil. (14) *Ibid.*, Verse 6. (15) *Ibid.*, Verse 9. (16) *Ibid.*, Verse 11. (17) *Ibid.*, Verse 18.

by terrors.[18] This resolves the problem of the prosperity of the wicked. A subsequent verse, *Nevertheless I am continually with Thee, Thou holdest my right hand,*[19] answers the question of the suffering of the righteous.[20] At the end of the psalm, he returns to this theme and states, *And as for me, the nearness of G-d is my good.*[21]

We find that David himself[22] mentioned this very theme. He said, *I say unto the arrogant: Deal not arrogantly, and to the wicked: Lift not up the horn.*[23] *For G-d is Judge; He putteth down one and lifteth up another.*[24] He is saying that the affluence of these arrogant ones, who are the rich and secure men of the world, has not come to them *from the east,* whence comes the sun, *or from the west,* or from their efforts in the mountains or the wilderness.[25] Their affluence has come only from G-d in reward for the few merits, *for G-d is Judge; He putteth down one, and lifteth up another.*[24] Thus, the psalmist says here, *The Eternal looketh from heaven,* etc.[1]

The prophet Jeremiah explained [the problem of] providence in two parts, [addressing himself first to] general and then to specific [providence]. *Great in counsel, and mighty in action, Whose eyes are open upon all the ways of the sons of men,* etc.[26] This verse expresses [the principle of] general providence. [The conclusion of this verse], *to give everyone according to his ways, and according to the fruit of his doings,*[26] expresses [the principle of specific or] individual providence. Solomon likewise said, *My beloved is like a gazelle or a young hart;*

---

(18) *Ibid.,* Verse 19.   (19) *Ibid.,* Verse 23.   (20) "The verse indicates the permanence of the righteous and the continuance of their lineage and their name, for Asaph, author of this psalm, included the righteous in his use of the prenominal first person" (Kithvei Haramban, Vol. I, p. 21).   (21) Psalms 73:28. The nearness of G-d is the psalmist's profound assurance that Divine Providence is a reality.   (22) Psalm 75, about to be quoted here, was also written by Asaph, as the first verse indicates. Rabbeinu Bachya credits it to David on the basis of the Sages' saying that "David wrote the Book of Psalms, including in it the work of the elders" (Baba Bathra 14 b).   (23) Psalms 75:5.   (24) *Ibid.,* Verse 8.   (25) See *ibid.,* Verse 7.   (26) Jeremiah 32:19.

behold, this One standeth behind our wall, He looketh in through the windows, He peereth through the lattice.[27] Note that Solomon began the verse in the third person, saying *My beloved is like,* not "You are like," but he continued in the second person, saying *this One standeth,*[28] not "He standeth." This teaches us that while G-d, Who is compared to the *beloved,* can be found [by him that seeks Him] and is near to the heart, He is nevertheless remote from [mortal] perception, as the poet[29] expressed it, "He is extremely far from the heaven of heavens and yet extremely near to me." In this sense, you will also find that the text of the benedictions consists of expressions in both the third and second person.[30]

Solomon stated, *This One standeth behind our wall,*[27] thus comparing the substance which intervenes between G-d and us to an earthen wall. Were it not for this intervening wall, we could say, *Behold, this is our G-d,*[31] and as Scripture explicitly states, *But your iniquities have separated between you and your G-d.*[32] Solomon is teaching us that the wall notwithstanding, G-d still watches from *the windows* of the heavens *and peereth through the lattice*[27] of the Throne of Glory. This refutes the opinion of those who say that because of the lowliness of man in relation to the loftiness of G-d, His providence does not extend to the [insignificant] lower world. Solomon's double expression—*He looketh in* and *peereth*—alludes to the two kinds of providence I have mentioned.[33]

---

(27) Song of Songs 2:9.   (28) The Hebrew word *zeh* (this one) is a second person pronoun because it is used to indicate something near the speaker. The alternate choice "He standeth" would indicate that "He" was at a distance from the speaker.   (29) I have been unable to identify this poet.   (30) Benedictions begin "Blessed art Thou etc.," thus acknowledging the sovereignty of G-d in the second person *Thou.* However, the benedictions then refer to G-d in the third person: "Who has sanctified us by His commandments." See Ramban, Commentary on the Torah, Exodus, pp. 214-215.   (31) Isaiah 25:9.   (32) *Ibid.,* 59:2.   (33) Thus, *He looketh in* refers to His providential care of the specific individual, and *He peereth* expresses His providence over the world in general.

Providence over a special individual is only associated with the rational faculty of that person[34] [which is the basis for reward and punishment].[35] This is clearly stated, *O Eternal, Thou hast ordained them for judgment, and Thou, O Rock, hast established them for correction,*[36] thus instructing you that the function of His care is to lead the individual in the ways of justice and to correct him with chastisement for sin.

The prophet Jeremiah cited the sea and the rain as two visible proofs of providence: Thus, he said, *Will ye not tremble at My presence? Who have placed the sand for the bound of the sea.*[37] The sand is not a high wall which can stand against the sea, yet though the waves roar and advance against it, *they cannot pass over it.*[37] Hence, you can understand that G-d watches over the lower world and that you are to fear Him. The prophet further stated, *Neither say they in their heart: Let us now fear the Eternal our G-d that giveth the former rain and the latter in their season, that keepeth for us the appointed weeks of the harvest.*[37] The rain comes in its time—the *former rain* in [the month of] Marcheshvan, and the *latter* rain in Nisan—not in the harvest season,[38] and the wind blows in accordance with the need [of the fields]. This is an example of providential care for an individual [nation], for [Israel], the recipient of this great blessing, is indeed distinguished thereby among the other nations. He specified *the appointed weeks of the harvest,* not "the appointed days," because we count seven weeks[39] until [*Shavuoth*], *the feast of harvest.*[40]

(34) This theory was developed by Maimonides in his Guide of the Perplexed III, Chapter 18.   (35) If not for his rational faculty, man would be as the beast which is irresponsible for its actions.   (36) Habakkuk 1:12.   (37) Jeremiah 5:22-24, The *former rain* comes in the Land of Israel towards the middle of the month Marcheshvan (October), and increases throughout the winter months. The *latter rain* are the heavy showers in the month of Nisan (April).   (38) Rain during the harvest season is not a sign of blessing (Taanith 12 b).   (39) See Deuteronomy 16:9.   (40) Exodus 23:16.

There is yet another distinguished and great book dedicated to the subject of providence, The Book of Job, which our Rabbis of blessed memory attributed to Moses our teacher, peace be upon him. Thus, they said,[41] "Moses wrote his book [the Pentateuch] and the Book of Job." The Sages' intent was to declare that just as the Almighty related the Book of Genesis to Moses on Sinai, so did He relate the subject of Job and his friends to him in the same form as it exists today. The Book of Job is thus like the Book of Genesis. The latter instructs us about the creation of the world out of nothingness, about providence, and about the truth of punishment and reward, [and the former also teaches us about these same themes]. Although the secret passages of the Book of Genesis deal with the esoteric Divine Chariot,[42] its overt passages cover the story of Creation. This is likewise true of the Book of Job. In all of the accounts in the Book of Genesis, you will find not the Divine Tetragrammaton, but the Name *Elokim* (G-d) or *Aleph-Dalet* or *Shin-Dalet*,[43] all of which indicate that He conducts the world with the attribute of justice. In the Book of Job, too, you will find that these Names are used [rather than the Tetragrammaton]. From these standpoints, it was fitting for the Sages to attribute the Book of Job to Moses our teacher.

I shall now explain to you the general subject of the Book of Job according to Ramban of blessed memory. Most of the explanation[44] consists of direct quotations from his distinguished commentary.

(41) Baba Bathra 15 a. Our author is following the line of thought developed by Ramban. See Kithvei Haramban, Vol. I, p. 22. (42) The term "Divine Chariot" is understood here as defined by Maimonides in his commentary on Chagigah, Chapter 2. It indicates the process of religious thought which treats of G-d, His attributes, the angels, the soul of man, etc. (43) *Aleph Daleth* are the first two letters of the Divine Name Ado-noy which is generally translated as "the Lord." *Shin Daleth* are the first two letters of the Divine Name *Sha-dai*, the Almighty. See Ramban, Commentary on the Torah, Genesis, p. 216. (44) Rabbeinu Bachya is the first to mention Ramban's commentary on the Book of Job. Here in Kad Hakemach, as well in his Commentary on the Torah (Genesis, p. 27, in my edition), our author clearly attributes this work to Ramban. A close contemporary of Rabbeinu Bachya, namely, Rabbi Menachem

Job denied [the existence of] providence because he experienced much suffering, and he wanted to engage in debate with the attribute of justice. He claimed that the sufferings and troubles which befell him, a righteous man, prove that there is no Divine Providence over the lower world. If there were, how could G-d possibly punish him unjustly and allow a perverted judgment to issue forth from Himself. Furthermore, Job saw many wicked people in the world living in peace and tranquility.

Job's friends—Eliphaz the Temanite, Bildad the Shuhite, and Zophar the Naamathite—argued that even if Job is [relatively] righteous, it is nevertheless impossible that he never sinned, *for there is not a righteous man upon earth, that doeth good, and sinneth not.*[45] Their contention was that a thoroughly righteous person who has intentionally transgressed some commandment of his Creator must certainly be punished for it. Now, even if G-d [punishes him by] depriving him of all the worldly favors and causes him to suffer all his life, this is still better than being punished in the World of Souls[46] with the sufferings of Gehenna[47] or diminishing his share in the World to Come,[46] which is the absolute and incomparable beneficence that is immeasurable by any physical standard. Accordingly, it is logical to lessen the punishment of the righteous man [in the World of Souls or to assuage the diminution of his reward in the World to Come] by

Ricanti of Italy, also quotes from this work of Ramban. Considering the fact that both of these authors were but one generation removed from Ramban, the authenticity of Ramban's authorship of the commentary on the Book of Job cannot be questioned. See further on this point in my Introduction to this work in Kithvei Haramban, Vol. I, pp. 12-14. — It shoulds be noted that a significant part of the explanation here, is also based upon Rabbeinu Saadia Gaon's commentary, as mentioned further. See Note 52 below. Rabbeinu Bachya was fluent in the Arabic language and undoubtedly drew directly from Saadia's commentary in its original form. (45) Ecclesiastes 7:20. (46) This is where a person's soul goes immediately following the death of the body. At the Resurrection, body and soul will be reunited in *Olam Haba*, (the Coming World, or the World to Come). (47) See Note 12 in *Orchim* (Hospitality).

punishing him in some minor matter, which is the body and in a limited time, which is [the life in] this world. Thus, he will be able to accept his reward in a distinguished manner and at a proper time. Similarly, in the case of the wicked man, it is unlikely that he never did some good deed for which he deserves reward. [Because of his numerous sins], the exquisite reward of the World to Come is withheld from him, and G-d requites him instead in a [relatively] minor and inferior way in this world.

With this explanation, one can avoid critics by saying that every prosperous wicked man must have done some good deeds and every suffering righteous man must have done something evil; they are judged accordingly. However, Job knew that he was absolutely righteous, and even *He that knoweth*[48] testified about him: *And thou [Satan] didst move Me to destroy him without cause.*[49] There are similar cases [of thoroughly righteous men who suffered]. For example, we have a tradition[50] that as the Romans were selling Rabbi Akiba's flesh in the meat markets, Moses thereupon said to G-d,[51] "Is this the reward for such [knowledge of the] Torah?" G-d replied, "Be silent, for thus have I decreed." These cases do not fall under the principle [discussed above], and the only answer to the problem posed by these instances lies in the words of Elihu, [which will be mentioned further].

G-d wanted to test Job because of the prompting of Satan, and He crushed Job with much suffering—first afflicting his wealth, then his children, and finally his body.

---

(48) Jeremiah 29:23.   (49) Job 2:3.   (50) Menachoth 29 b. See Ramban, Commentary on the Torah, Deuteronomy p. 73.   (51) Tractate Menachoth 29 b relates that when Moses was in heaven to receive the Torah, he noticed *tagim*, small crown-like decorations, atop many of the letters of the Torah. He asked G-d what the *tagim* represented. G-d answered, "Many generations from now, there will live a man named Akiba the son of Joseph, who will explain every dot and decoration of all [of the Torah's] letters." Moses then asked to be shown Rabbi Akiba's reward. G-d answered, "Turn around." Moses then saw how the Romans tortured the great scholar and sold his flesh in the markets, at which point he uttered his exclamation, quoted in the text.

There is a difference of opinion among the Sages as to the identity of Satan. Rav Saadia Gaon[52] explained[53] that Satan was a real person who accused Job out of hatred and jealousy over Job's success and the great results of his good deeds. Likewise, the *b'nei ha'elohim*[54] were Job's contemporaries. They were his enemies and were jealous of him. It was the custom of these people to gather on certain days of the year in a designated place to worship G-d, after which they would have a sumptuous feast. *B'nei ha'elohim* means "famous people," similar to the expressions, *Israel is My son, My firstborn*[55] and *Ye are the children of the Eternal your G-d.*[56] [Although all of these people were also Job's enemies], Scripture designates Satan as Job's accuser because he was the greatest among them and all followed his advice.

During one particular gathering and in the presence of the rest, *the Eternal said unto Satan, Whence comest thou?*[57] That is to say, the word of G-d came to this man, who was Job's greatest accuser, so that the others should hear and know that Job is a thoroughly righteous man. Although this accuser, a jealous, hateful, and angry man, was unworthy of being addressed by G-d, G-d spoke to him in honor of Job and for the sake of publicizing Job's distinction, the purity of his intention, and the perfection of his faith. There are similar instances of G-d addressing an unworthy person in honor of a righteous man. For example, G-d spoke to Abimelech for the sake of Abraham's honor,[58] and to Laban for the sake of Jacob,[59] and to Balaam for the sake of Israel's

---

(52) One of the greatest Jewish personalities of all times, Rav Saadia Gaon (892-942 C.E.) was head of the Academy of Sura. He translated the Scriptures into Arabic and wrote extensively on every aspect of Jewish learning, including Bible, Talmud, grammar, philology, and philosophy. He also composed polemics, etc. His work, Ha'emunoth V'hadeioth, the first of its kind in the field of Jewish religious philosophy, exercised a great influence on Jewish thought. (53) This explanation of Rav Saadia Gaon is mentioned only briefly by Ibn Ezra, but our author, who cites Rav Saadia's interpretation at length, must have drawn upon his commentary in the original Arabic. (54) Job 1:6. (55) Exodus 4:22. The term connotes importance and dignity. (56) Deuteronomy 14:1. (57) Job 1:7. (58) Genesis 20:3. (59) *Ibid.*, 13:24.

honor.[60] The people at this evil gathering exceedingly despised Job and were jealous of his success, and G-d delivered Job into the hands of the man called Satan in order to test Job in matters of his wealth and physical health, but not to kill him.

The proof that this Satan was a man is the language of the verse, *And the Eternal raised up Satan unto Solomon, Hadad the Edomite.*[61] It is further written, *And G-d raised up another Satan unto him* [Solomon], *Rezon the son of Eliada.*[62] In the case of Joshua the High Priest, it also says, *and Satan standing at his right hand,*[63] and it is known that this Satan refers to *Rehum the commander and Shimshai the Scribe,*[64] who accused Jeshua the son of Jozadak[65] [before the Persian government because of his efforts to complete the building of the Second Temple]. Thus, it is written, *And in the reign of Ahaseurus, in the beginning of his reign, they wrote 'sitnah' (an accusation).*[66] Saadia Gaon further wrote that it is impossible to believe that Satan was an angel, for angels go neither contrary to G-d's will nor against those who walk in His ways. Moreover, it is not their nature to be jealous, hateful, or envious, and they do not gather in places of fetes and mortal pleasures.

In the opinion of Ramban of blessed memory and most of the commentators,[67] this Satan and the *b'nei ha'elohim*[54] were angels. That they were jealous of Job's prosperity and manifested the physical desires of feasting and joy, should not be surprising.[68] Ramban wrote [in the Introduction to his commentary on the Book of Job]: "In our tradition, it is known that Satan, whose name is derived from the expression, *They wrote 'sitnah' (an accusation),*[66] is an angel created to accuse and

---

(60) Numbers, Chapters 22-24. (61) I Kings 11:14. (62) *Ibid.,* Verse 23. (63) Zechariah 3:1. (64) Ezra 4:9. These Samaritan leaders wrote of the rebelliousness of the Jews who with the permission of the Persian government had returned from the Babylonian captivity to build the Second Temple. (65) *Ibid.,* 5:2. (66) *Ibid.,* 4:6. (67) These commentators include Rashi and Ibn Ezra. (68) See Pirkei d'Rabbi Eliezer, 22.

harm people. Our Rabbis, in explaining his general task, said,[69] He is Satan, he is the evil inclination, he is the angel of death.'[70] The Sages thus attributed all these functions to him in addition to their believing that he is truly an angel and not some natural force or any physical power." Thus far is the language of Ramban. It is his opinion, then, that because G-d wanted to test Job and permitted Satan to bring about [his sufferings], a power emanated from Satan, the manifestation of which was a desire among the Chaldeans[71] and Sabeans[72] to attack [Job's servants] by the sword and capture his cattle. [Satan's power was further manifested when] the wind blew and the house fell upon Job's children. All of these mishaps were apparently natural, yet they were all the result of Divine intervention.

Job, a descendant of Abraham — he was one of his brother's [73] children — recognized his Creator. *He feared G-d* [74] and served Him by means of the rational commandments, by being *wholehearted and upright,*[74] by refraining from doing evil to his fellow man, and by worship with a sincere heart, which is the root of all things. His friends, Eliphaz, Bildad, and Zophar, were also of the same seed as Job. Elihu, too, was of this family, for he is called *the Buzite,*[75] which shows that he was related to Buz the son of Nahor.[76] Furthermore, it is written of Elihu that he was *of the family of Ram,*[75] which indicates that he was of the family of Abraham, who was called Ram and whose name indeed had been Abram. The Targum [on the Book of Job] also explains [that Job, *et al*], were "from the family of Abraham."

---

(69) Baba Bathra 16 a.   (70) The essential nature of Satan both as the inciter and the accuser are thus succinctly expressed here.   (71) See Job 1:17.   (72) See *ibid.,* Verse 15.   (73) In all manuscripts of Kad Hakemach the reading is "Edom," rather than *achiv* (his brother). In Ramban's commentary on Job the reading is also Edom. See Kithvei Haramban, Vol. I, p. 27. Edom, or Esau, was a grandson of Abraham. However, since Uz is mentioned as the son of Nahor, Abraham's brother (Genesis 22:21), and Job was of *the land of Uz* (Job 1:1), the reading *achiv* (his brother) is preferable.   (74) Job 1:1.   (75) *Ibid.,* 32:2.   (76) Genesis 22:21.

The general intent of the Book of Job is that Job, seeing the many troubles and evils befall him and knowing his own righteousness, began thinking that perhaps G-d has no knowledge and reckoning concerning the affairs of people and that His providence is removed from them. Job began by saying that man's destiny, whether for good or evil, is determined by the paths of the stars and constellations at the time of his birth and conception. This is the opinion of the foolish astrologers. Therefore, Job commenced with these words, *Let the day perish wherein I was born,*[77] and he cursed the day, the night, *the stars of the twilight,* and *the eyelids of the morning*[78] for having brought about his troubles. He claimed that due to man's lowliness, G-d in His loftiness pays no attention to him, and he is therefore under the rule of chance, which is determined by the arrangement of the stars and the powers of the earth. Job believed that man is like the other creatures upon the earth. They are afforded the protection of higher providence only for the sake of the existence of the species, but [the concept of] reward or punishment does not apply to any individual creature. This is Job's intent in his first dialogue, and he returns to it in the second dialogue, when he says, *What is man that Thou shouldest magnify him?*[79]

A further proof to this[80] is Eliphaz's answer to Job: *And thou [Job] sayest: What doth G-d know? Can He judge through the dark cloud?*[81] *Thick clouds are a covering to Him, that He seeth not.*[82] This is a denial of providence over the lower creatures. *And He walketh in the circuit of heaven,*[82] which means that His providence extends only over those heavenly powers that determine the fate of those born under their sway. *Wilt thou keep the old way which wicked men have trodden?*[83] Note how Job himself now expresses his regret by saying that he

(77) Job 3:3. (78) *Ibid.,* Verse 9. (79) *Ibid.,* 7:17. (80) I.e., Job believed that G-d withholds His providence from man because of his lowliness. (81) *Ibid.,* 22:13. (82) *Ibid.,* Verse 14. (83) *Ibid.,* Verse 15. Ramban in his commentary on this verse explained that Eliphaz here challenges Job and asks, "Will you, Job, keep the old way, saying that good or evil proceed not out of the Most High but only out of the stars and constellations in that sphere?"

never entertained such thoughts while he lived in tranquility: *If I beheld the sun when it shined, or the moon walking in brightness;*[84] *and my heart hath been secretly enticed, and my mouth had kissed my hand,*[85] as one who admits that they are gods, *This also was an iniquity in my eyes, for I should have lied to G-d Who is above.*[86] Everything comes from Him, not from the powers of the shining stars and the moon. This was Job's opinion while he lived in tranquility, but now that troubles befell him unjustifiably, they proved to him that there is no providence over lower creatures. However, he has not yet broached the problem of the righteous who suffer or the wicked who prosper.

Eliphaz then challenged Job for turning away from the Master, Who does all things in justice and righteousness, and ascribing the dominion [of the world] to the stars and constellations. Eliphaz said, *Remember, I pray thee, who ever perished, being innocent?*[87] That is to say, "Innocents do not perish, for you see that *they that plow iniquity reap the same.*[88] This is proof to me that *by the breath of G-d they perish*[89] and not by the power of the times and the stars. Only He causes the destruction of the wicked man who has taken root. As for righteous men like you [Job] who are stricken by evil, it is *the chastening of* G-d, *despise it not,*[90] for the purpose of such chastening is like that of the trials of the righteous. It is written, *As a man chasteneth his son, so the Eternal thy G-d chasteneth thee,*[91] and it further states, *That He might afflict thee, and that He might prove thee, to do thee good at thy latter end.*"[92] Eliphaz was the wisest of all of Job's friends, and therefore he replied first. At the end, he attained the distinction of prophecy.[93]

---

(84) Job 31:26. (85) *Ibid.*, Verse 27. (86) *Ibid.*, Verse 28. Thus, Job clearly stated that formerly, in the state of his tranquility, such thoughts of attributing man's fortune to the stars were far from him, as he would have considered them to be a denial of G-d Who is above. But now that troubles befell him, etc. (87) Job 4:7. (88) *Ibid.*, Verse 8. (89) *Ibid.*, Verse 9. (90) See, *ibid.*, 5:17. (91) Deuteronomy 8:5. As explained by Ramban (*ibid.*): "He (the father) places upon the son the yoke of instruction for his benefit, as it is said, *Chasten thy son, for there is hope, but set not thy heart on his destruction*" (Proverbs 19:18). (92) Deuteronomy 8:16. (93) See Job 42:7: *And the Eternal said to*

Job replied to Eliphaz: "If the discipline of G-d has come upon me, *what is my strength that I should wait*[94] until it will pass? The suffering is too great to be considered a mere trial." As for Eliphaz's other arguments that everything is done in justice, that there is no death without sin and no suffering without transgression, Job argued that there is *a time of hard labor for man upon earth, and his days are like the days of a hireling,*[95] and his merits do not save him from death. Thus, there are righteous men who are not saved by their righteousness. Hence, if they sin, they should rightfully be spared further punishment since the essential existence of man is likened to vanity, as it is written, *I loathe it, I shall not live always; let me alone, for my days are vanity.*[96]

Bildad the Shuhite answered: *Doth G-d pervert judgment? Or doth the Almighty pervert justice?*[97] *If thy children sinned against Him, He delivered them into the hand of their transgression.*[98] Bildad was more outspoken than Eliphaz, for he explicitly stated that the evils that befell Job and his children were all just in nature. He declared that Job's children were thoroughly wicked and deserved their death, and as for Job, his suffering served to cleanse him of some of his sins. If he would seek earnestly unto G-d, He would yet reward him for his righteousness.[99] Thus, Bildad was the first to declare that Job was wicked. He did not see fit to agree with Eliphaz that [Job's affliction] was a form of chastening, for Job had complained, *What is my strength, that I should wait? and what is mine end, that I should be patient?*[94]

Job replied by proving the lack of providence over man. [He argued that if we] assumed that everything is done by the Divine will and

---

Eliphaz. The Sages also counted Eliphaz among the seven prophets who prophesied among the nations of the world (Baba Bathra 15 b).   (94) Job 6:11.   (95) *Ibid.*, 7:1. In other words, the battle of life is wearisome and unabating, leading hopelessly to the grave, without regard to the righteousness of the person or not.   (96) *Ibid.*, Verse 16. "In view of the brevity of life, there is then no hope or meaning to my righteousness" (Ramban).   (97) *Ibid.*, 8:3.   (98) *Ibid.*, Verse 4.   (99) See *ibid.*, Verse 5-6.

desire, then *if the scourge slay suddenly*, killing people indiscriminately, and *He will mock at the calamity of the guiltless,*[100] [it is apparent,
that] *the earth is given into the hand of the wicked*[101] king, who covers
the faces of the judges so that they cannot administer justice while he
commits crimes at will. *And if it be not He, who then is it*[101] that
destroys all? *Now my days are swifter than a runner, they flee away,
they see no good.*[102] That is to say, it is far better to [believe that] providence is removed from the lower creatures because of the Creator's
exalted loftiness than to assert that there is providence but that justice
is perverted, as explained above.

[Job continued], *"I will speak, and not fear Him,*[103] for it is Adam
who sinned, not I."[104] The Sages commented,[105] *"For I am not so with
myself.*[103] [Job said], 'I am not like [Adam], the first man, who said,
*The woman whom Thou gavest to be with me, she gave me of the tree,
and I did eat.*[106] Therefore, I have no fear of the judgment.' "

[Job continued his reply], *"Is it good unto Thee that Thou shouldest
oppress, that Thou shouldest despise the work of Thy hands, and shine
upon the counsel of the wicked?*[107] One who takes anything which is
not his is called an oppressor. Now, there are three partners in the
creation of a person:[108] G-d, the [person's] father, and his mother.
When a person dies, G-d takes his part, and the part of the father and
mother lies before them." Job is saying, *"Is it good unto Thee that
Thou shouldest oppress* my body, which is not Your portion but that of
my parents? You renounced [Your claim to] that part when You said,
only spare his life.[109] You should have taken Your portion, the soul, so
that it would depart from my body and I would not have to experience
these sufferings."

---

(100) *Ibid.*, Verse 9:23. (101) *Ibid.*, Verse 24. (102) *Ibid.*, Verse 25.
(103) *Ibid.*, Verse 35.   (104) Adam heeded his wife when she gave him the fruit of
the tree of knowledge, but Job did not listen to his wife. See Job
2:9-10. (105) Bereshith Rabbah, end of Chapter 19. (106) Genesis
3:12. (107) Job 10:3. By His splendor upon the counsel of the wicked, He gives en-
couragement to their continuing deeds of evil.(108) Kiddushin 30 b.(109) Job 2:6.

Zophar the Noamathite now answered, intending to support his friends' contention that Job did sin and that is why all this evil befell him. However, Zophar expressed the novel thought that some of G-d's deeds are overt and others are hidden. Thus, he stated, *for sound wisdom is double to that which is in our possession*.[110] He explained thereby that the Torah is twofold in nature, for its open and hidden truths, as it is written, *Apples of gold in filigrees of silver*.[111] Furthermore, out of compassion for His works, G-d overlooks the transgression of the wicked, *and when He seeth iniquity He will not consider it*[112] at first, for perhaps the wicked perpetrators will return to Him. If He has mercy upon the wicked and deals kindly with them, He certainly would not do evil to the righteous. Therefore, the purpose of Job's suffering can only be to cause him to direct his heart in prayer to G-d, and ultimately he will enjoy tranquility.

Zohar thus transformed Job's question about the prosperity of the wicked into proof that G-d has compassion for his creatures and would surely not do evil to those who are good. As to the question of the suffering of the righteous, the problem is not at all self-evident. You could say that each person so affected deserved the punishment. The question applies only to the suffering person himself who knows that he is righteous. Even then, perhaps he is favoring himself egotistically. You will therefore note that after Zophar's response, Job's friends speak only of the [deserving] ultimate destruction of the wicked, which they consider the crucial issue as to why they prosper. Job, however, continues to elaborate on his own righteousness and as to why he suffers.

---

(110) *Ibid.*, 11:6.   "You [Job] should know that G-d's providence over the world is both visible and hidden. Visible in its goodness and hidden in that it is far more beneficial than we can possibly understand" (Ramban).   (111) Proverbs 25:11. The author undoubtedly had in mind Maimonides' explanation of this verse: "When a golden apple which is overlaid with a silver filigree is seen from a distance or observed superficially, it is mistaken for a silver apple, but when a keen-sighted person looks well at it, he will find what is within and see that the apple is gold, etc." The same is true of the Torah as a whole.   (112) Job 11:11. For G-d is slow to anger, affording the sinner an opportunity to repent.

Then was kindled the wrath of Elihu the son of Berachel the Buzite, of the family of Ram,[113] which means the family of Abraham, who was the founder of the faith [in One G-d]. Elihu's wrath was kindled against Job because in his opinion, Job had gone astray, as it is said, *Against Job was his wrath kindled, because he justified himself rather than G-d.*[113] *Also against his three friends was his wrath kindled, because they had found no answer, and yet had condemned Job.*[114] It is clear that Elihu was not condemning Job as a wicked sinner. His intention was to vindicate Job but not [at the expense of] having Job's righteousness surpass God's. [In other words, Elihu's argument] obviated the conclusion that G-d has perverted His judgment [by afflicting a righteous man]. Thus, Scripture did not say that Elihu's wrath was kindled against Job merely "because he justified himself." Instead it says, *because he justified himself rather than G-d.*[113] Elihu was saying that even though it is possible that Job is righteous, yet *G-d is greater than man.*[115]

Elihu next proceeded to explain the secret of the righteous man who suffers. *For G-d speaketh in one-way,*[116] *in a dream, in a vision of the night.*[117] That is to say, in visions of prophecy *He openeth the ears of men*[118] and sets His seal upon their affliction.[119] Then, while the body will be interred in the grave, the soul will exist forever. And what does the merciful G-d do to *hold him back from the pit*[120] so that man will not be destroyed forever because of his transgressions? He afflicts him with pain *upon his bed, and his bones grow stiff.*[121] *If there be for him an angel to vouch* for *his uprightness,*[122] that is, if he has done repentance, *then* G-d *is gracious unto him and saith* to the defending angel, *Deliver him from going down the pit, I have found a ransom.*[123]

---

(113) *Ibid.*, 32:2.   (114) *Ibid.*, Verse 3.   (115) *Ibid.*, 33:12.   (116) *Ibid.*, Verse 14.   (117) *Ibid.*, Verse 15.   (118) *Ibid.*, Verse 18.   (119) After the Divine judgment is given, there is still an opportunity for repentance, until "He sets His seal" upon it.   (120) Job 33:18. That is to save the sinner from ultimate destruction.   (121) *Ibid.*, Verse 19.   (122) *Ibid.*, Verse 23.   (123) *Ibid.*, Verse 24.

Thus, repentance and suffering[124] saved the sinner *from going down the pit,*[123] but he will not merit to see the Supreme Light[125] until the soul is reborn as at first. Thus, Elihu next said, *His flesh is more tender than a child's, He returneth to the days of his youth.* [126] When he grows up, he will pray to G-d, and through his repentance and suffering he will be accepted by G-d. His righteousness will then be restored [as at first] for he will not have sinned since the days of his rebirth. His afflictions will have ensued from his former transgressions, which should have brought about his utter destruction. However, G-d devised means so that he would not be banished from the World to Come, and he will then merit the Supreme Light,[125] as Elihu said. *So He redeemed his soul from going into the pit, and his life beholdeth the light,*[127] a reference to the Supreme Light. This device [of rebirth] can be repeated three times, as it says, *Lo all these things doth G-d work, twice, yea thrice, with a man.*[128] Thus, the paradox of the suffering of the righteous man has been clearly explained. The question is completely removed, and there remains no doubt about it. Similarly, the secret of the prosperity of the wicked may also be derived from the [above] solution, or perhaps we can attribute it [simply] to an act of Divine mercy.

You will note that Job did not offer any reply to Elihu, which indicates that Elihu's argument was novel and sufficiently answered Job's question. Hence, Job remained silent. In fact, Elihu said to him, *If thou hast anything to say, answer me,*[129] but Job did not stand up to challenge his words. Furthermore, G-d later censured Job's friends and said they would require a burnt-offering to atone for them *for ye have*

---

(124) Both elements — repentance and suffering — are thus required to mitigate the judgment. (125) A Cabalistic term signifying the summit of perfection in the World to Come. (126) Job 33:25. See Ramban, Commentary on the Torah, Genesis, pp. 469-470, where the doctrine of the transmigration of souls is indicated. (127) Job 33:28. (128) *Ibid.,* Verse 29. (129) *Ibid.,* Verse 32.

not spoken of Me the thing that is right.[130] However, He did not condemn Elihu and did not require such an atonement from him.[131]

Then the Eternal answered Job out of the whirlwind.[132] Job now attained the degree of prophecy because he was *wholehearted, and upright, and one that feared G-d, and shunned evil,*[74] and had been chastised by trial. Although in his lack of wisdom, he transgressed by doubting G-d's judgment, his trial brought him nearer to G-d, for he accepted Elihu's words and found them satisfactory. Thus, he was now one that feared G-d and was sincere in his righteousness.[133]

The expression *out of the whirlwind*[132] does not mean that the heavens were opened for him so that he could clearly envision G-d. Rather, [the expression teaches us that] he heard a great whirlwind and perceived what the prophets apprehended at the beginning of a vision, as it says of Ezekiel at the beginning [of his vision], *And I looked, and behold, a stormy wind came out of the north.*[134] Likewise, it says in the case of Elijah, *And, behold, the Eternal passed by, and a great and strong wind rent the mountains, and shattered the rocks before the Eternal; but the Eternal was not in the wind, and after the wind an earthquake,* etc.[135] Afterwards, the prophets perceived the prophecy. Job, too, heard the Divine Voice out of the whirlwind, and he knew that it was the Voice of G-d responding to his words.

In two responses,[136] the Holy One, blessed be He, informed Job how He conducts the world with the two attributes of mercy and justice. In the first answer, He mentioned the subject of the sea, to the waters of

---

(130) *Ibid.,* 42:7.   (131) This proves that Elihu did not reiterate the arguments of the other friends of Job but rather presented a new approach to the problem. (132) *Ibid.,* 38:1.   (133) Thus, Job's spiritual integrity was acknowledged at the end, while his friends needed atonement for speaking presumptuously of Job's suffering.   (134) Ezekiel 1:4.   (135) I Kings 19:11.   (136) G-d's first answer is contained in Job, Chapters 38-39, and the second one in Chapters 40-41.

which He set the sand as a boundary.[137] This constitutes an act of great
mercy and compassion to the world, for it enables inhabited regions to
exist and to avoid destruction. Afterwards, He informed Job of the
rain, which constitutes another act of mercy to the world, as it says,
*Who hath cleft a channel for the waterflood, or a way for the lightning
of the thunder*, etc.?[138] All of these acts of mercy and compassion serve
to make manifest His tender care over all His works.

In the second answer, G-d revealed His conduct [of the world]
through the attribute of justice.[139] Thus, He mentioned the two great
creatures [the behemoth and the leviathan], one of the land and one of
the sea. Their great and mighty physical proportions betoken the
quality of their strength. In short, He informed Job that His providential care extends over man in general and in particular, and that it extends over all other creatures only for the sake of the existence of the
species. In the midst of His words,[140] He also intimated that the secret
which Elihu revealed is true. Elihu, after all, had no compelling proof
to offer, and the subject could only be known by tradition.

Job then answered, *"I know that Thou canst do everything, and that
no purpose can be withholden from Thee*,[141] for Your wisdom is infinite. *It is I that have uttered words* to my friends *which I understood
not, and they are too wonderful for me, which I know not*[142] even now.
I had heard of Thee by the hearing of the ear.[143] I had adhered to
tradition concerning G-d, and now I have attained the degree of prophecy, and I know the truth of Your existence. I know that You are

(137) See Job 38:8-11. (138) *Ibid.*, Verse 25. (139) This distinction between
G-d's two answers—i.e., that the first represents His providence through the attribute
of mercy, and the second, His providence through the attribute of justice—is not
found in Ramban's commentary on the Book of Job. (140) Rabbeinu Bachya is
referring to Job 38:14, which in his opinion alludes to the dead man's soul, *It is changed as clay under the seal*, which means its rebirth. "This is an act of mercy and compassion so that all Israel can merit eternal life and be enlightened with the Supreme
Light and thus avoid destruction." (141) *Ibid.*, 42:2. (142) *Ibid.*, Verse 3.
(143) *Ibid.*, Verse 5.

omniscient and providential and that You are the Righteous Judge, Who abounds with mercy and truth. *Therefore I abhor* life and tranquility in this world. I had desired them until now, and I complained over their loss. *I repent seeing I am dust and ashes.* "[144]

And the Eternal said to Eliphaz the Temanite.[145] This man, who was the greatest among Job's friends, also reached the degree of prophecy because of his outstanding wisdom. Perhaps [the word of G-d came to him] in a dream at night, as in the cases of Abimelech and Laban.[146] G-d addressed Eliphaz because He desired [that Job's friends should] atone for their transgression, and He wanted to inform them that *"ye have not spoken of Me the thing that is right.*[145] Because of your arguments, I would have appeared as unjust in the eyes of all those who know themselves to be righteous."

[In the same verse],[145] G-d now referred to Job as *My servant,* for Job had confessed [his mistake]. Both Job and his friends had erred. Job, who was truly righteous but did not know why afflictions befell him, confessed his error after Elihu explained it to him. Thus, he was forgiven. However, Job's friends sought to justify G-d's deeds by condemning Job for his wickedness. They believed that they had done the right thing and therefore did not confess [their mistake]. Thus, they required expiation.

And the Eternal restored the fortune of Job.[147] In the opinion of Ramban, none of Job's children or livestock had died. Satan had originally taken Job's herds into the wilderness, and showed the messengers their apparitional loss, and they told Job about it. Satan knew that G-d's wish was only to test Job, and not to have his cattle destroyed. G-d now restored Job's fortune, his sons and daughters, his sheep and camels. Indeed, his wealth even doubled. Therefore, it does not say here that there were born unto him seven sons and seven daughters, as it originally stated.[148] G-d also extended henceforth Job's

---

(144) *Ibid.*, Verse 6.   (145) *Ibid.*, Verse 7.   (146) Genesis 20:3 and 31:24 respectively.   (147) Job 42:10.   (148) See *ibid.*, 1:2.

years doubly of a man's normal life span, as it says, *And after this, Job lived one hundred and forty years,* [149] while the normal span of a man's life is only seventy years.[150] Only then, Job *died, being old and full of days*[151] by merit of his wholeheartedness with the Eternal in health and in sickness, and by virtue of his fear of G-d both in wealth and in poverty.

Fear of G-d, a commandment that applies to the heart, is the principal aspect of Divine worship. Devotion of the heart is essential to all commandments, for it is the root of the faith and [belief in] the Unity of G-d, as it is written, *And lay it to thy heart, that the Eternal, He is G-d in heaven above and upon the earth beneath; there is none else.*[152] It is further written, *Let us lift up our heart with our hands, unto G-d in the heavens.*[153]

(149) *Ibid.,* 42:16. (150) See Psalms 90:10. (151) Job 42:17. (152) Deuteronomy 4:39. (153) Lamentations 3:41.

הלבנה

Shaming Someone

> The sense of shame instilled in the Jewish personality entails discretion and humility. It obligates one not to shame or embarrass his fellow man by word or deed / The very purpose of the Revelation on Sinai was to invest Israel with the quality of discretion and shame / One should be wary of embarrassing his fellow men, for one who adheres to this sinful practice loses his share in the World to Come / Shaming someone is semi-murder / Shaming is a most serious offense. The wicked are imprecated by it, and the righteous are blessed by not having to suffer it / The applicability of the expression, 'It would have been better for man not to have been born at all, etc.'

Shaming Someone

THEREFORE THUS SAITH THE ETERNAL, WHO RE-
DEEMED ABRAHAM, CONCERNING THE HOUSE OF
JACOB: JACOB SHALL NOT NOW BE ASHAMED, NEITHER
SHALL HIS FACE GO PALE[1]

It is known that a veil of shame has been placed upon the face of Israel, *the sacred seed,*[2] and it attests that they are the children of the patriarchs Abraham, Isaac, and Jacob.[3] In the account of the Giving of the Torah, Scripture has testified that G-d's Revelation [on Mount Sinai] amid those mighty and fearful visions was intended to invest Israel with the qualities of discretion and shame. This is expressed in the verse, *And Moses said to the people: Fear not, for G-d is come to prove you, and that His fear may be upon your faces that ye sin not.*[4] Moses should have said, "that His fear may be in your hearts," but as the Sages commented,[5] *"His fear may be upon your faces*[4] refers to shame [about sinning]." The Sages clearly said,[6] "The shamefaced are destined for the Garden of Eden."

(1) Isaiah 29:22. The patriarch Jacob will not be ashamed of his descendants any longer, for [as the prophecy continues] they will all shun evil and sanctify the Holy One of Jacob. (2) *Ibid.*, 6:13. (3) Yebamoth 79 a: "This nation [Israel] has three characteristics: they are merciful, they are ashamed [to commit a transgression], and they perform deeds of kindness." (4) Exodus 20:17. (5) Nedarim 20 a. (6) Aboth 5:25. The expression, "are destined" signifies that the road is open for them to reach eternal bliss in the "Garden of Eden," and they will be assisted from on high to reach their goal, but they must continue in that effort.

People will observe many commandments of the Torah out of shame, but when they are divested of that shame, they cast off the yoke of Torah and the fear [of G-d] from themselves and uphold injustice and pervert the truth. In fact, all the prophets admonished Israel concerning the loss of this sense of shame, as it is said, *Yea, they are not at all ashamed, neither know they how to blush.*[7]

Shame entails discretion and humility, as well as the aspects of scorn and disgrace. Discretion and humility require that one should be ashamed [to commit a transgression] before G-d and man, and the aspects of scorn and disgrace obligate one not to shame or embarrass his fellow man by word or by deed. One who is abashed before G-d will never shame others. Only sinfully wicked people who have no shame before G-d will shame others. We find the following in Midrash Tehillim:[8] "Rabbi Yehoshua the son of Levi said that Scripture imprecates the wicked only with shame. Moreover, it doubles the imprecation, as it says, *Let them be ashamed and abashed together.*[9] When it blesses the righteous, it doubles their blessing, as it is said, *Ye shall not be ashamed nor confounded forever and ever.*[10] It is further stated, *Fear not, for thou shalt not be ashamed, neither be thou confounded, for thou shalt not be put to shame.*"[11]

Since it has been explained that embarrassment and shame constitute *a grievous curse*,[12] a person should be wary of shaming his fellow man. If he persists in doing it, he loses his share in the World to Come. Thus, the Sages commented:[13] "A sage lectured before Rav Nachman, 'One who shames his fellow in public is considered as if he shed blood.' Rav Nachman said to him, 'Your statement is correct, for we see that when a man that is exposed to shame, his face loses its reddish complexion and becomes white.' Abaye asked Rav Dimi, 'What is strictly

(7) Jeremiah 8:12.   (8) Midrash Tehillim, end of Chapter 6.   (9) Psalms 35:26. The imprecation is repeated *ashamed and abashed*.   (10) Isaiah 45:17.   (11) *Ibid.*, 54:4.   (12) I Kings 2:6.   (13) Baba Metzia 58b-59a.

observed in the west [i.e., in the Land of Israel]?'[14] He answered, 'They carefully avoid making anyone's face pale [by embarrassing him], for Rabbi Chanina said that all of those who descent to Gehenna also ascend therefrom, but these three descend and never return: an adulterer, one who calls his neighbor by a nickname, and one who shames his fellow man in public. Although applying a nickname [to a fellow man] is equivalent to shaming him, [Rabbi Chanina's intent is that it is wrong to call someone by a nickname] even if he was accustomed to being so called. Mar Zutra the son of Tuvya—or according to some authorities, Rav Chama quoting Rabbi Shimon the Pious, and still in the view of still others, Rabbi Yochanan quoting Rabbi Shimon ben Yochai—said, It would be better for a person to throw himself into a burning furnace than to shame his fellow man in public. We derive this from Tamar, as it is written, *When she was brought forth, she sent to her father-in-law, saying,* etc.' "[15] Similarly the Sages expounded:[16] "[Before Joseph identified himself to his brothers, he commanded his servants], *cause every man to go out from me.*[17] Rabbi Shmuel the son of Nachmani said, 'Joseph greatly endangered himself at that moment, for had his brothers killed him, no one would discern the deed and no one would avenge him. Why then did he say, *Cause every man to go out from me?*[17] He said, Better that I be killed rather than expose them to public shame.' "

---

(14) The Talmud was written in Babylon, where the majority of Jewish communities flourished during the third, fourth, and fifth centuries of the Common Era. Simultaneously, however, Jewish community life also continued in the west, i.e., in the Land of Israel, which was then under Roman rule.   (15) Genesis 38:25. See *ibid.,* Verses 1-26, and Rashi there. Although condemned to death by burning for apparent harlotry, Tamar refused to name Judah as the man from whom she had become pregnant. Instead, she sent him certain items which could identify him, saying to herself, "If he confesses, well and good, but if not, I would rather die than disgrace him." Recognizing the items as his own, Judah thereupon admitted Tamar's innocence, declaring *She is more righteous than I (ibid.,* Verse 26).   (16) Tanchuma, *Vayigash,* 5.   (17) Genesis 45:1. Joseph ordered his servants to remove the Egyptians at the time

We find that shaming is a semi-murder. The murderer spills the victim's blood outside his body, and although the one who publicly shames his neighbor does not actually spill his blood, he stirs it to leave his neighbor's body. Therefore, the Rabbis said,[13] "One who shames his fellow in public is considered as if he sheds blood, " but he is not actually a murderer. A philosopher said, "Shaming is a minor form of death."[18]

From the preceding, we can appreciate the gravity of shaming. In fact, when G-d wishes to imprecate the wicked, He does so by shaming them, and when He desires to bless the righteous, He blesses them [by ensuring] that they will not be ashamed or disgraced. The prophet Isaiah said, *Thus saith the Eternal . . . concerning the House of Jacob,* etc.[1] Isaiah assured his contemporaries that G-d would chastise them through Sennacherib, King of Assyria, until they return [to G-d] penitently and become worthy of being saved from Sennacherib's power. [The prophet continued], *And Jacob shall not now be ashamed,*[1] meaning that [when they repent] the patriarch Jacob will no longer be ashamed of them, for when children persist in their rebelliousness, their father is ashamed of their evil deeds.

The expression *Who redeemed Abraham*[1] refers to G-d, according to the simple meaning of Scripture. In the Midrash,[19] it states: "*Who redeemed Abraham.*[1] Come and see that fathers are saved for the sake of their children. Abraham was saved from the furnace of Nimrod[20] by the merit of his grandson Jacob. Thus it is written, *Thus saith the Eternal, Who redeemed Abraham, concerning the House of Jacob,* for He redeemed Abraham for the sake of Jacob." One may ask: Were Abraham's merits insufficient that he had to be redeemed for his

---

he identified himself, so as not to embarrass his brothers on account of what has transpired between them. "But," asks the Midrash, "was not this a dangerous step on Joseph's part?" (Tanchuma, *Vayigash* 5). (18) I have been unable to identify the source of this quotation. (19) Tanchuma, *Toldoth,* 4. (20) See Ramban, Commentary on the Torah, Genesis, pp. 156-160.

grandson's sake rather than his own? Does this not indicate a lack of merit in Abraham? The apparent answer is that [salvation for Jacob's sake] would indeed have pointed to a lack of merit in Abraham if Jacob had not been his descendant. However, since Jacob was Abraham's grandson and a branch of his family, the merits of all Abraham's descendants are included in his merit and augment his distinction, for he was the founder of the family line. It is as if Scripture stated: "The merit of Jacob which Abraham contained redeemed him from the furnace. Since Abraham contained the merits of many [generations], he was worthy of salvation."

How grievous a sin shaming is! The Torah has warned us even when we must chastise our fellow man, we should not shame him at the same time, as it is said, *Thou shalt surely rebuke thy neighbor, and do not bear sin because of him.*[21] That is to say, chastise him in a way which will instruct him in the way of life, [but do not shame him]. Now, if the Torah instructed us to be cautious about shaming our fellow man when rebuking him for a good cause, it follows that for some unworthy purpose our sinful action would be heinous to be forgiven.

In *Ma'asei Torah,*[22] composed by Rabbeinu Hakadosh,[23] we find the following: "It would be better for a person not to have been born at all than to experience these seven things: the death of his children in his lifetime, economic dependence upon others, an unnatural death, forgetting his learning, suffering, slavery, and publicly shaming his fellow man."

The Sages' use of the term *halbanah,* [which literally means "making white"], is based upon the prophet's promise[1] that Jacob will not be

---

(21) Leviticus 19:17.   (22) *Ma'asei* (Deeds of) *Torah* deals with ordinary conduct according to the precepts of the Torah. See *Ma'asei Torah* under the letter *Mem* in *Rav P'alim* by Rabbi Abraham son of the Vilna Gaon.   (23) See Note 42 in *Ahavah* (Love).

ashamed, and that his face will not go pale [with embarassment], for his children will repent. G-d will then forgive them and show them His wonders, and the Name of G-d will be sanctified by them, as it is said, in the following verse, *When he* [Jacob] *seeth his children, the work of My hands that they sanctify My Name; Yea, they shall sanctify the Holy One of Jacob, and shall stand in awe of the G-d of Israel.* [24]

(24) Isaiah 29:23.

וידוי

Confession of Sin

Confession of sins is a positive commandment of the Torah. It affects atonement even in a case of a non-Israelite / The punishment for a known but unconfessed sin is grievous. Even if uncertain whether one committed a certain sin, the Torah requires a sacrificial offering because the individual will not have confessed thereto / When oral confession is impossible, as in the case of sickness, one should confess in his heart. Confession should always be tearful / After repentance and confession, one may be sure that all his sins have been forgiven. However one should still pray to G-d to reinstate him to the status he held before he sinned.

Confession of Sin

AGAINST THEE, THEE ONLY, HAVE I SINNED, AND DONE
THAT WHICH IS EVIL IN THY SIGHT, THAT THOU
MAYEST BE JUSTIFIED WHEN THOU SPEAKEST, AND BE
IN THE RIGHT WHEN THOU JUDGEST.[1]

It is known that confession of sin is a positive commandment of the
Torah,[2] as it is said, *When a man or woman shall commit any sin that
men commit, to commit a trespass against the Eternal, and that soul
be guilty,*[3] *then they shall confess their sin which they have done.*[4] The
intent of confession is that one should admit and say to G-d, "I have
sinned before You." Our Sages expounded:[5] "Once a person sins and
confesses, 'I have sinned,' no angel is permitted to harm him, for it is
said, *And Balaam said unto the angel of the Eternal: I have sinned, for
I knew not that thou stoodest in the way against me.*"[6] Similarly, we
find that when Israel spoke evil of the manna, they confessed to Moses,
*We have sinned, because we have spoken against the Eternal and
against thee.*[7] G-d immediately forgave them and Moses prayed for
them, as it is said, *and Moses prayed for the people.*[7]

---

(1) Psalms 51:6. The "sin" in the verse refers to the matter of Bath-sheba (II
Samuel, 11). The verse states: "If He accepts my confession of the sin I committed, He
will be adjudged right when He punishes the wicked that do not confess"
(Rashi). (2) See Maimonides, "The Commandments," Vol. I, pp.
83-86. (3) Numbers 5:6. (4) *Ibid.*, Verse 7. (5) Tanchuma, *Balak*, 10.
(6) Numbers 22:34. (7) *Ibid.*, 21:7.

Confession even atones for the wicked. Once they accept the Divine judgment upon themselves and make confession, they merit life in the World to Come. Confession even effects atonement among non-Israelites. We find that Adoni-bezek, a great lord among the kings of Canaan, had *threescore and ten kings, with their thumbs and their great toes cut off, gathering food under* his *table,*[8] but when he confessed his sin and mentioned G-d, it was forgiven him. Thus, it is written in the beginning of the Book of Judges, *And they* [the tribes of Judah and Simeon] *found Adoni-bezek in Bezek,* etc.[9] *But Adoni-bezek fled, and they pursued after him, and caught him, and cut off his thumbs and his great toes.*[10] *And Adoni-bezek said: Threescore and ten kings,* etc. *As I have done, so G-d hath requited me. And they brought him to Jerusalem, and he died there.*[8] Why does Scripture mention his death in Jerusalem? It teaches you that once Adoni-bezek confessed his sin and mentioned the Divine Name, blessed be He, in his confession, his death effected atonement because he accepted G-d's judgment as measure for measure.

Among the essential principles of confession is an avowal of words. One should regret his transgression in his heart and acknowledge it in words. The prophet stated, *Take with you words and return unto the Eternal; say unto Him, forgive all iniquity,* etc.[11] He thus explained that the crucial factor of repentance is an avowal of words. A sacrifice is unnecessary, for the words alone stand in place of the sacrificial offering, as it says, *So we will render for bullocks the offering of our lips.*[11]

One is obligated to confess each sin he has committed. The Torah states in the chapter on the offerings, *And it shall be, when he shall be guilty in one of these things, that he shall confess that wherein he hath*

---

(8) Judges 1:7.   (9) *Ibid.,* Verse 5.   (10) *Ibid.,* Verse 6.   (11) Hosea 14:3. *"Take with you words,* G-d does not require your wealth or your sacrifices, but only your sincere confession" (Ibn Ezra).

sinned.[12] Based upon this verse, the Sages commented,[13] "Each sin-offering requires [also] confession," for this is the intent of the phrase, *in one of these things.*[12]

There is a grievous punishment for one who does not confess a known sin regardless of whether he committed it unwittingly or wittingly. Even if one has no positive knowledge of a sin [but the possibility exists that he did commit it],[14] he will be punished if he does not confess thereto. Thus, in the section on the offerings, the Torah obligates one to bring a "sin-offering" if he knows he committed a sin,[15] but if he is uncertain that he sinned, Scripture obligates him to bring a "guilt-offering."[16]

One may wonder why Scripture calls the offering for a known transgression a "sin-offering" but designates [the sacrifice] for an unknown sin a "guilt-offering." Furthermore, the offering for a known sin is a female goat,[17] but for an unknown sin a ram,[18] which is more expensive than a goat! The explanation is that the person's heart is troubled and grieved over a known sin. Thus, his sorrow constitutes an altar of

---

(12) Leviticus 5:5.   (13) Sifre, *Naso,* 2. See Ramban, Commentary on the Torah, Leviticus, pp. 53-54.   (14) The following is a case in point as stated by Maimonides: "One has two pieces of fat before him. One is fat of the kidneys [which is Scripturally forbidden] and the other is fat of the heart [which is Scripturally permitted]. He eats one of the two, and the other is eaten by another person or lost. A doubt then arises in his mind whether the piece he ate was the permitted or the forbidden one. In this case, he must bring the suspensive guilt-offering because of the doubt that arose, but he must first confess the sin over which he is in doubt. If it is subsequently established that the piece he ate was indeed the fat of kidneys, it is confirmed that he has sinned unintentionally, and he additionally must bring a fixed sin-offering" ("The Commandments," Vol. I, pp. 79-80).   (15) This applies only if one unwittingly committed a sin which, if wittingly committed, would incur the punishment of *kareth* (extirpation). Because his transgression was unintentional, he must bring a sin-offering. See more on this subject in Ramban's Commentary on the Torah, Leviticus, pp. 55-58.   (16) Leviticus 5:17.   (17) *Ibid.,* 4:28.   (18) *Ibid.,* 5:18. Logically, it should have been the opposite: for a known sin, the offering should be more expensive than for an unknown, doubtful, sin, which may never have occurred.

atonement and is one of the forms of repentance, as David said, *For I do declare mine iniquity, I am sorry for my sin.* [19] However, in the case of an unknown sin, the person is neither troubled nor grieved and does not confess. Therefore, it is proper that the Torah be more strict in that case.

You may thus learn how grievous is the punishment of one who does not confess a known sin, for even when he is in doubt whether he had committed a sin, the Torah was strict with him because of his failure to confess. Therefore, King David confessed to G-d, saying, *Against Thee, Thee only, have I sinned*, etc. [1] "David said before G-d, 'Master of the universe! Forgive me that sin [i.e., the matter of Bath-sheba].' G-d said to him, 'It is forgiven you.' David requested, *'Do in my behalf a sign for good, that they that hate me may see it, and be put to shame.'* [20] G-d answered, 'In your lifetime, I will not let it be known [that I have forgiven you], but during the lifetime of your son Solomon, I will make it known.' When Solomon built the Sanctuary and wanted to bring the Ark into the Holy of Holies, the gates clove to one another. Solomon then recited twenty-four prayers, but was not answered. [The gates remained closed.] Solomon then said, *Lift up your heads, O ye gates, [and be ye lifted up, ye everlasting doors, that the King of Glory may come in].* [21] They [22] pursued him to swallow him. However, when he prayed, *O Eternal G-d, turn not away the face of Thine anointed, remember the good deeds of David Thy servant,* [23] he was answered forthwith, [and the gates opened]. At that time, the

---

(19) Psalms 38:19. (20) *Ibid.*, 86:17. (21) *Ibid.*, 24:7. (22) "They," the gates (Rashi, Shabbath 30a). It was thought that Solomon was referring to himself when he used the expression *King of Glory* (Rashi, *ibid.*), and therefore his life was endangered. This explains why Solomon concluded with the succeeding verses: *Who is the King of Glory? The Eternal strong and mighty,* (Psalms 24:8, and so on to the end of that psalm). (23) II Chronicles 6:42. This is the concluding verse in Solomon's prayer at the dedication of the Temple. That G-d hearkened only to the mention of *the good deeds of David Thy servant* is the fulfillment of His assurance to David that in Solomon's time, He would make known His favorable acceptance of David.

faces of David's enemies turned [black] like the bottom of a pot, and all Israel knew that G-d had favorably accepted David."[24]

Our Rabbis of blessed memory commented:[25] "When a person falls ill and is close to death, we say to him, 'Confess, for it is the way of those who have been condemned to death to make confession. There are many people who confessed and did not die, while others who did not confess died. There are many people walking the streets who confessed. Perhaps by merit of your confession, you will live.' " The Sages expounded in the Sifre,[26] "*And that soul be guilty.*[3] This [redundant] expression establishes the rule that all who are about to die need to make confession." If he can make a verbal confession, he should do so, and if he cannot, he should confess in his heart, provided that he is in possession of his mental faculties.

The Sages further commented[27] that we ask the dying man whether he is owed or owes money and whether he deposited anything with others or others deposited something with him. We find that the sons of Korach, [who joined their father in the rebellion against Moses], could not make verbal confession [as explained below] and confessed in their hearts. Their act of repentance was accepted [and they remained alive].[28] A great genealogical chain came forth from them. Among their descendants was the prophet Samuel[29] whom Scripture equated to Moses and Aaron, as it is said, *Moses and Aaron among His priests, and Samuel among them that call upon His Name.*[30] The Sages said in

(24) Sanhedrin 107 a. (25) The text quoted is in Ramban's Torath Ha'adam (Kithvei Haramban, Vol. II, p. 46). Ramban himself cites his source as Tractate Semachoth. However, the passage is not found in our editions of that tractate. From Ramban's work, the material was incorporated into the Tur and Shulchan Aruch Yoreh Deiah, 338:1. (26) Sifre, *Naso,* 2, and mentioned by Ramban. See preceding note. (27) Mentioned by Ramban in Torath Ha'adam (Kithvei Haramban, Vol. II, p. 16) in the name of Tractate Semachoth, in our editions of which the passage is not present. Ramban's words were incorporated into the Tur and Shulchan Aruch Yoreh Deiah, 338:7. (28) Numbers 26:11. (29) Tanchuma, *Korach,* 5. (30) Psalms 99:6.

Midrash Tehillim:[31] *"For the leader, upon 'shoshanim,'* [a psalm] *of the sons of Korach.*[32] *My heart is stirred with beautiful words.*[33] One who cannot confess orally should confess in his heart. The sons of Korach were unable to confess orally because they saw the pit [of Gehenna] open [suddenly] beneath them[34] and the flaming fire engulf them. Thus, they confessed in their hearts, as it is said, *My heart is stirred with beautiful words*[33] and G-d accepted their [repentance]. Why is the verse *My heart is stirred* expressed in the singular, when there were three?[35] It teaches you that the three brothers were of one will [in this matter. The psalm then continues], *I say: My work concerns a King.*[33] The brothers said, 'If our hearts have been stirred to repentance, we [are considered to] have already said our word to G-d.' Since they had no time for oral confession, they contemplated it in their hearts."

In Chapter *Seider Taanioth* (the Order of Prayers on Fastdays)[36] we find the following: "The Rabbis taught, that a man who sinned and confessed but does not change his ways is like a person who holds a [dead] reptile in his hand and ritually immerses himself in all the waters of the world. The immersion will be of no avail [in purifying him of the uncleanness conveyed to him by the dead reptile]. As soon as he throws it away, however, the immersion produces the effect he desires, as it is said, *But whoso confesseth and forsaketh* [his transgressions] *shall obtain mercy.*[37] It is further stated, *Let us lift our heart with our hands unto G-d in the heavens.*"[38]

---

(31) Midrash Tehillim 45. (32) Psalms 45:1. The "leader" was a Levite who directed the music in the Sanctuary. The content of the psalm that was to be sung provided him with instruction on the nature of its accompanying music. The *shoshanim* — a Hebrew word meaning lilies — were musical instruments shaped like lilies, from which they took their name (Metzudath Tziyon). (33) Psalms 45:2. (34) See Numbers 16:31. (35) *And the sons of Korach: Assir, and Elkanah, and Abiasaph* (Exodus 6:24). (36) Taanith 16 a. (37) Proverbs 28:13. (38) Lamentations 3:41.

Confession should be accompanied by tears, which are one of the essentials of repentance. The Sages said,[39] "[Since the destruction of the Sanctuary], all of the [heavenly] gates have been closed [to man] except the gates of tears, for David said, *Hear my prayer, O Eternal, and give ear unto my cry, keep not silence at my tears.*[40] It is also said, *Mine eyes run down with rivers of water.*[41] When King Hezekiah prayed [to recover from his sickness], we also find that *Hezekiah wept profusely.*[42] By crying, one becomes contrite and sincerely regrets each transgression he had committed. He rejects [the physical pleasures of] the life in this world, for he realizes that he is dust and ashes. Thus, his confession is accepted, and G-d takes those tears and places them in His treasury, for it is said, *Put Thou my tears into Thy skin-bottle.*[43]

Once a person has made an effort to repent in accordance with all the laws and statutes and then confessed, he can be certain that all of his sins have been forgiven. He must still plead for Divine mercy so that G-d will be with him now as He was before he sinned. When a servant of a mortal king sins numerous times before his master and was fogiven by him, the pardon means only that he will not be punished. He must still reconcile himself to the king so that the latter will be favorably disposed to him as he was previously. Certainly, [in the case of] the Sovereign King in Whose hand are all living beings, one must first repent and confess and then seek His favor and grace so that his soul will receive an everlasting salvation. Thus, we find that David repented and then prayed for G-d's favorable disposition towards him, as he said, *O Eternal G-d of hosts, restore us, cause Thy face to shine, and we shall be saved.*[44]

(39) Baba Metzia 59 a. (40) Psalms 39:13. (41) *Ibid.*, 119:136. (42) Isaiah 38:3. Hezekiah finally recovered from the illness (*ibid.*, Verse 21). (43) Psalms 56:9. Liquid, contained in a skin-bottle, does not evaporate. In this sense David is praying that the tears he shed in anguish and regret of his sin should ever be before the Merciful Judge, and he be spared punishment. (44) *Ibid.*, 80:20.

זנות הלב והעין
Lust of Heart and Eye

One of the wonders in man's creation is that G-d implanted in his body five doorways to the world. These are the five senses, three of which—sight, hearing, and smell—are spiritual—and two of which—taste and touch—are physical / The Sages ordained various blessings for each of these senses, except of the sense of touch / Each of these five senses bears certain permissible and forbidden aspects. Thus the fulfillment or voidance of the entire Torah depends upon these senses / The wonderful design in these five senses shows that man's perfection is attributable to his Maker.

Lust of Heart and Eye

THE LIGHT OF THE EYES REJOICETH THE HEART, AND
GOOD NEWS FATTENS THE BONES.[1]

This verse explains the distinction of the senses. It is known that the greater the eminence of the particular sense, the greater the obligation upon man to worship G-d with it, for the body is the palace of the soul. The soul dwells within the body like a king in his royal residence. The soul also hovers over the body. [The soul is thus] similar in nature to the Creator, blessed be He, Who is both in the world and outside thereof, as He constitutes the space occupied by the world, yet the world is not His place.

One of the wonders in man's creation is that G-d emplaced five doorways to the world in this palace [which is man's body]. He appointed five watchmen over these doorways from among His trustworthy servants. These [watchmen] are the eyes, the ears, the nose, the tongue and the hands. The doorways are the senses—sight, hearing, smell, taste, and touch—which comprise the perfection of the palace and its eminence.

The sense of sight is very important, yet the power of hearing is greater. The Sages said,[2] "If a man blinded another, he must pay him the value of the sight of an eye; if he deafened him, he must pay the

---

(1) Proverbs 15:30. At the end of this discourse our author will explain the significance of why Solomon singled out these two senses—sight and hearing—for specific mention, more than the other senses of man. (2) Baba Kamma 85 b.

value of the entire [person]."[3] We find that G-d, too, mentioned the sense of hearing before that of sight, as He said, *Who maketh a man dumb, or deaf, or seeing, or blind?*[4] Accordingly, the explanation of the aforementioned verse[1] is that hearing good news not only gladdens the heart as does the light of the eyes, but it also fattens the bones, which are the foundation of the body. Moses our teacher instructed Israel concerning these two senses and also mentioned hearing before seeing. Thus, he first said, *Hear, O Israel,*[5] and afterwards, *Behold, I set before you.*[6] Isaiah, too, mentioned these two senses in that order: *He that stoppeth his ears from hearing of blood, and shutteth his eyes from looking upon evil.*[7]

The important senses [of hearing, sight, smell, and taste] are located in the head, the primary limb of the body, the choicest and highest place. The sense of touch is concentrated in the hands and is present throughout the entire body, including the head. It is activated only by the direct contact of one body to another. Three of these [five] senses — sight, hearing, and smell — are spiritual, and two — taste and touch — are physical. Wisdom thus teaches us that the intent in man's creation is to have his rational side dominate his physical nature. Because of the [relatively] higher distinction of the three spiritual senses, you will find that Scripture ascribes them to G-d [Himself], as it is said: *And when the Eternal saw that he* [Moses] *turned aside to see;*[8] *And the Eternal heard the voice of your words;*[9] *And the Eternal smelled the sweet savor.*[10] However, you will never find the two physical senses ascribed to G-d. [Expressions such as] "G-d tasted" and "G-d touched" are non-existent [throughout Scripture].

---

(3) If deafened, "the injured is not fit for any work" (Rashi *ibid.*, and also in Mishneh Torah, *Hilchoth Choveil Umazik* 4:13). Hence, the sense of hearing is clearly more important to a person than that of sight. According to Tosafoth in Baba Kamma 85 b, however, this applies only to a person who has no trade or profession. A person of this kind, if deafened, is not fit for any work. The law is so finalized in Choshen Mishpat 420:25. (4) Exodus 4:11. (5) Deuteronomy 6:4. (6) *Ibid.*, 11:26. (7) Isaiah 33:15. (8) Exodus 3:4. (9) Deuteronomy 5:25. (10) Genesis 8:21.

We utilize these five senses in all our deeds and affairs, and we are not permitted to derive any benefit from them without first reciting a benediction, [except the sense of touch, as will be explained later]. Thus, the Sages said:[11] "One who enjoys the benefits of this world without reciting a blessing is considered as if he robbed G-d and the congregation of Israel,[12] for it is said, *Whoso robbeth his father and his mother, and saith, It is no transgression, the same is the companion of a destroyer.*"[13] Accordingly, the Sages instituted many blessings connected with the sense of sight. One is obligated to recite a blessing upon seeing the sun at its solstice,[14] the [monthly] renewal of the moon,[15] a friend after twelve months,[16] the Great Sea,[17] and trees blooming in the month of Nisan.[18] Based upon this principle, the Sages ordained the daily recitation of the blessing "Creator of the luminaries,"[19] for the sun renews itself and shines each day. One who built a new house or bought new garments is obligated to recite the benediction "Who has kept us in life [and hast preserved us and enabled us to reach this season]."[20] These blessings relate to the sense of sight.

With respect to the sense of hearing, too, the Sages instituted certain benedictions. Thus, they said,[21] "On hearing good tidings, one should recite the benediction 'Who art good and dispenseth good,' and on

---

(11) Berachoth 35 b.   (12) G-d is "robbed" of the benediction, and the congregation of Israel is deprived of the fruit crops, which will waste away because of sin (Rashi *ibid.*).   (13) Proverbs 28:24. In the verse, *father* refers to G-d and *mother* to the congregation of Israel (Berachoth 35 b).   (14) Solstice here is understood to mean that point in the ecliptic at which the sun was first assigned to its role in the heavens. The sun reaches this point in twenty-eight years when, with reference to the heavenly bodies, it is in the same location it was in at the time of Creation. See Berachoth 59 b and Shulchan Aruch, *Orach Chayim* 229:2.   (15) I have been unable to find the term "renewal" or any similar expression in the Talmud. Tractate Berachoth 59 b uses the phrase "at its strength."   (16) Berachoth 58 b.   (17) *Ibid.*, 59 b. This is the Mediterranean, but the same rule applies to the other major seas, which one has not seen for thirty days (Orach Chayim, 228).   (18) Berachoth 43 b.   (19) *Ibid.*, 12 a.   (20) *Ibid.*, 59 b.   (21) *Ibid.*, 54 a.

hearing evil tidings, one should recite the benediction 'Blessed be the true Judge.' "

With reference to the sense of smell, the Sages ordained the recitation of benedictions, [as follows]: over the fragrant odors of fruits such as the *ethrog*[22] and the apple,[23] "Blessed be He Who givest a goodly scent to fruits;" over aromatic vegetation such as lilies,[24] "Who createst aromatic plants;"[23] over the myrtle,[25] "Who createst fragrant woods," and over myrrh,[25] "Who createst diverse kinds of spices." The Sages also instituted blessings over the sense of taste. Thus, for the fruits of a tree, one must recite the blessing[26] "Who createst the fruit of the tree." If it is a vegetable of the earth and does not grow upon a tree, one should recite[26] "Who createst the fruit of the earth," and if it is an inorganic substance of the earth [such as salt, brine, etc.], one should recite the benediction[27] "By Whose word all things came into existence."

With respect to the sense of touch, the Sages ordained no blessings, for this faculty entails no part of the intellect; it is entirely physical, the opposite of the rational. Therefore, they instituted blessings only for the sensory activities in which a person's intellect participates.

You should be aware that all of man's actions, whether in the performance or transgression of a commandment, are accomplished with these five senses. Hence, we have been charged to use them only in a permissible manner and to avoid utilizing them sinfully. Thus, the sense of sight is divided into two parts, good and evil. The good aspect [of sight] is that we have been commanded to look at the creations of G-d in order to comprehend His majesty and His power, as David said, *When I behold Thy heavens, the work of Thy fingers, the moon and*

(22) See the subject of *Ahavah* (Love), Note 13.   (23) In Berachoth 43 b the apple is not singled out for this blessing, but it is Maimonides who mentions the *ethrog* and apple jointly, that one is obligated to recite a benediction for their fragrant odors (Hilchoth Berachoth 9:1).   (24) See my commentary in my Hebrew edition, p. 166.   (25) Berachoth 43 a.   (26) *Ibid.*, 35 a.   (27) *Ibid.*, 40 b.

the stars Thou hast established.[28] It is further written, *The heavens declare the glory of G-d, and the firmament showeth His handiwork.*[29] Isaiah too said, *Lift up your eyes on high, and see: Who hath created these?*[30] We have been directed to look at the heavenly bodies and comprehend that they are but G-d's messengers. They derive their powers from Him, and they have no power of their own to do either good or evil. We also have been warned against deriving any opposite conclusion from these heavenly bodies, as it says, *And lest thou lift up thine eyes unto heaven, and when thou seest the sun and the moon and the stars, even all the hosts of heaven, thou be drawn away, and bow down to them and serve them.*[31] Accordingly, we are commanded to look at a thing from which we may derive some physical or spiritual benefit. On the other hand, we have been warned against looking at those women who are sexually forbidden to us, as the Sages commented,[32] "The heart and the eyes are the two agents of sin, as it is written, *And ye go not astray after your own heart and your own eyes.*"[33] Based upon this thought, Isaiah praised the righteous man who *shutteth his eyes from looking upon evil,*[34] and Solomon said, *Let thine eyes look right in front, and let thine eyelids look straight before thee.*[35]

The sense of hearing also divides itself into good and bad aspects. The good part concerns our being commanded to hear words of Torah and to listen to the instruction of the wise, as Solomon said, *Incline thine ear, and hear the words of the wise.*[36] It is further written, *The ear that hearkeneth to the reproof of life abideth among the wise.*[37] The evil part concerns listening to evil gossip and slander, as well as to the kinds of music, songs, and levity which divert one from observing

---

(28) Psalms 8:4. Therefore, the psalmist continues, *What is man, that Thou art mindful of him, and the son of man that Thou thinkest of him?* (Verse 5). (29) *Ibid.,* 19:2. (30) Isaiah 49:26. *These,* the stars. The myriads of stars all attest to the Creator, to Whose command they all respond with unswerving obedience. (31) Deuteronomy 4:19. (32) Yerushalmi Berachoth I,5. (33) Numbers 15:39. (34) Isaiah 33:15. (35) Proverbs 4:25. (36) *Ibid.,* 22:17. (37) *Ibid.,* 15:31.

the Torah and commandments and from doing proper and chosen things.

The sense of smell also entails good and bad features. The good feature concerns the function of this faculty in the performance of commandments such as [the recitation of] the blessing "Who createst fragrant woods,"[38] instituted by the Rabbis in the *Havdalah,*[39] and the blessing recited on spices put on coals after dinner. It was an [ancient] custom to burn incense at the meal, so that the Grace should be recited amid the sweet scent of spices. Thus, the Sages commented,[40] "[The verse], *Sanctify yourselves,*[41] refers to the washing of hands before meals. *And be ye holy*[41] refers to the washing of hands [for Grace] after meals. *For I am holy*[41] refers to the [fragrant] pleasant oil [with which the people anointed their hands]. *I am the Eternal your G-d*[41] refers to the Grace [after meals]." The evil aspect of the sense of smell is the attractive fragrance of a transgression, such as that present in idolatry, against which we have been warned.

In the sense of taste, too, there are good and bad parts. The good part concerns our having been commanded to eat unleavened bread on the night of Passover and to recite the benediction over it. Similarly, on the night of Tabernacles, we are obligated to eat [a minimum of] an olive's size [of bread] in a *Succah* (booth). [The good aspect of] the sense of taste also entails that in order to sustain his body, a person should eat those permissible foods which he desires, as it is written, *The righteous man eateth to the satisfaction of his desire.*[42] The evil part [of

---

(38) We now recite, "Who createst diverse kinds of spices," a more inclusive blessing. See my commentary in my Hebrew edition, p. 167.   (39) At the conclusion of the Sabbath or festivals, the *Havdalah* (Distinction) prayer is recited to delineate between the Sabbath and the weekdays. The prayer thus marks the official ending of the Sabbath. Part of the ceremony entails the recitation of a benediction over fragrant spices, which serve to alleviate a person's dejection over the imminent departure of his "higher soul" which dwells within him throughout the Sabbath. In the *Havdalah* at the conclusion of a festival the blessing over spices is omitted. (40) Berachoth 53 b. (41) Leviticus 11:44. (42) Proverbs 13:25.

the sense of taste] concerns the prohibitions against eating the forbidden foods, as well as indulging in luxuries that destroy body and soul, as Solomon said, *He that doeth it would destroy his own soul.*[43] The Sages commented,[44] "Moderation in wine, sexual activity, and sleep is good, but indulgence therein is harmful."

The sense of touch, which is concentrated in the hands, also entails good and bad features. The good feature is that one should use his hands in the course of his work. The Sages commented:[45] "One who benefits from his labor is greater than one who fears Heaven, for it is written of the latter, *Happy is the man that feareth the Eternal,*[46] and it is written of one who benefits from his labor, *When thou eatest the labor of thy hands, happy shalt thou be, and it shall be well with thee.*[47] *Happy shalt thou be* in this world, and *it shall be well with thee* in the World to Come." The Torah also commanded us to distribute charity to the poor, as it is written, *And thou shalt surely open thy hand unto him.*[48] Thus, Solomon said [of the woman of valor], *She stretcheth out her hand to the poor,*[49] and he further stated, *A gift in secret pacifieth anger, and a present in the bosom strong wrath.*[50] The verse is explaining that giving a gift to the poor and bribing a judge are opposites. The charity *pacifieth* [G-d's] *anger,* and the bribe brings about [His] *strong wrath.* The bad feature [of the sense of touch] concerns our having been warned against touching prohibited things. For example, [it is forbidden] to touch one's own menstruant wife even with the small finger. One is also forbidden to touch anything not his, and one must avoid cheating, robbing, and taking a bribe, as the prophet said [of the righteous], *That shaketh his hands from holding of bribes.*[51]

---

(43) *Ibid.,* 6:32. (44) Gittin 70 a. However, in addition to the things enumerated here, the text in the Gemara lists five other things: traveling, riches, work, bathing in hot water, and blood-letting. (45) Berachoth 8 a. (46) Psalms 112:1. (47) *Ibid.,* 128:2. (48) Deuteronomy 15:8. (49) Proverbs 31:20. (50) *Ibid.,* 21:14. (51) Isaiah 33:15.

The sense of touch, although concentrated in the hands, also involves the feet. Here, too, it is divided into good and bad aspects. The good part concerns running to perform any commandment, such as attending synagogue services or [study sessions in a] house of learning, accompanying the dead to the burial ground, and joining the company of the wise, as Solomon stated, *He that walketh with wise men shall be wise.*[52] One should run to do these things even if they are far, and this is certainly so if they are near. It is written, *Seek peace, and pursue it,*[53] which means *seek peace* in the city *and pursue it* outside of the city even at a far distance. The bad part [of the sense of touch involving the feet] concerns our being warned against going to anything sinful, as Scripture states, *And he that hasteth with his feet sinneth.*[54] It is further stated, *Her feet* [i.e., those of the harlot] *go down to death.*[55] Therefore, we have been warned not to walk in the company of the wicked, as David said, *Happy is the man that hath not walked in the counsel of the wicked.*[56] Solomon, too, stated, *My son, walk not in the way with them, restrain thy foot from their path.*[57] Similarly, with reference to the activity of the feet, it is written, *The iniquity of my steps compasseth me about.*[58]

You may thus learn that one is obligated to use his five senses in the performance of the commandments and to restrict them from the commission of sin, for the fulfillment or abolition of the entire Torah depends upon the senses. Accordingly, [G-d implanted the five senses in man] to correspond to the five books of the Torah and to the five times the word "light" is mentioned in the chapter on Creation.[59] Because these five senses correspond to the five lights of above,[60] Scrip-

(52) Proverbs 13:20. (53) Psalms 34:15. (54) Proverbs 19:2. The mere running for the purpose to do evil is in itself considered a sinful act (Ralbag). (55) *Ibid.*, 5:5. (56) Psalms 1:1. (57) Proverbs 1:15. (58) Psalms 49:6. (59) Genesis, Chapter 1: *Let there be lights* (Verse 14), *and let them be for lights* (Verse 15), *the two great lights, the greater light . . . and the lesser light* (Verse 16). (60) As identified by Rabbeinu Bachya in his commentary to the Torah, Genesis 1:18, these five lights are: that of the [sunless] day, of the sun, of the moon, of the stars, and of the constellations.

ture deprecated idols for their lack of them. Without these five
faculties, the idols are powerless to save their supplicants and their
strength is nought. Moses our teacher mentioned four of the senses that
the idols lack: *Which neither see, nor hear, nor eat, nor smell.*[61] David
cited the fifth: *They have hands, but they handle not.*[62]

Philosophers have pointed out that these five senses are among the
wonders of Creation. The sense of touch pervades the entire body, and
the sense of smell extends outside the body. The sense of hearing goes
even farther because of man's greater need for its service, and the sense
of sight extends even farther due to its importance to man's physical
welfare. Thus, it is seen that these are the deeds of G-d, done with providential care by the Creator Who is sagacious, mighty in strength, and
wonderful in wisdom.

With regard [to the wonders manifested in man's senses], Solomon
said, *The light of the eyes rejoiceth the heart, and good news fattens
the bones.*[1] Solomon mentioned only two of the five senses—sight and
hearing—because these are the mainstay of a person's effort to acquire
wisdom. Although we have shown above[63] that hearing is a more vital
sense than sight, Solomon nevertheless mentioned sight first, for his intention coincides with that of our matriarch Leah, who named her
firstborn son Reuben because G-d had "seen" her affliction,[64] and her
second son Shimon because G-d had "heard" that she was hated.[65]
However, you will find that the Almighty Himself arranged the senses
in that order [of hearing first, then sight].[66] G-d first said, *Who
maketh a man . . . deaf,*[4] and subsequently stated . . . *or blind?*[4]

(61) Deuteronomy 4:28. (62) Psalms 115:7. (63) See Note 3
above. (64) Genesis 29:32. (65) See *ibid.*, Verse 33. (66) The thought expressed
is that although Solomon and Leah mentioned the sense of sight first, in truth, hearing
is more vital. This is proven by G-d's words, in which He mentioned the sense of hearing first and then sight, as the text continues.

חנופה

Flattery

Flattery is the most destructive force in the world. It is even more severe a sin than idolatry / Flattery is rebellion against G-d, for in deference to mortals, the flatterer forsakes his devotion to G-d / The harsh punishment incurred for the sin of flattery / It is an obligation to publicize the names of flatterers / To avoid harm, it is permissible to use flattery which is ambiguous in meaning.

Flattery

HE THAT SAITH UNTO THE WICKED: THOU ART
RIGHTEOUS, PEOPLE SHALL CURSE HIM, NATIONS
SHALL EXECRATE HIM.[1]

In this verse, Solomon cautioned us concerning the act of flattery in order to make it loathsome in the eyes of the people. A person who utilizes flattery brings about the destruction of the entire world, [for lacking all sense of honor, he strengthens the cause of injustice which leads to the ruination of the world]. Moreover, [as a punishment] for the sin of flattery, the crops of the world are diminished.

It is common knowledge that the flatterer is worse than the idolator[2] in four respects. First, the idolater has not been [personally] warned by a prophet about the harm his act brings to his mind. However, the flatterer who professes loyalty to the Divine Torah did accept upon himself the duty of worshipping G-d alone and was warned about serving anyone else. Second, the idolater gives his loyalty to something which never rebels against him, but the flatterer will show obeisance even to one who does rebel against him. Third, the idolater serves only the particular idol before him, but the flatterer humiliates himself before all people. Fourth, the act of idolatry is not hidden from people. Thus, they can avoid the sinner because his denial of G-d is exposed. However, the flatterer is not recognizable. Consequently, people can-

---

(1) Proverbs 24:24. The utter contempt of flattery in human affairs is hereby stated distinctly. In the long run, those who make use of it will be imprecated by people and nations. (2) Thus the flatterer is condemned in no uncertain terms.

232

not be wary of him, and they trust him. He can therefore harm them where others cannot.

Flattery is rebellion against G-d. When a servant knows his master but serves the interests of another, that is tantamount to rebellion. The flatterer, too, who is obeisant to mortals, abandons his worship of G-d and in effect rebels against Him.

How severe this sin of flattery is! "The enemies of Israel"[3] deserved destruction only for having flattered King Agrippa,[4] as the Sages recounted in Tractate Sotah:[5] "When Agrippa reached the verse, *Thou shalt in any wise set him king over thee, etc., one from thy brethren shalt thou set king over thee; thou mayest not put a foreigner over thee, who is not thy brother,*[6] his eyes immediately flowed with tears. The people said to him, 'Do not fear, Agrippa, for you are our brother.' " The Rabbis stated in the name of Rabbi Nathan,[7] "The Sages said, 'At that time, the enemies of Israel[3] were guilty of destruction because they had flattered Agrippa.' "

In the same tractate,[8] the Sages further said, "Four classes of people are not permitted to greet the Divine Presence: mockers, flatterers, liars, and those who engage in evil talk." With regard to this thought, Solomon warned, *He that saith unto the wicked: Thou art righteous,*[1] and praises his evil deeds, deserves to be rejected by people because he is an abomination to G-d. Similarly, Solomon warned, *He that justifieth the wicked, and he that condemneth the righteous, even they both are an abomination to the Eternal.*[9]

---

(3) A euphemism for Israel. (4) The Torah requires that every seventh year on the Festival of Tabernacles, all Israel should assemble to hear the king read certain sections from the Book of Deuteronomy. The Mishnah recounts what transpired at such an assembly during the reign of King Agrippa I. Agrippa was a descendant of Herod the Idumean, who had been appointed to the throne of Israel by the Romans. However, Agrippa was genuinely attached to the Jewish people and had won the love of the nation. During the said assembly as he read the verse forbidding the throne to a foreigner, he began to weep. The text continues the story. (5) Sotah 41a. (6) Deuteronomy 17:15. (7) Sotah 41 b. (8) *Ibid.,* 42a. (9) Proverbs 17:15.

Solomon further stated, *With his mouth the flatterer destroyeth his neighbor.*[10] When the flatterer praises his neighbor for his evil deeds and gives him his approval, the neighbor will then continue to act that way. *But through knowledge the righteous shall be delivered*[10] from the flatterer mentioned [in the first part of the verse]. Righteous people will not be misled into conceit because others praise them. Thus, the Sages commented,[11] "Be righteous and do not be wicked. Even if the entire world tells you that you are righteous, consider yourself wicked."

The Sages commented:[7] "One who flatters the wicked will ultimately fall into the hands of the latter, or of his son, or of his grandson, for it is said, *And the prophet Jeremiah said: Amen! the Eternal do so!*[12] Jeremiah was prophesying that the remaining vessels of the Sanctuary *shall be carried to Babylon, and there shall they be,*[13] while Hananiah the son of Azzur was prophesying that the vessels originally taken by Nebuchadnezzar would be returned *within two full years.*[14] [Hananiah claimed that] Nebuchadnezzar would certainly not take any more of the vessels. Although Jeremiah knew that Hananiah spoke falsely,[15] he

(10) *Ibid.*, 11:9.   (11) Niddah 30 b. The subject in the Talmud there, concerns the oath administered to every child before birth: "Be righteous, etc."   (12) Jeremiah 28:6.   (13) *Ibid.*, 27:22. Eleven years before the destruction of the Sanctuary, King Nebuchadnezzar of Babylon deposed King Yehoyachin of Judah, and took him captive to Babylon along with many of the sacred vessels of the Sanctuary. Nebuchadnezzar enthroned Zedekiah, the uncle of Yehoyachin, as King of Judah. When Zedekiah rebelled against Nebuchadnezzar, his action was opposed by the prophet Jeremiah, who warned that the rebellion would bring about the destruction of the Temple and the removal of its remaining vessels. Jeremiah, in turn, was opposed by Hananiah, a false prophet, as the text here continues.   (14) Jeremiah 28:3.   (15) Before the word of G-d comes to a certain prophet, all of the prophets of that generation are first made aware of the Divine message. Since Jeremiah did not know of the prophecy delivered by Hananiah, who until then had been a true prophet, he knew that Hananiah must be speaking falsely on this occasion. — Jeremiah's response *Amen! the Eternal do so,* may indeed be understood as meaning, "I wish indeed that it were as you said, that there will be no more plundering of the Temple's vessels." Yet, knowing that Hananiah spoke falsely, Jeremiah was obligated to tell him outrightly that he was lying (Maharsha, Sotah 41 b).

flattered him by saying, *Amen! the Eternal do so,* instead of clearly telling him, "You are prophesying falsely." Ultimately, [during the siege of Jerusalem], Jeremiah fell into the hands of Irijah the son of Shelemiah the son of Hananiah, as it is said, *And he laid hold on Jeremiah the prophet.* [16]

The prophet Jeremiah chastised Israel over the act of flattery. They came to the Sanctuary for prayerful prostrations, yet they continued to commit many sins, saying that the Sanctuary would protect them. Thus, it is said, *Amend your ways, and your doings, and I will cause you to dwell in this place.* [17] *Trust ye not in lying words, saying, The Temple of the Eternal, the Temple of the Eternal, the Temple of the Eternal, are these.* [18] *Nay, but if you thoroughly amend your ways and your doings; if ye thoroughly execute justice between a man and his neighbor,* etc. [19] He is thus saying that although the people proclaim *the Temple of the Eternal,* where they come three times a year for prostration, they are depending on false words. The prophet quoted them as saying *the Temple of the Eternal* three times [to indicate the three festival pilgrimages of Passover, Weeks and Tabernacles. The verse] is so rendered by Yonathan the son of Uziel. Some scholars[20] explain that the expression, *the Temple of the Eternal, the Temple of the Eternal, the Temple of the Eternal, are these,* means that the people believed that despite their sins, G-d would not cause the destruction of these three [sacred places] — the hall [leading into the interior of the Sanctuary], the Sanctuary proper, and the Holy of Holies — and He would not permit the desecration of His glory. However, the prophet

---

(16) Jeremiah 37:13.   (17) *Ibid.*, 7:3.   (18) *Ibid.*, Verse 4. The expression *these* refers, in the opinion of our author, to the three pilgrimage festivals when the people must come to the Temple of the Eternal. Another opinion, quoted in the text, is that it refers to the three divisions in the Temple: the hall [leading to the interior], the Sanctuary proper, and the Holy of Holies. The people are, in other words, saying to the prophet that G-d will not destroy His own Sanctuary.   (19) *Ibid.*, Verse 5.   (20) In his commentary to the Book of Jeremiah, Rabbi David Kimchi (R'dak) cites this explanation in the name of his father.

answered them, *O land, land, land [hear the words of the Eternal],*[21] meaning that if the people sin and rely upon false words, these are not Temples, but [unhallowed] *land* like any other land.

The Sages commented,[22] "We expose the flatterers because [their action involves] the profanation of G-d's Name, for it is said, *And when a righteous man doth turn from his righteousness and commit iniquity, I will lay a stumbling block before him,*[23] which Yonathan the son of Uziel rendered, "I will expose him." Since G-d publicly exposes him, we in turn are obligated to do so, for otherwise people would consider him a reputable person when he is indeed wicked.

Isaiah declared, *The sinners in Zion are afraid, trembling seized the flatterers.*[24] He mentioned fear in connection with the sinner. [However, he mentioned] trembling, which is worse than fear, in connection with the flatterer, for one who seeks to gratify another by blandishment is also impious towards G-d. This is why he is punished so harshly, as Isaiah continued to say, *Who among us shall dwell with the devouring fire? Who among us shall dwell with everlasting burnings?*[24] This is the same punishment as that mentioned in the case of the wicked: *For their worm shall not die, neither shall their fire be quenched.*[25]

However, under certain circumstances we find one form of flattery permissible, that one should conduct himself respectfully towards a wicked person. He should honor him and rise before him and tell him that he is his friend. This is permissible only when one finds it necessary to do so and when he fears him, for we find that Jacob said to wicked Esau, *For as much as I have seen thy face, as one seeth the face of G-d, and thou was pleased with me.*[26] This is the opinion of Rabbi Yochanan.[7] Rabbi P'dos maintains that it is forbidden to flatter the

(21) *Ibid.*, 22:29. R'dak quotes this explanation also in the name of his father (see his commentary *ibid.*, 7:4). (22) Yoma 86 b. (23) Ezekiel 3:20. (24) Isaiah 33:14. (25) *Ibid.*, 66:24. (26) Genesis 33:10, see also *Bitachon* (Trust in G-d), Note 9.

wicked even when one fears him, for it states, *He that speaketh falsehood shall not be established before Mine eyes.*[27] Jacob's flattery of Esau, however, was still permitted because his language could be interpreted in two ways. The word *ra'ithi* (I have seen) can also be used in a derogatory sense, as in the verse, *They gaze, 'they stare' at me.*[28] If the wicked one understands it in a laudatory sense, we do not mind it. This is similar to the Sages' statement,[29] "He deceived himself; I did not mislead him." This form of flattery is permissible even according to Rabbi P'dos in a case where fear is involved.

Since flattery causes a person to be an abomination to G-d,[30] one should keep himself far from this characteristic. He should not justify the wicked or condemn the righteous. All of his words should be truthful, and all of his deeds should be done in truth and sincerity, for a person only merits eternal life among the angels if he conducts himself with sincerity. This is the quality with which the righteous people and the patriarchs were lauded. It is written of Noah, *He was a righteous man and wholehearted.*[31] Regarding Abraham, it is written, *Walk before Me, and be wholehearted,*[32] and you will find it written of Jacob, *And Jacob was a wholehearted man.*[33] Solomon also said, *He that walketh uprightly walketh securely*[34] towards the World to Come. David, too, mentioned, *O Eternal, who shall sojourn in Thy tabernacle, etc.?*[35] *He that walketh uprightly,* etc.[36] It further says, *And as for me, Thou upholdest me because of mine wholeheartedness, and settest me before Thy face forever.*[37]

---

(27) Psalms 101:7. (28) *Ibid.*, 22:18. *They stare at me* in malicious delight over their victim. (29) Chullin 94 b. (30) As it is said, *Lying lips are an abomination to the Eternal* (Proverbs 12:22). (31) Genesis 6:9. (32) *Ibid.*, 17:1. (33) *Ibid.*, 25:27. (34) Proverbs 10:9. (35) Psalms 15:1. (36) *Ibid.*, Verse 2. (37) *Ibid.* 4:13.

חלול השם
Profaning G-d's Name

The profaning of G-d's Name is an extremely serious sin, the punishment for which is most severe / This sin begins with small things and permeates all aspects of life / The greater a person's distinction, the more severe his degree of commission of this sin / The Hebrew term 'chillul Hashem' stems from the root 'chol' (secular, profane), for one who profanes G-d's Name, causes people to desecrate that which is holy / The prophet Isaiah mentioned that in the future, G-d's Name will be sanctified. However, while we of Israel are in exile, the nations who deprecate us, profane that which is holy / To atone for profaning G-d's Name, one should sanctify G-d under the same circumstances that existed when he committed the profanation.

Profaning G-d's Name

FOR MY NAME'S SAKE WILL I DEFER MINE ANGER, AND
FOR MY PRAISE WILL I REFRAIN FOR THEE, THAT I CUT
THEE NOT OFF.¹ BEHOLD, I HAVE REFINED THEE, BUT
NOT AS SILVER, I HAVE TRIED THEE IN THE FURNACE OF
AFFLICTION.² FOR MINE OWN SAKE, FOR MINE OWN
SAKE, WILL I DO IT, FOR HOW SHOULD IT BE PROFAN-
ED? AND MY GLORY WILL I NOT GIVE TO ANOTHER.³

It is common knowledge that the entire world and all it contains were created only for the glory of G-d, as it is said, *Everything that is called by My Name, it is for My glory that I have created it, I have formed it, yea, I have made it.*⁴ It is therefore unbefitting for any person to desire honor in this world unless it is for G-d's glory. One should strive to make his deeds sanctify and not profane G-d's Name, for the profanation of His Name constitutes an extremely serious sin, the punishment for which is most severe. Sacrificial offerings are insufficient to atone for this sin, and repentance and the Day of Atonement are impotent to effect forgiveness.

The Sages commented in Tractate Yoma:⁵ "Rabbi Masya the son of Charash⁶ asked Rabbi Eleazar the son of Azaryah in Rome, 'Have you

---

(1) Isaiah 48:9. Israel's survival is thus assured, for if the existence of G-d's people were to be cut off, it would be a profaning of His Name. (2) *Ibid.,* Verse 10. (3) *Ibid.,* Verse 11. (4) *Ibid.,* 43:7. (5) Yoma 86 a. (6) Rabbi Masya the son of Charash was one of the few Tannaim who lived outside the Land of Israel. He is

heard the four distinctions in atonement expounded by Rabbi Yishmael?' He answered him, 'There are only three categories, and each one also requires repentance. Thus, if one transgressed a positive commandment and repented, he is forgiven immediately, for it is said, *Return, ye backsliding children, [I will heal your backslidings].*[7] If one transgressed a negative commandment and repented, the repentance suspends his punishment and the Day of Atonement effects expiation, for it is said, *For on this day shall atonement be made for you.*[8] If one transgressed a negative commandment, the punishment for wanton violation of which is extirpation or death by the hands of the court, and then repented, his repentance coupled with the Day of Atonement suspend his punishment, and suffering completely cleanses him [of the sin], for it is said, *Then will I visit their transgression with the rod, and their iniquity with strokes.*[9] However, if one has profaned G-d's Name, all of these factors—repentance, the Day of Atonement, and suffering—merely suspend [his punishment]. Death is his expiation, for it is said, *And the Eternal of hosts revealed Himself in mine ears: Surely this iniquity shall not be expiated till ye die.'*"[10]

The sin of profaning G-d's Name constitutes a negative commandment, for it is said, *And ye shall not profane My holy Name.*[11] It is known that this sin begins with some small matter and diffuses to include any act which constitutes disrespect for G-d and His commandments, such as worshipping idols and swearing falsely. [With regard to the latter], it is said, *And ye shall not swear by My Name falsely, so that thou profane the Name of thy G-d,*[12] and with reference to the idol-worship of Molech, it is stated, . . . *to defile My Sanctuary,*

mentioned several times throughout the Mishnah. When a delegation headed by Rabbi Eleazar the son of Azaryah came to Rome, where Rabbi Masya lived, to intercede with the government on behalf of the Jewish communities in the Land of Israel, Rabbi Masya asked the question mentioned here. (7) Jeremiah 3:22. The verse thus clearly intimates that repentance alone is sufficient for the sinner to be healed (Maharsha). (8) Leviticus 16:30. The verse is in reference to the Day of Atonement, when repentance effects forgiveness of sin. (9) Psalms 89:33. (10) Isaiah 22:14. (11) Leviticus 22:32. See "The Commandments, Vol. II, pp. 61-63. (12) Leviticus 19:12.

and to profane My holy Name.[13] Similarly, there are certain distinguished and outstanding individuals whose actions unintentionally cause the spurning of the Torah and commandments. This, too, is termed a profanation of G-d's Name. The Sages commented in Tractate Yoma,[14] "What constitutes profanation of G-d's Name? Rav said, 'For instance, if I take meat from the butcher and do not pay him at once.'[15] Rabbi Yochanan said, 'In my case, [it is a profanation if] I walk four cubits without uttering words of Torah or without wearing phylacteries.' Rav Nachman the son of Yitzchak said, '[Profanation occurs] if people say [of a certain individual], May his Creator forgive him for his actions.' Rav Yitzchak the son of Avdimi said, '[Profanation occurs] if his friends are embarrassed upon hearing the reports about him.' "

You can thus appreciate the gravity of this sin, which applies even more to scholars. If one is learned and people suspect him of any wrongdoing, G-d's Name is profaned even if there is no truth to the matter, for people who are unable to discern between truth and falsehood believe anything. Thus, they censure him and his learning, *and there arises enough contempt and wrath.*[16] This is all the more the case if the report turns out to be true, for based on this scholar's actions, people may no longer hold sin in contempt. Thus, the Name of G-d is profaned. It is therefore clear that the greater a man is, the more scrupulous his actions must be to avoid sin, and the greater his status in learning Torah, the more severe will the commission of his sin be with respect to profanation of G-d's Name. We find that Moses our teacher, master of all the prophets, was punished sternly for the inadvertent sin which he committed at the rock.[17] His act was considered

(13) *Ibid.,* 20:3.   (14) Yoma 86 a and quoted in "The Commandments," cited in Note 11 above.   (15) If Rav delays paying him, the butcher would learn from his action to treat his own debts lightly, first by delaying payment and then by failing to pay it altogether.   (16) Esther 1:18.   (17) See Numbers 20:11. The occasion was the smiting of the rock to give forth its water, when G-d had told him to speak to the rock.

as if he had done it intentionally, as G-d said, *Because ye believed not in Me, to sanctify Me in the eyes of the children of Israel, [therefore ye shall not bring this assembly into the Land which I have given them].*[18] Thus, it is said in the Book of Ecclesiastes, *For in much wisdom is much vexation.*[19] That is to say, the greater the person's wisdom and position, the greater [G-d's] vexation against him in case of sin.

The sin of profaning G-d's Name is so severe that there is no distinction made between its inadvertent or wanton commission. The Sages taught,[20] "They do not withhold requital for profanation of G-d's Name whether it was done inadvertently or wantonly." That is to say, there is no forbearance of the punishment thereof. It is not meted out partially in the manner of a storekeeper who collects his debts piecemeal. The punishment is wholly exacted at one time. Because of the gravity of the sin, the inadvertent act is considered as having been committed wantonly. In the P'sikta, the Sages expounded:[21] "*Two things have I asked of Thee.*[22] We find that G-d was indulgent concerning the sin of idolatry but not concerning the profanation of His Name, as it is said, *As for you, O House of Israel, thus saith the Eternal G-d: Go ye, serve every one his idols, even because ye will not hearken unto Me, but My holy Name shall ye no more profane with your gifts, and with your idols.*"[23]

You can see the severity of the sin of profaning G-d's Name [from the following]. Even when Israel deserved destruction according to the attribute of justice, G-d promised to save them in order to avoid profaning His Name! Thus, Isaiah stated here [in the verses quoted above]: *For My Name's sake will I defer Mine anger, and for My praise*

---

(18) *Ibid.*, Verse 12.   (19) Ecclesiastes 1:18.   (20) Kiddushin 40 a.   (21) P'sikta Rabbathi 25:3.   (22) Proverbs 30:7. As the Biblical text continues, the author is asking G-d's help to be spared from the sins of idolatry and of profaning His Name. The P'sikta raises the question as to which of the two sins is the more serious one. The answer follows in the text.   (23) Ezekiel 20:39.

will I refrain for thee, that I cut thee not off.[1] He is saying: "You do not deserve that I be long-suffering with you, but I will nevertheless be so for the sake of My Name. For the sake of My praise, I will tolerate your evil deeds. You deserved to be extirpated because of them, but I will not cut you off." This is similar to Joshua's statement, *And they* [the inhabitants of the land of Canaan] *will cut off our name from the earth, and what wilt Thou do for Thy great Name?*[24]

The term *chillul Hashem* (profaning G-d's Name) stems from the root *chol* (secular, profane). One who profanes the Divine Name by word or deed causes people who see or hear him to entertain impure thoughts about desecrating that which is holy. Regarding the future, the prophet mentioned, *And I will sanctify My great Name, which hath been profaned among the nations.*[25] While Israel is in absolute dejection in exile, the nations have a reason to make that which is holy profane. Therefore, G-d promised that in the future, He would assure the sanctification of His Great Name, which has been desecrated by the nations.

The Sages mentioned that although the sin of profaning G-d's Name is most severe, there is a means of atoning for it, namely, that G-d's Name should be sanctified under the same circumstances that existed when the profanation took place. This thought is expressed in the verse, *And ye shall not profane My holy Name, but I will be hallowed among the children of Israel.*[26] Scripture thus teaches you that by sanctifying G-d's Name, you can atone for the profanation.

The Sages clearly expressed it as follows:[27] If a person sinned by engaging in evil talk, he should occupy himself with the study of Torah. If he sinned by engaging in forbidden sexual relations, he should restrain himself even from permissible relations. If he sinned

---

(24) Joshua 7:9.   (25) Ezekiel 36:23.   (26) Leviticus 22:32.   (27) See Vayikra Rabbah 21:4, which contains the general thought expressed here. I have been unable to locate the source of the exact wording cited by the author in the text.

with his eyes, he should be overcome with sorrow to the point where tears flow from his eyes, as David said, *Mine eyes run down with rivers of water, because they observe not Thy Torah.*"[28] The purport thereof is that sin is a malady of the soul. Like a sickness of the body, it can be healed only by its antithesis, and a proficient doctor cures the illness by employing an antithetical countermeasure.[29] Thus Solomon said, *By mercy and truth iniquity is expiated,*[30] which means that the sins of wickedness and falsehood are expiated by their opposites, mercy and truth. The Sages related that King Herod[31] asked Baba the son Buta[32] if he could possibly atone for having killed many of the Sages of Israel. The Sage answered him affirmatively, saying, "You extinguished the lights of the world, therefore go and engage yourself in the light of the world." Thereupon, Herod went and rebuilt the Sanctuary,[33] which we find is called the light of the world, as it is said, *And nations shall walk at thy light, and kings at the brightness of thy rising.*[34]

(28) Psalms 119:36.   (29) See Maimonides' "Eight Chapters," Chapters 1 and 4, where he develops this theory at length.   (30) Proverbs 16:6.   (31) Herod, King of Judea, was a tyrant appointed by the Romans. He ruled with an iron hand, suppressing all resistance against him. He especially vented his anger against the Sages of Israel, who refused to acknowledge him as king because of his Idumean descent. According to Tractate Baba Bathra 3 b, he left only the Sage Baba the son of Buta as his counsellor.   (32) To test the Sage's loyalty, Herod first blinded him so that he would be unable to recognize the king when the latter asked for advice. When confronted by his unknown questioner the sightless Baba refused even to verbally disparage the king, and so Herod was convinced of the Sage's loyalty and integrity (Baba Bathra 4 a).   (33) Regarding Herod's Sanctuary, the Rabbis said, "One who has not seen the Sanctuary in its finished state, has not seen a glorious structure (Succah 51 b).   (34) Isaiah 60:3. The author's interpretation of *thy light* as an allusion to the Sanctuary is novel. Note that our editions of Tractate Baba Bathra 4 ᴧ quote Isaiah 2:2: *And all nations shall flow unto it.* See my commentary in my Hebrew edition, p. 176, Note 40.

חֶמְדָה

Covetousness

Coveting is an evil characteristic which results from the pursuit of vacuities by idle people / Idleness causes the avaricious desire for money, and an avaricious person is called 'wicked' / Coveting leads to robbery, murder, and other serious transgressions / Why coveting is mentioned last in the Ten Commandments / The best remedy for coveting is work / Just as farming, the source of the body's sustenance, entails much effort, so does the study of Torah, the source of the soul's sustenance, require much effort / Coveting is permissible only in the study of Torah and in the service of G-d.

Covetousness

HE THAT TILLETH HIS GROUND SHALL HAVE PLENTY
OF BREAD, BUT HE THAT FOLLOWETH AFTER VAIN
THINGS IS VOID OF UNDERSTANDING.[1] THE WICKED
DESIRETH THE PREY OF EVIL MEN, BUT THE ROOT OF
THE RIGHTEOUS YIELDETH FRUIT.[2]

Solomon warned us here against coveting, for it is a characteristic implanted in the heart through passion and the evil inclination. It is known that the first sin arose from desire, as it is said, *And that the tree was to be desired to make one wise.*[3] Thus, Solomon said, *He that tilleth his ground shall have plenty of bread,*[1] meaning that whoever earns his livelihood by the toil of his hands will be satisfied with all things. However, one who pursues vacuities, goes idle, and attaches himself to worthless unemployed fellows, will not only lack bread but will also be *void of understanding.*[1]

The Sages said,[4] "Idleness leads to dullness." Idleness also leads to an avaricious desire for easy money. Therefore, Solomon mentioned in the following verse, *The wicked desireth the prey of evil men.*[2] Once a person covets, he is called "wicked," for it is forbidden to desire the legitimate wealth of one's friend, [even in order to acquire it in a legal

---

(1) Proverbs 12:11. While the intent of the verse is to praise work which gives one assurance of his material needs, it also gives special praise to agriculture as a source of secure livelihood. (2) *Ibid.*, Verse 12. (3) Genesis 3:6. (4) Kethuboth 59 b.

248

way], and it is surely true of the wealth of the wicked which was acquired through robbery and violence. At the end, possessions so acquired through coveting will be momentarily lost, as it is written, *Evil shall kill the wicked.*[5] The righteous man, however, constantly takes root and exists forever. He avoids pitfalls and destruction even in the face of many misfortunes, *for a righteous man falleth seven times, and riseth up again.*[6] He is like a well rooted tree planted alongside streams of water. No wind can ever uproot him, as it is written, *And he shall be like a tree planted by streams of water,* etc.[7] *Not so the wicked.*[8]

The prohibition against coveting is considerable indeed, for it will lead one to rob. Gehazi, the servant of Elisha, was stricken with leprosy because he desired Naaman's wealth. When Naaman[9] came to Elisha with a gift and said to him, *Behold now, I know that there is no G-d in all the earth, but in Israel; now, therefore, I pray thee, take a present of thy servant.*[10] But he [Elisha] *said, As the Eternal liveth, before Whom I stand, I will receive none.*[11] Thereupon, the selfish and avaricious Gehazi followed Naaman and said to him, *My master hath sent me, saying: Behold, even now there are come to me from the hill-country of Ephraim two young men of the sons of prophets; give them, I pray thee, a talent of silver, and two changes of raiment.*[12] *And Naaman said: Be content, take two talents. And he* [Naaman] *urged him*[13] to swear [that Elisha had sent him], and he swore *and took them*[14] from Naaman. What did he take? [He took] the leprosy of Naaman, which has clung to Gehazi and his seed forever, as Elisha said

(5) Psalms 34:22. The word *ra'ah* (evil) is in the singular, in order to indicate that one stroke of evil is sufficient to ruin the wicked (Ibn Ezra). The righteous man, however, etc. (6) Proverbs 24:16. (7) Psalms 1:3. (8) *Ibid.,* Verse 4. (9) Naaman, captain of the host of the King of Aram (Syria), had been stricken with leprosy. When told that he could be healed by the prophet Elisha in Israel, he went there and was indeed healed by the prophet (II Kings 5:14). He then brought Elisha a gift and said to him, *Behold, now,* etc. (10) II Kings 5:15. (11) *Ibid.,* Verse 16. Since Elisha healed Naaman only to sanctify G-d's Name, he did not want to derive any personal benefit from it. (12) *Ibid.,* Verse 22. (13) *Ibid.,* Verse 23. (14) *Ibid.,* Verse 24.

to Gehazi; *And the leprosy of Naaman shall cleave unto thee, and unto thy seed forever.*[15] This indeed befell Gehazi, as it is written, *Now there were four leprous men at the entrance of the gate.*[16] "Who were they? They were Gehazi and his three sons."[17]

Coveting leads to murder. King Ahab of Israel desired the vineyard of Naboth, the Jezreelite, [and failing to obtain the latter's consent for the sale of the property, he falsely accused Naboth of having blasphemed G-d and the king, and had him killed]. Elijah then related the word of G-d to Ahab, *Hast thou killed and also taken possession, etc.? In the place where dogs licked the blood of Naboth shall dogs lick thy blood, even thine.*[18] However, Ahab's self-humiliation at the word of G-d saved him [from this punishment], for it is written there, *Seest thou [Elijah] how Ahab humbleth himself before Me?*[19] Jezebel, [Ahab's wife], who had hired the two false witnesses against Naboth and was therefore responsible for his murder, her blood was licked by dogs on the property belonging to Naboth the Jezreelite.[20]

Thou shalt not covet,[21] the prohibition of coveting, is stated in the Ten Commandments. The prohibition of robbery is not enumerated in the Ten Commandments because it is included in [the definition of] coveting.[22] We may thus reason *a fortiori* that if coveting has been forbidden even though it is only an emotion, robbery, which involves an action, is certainly prohibited.

Coveting causes a person to betray the precepts of the Torah. If he wrongfully desires the wealth of others, he will assuredly desire to retain his own wealth. He will thus refuse to give charity and the other

(15) *Ibid.*, Verse 27. The sons had connived with the wrong-doing of their father, and hence their inclusion in the punishment (R'dak). (16) *Ibid.*, 7:3. (17) Sanhedrin 107 b. (18) I Kings 21:19. (19) *Ibid.*, Verse 29. (20) See II Kings 9:33-37. (21) Exodus 20:14. (22) "Since a person does not rob unless he first covets, it was unnecessary to mention robbery, for it is already included in the prohibition of coveting" (Rabbeinu Bachya in his commentary on Exodus 20:14). The prohibition against open and forceful robbery is stated in Leviticus 19:13.

gifts for the poor, such as gleanings [the ears of corn which fall from the hand of the reaper], the forgotten sheaf, the corner of the field [to be reaped], and tithes [to the Levite and the poor]. For this reason, the Torah stated *Thou shalt not covet*[21] as the tenth commandment, thereby cautioning people about giving tithes so that they should not covet their own wealth. Rather, tithes should be set aside properly, as well as all the other gifts ordained by the laws of the Torah.

It is also possible that the Torah placed coveting last in the Ten Commandments because it is equal to all other commandments. One who is unwary of the wrongful desire of another man's property will ultimately stumble and transgress all of the commandments, [as follows]: Through coveting, he will come to steal and transgress [the prohibition], *Thou shalt not steal.*[23] When he will be taken to court [by his victim], he will deny the charge and swear falsely, thus violating the commandment, *Thou shalt not take the Name of the Eternal thy G-d in vain.*[24] Occasionally, he will steal on the Sabbath, thus violating the charge to *remember the Sabbath-day, to keep it holy.*[25] Fearful of the punishment for stealing [on the Sabbath], he will apostatize, thus transgressing the command, *Thou shalt have no other gods before Me.*[26]

Although coveting is only an emotion which is beyond the control of man, the purport of the prohibition, *Thou shalt not covet,*[21] has been explained by the scholar Rabbi Abraham ibn Ezra[27] as meaning that one should consider the object of his unlawful desire as unattainable. Just as a peasant never entertains any thought of marrying a princess, [so too should every rational person consider those objects belonging to another person, as unattainable]. Were this not the case, how could the Torah punish a man for the emotion he feels, when [for example] he suddenly sees and covets a princess?

---

(23) Exodus 20:13.   (24) *Ibid.*, Verse 7.   (25) *Ibid.*, Verse 8.   (26) *Ibid.*, Verse 3.   (27) In Ibn Ezra's commentary on Exodus 20:14.

It is also possible that by placing the prohibition of coveting at the end of the Ten Commandments, the Torah intended to compare the last commandment to the first, [i.e., *I am the Eternal thy G-d Who brought thee out of the land of Egypt*].[28] Both commandments concern an emotion. One is a positive commandment, and the other is a negative commandment. The Torah thus teaches us that when one observes the prohibition of coveting, he thereby fulfills the commandment of believing in the existence of G-d.[29] When one violates the prohibition of coveting, he thereby denies the first commandment, for by wrongfully desiring that which is not his, he demonstrates the flawed quality of his trust in G-d. This, in my opinion, is the meaning of the verse, *But he that hateth gifts shall live.*[30] It is known that one's love of gifts stems only from the inordinate desire of gain which is implanted in his heart, while he that despises gifts shows that he has freed himself of that desire. Therefore, *he shall live*[30] without them, for G-d will supply his needs and livelihood from other sources and he will not need gifts.

Since the blessings of man's work are manifold and help him to avoid the sin of coveting, Solomon stated [in the aforementioned verse], *He that tilleth his ground shall have plenty of bread.*[1] Solomon thus urged that one should strive to be engaged in work, for thereby he will be satisfied and not be impoverished and in need of the gifts of other men. Solomon further warned, *Love not sleep, lest thou come to poverty; open thine eyes, and thou shalt have bread in plenty.*[31] In other words, "you who have plenty, open your eyes and do not sleep, lest you become impoverished," for one must certainly [remain vigilant] in order to retain his wealth and avoid poverty.

(28) Exodus 20:2. (29) In shunning coveting the possession of his neighbor, one demonstrates his belief in the existence of G-d and His providence, Who affords each one his due. The contrary is true of one who longs for the possessions of anything that is his neighbor's. (30) Proverbs 16:27. (31) *Ibid*. 20:13.

In the Midrash,[32] we find [the following]: *"He that tilleth his ground shall have plenty of bread.*[1] If a person toils in the study of Torah, he shall have plenty of bread, as it is said, *Come, eat of my bread.*[33] But *he that followeth after vain things is void of understanding,*[1] for it is said, *If it concerneth the scorners, He scorneth them.* "[34] The purport of this Midrash is that the Torah is called "bread" because it nourishes the soul just as real bread sustains the body. Just as farming requires toil in order to obtain bread, the study of Torah requires toil in order to sustain the soul. One who toils therein will undoubtedly find his reward, as the Sages said,[35] "[If anyone tells you], 'I have toiled [in Torah] and found it,' believe him." *But he that followeth after vain things*[1] does not toil in Torah but sits idle. He will [eventually] become devoid of understanding like other idle people and will turn to evil deeds. He will covet, rob, and be as scornful as other wicked people. Therefore, Solomon adjoined [the following to the first verse],[1] *The wicked desireth the prey of evil men.*[2] His intention was to say that because of idleness, one becomes attracted to evil men. This in turn will induce him to commit the transgression of coveting, which is the root of all sins.

If one toils in the study of Torah, however, he will find his satisfaction therein and will be gratified with moderation. He will not covet the luxuries of wealth, and he will find satisfaction in the bread he eats and the garment he wears. He will lead a life of honor rather than one of disgrace, and he will conduct himself in a permissible rather than a prohibited manner.

---

(32) I have been unable to locate this Midrash. (33) Proverbs 9:5. In other words, if one toils in the study of Torah, its wisdom will satisfy all his needs and he will find all gates of understanding open to him. (34) *Ibid.*, 3:34. If a person aims to scorn the words of the Torah, or lead an evil life, he has the opportunity to do so, for G-d neither assists nor impedes him in his course of action. (35) Megillah 6 b.

Therefore a person should carefully avoid violating the prohibition of coveting anything in this lowly world. Instead, he should desire only Torah and good deeds, of which it is written, *More to be desired are they than gold, yea, than much fine gold.*[36] Only this kind of coveting is permitted, as the Sages said,[37] "Jealousy among scholars increases wisdom." Similarly, it is permissible to desire and yearn to be among those who [strive to] perceive G-d and who search for knowledge of Him. It is also permissible to desire to sit in G-d's shadow and to be in proximity to Him, as Solomon said, *As an apple-tree among the trees of the wood, so is my Beloved among the sons. Under His shadow I delighted to sit, and His fruit was sweet to my taste.*[38]

(36) Psalms 19:11.   (37) Baba Bathra 22 a.   (38) Song of Songs 2:3.

חתן בבית הכנסת
The Bridegroom in the Synagogue

*Isaiah's prophecy 'Thine eyes shall see the King in His beauty,'
is a vision of the future which has not yet been fulfilled. In the
era of the Messiah, the understanding and knowledge of G-d
will increase so that we will merit to 'see the King in His beauty'
when the Divine Presence returns to the Holy of Holies / At
that time, Israel's relationship to G-d will be in a state of
perfection / Just as the perfection of the world will be achieved
only in the days of the Messiah, which is symbolized by a marriage, so the individual can attain his perfection only through
marriage / The purposes of marriage and the Divine help
needed therein / The various allusions in the gifts given by
Eliezer to Rebekah / Marriage is analogous to the creation of
the world. The Sages ordained various benedictions to indicate
that analogy.*

The Bridegroom in the Synagogue[1]

THINE EYES SHALL SEE THE KING IN HIS BEAUTY, THEY
SHALL BEHOLD A LAND STRETCHING AFAR.[2]

Isaiah mentioned this verse in connection with the reward of the righteous who are destined to enjoy the splendor of the Divine Glory. His intent was to affirm that the worship of G-d and the capacity to greet the Divine Presence are accessible to all people who aspire thereto.

However, these things are far removed from the wicked, to whom Divine worship is considered laborious and unattainable. Therefore, the prophet first mentioned, *The sinners in Zion are afraid; trembling hath seized the ungodly: Who among us shall dwell with the Devouring Fire? Who among us shall dwell with everlasting burnings?*[3] These are

---

(1) According to custom, a bridegroom was called up to the Torah prior to his wedding. After the reading of the appropriate portion for that day, the Torah would be rolled to Genesis, Chapter 24, which relates how Eliezer, the servant of Abraham, chose Rebekah as the wife of Isaac. This chapter with the accompanying Targum was read to the bridegroom. In his commentary on Genesis 24:3, our author explained that this custom served "to remind people of the importance of a suitable marriage." In the present work Rabbeinu Bachya expresses the wider significance of this custom as it applies to Israel as G-d's people. — This custom has persisted to this day, though in a weakened form, for the bridegroom who is called up to the Torah prior to his wedding is just read part of the current portion of that day. (2) Isaiah 33:17. Our author opens the theme of the wedding with the ultimate reward of the righteous, and describes the struggle between good and evil in this world, and the final victory of truth. Then will true happiness, symbolized by the wedding, be possible. Thus, the happiness of the individuals about to enter into marriage is illumined by the part of Israel's role in the world. (3) *Ibid.*, Verse 14.

the words of the sinners and the flatterers, who say, "Who can dwell in Zion with G-d, Who is a Devouring Fire,[4] and worship Him and fulfill His commandments? Who can live in the place of the altar, which contains *the everlasting burnings,* as it is written, *Fire shall be kept burning upon the altar continually; it shall not go out?*"[5] G-d, however, answers them, *He that walketh righteously, and speaketh uprightly; he that despiseth the gain of oppressions, that shaketh his hands from holding of bribes, that stoppeth his ears from hearing of blood, and shutteth his eyes from looking upon evil.*[6] *He shall dwell on high; his place of defense shall be the fastnesses of rocks; his bread shall be given, his waters shall be sure.*[7] *Thine eyes shall see the King in His beauty, they shall behold a land stretching afar.*[2]

The wicked spoke of G-d as *the Devouring Fire,*[3] thus negating the possibility of serving Him, [for they wished to remove themselves from G-d] just as one would remove himself from a fire in order not to be burnt. Therefore, the prophet speaks of *the King in His beauty,*[2] as if to say that serving G-d is not unfeasible but is easy and possible. Through his rational mind, the worshipper can come near to G-d and can rejoice at His Presence as one rejoices when seeing a king in his splendor.

The expression, *they shall behold a land stretching afar,*[2] means that the righteous will witness the punishment of the sinners and the flatterers who maintained that serving Him was impossible. In his Targum, Yonathan [the son of Uziel] rendered the meaning of the verse as follows: "They [the righteous] shall see the splendor of the Divine Presence, the Eternal King is His glory; they shall behold the wicked going to the Gehenna."

In the opinion of the commentators,[8] this [thirty third] chapter [of the Book of Isaiah] is a prophecy of the future. It refers to King

---

(4) The same appellation appears in Deuteronomy 4:24: *For the Eternal thy G-d is a Devouring Fire.*   (5) Leviticus 6:6.   (6) Isaiah 33:15.   (7) *Ibid.,* Verse 16.   (8) I have not been able to identify these commentators.

Messiah. Indeed, all erudite persons will find in the expressions *King* and *land* an intimation that this chapter speaks of the future and has never been fulfilled. It was not fulfilled during the era of the First Temple, for although the Divine Presence dwelt therein [while it existed, the Temple's] pegs were plucked up and its cords were broken [by the enemy, when it was destroyed. In his prophecy], however, Isaiah assured us [that the Temple is] *a tent that shall not be removed, the pegs whereof shall never be plucked up, neither shall any of the cords thereof be broken.*[9] Needless to say, the prophecy was not fulfilled during the era of the Second Temple when the Divine Presence did not dwell there.[10] Furthermore, it is known that Isaiah, who proclaimed this prophecy was a contemporary of King Hezekiah who reigned during the era of the First Temple when the Divine Presence dwelt therein. Nevertheless, Isaiah spoke in terms of the future: [*Thine eyes 'shall see' the King in His beauty*]. Therefore, we can only conclude that the chapter contains a prophecy for the future. *The King* and *the land* which he mentioned here are synonymous with the light and the glory about which he prophesied at the end of his book, *Arise, shine, for thy light is come.*[11]

Thus, you can see that this entire [thirty-third] chapter [in the Book of Isaiah] is dedicated to the future in the time of King Messiah when we will be privileged to see *the King in His beauty,* the Holy One, blessed be He. At that time the Divine Presence will return to the Holy of Holies,[12] and the *children shall return to their own border.*[13] The understanding and knowledge of G-d will be attained to a greater degree than that of the generation which received the Torah in the

---

(9) Isaiah 33:20.   (10) The Second Temple lacked five things: the Ark with the cover and the cherubim, the Divine fire upon the altar, the Divine Presence, the Holy Spirit, and the Urim and Thummim (Yoma 21 b). See more on this topic in Ramban, Commentary on the Torah, Leviticus, pp. 470, 473.   (11) Isaiah 60:1.   (12) The Ark containing the Tablets of the Law which were hidden, will then be restored to the Holy of Holies.   (13) Jeremiah 31:16.

wilderness.[14] The world will be in a state of perfection, and Israel's relationship to G-d will be, [so to speak], matrimonial, although it is presently only in the stage of betrothal. This [concept] is clarified in the Midrash:[15] "This [relationship between G-d and Israel] can be compared to a king who betrothed a woman and sent her a few gifts. When he came to wed her, he presented her with many gifts. In this world, too, G-d 'betrothed' Israel, as it says, *And I will betroth thee unto Me forever,*[16] and He gave them only the moon,[17] as it says, *This month shall be unto you.*[18] In the days of the Messiah, the 'wedding' will occur, for it says, *For thy Maker is thy husband.*[19] At that time, G-d will give them everything, as it says, *And they that are wise shall shine as the brightness of the firmament, and they that turn the many to righteousness as the stars, forever and ever.*"[20] Elsewhere, the Sages commented:[21] "This can be compared to a king who betrothed a woman with five rings, as it says, *And I will betroth thee unto Me in righteousness, and in justice, and in lovingkindness, and in compassion. And I will betroth thee unto Me in faithfulness, and thou shalt know the Eternal.*"[22] The "five rings" which the Sages mentioned refer to the five books of the Torah, which correspond to these [five] attributes.[23]

Just as the world will attain perfection only at the time of the [aforementioned] "wedding," which is the era of the Messiah, so man can attain perfection only when he is united [with his spouse] in marriage. Thus, in the case of Adam, the first man, who was created

(14) The generation of the wilderness is deemed as a *dor dei'ah* (generation of knowledge), as the people were witnesses to the Revelation on Mount Sinai, and all the wonders that transpired in the wilderness. (15) Shemoth Rabbah, end of Chapter 15. (16) Hosea 2:21. (17) When the new moon appears, it betokens the beginning of the month for Israel. Since the sanctification of the month is the first commandment given to Israel in Egypt, the Midrash considers this to be the gift for Israel's betrothal to G-d. (18) Exodus 12:2. (19) Isaiah 54:5. (20) Daniel 12:3. (21) I have been unable to locate the source of this quotation. (22) Hosea 2:22-23. (23) I.e., righteousness, justice, lovingkindness, compassion, and faithfulness.

alone, Scripture states, *It is not good [that man should be alone],* [24] and a thing that is *not good* is imperfect. Therefore, Adam was commanded to take to himself a wife and to cleave to her in order to bear children who would worship G-d. In this manner, Adam became a perfect entity. It is thus written, *Therefore shall a man leave his father and his mother, and he shall cleave unto his wife.* [25] Scripture informs us here of the two primary purposes of marriage. First, marriage ensures the continuation and the multiplication of the human species so that the world will be inhabited, as it is written, *He created it not in a waste, He formed it to be inhabited.* [26] Second, marriage ensures that children will be raised to worship G-d, to know Him and to recognize Him. [27]

Scripture specifies, *And he shall cleave unto 'his' wife,* [25] to indicate [that he should marry] a woman of his kind who is suitable for him and who will raise children in his pattern of life. Since it is known that children follow the nature of their mother's family, [28] a person should therefore take care not to marry a woman just for her beauty, for it is written, *Grace is deceitful, and beauty is vain.* [29] Nor should he marry for money, as it is written, *For riches certainly make themselves wings, like an eagle that flieth toward heaven.* [30] Instead, all his thoughts and intentions should be directed toward satisfying G-d's will.

To be successful, a marriage needs G-d's help. We learn this from the Torah, from the Prophets, and from the Writings. We learn it from the Torah, for in the chapter dealing with the conjugal destiny of

---

(24) Genesis 2:18.   (25) *Ibid.,* Verse 24.   (26) Isaiah 45:18.   (27) It shoulds be noted that the marital duty requires man and wife to live together regardless of whether the birth of children results therefrom or not (Exodus 21:11). Our author, on the other hand, addressing himself to the bridegroom about to be married, stresses the normal functions thereof, which result in child-bearing and the raising of a family to continue the worship of G-d.   (28) Baba Bathra 110 a: "The majority of children resemble the mother's brothers."   (29) Proverbs 31:30.   (30) *Ibid.,* 23:5.

Isaac and Rebekah, it is written, *The thing proceedeth from the Eternal*,[31] as proven by the events which you have experienced.[32] We derive it from the Prophets, for when Samson [decided to marry a Philistine woman despite the objection of his parents], it is written, *But his father and his mother knew not that it was of the Eternal.*[33] [It is also known] from the Writings, as Solomon said, *House and riches are the inheritance of fathers, but a prudent wife is from the Eternal.*[34] This means that parents can bequeath to their son only property and money, but they cannot provide him with a prudent wife, who is from G-d. Scripture thus informs us that a prudent wife is to be prized more than a house or wealth, as it is written, *Who can find a woman of valor?*[35]

Returning to the chapter which relates how Eliezer [chose a wife for Isaac], one may ask: Why was it necessary for Scripture to inform us of the gifts Eliezer gave to Rebekah, and why did the Torah emphasize the weight [of those gifts] — as it is said, *And the man took a golden ring of a 'beka' (half-shekel) weight, and two bracelets for her hand of ten shekels weight of gold*[36] — when there is nothing extraordinary about their weights or value? In my opinion, these gifts allude to the acceptance of the Torah by the blessed offspring of Isaac and Rebekah. [Those descendants] would bring *shekels* [for the building of

---

(31) Genesis 24:50.   (32) This refers to the events which Eliezer, the servant of Abraham, experienced in his quest for a suitable wife for his master's son Isaac. Upon meeting Rebekah at the water well, Eliezer requested some water from Rebekah's pitcher, and she responded with her natural kindness, indicating to Eliezer that she was the designated wife for Isaac. Bethuel and Laban, Rebekah's father and brother, later said to Eliezer, *"The thing proceedeth from the Eternal,* as proven by the events which you [Eliezer] have experienced [at the well]."* — The expression "which you have experienced" may possibly be understood as a direct reference to the bridegroom. The author is thus suggesting to him that his request for a suitable marriage partner has been granted to him by G-d.   (33) Judges 14:4. The verse continues, *for he* [Samson] *sought an occasion against the Philistines.*   (34) Proverbs 19:14.   (35) *Ibid.,* 31:10.   (36) Genesis 24:22.

the Tabernacle], of which it is written, *a 'beka' (half-shekel) a head.*[37] They would receive the Ten Commandments inscribed on the two Tablets of the Covenant, as alluded here in the verse, . . . *and two bracelets for her hand ten shekels weight of gold.*[36]

[Knowing the significance of "ten"], wicked Haman said to King Ahaseurus, And I will pay ten thousand talents of silver.[38] It was Haman's evil intention *to destroy, to slay, and to cause to perish*[39] Israel's enemies,[40] and with his "ten" [i.e., the ten thousand talents of silver], he sought to nullify the Ten [Commandments], which were proclaimed through the fire by the Divine Voice.[41]

These [aforementioned] gifts were given to Rebekah by the servant [Eliezer], thus alluding that her offspring would receive the Torah through the hand of the trusted servant Moses.[42] Regarding Eliezer, Scripture states that he came *having all goodly things of his master's in his hand.*[43] Similarly, it states of Moses, *I will make all My goodness pass before thee.*[44] Just as Eliezer gave Rebekah gifts in her home in addition to those which he gave her at the well — as it is said, *And the servant brought forth jewels of silver, and jewels of gold,* etc.[45] — so did Rebekah's offspring receive many commandments in the land of Moab just before they entered [their home], the Land of Israel, as it is written, *These are the words of the covenant which the Eternal commanded Moses to make with the children of Israel,* etc.[46] The Sages also commented,[47] "The Torah was written in sections."[48] [Finally], just as

---

(37) Exodus 38:26. This is alluded to by Eliezer giving Rebekah *the golden ring of a 'beka' weight.* (38) Esther 3:9. (39) *Ibid.,* Verse 13. (40) A euphemism for Israel itself. (41) See Deuteronomy 4:36. (42) See Numbers 12:7. (43) Genesis 24:10. (44) Exodus 33:19. (45) Genesis 24:53. (46) Deuteronomy 28:69. (47) Gittin 60 a. (48) Tractate Gittin *ibid.,* relates that when the laws of a certain section of the Torah were revealed to Moses, he recorded them immediately. At the end of his life, he joined these separate sections into one Torah. Based upon this viewpoint, Rabbeinu Bachya's analogy between Israel receiving the Torah piecemeal and Rebekah gradually receiving gifts from Eliezer is complete. It should be noted, however, that according to another opinion in the Talmud, the Torah was given as one

the episode of Eliezer is first stated when it happened and then repeated [by Eliezer] as he recounted it [to Rebekah's family], so did Rebekah's offspring receive the Torah twice, i.e., the first Tablets and the second Tablets. Moreover, [in the land] beyond the Jordan, Moses, *the servant of the Eternal*[49] reviewed all the events that transpired in connection with the first Tablets.

Marriage is analogous to creation of the world. Just as the world was created with ten Sayings, [50] so the Sages ordained that the benedictions for the wedding rite be recited in the presence of a quorum of ten men, as the verse states, *And he* [Boaz] *took ten men.*[51] The Sages likewise formulated ten expressions of joy[52] in "Who has created," [one of the wedding] benedictions. Further, just as there were seven days — including the Sabbath — at the creation of the world, so the Sages ordained seven wedding blessings, including the blessing over wine. The latter corresponds to the Sabbath, for wine is used in proclaiming the sanctity of the Sabbath both at the commencement and the conclusion of that day. Furthermore, there are seven days of rejoicing [immediately succeeding the wedding day itself]. Because there is no perfect joy in this world, the Sages ordained that the person who leads the Grace at a wedding feast should say, "We will bless our G-d in Whose abode there is joy." That is to say, the true rejoicing of the bridegroom and bride comes not from us but only from His abode, the source of joy and gladness.

May the Holy One, blessed be He, enable us to reach the time when the relationship of all Israel towards Him will be matrimonial in

complete unit, and Moses recorded all of its laws at the same time. (49) Deuteronomy 34:5. (50) Genesis, Chapter 1, which deals with the Creation, the expression *and G-d said* occurs nine times. The verse, *In the beginning G-d created* is understood as the tenth Saying, in accordance with Psalms 33:6. (51) Ruth 4:2. (52) The ten expressions are: joy, gladness, mirth, exultation, pleasure, delight, love, brotherhood, peace, and fellowship. In the "Discourse on a Wedding," Writings and Discourses, Vol. I, p. 22, Ramban speaks of twelve terms, adding "bridegroom and bride" to the ten above.

nature. We will then rejoice with that perfect happiness of which it is written, *And the ransomed of the Eternal shall return, and come with singing unto Zion, and everlasting joy shall be upon their heads.*[53] May G-d consider us worthy of eternal life and the distinction of the [Divine] light and joy, as David said, *Light is sown for the righteous, and gladness for the upright in heart.*[54]

(53) Isaiah 35:10.   (54) Psalms 97:11.

חתן על השלחן
The Bridegroom at the Wedding Feast

In the Song of Songs Solomon compared the Torah to food and drink, thus teaching us that just as food and drink sustain the body, so do Torah and wisdom nourish the soul / There is a profound connection between Torah and wisdom on one hand, and material concerns on the other, for one enters the rational domain only through the physical one. Therefore, Scripture compares Torah and Wisdom, the soul's nourishment, to bread, which provides nourishment of the body / This thought is alluded to by the apposition of the Candelabrum and Table of Showbread in the Sanctuary / It was also alluded to during the Giving of the Torah, the dedication of the Sanctuary, and other significant events at which a feast was held / The intent of the feast in the Garden of Eden which G-d will prepare for the righteous.

I AM COME INTO MY GARDEN, MY SISTER, MY BRIDE; I
HAVE GATHERED MY MYRRH WITH MY SPICE; I HAVE
EATEN MY HONEYCOMB WITH MY HONEY; I HAVE
DRUNK MY WINE WITH MY MILK; EAT, O FRIENDS,
DRINK, YEA, DRINK ABUNDANTLY, O BELOVED.[55]

Solomon stated this verse in Song of Songs, which is holy of holies.[56]
He was speaking to the soul, which he called *bride,* and he referred to
people as *friends* and *beloved* in his desire to justify them and bring
them near to the Torah, which he calls *garden.*

Solomon mentioned six items — myrrh, spice, honeycomb, honey
wine, and milk — all of which are included in three areas of physical
pleasure, smelling, eating, and drinking. Corresponding to these six
items, David had described the Divine character of the Torah in six
ways: *The law of the Eternal is perfect;*[57] *the testimony of the Eternal is
reliable;*[57] *the precepts of the Eternal are right;*[58] *the commandment of
the Eternal is clear;*[58] *the fear of the Eternal is pure;*[59] *the ordinances of
the Eternal are true.*[60] All of these are included within three categories:
testimonies, statutes, and ordinances, as it is written, *What mean the
testimonies, and the statutes, and the ordinances?*[61]

The sense of smell corresponds to the *testimonies.* These are the
traditional precepts[62] that are drawn from the Higher Wisdom even as
the fragrant scent is drawn forth from the *ethrog.*[63]

Eating corresponds to the *ordinances,* the rational commandments
that are sweeter to the people than honey and the honeycomb. They

(55) Song of Songs 5:1. (56) See *Emunah* (Faith), Note 22, on the significance of
this remark, which is based on Yadayim 3:5. (57) Psalms 19:8. (58) *Ibid.,* Verse
9. (59) *Ibid.,* Verse 10. In his commentary on this verse, Ibn Ezra explains that this
refers to the negative commandments, the observance of which guard the purity of the
individual. (60) Psalms 19:10. (61) Deuteronomy 6:20. (62) These precepts are
unfathomable by human reason. We are entirely dependent upon tradition for the
manner of their observance. (63) See *Ahavah* (Love of G-d), Note 13.

contain the framework for the existence of the world and the civiliza-
tion of countries, and their benefits are recognizable and apparent to
one and all. Thus, after David mentioned *the ordinances of the Eternal,*[60] he immediately stated, *They are more to be desired than gold,
than much fine gold, sweeter also than honey and the honeycomb.*[64]
The term eating alludes to the *ordinances* because eating is a more
physical act [than smelling], just as the ordinances [relate more to the
earthly matters than do the *testimonies*].

The act of drinking corresponds to the *statutes* to which the wine
and milk allude, as it is said, *I have drunk my wine with my milk.*[55]
[This verse] refers to the commandment of [not cooking] meat in milk
and is one of the statutes [the reason for which is not disclosed].

Addressing his soul, Solomon said, *I am come into my garden,*[55]
meaning that he came to the Torah and attained all of its commandments in their three aspects [i.e., testimonies, statutes, and or-
dinances]. After completing this address, Solomon then advised people
to engage themselves in the study of Torah, as he said, *Eat, O friends,
drink, yea, drink abundantly, O beloved.*[55]

Solomon's analogy of the study of Torah to eating and drinking
teaches you that just as eating and drinking sustain the body, so do
Torah and wisdom nourish the soul. We can perceive the profound
connection between Torah and rational matters on the one hand and
material concerns on the other, for one enters the intellectual domain
only through the physical one. A child, [for example], does not want to
learn [Torah] unless he is given sweets, and in his consideration, these
are more precious than the entire Torah. As he grows older, he desires
fine clothes as the price of his learning. Still later, his goal in learning is
the honor attached to the titles "scholar and Rabbi." When the eyes of
his mind are finally opened, however, and he realizes that all physical

(64) Psalms 19:11.

pleasures and pursuits are *things of nought and vanity*,[65] he then strives to study only for the sake of the Holy One, blessed be He. All his deeds and desires are directed only to G-d, as it is said, *Eternal, all my desire is before Thee*.[66] Thus, you see that this individual can achieve this intellectual status only through material means.

The same principle applies to all other human endeavors. One cannot raise progeny for the worship of G-d except through marriage and other material concerns, nor can one attain the distinction of the higher world except through this material world. Therefore, Scripture compares Torah and wisdom, the soul's nourishment, to bread, which provides the nourishment of the body.

We find, too, that the Candelabrum and the Table of Showbread stood opposite one another in the Sanctuary, the Candelabrum at the south and the Table of Showbread at the north.[67] The Candelabrum symbolized wisdom, which is the soul's nourishment, and the Table symbolized royalty and wealth, which are the body's nourishment. Candelabrum and the Table of Showbread faced each other to teach us that the material blessings of the world can be attained only through wisdom, and wisdom can thrive in mortals only through the sustaining power of food and drink.

One is therefore obligated to speak words of Torah at a feast for several reasons. First, doing so indicates that the adequacy and blessings [which mankind finds] in the world exist only for the sake of Torah. Second, any table at which words of Torah are spoken is preferred and beloved by G-d. The Sages commented,[68] "When three people have eaten at one table and words of Torah are among them,[69] it is considered as if they had eaten at G-d's table, as [Ezekiel] said, *And he spoke unto me, This is the table that is before the Eternal.*"[70]

---

(65) Isaiah 40:17.   (66) Psalms 38:10.   (67) See Exodus 26:35.   (68) Aboth 3:4.   (69) Our editions of the Mishnah explicitly state "are 'spoken' among them."   (70) Ezekiel 41:22. The prophet Ezekiel is speaking there of the altar in the

Third, preoccupation with food and drink can induce a sense of arrogance in the individual and can cause him to forget the essential principle of life, as the prophet said, *They were filled, and their heart was exalted, therefore have they forgotten Me.*[71] For these reasons, a person is obligated to engage in the study of Torah and to recall that which is essential whenever there is a possibility that such things will be forgotten.

We find that *the nobles of the children of Israel*[72] — i.e., the seventy elders[73] led by Moses, Aaron, Nadab and Abihu — made a feast [after the Revelation on Sinai]. As they were eating and drinking, they contemplated and perceived the Divine Glory, as it is written, *And they beheld G-d, and did eat and drink.*[72]

We also find feasting in connection with many sacred places and prophetic events. Thus, when Solomon completed the Sanctuary, he dedicated it with a feast, as it is said, *And the King, and all Israel, offered sacrifice before the Eternal.*[74] Our patriarch Jacob received the blessings [from his father Isaac] only through a feast consisting of *the savory food*[75] which he brought his father. The redemption in the time of Esther was accomplished through a feast, as it is said, *Let the king and Haman come to the banquet.*[76] At that feast, the king granted Esther her request, and as a result Israel was saved from destruction. With regard to the miracle of Chanukah, too, the Sages commented that it occurred by means of a feast.[77]

Sanctuary and he continues to state that he was told *This is the table* etc., when he should have been told "This is the altar etc." The Mishnah therefore derives from it the following thought: "*This* altar *is* itself *the table before the Eternal.* Just as the priests who eat of the offerings brought upon the altar complete the atonement, so are those who eat at one table and discuss words of Torah considered as if they had eaten at G-d's table." In other words, the table nowadays takes the place of the altar in the Sanctuary. The recitation of Grace which contains verses from the Torah is held to be sufficient for the fulfillment of this Mishnah. (71) Hosea 13:6. (72) Exodus 24:11. (73) This follows the explanation of Rashi and Ramban on Exodus 24:1. See also Verse 9 in that chapter. (74) I Kings 8:62. (75) Genesis 27:17. (76) Esther 5:8. (77) The only reference thereto I found in Midrash Chanukah. See Eisenstein's Otzar

The Sages also expounded,[78] "In the future, G-d will make a feast for the righteous." We are to believe that this feast will be an actual material one, for the pure foods [which will be served at that time] have been prepared since the time of Creation. Perhaps they are products of the Higher Light,[79] as was the manna in the wilderness.[80] Following these feasts at the end of time, the era of the Resurrection will begin. The resurrected will be sustained by the Glory of the Divine Presence, and they will never again return to the earth. The Sages said,[81] "The dead which the Holy One, blessed be He, will resurrect will never die again. They will exist forever like the ministering angels." They will be rejuvenated under seven canopies, as it is said, *And the Eternal will create over the whole habitation of Mount Zion, and over her assemblies, a cloud and smoke by day, and the shining of a flaming fire by night, for over all the glory shall be a canopy.*[82]

Hamidrashim p. 192.   (78) Pesachim 119 b.   (79) See *Orchim* (Hospitality), Note 51. (80) See Ramban, Commentary on the Torah, Exodus, pp. 224-229.   (81) Sanhedrin 92 a.   (82) Isaiah 4:5. — The seven canopies are: a cloud, smoke, shining, fire, flaming, glory, and canopy. (Rashbam, Baba Bathra 75 a). These terms have mystical connotations.

טהרת הלב
Purity of Heart

Purity of heart is one of the five rational traits which serve to purify man's thoughts / Purity of thought, together with the four physical traits which serve to purify man's deeds, will lead a person to the tenth characteristic—the gift of the Holy Spirit / The explanation of each of these qualities / In the language of the Torah, one who possesses purity of heart is called 'tamim' (wholehearted) / The spiritual loss engendered by impure thoughts / Various explanations of the Sages' adage, 'Sinful thoughts are more injurious than the sin itself' / The possession of purity of thought is dependent upon the choice of the individual. Whoever attempts to purify his thoughts, will be assisted by Heaven.

Purity of Heart

CREATE IN ME A CLEAN HEART, O G-D, AND RENEW A
STEADFAST SPIRIT WITHIN ME.[1]

In this verse David prayed for purity of thought, which is known to
be a rational trait. All traits of character fall into one of the two
categories: physical or rational. Physical traits correct one's deeds.
Without this correction, there can be no perfection of wisdom. It is
said, *A good understanding have all who practice it,*[2] upon which the
Sages commented,[3] "It does not say 'all who study it,' but it states, *all
who practice it.*"

The rational traits serve to purify one's thought, so that it is used exclusively in the service of G-d. Thus, it is written, *He that hath clean
hands, and a pure heart.*[4] *Clean hands* include the physical traits,
which correct one's deeds. *A pure heart* includes the rational traits,
which purify one's thought so that his inner personality will match his
outer appearance and his covert nature will suitably correspond to his
outward actions. The Sages commented,[5] "It is written [of the Torah],
Gold and glass cannot equal it.[6] The Torah is compared to gold and

---

(1) Psalms 51:12. The verse expresses the two elements required for the good life: *a
pure heart* to repel everything base and ignoble, and *a steadfast spirit* to be unwavering
in the constant pursuit of goodness. (2) *Ibid.*, 111:10. The beginning of the verse
reads: *The fear of the Eternal is the beginning of wisdom. A good understanding*
etc. (3) Berachoth 17 a. It is thus shown that the pursuit of wisdom is not an end in
itself, inasmuch as it must be accompanied with good deeds. (4) Psalms
24:4. (5) Chagigah 15 a. (6) Job 28:17.

glass, because like gold, its words are difficult to attain and like glass, it is easily lost [if not constantly guarded against forgetfulness]. Rabbi Akiba says, 'The words of the Torah are compared to glass to teach you that just as glass is transparent, so a scholar should reveal in his speech whatever is in his heart.' " Similarly, it is written of the Ark of the Covenant, *And thou shalt overlay it with pure gold, within and without shalt thou overlay it.*[7]

In the language of the Torah, one who possesses this trait of character, [i.e., one whose lips express the thoughts of his heart], is called *tamim* (wholehearted), a quality designating the righteous. It is written of Noah, *he was a righteous and wholehearted man.*[8] It is written of Abraham, *Walk before Me, and be thou wholehearted,*[9] and it is said of Jacob, *And Jacob was a man of integrity.*[10]

You may thus conclude that purity is a rational quality which comprises many excellent characteristics. Therefore, David prayed for it when he said, *Create in me a clean heart, O G-d.*[1] He asked G-d to help him fulfill the Torah and the commandments, since purity is eternally inseparable from the Torah. The Sages said,[11] "Words of Torah do not contract impurity, for it is written, *Is not My word like fire? saith the Eternal.*"[12] The Divine assistance requested by David is that G-d confer upon him a spirit of pure thought and desire. This is the renewed *steadfast spirit within*[1] him for which he yearned.

The trait of purity leads to holiness, as it is written, *And he shall purify it, and hallow it.*[13] The Sages commented,[14] "What is the mean-

---

(7) Exodus 25:11.—The actions of a person must then be a true reflection of his inner convictions. (8) Genesis 6:9. (9) *Ibid.*, 17:1. (10) *Ibid.*, 25:27. (11) Berachoth 22 a. Accordingly, a person who is impure may still recite the *Sh'ma* or other words of Torah, "since words of Torah do not contract impurity." (12) Jeremiah 23:29. "Just as fire does not contract impurity, so the words of Torah do not contract impurity." (Berachoth 22 a). (13) Leviticus 16:19. (14) Abodah Zarah 20 b, with textual variations.—The thought conveyed is that just as one evil deed brings on another, so do the virtues of character follow one

ing of the verse, *And thou shalt keep thee from every evil thing?*[15] It means that one should guard against sinful thoughts during the day in order to avoid impurity at night. Based upon this verse, Rabbi Pinchas ben Ya'ir said, Heedfulness leads to alertness, alertness leads to cleanliness, cleanliness leads to restraint, restraint leads to purity, purity leads to holiness, holiness leads to fear of sin, fear of sin leads to humility, humility leads to saintliness, saintliness leads to the gift of the Holy Spirit, as it is said, *Then Thou spokest in vision to Thy saintly ones.*"[16]

Of these ten characteristics,[17] the first five — heedfulness, alertness, cleanliness, restraint, and purity — are spiritual, and serve to purify man's thoughts. Heedfulness applies to the observance of negative commandments; one must beware of committing certain forbidden acts. Alertness applies to the fulfillment of positive commandments which one must attentively perform. Alertness also leads to [physical] cleanliness, keeping the body unsoiled, and free of any impurity. Cleanliness leads to restraint, for one will check all evil thoughts and desires. Restraint, in turn, leads to purity of thought.

[The traits of holiness, fear of sin, humility, and saintliness, are physically oriented and serve to perfect one's actions.] Holiness entails abstention not only from forbidden foods but from permissible ones as well. One who disciplines himself by abstaining from permissible things beyond those necessary for sustenance is called "holy." This

---

from another. Thus, "heedfulness leads to alertness," for he who is heedful of the consequences of his deeds, and acts with caution against committing a sin, will develop a vigilant attentiveness to fulfilling his positive duties. The same reasoning applies to all the other moral excellences mentioned by Rabbi Pinchas ben Ya'ir. (15) Deuteronomy 23:10. (16) Psalms 89:20. Rashi, *ibid.*, explains, "It does not say 'to those who fear Thy Name,' or 'to Thy humble ones.' " It is thus clear that G-d communicates through visions only with saintly ones. (17) I.e., heedfulness, alertness, cleanliness, restraint, purity, holiness, fear of sin, humility, saintliness, and the gift of the Holy Spirit.

thought motivated the Sages to say,[18] "Sanctify yourself with that which is permissible to you." Such abstinence for the sake of holiness leads to fear of sin. The individual will abstain from evil conversation, as it is written, *A wise man feareth, and departeth from evil.*[19] The fear of sin leads to humility, for one will not only avoid speaking about others, but will refrain from retorting even if others speak evil of him. A person who hears himself being humiliated and remains silent is called "humble." Humility leads to saintliness. Since one will avoid retorting to those who humiliate him, he will also tend to overlook his precise rights in his dealings with other people and will act liberally beyond strict legal requirement. Thus, after purifying his thoughts and correcting his deeds [through the aforementioned traits], he will then be worthy of the tenth characteristic, the gift of the Holy Spirit.

The reason David prayed for *a clean heart,*[1] [which as explained above is a prayer for purity of thought][20] is that by means thereof he knew he would find grace *in the sight of G-d and man,*[21] and he would be assured of never sinning. Solomon, too, said, *Who can say: I have made my heart clean, I am pure from my sin?*[22] That is to say, since purity of heart cannot be attained unless one is clean from sin, who can say that he is pure from sin? Similarly, Solomon said, *He that loveth pureness of heart, that hath grace in his lips, the king shall be his friend,*[23] which means that when one has genuine feelings towards the person that loves him, his words will always be graceful to that person, and, in turn, he will be worthy of royal recognition to be appointed overseer over the king's house. This verse speaks of a mortal king and alludes to the Supreme King, blessed be He. The verse is thus saying that one who loves G-d and is sincere in his thoughts will always find grace in His sight and will have his prayer accepted. The message of

(18) Yebamoth 20 a. See also Ramban, Commentary on the Torah, Leviticus, pp. 282-284, for development of this thought. (19) Proverbs 14:16. (20) David singled out *a clean heart* above any other virtues of character, for "he knew etc." (21) Proverbs 3:4. (22) *Ibid.*, 20:9. (23) *Ibid.*, 22:11.

the verse is that if mortal kings elevate a person for his purity of heart, G-d will assuredly raise and exalt such a person and designate his reward, as it is said, *Behold, His reward is with Him, and His recompense before Him.*[24]

It is necessary to understand that the importance of purity of thought is attributable to its origin in the individual's rational faculty, which is of Divine essence. Thought and the rational soul thus have a common root. It is therefore possible for a person to elevate the lowly ones or to lower the exalted in his thought. This concept should bestir the sinner who defiles his pure thought with his sinful ideas, thus committing many sins and transgressions. Concerning this offense, the Sages said,[25] "Sinful thoughts are more injurious than the sin itself." That is to say, they are more injurious to the soul, for thoughts depend upon the heart, the seat of the soul. Therefore, when one renders the soul impure with evil thought, that is more injurious than the sin itself which does not preoccupy the soul as much. There are scholars who explain that the expression "more injurious than the sin itself" means that it is more difficult to withdraw from sinful thoughts, for habitually thinking about a sin will ultimately lead to its commission. Other scholars explain the adage to mean that when one plans to commit a certain sin, he actually prepares himself to do more than one sin. For example, if one thinks of stealing or robbing, he prepares himself even to kill in order to accomplish his desire. Thus, when he actually perpetrates the theft or robbery, he will have committed only one sin, but his sinful thoughts will be even worse than the crime itself because he was prepared to injure or even kill others to accomplish his goal.

The great Rabbi, the Ramban[26] [Rabbi Moshe ben Nachman] of blessed memory explained the saying as follows: "After the commission

(24) Isaiah 40:10.   (25) Yoma 29 a.   (26) Although other manuscripts designate Maimonides as "the great Rabbi," the correct reading is "Ramban." In Rabbeinu Bachya's commentary on Deuteronomy 29:18, he mentions a number of explanations

of the sin, sinful thoughts are more injurious than the sin itself." Even though the individual has already committed the sin and still entertains thoughts of it in his mind, it is more injurious than the act itself. However, before he committed the sin, he incurred no punishment for the mere imagination thereof, for the Rabbis said,[27] "G-d does not combine an evil intention with the deed," and no punishment is incurred for such thought. Scripture, too, states, *If I had regarded iniquity in my heart, the Eternal would not hear.*[28] The exception to this is a thought of idolatry, of which it is written, *That I may take the House of Israel in their own heart because they are turned away from Me through their idols.*[29]

From Ramban's opinion, it appears that inasmuch as a person has no control over his imagination, he incurs no punishment for it before commission of the sin. This, however, is surprising. Why should one not be punished for the sinful thought alone since he is defiling his rational soul thereby, as I mentioned above? Rather, we must turn to the following clarification [of Ramban's explanation]. Sinful thoughts in a person betoken deficient rational preparedness. Just as man has freedom of action—as it is said, *See, I have set before thee this day life and good, and death and evil*[30]—so does he have the freedom of thought after proper rational preparations. These preparations require that one direct his heart and thoughts to G-d and that he think only good thoughts and of appropriate deeds. If an evil thought occurs

of this adage of the Sages, among them that of Maimonides, as stated in the Guide of the Perplexed III, Chapter 5. After these various interpretations, our author continues, "There is yet another explanation," which coincides with the one mentioned in our text here. This is the explanation of Ramban, as found in the *Igereth Hakodesh* (The Sacred Letter), Kithvei Haramban, Vol. II, pp. 333-334. See also Kad Hakemach, p. 191, Note 39. (27) Kiddushin 40 a. (28) Psalms 66:18. The psalmist is thus stating that for the mere thought of sinning he would not be punished. See in the text that follows for the explanation of this principle. (29) Ezekiel 14:5. (30) Deuteronomy 30:15.

to him, he should drive it away so that it should not be brought to completion in his heart. If he does not drive it away and it is consummated in his heart, he will be punished for it. When the individual will discipline his mind in this way for a long time and will prepare his heart to love G-d, to come near Him, and to follow in His ways, G-d will recompense him according to his righteousness and will protect him from any evil thought. His mind will then be preoccupied only with good things.

In consonance with this thought, the Sages said,[31] "One who attempts to purify himself is assisted by Heaven." There are many verses that set forth this principle, such as: *The Eternal searcheth all hearts*[32] and *The Eternal weigheth the hearts.*[33] These verses teach you that when man directs his heart towards G-d, blessed be He, G-d prepares man's heart and properly guides it. Thus, it is written, *Eternal, Thou hast heard the desire of the humble; Thou wilt direct their heart, Thou wilt cause Thine ear to attend.*[34] It is further stated, *O Eternal, the G-d of Abraham, of Isaac, and of Israel, our fathers, keep this forever, even the imagination of the thoughts of the heart of Thy people, and direct their heart unto Thee.*[35]

(31) Yoma 38 b.   (32) I Chronicles 28:9.   (33) Proverbs 21:2.   (34) Psalms 10:17.   (35) I Chronicles 29:18.

יראה

Fear of G-d

To attain fear of G-d, one must train himself to regard mundane matters as vanity and to consider the transgression of any
of G-d's commandments absolutely impossible / The fear of
G-d is incomplete if one fears another person. The exception to
this is that we have been commanded to fear the king, the
public, and the learned scholar / The fear of G-d as reflected
in the sayings of the Sages / The fear of G-d consists of two
parts, both of which are essential to worshipping Him. First,
there is the fear of reward and punishment in this world and in
the World to Come. Second, there is the realization of His majesty and power, from which awareness will ensue man's fear
and shame of transgressing G-d's will.

Fear of G-d

THOU SHALT FEAR THE ETERNAL THY G-D; HIM SHALT
THOU SERVE, AND TO HIM SHALT THOU CLEAVE, AND
BY HIS NAME SHALT THOU SWEAR.[1]

Fear of G-d will lead one to the excellent quality of humility, which
in turn will engender the desire to cleave to G-d. The individual will
then be worthy of swearing by G-d's Name. To attain fear of G-d, one
must first regard mundane matters as vanity and emptiness. He should
reckon himself dust and ashes in his lifetime and worms and maggots
after his death, and he should consider the transgression of any of the
commandments of the Master of the entire world as an absolute impossibility. The fear of G-d cannot be attained without such thought.

This principle is the theme of the Book of Ecclesiastes, which begins
with the words, *Vanity of vanities,*[2] and closes with the topic of fear of
G-d, as it is said, *The end of the matter, all having been heard: fear
G-d, and keep His commandments, for this is the whole* [duty of]
man.[3] Solomon thus teaches you that it is impossible to achieve the fear
of G-d unless one first disregards worldly matters. Only by doing so will

---

(1) Deuteronomy 10:20. The fear of G-d is thus declared to be the central requirement among all the other duties—serving Him, cleaving to Him, and swearing by His
Name. Only where the fear of G-d is the foundation of human character can a secure
society thrive. (2) Ecclesiastes 1:2. Apparently, Rabbeinu Bachya, like Ramban,
understands that this verse expresses a command: "Solomon bids man to nullify the
vanities of this world and neither make them a mainstay of his thoughts nor think that
he can give much substance to them" (Ramban, "Discourse on the Words of
Koheleth," Writings and Discourses, Vol. I, p. 162). (3) Ecclesiastes 12:13.

one's worship of G-d be complete. His sincere intentions will be acceptable to G-d, for they will be free of the arrogance which would render
them abominable, as it is written, *Everyone that is proud in heart is an
abomination to the Eternal.*⁴

Scripture states, *Thou shalt fear the Eternal thy G-d; Him shalt thou
serve, and to Him shalt thou cleave.*¹ This means that you should rationally cling to G-d according to the degree of your understanding
and knowledge of Him. Scripture then says, *And by His Name shalt
thou swear.*¹ This is not to be construed in any way as a positive com-
mandment.⁵ Instead, it means that if it will be necessary to swear by
G-d's Name, blessed be He, in order to sanctify Him, you will be worthy to do so. You will thus act as did the righteous and the prophets,
for after having perfected themselves with the aforementioned
characteristics, they swore by His Name according to the needs of the
times in order to sanctify Him. For example, Elijah said to Ahab, *As
the Eternal, the G-d of Israel, liveth, before whom I stand, there shall
not be dew, nor rain these years, except according to my word.*⁶
Similarly, the Sages relate that Choni *Hama'agal*⁷ "drew a circle and
stood in its center" as Habakkuk the prophet had done, as it is said, *I*

(4) Proverbs 16:5.   (5) Among his list of the 248 positive commandments of the
Torah, Maimonides enumerates the injunction to invoke G-d's Name whenever a con-
firmation or denial on oath is required. See "The Commandments," Vol. I, pp. 10-11.
However, our author follows the opinion of Ramban whose position against including
this injunction among the positive precepts is explained in his Commentary on the
Torah, Deuteronomy, pp. 84-86, as well in his Critical Notes to Maimonides' Book of
the Commandments.   (6) I Kings 17:1. The idolatrous King Ahab of Israel mocked
the words of the Torah which declare that there will be no rain because of the sin of
idol-worship. See Deuteronomy 11:17. Therefore, in order to sanctify G-d's Name, Elijah swore that neither dew nor rain would fall until he so commanded.   (7) Choni
Hama'agal (the circle maker) lived during the era of the Second Temple. He was a
famous sage known for his saintliness. In moments of distress, people would ask him to
pray on their behalf. On one occasion, he was asked to pray for rain, but when he did,
no rain fell. "He then drew a circle and stood in its center, etc.," as the text here continues. Because of this event, which is recorded in Taanith 23 a, *Hama'agal* (the circle
maker) was added to his name.

will stand upon my watch, and set me upon the tower.[8] Choni said to
G-d, "Master of the world! Your children have turned to me because I
am looked upon as one of Your household. I swear by Your great
Name that I will not move from here until You have mercy upon Your
children." [Elijah, Choni *Hama'agal*], and others like them reached
this stage of which Scripture says, *And by His Name shalt thou swear.*[1]

To properly fear G-d, we must fear Him alone, not any mortal
creature. The Torah has warned us, *And thou seest horses, and
chariots, and a people more than thou, thou shalt not be afraid of
them.*[9] As long as man fears the strength of another human being, his
fear of G-d remains incomplete since a measure of his fear is given
elsewhere. Similarly, the Torah commanded that he who *is fearful and
fainthearted*[10] should return home before the commencement of battle. The reason for this exhortation is that in all its wars, Israel's victory
was based upon the merit of its fighters. If one's fear of G-d was imperfect, his merit was imperfect. [Thus, he should return to his house].

Isaiah warned about this imperfection when he said, *Who art thou,
that thou art afraid of man that shall die,*[11] *and thou hast forgotten the
Eternal thy Maker?*[12] He thus explained that when one assigns part of
his fear to mortal man, it is as if he has forgotten G-d, blessed be He.
With regard to the fear [of an oppressive enemy], Isaiah said afterwards, *For I am the Eternal thy G-d, Who stirreth up the sea, that the
waves thereof roar, the Eternal of hosts is His Name.*[13] That is to say, "I
have the power to stir up the rage of the sea and to allay it, for I am the
Master of all hosts, above and below. Certainly, I have the power to
assuage the fury of the oppressor."

Although the way of the Torah is not to fear mortal man, we are
nevertheless commanded to fear the king, the public, and the learned

---

(8) Habakkuk 2:1. "The prophet drew a circle and placed himself in its center and
said [before G-d] 'I will not move from here until I will hear Your answer on the question, Why do the wicked succeed?' " (Rashi *ibid.*). (9) Deuteronomy
20:1. (10) *Ibid.*, Verse 8. (11) Isaiah 51:12. (12) *Ibid.*, Verse 13. (13) *Ibid.*,
Verse 15.

scholar. Concerning the king, it is written, *Thou shalt indeed set him king over thee,*[14] to which the Sages added,[15] " . . . so that his fear will be upon you." The reason for this is that the king represents the existence of the country, as it is written, *The king by justice establisheth the land,*[16] and the Sages said,[17] "If not for the fear of the government, men would swallow each other alive." Fear of the king is entailed in the fear of G-d, since it is G-d Who has commanded us thereon. We also find that the fear of the king has been compared to the fear of G-d, as Solomon said, *My son, fear thou the Eternal and the king.*[18] This means that just as you must fear G-d and thereby avoid sin although you do not see Him, it is equally imperative that you fear the reigning king of the land, whose image should always be before you although you do not physically see him. [You will thereby be forewarned against committing any capital crime, and] you will thus be spared mortal punishment by the government. Alternatively, Solomon may be saying [that one owes allegiance first to G-d, then to the king, or in his words], *"My son, fear the Eternal* first, *and* after Him, fear *the king."* [In the conclusion of that verse], Solomon further exhorted us not to join the company of those *that are given to change.*[18] That is, they put the fear of the king first and the fear of G-d second.

Concerning the public, the Sages commented,[19] "The awe of the public should always be upon you, for when the priests bless the public, they face the people while their backs are towards the Sanctuary."[20] It is surprising that they should turn their backs to the Sanc-

---

(14) Deuteronomy 17:15. (15) Kethuboth 17 a. The use of the verb *som* (set), the infinitive, with the word *thasim* — translated, *thou shalt indeed set him* . . . — means a resolute acceptance of the authority of the kingdom (Rashi, *ibid.*). (16) Proverbs 29:4. (17) Aboth 3:2. (18) Proverbs 24:21. (19) Sotah 40 a. (20) Instead of "Sanctuary," the reading in our editions of the Gemara *(ibid.)* is "Divine Presence." When the Priestly Blessing was invoked during the Temple era the priests faced the public with their backs to the Sanctuary. Nowadays, their backs are turned to the synagogue's Holy Ark. The priests are permitted to do so out of the awe they must have of the public. See further in the text for Rabbeinu Bachya's explanation of this practice.

tuary, [for such an act is obviously disrespectful]! However, the explanation of the matter is that when the priest lifts his hands to invoke the blessing, the Divine Presence rests upon his hands, as the Sages commented, *He looketh in through the windows, He peereth through the lattice.*[21] Since the Divine Presence rests between the priest's two hands as *from between the two cherubim,*[22] we should not be concerned about their backs being turned towards the Sanctuary, for the sanctity of even the Holy of Holies stems only from the Divine Presence. The verse, *And when ye spread forth your hands, I will hide Mine eyes from you,*[23] which was said by G-d in a moment of anger, proves that when the priests spread their hands for the Priestly Blessing in a time of Divine acceptance, His eyes are set upon them and the Divine Presence rests upon their hands.

The Sages derived that we are to fear learned scholars from this verse:[24] "*Thou shalt fear 'eth' (the) Eternal thy G-d.*[1] The word *eth* includes the learned scholars," for the fear of them is truly the fear of Heaven. One who is careful with respect to the fear of scholars certainly stands in true awe of G-d, for it is known that the Sages are G-d's messengers on earth. They are the teachers of Torah and the sole source of instruction in the performance of the commandments. One who fears them, therefore, of necessity fears G-d. It is also known that this fear of scholars includes not talking in their presence without first having obtained leave from them. We find this in the case of King David, who refrained from expounding in public in his teacher's presence.[25]

***

(21) Song of Songs 2:9. Midrash Shir Hashirim Rabbah comments on this verse: "*He looketh in through the windows,* that is, from between the shoulders of the priests. *He peereth through the lattice,* that is, from between the fingers of the priests." This last statement refers to the priestly practice of dividing the fingers of each hand into two groups with a space between them. The priests do this as they raise their hands for the blessing. When their hands are joined together, three open spaces are thus formed. (22) Numbers 7:89. (23) Isaiah 1:15. (24) Pesachim 22 b. (25) Shir Hashirim Rabbah 1:17.

Great is the power of the fear of G-d, for having wisdom without fear is like having some injury for which there is no cure. Wisdom in itself can be repulsive, as the prophet said, *Lo, they have rejected the word of the Eternal, and what wisdom is in them?*[26] However, having wisdom in combination with the fear of G-d is like having a cure without an injury. Therefore, the Torah has been compared to fire, as it is said, *Is not My word like fire? saith the Eternal.*[27] Fire damages as it burns, but it also cures as one enjoys its warmth. Thus, Scripture states, *The commandment of the Eternal is pure, enlightening the eyes,*[28] and it is further written, *Thy word is a lamp unto my feet.*[29]

In Midrash Tehillim, the Sages stated,[30] "*The law of the Eternal is perfect.*[31] It is perfect when it comes forth from the mouth of a perfect one. *The testimony of the Eternal is reliable.*[31] It is reliable when it comes forth from the mouth of a reliable person." The Sages commented,[32] "Rabbi Shimon the son of Lakish said, 'What is the meaning of the following verse: *And the steadfastness of thy times shall be a wealth of salvation, wisdom and knowledge, and the fear of the Eternal which is His treasure?*[33] *Steadfastness* is the Order of *Zeraim* (Seeds);[34] *thy times* is the Order of *Mo'eid* (Appointed Season);[35] *Wealth* is the Order of *Nashim* (Women);[36] *salvation* is the Order of *Nezikin*

(26) Jeremiah 8:9. (27) *Ibid.*, 23:29. (28) Psalms 19:9. (29) *Ibid.*, 119:105. (30) Midrash Tehillim 19. (31) Psalms 19:8. (32) Shabbath 31 a. (33) Isaiah 33:6. (34) The verse quoted is interpreted with respect to the six major sections or orders into which the entire body of Mishnayoth is divided. The overall thought conveyed by this interpretation of the verse is that besides the laws set forth in the six orders, the final determining factor in a person's character is his fear of G-d. *Zeraim* (seeds), the first order of the Mishnayoth deals principally with agricultural laws and related subjects. It is alluded to in the word *steadfastness* because the farmer's activities in plowing, planting, etc., are based upon his steadfast faith that G-d will send the rain, etc., for his crops. (35) This second order of the Mishnayoth deals with the laws of the Sabbath and festivals. (36) Wealth alludes to *Nashim* because a man's wealth comes through his wife and family. In this order all the laws pertaining to marriage and divorce are discussed.

(Damages);[37] *wisdom* is the Order of *Kadoshim* (Sacred Matters);[38] and *knowledge* is the Order of *Taharoth* (Purities).[39] Yet *the fear of the Eternal is His treasure.*"[40] In Tractate Yoma, the Sages said,[41] "The verse, *Why is there a price in the hand of a fool?*[42] means 'Woe unto the learned scholar who engages in the study of the Torah but has no fear of G-d.' Rabbi Yanai said that it means 'Woe unto him who has no house and builds a gate.'[43] Rava said to his disciples, 'I beg of you not to inherit the two forms of Gehenna.' "[44]

The fear of G-d consists of two parts. First, there is the fear of reward and punishment in this world and in the World to Come. Second—and this constitutes a very high standard—there is the realization by the soul of the majesty, power, and wonders of G-d. This awareness will lead the soul to experience great fear, shame, and humility before G-d; it will make it impossible to ever violate G-d's command. These two essential aspects of the fear of G-d are mentioned in one verse: *For calamity from G-d was a terror for me, and by reason of His majesty I could do nothing.*[45]

Because the fear of G-d is the foundation of the entire Torah, we find that at the Revelation on Sinai, there was the sight of *thunderings*

(37) The laws of guarding against physically or financially injuring one's neighbor, making restitution for such damages, etc., are discussed in this order of the Mishnayoth, and constitute the foundations of society. They are the *salvation* of a peaceful world.   (38) This order of the Mishnayoth contains the laws pertaining to all matters concerning the offerings, the priests, the Sanctuary, etc.   (39) The laws of purity and impurity, and the means of attaining purity after having contracted impurity, are discussed in this sixth order of the Mishnayoth.   (40) "This is G-d's principal concern, which He keeps as a treasure to be remembered" (Rashi, Shabbath 31 a).   (41) Yoma 72 b.   (42) Proverbs 17:6.   (43) The fear of G-d is considered the house in which one lives, while the study of Torah is the gate through which one enters the house. It is senseless for one to build the gate if he has no house in which to live.   (44) "If you take pains to study Torah in this world but do not fulfill it, you will not only inherit Gehenna upon your death, but you will have lost the enjoyment of this world because of your arduous studies in your lifetime" (Rashi, Yoma 72 b).   (45) Job 31:23. The awareness of G-d's majesty made Job powerless to commit any wrongful deed.

and lightnings, and the voice of the Shofar,[46] and all the other great and fearful wonders. All of them were unveiled to the people so that their hearts would be invested with trembling and fear before G-d and so that they would be strong and alert in practicing the trait of fear. Thus, at the conclusion of the Revelation, Moses said to the people, *For G-d is come to prove you, and that His fear may be before you.*[47] Solomon, too, in his wisdom, ended the Book of Ecclesiastes with the trait of fear, the root of all the commandments, as he said, *The end of the matter, all having been heard: fear G-d, and keep His commandments, for this is the whole* [duty of] *man.*[3]

(46) Exodus 20:15.   (47) *Ibid.*, Verse 20.

יחוד השם
Unity of G-d

The reason that the section of the 'Sh'ma' is written after the Ten Commandments in the Book of Deuteronomy / The explanation of the 'Sh'ma' and the intent of the word 'One' / The Unity of G-d as explained by Bachya ibn Pekuda, and the definition of G-d's Unity / The Sages ordained the saying of 'Blessed be the Name, etc.' after the 'Sh'ma' / The arrangement of the passages in the reading of the 'Sh'ma,' and the reason for their recitation at the rising of the sun and the emerging of the stars / Why the Ten Commandments are alluded to in the reading of the 'Sh'ma' / The extent to which one must have proper intention in the reading of the 'Sh'ma' and the laws regarding the exact pronunciation of its letters / The main principle of G-d's Unity will be realized in the Messianic era, for the signs of the Unity are not recognized in the exile. Only in the era of Messiah will all creeds return to the One Faith.

Unity of G-d

HEAR, O ISRAEL: THE ETERNAL OUR G-D, THE ETERNAL IS ONE.[1]

The Torah mentioned the section of the *Sh'ma*[2] after the Ten Commandments[3] in order to explain that the Unity of G-d[4] is expressed in the utterance, *I am the Eternal thy G-d.*[5] The Sages commented:[6] "Rabbi Nathan says, 'This verse[5] constitutes a refutation to those heretics who say that two powers govern the universe. When the Holy One, blessed be He, stood on Mount Sinai and proclaimed, *I am the Eternal thy G-d,*[5] who protested against Him?'"

According to the plain meaning of Scripture, the verse mentions the Divine Name three times: *the Eternal our G-d, the Eternal is One.*[1] Had Scripture said, "Hear, O Israel: the Eternal is One," the nations of

---

(1) Deuteronomy 6:4. As explained by Rashi: "The Eternal, Who is [now, only] our G-d and not the G-d of [other] nations, will eventually be acknowledged as the One [and only] Eternal, as it is said, *On that day, shall the Eternal be One, and His Name One*" (Zechariah 14:9). See Ramban, Commentary on the Torah, Deuteronomy, pp. 76-77. (2) See above in *Eivel* (Mourning), Note 42 for an explanation of the term *Sh'ma.* (3) Our author is referring to the Ten Commandments in Deuteronomy 5:6-18. The section of the *Sh'ma* is stated *ibid.*, 6:4-9. (4) This is in consonance with the opinions of Ramban, who explained in his Commentary on the Torah, Deuteronomy, p. 76: "Contained in the commandment *I am the Eternal thy G-d* is the principle of the Unity of G-d." This interpretation contrasts with the opinion of Maimonides, who maintained that this verse is the source of the commandment to believe in G-d, the Creator of everything in existence. Maimonides contended that G-d's Unity is derived from the verse of *Sh'ma* itself. See "The Commandments," Vol. I, pp. 1-3. (5) Deuteronomy 5:6. (6) Mechilta, *Bachodesh,* 5. It is quoted also by Ramban, Commentary on the Torah, Deuteronomy, p. 76.

the world could have countered that this verse refers to their own deity. Therefore, it was necessary to state *our G-d* to specify the G-d of Israel. Had the Torah said, "The Eternal our G-d is One," the nations could have countered, "It is true that the G-d of Israel is One, but our deity is also one." Therefore, it was necessary to state, *The Eternal our G-d, the Eternal is One,* thus teaching that only the Eternal, Who is the G-d of Israel, is One and there is nothing like Him either in the heavens above or on the earth below. That Moses said, *Hear, O Israel: the Eternal our G-d,* rather than "your G-d" as he does elsewhere,[7] is because he wanted to include himself [in the charge directed to all Israel].

The matter of G-d's Unity is called "the worship of the heart," similar to the statement, *And to serve Him with all your heart.*[8] Thus, the verse[1] uses the expression *Sh'ma* because it connotes both hearing and understanding. That is to say, one should direct his heart to the Unity he is proclaiming to his ear. Since no one can tell whether his heart and lips are speaking the same language or he is merely proffering lip service, the letters *ayin* and *dalet,* the last letters in the words *Sh'ma* (Hear) and *Echad* (One) respectively, are written large to constitute the word *eid* (witness). This signifies that G-d is witnessing the proclamation, as it is written, *And I am He that knoweth, and am witness, saith the Eternal.*[9] Accordingly, a person should take heed to remove from his heart all material thought when he proclaims the Unity of G-d.

This verse has still another meaning, which is to be included among its select and excellent interpretations. The great Rabbi Eliezer of Worms[10] wrote: *"The Eternal our G-d, the Eternal is One.*[1] *The Eternal* before the world's creation, *our G-d* in this world, *the Eternal* in the World to Come—He is *One* in all the worlds."

---

(7) E.g., *Hear, O Israel: thou art to pass over the Jordan this day . . . Know therefore that the Eternal thy G-d,* etc. (Deuteronomy 9:1-3). (8) *Ibid.,* 11:13. This verse is stated after the section dealing with the Unity of G-d, and is recited in the second section of the *Sh'ma.* (9) Jeremiah 29:23. (10) Rabbi Eliezer of Worms was a disciple of the famous Rabbi Yehudah the Pious, author of the *Sefer Hachasidim*

The subject of the Unity of G-d is divided into four stages.[11] "The first stage is attained by the young and simple-minded who do not know the meaning of faith. Consequently, the true meaning of G-d's Unity is not established in their hearts. The second stage is one's acceptance of the Unity of G-d as defined by tradition. However, one's true knowledge thereof is thus not based on his own intellect and understanding, and he is like a blind man who, following a sighted person may stumble or go astray after him. By the same token, one who accepts G-d's Unity based only on tradition may fall victim to the belief in duality, for upon hearing the arguments and misconceptions of. the heretics, he might change his opinion or unwittingly be led astray. It was for this reason that the Sages said,[12] 'Be diligent in the study of the Torah, and know what to answer the disbeliever.' The third stage is the declaration of G-d's Unity in one's thought and speech when one who is still unable to distinguish between the true Unity and mere transitory unity can nevertheless rationally prove G-d's true Existence. This type of person is like a traveler who has a far distance to go. Upon arriving at a crossroad he does not recognize the correct road to his destination. He will never reach his goal because of his lack of knowledge. The fourth stage is the declaration of G-d's Unity in thought and speech when one is able to bring proofs and verify the truth thereof by rational thinking and correct arguments. This stage is the most perfect and acceptable. With regard thereto, Scripture has charged us, *Know this day, and lay it to thy heart, that the Eternal, He*

(Book of the Pious). Rabbi Eliezer wrote many works on the esoteric teachings of the Cabala, some of which are cited by Ramban in his "Letter to the French Rabbis." See Writings and Discourses, pp. 399-400. (11) From this point until the end of the paragraph, our author quotes from Rabbeinu Bachya ibn Pekuda's *Chovoth Halevavoth* (Duties of the Heart), one of the classic works on the philosophy of Judaism. Ibn Pekuda wrote his work about the year 1040 Common Era, 250 years before Rabbeinu Bachya ben Asher was engaged in the writing of Kad Hakemach. On the general significance of these two sages, see my article in Shanah B'shanah, 5732, pp. 232-242. (12) Aboth 2:14.

is G-d in heaven above and upon the earth beneath; there is none else."[13] This is what the great scholar, Rabbi Bachya ibn Pekuda of blessed memory, wrote in his Chovoth Halevavoth.[11]

The law requires mental affirmation of G-d's Unity. One must proclaim in his heart and mind that G-d is the Sole Master of heaven, earth, and the four corners of the world. The Sages commented in Tractate Berachoth,[14] "Rabbi Yirmiyah was sitting before Rabbi Zeira[15] and noticed that the latter was considerably prolonging the word *Echad* (One).[1] Rabbi Yirmiyah asked him, 'Why is all this prolonging necessary?' Rabbi Zeira retorted, 'To what extent should it then be prolonged?' Rabbi Yirmiyah answered, 'It should be sufficiently prolonged to acknowledge His Kingdom in heaven, upon the earth, and in the four corners of the world.' "

In Tractate Berachoth,[14] it is also written, "One who prolongs the utterance of the word *Echad* (One) shall have his days and years prolonged for him. Rabbi Acha bar Yaakov[15] said, 'He should prolong the word *Echad* at the letter *dalet*.' Rav Ashi said, 'This is true, but he should not hurry the utterance of the letter *cheth*, as he should the letter *aleph*.' " If he hurries the letter *cheth*, the entire word *Echad* will be disarranged and he will not have uttered it properly. The mystics possess a great secret concerning [the three letters of the word *Echad*], which explains why we hurry the utterance of the *aleph* and not the *cheth*, and why we prolong the *dalet*. Each letter [of the word *Echad*] contains an essential principle and profound doctrine in the root of the Unity.

After the utterance of the *Sh'ma*, the Sages added the statement, "Blessed be the Name of His glorious Kingdom forever and ever." Since this statement was not mentioned by Moses in the Torah, why was it ordained by the Sages? The answer is stated in Tractate

---

(13) Deuteronomy 4:39.   (14) Berachoth 13 b.   (15) "Zeira," is the reading in the Talmud manuscript, but our editions of the Gemara have "Chiya bar Abba."

Berachoth[16] and Tractate Pesachim:[17] *"And Jacob called to his sons.[18]* Jacob desired to reveal the end,[19] but the Divine Presence departed from him. Jacob then said, 'Perhaps one or more of my children are unworthy, just as my father Abraham begot the unworthy Ishmael, and my father Isaac begot the wicked Esau.' His sons then proclaimed, *'Hear, O Israel: the Eternal our G-d, the Eternal is One.* Just as there is only the One G-d in your heart, so is there only the One G-d in our hearts.' At that moment, the patriarch exclaimed, 'Blessed be the Name of His glorious Kingdom forever and ever.' The Rabbis said: 'What shall we do [regarding Jacob's exclamation]? Shall we say it [immediately after the *Sh'ma* as he did]? Moses did not. Shall we then not say it? Yet our patriarch Jacob did!' Therefore, the Rabbis ordained that it should be recited silently." The explanation of [this difference in behavior between Jacob and Moses] is that our patriarch Jacob required the Holy Spirit to rest upon him [in order for him to prophesy]. Since it had departed from him, he exclaimed, "Blessed be the Name of His glorious Kingdom," [in an effort to have it restored]. Moses our teacher, however, was always prepared for prophecy and invested with "garments of royalty." Therefore, he did not need to mention "Blessed be the Name of His glorious Kingdom." This is clear to all who have knowledge of the mystic teachings of the Torah.

Of the three sections contained in the *Sh'ma*, the first two—*Hear, O Israel,*[1] *And it shall come to pass, if ye shall hearken*[8] — are in sequential order as they appear in the Torah. However, the third section of the *Sh'ma—And the Eternal spoke*[20]— is stated in the Torah prior to

---

(16) The passage quoted is not found in our editions of Tractate Berachoth. (17) Pesachim 56 a. (18) Genesis 49:1. (19) The reading in our editions of the Gemara is "the end of [the servitude of] the Right Hand," which Rashi explains as the end of time "when His Right Hand will be restored [in defense of His people] which [in the absence of the Temple] *He hath drawn back His Right Hand from before the enemy"* (Lamentations 2:3). In other words, Jacob was about to reveal to his children the time when the Messianic era would occur, but at that point the Divine Presence departed from him and he began to speak of other things. (20) Numbers 15:37.

the first two. The reason for this order, as explained by the Sages,[21] is that the section *Hear, O Israel* precedes the others because first, it contains the duty of accepting the yoke of the Kingdom of Heaven, and second, it contains the commandments of studying the words of Torah, teaching them to our children, and fulfilling them— *Tefillin*[22] and *Mezuzah.*[23] The second section, *And it shall come to pass, if ye shall hearken,*[8] contains the commandments to teach the Torah to our children and to fulfill the precepts. The section, *And the Eternal spoke,*[20] contains only the duty of fulfilling the commandments, as it is said, *And they should make them fringes in the corners of their garments.*[24]

At the end of the first chapter in Tractate Berachoth, the Sages said,[25] "The section of *Tzitzith*[20] was incorporated in the reading of the *Sh'ma* because it embodies these five topics: the commandment to wear *Tzitzith,* the Exodus from Egypt,[26] the yoke of the commandments,[27] and the exhortations against unchaste thoughts, and idolatrous ideas. We have been taught: The verse, *And that ye go not about after your own heart,*[28] refers to heresy, as it states, *The fool hath said in his heart, There is no G-d.*[29] The verse, *And after your own eyes,*[28] refers to unchaste thoughts, as it states, *And Samson said unto his father: Get her for me, for she pleaseth me well.*[30] The verse, *After which ye use to go astray,*[28] refers to idolatrous ideas, as it is said, *And they went astray after the Baalim.*"[31]

The times designated for the reading of the *Sh'ma* are in the morning at the rising of the sun,[32] and in the evening when the stars appear.

---

(21) Berachoth 13 a. (22) Deuteronomy 6:8. (23) *Ibid.,* Verse 9. (24) Numbers 15:38. (25) Berachoth 12 b. (26) Numbers 15:41. (27) *Ibid.,* Verse 40. *That ye may remember and do all My commandments.* (28) *Ibid.,* Verse 39. (29) Psalms 14:1. (30) Judges 14:3. The literal expression *for she pleaseth 'mine eyes'* is the source for the Talmudic saying, although the following verse clearly states, it was *at the prompting of G-d that he was seeking an occasion to quarrel with the Philistines.* (Verse 4). However, Samson's words *'she pleaseth mine eyes'* is considered an unchaste expression. (31) *Ibid.,* 8:33. (32) This is in accordance with the custom of "the conscientiously pious men

The Torah established the time of the reading of the *Sh'ma* in accordance with the appearance of these lights to teach us that the luminaries
have a Supreme Master. We have been commanded to proclaim G-d's
Unity by reciting the *Sh'ma* at these times when night changes to day
and day to night because G-d is the Supreme One Who never changes.
Accordingly, the reading of the *Sh'ma* in the morning takes place when
the sun begins to shine. According to our Rabbis, this is the time when
the conscientiously pious people³³ "used to finish the reading of the
Sh'ma with the first sparklings of the rising sun, as it is said, *They shall
fear Thee at* [the appearance of] *the sun.*"³⁴ The reading of the *Sh'ma*
in the evening takes place when stars appear. This is Scripturally supported by the verse, *Lift up your eyes on high, and see: Who hath
created these?*³⁵ This is why Scripture says on the fourth day of Creation, *And they* [the luminaries] *shall be for signs, and for seasons,*³⁶
meaning that they will serve as signs for the reading of the *Sh'ma*.
When they come forth to shine upon the world, men will give thanks to
G-d, Who created them and the world with ten Sayings³⁷ and Who
took us out of Egypt and proclaimed the Ten Commandments to us at
Sinai.

For this reason, the Ten Commandments are alluded to in the sections of the *Sh'ma*³⁸ as follows: "The First Commandment, *I am the
Eternal thy G-d,*³⁹ corresponds to Hear, *O Israel: the Eternal our G-d,
the Eternal is One.*¹ The Second Commandment, *Thou shalt have no
other gods,*⁴⁰ corresponds to *Lest ye turn aside, and serve other gods.*⁴¹

---

who conclude the reading of the *Sh'ma* with the first sparklings of the rising sun"
(Berachoth 9 b). (33) The Talmudic term for "conscientiously pious people" is
vathikim, which Rashi interprets to mean "humble people who cherish the fulfillment
of a commandment." (34) Psalms 72:5. So explained by Rashi in Berachoth 9 b.
(35) Isaiah 40:26. At the appearance of the stars, one is to be reminded of Him Who
created them. (36) Genesis 1:14. (37) See above in *Chathan* (The Bridegroom),
Note 50. (38) Yerushalmi Berachoth I, 8 with certain variations. (39) Exodus
20:2. (40) *Ibid.*, Verse 3. (41) Deuteronomy 11:16.

The Third Commandment, *Thou shalt not take the Name of the Eternal thy G-d in vain,*[42] corresponds to *Thou shalt love the Eternal thy G-d,*[43] for one who loves a king will not swear falsely by his name. The Fourth Commandment, *Remember the Sabbath-day,*[44] corresponds to the verse, *That ye may remember and do all My commandments.*[45] Rabbi[46] says, This verse alludes to the Sabbath, the observance of which is equal to all the commandments, as it is said, *Thou camest down also upon Mount Sinai and gavest* to Thy people *Torah and the commandments,*[47] *and madest known unto them Thy holy Sabbath.*[48] Rabbi Eleazar bar Avina says, This verse informs us that the observance of the Sabbath is equal to all the commandments. The Fifth Commandment, *Honor thy father and thy mother that thy days be long*[49] corresponds to the assurance *that your days may be multiplied.*[50] The Sixth Commandment, *Thou shalt not murder,*[51] corresponds to the expression, *ye shall perish quickly,*[52] for one who murders will himself be killed. The Seventh Commandment, *Thou shalt not commit adultery,*[53] corresponds to the statement *That ye go not about after your own heart and your eyes.*[28] Rabbi Levi said that the heart and the eye are the two agents of sin. It is thus written, *My son, give me thy heart, and let thine eyes observe my ways.*[54] The Holy One, blessed be He, said, 'If you give Me your heart and your eye, then I know that you are Mine.' The Eighth Commandment, *Thou shalt not steal,*[55] corresponds to *You shall gather in 'thy' corn,*[56] which excludes the corn of your neighbor. The Ninth Commandment, *Thou shalt not bear false witness,*[57] corresponds to *I am the Eternal thy G-d.*[26] It is further written, *And the Eternal G-d is the true G-d, He is the living G-d.*[58] Rabbi

(42) Exodus 20:7.   (43) Deuteronomy 6:5.   (44) Exodus 20:8.   (45) Numbers 15:40.   (46) See above in *Ahavah* (Love of G-d), Note 42.   (47) Nehemiah 9:13.   (48) *Ibid.,* Verse 14. The Sabbath is thus singled out of all the commandments, indicating that it is equal to all of them.   (49) Exodus 20:12.   (50) Deuteronomy 11:21.   (51) Exodus 20:13.   (52) Deuteronomy 11:17.   (53) Exodus 20:14.   (54) Proverbs 23:26.   (55) Exodus 20:15.   (56) Deuteronomy 11:14.   (57) Exodus 20:16.   (58) Jeremiah 10:10.

Levi said that the Holy One, blessed be He, said, 'If you have testified falsely against your neighbor, I consider it as if you have testified against Me that I have not created heaven and earth.' The Tenth Commandment, *Thou shalt not covet thy neighbor's house,*[59] corresponds to *Thou shalt write them upon the doorposts of 'thy' house, and upon 'thy' gates,*[23] which excludes the house of your neighbor." Thus far the Yerushalmi.[38]

It was Rabbi Akiba's opinion[60] that the proper intention of heart is required throughout the entire first section of the reading of the *Sh'ma.* His view was based upon the verse, *And these words, which I command thee this day, shall be upon thy heart.*[61] The expression *and these words* refers to the love of G-d, which was mentioned in the preceding verse, and His Unity. The additional words *which I command you this day* lead one to understand that this entire section requires proper intention of heart. The Rabbis, however, concluded that proper intention is principally needed for the utterance of the first verse only, as the Gemara states,[60] "*Hear O Israel: the Eternal our G-d, the Eternal is One.*[1] Intention of the heart is required for this verse only. This is the opinion of Rabbi Meir, and Rava said that Rabbi Meir's view prevails." We consequently decide the law in accordance with Rava,[62] for he was of a later generation.[63]

It is furthermore said there,[60] "*Hear, O Israel: the Eternal our G-d, the Eternal is One.*[1] This was the reading of the *Sh'ma* of Rabbi

---

(59) Exodus 20:17.   (60) Berachoth 13 b.   (61) Deuteronomy 6:6.   (62) So stated by Maimonides in *Hilchoth K'riath Sh'ma* 2:1, and in Shulchan Aruch Orach Chaim 60, 5.   (63) This reason is stated in Tosafoth Berachoth 13 b. — Beginning with the generation of Abaya and Rava — the leading Sages of the fourth generation of Babylonian Amoraim [flourished in the second half of the fourth century, Common Era] — a decision is rendered in accordance with the opinion of a Sage of a later generation, even if it goes contrary to an opinion of a Sage of a former generation. The reason for this principle is that the Sages of the later generation in formulating their opinion, were already familiar with the one of the former generation, and if notwithstanding decided against it, the opinion of the Sage of the later generation prevails. See Yad Malachi, Nos. 167-169.

Yehudah Hanasi."[46] This statement means that Rabbi[46] interrupted his study of the Torah only for the first verse of the *Sh'ma*,[1] for it contains the essential expression of G-d's Unity and is thus the principal object of proper intention of heart. In view of the Sages' statement,[64] "One who reads 'the *Sh'ma* in its designated time will receive a reward greater than that of one who reads the Torah," Rabbi Yehudah Hanasi[46] should have interrupted his Torah study [to read all three sections of the *Sh'ma*]. However, this saying of the Sages applies only to an individual's study of Torah. The reward for public study of Torah exceeds that of the timely recitation of the *Sh'ma*, and the study of Torah by Rabbi Yehudah Hanasi, was public study. An alternative explanation is that this saying of the Sages applies only to the first verse,[1] while the rest of the *Sh'ma* is equivalent to the reading of Torah. Hence, even an individual whose sole occupation is the study of Torah need not interrupt his studies except for this first verse alone. Certainly, then, a great man in Israel such as Rabbeinu Hakadosh,[46] whose Torah study was public, [need not interrupt his studies for anything more than the utterance of the first verse].

Our Sages directed that a person should properly enunciate the letters of the three sections of the *Sh'ma*, as it is said, *"V'limad'tem (And ye shall teach them),*[65] meaning that the teaching should be *tamah* (whole). That is to say, one must allow an interval between those words which may otherwise run into each other."[66] Similarly one should carefully utter each of the 248 words contained in the *Sh'ma*, which correspond to the 248 limbs of the body.

The Sages commented[67] that the reading of the *Sh'ma* is like the signed order of a king. When a mortal king sends his signed dictate to his subjects, all stand to hear it, [and uncover their heads]. Yet reading

---

(64) Berachoth 10 b.   (65) Deuteronomy 11:19.   (66) Berachoth 15 b. An example of letters which may run into each other is *al levavcha* (upon thy heart). Reading it hurriedly, one may omit one *lamed* from either the first or the last word.   (67) Vayikra Rabbah 27:6.

the *Sh'ma* requires no such civilities. Only proper intention of heart and attentiveness to its letters are required, and thus people fulfill their obligation.

The reward of reciting the *Sh'ma* is great. The Sages have established[68] that one inherits both this world by virtue of his recitation of the *Sh'ma*, and the World to Come by his utterance of the Eighteen Benedictions which follow the *Sh'ma*.

It is well known that the principle of G-d's Unity will be universally recognized in the era of the Messiah. Presently, in the era of the exile and its subjugation, the signs of G-d's Unity are not discernible, for one person worships the sun, and another the moon or the stars and constellations. One worships fire, and another worships water. Thus, heresy increases in the world as the truth is denied, and opinions are altered as the religions change. In the Messianic era, however, many of the kingdoms will be abolished and all creeds will turn to the One Faith. The world will exist in perfection under the Kingdom of G-d, and all will agree to worship G-d alone *that they may all call upon the Name of the Eternal, to serve Him with one consent.*[69] The Unity of our G-d will then be made known to all nations, as the prophet assured us of the future, *And the Eternal will be King over all the earth; in that day shall the Eternal be One, and His Name One.*[70]

---

(68) Berachoth 16 b.   (69) Zephania 3:9.   (70) Zecharia 14:9.

יצר הרע
The Evil Inclination

The harm caused by the evil inclination, which is implanted in man while in his mother's womb, is like the damage wrought by leprosy or fire. It begins trivially and spreads widely / A person should be extremely vigilant regarding the evil inclination and even more so regarding matters of immorality / The seven names of the evil inclination / The Men of the Great Assembly nullified the evil inclination of idolatry, but they did not void the desire for sensuality / One who is careful to worship G-d sincerely will be able to ward off the power of the evil inclination and even the angel of death, for Satan, the evil inclination, and the angel of death are all one and the same.

The Evil Inclination

IF THE SPIRIT OF THE RULER RISE UP AGAINST THEE,
LEAVE NOT THY PLACE, FOR GENTLENESS ALLAYETH
GREAT OFFENSES.[1]

This verse warns man not to follow the evil inclination. Even if it entices and allures him with its vanities, even if it entreats him, he should not heed it. Scripture calls the evil inclination *ruler* in the above verse and also refers to it as *king*, as it is said, *Better is a poor and wise child than an old and foolish king,*[2] for the evil inclination is the reigning power on the earth and ruler of all the lower creatures. Its power is invested in man while he is in his mother's womb. The Sages expounded[3] *"There shall be no strange god in thee.*[4] What *strange god* is there in the body of man? I must say that it is the evil inclination."

It is common knowledge that the harm caused by the evil inclination is like the damage wrought by leprosy or fire. They begin trivially and spread widely, and so it is with the evil inclination. If one hearkens to it regarding a minor transgression, he will eventually commit increasingly severer sins. Ultimately, the evil inclination will lead him to idolatry. The Sages commented,[3] "This is the way of the evil inclination. Today,

---

(1) Ecclesiastes 10:4. The way of gentleness to allay a ruler's anger — or the wisdom to abate the temptations of sin by the evil inclination — are here clearly suggested. Our author uses this verse as a basis to illustrate how a wise heart brings its possessor a judicious enjoyment of the right mode of life. (2) *Ibid.*, 4:13. The *wise child* is the good inclination which comes to a person until he is thirteen years of age. He is *poor,* because the members of his body reject his authority (Rashi *ibid.*). (3) Shabbath 105 b. (4) Psalms 81:10.

it tells man, 'Commit that minor sin,' Tomorrow, it will tell him, 'Go and worship idols,' and he will do so." Therefore, Scripture states, *If the spirit,* which is *the ruler,*[5] *rise up against thee,* etc.[1]

Perhaps Scripture designates the evil inclination as the spirit to intimate what the Sages said,[6] "Satan, the evil inclination, and the angel of death are all one and the same." The verse is thus stating: If the evil inclination seeks to overpower you and to constrain you from doing something which is proper, *leave not thy place.*[1] That is to say, do not cease your study of the Torah and the good deeds in which you were engaged, for your intellect will regain mastery over your desire and you will *allay great offenses.*

Alternatively, *leave not thy place*[1] may refer to G-d. In that case the verse is saying: If the evil inclination wishes to overwhelm you, do not leave the service of G-d, the *Makom* (Existence or Preserver) of the world.[7] Instead, you should strengthen yourself in His service and free yourself from the grip of the evil spirit. Thus, you will *allay great offenses.*

A person should be exceedingly vigilant regarding the evil inclination and even more so regarding matters of immorality.

The Sages commented in Tractate Succah[8] "Scripture designates the evil inclination by these seven terms: the evil one, the unclean one, the uncircumcised one, the enemy, the stumbling block, the stone, and the waiting one. G-d called it evil, as it is said, *The bent of man's heart is evil from his youth.*[9] Moses called it the uncircumcised one, as it is said,

(5) Here, *ruler* is understood as the mortal monarch of the land. If the monarch rises against you, enticing you to commit a sin etc. — At the time of the writing of this work, this was indeed a point to remember. Very often the state powers would use all their efforts to have the Jews give up their religion. See Ramban, Writings and Discourses, pp. 653-655. Our author uses this theme to remind his audience to remain steadfast in their loyalty to the Jewish faith by rejecting the temptations of the king of the land.   (6) Baba Bathra 16 a.   (7) *Makom* literally means "place." The verse is thus advising that if the evil inclination entices you to sin, *do not leave thy Place,* do not abandon the service of G-d.   (8) Succah 52 a.   (9) Genesis 8:21.

And ye shall circumcise the foreskin of your heart.[10] David called it the unclean one, as it is said, *Create in me a clean heart,*[11] which implies that there is an unclean heart. Solomon called it the enemy, as it is said, *If thine enemy be hungry, give him bread to eat, and if he be thirsty, give him water to drink.*[12] *For thou wilt heap coals of fire upon his head, and the Eternal 'y'shaleim lach' (will reward thee).*[13] Read *y'shaleim lach* (will reward thee) as *yashlimeno lach* (He will assist thee) [in overcoming the evil inclination]. Isaiah called it the stumbling block, as it is said. *Take up the stumbling block out of the way of My people.*[14] Ezekiel called it the stone, as it is said. *And I will remove the stony heart out of their flesh.*[15] Joel called it the hidden one [which constantly lies in wait in the heart of man], as it is said, *And I will remove far off from you the hidden one.*[16] Rabbi Shimon ben Lakish said, 'The evil inclinations renews its struggle against man every day and desires to slay him, as it is said, *The wicked watcheth the righteous, and seeketh to slay him.*[17] Were it not for the help of G-d, man would not be able to resist the evil inclination, as it is said, *The Eternal will not leave him in his hand.*'[18] In the academy of Rabbi Yishmael, it was taught, 'If the offensive one [i.e., the evil inclination] meets you, drag it along into the house of learning. If it is of stone, it will melt; if it is of iron, it will shatter, as it is said, *Is not My word like as fire? saith the Eternal, and like a hammer that breaketh the rock in pieces?*'[19] Rabbi Shmuel bar Nachmani said in the name of Rabbi Yonathan, 'At first, the evil inclination entices man to sin. Ultimately,

(10) Deuteronomy 10:16.   (11) Psalms 51:12. See above *Taharath Haleiv* (Purity of Heart).   (12) Proverbs 25:21. Rashi, *ibid.*, elucidates: "If your evil spirit entices you to sin, give him *bread.* That is, redouble your efforts in the study of Torah. *Give him water to drink* refers to the waters of the Torah."—Torah is compared to bread, for just as bread is the staff of physical life, so is the Torah the support of the spiritual life. It is also likened to water, for just as water runs from a high to a low place, so is the Torah sustained only in a humble person (Taanith 7 a).   (13) Proverbs 25:22.   (14) Isaiah 57:14.   (15) Ezekiel 11:19.   (16) Joel 2:20.   (17) Psalms 37:32.   (18) *Ibid.*, Verse 33.   (19) Jeremiah 23:29.

it bears witness against him for those same sins.' Rabbi Asi said,[20] 'At first, the evil inclination appears as thin as the strand of a cobweb, but at the end, it is as thick as a wagon rope, as it is said, *Woe unto them that draw iniquity with cords of vanity, and sin as it were with a cart rope.'* "[21] Thus far from Tractate Succah.

Elsewhere, the Sages commented,[22] "Rabbi Yitzchak said, 'At first, the evil inclination is called a stranger, then a guest, and ultimately, is called master of the house. Thus, [Nathan the prophet said to King David], *And there came a traveler unto the rich man, and he spared to take of his own flock [and of his own herd to dress for the wayfaring man that was come to him].'* "[23] In Midrash Tehillim, the Sages said,[24] *"For He knoweth our inclination.*[25] Woe unto the dough that the baker declares as bad."[26]

Because the serpent was the evil inclination's instrument in misleading Eve, the Sages commented that the serpent will have no cure in the World to Come. It is said in Midrash Tehillim:[27] *"And he shall be like a tree planted by streams of water.*[28] This refers to Adam, the first man, whom G-d took and placed in the Garden of Eden. *That bringeth forth its fruit in its season.*[28] This refers to Cain. *And whose leaf doth not wither.*[28] This refers to Abel. *And in whatsoever he doeth*

---

(20) Succah 51 a. (21) Isaiah 5:18. (22) Bereshith Rabbah 22:11. Essentially, this text is also found in Succah 52 b, but our author apparently preferred this particular passage because it presents the same thought more lucidly. (23) II Samuel 12:4. Thus, the stranger is first the *wayfaring man* and finally becomes *the man that was come to him* to stay. (24) Midrash Tehillim, 103. (25) Psalms 103:14. (26) This Midrash compares a human being to dough, because he is fashioned by G-d out of two inclinations — one evil and the other good — just like dough, which is basically composed of two ingredients, water and flour. (27) Midrash Tehillim, 1. In view of the statement with which the author precedes this text of Midrash Tehillim — namely, "Because the serpent was the evil inclination etc." — the main thought behind the teaching that the serpent will have no cure in the World to Come may thus be a restatement of the fact that a person who is instrumental to make another person sin, will have no share in the future world. (28) Psalms 1:3.

he shall prosper.[28] This refers to Seth.[29] *Not so the wicked.*[30] This refers to the serpent. *Therefore the wicked shall not stand in judgment.*[31] All but the serpent will have a cure [at the time of resurrection] in the World to Come."

In the days of the Men of the Great Assembly,[32] the Sages prayed for the abolition of the evil inclination, as it is related in Tractate Sanhedrin.[33] It means that the power of the evil inclination in matters of idolatry was nullified.[34] However, they did not want altogether to abolish sensuality. Had they done so, propagation would have ceased and the existence of mankind would have been endangered. Hence, they allowed sensuality to continue to exist for the sake of the procreation of the human race and for the sake of reward [for withstanding the evil inclination for forbidden sexual activity].[35]

One who is careful to worship G-d sincerely will be able to ward off the evil inclination, whose power is deadly. Instead, he will rule over the power of death, as the Sages commented in Tractate Kethuboth,[36] "Rabbi Yehoshua ben Levi was host to the angel of death," It is related there in the Gemara that Rabbi Yehoshua took away the angel of death's knife. In other words, the angel's power was given over into the

(29) Since mankind was founded by Adam's son Seth—Noah was his direct descendant—the Midrash appropriately applied the verse, *And in whatsoever he doeth he shall prosper,* to him. On the other hand, Adam's first son, Abel, was killed by his brother Cain, and the latter's descendants all perished in the Flood. (30) Psalms 1:4. (31) *Ibid.,* Verse 5. (32) When the Jews returned from the Babylonian captivity to rebuild the Second Temple, the leadership of the nation was assumed by this body of 120 men. Successors to the prophets, they abolished the evil inclination which led to idolatry. They further established many fundamental regulations, such as the text of the daily liturgy which is still in use today. They were active through the Persian period and were eventually supplanted by the Tannaim at the beginning of the Grecian period (333 Before Common Era). The era of the Tannaim lasted for 500 years, until the Writing of the Mishnah by Rabbi Yehudah Hanasi. (33) Senhedrin 64 a. (34) Thus, the history during the Second Temple is completely free of any trace of idolatry among the masses of Jewish people. (35) However, their efforts in this respect were of avail that one is not sensually aroused toward relatives. (36) Kethuboth 77 b.

Rabbi's hand, so that he was powerless to slay. G-d then told the Rabbi, "Return it to him, for death is necessary for mankind." Had G-d not so directed, Rabbi Yehoshua would have abolished death forever. The Sages explicitly stated,[6] "Satan, the evil inclination, and the angel of death are all one and the same." We have been assured that in the World to Come, G-d will remove Satan from the world and death will be swallowed up forever. Thus, the prophet says, *And I will remove far off from you the hidden one.*[16] The Sages interpreted this verse as follows:[8] "*The hidden one* refers to the evil inclination, which lies in wait for man. *G-d will drive him into a land barren and desolate,*[16] a place where there are no people for Satan to tempt. *With his face toward the eastern sea.*[16] This alludes to the fact that Satan set his eyes on the First Temple and destroyed it. *And his hinder part toward the western sea.*[16] Satan set his eyes on the Second Temple and destroyed it, and he also killed the scholars who lived at that time . . . *That his foulness may come up, and his ill savor may come up.*[16] This means that Satan does not trouble the nations of the world but tempts only the Israelites."[37]

The Sages commented in Tractate Sanhedrin,[38] "One who slays his evil inclination and confesses [his sins][39] is considered as if he honored G-d both in this world and in the World to Come, for it is said, *Whoso offereth the sacrifice of thanksgiving honoreth Me, and to him that ordered his way aright will I show the salvation of G-d.*"[40]

---

(37) The thought suggested is that Satan who tempts people to sin is mainly concerned with those people who are under the obligation to observe the commandments. Hence, his chief concern is with the Israelites who are duty bound to observe all the 613 commandments, whereas such an obligation does not rest upon the nations of the world.   (38) Sanhedrin 43 b.   (39) That is, "he slays his evil inclination altogether and confesses his sins of the past" (Maharsha, *ibid.*).   (40) Psalms 50:23. In Hebrew, the word *y'chabdan'ni (honoreth Me)* repeats the letter *nun*, to indicate the double honor conferred upon G-d when one slays his evil inclination altogether and confesses his sins of the past.

כבוד אב ואם
Honoring Father and Mother

This precept is one of the rational commandments. Scripture, however, has not explained the precise meaning of this honor. We must therefore derive its requirements from the honor we owe our Supreme Father, concerning which we are directed in the commandment, 'I am the Eternal thy G-d' / The duties entailed in this commandment as designated by the Rabbis / The great importance attached to the fulfillment of this precept / The reason the Torah promises longevity is only the by-product of the fulfillment of this obligation. The essential reward for its fulfillment will be conferred in the World to Come.

Honoring Father and Mother

HONOR THY FATHER AND THY MOTHER, THAT YOUR
DAYS MAY BE LONG UPON THE LAND WHICH THE ETER-
NAL THY G-D GIVETH THEE.[1]

This is one of the rational commandments of the Torah. Scripture, however, has not explained the precise meaning of this honor. We must therefore derive its requirements from the honor we owe our One Supreme Father, concerning which we are directed in the commandment, *I am the Eternal Thy G-d.*[2] The Eternal is thus stating: "Just as I have first commanded you with respect to My honor, so do I command you concerning the honor of your father and mother, my partners in your formation." His intention is to establish that just as we are commanded to acknowledge the One Father and His existence, so we are obligated to acknowledge our father and mother, who begot us. Just as one is charged by G-d, *Thou shalt have no other gods before Me,*[3] in order not to deny Him, one is similarly obligated not to deny his father and mother by saying that some other person is his parent. Just as it says, *Thou shalt not take the Name of the Eternal thy G-d in vain,*[4] thus prohibiting swearing in G-d's Name falsely or in vain, one is

(1) Exodus 20:12. This is the fifth of the Ten Commandments, and is engraved at the end of the first Tablet which deals specifically with our duties towards G-d. Honor of parents is thus the bridge leading from duties towards G-d to those we owe to our fellow man, being the theme of the commandments mentioned on the second Tablet. Thus, only where parents are honored can a society safe from crime exist and the blessing of longevity be assured. (2) *Ibid.*, Verse 2. (3) *Ibid.*, Verse 3. See Ramban, Commentary on the Torah, Exodus, pp. 318-319. (4) *Ibid.*, Verse 7.

similarly obligated not to swear by the life or name of his parents falsely or in vain. Furthermore, one must not serve his parents for the sake
of an eventual inheritance, for some honor which may be derived from
such service, or for any other selfish consideration.

There are many duties entailed in this commandment, as our Rabbis explained. Thus they said,[5] "One is obligated to give his parents
food and drink, to clothe them, to shelter them, to take them out and
to bring them in." The expression *honor* also applies to financial
assistance for it is said, *Honor the Eternal with thy substance.*[6] One can
honor G-d by financial means in giving charity to the poor and by set-
ting aside heave-offerings, tithes,[7] gleanings, the forgotten sheaf, and
corners of the field. Similarly, one is obligated to give money to his
parents for their needs, if they have none. If the son has no money [to
spare for this purpose], he must strive and even toil to support them.
The Sages commented,[8] "The duty towards a parent is greater than
that towards G-d. Concerning G-d, it is said, *Honor the Eternal with
thy substance*[6] — if you have the means to do so. However, regarding
the honor due a father and mother, Scripture does not express the
obligation in that way, for even if you must go begging from door to
door, you are obligated to provide them with support."

In Tractates Kiddushin[8] and Abodah Zarah,[9] the Sages related:
"Rabbi Eliezer was asked to define the extent of the duty of honoring a
father and mother. He replied, 'Go and see what a non-Jew, Dama the
son of Nesina of Ashkelon, did to honor his father. The Sages once
desired to purchase from him certain precious stones for the High

---

(5) Kiddushin 31 b.   (6) Proverbs 3:9. Thus one should use his wealth in a manner
approved by G-d, such as helping the poor, etc., as the text continues, or in a manner
bestowing glory to the Creator. Similarly, one is to use his bounty in a manner to provide for the welfare and dignified way of life of his parents.   (7) This is a general term
which includes the first tithe of the Levites, the second tithe which had to be consumed
by the owner in Jerusalem, and the poorman's tithe. See Ramban, Commentary on the
Torah, Exodus, pp. 399-400, and Deuteronomy pp. 311-312.   (8) Kiddushin
31 a.   (9) Abodah Zarah 23 b-24 a.

Priest's ephod.[10] They offered him a profit of 600,000 dinars. Rav Kahana taught that the sum was 800,000. However, the key [to the safe where the stones were kept] was under the pillow upon which his father was sleeping. Since Dama would not disturb his father, the sale was lost. In the following year, Dama was rewarded by the birth of a red heifer[11] among his herds. The Sages of Israel came to buy it for him. He said to them, 'I know that you will pay any amount of money I ask for the red heifer, but I only wish you to make good the money I lost on account of [the honor I gave to my] father.' "

One who honors his father and mother thereby honors G-d, and one who spurns them dishonors the Glory of G-d. The Sages expounded in Tractate Kiddushin:[12] "Scripture has compared the fear of parents to the fear of Heaven. In the case of parents, it states, *Every man shall fear his mother and his father*,[13] and it is further said, *Thou shalt fear the Eternal thy G-d*.[14] Scripture compares the blasphemy of parents to that of Heaven. It is stated, *And he that curseth his father or his mother*,[15] and it is further said, *Whoever curseth his G-d*.[16] In the case of striking, the comparison is impossible.[17] It is furthermore logical that in respect of honor and fear, these three partners in the formation of the child—G-d and the person's father and mother—should be alike."

The Sages commented in Tractate Niddah,[18] "There are three partners in the formation of a child: G-d and the child's father and mother.

---

(10) Exodus 28:6-12. The ephod was a kind of apron which fastened at the back. The precious stones were inset upon its two shoulder straps.   (11) For the significance of the Red Heifer, see Numbers 19:2-22. Since the birth of a red heifer is a natural rarity, the owner could of course ask any price for it. (12) Kiddushin 30 b. (13) Leviticus 19:3. (14) Deuteronomy 6:13. (15) Exodus 21:17. (16) Leviticus 24:15. (17) "It is impossible to compare parents to Heaven in this respect, since smiting cannot apply to Heaven" (Rashi, Kiddushin 30 b). The thought suggested is as follows: Surely the comparison between G-d and parents cannot be completely alike, but logically they should be equated, for each has a share in the creation of the child, and therefore to honor and fear one's parents is to honor and fear G-d. (Maharsha, *ibid.*).   (18) Niddah 31 a.

The father provides the white substance out of which are formed the bones, sinews, nails, brain, and the white of the eyes. The mother provides the red substance for forming skin, flesh, blood, hair, and the black substance in the eye. G-d provides the spirit, the soul, physical appearance, the faculties of sight, hearing, and speech, the ability to walk, knowledge, understanding and reason." There are thus a total of ten things which are given each child by his father and mother, each of whom provide five. G-d provides ten, a quantity equal to the sum provided by both parents.

[The Sages cited instances to demonstrate the eminence accorded to this precept.] "When a man honors his father and mother, G-d says, 'I consider his act as if I were living among them and he honored Me.' "[12] Expressing the weightiness of the obligation to honor parents, Rabbi Tarphon[19] often said,[20] "Happy is the one who has not seen his parents,"[21] for it is impossible for a child to entirely fulfill his duty towards his parents, and he might thus be found at fault and guilty of sin on account of his parents. However, one who has not seen his parents and thus never incurred the obligation to honor them, will not be held accountable on the day of judgment. Finally, the Sages relate,[20] "As soon as Rav Yoseif heard the sound of his mother's footsteps, he would say, 'I will rise before the Divine Presence that is approaching.' "[22]

(19) Rabbi Tarphon was one of the leading Tannaim in the second century, Common Era. — Our versions of the Gemara attribute this saying to Rabbi Yochanan, an Amora of the first Palestinian Amoraim who were active at the beginning of the third century. The Amoraim were the Sages who interpreted the Mishnah after its redaction in the year 200. Together with their Babylonian colleagues, this era continued for about 300 years when the Gemara was written down by Rav Ashi and Ravina. The Mishnah and Gemara together constitute the Talmud. (20) Kiddushin 31 b. (21) Rabbi Yochanan was orphaned of his father and mother at his birth (*ibid.*). (22) This statement is to be understood in the light of the preceding saying, "When a man honors his father and mother, G-d says, 'I consider his act as if I were living among them and he honored Me' " (Maharsha, *ibid.*). Rav Yoseif therefore welcomed his mother's coming by greeting the Divine Presence that accompanies her.

Great is the power of the commandment of honoring parents. Its reward is certainly assured, and people can see its reward manifested in material benefits in this world. G-d will either add tranquility and success to all one's endeavors, or He will bless him with longevity, the usual reward for fulfilling this commandment. The Gaon Rav Saadia[23] explained why the Torah established longevity as the reward for this commandment. Parents sometimes live a long time and become a burden upon their children. G-d therefore proclaimed that in reward for fulfilling this commandment, *thy days may be long.*[1] That is to say: "you are to honor them and live with them. If you will begrudge their years, know that you are begrudging your own life."

The Sages commented in Midrash Mishlei:[24] *"The hoary head is a crown of glory, it is found in the way of righteousness.*[25] You derive this principle from the righteous Joseph. Because he exerted himself for the sake of his father's honor in Egypt, he merited the crown of ripe old age, as it is said, *And Joseph saw Ephraim's children of the third generation.*[26] Whence do we know that Joseph did charity? We know it from the verse which says, *And Joseph sustained his father, and his brethren."*[27]

It is common knowledge that the reward of longevity which G-d established for the fulfillment of this precept is only the by-product of the commandment which a man enjoys in this world. The essential reward for its fulfillment will be conferred in the World to Come. The Sages received a tradition:[28] *"That thy days may be long.*[1] This refers to the World to Come which will endure for eternity." In the Ten Commandments as stated in the Book of Deuteronomy, Scripture added: *and that it may go well with thee,*[29] to the commandment of honoring parents. The Sages[28] interpreted this as a reference to the "World to

(23) See above in *Hashgachah* (Divine Providence), Note 52. (24) Midrash Mishlei, end of Chapter 16. (25) Proverbs 16:31. It should be noted that the Hebrew word *Tz'dakah* here translated as *righteousness,* also means "charity." It is this latter meaning that is referred to in the text. (26) Genesis 50:23. (27) *Ibid.,* 47:12. (28) Kiddushin 39 b. (29) Deuteronomy 5:16.

Come, which is entirely good." Hence, the essential reward for fulfilling this commandment is not in this world.

The Sages commented in Tractate Chullin:[30] "Rabbi Yaakov says, 'There is no commandment in the Torah accompanied by a promise of reward to which resurrection is not appended. Concerning the honor we must give our father and mother, it is written, *That thy days may be long, and that it may go well with thee.*[29] Concerning the commandment to release the mother bird when her nest is taken, it is written, *That it may be well with thee, and that thou mayest prolong thy days.*[31] Suppose that a father sent his son to the top of a certain building to fetch the doves nesting there, and the son did go up and sent away the mother bird and took the nestlings. If, however, he fell off the building as he was returning and died as a result, where is this individual's reward of longevity and well-being? You must therefore conclude [that Scripture is assuring you] *that thy days may be long*[1] in the world that will endure eternally, *and that it may go well with thee*[29] in the world that is entirely good.' 'Perhaps,' suggests the Gemara, 'the event supposed by Rabbi Yaakov never occurred, [and if that is the case, his conclusion is unfounded]!' However, Rabbi Yaakov actually witnessed such an incident himself. The Gemara again counters, 'But perhaps the person who was killed thought of some sin, [and thus did not deserve longevity and well-being in this world]!' The explanation is that G-d does not combine the intention to sin with the sinful deed itself. 'But' persists the Gemara, 'the individual who was killed intended to worship idols. [In that case, intention is punishable], as it is written, *That I may take the House of Israel in their own heart!*[32] Rabbi Yaakov, however, reasoned as follows: 'If there is reward in this world

(30) Chullin 142 a. The thought suggested is that all commandments which are accompanied by a promise of reward must necessarily allude to reward in the hereafter. (31) Deuteronomy 22:7. (32) Ezekiel 14:5. The prophet there dealt with the sin of idolatry, declaring that sinners will be punished even if their idolatry will be *in their own heart* only.

for performing commandments, that reward should have benefited him and protected him from such sinful thought as idolatry. Hence, no harm would have befallen him. Since this was not the case, you must conclude that reward for the observance of the commandments is not conferred in this world.' The Gemara argued further, 'Did not Rabbi Eleazar say that messengers on a religious mission will not be harmed either upon going or upon their return?' The explanation is that this incident involved a broken ladder, and where danger is imminent, Rabbi Eleazar's rule does not apply, for it is written, *And Samuel said to G-d: How can I go to anoint David? If Saul will hear it, he will kill me.*[33] Rav Yoseif said, 'If Acheir (the Other One)[34] had interpreted the verse *[that it may be well with thee]*[31] as his nephew Rabbi Yaakov did, he would not have sinned.' What did Acheir see that caused him to commit apostasy? Some say that he saw an incident such as Rabbi Yaakov described, and some say that he saw the tongue of Rabbi Chutzpith the Interpreter[35] lying upon a dunghill. Acheir exclaimed, 'Oh that the mouth which brought forth pearls should now be licking dust!' He did not know, [however, that Scripture's promise of reward meant] *that it may go well with thee*[29] in the world that is entirely good, *and that thy days may be long*[29] in the world that will endure for eternity."

Commenting upon the word *'eth'* in the expression, *Honor 'eth' thy father and 'eth' thy mother,*[1] the Sages said in Tractate Kethuboth,[36] " *'Eth' thy father* refers to your stepmother. *'Eth' thy mother* refers to your stepfather. The extra *vav* in *v'eth (and) thy mother* includes your older brother."

(33) I Samuel 16:2.   (34) Acheir, was the pseudonym given by the Sages to Elisha ben Abuyah, a contemporary of Rabbi Akiba. Living in the times of the cruel persecutions by Emperor Hadrian in the middle of the second century C.E., Acheir was disturbed by problems involving Divine Providence as the text here suggests. Consequently, he turned against his faith.   (35) Rabbi Chutzpith was one of the ten martyred Sages sentenced by the Romans to death by barbaric torture for practicing their religion, which was then under Hadrian's imperial proscription.   (36) Kethuboth 103 a.

"Come and see how much G-d loves this commandment, for He does not withhold His reward[37] for its performance from anyone, whether he is righteous or wicked. We know this from wicked Esau. Because he honored his father Isaac, G-d rewarded him with all this power [in this world]. Now, if that wicked Esau was so extensively repaid by G-d because he honored his father, a righteous man who honors his parents will certainly be rewarded. G-d said, *'Who hath given Me anything beforehand, that I should repay him?*[38] Who has given honor to his father that I should not have given him children?' "[39]

The commandment to honor parents is the fifth commandment, and it concludes the first of the two Tablets. The first Tablet began with *I am the Eternal,*[2] which concerns the honor of the True Father, and concludes with *Honor thy father,*[1] who is the natural father. The true purpose of this commandment to honor parents is that we must honor G-d, our True Father. Just as the person who begets the child is called the father, so the Creator, Who brings forth the soul from His sacred spirit, and blows it into the child, is called Father. The mercies of the True Father toward His creatures are far greater than those of the natural father toward his child, as David said, *For though my father and my mother have forsaken me, the Eternal will take me up.*[40] This thought was similarly expressed by Isaiah: *For Thou art our Father, for Abraham knoweth us not, and Israel doth not acknowledge us; Thou, O Eternal, art our Father, our Redeemer from everlasting is Thy Name.*[41] He is saying: "Abraham did not know us in the Egyptian exile, nor did Jacob know us in the wilderness, for they had already passed away. Hence, You are our True Supreme Father; *our Redeemer from everlasting is Thy Name,*[41] for You have redeemed us from Egypt." Thus, Moses stated, *Is He not thy Father that hath gotten thee? Hath He not made thee, and established thee?*[42]

---

(37) The reward spoken of here is only the by-product of the commandment which a person enjoys in this world, while its true reward is reserved for the World to Come. (38) Job 41:3. (39) This entire paragraph is found in Tanchuma, *Kedoshim,* 15. (40) Psalms 27:10. (41) Isaiah 63:16. (42) Deuteronomy 32:6.

כפורים

Atonement

Part One

Suffering is an atonement for sins. The righteous are made to suffer in order for them to be completely worthy of the World to Come / The meaning of 'affliction of love' / There are afflictions of the body and those affecting property. Both serve to absolve sins in this world / Just as the suffering of the righteous is for their welfare, the tranquility enjoyed by the wicked in this world is for their detriment / The enigma of the righteous who suffer and the wicked who prosper / G-d teaches repentance to wicked men, such as Cain, et al / The explanation of the Book of Jonah.

Atonement

BEHOLD, G-D DOETH LOFTILY IN HIS POWER, WHO IS A
TEACHER LIKE HIM?[1]

Scripture is stating that G-d gives strength to the righteous and gives them fortitude to bear suffering, which is an atonement for sins. Rabbi Akiba said,[2] "Suffering is beloved."[3] It is also stated in the first chapter of Tractate Berachoth:[4] "The Holy One, blessed be He, crushes the one He loves with affliction, for it is said, *It pleased the Eternal to crush him by disease.*"[5]

Afflictions befall a person to cleanse him of his sins so that consequently, he will be completely worthy of the World to Come. Thus, for the few sins committed by the righteous, suffering befalls them for an insignificant amount of time in this temporal world and they are made to suffer physically, which is of no consequence. As a result, they will be fully worthy of being rewarded for their good deeds in the venerable era of the eternal World to Come. Moreover, their soul, a superior form to the body, will receive that reward. This was the intent of Rabbi Akiba's saying,[2] "Suffering is beloved." Through suffering, he can exchange the benefits of this world for those of the World to Come.

(1) Job 36:22. These are Elihu's words to Job, that G-d in His power does loftily for man to save him from impending doom, teaching him the good way of life in order to avoid evil (Ralbag). Our author will use the theme of this verse on the lofty purpose of Divine Providence in the suffering of the righteous as an atonement for sins. (2) Sanhedrin 101 a. (3) See Ramban, Writings and Discourses, pp. 442-443, for a full discussion of this concept and related topics. (4) Berachoth 5 a. (5) Isaiah 53:10.

320

If one cannot ascribe his afflictions to any sin he might have committed, he should consider his suffering as resulting from his neglect of the study of Torah. If he finds no such shortcoming in himself because he studies the Torah continuously and is nevertheless afflicted with suffering, he should know that these are "afflictions of love."[6]

In the first chapter of Tractate Berachoth,[4] the Sages differed over whether "afflictions of love" include those which are so severe that they prevent the sufferer from studying Torah and praying. The Rabbis came to the conclusion that both types of suffering—that which does prevent study and prayer and that which does not—are still "afflictions of love." They derived this from the verse, *"Happy is the man whom Thou chasteneth, and out of Thy law 't'lamdenu' (he should be able to study).*[7] Read the word, not as *t'lamdenu* (he should be able to study), but as *t'lamdeinu* (Thou teachest us). That is to say, out of Thy Torah, You teach us *a fortiori* that chastisement is good. It is written, *And if a man smite the eye of his bondman, or the eye of his bondwoman, and destroy it, he shall let him go free for his eye's sake.*[8] If the loss of a tooth or an eye, which is only one organ of the body, imparts freedom to the bondman, how much more do afflictions which affect all limbs of the body impart freedom and absolution from sin!"

There are afflictions of the body and those of property. Bodily afflictions are like those mentioned by the Sages in connection with Rabbeinu Hakadosh,[9] who suffered from toothache for six years.[10] Afflic-

(6) "Nevertheless, even these afflictions come for atonement and for purification from sin" (Ramban, Writings and Discourses, p. 440. (7) Psalms 94:12. (8) Exodus 21:27. The law is that a non-Israelite bondman or bondwoman regains freedom, if on account of being smitten one looses an eye, tooth, or any limb. (9) Rabbeinu Hakadosh, also called "Rabbi," refers to Yehudah Hanasi. See above in *Ahavah* (Love of G-d), Note 42. (10) Baba Metzia 85 a. The Gemara there relates that a young calf which was about to be slaughtered ran up to Rabbi for protection. Rabbi said, "Go, for you were created for that purpose." Thereupon, it was said in Heaven, "Since he showed no compassion for the calf, suffering shall come upon him." Sometimes later, the maidservant who was cleaning Rabbi's house wanted to throw out some kittens. Rabbi said to her, "leave them, for it is written, *And His tender mercies are over all His*

tions which affect one's property are like those related by the Sages,[11] as follows: "Rav Huna had four hundred barrels of wine which had turned into vinegar. [Hearing of his misfortune], the Rabbis came to visit him and said, 'Let the master look into his affairs, [for this may have happened to him because of some wrongdoing].' He replied, 'Do you suspect me of having done anything wrong?' They retorted, 'Should we suspect the Holy One, blessed be He, of having rendered judgment against you unjustly?'[12] Rav Huna then said, 'If you have heard anything against me, do tell it to me.' They said to him, 'We have heard that you did not allow your tenant to share in the prunings of the vines.' Rav Huna replied, 'Has he left me anything? He has been constantly stealing from me! [Therefore, I did not allow him to share in the prunings.]' They replied, 'There is a common saying: One who steals from a thief also smells like a thief. [Because he has sinned by stealing from you, do you wish to sin too in retaliation?]' Immediately, Rav Huna took it upon himself to give [the tenant his share of the prunings]. Some report that his vinegar turned back to wine, and others maintain that the price of vinegar rose and equaled that of wine."

You may learn from this episode that when one sincerely decides [to correct some wrongdoing] by performing a favorable deed, he is immediately forgiven for his sin even though he has not yet performed the deed. In fact, this is clearly stated in Scripture: *From the first day that thou* [Daniel] *didst set thy heart to understand, and to humble thyself before thy G-d, thy words were heard.*[13]

---

works" (Psalms 145:9). It was then said in Heaven, "Since he showed mercy to the kittens, mercy will be shown to him," and he was healed. (11) Berachoth 5 b. (12) Although there are righteous people who are afflicted in body and property, yet knowing that there was a claim against him from his tenant they wanted to apprise him thereof in order that it should not happen again. (Tosafoth, *ibid.*). (13) Daniel 10:12.

Thus, we derive the principle that all afflictions, whether physical or pecuniary, come upon man to atone for his sins in this world so that he might be perfectly worthy of the World to Come. This is expressed in the verse here, *Behold, G-d doeth loftily in His power, who is a Teacher like Him?*[1] G-d assays the righteous for their own good, as it is written, *The Eternal trieth the righteous.*[14] G-d supports the strength of the righteous so that they will endure the suffering and deserve life in the World to Come. All of this is done for the welfare of the righteous man, as it is written, *And though thy beginning was small, yet thy end will greatly increase.*[15]

Just as the suffering of the righteous is for their welfare, the tranquility and success enjoyed by the wicked are for their detriment. Even an utterly wicked person must have done some good. G-d therefore wants to reward him in the insignificant transience of this world and in the triviality which is the body so that he will be completely denied life in the World to Come. Thus, Scripture states, *He repayeth them that hate Him to their face, to destroy them.*[16] The Rabbis also expounded,[17] "*It is not good to respect the person of the wicked.*[18] That the wicked is shown favors in this world is not going to be good for him in the World to Come."

In the first chapter of Tractate Berachoth, the Sages expounded:[19] "The verse states, *Show me now Thy ways.*[20] Moses asked G-d, 'Master of the universe, why do some righteous men prosper while other righteous men suffer? Why do some wicked men prosper while other wicked men suffer?' G-d answered Moses, 'The righteous man who prospers is thoroughly righteous, while the righteous man who suffers is

---

(14) Psalms 11:5. (15) Job 8:7. (16) Deuteronomy 7:10. As rendered by Onkelos: "He repays them their recompense in this world." See also Ramban, Commentary on the Torah, Deuteronomy, pp. 91-93. (17) Yoma 87 a. (18) Proverbs 18:5. (19) Berachoth 7 a. (20) Exodus 33:13.

not thoroughly righteous. The wicked man who prospers is not thoroughly wicked, while the wicked man who suffers is thoroughly wicked.' This text conflicts with the opinion of Rabbi Meir, who said, 'Only two of Moses' requests[21] were granted to him. However, his request [that he be explained the principle which governs reward and punishment in each individual case] was not granted to him. It is said, *And I will be gracious to whom I will be gracious*[22] even though the individual is undeserving of G-d's graciousness; *and I will show mercy on whom I will show mercy*[22] even though the individual does not deserve it."[23]

Who is a Teacher like Him,[1] instructing the wicked in the way of repentance? Scripture states, *Good and upright is the Eternal; therefore doth He instruct sinners in the way.*[24] "It was asked of Prophecy,[25] 'What punishment should be meted out to the sinner?' Prophecy answered, *'The soul that sinneth, it shall die.*[26] It was asked of the Torah, 'What punishment should be meted out to the sinner?' The Torah answered, 'Let him bring a guilt-offering and he will be forgiven.' It was asked of G-d, and He answered, 'Let him repent and he will be forgiven.' Thus, it is written, *Good and upright is the Eternal; therefore doth He instruct sinners in the way.*"[24] It is further stated, *Return, O Israel, unto the Eternal thy G-d,* etc.[27] *Take with you words, and return unto the Eternal.*[28]

Whence do we know that G-d has instructed sinners in the way of repentance? We derive it from the Torah. Cain killed his brother and Divine judgment was decreed upon him. Yet, he repented, saying, *My*

(21) Moses asked that the gift of prophecy be conferred upon Israel, and that it not be bestowed upon any other nation (Berachoth 7 a). Only these two requests were granted to Moses. However, his request etc. (see text). (22) Exodus 33:19. (23) "This means that the matter   [of G-d's dispensation of punishment and reward] is not meant for human knowledge, thus declaring that this principle was not made comprehensible to man" (Ramban, Writings and Discourses, p. 451). (24) Psalms 25:8. (25) Yerushalmi Makkoth II, 6, with textual variations. (26) Ezekiel 18:4. (27) Hosea 14:2. (28) *Ibid.*, Verse 3. *Words* of sincere confession of sin.

punishment is greater than I can bear.[29] It is further written, *Behold, Thou hast driven me out of the land.*[30] G-d accepted Cain's repentance, as it is said, *And the Eternal set a sign for Cain, lest anyone finding him should smite him.*[31] It is further stated, *And Cain went out from the presence of the Eternal.*[32] The Sages interpreted this to mean that "he went out happily because his repentance was accepted."[33]

We also find [that G-d has instructed sinners in the way of repentance] in the case of Menasheh son of Hezekiah. He erected a statue of four faces[34] in the Sanctuary, thereby causing the King of Glory to leave the Sanctuary in ten stages, as the Sages said,[35] "The Divine Presence left [Israel] in ten stages." It is also written of Menasheh that *he reared altars for the Baalim, and made Asheiroth, and worshipped all the host of heaven, and served them.*[36] Notwithstanding the above, when the King of Assyria attacked and defeated Menasheh and led him away captive in a copper caldron, under which a fire was kindled,[37] what does Scripture relate of that incident? *And when he was in distress, he besought the Eternal his G-d, and humbled himself greatly before the G-d of his fathers.*[38] *And he prayed unto Him, and He was entreated of him and heard his supplication.*[39] Menasheh said, "I remember that during my father's reign, I read in the Torah of Moses, *In thy distress, when all these*

---

(29) Genesis 4:13. (30) *Ibid.*, Verse 14. Since "I am a fugitive and a wanderer unable to stay in one place, *whosoever findeth me shall slay me (ibid.),* and You in Your manifold loving-kindness did not decree death upon me" (Ramban, Commentary on the Torah, Genesis, p. 91). (31) Genesis 4:15. (32) *Ibid.*, Verse 16. (33) Bereshith Rabbah 22:28. (34) The four faces corresponded to the four directions of the world (Devarim Rabbah 2:20). (35) Rosh Hashanah 31 a. Reference is to the destruction of the First Temple. The ten stages are: "from the Ark-cover to the Cherub, from one Cherub to the other, from the Cherub to the threshold [of the Temple], from the threshold to the court, from the court to the altar, from the altar to the roof [of the Temple], from the roof to the wall [of the court], from the wall to the city [of Jerusalem], from the city to the mountain [of Olives], and from the mountain to the wilderness" (*ibid.*). (36) II Chronicles 33:3. (37) Devarim Rabbah 2:13. (38) II Chronicles 33:12. (39) *Ibid.*, Verse 13.

things are come upon thee, etc., *thou wilt return to the Eternal thy G-d.*[40] It is further stated, *For the Eternal thy G-d is a merciful G-d, He will not fail thee, neither destroy thee,* etc.[41] If You will help me now from this distress, I will know and acknowledge that You are G-d and that all the statues I worshipped are false. If You will not help me, You are one of them." Thereupon, G-d had pity on Menasheh, and He commanded the ministering angels to save him. However, they said to G-d, "Master of the universe, are You showing compassion for this man who has sinned so much before You!" He said to them, "If I do not accept his repentance, I will lock the gates of repentance in the face of all sinners." At that instant, the enemy removed Menasheh from the caldron, *and He brought him to Jerusalem into his kingdom,*[39] and he removed the idols from the House of G-d.[42]

Ahab, too, committed a number of grave sins. Because he coveted the vineyard of Naboth, Jezebel, Ahab's wife, commanded that Naboth be slain on the strength of testimony by false witnesses [that Naboth blasphemed G-d and the King]. It is written, *And it came to pass, when Ahab heard that Naboth was dead, that Ahab rose up to go down to the vineyard of Naboth the Jezreelite, to take possession of it.*[43] On that day, Elijah said to him, *Thus saith the Eternal: Hast thou killed and also taken possession? . . . In the place where dogs licked the blood of Naboth shall dogs lick thy blood, even thine.*[44] Still, Ahab repented and G-d accepted it, as it is written, *And it came to pass, when Ahab heard these words, that he rent his clothes, and put sackcloth upon his flesh, and fasted, and lay in sackcloth, and went softly.*[45] He fasted only from the time that Elijah spoke to him until that evening.[46] Immediately thereafter, it is written, *And the word of the Eternal came to Elijah the Tishbite, saying:*[47] *Seest thou how Ahab humbleth himself before Me?*[48]

---

(40) Deuteronomy 4:30.   (41) *Ibid.,* Verse 31.   (42) In II Chronicles 33:13, Scripture concludes, *Then Menasheh knew that the Eternal was G-d.*   (43) I Kings 21:16.   (44) *Ibid.,* Verse 19.   (45) *Ibid.,* Verse 27.   (46) Taanith 28 b.   (47) I Kings 21:28.   (48) *Ibid.,* Verse 29.

The case of Coniah[49] the son of Yehoyakim is another [example of G-d instructing sinners in the way of repentance]. G-d had decreed that Coniah be exiled from Jerusalem to Babylon together with his mother and servants, and that they should die there.[50] Regarding Coniah,[49] Scripture states, *Thus saith the Eternal: Write ye this man as childless, a man that shall not prosper in his days,*[51] which means that he will leave no children. Still, when Nebuchadnezzar slew Zedekiah's children,[52] Coniah alone, of all the seed of David, was left alive and did leave a son, as it is said, *And the sons of Yeconiah:*[49] *Assir-Shealtiel his son,* etc.[53] He was called *Assir* (prison) because he was begotten in prison.

The people of Anathoth[54] also had incurred the decree of punishment, as it is said, *The young men shall die by the sword, their sons and their daughters shall die by famine.*[55] However, when they repented, G-d accepted their penitence, the decree was annulled, and they were privileged to have their genealogy recorded in Scripture, as it is written, *The men of Anathoth, a hundred twenty and eight.*[56]

(49) Coniah, also known as Yehoyachin and Yeconiah, was King of Judah. He was exiled to Babylon eleven years before the destruction of the First Temple in the year 586 B.C.E.   (50) See Jeremiah 22:26.   (51) *Ibid.*, Verse 30.   (52) II Kings 25:7. Zedekiah was the last King of Judah.   (53) I Chronicles 3:17. The original decree that Yehoyachin die childless was annulled for the following reason. Fearing that the line of the House of David would become extinct upon Yehoyachin's death, members of the Sanhedrin successfully interceded with Nebuchadnezzar to permit Yehoyachin's wife to be with him during his imprisonment. However, because of the woman's state of ritual impurity, Yehoyachin forwent having relations with her until she properly regained her ritual purity. Because Yehoyachin restrained his sensual desires in order to comply with the laws of the Torah, the decree against him was annulled and he begot a son, Assir-Shealtiel. The latter's son Zerubabel was a leader in the rebuilding of the Second Temple. Thus we derive the greatness of repentance, for Yehoyachin's act of self-restraint from committing a sin effected salvation of the entire House of David.   (54) Anathoth was a city in the holding of the tribe of Benjamin. It was the home town of the prophet Jeremiah. Because the citizens of Anathoth persecuted the seer for his adverse prophecies, punishment was decreed upon them.   (55) Jeremiah 11:22.   (56) Ezra 2:23. This chapter of Ezra lists those who were privileged to return from the Babylonian captivity and to participate in the rebuilding of the Second Temple.

Similarly, because of the wickedness, robbery, and violence
perpetrated by the men of Nineveh, which was as grievous as that of
the generation of the Flood, it was decreed that punishment would
come upon them in forty days,[57] just as the rains of the Flood lasted
forty days.[58] Although the people of Nineveh were non-Jews, when they
repented and *every one turned from his evil way and from the violence
that was in their hands,*[59] G-d accepted their repentance and the
decree was annulled.

The following is the interpretation of the Book of Jonah:[60]

*Now the word of the Eternal came unto Jonah the son of Amittai,
saying:*[61] *Arise, go to Nineveh, that great city, and proclaim 'aleha'
(against it).*[62] The size of Nineveh is mentioned in the Torah: *And
Resen between Nineveh and Calah—the same is the great city.*[63] This
verse is stating that Resen was moderate in size relative to the great city
of Nineveh and Calah, the smallest of the three cities.

And proclaim 'aleha' (against it). The expression *proclaim* in combination with the Hebrew word *al* (against) signifies punishment, as it
is written, *He hath proclaimed a solemn assembly 'alai' (against me).*[64]
Proclaim against it, for their wickedness is come up before Me.[62] Their
sin equaled that of the generation of the Flood, of which it is written,
The wickedness of man was great on the earth.[65]

---

(57) See Jonah 3:4.   (58) See Genesis 7:12.   (59) Jonah 3:8.   (60) The commentary presented here is essentially the same as that of Abraham ben Chiya, a famous
mathematician and astronomer of the eleventh century. Ramban refers to him as
Sahib al Schurta (Foreman of the Troop), and he is also known as Savasorda, a muta-
tion of the Arabic title. See Ramban Writings and Discourses, p. 85, Note 298.
Abraham ben Chiya's book is entitled *Higayon Hanefesh* (Meditations of the Soul),
and the commentary on the Book of Jonah is found on pp. 21-30 in Yitzchak Freiman's
edition. Rabbeinu Bachya fitted the commentary to his own literary
style.   (61) Jonah 1:1. Nineveh was the capital city of the Kingdom of Assyria, a city
destined to play a great role in the history of Israel. It was Assyria that later destroyed
the Kingdom of Israel, comprising of the ten tribes.   (62) *Ibid.,* Verse
2.   (63) Genesis 10:12.   (64) Lamentations 1:15. And as the verse continues, *to
crush my young men.*   (65) Genesis 6:5.

But Jonah rose up to flee unto Tarshish from the presence of the Eternal. [66] Jonah did not think that a person could escape the presence of G-d, for David said, *Whither shall I go from Thy spirit? or whither shall I flee Thy presence?* [67] *If I ascend up into heaven, Thou art there,* etc. [68] *If I take the wings of the morning,* etc., [69] *even there would Thy hand lead me.* [70] Instead, Jonah intended to flee to Tarshish, where the Glory of G-d had not been revealed. The expression *from the presence of the Eternal* [66] thus means "from the place where the Glory of G-d was revealed." Jerusalem is called *the valley of vision,* [71] for just as a valley receives the rainfall, so did Jerusalem receive the flow of prophecy, as the Sages commented, [72] "Jerusalem is the valley from which all prophets come." Thus, Jonah left the place where the spirit of prophecy was constant and fled outside the Land of Israel, where he would be unable to prophesy. G-d would then accomplish His purpose through someone else.

Out of his humility and wholeheartedness, Jonah declined to execute G-d's mission. He reasoned: "If Moses, who was sent by G-d to bring forth righteous Israel from Egypt, refused his mission, I who am sent to admonish the wicked am certainly entitled to decline. Therefore, I should flee the place of prophecy so that I should not receive the vision which would require me to execute that mission." [73]

You may ask: "If so, Jonah's intention was good. Why then was he punished by being thrown into the sea?" The answer is that he was not punished for this thought. He was punished because he failed to warn the people of Nineveh as G-d had commanded him. It is the way of the Torah that the righteous and the prophets are obligated to admonish the wicked. [74] Since G-d had told him, *Arise, go to Nineveh, that great*

(66) Jonah 1:3. (67) Psalms 139:7. (68) *Ibid.,* Verse 8. (69) *Ibid.,* Verse 9. (70) *Ibid.,* Verse 10. (71) Isaiah 22:1. (72) P'sichta Eichah Rabbah, 24. (73) Jonah had not as yet been told to proclaim the impending doom of Nineveh if they do not repent of their evil deeds (Ibn Ezra). He was only told, *for their wickedness is come up before Me* (Jonah 1:2). Therefore Jonah thought that there was still an opportunity for his refusal to accept the mission. — On Moses' refusal, see Exodus 3:11 and 4:13. (74) See Ezekiel 3:18-19.

city, and proclaim against it,[62] he was in effect appointed as their
guardian and was obligated to warn them. When he did not warn
them, he incurred the responsibility for their lives not for their sake,
but for the honor of G-d, the fulfillment of Whose word was deterred.
Jonah's declination of his mission was therefore dissimilar to that of
Moses, for G-d sent Moses not merely to warn Pharaoh but to take
Israel out of bondage, [hence, he first refused, claiming that the task
be given to someone more suitable for the great mission]. This is the
reason that Jonah was punished, as it is written, *And the Eternal hurl-
ed a great wind into the sea.*[75] This is G-d's way with the righteous. He
brings some natural distress upon them and saves them through a
supernatural miracle.

And the mariners were afraid, and every man cried unto his god,[76]
which is natural for all sea voyagers in a stormy sea. These mariners
did not believe strongly in their deities, for immediately after they had
prayed, *they cast forth the wares in the ship into the sea*[76] and did not
wait for their gods to save them. Therefore, they did not pray again.
Jonah, on the other hand, justified the Divine judgment against him.
However, he trusted that G-d would save him as He saves all righteous
men, as it is written, *Many are the ills of the righteous, but the Eternal
delivereth him out of them all.*[77] [During the storm], *Jonah was gone
down into the innermost parts of the ship, and was fast asleep.*[76] His
action proves that he did not flee the place of prophecy for some evil
purpose, for he was fast asleep and had no fear at all.

*So the shipmaster came to him, and said unto him: What meanest
thou that thou sleepest?*[78] The shipmaster, who was a man of great
wisdom, said to him, "Is this the time to sleep when we are in this great
storm? If your confidence is based upon your righteousness, you are
obligated to pray for mercy. *Arise, call upon thy G-d.*"[78] The shipmaster thus informed Jonah that if one can save himself by praying for
salvation from his distress, G-d will accept his prayer and save him
from the violence which might otherwise be his lot.

(75) Jonah 1:4.   (76) *Ibid.*, Verse 5.   (77) Psalms 34:20.   (78) Jonah 1:6.

And they said everyone to his fellow: Come, and let us cast lots.[79]
They sought to determine the one who had not prayed, for perhaps he
was the one who was the cause of this evil. *And the lot fell upon
Jonah,*[79] for the lots of the others had demonstrated that all had prayed
except Jonah. *They then said unto him: Tell us, we pray thee, for
whose cause this evil is upon us: what is thine occupation? and whence
comest thou? what is thy country? and of what people art thou?*[80] They
asked him four questions which would enable them to discern if he was
the cause of their misfortune. They first asked him about his occupation, lest he be a magician or wizard who precipitated the storm with
his magic. They next asked him about his destination, for perhaps he
was on a mission for magicians and enchanters. Then they asked him
about his country of origin to determine if it is some evil land or a
country despised by them.[81] Finally, they asked him about his people,
for perhaps he was a member of a nation which caused evil.

Jonah answered: *I am a Hebrew.*[82] He answered their last question
first, as if to say that they have nothing to fear from him. "I am of a
people to whom all activities and sciences harmful to man are forbidden. *I fear the Eternal, the G-d of heaven,*[82] and it is not the way of one
who fears Heaven to engage in an evil matter."

*Then were the men exceedingly afraid, and said unto him: What is
this that thou hast done? For the men knew that he fled from the
presence of the Eternal, because he had told them.*[83] From his
answer — *I fear the Eternal, the G-d of heaven*[82] — they understood that
he was fleeing from G-d's presence and considered themselves as having sinned by accepting his payment for passage,[84] which was the cause

(79) *Ibid.*, Verse 7. According to Pirkei d'Rabbi Eliezer [mentioned by Rashi] the
raging storm was only upon the boat. Therefore the people knew that there must be
someone guilty on the boat, on whose account the storm raged. (80) Jonah
1:8. (81) That is, despised by magicians. If Jonah were a citizen of such a country,
the magicians may have brought about the storm because of him. (82) Jonah
1:9. (83) *Ibid.*, Verse 10. The question asked of Jonah, *What is this that thou hast
done?* was not an inquiry but rather in bewilderment, as if to say: "How could you have
done this, to rebel against the word of G-d!" (Metzudath David). (84) See Jonah 1:3.

of all this evil. However, Jonah assured them, *For my sake this great tempest is upon you.*[85]

When they heard Jonah's admission and his declaration of readiness to be cast into the sea,[85] they had compassion upon him, *and the men rowed hard to bring it to the land.*[86] Realizing that they could not reach shore, they prayed to G-d for mercy, saying, *We beseech Thee, O Eternal, let us not perish for this man's life.*[87] They actually prayed for two things. One was that G-d should save them from the tempestuous sea, and the other was that He should save them from the sin [of throwing Jonah into the sea]. *So they took up Jonah, and cast him forth into the sea, and the sea ceased 'mizapo.*'[88] The raging which ceased was not that of the sea, but rather G-d's raging, as it is written, *I will bear the indignation of the Eternal.*[89]

Then the men feared the Eternal exceedingly.[90] This "fear" was unlike the one mentioned above, *Then were the men exceedingly afraid.*[83] In that verse, it means they were afraid of the sea's tempest and of what might befall them only in this world. Here, however, it means they feared G-d and His punishment in the World to Come.[91] *And they offered a sacrifice unto the Eternal.*[90] This does not mean that they brought sacrifices. Being at sea, they did not have animals available. Rather, the meaning of this *sacrifice* is that their spirits became contrite and their hearts submissive, for these are the essential requirements of repentance, as it is written, *The sacrifices of G-d are a broken spirit.*[92] *And they made vows,*[90] all agreeing that when they would return to their countries, they would devote themselves to the fear of Heaven.

---

(85) *Ibid.*, Verse 12.   (86) *Ibid.*, Verse 13.   (87) *Ibid.*, Verse 14. *They cried unto the Eternal, and said: We beseech Thee, O Eternal* etc. The verse indicates that they now believed in the True G-d of Jonah (Ibn Ezra).   (88) *Ibid.*, Verse 15. The word *mizapo* is generally translated "from its raging," that is, from the raging of the sea. Our author will explain it as referring to G-d, meaning that the sea ceased from His raging, as explained in the text.   (89) Micah 7:9.   (90) Jonah 1:16.   (91) In Higayon Hanefesh—see above, Note 60—Abraham ben Chiya adds, "They turned to the way of truth." The verse in the text then follows: *"And they offered a sacrifice unto the Eternal,* as explained further on.   (92) Psalms 51:19.

Jonah himself did not pray during the tempest because he was accepting the affliction willed by G-d for his transgression. Jonah trusted in G-d and was certain He would not punish him with death. He knew that G-d would perform miracles and wonders in his behalf. Therefore, he deferred his prayer until later when he was in the fish's belly.

And the Eternal prepared a great fish to swallow up Jonah.[93] The term *great* does not mean great in size, for the ocean contains fish which are larger than the one which swallowed Jonah.[94] Instead, the verse refers to the fish's great age, for since Creation it had been prepared by G-d to save the life of a righteous man like Jonah. Thus, Scripture does not state, "and it swallowed Jonah." Rather, it relates that G-d *prepared a great fish to swallow up Jonah,* which indicates that it had been prepared for this task from the time of its creation.

And Jonah was in the belly of the fish three days and three nights.[93] It is subsequently written, *Then Jonah prayed unto the Eternal his G-d out of the fish's belly.*[95] During the first three days, Jonah was ashamed to pray because he felt chided by G-d and accepted the afflictions willed upon him by the Creator. After the first three days, which were like the three days of darkness that fell upon the Egyptians,[96] he began to pray and was sure that G-d would help him even as He delivered Israel in Egypt. It may be suggested that Jonah enjoyed a great light while in the fish's belly just as the Israelites had light in their dwellings while the rest of Egypt was in darkness.[97] Thus, Jonah prayed and G-d accepted

---

(93) Jonah 2:1.   (94) "Besides, the size of the fish has no bearing upon the story" (Higayon Hanefesh).   (95) Jonah 2:2.   (96) See Exodus 10:22.   (97) See *ibid.,* Verse 23. In Higayon Hanefesh the author finds an allusion for this thought in the expression while Jonah was in the belly of the fish *three days and three nights* (Jonah 2:1). Ordinarily the day follows the preceding night and therefore it should have said "three nights and three days." However, the days are mentioned first in order to indicate a comparison to the three days of darkness that fell upon the Egyptians while the Israelites were not affected. The thought suggested then is that just as in Egypt the Israelites enjoyed the light both at night and day continuously, so was Jonah enjoying the great light for a period of three days uninterruptedly just as if it were at daytime.

his prayer. *And the Eternal spoke unto the fish and it vomited out Jonah upon the dry land.*[98]

And the word of the Eternal came unto Jonah the second time.[99] The verse mentions *the second time* because this was another message unlike the original prophecy. At first the people of Nineveh deserved immediate punishment, but since the effectuation of the decree had been delayed [due to Jonah's flight], the gates of repentance were opened to the people of Nineveh and the decree was postponed for forty days.[57]

And Jonah began entering the city by a day's journey.[57] During that first day, Jonah awaited the word of G-d which He had told him to expect, as He had said, *And make unto it the proclamation that I will bid thee.*[100] At the beginning of the second day,[101] Jonah was informed of the proclamation he was to make, namely, *Yet forty days, and Nineveh shall be overthrown.*[57] The proclamation was delayed until he was in the midst of the city so that the people would realize the truth of his message because he was risking his life by declaring G-d's message of doom in the heart of the city. The delay also allowed the news of his mission to reach the attention of the ruler more speedily.

And the people of Nineveh believed in G-d.[102] They believed that it was within the power of the Creator to punish them just as any king and ruler could do to his subjects. However, they did not believe in G-d out of sincere faith. The fast they proclaimed and the sackcloth they donned were but expressions of their fear for their own lives, not the fear and awe of G-d or expressions of sincere belief.

And the tidings reached the king of Nineveh,[103] and he ordered a fast for *both man and beast, and let them cry mightily unto G-d.*[104]

(98) Jonah 2:11.   (99) *Ibid.*, 3:1.   (100) *Ibid.*, Verse 2.   (101) This is evidently derived from the verse, *And Jonah began entering the city by a day's journey*—and he proclaimed and said, *Yet forty days* etc. (*ibid.*, Verse 4)—which indicates that after the completion of the day's journey into the city then the prophet was informed of the message he was to deliver.   (102) *Ibid.*, Verse 5.   (103) *Ibid.*, Verse 6.   (104) *Ibid.*, Verse 8.

Throughout this entire episode, you will not find that the men of Nineveh prayed to G-d themselves. Instead, they had mutually agreed and planned to proclaim a fast in order to cause suffering to their children and beasts by depriving them of their food and drink. It was their hope that G-d would have compassion upon them for the sake of the innocent little ones and senseless beasts. They themselves did not pray because that was not their habit.[105] Yet, when they turned from their evil way and the violence they had been committing, G-d had pity on them. Our Sages said[106] that their restitution of stolen property constituted a great and mighty repentance, as follows: "If one had stolen a beam and used it in the building of a castle, he would demolish the entire castle in order to restore the beam to its owner" although reimbursing the owner for its value would have been sufficient.

The King of Nineveh wondered, *"Who knoweth whether G-d will turn and alter* [His decree]?[107] Who knows whether He will annul His decree of destruction or not?" Although they were not certain that their repentance would nullify the decree against them, the G-d of compassion nevertheless did not hide His face from them. Note that the people of Nineveh did not ask for forgiveness and atonement so that they might acquire life in the World to Come; they only asked *that we perish not*[107] from this world.

And it displeased Jonah exceedingly[108] when his prophecy was not fulfilled. *And he prayed unto the Eternal, and said: "I pray thee, O Eternal, was not this my saying,* etc., *for I knew that Thou art a gracious G-d, and compassionate.*[109] Because I knew this, *therefore I fled beforehand unto Tarshish.*[109] I believed that with Your good attributes, Your long-suffering, and Your abundant mercy, You would forgive my sin and not punish me. *And now, O Eternal, take I beseech*

(105) "They did not rely on prayer because they were aware of their wickedness. The scholar who judges them favorably would say that they did not pray because due to their numerous sins, they were ashamed to lift their eyes in prayer to G-d" (Higayon Hanefesh). (106) Taanith 16 a. (107) Jonah 3:9. (108) *Ibid.*, 4:1. (109) *Ibid.*, Verse 2.

Thee, my life from me,[110] for You have decided against the evil which
You planned against the men of Nineveh, whose repentance was not
for the sake of Your honor. You have commissioned me to go to them,
however, and I will thus be a liar in their eyes. Therefore do I say that
it is better for me to die than to live."[110]

G-d strengthened Jonah's argument by saying, *Art thou greatly
angry?*[111] This question, which has the force of an affirmation, means
"this matter should indeed cause you indignation." We derive this interpretation from the fact that Jonah did not respond at all, for he was
grateful to G-d for confirming his complaint and hoped that perhaps
his prophecy would be fulfilled. Therefore, it states immediately afterward, *Then Jonah went out of the city, and sat on the east side of the
city, and there made himself a booth, and sat under it in the
shadow.*[112] He made himself a booth, metaphorically speaking, out of
his trust and hope in G-d. *He sat under it in the shadow,* finding refuge
in the shadow of his hope about what would happen to the city at the
end of the forty days. He would see whether the people of the city
would be saved from destruction or not.

G-d then relayed to Jonah the secret of the matter and made it
known to him that his thought could not materialize. G-d illustrated
this through the gourd which came up over Jonah *that it might be a
shadow over his head.*[113] Jonah's rejoicing over the gourd was like the
joy people have with material acquisitions. These are transitory in
nature, and thus are undeserving of any joy upon their acquisition or
grief upon their loss. To indicate the insignificance of their benefit,

---

(110) *Ibid.*, Verse 3.   (111) *Ibid.*, Verse 4. Since Scripture does not mention
Jonah's answer to this question, we are forced to interpret it as an affirmation, of G-d
confirming his complaint as explained in the text. Further in Verse 9 where the same
question appears together with Jonah's reply, it is clear that it should be interpreted as
a real question, not an affirmation.   (112) *Ibid.*, Verse 5. In Higayon Hanefesh, the
verse is more fully explained: "*Then Jonah went out of* the grief caused to him [regard-
ing the outcome of the decree on] *the city, and sat,* etc."   (113) Jonah 4:6.

Scripture states, *But G-d prepared a worm.*[114] This worm symbolizes the days and nights which gnaw at man's existence and destroy his life. Man remains unaware of their pernicious effect until his end suddenly comes upon him. Thus, it says that *when the morning rose the next day,*[114] the worm was ready to smite the gourd just at that time when man requires the shades. *And the sun beat upon the head of Jonah, and he fainted,*[115] for he was concerned about the dryness of the gourd and the lack of shade in the booth. Therefore, he said, *It is better for me to die than to live.*[115]

When G-d saw his grief, He asked Jonah about the cause thereof, saying, *Art thou greatly angry for the gourd?*[116] This is a real question, not an affirmation as in the case above.[111] Jonah answered this question, I am greatly angry, even unto death.[116] And the Eternal said: *Thou hast had pity on the gourd, for which thou has not labored, etc.,*[117] *and should I not have pity on Nineveh, that great city, wherein there are more than sixscore thousand persons, that cannot discern between their right hand and their left hand, and also much cattle?*[118]

(114) *Ibid.*, Verse 7.   (115) *Ibid.*, Verse 8.   (116) *Ibid.*, Verse 9.   (117) *Ibid.*, Verse 10.   (118) *Ibid.*, Verse 11. Our author ends the topic abruptly, just as the Book of Jonah ends precipitously. The message, however, for the Day of Atonement is clear. G-d's abundant mercy is extended to all living creatures to return from their evil ways and thus be worthy of His forgiveness.

Part Two

Purity of thought leads to holiness / Through the traits of purity of thought and holiness, Israel was sanctified at Sinai / In the matter of holiness, Israel is compared to the sacred ministering angels. This is especially true on the Day of Atonement / The reason for the Torah's prohibition of eating and drinking on the Day of Atonement / The sacred Divine Name which the High Priest uttered on the Day of Atonement / The interpretation of the Thirteen Divine Attributes.

AND HE SHALL PURIFY IT, AND HALLOW IT.[119]

"We have been taught:[120] 'Rabbi Pinchas ben Ya'ir says that purity leads to holiness, for it is said, *And he shall purify it, and hallow it.'*"[119]

It is common knowledge that qualities of character affect our physical behavior as well as our rational processes. Those which affect physical behavior serve to rectify one's deeds, for there can be no perfection in wisdom without the mending of one's deeds. Those characteristics which affect rational processes serve to purify one's thought so that his inward feelings will be accurately reflected by his

---

(119) Leviticus 16:19. The verse refers to the High Priest's service at the Golden Altar of Incense in the Sanctuary on the Day of Atonement. Scripture means to say, *"Purify it* from its past defilement, and then *hallow it* for its future use." Thus, Scripture indicates that purity leads to holiness. (120) Yerushalmi Shekalim, end of Chapter 3. See above, *Taharath Haleiv* (Purity of Heart) where the entire Beraitha is quoted. Here, our author cites only that segment which has a direct bearing upon the nature of the sanctity of the Day of Atonement.

external appearances and his inner thoughts will correspond to his overt actions.[121] A person who succeeds in purifying his thought to this extent will be led to holiness. It is known that both purity and holiness are found only when one fulfills the Torah and the commandments,[122] for purity cleaves to the Torah, as it is said, *The fear of the Eternal is pure, enduring forever.*[123] That is to say, it remains pure forever; purity is never separated from it. Thus, the Sages commented,[124] "The words of Torah do not contract impurity, for it is said, *Is not My word like as fire? saith the Eternal.*"[125]

Through the traits of purity of thought and holiness, Israel was sanctified at Sinai when they heard the Ten Commandments from the mouth of the Eternal, something no other nation or ethnic group heard. It is thus written, *Did ever a people hear the voice of G-d?*[126] Our Sages commented:[127] "The *voice* was heard from one end of the world to the other. The elders and the younger people, each heard and understood the *voice* according to his or her individual ability."

[We know that Israel was sanctified at Sinai through] purity, for a proselyte who seeks shelter under the wings of the Divine Presence must fulfill three requirements. He must be circumcised, he must have immersed himself in a ritual pool, and he must bring an offering.[128] The latter is the most essential of the three.[129] Circumcision is required because the general name for the prepuce is impurity. Therefore, the proselyte must be circumcised to be pure. He must also undergo ritual

---

(121) See above, *Taharath Haleiv* (Purity of Heart), for a fuller discussion of this point, which is restated here. (122) "Torah and the commandments," see above, *Emunah* (Faith), Note 2, for the explanation of this term. (123) Psalms 19:10. *The fear of the Eternal* is a synonym for the Torah. The verse's meaning is: "The fear of G-d, as expressed in the Torah, etc." This is apparent from Verse 8 in this psalm, which reads, *The Torah of the Eternal is perfect,* etc. (124) Berachoth 22 a. (125) Jeremiah 23:29. See above, *Taharath Haleiv* (Purity of Heart), Note 12. (126) Deuteronomy 4:33. (127) Shemoth Rabbah 5:9. (128) Kerithoth 9 a. In the Gemara there, it is clearly stated that just as our ancestors at Sinai entered the covenant with G-d through fulfilling these three requirements, so is every proselyte required to do the same. See further, Note 130. (129) As explained further in the text, "One who achieves expiation through his offering attains purity."

immersion, for true purity comes through [immersion in] water. Finally, he must bring an offering[130] because sin is termed impurity, and one who achieves expiation through his offering attains purity. [We also know that Israel attained] holiness at Sinai, as it says, *And ye shall be unto Me a kingdom of priests, and a holy nation.*[131]

It is common knowledge that the people of Israel are divided into three categories: priests, Levites, and Israelites. [As a descendant of Aaron], the priest is holy in his own right as well as through the holiness of Levi, the founder of his tribe. [As a member of the tribe of Levi], the Levites are holy in their own right as well as through the holiness of G-d, [Who conferred of His holiness upon them. Priests, Levites, and Israelites] are all sanctified by G-d, the Source of holiness, as it is said, *Lift up your hands to 'Kodesh,'*[132] *and bless ye the Eternal.*[133] Note that Scripture states, *And ye shall be men of 'Kodesh'*[132] *unto Me;*[134] it does not say, "And ye shall be *anashim k'doshim* (holy men) unto Me." This designation by Scripture necessarily suggests that Israel is like the sacred ministering angels, whose sanctity flows directly from the Source of holiness, for it is written, *And He came* to Sinai *with myriads of* [angels from the] *'Kodesh.'*[135] The Sages commented,[136] "Just as the ministering angels are holy and pure, so is Israel holy and pure on the Day of Atonement. Just as the ministering angels are barefooted, so is Israel barefooted on the Day of Atonement. Just as the ministering angels do not eat or drink, so does Israel not eat or drink on the Day of Atonement."

The Torah has prohibited eating and drinking on the Day of Atonement because partaking of food leads a person to presumptuousness

---

(130) This requirement applies only during the existence of the Sanctuary. "At present, when no offerings can be brought, the proselyte is required to undergo circumcision and immersion only. In the future, when the Sanctuary will be built, he will bring his offering" (Mishneh Torah, *Hilchoth Isurei Biah* 13:5). (131) Exodus 19:6. (132) Generally translated as "the Sanctuary," the word *Kodesh* here obviously means G-d, Who is "the Source of holiness." (133) Psalms 134:2. (134) Exodus 22:30. (135) Deuteronomy 33:2. (136) Pirkei d'Rabbi Eliezer, 46.

and conceit. These in turn, lead to forgetfulness of G-d, the Essential Principle of all, as it is written, *Lest when thou hast eaten and art satisfied,* etc.,[137] *[and thou forget the Eternal thy G-d].*[138] Similarly, the prophet said, *When they were fed, they became full, they were filled and their heart was exalted, therefore they have forgotten Me.*[139] Our Sages also said,[140] "One who has eaten and drunk should not render legal decisions." This restriction is based on the requirement that a judge should decide cases only in the morning, as it is said, *Execute justice in the morning.*[141] If the judge is forbidden to eat and drink [before rendering a decision] in mere monetary matters, we may conclude *a fortiori* that eating and drinking should certainly be forbidden on the Day of Atonement, the day of judgment when the entire world is suspended between life and death. On the other hand, when a person fasts, his heart becomes submissive and contrite, his physical strength is diminished, and his rational powers are heightened. This, then, was the Torah's intention in saying, *Ye shall afflict your souls,*[142] which has traditionally been interpreted to mean[143] "affliction by abstaining from eating and drinking."

"Just as the ministering angels stand upon their feet,[144] so does Israel stand on the Day of Atonement. Just as there is peace among the ministering angels, as it is said, *He maketh peace in His high places,*[145] so is [there peace among the people of] Israel on the Day of Atonement.[146] Just as the ministering angels extol and praise G-d in four

(137) Deuteronomy 8:12. (138) *Ibid.*, Verse 14. (139) Hosea 13:6. (140) I have been unable to locate the source of this quotation. It appears to be a combination of two sayings in Kethuboth 10 b: "If one has eaten dates, he should not render legal decisions [because his mind becomes confused (Rashi)]. One who drinks a quarter of a *log* of wine should not render legal decisions." (141) Jeremiah 21:12. (142) Leviticus 16:29. (143) Yoma 74 b. (144) "They have no joints in their feet." (Pirkei d'Rabbi Eliezer, 46). Therefore, the angels cannot bend their knees; they minister only standing. — A major part of the Services on the Day of Atonement is likewise recited while the congregation is standing. There are certain devout people who remain standing throughout the entire Services, and others even stand the whole day. (145) Job 25:2. (146) The law obligates each person to make peace on the eve of the Day of Atonement with anyone he might have offended during the year.

groups,[147] so does Israel praise G-d in the four Services of the Day of Atonement: the Morning Service, the Additional Service, the Afternoon Service, and the Closing Service."[136] In regard to this, the Sages said in the Midrash: *"I rose up to open to my Beloved, and my hands dripped with myrrh, and my fingers with flowing myrrh, upon the handles of the bolt.*[148] *I rose up to open to my Beloved:* this refers to the Morning Service. *And my hands dripped with myrrh:* this refers to the Additional Service. *And my fingers with flowing myrrh:* this refers to the Afternoon Service. *Upon the handles of the bolt:* this refers to the Closing Service."

These four Services correspond to the four categories of people who praise the Divine Presence: the thoroughly righteous who have never sinned, the righteous proselytes, the penitents, and those who fear Heaven. These four groups are alluded to in one verse. Isaiah said: *One shall say, I am the Eternal's, and another shall call himself by the name of Jacob, and another shall subscribe with his hand unto the Eternal, and surname himself by the name of Israel.*[149] Commenting on this verse, the Sages said in the Midrash:[150] *"One shall say, I am the Eternal's:* this is the one who has never sinned. *And another shall call himself by the name of Jacob:* this refers to the proselytes. *And another shall subscribe with his hand unto the Eternal:* this refers to the penitents. *And surname himself by the name of Israel:* this refers to those who fear Heaven."

Each of these four groups has its own unique distinction, and appropriate recognition is given to each. This can be compared to the following:[151] A king and his troops entered a city through one gate and each of the troops was assigned a place of lodging in accordance with

(147) Batei Midrashoth, Vol. I, p. 59. — The four camps of the Israelites encamped around the Tabernacle in the wilderness, were symbolic of those four group of angels (Rabbeinu Bachya, in his commentary on Numbers 1:2, p. 8 in my edition). (148) Song of Songs 5:5. — I have been unable to locate this Midrash. (149) Isaiah 44:5. (150) Mechilta, *Nezikin*, 18. (151) A similar comparison is found in Koheleth Rabbah 12:5.

his status. Some stayed in the king's castle, others in the courtyard, still others at the gate, and others in the adjoining house next to the king. Thus, David said, *Happy is the man whom Thou choosest, and bringeth near, that he may dwell in Thy courts.*[152] In the Midrash Tanchuma, the Sages commented upon this verse:[153] "Happy is the one who has been chosen by G-d even though he has not been brought near to Him, and happy is the one who has been brought near to G-d even though he has not been chosen by Him. Happy is the one who has been chosen even though he has not been brought near, as is the case of Abraham, of whom it is said, *Who didst choose Abram.*[154] Happy is the one who has been brought near to G-d even though he has not been chosen by G-d, as is the case of Jethro and Rahab."[155]

The Day of Atonement is designated as holy, for it is said, *And call . . . the holy of the Eternal honorable.*[156] The High Priest is designated as holy, for it is said, *He is holy unto his G-d.*[157] In the Sanctuary on the Day of Atonement, the High Priest uttered the sacred Divine Name ten times[158] in holiness and purity. For this reason, [when we repeat the Additional Service on the Day of Atonement, we recite] the High Priest's prayer [and what is related thereon in the

---

(152) Psalms 65:5. (153) Tanchuma, *Tzav*, 8. (154) Nehemiah 9:7. The Eitz Yoseif, *ibid.*, comments that Abraham was not brought near to G-d by anyone; he brought himself near to G-d. (155) The case of Jethro is known as the perfect example of a non-Jew who comes from afar to accept the faith of Israel (Exodus, Chapter 18). — Rahab was the innkeeper in Jericho who saved Joshua's two spies from being captured by the soldiers of the king of the city. According to tradition, she later married Joshua (Megillah 14 b). (156) Isaiah 58:13. "This refers to the Day of Atonement, on which there is no eating or drinking. The Torah charges you, 'Honor it by wearing a clean garment' " (Shabbath 119 a). (157) Leviticus 21:7. (158) The High Priest recited the confession of sins three times during the special Service on the Day of Atonement: once for the confession of his own sins and those of his household, once for those of the other priests, and once for those of Israel in general. In each of these confessions, he uttered the Divine Name three times, as will be explained further in the text, thus totaling nine utterances. The tenth utterance of the Divine Name occurred when he cast lots over the two goats (see Leviticus 16:8-9) and proclaimed, "A sin-offering unto the Eternal."

Mishnah]:[159] "And when the priests and the people who stood in the court heard the Divine Name pronounced by the High Priest in holiness and purity, they knelt and prostrated themselves, fell on their faces, and said, 'Blessed be the Name of His glorious Kingdom forever and ever.' Thus did the High Priest say: 'O G-d, I have sinned, I have committed iniquity, I have transgressed against Thee. I beseech Thee, O G-d, make Thou atonement for the sins, and for the iniquities and for the transgressions, etc.' The High Priest then said to them, *'Before the Eternal ye shall be clean.' "*[160]

When the High Priest uttered the Divine Name, he did not raise his voice. In fact, as soon as he began pronouncing it, the assembly responded loudly, "Blessed be the Name of His glorious Kingdom forever and ever," so that the pronouncing of the Divine Name should not be heard.[161] The High Priest likewise did not outrightly pronounce it but absorbed it in his heart. This is the meaning of the expression [that he pronounced the Divine Name] "in holiness and purity," for the Divine Names cannot be pronounced in holiness outrightly. [The required holiness can be achieved] only in thought. If the Divine Names would be pronounced orally, they would be absorbed in the air, which can become impure, and they would thus be profaned. Therefore, the High Priest completed his utterance of the Divine Name by absorbing it in his heart.

I will now explain the Thirteen Attributes,[162] which assist us in times of prayer and in periods of affliction. They are *an inheritance of the congregation of Jacob.*[163] Although we in these generations do not know how to attain G-d's favor, His attributes of mercy nonetheless in-

---

(159) Yoma 66 a.   (160) Leviticus 16:30.   (161) This was done in order that the indiscreet should not have a knowledge of the Divine Name and use it on occasions which would constitute a desecration thereof. (162) These are the thirteen characteristic qualities of the Divine Nature in governing the world. G-d taught them to Moses when He gave him the second Tablets of the Law (Exodus 6-7): *And the Eternal passed by before him and proclaimed: The Eternal, the Eternal, G-d,* etc. The Thirteen Attributes are recited in all prayers of repentance. (163) Deuteronomy 33:4.

tercede for us, for G-d assured Moses on Sinai,[164] "Whenever Israel
sins, let them perform this service of the Thirteen Attributes before
Me, and I will forgive them." The Sages commented,[164] "G-d has made
a covenant with the Thirteen Attributes that they will not be turned
away empty-handed, for it is said there, *Behold, I make a
covenant.*"[165] Thus, in every generation, these attributes are of paramount importance in praying before the Gates of Mercy. This is true
for an individual as well as the public, and it is especially true in our
times when we are in exile and have no High Priest to atone for our
sins, no altar for sacrificial offerings, and no Sanctuary in which to
pray. We have no recourse left to us before G-d except our prayer and
these Thirteen Attributes.

The following is their interpretation: *The Eternal, the Eternal.*[166]
These are two characteristics of Divine mercy. They are considered one
inseparable attribute, for both are alike in spelling and pro-
nounciation. The first Name is the great attribute of unsought mercy.
G-d is merciful; He does not withhold the reward of any creature, nor
does He thrust away the wicked. Scripture states, *For He hath not
despised nor abhorred the lowliness of the poor, neither hath He hid
His face from him.*[167] He also has compassion upon the wicked, as it
states, *The Eternal is good to all, and His tender mercies are over all
His works,*[168] including the nations of the world. Thus, the Sages expounded, "My handiwork is drowning in the sea, and you offer to
recite songs."[169] G-d's mercy also extends over cattle, as it is said, *Man
and beast Thou savest, O Eternal.*[170] A great proof that G-d does not

---

(164) Rosh Hashanah 17 b. The obvious intention is of course not the mere recitation of the Thirteen Attributes, but rather their recitation when accompanied by deeds
which are favorable in the presence of G-d (Ein Yaakov). (165) Exodus 34:10.
(166) *Ibid.*, Verse 6.   (167) Psalms 22:25.   (168) *Ibid.*, 145:9.   (169) Sanhedrin
39 b. Upon the drowning of the Egyptians in the Red Sea, the angels desired to recite
their usual hymn. G-d, however, said to them, "My handiwork is drowning, etc." G-d
therefore hindered them from singing at that time. On the other hand, Israel, which
had personally suffered at the hand of the Egyptians, was permitted to sing the Song at
the Red Sea.   (170) Psalms 36:7.

thrust away the wicked may be derived from the people of Nineveh, who were extremely wicked and perpetrated many sins. Nevertheless, when they turned from their evil ways, G-d accepted their repentance and the decree against them was annulled.

The second Divine Name is also one of compassion, but it is unlike the first, which indicates mercy given without being sought, as a father has compassion upon his children without their asking for it. In the second Divine Name, G-d bestows His compassion when the person asks forgiveness or anything else he needs, such as sustenance, healing, salvation, etc. It is thus said, *O Eternal, hear, O Eternal, forgive, O Eternal, attend and do.*[171] G-d mentioned this attribute in regard to all of man's needs, for He has compassion upon all things.

G-d.[166] This Divine attribute applies only to two specific matters: forgiveness for sin and healing, as it is said, *O G-d, heal her now, I beseech Thee.*[172] One is answered by this attribute only upon tearful request and supplication.

Merciful and gracious.[166] These attributes are alike in compassion. However, *merciful* indicates that G-d grants an urgent request for sustenance or healing even though the supplicant does not ask forgiveness for his few sins. *Gracious* applies to G-d's hearing one's request for satisfaction upon being humiliated by his fellow man, as it is written, *And it shall come to pass, when he* [the poor man] *crieth unto Me, that I will hear, for I am gracious.*[173]

Long-suffering[166] comprises the fifth and sixth Divine attributes.[174] All of the preceding attributes referred to one who is mostly righteous. Here, we encounter one who does not ask forgiveness for his few sins.[175]

---

(171) Daniel 9:19. (172) Numbers 12:13. (173) Exodus 22:26. (174) The Hebrew term *erech apayim* is in the plural, denoting that G-d is long-suffering with both the righteous and the wicked. Therefore, our author considers *long-suffering* as two attributes, as the text continues to explain. (175) In the attribute *Merciful*, as explained above, the supplicant likewise has not asked forgiveness for his few sins. Here, in *Long-suffering* the sinner is not a supplicant at all in addition to not asking forgiveness for his sins.

By this attribute, G-d does not hasten to punish such a person. Thus the Sages said,[176] "G-d is *long suffering*, to the righteous and the wicked."

Abundant in goodness[166] applies to one whose sins equal his good deeds. G-d, Who is *abundant in goodness*, inclines the scales of judgment towards grace, and the individual is judged like one who has a majority of good deeds. When he asks for mercy, G-d answers him accordingly.

And truth.[166] This refers to one whose deeds are mostly sinful. When he repents, G-d forgives him for all his sins except that of failing to study Torah, being that the attribute of *truth* is one of justice. Therefore, *truth* does not call for treatment beyond the line of justice.[177]

Keeping mercy to thousands of generations.[178] This attribute concerns one who is predominantly righteous. G-d remembers his good deeds and for thousands of generations [deals kindly with his descendants] who may have but few good deeds of their own. This benefit applies only to an ancestor who has worshipped G-d out of love, but if he worshipped out of fear, his good deeds are remembered only for a thousand generations.[179]

Forgiving iniquity[178] refers to one who is principally wantonly sinful. If he repents and asks forgiveness, G-d pardons him completely. *And transgressions.*[178] This concerns one who has acted rebelliously. Upon repenting, he is forgiven. *And sin.*[178]. This refers to acts committed unintentionally, for even unintentional sins require repentance when one becomes aware of having committed them.

---

(176) Sanhedrin 111 a.   (177) The apparent thought here suggested is that the study of Torah is the source of knowledge of the truth. Therefore, having failed to take advantage of this source of truth, he may be forgiven for all sins, except for that of not studying the Torah.   (178) Exodus 34:7. The Hebrew *alaphim* (thousands) denotes at least two thousand generations. See text further.   (179) Deuteronomy 7:9.

And He will clear the guilty. [178] This attribute regards one who sins again after having repented some former sin and having been forgiven by G-d. Although he now sins again, G-d does not count the former sins together with this sin. Upon his repentance, G-d clears him again. [180]

May G-d cleanse us from iniquity and grant us life in the World to Come. May He forgive our iniquities on this Day of Atonement, as He has assured us in His perfect Torah, *For on this day shall atonement be made for you, to cleanse you; from all your sins shall ye be clean before the Eternal.* [160]

---

(180) In summary, these then are the Thirteen Attributes according to Rabbeinu Bachya: 1) *The Eternal, the Eternal,* 2) *G-d,* 3) *Merciful,* 4) *Gracious,* 5-6) *Long-suffering*—see Note 174, 7) *Abundant in goodness,* 8) *and truth,* 9) *Keeping mercy to thousands of generations,* 10) *Forgiving iniquity,* 11) *and transgression,* 12) *and sin,* 13) *and He will clear the guilty.*

לשון הרע
The Evil Tongue

The positive commandment of remembering what happened to Miriam when she spoke evil of Moses / The reason the Torah forbids us to join those idle people who gather for purposeless chatter / The great severity of the sin of slander and its punishment / Slander and shade of slander / The sin of slander is as severe as committing a sinful act / Slander of quarrelsome people / The great obligation to guard oneself in his speech, since the power of speech stems from the rational soul.

The Evil Tongue

REMEMBER WHAT THE ETERNAL THY G-D DID UNTO
MIRIAM, ON THE WAY YE CAME FORTH OUT OF EGYPT.[1]

This constitutes a positive commandment of the Torah[2] and is included among the *taryag*[3] commandments. It is similar in expression to
the positive commandments, *Remember this day, in which ye came
out of Egypt,*[4] and *Remember the Sabbath-day, to keep it holy.*[5] Moses
our teacher thus warns us in the above verse[1] that slander is extremely
loathsome and that those who engage in it are not worthy of receiving
the Divine Presence [as explained further on].

With regard to this abhorrent practice, the verse is stating what happened to Miriam the prophetess because of slander. She spoke only

---

(1) Deuteronomy 24:9. Miriam compared Moses to other prophets. She also implied
criticism of Moses' separation from marital life, something which other prophets did
not do. For this mistaken slander, Miriam was stricken with leprosy. The verse here
thus serves to remind us of the abhorrence which G-d has for slander, and that we
should guard ourselves against it. See Numbers, Chapter 12. (2) This is in accord
ance with the opinion of Ramban. See Commentary on the Torah, Deuteronomy, pp.
298-300, and "The Commandments," Vol. I, p. 264. (3) See above, *Emunah* (Faith
in G-d) Note 32. (4) Exodus 13:3. This constitutes a positive commandment to
remember daily the Exodus from Egypt (Rabbeinu Bachya, *ibid.,* – p. 100 in my edition). (5) *Ibid.,* 20:8. This commandment enjoins us "to recite certain words at the
commencement and the end of the Sabbath, thereby mentioning the greatness and
high dignity of the day and its distinction from the weekdays which have preceded and
are to follow (Maimonides, "The Commandments," Vol. I, p. 181).

about her brother Moses whom she herself had raised.[6] She did not mention the matter to other people but only discussed it privately with her brother Aaron, and she did not repeat it in the presence of Moses who might have been ashamed and embarrassed by her talk. Nevertheless, she was punished with leprosy;[7] all her good deeds could not protect her from punishment. This is certainly an *a fortiori* lesson for other people. Miriam, Moses' elder sister, risked her life for his sake in the affair at the Nile.[6] Moreover, Moses did not mind her words. Furthermore, her words were not really slander; she only mistakenly compared Moses to other prophets.[7] If, notwithstanding all this, Miriam was still punished with leprosy for her sin, it is certainly logical that an extremely severe punishment will be incurred by people who really slander those superior in wisdom and age, and those who are sensitive to slanderous statements.

For this reason, the Torah has prohibited us from joining those idle people who gather for purposeless chatter. It is stated, *For a dream cometh through a multitude of business, and a fool's voice through a multitude of words.*[8] That is to say, just as most dreams are worthless and devoid of meaning, so are most of the words of a fool. By engaging in vain talk, one will eventually slander common people and ultimately even the righteous and the prophets. This will lead him to scorn their words, as it is said, *But they mocked the messengers of G-d.*[9] Finally, once he has become accustomed to disparaging people, he will then belittle Heaven by denying the fundamental principle of religion. It is thus written, *They have set their mouth against the heavens, and their tongue walketh through the earth,*[10] for their slander of mortals upon the earth has brought them to defy G-d Who is in heaven.

---

(6) Miriam, the eldest child in the family, helped her mother raise Moses. In fact, it was she who helped save the infant Moses from the Nile. See Exodus 2:7. Ramban, in his Commentary on the Torah, Deuteronomy, p. 299, expresses the same thought about Miriam's relationship to Moses, and he adds that it was upon Moses that "she bestowed her mercy and whom she loved as herself." (7) See Numbers 12:6-7. (8) Ecclesiastes 5:2. (9) II Chronicles 36:15. (10) Psalms 73:9.

Because of the severity of the sin of slander, those guilty thereof will not be permitted to receive the Divine Presence [in the World to Come]. The Sages commented,[11] "Four categories of people will not receive the Divine Presence: flatterers, liars, slanderers, and scorners." We find that David classified the slanderer among thieves and adulterers and said that the slanderer is not fit to study the Torah. Thus, he stated, *When thou sawest a thief, thou hadst company with him, and with adulterers was thy portion.*[12] He concluded, *Thou hast let loose thy mouth for evil, and thy tongue frameth deceit.*[13] Thus, he compared the slanderer to the thief and adulterer.

Solomon, too, spoke of the need to guard the tongue, saying, *A man's belly shall be filled with the fruit of his mouth.*[14] *Death and life are in the power of the tongue.*[15] In these two verses, Solomon thus informed us of the power of the tongue to achieve either good or evil. If one uses his speech in the study of Torah, instructing and causing the multitude to be righteous, *behold, His reward is with Him and His recompense before Him.*[16] However, if one uses his speech for gossip and slander, his punishment is ready and prepared for him. Hence, the beginning of the verse, *A man's belly shall be filled with the fruit of his mouth,*[14] addresses itself to the punishment meted out to the slanderer, and the end of that verse, *with the increase of his lips shall he be satisfied,*[14] speaks of the reward of the righteous man who causes the multitude to be righteous and who causes a community to do good through the power of his speech. The following verse, *Death and life are in the power of the tongue,*[15] is thus connected to the preceding one. It is stating that since death and life lie in the power of the tongue, one who loves to speak should ensure to limit himself to words of wisdom, instructions for moral living, truth, and peace. His reward

---

(11) Sotah 42 a. (12) Psalms 50:18. (13) *Ibid.,* Verse 19. (14) Proverbs 18:20. The way a person speaks, so will he be compensated. If he answers softly, it will turn away wrath, but if he answers harshly, it will stir up anger (Ralbag). In other words, speech is a powerful factor in a person's life, and one should use it responsibly. (15) *Ibid.,* Verse 21. (16) See Isaiah 40:10. In other words the reward of that person is assured by G-d.

will then be great, and the more he speaks, the greater his reward. The opposite is true of the slanderer.

We find this statement in the Midrash:[17] *"Death and life are in the power of the tongue.*[15] Everything is dependent upon the tongue. If a man has used his faculties in the study of Torah, he has merited life, for the Torah is a tree of life, as it is said, *She is a tree of life to them that lay hold upon her.*[18] The Torah is the remedy for slander, as it is said, *A healing tongue is a tree of life.*[19] However, if one has engaged in slander, he is liable to death, for slander is more grievous than murder. In case of murder, only the victim is killed, but one who slanders, kills simultaneously three people: himself [by incurring the punishment of death], the one who [listens to and] accepts the slander, and the slandered party. Is it more grievous to kill with a sword or with an arrow? To kill with a sword requires close proximity to the victim, but not so with the arrow. Therefore, the slanderer is likened to the arrow, as it is said, *Their tongue is a sharpened arrow, it speaketh deceit.*[20] It is similarly stated, *Even the sons of men, whose teeth are spears and arrows, and their tongue a sharp sword.*[21] To slander is to deny the fundamental principle of our religion, for it is stated, *Who have said, Our tongue we will make mighty, our lips are with us; who is lord over us?*[22] Slander is more grievous than bloodshed, immorality, and idolatry. In the case of bloodshed, it is written, *And Cain said unto the Eternal: Is my sin too great to be borne?*[23] Regarding immorality, it is written [that Joseph said to Potiphar's wife], *How then can I do this great wickedness?*[24] Regarding idolatry, it is written [that Moses said to G-d], *Oh, these people have sinned a great sin.*[25] However, it is written of slander, *May the Eternal cut off all flattering lips, the tongue that speaketh great words.*[26] It is therefore written, *Death and life are in the power of the tongue.*"[15]

---

(17) Tanchuma, *Metzora*, 2. (18) Proverbs 3:18. (19) *Ibid.*, 15:4. (20) Jeremiah 9:7. (21) Psalms 57:5. (22) *Ibid.*, 12:6. (23) Genesis 4:13. (24) *Ibid.*, 39:9. (25) Exodus 32:31. (26) Psalms 12:4. Scripture refers to each of the other three transgressions—bloodshed, immorality, and idolatry—as a *great* sin, which is in the singular. In case of slander, Scripture uses the plural *g'doloth*

In Midrash Tehillim, the Sages expounded:[27] *"I said: I will take heed in my ways, that I sin not with my tongue.*[28] Slander is more grievous than idolatry. When Israel sinned [on occasions] in the wilderness, the Heavenly decree of their punishment was not finalized until they sinned by speaking [evil against the Land of Israel], for it is said, *And the Eternal heard the voice of your words.*[29] It is further written, *Ye have wearied the Eternal with your words.*[30] It does not say 'with your deeds,' but *with your words.* Similarly, it states, *For Jerusalem is ruined, and Judah is fallen, because their tongue and their doings are against the Eternal.*[31] It is also written, *My heritage* [Israel] *is become unto Me as a lion in the forest; she has uttered her voice against Me, therefore have I hated her.*[32] Has G-d indeed hated Israel because of *her voice?* Has He not loved Israel's voice, as it is said, *Let Me hear thy voice?*[33] Rather, we must say that G-d both loved and hated Israel because of her voice. He loved her because of her voice, as it is said, *Let Me hear thy voice,*[33] And He hated her because of her voice, as it said, *She has uttered her voice against Me, therefore have I hated her.*[32] You must therefore admit that *death and life are in the power of the tongue.* "[15]

Certain types of speech constitute slander and others constitute a shade of slander. The Sages defined an expression of slander as follows:[34] "What is an instance of slander?[35] One who says, 'There is fire only in that house.' "[36] In Tractate Baba Bathra, the Sages commented,[37] "There are three sins mankind encounters daily and cannot

---

(great words), thus indicating that slander is equal to all those other sins which Scripture describes as *great.* (27) Midrash Tehillim 39. (28) Psalms 39:2. (29) Deuteronomy 1:34. (30) Malachi 2:17. (31) Isaiah 3:8. (32) Jeremiah 12:8. (33) Song of Songs 2:14. (34) Arakhin 15 b. (35) I.e., "what is an instance of a shade of slander?"—Slander itself is known. The question then must be understood as referring to a shade of slander. See also the following note. (36) Rashi *ibid.*, explains the implication of this statement: "In that house, which is occupied by a rich man, there is always a fire burning for the preparation of meals." This is an example of a shade of slander. See Rashbam, Baba Bathra, 165 a. (37) Baba Bathra 164 b.

avoid them: impure thoughts, lack of devotion in prayer, and slander. Do you really mean slander?[38] You must rather say, a shade of slander."

There are many people who think that the sin involving speech is not as grave as the commission of a sinful act. Therefore, King Solomon said, *As a maul, and a sword, and a sharp arrow, so is a man that beareth false witness against his neighbor.*[39] He is stating: "Do not suppose that the damage wrought by the tongue extends only to the sphere of speech and not to that of deed. On the contrary, it is as severe as if one takes a maul, sword, or sharp arrow, and smites someone with it. If you testify [falsely] that someone is liable to stripes, you have used your tongue as a maul; if you charge him by a crime punishable by death, your tongue acts like a sword; and if [you charge him with a crime punishable] by stoning, your tongue acts like a sharp arrow."

It is permissible to slander quarrelsome people, for it is said, *But me, even me thy servant, and Zadok the priest,* [etc., *hath he not called*].[40] One who fails to discredit people who are not conducting themselves properly is himself liable to punishment.

A person is obligated to beware sinning with his power of speech, for that faculty in man originates in his rational soul and distinguishes him from other living creatures. Therefore, one should take heed to save his soul by avoiding sinful speech. Thus, Solomon said, *Whoso guardeth his mouth and his tongue guardeth his soul from trouble.*[41]

---

(38) That is, why should you say that a person cannot escape slander daily? It is certainly possible to do so!   (39) Proverbs 25:18.   (40) I Kings 1:26. This was part of the prophet Nathan's report to King David of Adoniyahu's plans to assume the throne after David's death. Nathan had promised Bath-sheba, Solomon's mother, that after she would first inform the King of Adoniyahu's plans, Nathan would then appear before David *and confirm* her *words* (Verse 14). Based on the expression, *and confirm thy words,* the Yerushalmi, Peiah I, 1, derives the principle that it is permissible to discredit quarrelsome people.   (41) Proverbs 21:23.

לולב
The Lulav

The center of the earth is Zion, the point from which the earth was founded. Similarly, the essential strength of every individual object is concentrated in the center thereof / G-d's delight in Israel surpasses His delight in all other creatures of heaven and earth / The purpose and goal of all of the commandments of the Torah is to acknowledge the Creator. The palm branch thus alludes to G-d, Who is higher than the high / Various Talmudic and Midrashic interpretations of the Four Species / The importance of performing the commandment of taking the palm branch, which has been compared to an offering. An offering can be brought only in the city of Zion, thus intimating that all blessings and consolations originate from Zion.

The Lulav

OUT OF ZION, THE PERFECTION OF BEAUTY, G-D HATH
SHINED FORTH.[1]

This verse speaks of the resurrection, for it is written in the preceding verse, *G-d, the Eternal hath spoken, and called the earth.*[2] The purport of this verse[2] is that "G-d *called* those resting in *the earth,*" as it says of the resurrection, *All ye inhabitants of the world, and ye that rest in the earth.*[3] This is also similar to the statement, *Awake and sing, ye that dwell in the dust.*[4] Therefore, [in speaking of the resurrection] the psalmist subsequently states here, *He will call to the heavens above*[5] — a reference to the soul — *and to the earth, that He may judge His people*[5] — a reference to the body. This theme is the basis of this entire psalm.

Accordingly, the intent of this verse[1] is to state that the great miracle of resurrection will begin at Zion. The reason [that Zion was chosen as the site of the resurrection is] that the world was created and perfected from Zion. Scripture is thus stating that the first call to the dead, who dwell in the earth, will be from Zion, *the perfection of beauty,*[1] the place from which the beauty of the world was perfected.

---

(1) Psalms 50:2. After the Revelation on Sinai, the Divine Glory also revealed itself *out of Zion, the perfection of beauty,* manifesting G-d's pleasure in Israel. Our author uses the verse in the sense that in the future, likewise, the Glory of G-d will reveal itself out of Zion as explained in the text. From the centrality of Zion, the author's thought leads to the Four Species used on the Festival of Tabernacles. (2) *Ibid.,* Verse 1. (3) Isaiah 18:3. (4) *Ibid.,* 26:19. (5) Psalms 50:4.

It is common knowledge that the center of the inhabited world is Zion, the point from which the world was founded. Similarly, the essential strength of every individual object is concentrated in the center thereof. For example, the Tent of Meeting was located in the midst of the four camps of Israel.[6] Likewise, the formation of a person from the embryonic stage starts from the center, the navel. Thus, [a person's physical development is] similar to a tree, the branches of which spread in all directions. As soon as the child is born, the umbilical cord is cut. The Sages commented,[7] "Just as the navel is at the center of the body, so is the Land of Israel situated at the center of the world. Jerusalem lies at the center of the Land, and the Temple is located in the center of Jerusalem. The Sanctuary[8] is in the center of the Temple, and the Ark stood in the center of the Sanctuary. The Foundation Stone, from which the world was founded, was before the Ark."[9]

This design is reflected in the human eye, for man is a microcosm, reflecting the great world. The Sages commented in Pirkei d'Rabbi Eliezer:[10] "Abba Yosei ben Chanan says in the name of Shmuel Hakatan, 'This world is like the human eye. The white thereof is like the Atlantic Ocean, which encompasses the entire world. The iris resembles the world. The pupil is typical of Jerusalem, and the image in the pupil symbolizes the Sanctuary.' "[8]

The aforementioned statement[7] that the world was founded from the Foundation Stone is further corroborated by this comment of the

---

(6) See Numbers 2:2. This indicated that the essential strength of Israel was in the Tabernacle and all it stood for. (7) Tanchuma, *Kedoshim*, 10. (8) That is, the Temple structure proper. The term "Temple," as employed here, applies to the environs amid which the Temple structure stood. (9) In Hilchoth Beth Habchirah 4:1, Maimonides clearly states that the Ark of Testimony stood upon the Foundation Stone. The expression here, cited from the Midrash, should be understood accordingly. (10) Pirkei d'Rabbi Eliezer Zuta, end of Chapter 9. See also Maimonides, Guide of the Perplexed, I, Chapter 72, which is devoted entirely to this theme.

Sages:[11] "The heavenly beings and the earthly creatures all stem from Zion." It is needless to say the lower world [was created from Zion], for it is said in the Midrash:[11] "Rabbi Eliezer the Great says, '*These are the generations of the heaven and the earth when they were created.*[12] This verse teaches us that heavenly things were created from the heavens, and earthly creatures were created from the earth.' The Sages say, 'Both were created from Zion, for it is said, *Out of Zion, the perfection of beauty, G-d hath shined forth,*[1] which means that out of Zion, the beauty of the world has been perfected.' " Similarly, we find that our Rabbis said:[13] "The chief dwelling of the Divine Presence was among the earthly creatures," for despite their physical and rational powers, the spheres and all their hosts were created to serve man. It is thus written, *And let them* [the luminaries] *be for lights in the firmament of the heaven to give light upon the earth.*[14]

Philosophers object to this [idea that the spheres and all their hosts were created to serve man]. They claim that it is not in consonance with the wisdom of a great architect to build a mighty and fortified palace in order to hide therein a single berry. Notwithstanding this argument, we have nothing on which to rely except the truth of the Torah, which is justified in all its words, and the Torah tells us that a righteous man is more important and more distinguished than all the spheres and angels. The Sages clearly enunciated this concept:[15] "The righteous are greater than the ministering angels." They bring proof thereto from Scripture, which states, *And the appearance of the fourth is like an angel of G-d.*[16] A further proof is provided by the Sages' exposition in Midrash Tanchuma:[17] "*And the Eternal uttered His voice*

---

(11) Yoma 54 b. (12) Genesis 2:4. (13) Bereshith Rabbah 19:13. (14) Genesis 1:15.—The fact that the heavenly luminaries were created to serve the inhabitants of the earth, as the verse indicates, shows that the Divine Presence intended essentially to dwell upon the earth. (15) Sanhedrin 93 a. (16) Daniel 3:25. After first mentioning the appearance of three righteous men who were unharmed by fires of the furnace, Nebuchadnezzar mentioned that he saw *the fourth* being who was *like an angel of G-d.* It is obvious from this verse that the righteous men are more important than angels, since Nebuchadnezzar mentioned the three righteous men first and then the angel. (17) Tanchuma, *Vayikra*, 1.

before His army. [18] *Army* refers to the angels, as it is said, *This is G-d's camp.* [19] The verse[18] continues, *He that fulfilleth His word is powerful.* This refers to the righteous person, who is mightier than the angels because he fulfills the command of G-d, as it is said, *Ye mighty in strength, that fulfill His word.* [20] This latter verse alludes to the people of Israel, who declared, *We will do, and we shall hear.* [21] [They thus expressed their determination to fulfill G-d's directive even before they would understand the reason for it.]"

It appears to me that the words of Moses also provide somewhat of a proof in this matter. Moses said, *Behold, unto the Eternal thy G-d belongeth the heaven, and the heaven of heavens, the earth, with all that is therein.* [22] *Only the Eternal had a delight in thy fathers to love them.* [23] This indicates that G-d's delight in Israel surpasses the delight He has in all His creations of heaven and earth. If Moses intended only to extol Israel's importance over other earthly creations, he should have said, "Behold, unto the Eternal thy G-d belongeth the earth." [There would have been no need to mention *the heaven, and heaven of heavens.*]

David, too, mentioned all creation in his psalm, *Praise the Eternal from the earth.* [24] David concluded, *And He hath lifted up a horn for His people.* [25] Isaiah also said, *Thus saith the Eternal: The heaven is My throne,* etc.[26] *For all these things hath My hand made, and so all these things came to be, saith the Eternal, but on this man will I look, even on him that is poor and of a contrite spirit.* [27] This is the humble righteous man, the essence of everything in creation.

Contemplate the high distinction of man. In His Torah, G-d commanded that material vessels be made for the Tabernacle and Sanctuary, all of which were designs and similitudes of rational things in the Higher World,[28] so that His Divine Presence would dwell among the

---

(18) Joel 2:11. (19) Genesis 32:3. (20) Psalms 103:20. (21) Exodus 24:7. (22) Deuteronomy 10:14. (23) *Ibid.,* Verse 5. (24) Psalms 148:7. The first verse of this psalm states, *Praise ye the Eternal from the heavens.* (25) *Ibid.,* Verse 14. (26) Isaiah 66:1. (27) *Ibid.,* Verse 2. (28) See Rabbeinu Bachya's commentary on Exodus, Chapters 25-26, where he elaborates on this theme.

earthly creatures. Moreover, the earthly creatures are more dearly loved by Him than those above, for He left the latter and came to dwell
among those on the earth, as it is said, *And they shall make Me a Sanctuary, that I may dwell among them.*[29] It is indeed a great distinction
for Israel to have had such a great attachment to G-d, blessed be He.
With regard to this, Scripture alludes, *And ye shall be Mine own
's'gulah' (treasure).*[30] The word *s'gulah* is applied to those objects
which contain some hidden power like that in certain vegetations and
pearls.

Because of Israel's close attachment to G-d, you will find that He
distinguishes them and praises them as being one nation. The Sages
commented,[31] "It is written in the phylacteries of the Creator of the
world, *And who is like Thy people Israel, a nation one in the earth.*"[32]
This is similar to Israel's praise of G-d by the proclamation of His Unity, *Hear, O Israel: the Eternal our G-d, the Eternal is One.*[33]

It is common knowledge that G-d's Unity is the essential principle of
the commandments of the Torah and of the worship of G-d. Although
His creations in the heavens and on earth are many, He is nevertheless
One and supreme above them. We can prove this from mathematics.
The number "one" does not begin a computation. Instead, it is the
cause of the computation.[34] Now, just as "one" is the cause of computation [of the numbers which succeed it] but in itself is not a part
thereof, so the Creator is the Cause of the existence of the world but is
not part of it. Just as all numbers would be nullified by the removal of
the power of "one" — they exist as numbers only because of "one" — so

---

(29) Exodus 25:8. (30) *Ibid.,* 19:5. (31) Berachoth 6 a. (32) I Chronicles
17:21. (33) Deuteronomy 6:4. (34) Although you have the number "one," no computation can be made with that integer alone. However, computations can begin when
you have the numbers "two," "three," etc. Thus, the number "one" does not begin the
computation but is the cause of it. This entire argument is developed at greater length
by our author in the next essay, *Metziuth Hashem Yithbarach* (Existence of G-d). See
Note 23 there.

would all that exists in heaven and on earth cease to be if the power of the Creator, blessed be He, were withdrawn. Furthermore, the power of "one" would remain even if you removed all other numbers, for "one" is like a tree and the other numbers are its fruits. The tree does not necessitate the existence of the fruits, but the fruits require the tree. So it is with the Creator. If all things would disappear, His power would not disappear; He would continue to exist forever and ever. This is an incontrovertible analogy from mathematics that the world needs G-d but He does not need the world. Just as "one" is the cause of "two," through which it causes "three," etc., until "nine," the last of the units, so the One G-d is the Cause of all things through the intermediary powers which exist between Him and them, each one of which is higher than the other. The power of the One, however, Who is the Cause of all of them, extends throughout the entire universe, for He is the Cause of everything and the Most High over all, as Solomon said, *For One higher than the high watcheth over them, being the Highest Power.*[35]

This great theme is alluded to in the commandment of the palm branch. The palm branch has many leaves, each higher than the other and all are attached to the spine of the palm branch. This arrangement intimates that all things have come into existence by cause upon cause, until you reach the First Cause, Who is G-d, Creator of everything. Therefore, it is proper to take the palm branch in the right hand and recite the benediction over it, as the Rabbis said,[36] "The palm branch is the highest of the Four Species, [which, in addition to the palm branch, include the *ethrog*, the myrtle, and the willow]." We have explained here that the palm branch alludes to the One Who is higher than the high. Thus, the verse states, *And ye shall take you on the first day* [of the Feast of Tabernacles] *the fruit of a goodly tree, a branch of palm trees, and the thick bough of a tree, and willows of the brook,* etc.[37]

(35) Ecclesiastes 5:7.   (36) Succah 37 b.   (37) Leviticus 23:40.

Our Rabbis have taught:[38] "Rabbi Yishmael says, 'Three myrtle branches, two willow branches, one palm branch, and one *ethrog*' "[39] [combine to make up the Four Species ordained in the Torah, as will be explained]. *The fruit of a goodly tree*[37] is in the singular, [thus teaching that only one *ethrog* should be taken]. *Kapoth (a branch of) palm trees*[37] is likewise in the singular, since the Hebrew word is written [in Scripture]: *kaph, pei,* and *thav,* [omitting the *vav* between the *pei* and *thav,* which would mean "branches of" in the plural]. It thus teaches us that there should be but one palm branch. *Palm trees* is written in the plural because there are two types: male and female. Were it not for the two of them, they would not grow, for it is the natural way of plants as well as precious stones to be either masculine or feminine. In the phrase, *the thick bough of a tree*[37] the word *thick* refers to the *bough.* It is thus saying that the boughs should be thick and covered with leaves. If not, it cannot be classified as a *bough* but must be considered the tree itself. [It would thus be invalidated], for the Torah has specified *bough of a tree.*[37] The word *thick* means that there must be at least three leaves. The size of each of the three myrtle branches must be a minimum of three hand-breadths in length. However, this requirement is Rabbinical in origin; by law of the Torah, three moist leaves would suffice, provided that they are at the top of each branch. The Torah has written the word *avoth* (thick) diminutively, [it lacks the pluralizing *vav* between the letters *beth* and *thav*]. We thus learn that the three leaves must come out from one root. For this reason, the Sages said,[40] "Three leaves close together on one stem." Finally, *willows of the brook*[37] denote a minimum of two.[41]

The Sages expounded in the Midrash:[42] "*The fruit of a goodly tree*[36] represents Abraham. *A branch of palm trees* is Isaac. *The thick bough of a tree* is Jacob, *and willows of the brook* represent Joseph." The in-

---

(38) Succah 34 b.   (39) See above, *Ahavah* (Love of G-d), Note 13.   (40) Succah 32 b.   (41) This concludes the explanation of the brief Mishnah, "Rabbi Yishmael says, etc." The laws cited here are the accepted rule of practice.   (42) Vayikra Rabbah 30:10.

terpretation of this Midrash is as follows: *Fruit* is in the singular, for Abraham declared the Unity of G-d in the world and proclaimed His Divinity. Abraham's words bore fruit, for it is written, *And the souls they had gotten in Haran.*[43] It is further stated, *Abraham was one.*[44] Scripture uses the term *tree* [with regard to Abraham], for just as a tree which lacked water did not bear fruit until it was watered, so did Abraham despair of having offspring and then begot a son when he was a hundred years old. Scriptures uses the adjective *goodly,* for G-d crowned Abraham with hoary age, as the Sages said,[45] "Until Abraham, there was no old age, as it is said, *And Abraham was old, well advanced in age.*[46] It is further stated, *And the beauty of old men is the hoary head.*"[47]

"*A branch of palm trees* is Isaac." The word *kapoth* (branch of) also denotes "bound." [Thus, the phrase *a branch of palm trees* is indicative of Isaac], who was bound upon an altar as an offering. The word *t'marim* (palm branches) also suggests a connection with the phrase *k'thimroth ashan (like pillars of smoke).*[48] Isaac was considered an unblemished burnt-offering, and it is stated, *Who is this that cometh up out of the wilderness like pillars of smoke?*[48]

"*The thick bough of a tree* is Jacob." Just as a bough is covered with leaves, so Jacob is "covered" by the twelve tribes. "*And willows of the brook* represent Joseph." The willow can be moist, withered, or dry. Joseph, too, was at first fresh when he was viceroy to the King of Egypt and ruler of the land. When his father Jacob died, Joseph's strength was sapped and his great merit dried up, as he died before his brothers.[49]

---

(43) Genesis 12:5. (44) Ezekiel 33:24. (45) Baba Metzia 86 a. It is true that there were other old people before Abraham, but not in the sense that the more they advanced in age they grew more stable in understanding. In that perspective Abraham was the first to achieve this blessing. (46) Genesis 24:1. (47) Proverbs 20:29. (48) Song of Songs 3:6. (49) See Genesis 50:24-26. In our text of Vayikra Rabbah 30:10, the reading is: "Just as the willow of the brook is first of the Four Species to wither, so was Joseph first to die before his brothers." The intent of the Midrash is not to degrade Joseph as a person but rather to minimize the glamor of his

The purport of this Midrash[42] is that by our performance of the commandment of the palm branch, we are alluding to the merits of the patriarchs and asking G-d in His mercy to protect us by virtue of those merits. We find that Moses our teacher, master of all prophets, included the merit of the patriarchs in his prayer and supplication for G-d's mercy. He said, *Remember Abṛaham, Isaac, and Israel, Thy servants,*[50] meaning that their merits should act as shield and buckler for Israel.

There is another Midrash [concerning the commandment of the palm branch]:[51] *"The fruit of a goodly tree.*[37] The *ethrog,* is edible and has a pleasant taste and fragrance. *A branch of palm trees.* The palm tree has no fragrance, but it does bear edible dates, which have taste. *The thick bough of a tree.* The myrtle has fragrance but it does not yield any edible substance. Finally, the willows of the brook are inedible and have neither taste nor fragrance. The *ethrog* thus alludes to the righteous person who possesses both erudition and good deeds. The palm branch represents those who have knowledge of the Torah but do not practice good deeds. The myrtle symbolizes one who practices good deeds but is ignorant of the Torah. Finally, the willow stands for one who is ignorant of the Torah and does not practice good deeds. G-d said, 'Let all those types of people come before Me as one brotherhood, and I will forgive them all their sins.' " A similar concept is suggested with reference to the ingredients of the incense, [which was burnt daily in the Sanctuary]. All ingredients were aromatic except galbanum, the smell of which is offensive. [It was intentionally included in the incense] to teach us that the wicked of Israel should be counted with the righteous in prayer so that G-d would accept their repentance.

---

wordly powers, that his position did not bestow upon him longevity over that of his older brothers. (50) Exodus 32:13. (51) Vayikra Rabbah 30:11, with textual variations. It should be noted that the intent of the Midrash as a whole is to derive moral principles from the Scriptural text. Each section is therefore to be independent of the thought developed in another section.

A further interpretation of the Four Species is that they symbolize the four organs of the body which represent the individual's essential activities regardless of their good or bad purpose. The four organs are: the eyes, the heart, the lips, and the spine. "The eyes and the heart are two agents [most vulnerable] to sin."[52] The lips, likewise, are in that category, since fulfillment of many of the commandments, as well as their transgression, depend upon speech. The spine, the backbone of the body, constitutes the natural strength thereof, the source of which is the brain. The *ethrog* is like the heart, the palm branch like the spine, the myrtle like the eyes, and the willow like the lips. The intent of the commandment is to remind the individual that if he has stumbled in sin effected by these four organs of the body, he can redeem himself by doing something favorable with those same organs. For example, if a person sinned by profaning G-d's Name, even repentance and the Day of Atonement cannot expiate his sin. Affliction, too, cannot expunge his transgression, [which remains with him] until the day of his death. However, if he later sanctifies G-d's Name, he will have atoned for his sin. The Sages clearly said,[53] "If a person has sinned through slander, he should engage in the study of Torah." Sin is a sickness of the soul. Just like a sickness of the body, it can only be healed by its antithesis. A proficient physician will heal his patient by prescribing that which is antithetical to his sickness. Regarding King Herod, who asked Baba ben Buta whether there is a remedy for him for having killed many of the scholars of Israel, the Sages report that Baba answered,[54] "Herod extinguished the light of the world. Let him go and engage in reestablishing the light of the world by rebuilding the Sanctuary." It is enlightening to one's heart to know that sin can be remedied by offsetting it with the performance of a similar deed in connection with some commandment.

---

(52) Yerushalmi Berachoth I, 8.   (53) I have not found the source of this saying. The thought, however, is explicitly expressed in Arakhin 15 b: "What is the slanderer's remedy? If he is learned, he should engage in the study of Torah."   (54) Baba Bathra 4 a. See also in *Chillul Hashem* (Profaning G-d's Name), where our author quotes the same text.

Through their power of growth, the Four Species retain their freshness throughout the year. Their moistness, which is their life, lasts longer than that of other fruits, and the moisture in a fruit is like the blood in a living person. Because of their beauty, we are commanded to take these Four Species and to make them a sign and symbol for the ways of our life. Our Torah is called *the path of life.*[55] It contains *life and goodness, death and evil,*[56] and we have been commanded, *Therefore choose life.*[57] We who cleave to the Torah are called "alive," as it is said, *And ye that did cleave unto the Eternal your G-d are alive every one of you this day.*[58] In light of the foregoing, if the Four Species would become dry, they would no longer serve as a sign and symbol for our ways of life. Therefore, the Sages said on the Yerushalmi,[59] "If it is dry, it is invalid, for it says, *The dead praise not the Eternal.*"[60]

Through prayer,[61] Moses our teacher was instrumental in effecting the acknowledgment by the nations of the world that G-d is the Master of all, the Life of all worlds. By taking the Four Species, which, by their moistness, are a token of the Living G-d, we too are instrumental in proclaiming G-d's Divinity to the world and that He lives and exists forever, for all life comes only from Him.

Moses' accomplishment was explained by the Sages as follows: Moses had interceded [on behalf of Israel in the affair of the spies. He prayed that the intended punishment should not be carried out, for the nations would interpret Israel's destruction as G-d's inability to bring them into the Land].[62] G-d said to Moses, *"But in very deed, as I live,*[63] Moses you have revived Me with your words."[64] If not for your prayer, Israel would have been punished with destruction. Now, that you have nullified the punishment, you have revived Me in the sense that you

---

(55) Proverbs 5:6.   (56) Deuteronomy 30:15.   (57) *Ibid.,* Verse 19.   (58) *Ibid.,* 4:4.   (59) Yerushalmi Succah III, 1. Reference is to a dry *lulav.*   (60) Psalms 115:17.   (61) This is explained further on in the text.   (62) Numbers 14:16.   (63) *Ibid.,* Verse 21.   (64) Berachoth 32 a.

have made the nations aware of My Presence. They now know that I live and exist and that I am the Master of all. If Israel were destroyed, there would be no one to proclaim My existence to the world, and the denial of the truth would increase.

The commandment of the palm branch is important,[65] for Scripture compared it to an offering.[66] The Sages said,[67] "One who fulfills the commandment, [that is] the palm branch properly tied [to the myrtle and willow branches] and the myrtle in its correct thickness is considered by Scripture as if he built the altar and brought an offering upon it, for it is said, *Bind the festival procession with boughs, [even unto the horns of the altar].* "[68] You are aware that the offerings assure the existence of the world.[69] Offerings were brought only in the Land of Israel and were slaughtered on the northern side of the altar. Scripture therefore states, *Even Mount Zion, the uttermost parts of the north.*[70] Thus you learn that everything stems from Zion. The world was created from Zion, as we have said at the outset: *Out of Zion, the perfection of beauty, G-d hath shined forth.*[1] All blessings and consolation come from Zion, as the Sages said in Midrash Tehillim,[71] "All Divine blessings and bestowals of favor which G-d confers upon Israel stem from Zion. Blessings come from Zion, as it says, *The Eternal bless thee out of Zion.*[72] Succor comes from Zion, as it says, [The Eternal]

(65) Our author is now proceeding to link the subject of the Four Species to the centrality of Zion. By pointing out that the importance of the commandment of the palm branch is equal to that of bringing an offering, which as is known, can only be brought in the Sanctuary at Zion, the two subjects are thus united. (66) The Sages thus depict the Jew's privileged relationship to G-d: by taking the Four Species, he renews the covenant G-d made with Israel that His Presence will forever dwell only in the Sanctuary at Zion. (67) Succah 45 a-b. (68) Psalms 118:27. Rashi, in Succah 45 a-b, explains the verse to mean, "Bind the palm branch *with bough,* i.e., with the myrtle, which has the thickness of three leaves on each [of its three branches]." (69) Taanith 27 b. (70) Psalms 48:3. Thus, our author returns to the theme with which he opened this discussion—the centrality of Zion in Jewish thought—and concludes with various manifestations of blessings. (71) Midrash Tehillim, 14. (72) Psalms 134:3.

sent forth thy help from the Sanctuary, and support thee out of Zion.[73]
Life comes from Zion, as it says, *For there* [in Zion] *the Eternal commanded the blessing, even life forever.*[74] Greatness comes from Zion, as it says, *The Eternal is great in Zion.*[75] Salvation stems from Zion, as it says, *Oh that the salvation of Israel were come out of Zion.*[76] Torah comes from Zion, as it says, *For out of Zion shall go forth the law, and the word of the Eternal from Jerusalem.*"[77]

(73) *Ibid.,* 20:3. (74) *Ibid.,* 133:3. (75) *Ibid.,* 99:2. (76) *Ibid.,* 14:7. (77) Isaiah 2:3.

מציאות השם יתברך
The Existence of G-d

The primary principle of the Torah is belief in the existence of G-d / This principle entails the belief in His dominion in the past, present, and future / The different connotations of the names Jacob and Israel / Absolute existence and acquired existence / What the philosophers have derived from the numeral 'one.'

The Existence of G-d

HEARKEN UNTO ME, O JACOB, AND ISRAEL MY CALLED
ONE: I AM HE, I AM THE FIRST, I AM ALSO THE LAST.[1]

The primary principle of the Torah is belief in the existence of G-d, blessed be He, *for this is the whole* [duty of] *man.*[2] Man was created so that he should believe that there exists a Primordial Creator, Who is One and Who preceded the first of all things in existence and Who will succeed the last of all things in existence. His existence is absolute[3] and unlike the existence of all other things, which were created by Him. Their existence [being dependent on G-d], is only possible, not absolute like His.

This concept is the underlying explanation of the Divine Name, *Eh'yeh Asher Eh'yeh (I Will Be that which I Will Be),*[4] which was revealed to Moses at the burning bush. The Name denotes existence, and the purport thereof is that G-d is the existing Being in past, present, and future. That is to say, His existence is absolute, for He has never been and never will be without existence, as Maimonides explained.[5]

---

(1) Isaiah 48:12. The eternal existence of G-d is thus indicated: *I am He* in the present, *I am the first* in the past, *I am also the last* in the future. There can be, therefore, no comparison between G-d and His creatures, since they are all subject to the properties of time.   (2) Ecclesiastes 12:13. This is the whole purpose in the creation of man, that he recognize his Creator, and not live merely as any of the other lower creatures (Sforno).   (3) See above, *Emunah* (Faith) Note 4.   (4) Exodus 3:14.   (5) Guide of the Perplexed, I, Chapter 63. See also Ramban, Commentary on the Torah, Exodus, pp. 37-39.

This principle of G-d's existence is the first of the two commandments we heard at Sinai from the Almighty Himself when all Israel attained the degree of prophecy, the kind Moses our teacher possessed.[6]
It is thus stated, *I am the Eternal, thy G-d,*[7] which constitutes a
positive commandment of the Torah to believe in His existence, for He
brought us out of Egypt, *out of the house of bondage.*[7] As proof of His
existence, we also have seen with our own eyes those great signs and
wonders which followed the Exodus.

This primary principle concerning the belief in His existence entails
our belief in His dominion in the past, present, and future. You will
find that in the episode of the burning bush, G-d mentioned to Moses
the Name *Eh'yeh (I Will Be)*[4] three times in one verse in order to
establish this principle in our hearts. [In the verse cited above],
therefore, Isaiah mentioned, *Hearken unto Me, O Jacob, and Israel
My called one: I am He, I am the first, I also am the last.*[1]

In that verse, the people of Israel are referred to by the names of
Jacob and Israel, for when the Torah was given on Sinai, at which time
they accepted this principle of the belief in His existence and His dominion, these two names are used, as it is said, *Thus shalt thou say to
the house of Jacob, and tell the children of Israel.*[8] The name Jacob applies to material matters, based on the verse, *And his* [Jacob's] *hand
holding on to Esau's heel, and he* [his father Isaac] *called him Jacob.*[9]
For this reason, Scripture applies the name of Jacob to material matters, as the prophet states: *Thus said the Eternal that created thee, O
Jacob, and He that formed thee, O Israel.*[10] He mentioned Jacob in

(6) See Ramban, *ibid.*, pp. 304-305. (7) Exodus 20:2. (8) *Ibid.*,
19:3. (9) Genesis 25:26. *Yaakov,* the Hebrew name for Jacob, means "one who takes
by the heel" or "one who supplants." (10) Isaiah 43:1. The definition of the terms
creation and formation as given by our author are to be understood as follows: After a
physical entity has been "created," it is then shaped into "form." In this sense the name
Jacob represents the physical existence of the nation, while the name Israel denotes its
spiritual qualities. Hence the verse, *Thus said the Eternal that 'created' thee, O Jacob,
and He that 'formed' thee, O Israel.*

connection with creation and Israel in connection with formation. It is similarly written, *I form the light, and create darkness,* [11] thus explaining that the term "creation" applies to the physical realm and "formation" to the rational realm.

This differentiation explains the verse, *Yet thou hast not called upon Me, O Jacob, but thou hast been weary of Me, O Israel.* [12] The verse is stating that "when you pursue material quests, *thou hast not called upon Me, O Jacob,* but when you weary yourself about Me and you pursue rational matters, then you are Israel." Similarly, the prophet mentioned, *Hearken unto Me, O Jacob, and Israel My called one: I am He, I am the first, I also am the last.* [1] He mentioned Jacob, the name which his father and mother called him, and he mentioned Israel, the name which G-d called him. [13] Thus, he said, *My called one,* [1] meaning "the name which I called him," as it is said, *And He called his name Israel.* [13]

According to the Midrash, [14] *My called one* [1] is associated with the expression *the invited ones,* [15] for in the future, G-d will make a feast for the righteous at which Israel alone will merit attendance.

I am He, I am the first, I am also the last. [1] In this verse, G-d mentioned His dominion in the present, past, and future. He mentioned the present first by saying *I am He,* for the past and the future are both in the present with respect to G-d, Who is above time, as David said, *Thou art the selfsame, and Thy years shall have no end.* [16] We express a similar thought in our supplications for mercy and forgiveness: "The Eternal reigns, the Eternal has reigned, the Eternal shall reign forever and ever." [17] Of course, the latter is not one specific verse but a com-

---

(11) *Ibid.,* 45:7. (12) *Ibid.,* 43:22. (13) Genesis 35:10. See Ramban, Commentary on the Torah, Genesis, pp. 424-425. (14) Midrash Tehillim, 14. (15) II Samuel 15:11. (16) Psalms 102:28. (17) This is a combination of three verses, as will be elaborated by the author: *The Eternal reigns* (Psalms 10:16); *The Eternal has reigned (ibid.,* 93:1); *The Eternal shall reign forever (ibid.,* 146:10). The combination is recited in the Morning Service in the paragraph entitled *Yehi Ch'vod* ('Let the glory

bination of several verses which were mentioned by David in the order shown here. He first stated, *The Eternal reigns forever and ever; the nations are perished out of the earth.*[18] He next mentioned, *The Eternal has reigned, He has robed Himself in majesty.*[19] Finally, at the end of the Book of Psalms, he mentioned, *The Eternal shall reign forever, thy G-d, O Zion.*[20]

In order to implant in our hearts this principle of faith that all times are considered the present with respect to G-d, He said to Abraham at the time of the Binding of Isaac,[21] *Now I know that thou art a G-d-fearing man.*[22] That is to say, "Your good heart has already been tested before Me. I have known its quality before your actions were manifested as they now have been. However, I desired that your devotion to Me should be made known to mankind and the purity of your heart should be publicized among all nations."

It is known that the existence of G-d is absolute, while that of all other things is acquired. The meaning of "absolute existence" is that if it were possible for G-d's existence to be negated, everything else would disappear. Therefore, His existence is termed absolute because it is completely self-sufficient and independent of everything else. "Acquired existence," on the other hand, refers to the existence of all other things besides G-d. Their existence is not self-sufficient but is acquired from Him. Thus, everything is in need of His existence, while He has no need of theirs.

From the science of mathematics, philosophers have proven that G-d has no need of the existence of all other things, as follows: Just as the numeral "one" is the cause of calculation and is not in itself a part

---

of the Eternal endure forever). — It should be noted why the present is mentioned first, when in the order of time the past should have come first. The answer is as follows: The worshipper is aware of G-d's existence and dominion at present. From this awareness of G-d he derives a sense of certitude about the Creator in the past, and from both the present and the past comes his belief in Him in the future (Meshech Chochmah, Numbers 23:2). (18) Psalms 10:16. (19) *Ibid.*, 93:1. (20) *Ibid.*, 146:10. (21) Genesis, 22:1-19. (22) *Ibid.*, Verse 12.

thereof,[23] so the Creator, blessed be He, is the cause of all existing things in the world and is not a part thereof. Just as the removal of the numeral "one" would render all other integers inconceivable, so the negation of the Creator's existence would cause the extinction of all things. Just as the removal of all other digits has no effect upon "one," so the removal of all things extant would have no effect on His existence. Just as all integers acquired their existence from "one" without [their own] movement in time, or place, and "one" required nothing besides itself in order to make the other integers possible, so all created things were brought into existence by the Creator without [their] movement in time, place, or anything whatsoever. Just as the unity of "one" remains unchanged despite the increase of other numbers, which neither increase nor alter the essence of "one," so the manifold aspects of the created world do not effect any change in the Unity of the Creator or in His essence.

Thus, the existence of G-d is absolute and unlike the unity of the created higher powers. Although there are philosophic proofs which rationally demonstrate the truth of this principle, the Torah, which itself is an embodiment of reason, teaches us that G-d, blessed be He, exists, that He is One, and that He rules at all times. The prophets attest to this, as it is written, *Ye are My witness, saith the Eternal, and My servant whom I have chosen; that ye may know and believe Me, and understand that I am He; before Me there was no god formed, neither shall any be after Me.*[24]

(23) The numeral "one" is prerequisite for the process of addition. With it, you will be able to proceed to "two," "three," and all other integers. Yet "one" always remains aloof, as it were, from the other numbers. If you subtract from the other numbers, you will always have at least "one." However, "one" itself cannot be negated, for beyond it lies "zero," which denotes nothingness and non-existence. The independent integer "one" is thus the cause of all calculations, but of necessity, it itself always exists. If it were negated, all further calculations would be impossible. The analogy of the numeral "one" to the Creator is obvious.   (24) Isaiah 43:10.

מזוזה
The Mezuzah

The extra protection afforded Israel by G-d / To implant in
our hearts the principle of this Divine protection, the Torah
has commanded us to affix the 'Mezuzah' on the doorpost / Laws pertaining to the writing and affixing of the
'Mezuzah' / Why G-d's Name is mentioned inside the
'Mezuzah' and the Name 'Sha-dai' (Almighty) is inscribed outside / The great significance of this commandment.

The Mezuzah

THE ETERNAL WATCHETH OVER ALL THOSE WHO LOVE
HIM, BUT ALL THE WICKED HE WILL DESTROY.[1]

It is known that Divine Providence pervades the life of all mankind in general and each individual in particular, and that G-d's protection hovers over them. Were it not for the Divine vigilance, we would be subject to chance happenings. Due to this protection, G-d is called "The Guardian of Israel," as it is said, *Behold, He that guardeth Israel doth neither slumber nor sleep.*[2] It further states, *The Eternal is thy guardian, the Eternal is thy shade upon thy right hand.*[3] Since G-d is supreme above all and rules over the six ends [of the universe, i.e., above, below, east, west, north, and south], the psalmist mentioned the expression "guarding" six times in that psalm.[4]

Because G-d took Israel as His inheritance, His protection applies to Israel more than it does to the other nations, as it has been stated, *For let all the peoples walk each one in the name of its god, but we will*

---

(1) Psalms 145:20. In time of trouble G-d saves those who serve Him out of fear. However, those who serve Him out of love, G-d protects from encountering trouble. On the other hand, the wicked are at the end destroyed (Ibn Ezra). Before delving into the subject of *Mezuzah*, our author first broadens the theme of the love of G-d, and then comes to the *Mezuzah* which is the sign of G-d's guardianship of those who serve Him out of love. (2) *Ibid.*, 121:4. (3) *Ibid.*, Verse 5. (4) *Ibid.*, Verse 3: *He that guardeth thee will not slumber;* Verse 4: *He that guardeth Israel;* Verse 5: *The Eternal is thy guardian;* Verse 7: *The Eternal shall guard thee from all evil; He shall guard thy soul;* Verse 8: *The Eternal shall guard thy going out.*

walk in the Name of the Eternal our G-d forever and ever.[5] Therefore, David said here, *The Eternal preserveth all them that love Him,*[1] meaning the people of Israel, who love Him. They are the descendants of Abraham, who was praised for the quality of love, as the prophet mentioned, *The seed of Abraham My friend.*[6] That is to say, the people of Israel are like their ancestor with respect to the attribute of love.

Our Rabbis stated:[7] "The verse, *Of them that love Me,*[8] refers to those who observe the commandments out of love.[9] 'Why are you being led out to be executed?' 'Because I have circumcised my son.' 'Why are you being led out to be stoned?' 'Because I performed the commandment of taking the palm branch.' 'Why are you being led out to be burned?' 'Because I ate the unleavened bread.' 'Why are you being lashed with the whip?' 'Because I have complied with the will of my Father in heaven.' *What are these wounds between thy hands? Then he shall answer: Those with which I was wounded in the house of my friends.*[10] 'These are the wounds which have caused me to become beloved by my Father in heaven.' " Similarly, David said, *But for Thy sake are we killed all the day.*[11] *The seed of Abraham*[6] refers only to the people of Israel; it excludes the descendants of Ishmael and Esau. It is written, *And He chose their seed after them* [the patriarchs], *even you,*[12] meaning *even you* who are the descendants of Jacob.

---

(5) Micah 4:5. (6) Isaiah 41:8. (7) Mechilta, *Yithro,* end of Chapter 6, and quoted by Ramban, Commentary on the Torah, Exodus, pp. 301-302. (8) Exodus 20:6. (9) In Ramban's version of the Mechilta—see Note 7 above—this verse "refers to those who dwell in the Land of Israel and give their lives for the commandments." The text in the Mechilta is describing the period of cruel persecutions during the reign of Hadrian (117-118 C.E.), when the Jews in the Land of Israel were forbidden to practice their religion. Their determination to remain in the Land and to adhere to the tenets of the Torah is held by the Mechilta as a special manifestation of their love of G-d. (10) Zechariah 13:6. As explained further in the Mechilta: "These wounds that I have sustained for the sake of my religion have earned me a place of honor in the House of my Friend, to become His beloved one." (11) Psalms 44:23. Our devotion to His Torah, at times, calls even for the supreme sacrifice, for which Israel has ever been ready. (12) Deuteronomy 10:15.

To implant in our hearts the principle that Divine protection pervades Israel at all times, day and night, the Torah has commanded us to place the *Mezuzah*[13] at the entrance of our homes. We will thus be cognizant of this principle of Divine protection whenever we enter a home and we will be mindful that this protection is constantly with us. Even at night His protection surrounds us outside our house and protects us while we sleep. Therefore, we are commanded to write in the first section[14] of the *Mezuzah* the subject of G-d's Unity and the obligation to study Torah, and in the second section,[15] the veracity of reward and punishment. These topics attest to and signify three things: the truth of prophecy, the creation of the world, and Divine Providence, as the remembrance of the Exodus from Egypt, which was replete with wonders, obliges one to arrive at the above principles and to attest to their truth. Thus, when one buys a *Mezuzah* and affixes it in the doorway through which he enters and leaves his home, he demonstrates thereby his approval and admission of belief in these three principles, which constitute the essentials of the Jewish faith and the Torah.

A person should not regard lightly the commandment of affixing a *Mezuzah,* nor should he be negligent about fulfilling this precept even at great monetary expense. We see the great benefit and reward which result from its fulfillment. [In light of this, consider] how severe a punishment is deserved, when one is negligent in its fulfillment when the cost of the *Mezuzah* is minimal.

The law of the *Mezuzah* requires that it be inscribed with the two sections of the Torah which begin with *Sh'ma (Hear)*[16] and *V'haya im shamo'a (And it shall come to pass if ye shall hearken)*[17] The *Mezuzah* must be written in twenty-two lines[18] corresponding to the twenty-two

---

(13) The *Mezuzah* is a small scroll of parchment on which two sections from the Book of Deuteronomy (6:4-9 and 11:13-21) are written. It is fastened to the right-hand doorpost upon the entrance to the house. (14) *Ibid.,* 6:4-9. (15) *Ibid.,* 11:13-21. (16) *Ibid.,* 6:4. (17) *Ibid.,* 11:13. (18) In Shulchan Aruch, Yoreh Deiah, *Hilchoth Mezuzah,* 288:11: "It is the practice of the scribes to write it in twenty-two lines."

letters [of the alphabet].[19] The concluding words, *above the earth*,[20] must begin the last line; they should not be written at the end of the line.[21]

Regarding whether the *Mezuzah* should be written on the inward or outward side of the parchment, Rabbeinu Hai of blessed memory[22] wrote: "The inward side of the parchment and its outward side are alike as far as the writing of the *Mezuzah* is concerned. The *Mezuzah* may be written on both sides. This is the law, and this is the practice."

Some of the Gaonim[23] require that like a Scroll of the Law, the *Mezuzah* must be written on parchment prepared and ruled especially for the purpose of a *Mezuzah*.[24] The writing should be done with a reed, for the Rabbis said,[25] "Therefore,[26] the reed has merited to be

---

(19) In the Rome manuscript: "corresponding to the twenty-two letters in the Torah." (20) Deuteronomy 11:21. (21) The Taz, commenting on Yoreh Deiah, *Hilchoth Mezuzah*, 288:5, explains the reason for this rule as follows: The preceding line in the *Mezuzah* thus concludes with the word *heavens: as the days of the heavens—above the earth*. By placing the words *above the earth* at the beginning of the next line, the words *heavens* and *earth* are separated from each other as much as possible. This arrangement intimates that *your days will be multiplied, and the days of your children* (Deuteronomy 11:21) to an extent equal in magnitude to the distance between *heavens* and *earth*. (22) Rabbeinu Hai Gaon (939-1038 C.E.) was a world authority on all aspects of Jewish law, and he wrote thousands of responsa to all parts of Jewry. His death ended the period of the Gaonim, who were centered in Babylonia. (See following note). Thereafter, the academies in Europe assumed the leadership of Jewry. (23) Following the redaction of the Talmud in the year 500 C.E., the recognized spiritual leaders of Jewry were the heads of the academies at Sura and Pumbeditha in Babylon. These leaders were known as the Gaonim. Recipients and interpreters of the tradition of the Rabbis of the Talmud, the Gaonim flourished for over five hundred years during the height of the Moslem empires. The period of the Gaonim closed with the death of Rabbeinu Hai Gaon 1038 C.E. See Note 22 above. (24) In Shulchan Aruch, Yoreh Deiah, *Hilchoth Mezuzah*, 288:5, the law is rendered: "Preferably, the *Mezuzah* should be written on parchment prepared especially for that purpose, but post factum, the *Mezuzah* is valid even if the skin was not so prepared." (25) Sanhedrin 106a. (26) The reed reminds one that he "must at all times be yielding like a reed and not unbending like a cedar." For this reason, it was chosen as the instrument of writing these sacred objects. In our text of the Gemara, the word "therefore" is not found; the thought is simply stated, " . . . and the reed has merited to be taken, etc."

taken as a pen with which to write a Scroll of the Law, *Tefillin,* and
Mezuzoth." The *Mezuzah* must be written with ink, not with other
dyes, in the quadrilateral script, for the Rabbis said,[27] "[*Tefillin* and
Mezuzoth] must be written in the Assyrian script."[28] It should be affixed on the right-hand doorpost, for it is said, [*And thou shalt write
them upon the doorposts of]* '*beithecha*' *(thy house)*[29] which means
"the way *bi'athcha* (you enter) your house, for when a person lifts his
foot in order to go somewhere, he does so with his right foot first."[30]

Regarding the exact position of the *Mezuzah* on the right-hand
doorpost, the Sages said:[31] "It must be placed within the handbreadth
nearest to the doorway.[32] For what reason? Rava said, 'One will thus
immediately encounter the commandment.' Rav Chanina of Sura said,
'It will thus protect [the entire house from any mishap].' Shmuel said,[33]
'The *Mezuzah* must be affixed at the beginning of the upper third of
the doorpost.' " This does not mean that it must be placed precisely at
that point, [for it is also valid if it is placed higher. However, any lower
position would render it invalid].[34] One who does not affix a *Mezuzah*
to his doorpost violates two positive commandments, for it is said, *And
thou shalt write them,*[29] and it is said again, *And thou shalt write
them.*[35]

You should contemplate the significance of the fact that the Divine
Tetragrammaton is written in the inside of the *Mezuzah* and the Name
Sha-dai (Almighty) is written on the outside.[36] This arrangement
counteracts the foreign opinion that the success of a home is dependent

(27) Megillah 8 b.   (28) The Assyrian script is the name given the quadrilateral
style of writing Hebrew characters. It is called *Ashurith* (Assyrian) because of "the
erectness of its square formations."   (29) Deuteronomy 6:9.   (30) Menachoth
34 a.   (31) *Ibid.,* 33 b.   (32) Our texts of the Gemara indicate that the *Mezuzah*
should be placed "nearest to the street," and the Shulchan Aruch (Yoreh Deiah 289:2)
likewise indicates "nearest to the outside." This is in consonance with the reason stated
by Rava as quoted in the text here. Rabbeinu Bachya's reading "nearest the doorway,"
refers to one's exit from the home. The reason would then be that one encounters the
Mezuzah as soon as one leaves his home.   (33) Menachoth 33 a.   (34) Yoreh Deiah
289:2.   (35) Deuteronomy 11:20.   (36) Maimonides, *Hilchoth Tefillin Umezuzah*
8:4, and Yoreh Deiah 288:15.

upon the influence of the stars that control this lower world. This opinion is manifested by those who say, for example, "Since I bought this house or married this woman, I have become rich, for my fortune rose in accordance with the constellation which was in its ascendancy at that time." However, it is known that this kind of thinking is erroneous. The moments and times of the day are under the control of G-d, as David said, *My times are in Thy hand.*[37] Similarly, those people who say, "One who works on a certain day will not succeed," violate the prohibition, *V'lo th'oneinu (Neither shall ye practice soothsaying),*[38] for in effect, they are saying, "This time is auspicious, and that time is inauspicious."

The popular custom of marrying only when there is a full moon[39] is not included in this prohibition and has no relevance to it, for this custom is intended only as a good sign of the fullness of blessings rather than a lack thereof. It is akin to our custom, which originated with the Gaonim,[23] to place a *karkasath*[40] upon the table on the night of Rosh Hashanah. Similarly, the Sages said,[41] "Kings are anointed only near a spring," for it serves as a good sign that the monarch's reign will extend like running water. We find that David explicitly said, *Take with you the servants of your lord, and cause Solomon my son to ride upon mine own mule, and bring him down Gihon.*[42] *And let Zadok the priest and Nathan the prophet anoint him there king over Israel, and blow ye with the horn, and say: Long live King Solomon.*[43] However, one who regards matters of marriage and buying a home as anything but a mere token violates this prohibition because his action has the appearance of a superstitious practice.

(37) Psalms 31:16. (38) Leviticus 19:26. Rashi, *ibid.*, explains that expression *V'lo th'oneinu* is etymologically related to the Hebrew word *on* (period or time). Thus, a *m'onein* is one who says, "This on that day is auspicious or inauspicious for beginning a particular task or journey." (39) This custom is cited by R'ma in Shulchan Aruch, Eben Ha'ezer, *Hilchoth Kiddushin*, 64:3. (40) *Karkasath*, a word of Spanish origin, means "pumpkin" or "gourd." Because of its rapid growth, the *karkasath* symbolizes a speedy inscription on the day of judgment for a good year. See Kerithoth 6 a and Rashi there. (41) Horayoth 12 a. (42) I Kings 1:33. (43) *Ibid.*, Verse 34.

Accordingly, the commandment of the *Mezuzah* has been given to us to teach us that the success of the home depends solely on the One Who brought us out of Egypt and on the Name *Sha-dai* (Almighty), which indicates that He controls and prevails over the power of the constellations. He can nullify them and revert them to nothingness, and He can certainly diminish their power. The Sages alluded to this thought in their statement regarding Abraham:[44] "G-d said, I have created My world with the letter *hei*,[45] and with the letter *hei* I nullify the power of your constellation [which hitherto denied you children]."

The power of the commandment of the *Mezuzah* is great because it protects man, similar to what is written, *When thou walkest, it shall lead thee, when thou liest down, it shall watch over thee, and when thou wakest, it shall talk with thee.*[46] Similarly, the Sages said in Yerushalmi Pei'ah:[47] "Artaban[48] sent Rabbi[49] a pearl, saying, 'Send me something of equal or greater value.' Rabbi sent him a *Mezuzah.* Artaban objected, 'I sent you a priceless jewel, and you sent me something worth a small coin.' Rabbi answered, 'Mine is more precious than yours. Yours has a fixed value, but mine will watch over you, for it is said, *When thou liest down, it shall watch over thee.* '"[46] The Sages further commented,[31] "A mortal king sits within his palace, and his servants stand guard outside. However, G-d does not do so. The people of Israel dwell within their homes, and G-d protects them from the outside, as it is said, *Behold, He that guardeth Israel doth neither slumber nor sleep.*[2] It is further stated, *The Eternal is thy guardian, the Eternal is thy shade upon thy right hand.* "[3]

(44) Bereshith Rabbah 39:17.   (45) The letter *hei* is often pronounced silently and effortlessly. G-d created the world without any effort and exertion, so He can change easily anyone's natural endowments.   (46) Proverbs 6:22. The verse speaks of the power of all commandments, that their observance offers protection in this world and in the life hereafter. The *Mezuzah* shares equally with all commandments in this quality of theirs, and additionally offers yet a unique form of guardianship as the story that follows illustrates.   (47) Yerushalmi, Pei'ah I,1, with minor textual changes.   (48) Identified by P'nei Moshe, *ibid.*, as a certain distinguished Jew.   (49) See above in *Ahavah* (Love of G-d), Note 42.

מילה
Circumcision

Abraham was the first to be privileged to enter into G-d's covenant / The symbolism of circumcision and the Sabbath / The reason for circumcision / The feast which is made when this commandment is fulfilled / Circumcision is like a sacrificial offering / The beneficial results of the fulfillment of this commandment.

Circumcision

GATHER MY SAINTS TOGETHER UNTO ME, THOSE THAT
HAVE MADE A COVENANT WITH ME BY OFFERING.[1]

It is known that our patriarch Abraham was the first person to enter
into a covenant with G-d and to proclaim G-d's Unity to the world.
Although the sons of Noah had been charged with seven command-
ments,[2] the Noachides nevertheless remained impure until the advent
of Abraham, for in their generations, no one called upon the Name of
G-d to stir people to serve Him and to be worthy of entering into His
covenant. However, due to his great wisdom, Abraham recognized his
Creator when he was just three years old.[3] He was aware of the
Creator's Unity and G-dliness and proclaimed these principles to all.
He thereby firmly established faith in the hearts of people, as it is said,
And Abram called there in the Name of the Eternal.[4] The Sages com-
mented,[5] "[Abram strengthened faith] as one strengthens a ceiling. It
is writen here, *'Vayikra' Abram (And Abram called),*[4] and elsewhere it

---

(1) Psalms 50:5. The covenant of circumcision is one that is made in every generation of Israel, and follows in the footsteps of our patriarch Abraham, who was first
commanded to fulfill this precept. Its performance is accompanied with a festive occasion, expressing the joy of fulfilling the commandment (R'dak).   (2) See above in
G'zeilah (Robbery),   Note 2. "The sons of Noah" or "Noachides" is a general term for
the human race.   (3) Nedarim 32 a.   (4) Genesis 13:4. This event occurred before
Abram's name was changed to Abraham.   (5) This homiletic interpretation is
evidently our author's. See my Hebrew edition p. 246, Note 8.

states, *'Ham'kareh' (Who layest the beams) of Thine upper chambers in the waters.*"[6]

[Because of Abraham's devotion to this principle], he was deemed worthy to enter into the covenant with G-d when commanded to do so, as it is said, *And as for thee, thou shalt keep My covenant,*[7] *And I will make My covenant between Me and thee.*[8] Although Abraham was ninety-nine years old at that time,[9] he was zealous and did not at all delay fulfillment of this commandment [of circumcision]. When he was one hundred years old[10] in the following year, Isaac was born to him. [Now, at the time of Isaac's birth], Abraham had already been sanctified with this sacred commandment. This was not the case at the time of Ishmael's birth [when Abraham was eighty-six years old].[11] This [sanctity was conferred upon Abraham only shortly before Isaac's birth] because Isaac was his main descendant, as it is written, *For in Isaac shall seed be called to thee.*[12] Consequently, Jacob and all his seed were sanctified and would be worthy to receive the holy Torah.

The expression *between Me and thee*[8] indicates the existence of a great secret in this commandment. When a king issues some command to his son or his trustworthy servant, telling him, "Remember the things that were spoken between me and you," there is no doubt that he is referring to some secret matters which were not recorded. You will find the very same language concerning the commandment of the Sabbath, stating, *It is a sign between Me and the children of Israel forever,*[13] thus indicating that this commandment too contains a hidden matter. Therefore, the Sages expounded in Tractate Beitzah,[14] "Rabbi Shimon ben Yochai said, 'G-d gave all the commandments to

(6) Psalms 104:3. The word *vayikra* is etymologically associated with the word *ham'kareh*. Thus *'Vayikra' Abram* connotes, "And Abram laid the beams [i.e. strengthened the world with the Name of the Eternal." (7) Genesis 17:9. (8) *Ibid.*, Verse 2. (9) See *ibid.*, Verse 24. (10) See *ibid.*, 21:5. (11) See *ibid.*, 16:16. (12) *Ibid.*, 21:12. (13) Exodus 31:17. The Sabbath and Circumcision are thus two "signs" of our belief in G-d as the Creator of the universe, and of His covenant with Abraham to make his seed a holy people. See also Note 21. (14) Beitzah 16 a.

Israel publicly, except for the commandment of the Sabbath, which He gave them privately.' " You may ask: "How was it given privately? The commandment of the Sabbath is part of the Ten Commandments, which were heard by all the nations of the world, as Scripture states, *From the beginning I have not spoken in secret!*[15] Moreover David too said, *All the kings of the earth shall give Thee thanks, O Eternal, for they have heard the words of Thy mouth!*"[16] However, the Sages' comment that it was given "privately" was intended to allude to an esoteric matter in the commandment of the Sabbath. That is why Scripture uses the expression *between Me and you.*[17] The same reasoning applies here to the commandment of circumcision, as the Sages clearly said,[18] *"The secret counsel of the Eternal is with them that fear Him, and His covenant, to make it known to them.*[19] This refers to the covenant of circumcision."

According to the simple meaning of Scripture, the reason for this commandment is that we must make a definite sign in our flesh concerning our belief in G-d's immutable Unity, in life or in our death. This is the meaning of the verse, *And ye shall be circumcised in the flesh of your foreskin, and it shall be a token of a covenant,*[20] which teaches you that this constitutes a definite sign in the flesh, *a token of a covenant [between Me and you].*[20] That is why this commandment is called "a sign" as are the commandments of the Sabbath[13] and the *Tefillin.*[21] Only these three precepts have been designated as "signs." Thus, in the benediction over the rite of circumcision,[22] we say, "Who didst seal his [Abraham's] offspring with the sign of the holy covenant."

(15) Isaiah 48:16. At Sinai G-d's word was not spoken in secret, but in fact reverberated throughout the world. (16) Psalms 138:4. (17) Exodus 31:13. (18) Tanchuma, *Lech Lecha,* 19. (19) Psalms 25:14. (20) Genesis 17:11. (21) See Exodus 13:9. The *Tefillin* (phylacteries) are thus the third "sign," reminding us of the Unity of the Creator, and of the Exodus from Egypt, proclaiming His dominion in the affairs of man. See Note 13 for the other two "signs." (22) Shabbath 137 b.

In the Midrash Shir Hashirim, the Sages of the truth said,[23] *"I adjure you, O daughters of Jerusalem, 'bitzva'oth' (by the hosts),*[24] i.e., it is a *tzava* (host) in whom I have an *oth* (sign)."[25] This is the sign for which man is called *wholehearted* as it is written of Abraham, *Walk before Me, and thou shalt be wholehearted.*[26]

Whoever is circumcised joins the belief in G-d's Unity and enters into the covenant of our patriarch Abraham, as it is written, *. . . to be a G-d unto thee and to thy seed after thee.*[27] He should not engage in forbidden sexual relations, as David said, *And I was wholehearted with Him, and I kept myself from mine iniquity.*[28]

We find in Scripture that Isaac was circumcised when he was eight days old.[29] On that day, Abraham made a great feast, for the Sages commented,[30] *"And Abraham made a great feast on the day Isaac 'higameil' (was weaned). On the hag (eighth) day, mal (he circumcised) Isaac."*[31] This constitutes a Scriptural basis for our custom of making a feast on the day of circumcision, for according to this Midrash, Abraham made a feast on the day of Isaac's circumcision.

The commandment of circumcision constitutes a sacrificial offering brought in the honor of G-d to fulfill His commandment. Just as the blood of the offering atones for sin, so does the blood of circumcision [atone for the parents]. Therefore, this commandment is essentially observed on the eighth day [after the birth of the child], just as an offering is not accepted before the eighth day after its birth, as it is said,

---

(23) Shir Hashirim Rabbah 2:18. The Expression "Sages of truth" signifies "men of the true traditional wisdom of the Torah." It does not refer to those learned in the mystic teachings of the Cabala. (24) Songs of Songs 2:7. (25) The Midrash is explaining that the word *bitzva'oth* is a combination of two words: *tzava* (host) and *oth* (sign). Israel is thus G-d's host, carrying the sign of His covenant with them. (26) Genesis 17:1. (27) *Ibid.*, Verse 7. (28) Psalms 18:24. (29) See Genesis 21:4. (30) P'sikta Zutratha, Genesis 21:8. (31) The word *higameil* is divided into two words: *hag* and *mal. Hag* is comprised of the letters *hei* and *gimel,* which are numerically equivalent to five and three respectively, making a total of eight. *Mal* means "he circumcised." Scripture is intimating that a feast should be given on the day of a child's circumcision.

*And from the eighth day and thenceforth it may be accepted for an of-
fering.*[32] Just as it is written with regard to an offering, *And they* [the
priests] *shall eat those things wherewith atonement was made,*[33] so it is
the custom among the people of Israel to make a feast on the day of circumcision at which all people gather. It is a fitting custom. Accordingly, David mentioned, *Gather My saints together unto Me, those that
have made a covenant with Me by offering,*[1] thus teaching you that it is
proper for relatives and friends to rejoice and participate in the feast
over this commandment.

By virtue of the fulfillment of this commandment, the world exists.
The Sages said in the Midrash:[18] "G-d said to Abraham, 'When I
created My world, I tolerated twenty generations[34] waiting for someone
with your merits to come and accept circumcision. If you will not accept it, *I am G-d Almighty,*[26] and I will say to My world: Enough until
here. I will then turn it back to a state of void and chaos.' "

By virtue of the fulfillment of this commandment of circumcision,
man receives the Divine Presence. In the case of our patriarch
Abraham, we find that the Torah mentions, *In the selfsame day was
Abraham circumcised.*[35] Immediately following this, it states, *And the
Eternal appeared to him,*[36] even as it says, *In the light of the King's
countenance is life.*[37] G-d appeared to Abraham *in the oaks of
Mamre*[36] because Mamre, one of Abraham's three friends,[38] advised
him on circumcision. Aner and Eshcol[38] advised Abraham against it.
Mamre said to him: "If G-d would desire your life, would you not give
it to Him? You should therefore certainly comply with His request for
merely one part of your body! Moreover, G-d, Who saved you from the
four kings,[39] from famine, and from Ur of the Chaldees,[40] will certainly help you now [in circumcising yourself at the age of ninety-nine]."

---

(32) Leviticus 22:27. (33) Exodus 29:33. (34) Ten generations from Adam to
Noah, and ten from Noah to Abraham. (35) Genesis 17:26. (36) *Ibid.,*
18:1. (37) Proverbs 16:15. The Divine visit thus restored Abraham's
health. (38) See Genesis 14:13. (39) See *ibid.,* Verse 1. (40) See Ramban, Commentary on the Torah, Genesis, pp. 159-160.

By virtue of the fulfillment of this commandment, Israel has been assured of salvation from the judgment of Gehenna. This is expressed in the Midrash:[41] *"And the flaming sword which turned every way.*[42] *The flaming* refers to Gehenna, which consumes man from head to foot. The *sword* refers to circumcision. G-d said, 'What will save My children from the flaming fire?' I must say it is circumcision." In Pirkei d'Rabbi Eliezer, the Sages commented:[43] "Abraham circumcised himself on the Day of Atonement, for it is written, *And ye shall do no manner of work in 'the selfsame day,'*[44] and here too it is written, *In 'the selfsame day' was Abraham circumcised.*[35] Each year on the Day of Atonement, G-d recalls the blood of the covenant of Abraham and forgives all the sins of Israel, as it is said, *For on this day shall atonement be made for you, to cleanse you from all your sins."*[45] The Sages commented elsewhere,[46] "The power of the commandment of circumcision is great, for one who is circumcised does not descend to Gehenna [for final destruction]."

By virtue of the fulfillment of this commandment, our patriarch Abraham was assured [that his descendants would receive] three gifts. The first gift is that the Kingdom of the House of David would never cease.[47] Thus, G-d said, *And I will make nations of thee, and kings shall come out of thee.*[48] The second gift is that the Land will be given to Abraham's descendants forever, and the third gift is that the Divine Presence will rest among the people of Israel. We find that a covenant was declared with the Kingdom of the House of David, as it is said, *I have made a covenant with My chosen, I have sworn unto David My*

---

(41) Bereshith Rabbah 21:14. (42) Genesis 3:24. When Adam was driven from the Garden of Eden because of his sin, G-d emplaced *the flaming sword which turned every way, to guard the way to the tree of life.* (43) Pirke d'Rabbi Eliezer 29. (44) Leviticus 23:28. (45) *Ibid.,* 16:30. (46) Tanchuma, *Lech Lecha,* 20. (47) The meaning, as set forth by Ramban in his Commentary on the Torah, Genesis, pp. 586-590, is that while the Kingdom of the House of David may be interrupted temporarily, it will never be permanently abolished. Thus, after the exile, the Kingdom of David will be reestablished by Messiah. (48) Genesis 17:6.

servant:[49] *Forever will I establish thy seed, and build up thy throne to all generations.*[50] The gift of the Land is expressed in the verse, *And I will give unto thee, and to thy seed after thee, the Land of thy sojournings.*[51] This means that the Land will be inherited and settled only by them. Even if they will be exiled from it, they will return thereto, for it is their eternal inheritance and not that of another nation. This constitutes a great sign for Israel. Since they have been exiled from the Land, no nation has ever permanently settled there, nor will it be settled until its children return to it. The Divine Presence will then dwell among the people of Israel, as it is said, *And I will be their G-d.*[51]

Happy are the people who have been assured of these three gifts: the unending Kingdom of the House of David, the eternal inheritance of the Holy Land for the people of Israel alone, and the resting of the Divine Presence among them. No other nation, or ethnic group has merited even one of those gifts. *Happy is the people, whose lot is thus. Yes, happy is the people, whose G-d is the Eternal.*[52]

(49) Psalms 89:4.   (50) *Ibid.*, Verse 5.   (51) Genesis 17:8.   (52) Psalms 144:15.

מטר
Rain: Heaven's Lifeline to Man

Being in exile, Israel should be more concerned than other nations about disorders that agitate the world / It is the way of the Torah to attribute success to G-d's mercies, and troubles to man's sins, and not to mere chance / Prayer should be tearful / Prayer shields Israel from troubles / The purport of the adage, 'Afflictions are beloved' / When trouble ensues, one should first purify himself inwardly and then outwardly by fastings and ritually immersing the body / Drought betokens the sins of man, and at such a time, Israel should return to G-d and ask for His mercies.

Rain: Heaven's Lifeline to Man

O ETERNAL, IN TROUBLE HAVE THEY SOUGHT THEE, SILENTLY THEY POURED OUT A PRAYER WHEN THY CHASTENING WAS UPON THEM.[1]

Isaiah said, "When Israel is in trouble, they seek Thee with fasting and prayer." It is known that since Israel has been exiled, they suffer more than any nation. The Sages commented,[2] "When the master enters the schoolhouse with the strap in his hand, the pupil who is usually beaten, worries." Similarly, since the people of Israel have been in exile, they have been accustomed to experiencing troubles. Therefore, they should be more concerned than other nations when disorders agitate the world and this is of course true if disorders affect Israel directly.

Regarding such crises, Scripture states, *The Eternal answer thee in the day of trouble, the Name of the G-d of Jacob set thee up on high.*[3] No other righteous person has been in more distress than Jacob. He experienced anguish over Esau, Laban, Rachel, Dinah, and Joseph. Therefore, the psalmist mentioned Jacob here[3] rather than any of the

---

(1) Isaiah 26:16. The verse expresses a fundamental truth of deepest significance. In a moment of trouble it is of incalculable importance not to quarrel or disparage, but rather to seek the help of Him Who alone is the source of all assistance. A case in point is rain. When there is a need for it, nothing is of any avail except prayer. Before starting with the actual theme of rain, the author first clarifies certain essential principles. (2) Succah 29 a. (3) Psalms 20:2.

other patriarchs [so that the mention of his name would be an incentive] to make one's heart submissive for repentance and prayer.

The Sages clearly said,[4] "Visitations come upon the world only for the sake of Israel, as it is said, *I have cut off nations, their corners are desolate, etc.*[5] *I said: Surely thou* [Israel] *wilt fear Me, thou wilt receive correction.*"[6] This is logical. Since G-d chose the people of Israel over other nations and they thus constitute the basis of the world, it is fitting that the world be maintained or destroyed according to their deeds. These visitations [which befall the world] should not be attributed to chance, for Scripture states, *And if ye walk with Me by chance, etc.*[7] That is to say, "When I agitate My world and bring about new decrees and you judge them to be mere ordinary events which have occurred without My specific design and special intent, *then will I also walk with you by chance.*[8] I will increase such 'chance' occurrences and allow them to run their course completely uncontrolled."

It is the way of the Torah and an essential tenet of our faith to attribute a person's real success to G-d's mercies, not to the individual's merits and good deeds. When troubles come upon an individual, he should likewise ascribe them to his sins, not to chance, which is the way of atheism and a criminal sin. One should believe that successes and troubles have been specifically designed by providence so that the individual will return from his sinful ways and humble his heart.

We find that while the Sanctuary existed, a leprous lesion would appear in the walls of a sinful person's house. This signified the distinction and sanctity of the Land and was a sign of providence, as it is written, *The eyes of the Eternal thy G-d are always upon it.*[9] The lesion would first appear in the house. If the sinner repented, well and good. If not, it appeared in his garments. If he repented, well and good. If not, it appeared upon his body, at which point he would undoubtedly scrutinize his deeds and repent. Thus, anyone who finds himself in

(4) Yebamoth 63 a. (5) Zephania 3:6. (6) *Ibid.*, Verse 7. (7) Leviticus 26:21. (8) *Ibid.*, Verse 24. (9) Deuteronomy 11:12.

distress should be stirred to perfect repentance. If he does not do so, he is not included among those of whom Isaiah said, *O Eternal, in trouble have they sought Thee.*[1] Rather, he is categorized among those of whom the prophet said, *And it set him on fire round about, yet he knew not, and it burned him, yet he laid it not to heart.*[10] This, then, is the intent of his words, *O Eternal, in trouble have they sought Thee, silently they poured out a prayer,*[1] i.e., when Israel is in trouble and anguish, they pray silently.

It is known that prayer should be tearful, for tears come from the anguish of cherished aspirations. They attest that the person's heart is broken and contrite and that his spirit is humbled. Thus, his prayer will be favorably accepted by G-d. Similarly, David said, *Hear my prayer, O Eternal, and give ear unto my cry, keep not silence at my tears.*[11] Our Sages commented:[12] "The gates of tears have not been locked."

Prayer shields Israel from trouble. The Sages said,[13] "A person should always pray before trouble comes. Had Abraham not done so,[14] not even a remnant of Israel's enemies[15] would have remained," as it is said, *And he* [Abraham] *went on his journeys.*[16] Immediately following that, it states, . . . *unto the place of the altar, which he had made there at first, and Abram called there on the Name of the Eternal.*[17] The Sages also stated explicitly that prayer has helped us throughout

---

(10) Isaiah 42:25.   (11) Psalms 39:13.   (12) Baba Metzia 59 a. — The following thought is brought out: Since the destruction of the Temple at Jerusalem "the Gates of Prayer" for an individual have been "locked," so to say, "except for the Ten Days of Penitence [between Rosh Hashanah and Yom Kippur], when they are opened." However, the gates of tearful prayer are never "locked" during the entire year, and one will find uninterrupted access to the Divine Throne of mercy (Rif).   (13) Sanhedrin 44 b.   (14) I.e., in his prayer between Beth-el and Ai. See Genesis 12:8.   (15) The phrase "Israel's enemies" is a euphemism for Israel itself. When the first battle of Ai was fought in the days of Joshua, Israel lost thirty-six men. See Joshua 7:5. However, were it not that Abraham had prayed there at first, thus shielding them from greater harm, they would have suffered complete destruction.   (16) Genesis 13:3.   (17) *Ibid.*, Verse 4.

the exile. By its merit, we have been saved from the sword of Esau, as it is said, *The voice is the voice of Jacob, but the hands are the hands of Esau.*[18] Jacob has power only with his voice, and Esau rules only with his hands.[19] "Isaac said to his son Jacob, 'Your power is greater than that of Esau. When Esau seizes a person, he has him in his power, but when the person runs away from him, Esau cannot harm him. You, however, retain your power even if the escapee is at the end of the world, since your strength lies in your voice. You pray in the synagogue, and he comes of his own volition.' "[20] Thus, you learn that the merit of prayer shields against troubles.

Thy chastening was upon them.[1] This means that the afflictions to which G-d has subjected them are for their own good, as the Sages said,[21] "Afflictions are beloved." The Sages stated,[21] "When Rabban Yochanan ben Zaccai[22] became ill, four elders — Rabbi Tarphon, Rabbi Yehoshua, Rabbi Eleazar ben Azaryah, and Rabbi Akiba — came to visit him. Rabbi Tarphon said, 'You are more beneficial to Israel than rain, for rain is helpful only in this world, but the Rabbi is a source of blessing in this world and the World to Come.' Rabbi Eleazar ben Azaryah said, 'You are more beneficial to Israel than the celestial sphere of the sun, for the sun is a boon only for this world, while the Rabbi is a source of blessing in this world and the World to Come.'

---

(18) *Ibid.*, 27:22. (19) Bereshith Rabbah 65:16. (20) Tanchuma-Buber, Toldoth, 15. In answer to the prayer, the desired person returns of his own volition. (21) Sanhedrin 101 a. (22) Rabban Yochanan ben Zaccai lived during the period of the destruction of the Second Temple in the year 70 C.E. As the title Rabban indicates he was the head of the Sanhedrin. It was he who went to the Roman general Vespasian and obtained permission to open an academy at Jabneh, which after the destruction of the Temple, became the seat of the supreme religious authority of the Jewish people. In historical perspective. Jabneh saved the Jewish people from extinction after the great calamity of the destruction. With this thought uppermost in their minds, the Rabbis came to visit the ailing Rabban Yochanan ben Zaccai. Their praise reflects his great accomplishment. — "Rabban Yochanan ben Zaccai." In our editions of the Talmud, the reading is "Rabbi Eliezer." Our author's reading is confirmed by manuscripts of the Talmud. See my Hebrew edition, Kad Hakemach, p. 251, Note 35.

Rabbi Yehoshua said, 'You are more beneficial to Israel than a father
and mother, for their beneficence is only in this world, while the Rabbi
is a source of blessing for this world and the World to Come.' Rabbi
Akiba said, 'Afflictions are beloved.'[23] Upon hearing Rabbi Akiba's
words, Rabban Yochanan said, 'Support me so that I can hear the
words of Akiba my disciple.' Rabbi Akiba continued, 'Rabbi, I am expounding a Scriptural text. It is written, *Menasheh was twelve years
old when he began to reign, and he reigned fifty-five years in
Jerusalem.*[24] *And he did that which was evil in the sight of the
Eternal.*[25] It is also written, *These also are proverbs of Solomon, which
the men of Hezekiah, King of Judah, edited.*[26] Is it possible that
Hezekiah taught everyone Torah and did not teach his own son?
Rather, we must say that all of the trouble and toil that Hezekiah en-
dured on behalf of his son [to teach him Torah], he failed to direct
Menasheh to the good path of the Torah. Afflictions alone achieved
this goal, as it is said, *And the Eternal spoke to Menasheh, and to his
people, but they gave no heed.*[27] *Wherefore the Eternal brought upon
them the captains of the host of the King of Assyria, who took
Menasheh with hooks, and bound him with fetters, and carried him to
Babylon.*[28] It is further written, *And when he [Menasheh] was in
distress, he besought the Eternal his G-d and humbled himself greatly
before the G-d of his fathers.*[29] *And he prayed unto Him, and He was*

---

(23) Each of the three comparisons provides additional dimensions to the blessings
bestowed upon the generations by Rabbi Yochanan ben Zaccai. Rabbi Tarphon likened him to the rain; yet there are times when rain is unwelcome, as in a period of
overabundant precipitation. Rabbi Eleazar ben Azaryah compared him to the sun; yet
the sun's blessings do not function at night. Rabbi Yehoshua then compared him to the
blessings bestowed by parents upon their children, for parental blessings are constant
through the day and night (Margoliuth Hayam). Rabbi Akiba's remark that "Afflictions are beloved" expresses the thought that there is a beneficent element in all afflictions, and therefore one is to accept them joyfully. (24) II Chronicles 33:1.
Menasheh was a son of King Hezekiah, one of the most righteous monarchs of
Judah. (25) *Ibid.,* Verse 2. (26) Proverbs 25:1. (27) II Chronicles
33:10. (28) *Ibid.,* Verse 11. (29) *Ibid.,* Verse 12.

entreated of him, and heard his supplication, and brought him to Jerusalem to his kingdom.' "[30]

As a result of the afflictions which come upon him, man improves his ways, as the Sages commented in Shir Hashirim Rabbah:[31] *"Behold, thou art fair, my beloved, yea pleasant.*[32] Even if You bring afflictions upon me, it is pleasant. Why? They cause me to improve my ways." A person's repentance is complete only when he has experienced affliction, for repentance, which entails the improvement of deeds and qualities of character, cannot be accomplished by merely fasting, rolling in ashes, and immersing oneself in a ritual pool while continuing to be inwardly soiled with numerous sins and evil thoughts. The prophet said, *Is such the fast that I have chosen? The day for a man to afflict his soul? Is it to bow down his head as a bulrush, and to spread sackcloth and ashes under him? Wilt thou call this a fast, and an acceptable day to the Eternal?*[33] *Is not this the fast that I have chosen? To loose the fetters of wickedness, to undo the bands of the yoke.*[34] In the case of the people of Nineveh, it is written, *And G-d saw their deeds,*[35] upon which our Sages commented[36] that they did as follows: "If one had robbed a beam and used it in the building of a castle, he would pull down the entire castle and restore the beam to its owner [although returning the value of the beam would have been sufficient]."

The way of the nations is to wash their bodies and exhibit their cleanliness. They fast and afflict themselves while inwardly their hearts remain impure and defiled. Therefore, the prophet said, *They that sanctify themselves and purify themselves, to go unto the gardens,*[37] i.e., they affect holiness and purity, yet they *eat swine's flesh, and the detestable thing, and the mouse.*[37] Similarly, Solomon said, *There is a*

---

(30) *Ibid.,* Verse 13. See above *Kippurim* (Atonement), beginning with Note 36 in text, for further details on Menasheh's repentance. (31) Shir Hashirim Rabbah 1:66. (32) Song of Songs 1:16. (33) Isaiah 58:5. (34) *Ibid.,* Verse 6. (35) Jonah 3:10. (36) Taanoth 16 a. See above *Kippurim* (Atonement), where the same text is quoted and more fully explained. (37) Isaiah 66:17.

*generation that are pure in their own eyes, and yet are not washed
from their filthiness.*[38] *There is a generation, Oh how lofty are their
eyes! and their eyelids are lifted up.*[39] *There is a generation whose teeth
are as swords, and their great teeth as knives, to devour the poor off the
earth.*[40]

The intent of the Torah, however, is that a person should first
cleanse himself inwardly. He should remove from his heart the
abominations of sin, and he should return things which he has il-
legitimately acquired. He should also seek forgiveness from his friend if
he has sinned against him. After one has purified his heart, he can
then outwardly purify himself by fasting and immersing his body in a
ritual pool. Thus, the prophet said, *And rend your heart, and not your
garments, and turn unto the Eternal your G-d.*[41] The intent of this
verse is that inward purification takes precedence. Therefore,
whenever trouble ensues, all the people of Israel should humble their
hearts and pray to G-d. They should first engage in inward purification and then concern themselves with outward purification.

There is no greater affliction than drought, as a result of which people better their ways and pray silently. Thus, the verse mentioned
above states, *O Eternal, in trouble have they sought thee, silently they
poured out a prayer.*[1] By the virtue of prayer, G-d grants rain, for it is
known that G-d is the source of rain. G-d said to Job, *Hath the rain a
father? or who hath begotten the drops of dew.*[42] He is saying: *"Hath
the rain a father* other than Me? It is in My power to grant rain, and I
have not appointed any other power or ruler over it?" The Sages also
commented,[43] "Three keys have never been entrusted by G-d to any
agent: the key of a woman to bear children [naturally], the key of rain,
and the key of Resurrection."

(38) Proverbs 30:12.   (39) *Ibid.*, Verse 13.   (40) *Ibid.*, Verse 14.   (41) Joel
2:13.   (42) Job 38:28.   (43) Taanith 2 a.

Drought is a sign and attestation of sins. We find that when G-d informed the prophet Jeremiah of the coming famine in the Land[44] and its tragic consequences, Jeremiah said, *"Though our iniquities testify against us, O Eternal, do Thou for Thy Name's sake,* which is called upon us, *for our backslidings are many.*[45] That is to say, we are guilty of many sins, such as idolatry, violence, conceit, heeding false prophets rather than true prophets." Accordingly, our Sages said,[46] When rain is withheld, Israel should return to G-d and pray before Him, for the prophet Jeremiah said, *And the showers have been withheld, and there hath been no latter rain.*[47] Immediately thereafter, it is written, *Didst thou not just now cry unto Me: My Father, Thou art the friend of my youth.*[48] That is to say, "When rain is withheld, call me 'Father' so that I will restore it to you."

---

(44) See Jeremiah 14:1.   (45) *Ibid.*, Verse 7.   (46) Taanith 7 b.   (47) Jeremiah 3:3.   (48) *Ibid.*, Verse 4

נחמו

The Comforting of Israel

Among the Divine laws which govern the world is the rule of 'measure for measure' / The connection between the prophetic message of 'Nachamu' and the section preceding it in the Book of Isaiah / The explanation of the section 'Nachamu,' according to Rabbi David Kimchi, with some additional comments.

The Comforting of Israel

NACHAMU[1] (COMFORT YE), COMFORT YE. MY PEOPLE,
SAITH YOUR G-D.[2]

Among the Divine laws which govern the world is the rule of
"measure for measure."[3] This is evident from the section preceding
Nachamu[1] in the Book of Isaiah. It is mentioned there that the King of
Babylon *sent a letter and a present to Hezekiah.*[4] Although the King of
Babylon was an idolater, G-d nevertheless rewarded him measure for
measure for the honor he bestowed upon Him, as the Sages related in
Midrash Shir Hashirim:[5] "Merodach-baladan was a worshipper of the
sun, and he was wont to eat at the sixth hour of the day and rest until
the ninth hour. During the reign of Hezekiah, on the day *when the sun
turned backward* [*ten degrees* on the sun-dial],[6] Merodach-baladan

---

(1) *Nachamu* (Comfort ye). Following the ninth day of Ab, the day on which both,
the First and Second Temple were destroyed, a period of "seven weeks of consolation"
starts. The first Sabbath is called *Shabbath Nachamu*, since the *Haftarah*, the
Readings from the Prophets (Isaiah 40:1-46) starts with *Nachamu*. During these "seven
weeks of consolation," each Sabbath, a section from the Book of Isaiah is read, and the
theme of each *Haftarah* is G-d's comforting Israel with the assurance of the coming
Redemption.   (2) Isaiah 40:1. G-d instructed His prophets to console His people with
these words after the suffering of the destruction of the Temple and the devastation of
the Land of Israel.   (3) Sotah 8 b. "With whatever measure a man metes out to
others, in a like manner shall he be requited" (*ibid.*).   (4) Hezekiah, King of Judah,
had been gravely ill and was miraculously restored to health, as will be explained further (see Note 6).   (5) Shir Hashirim Rabbah 3:3.   (6) Isaiah 38:8. When Isaiah

arose early from sleep and wanted to slay all his attendants, saying, 'You have let me sleep all day and all night.' They answered, 'The day went backward.' 'And which deity turned it backward?' he asked. They replied, 'The G-d of Hezekiah.' Thereupon *he sent a letter and a present to Hezekiah.*[4] What was written in the letter? 'Peace to Hezekiah, peace to the Great G-d, peace to Jerusalem.' As the letter was about to be dispatched, the King thought: 'I did not act properly in mentioning the name of Hezekiah first and then the name of his G-d.' He immediately arose from his throne, took three steps, and retrieved the letter. In its place, he wrote: 'Peace to the Great G-d of Hezekiah, peace to Hezekiah, peace to Jerusalem.' G-d then said, 'You rose from your throne and took three steps for My honor. I swear that I will therefore cause three kings to arise from you who will rule the world from end to end.' The three kings are Evil-merodach,[7] Nebuchadnezzar, and Belshazzar."[8]

Now, Hezekiah rejoiced over the letter and showed the messengers of the King of Babylon all of his treasures, as it is written, *And Hezekiah was glad of them, and showed them his treasure-house, the silver and the gold,* etc.[9] However, G-d was displeased [with Hezekiah's haughty demeanor, ascribing their visit to his own honor, and not to the glory of G-d]. Therefore, G-d sent him word through Isaiah: *Behold, the days come, that all that is in thy house, and that which thy fathers have laid up in store until this day, shall be carried to Babylon; nothing shall be left, saith the Eternal.*[10] This refers to the Babylonian exile.

---

brought the news to Hezekiah that he will recover from his illness, he asked him for a sign that G-d *will do the thing that He has spoken* (II Kings 20:8). The prophet replied that G-d will bring the shadow on the sun-dial of King Ahaz ten degrees backward (*ibid.*, Verse 11). — That day, being elongated ten hours, upset Merodach-baladan's day of activity, and he sent a letter of inquiry about the miracle and a gift to Hezekiah, as explained in the text. (7) II Kings 25:27. (8) See Daniel 5:1. Belshazzar was slain, and with him ended the Kingdom of the Babylonians (*ibid.*, Verse 30). — Nebuchadnezzar was the Babylonian king who destroyed the First Temple. (9) Isaiah 39:2. (10) *Ibid.*, Verse 6. See R'dak to II Kings 20:30, for the source of the explanation of G-d's displeasure with Hezekiah.

*And of thy sons that shall issue from thee, whom thou shalt
beget*[11] — i.e., Hananiah, Mishael, and Azariah[12] — *and they shall be
officers in the palace of the King of Babylon.*[11] Hezekiah replied, *Good
is the word of the Eternal which thou hast spoken that there shall be
peace and truth in my days.*[13]

This, then, is a case of measure for measure. Because of the three
steps which Merodach, King of Babylon, took from his throne, G-d
raised three kings from him. Similarly, [*Nachamu,*[1] the message of
comfort], is a case of measure for measure. G-d said, *Comfort ye, comfort ye My people.*[2] The repetition is due to their having sinned
grievously, as it said, *Jerusalem hath grievously sinned.*[14] Since they
were doubly punished, as it said, *That she hath received of the
Eternal's hand double for all her sins,*[15] it is therefore proper that they
now be doubly consoled [by the expression, *Comfort ye, comfort ye*].

In the Midrash, the Sages said:[16] "G-d said to Hezekiah, 'When
Isaiah foretold Israel's exile, you should have comforted My children.
Instead, you were concerned only for yourself, as you said, *That there
shall be peace and truth in my days.*[13] As their leader, you should have
comforted them. Since you did not, I Myself will comfort them.' It is
thus written, *Comfort ye, comfort ye My people, saith your G-d.*"[2]

This verse is addressed to the prophets so that they should comfort
Israel. Alternatively, its purport may be: "My people, comfort
Jerusalem," as He said, *Bid Jerusalem take heart.*[17] In general, the
prophet is comforting Israel by foretelling the ingathering of the exiles,
as follows: *Her time of service is accomplished,*[17] meaning her time of
exile is over. *Her guilt is paid off,*[17] her punishment has ended. *She
hath received of the Eternal's hand double for all her sins.*[17] The term
double may mean [that she was punished] several times, or it may be a
reference to the two exiles, that of Babylon and that of the present era.

---

(11) Isaiah 39:7.   (12) See Daniel 1:6.   (13) Isaiah 39:8.   (14) Lamentations
1:8.   (15) Isaiah 40:2. The meaning of the word *double* will be explained further in
the text.   (16) Yalkut Shimoni, Isaiah, 442.   (17) Isaiah 40:2.

And the glory of the Eternal shall be revealed.[18] When they will go forth from the exile with an outstretched arm and will find water and all their necessities even in the desert, then *the glory of the Eternal shall be revealed* in the presence of all the nations. *All flesh shall see it together.*[18] This refers to the understanding of the heart. *The mouth of the Eternal hath spoken it.*[18] When the nations will see the fulfillment of the prophecies, they will know that the prophets uttered the consolations by the command of G-d.

Get thee up into the high mountain.[19] This is a metaphorical expression. When one wishes to make his voice heard, he ascends a high place. Because Jerusalem is the essential part of the Land of Israel, as is Zion—both are one city—the prophet therefore calls upon them to bring the news [of the coming Redemption] to the other cities. Thus, the meaning of the verse is: "Thou, Zion, that tellest good tidings, and likewise thou, Jerusalem, that tellest good tidings, *lift up thy voice with strength, lift it up, be not afraid, say unto the cities of Judah, Behold, your G-d,*[19] for by all means, His glory will return to Jerusalem."

Even as a shepherd that feedeth his flock, that gathereth the lambs in his arm, and carrieth them in his bosom, and gently leadeth those that give suck.[20] As a good shepherd gathers the young suckling lambs that are unable to walk and carries them in his bosom, gently leading their mothers to them, so will G-d gently lead Israel out of the exile and will support all who are sick and infirm.

Who hath measured the waters in the hollow of his hand, and meted out heaven with the span, and comprehended the dust of the earth in a measure?[21] The prophet is saying: "In light of G-d's might which was made apparent in Creation, the nations of the world should believe in His ability to gather the exiles and to liberate Israel from their oppression. G-d, Who created the world, will find it easy to do so." The prophet presented further analogy for the gathering of the exiles from

(18) *Ibid.*, Verse 5.   (19) *Ibid.*, Verse 9.   (20) *Ibid.*, Verse 11.   (21) *Ibid.*, Verse 12.

Creation. Just as the deeds of Creation are hidden and sealed from us, so is the matter of the end [of the exile] hidden and sealed. Similarly, it was told to Daniel, *For the words are shut up and sealed till the time of the end.*[22]

Isaiah foresaw the length of the present exile and perceived Israel would sink "in the deep mire" and despair over its many troubles and its dispersion from one end of the earth to the other. Therefore, he comforted them, bid them to take heart, and brought them proof for his comfort from the deeds of Creation.

Note that this verse[21] mentioned three elements — fire,[23] water, and earth — but did not cite the wind, for these three elements are visible while the element of wind is not. This verse is stated only for the sake of the spiritually foolish people who believe only what their eyes see. However, those who are wise will not wonder at all whether G-d will bring forth the people of Israel out of the exile, for they know in their wisdom that G-d is unlimited in His power to help them.

Know ye not? hear ye not? hath it not been told to you from the beginning?[24] He mentions three functions[25] by which a person discerns or understands on his own. Thus, *"Know ye not* on your own Who is the Master of the world? *Hear ye not?* Is there no one from whom you could have heard that? *Hath it not been told to you from the beginning?* This refers to tradition which goes back to the beginning of human existence. *Have ye not understood the foundations of the earth?"*[24] The above is said in order to nullify idolatry. If you are capable of reasoning, you can understand that the world has a Creator Who rules the earth's foundations. These are the four elements: fire, wind, water, and earth. From an analysis of these four elements, you can conclude that there is a definite order in the world and that

---

(22) Daniel 12:9. See Ramban, Writings and Discourses, pp. 628-650, for full discussion of the subject. (23) Fire is included in the term *heaven,* for in the opinion of many philosophers, fire is the element out of which the heaven is made (R'dak on Isaiah 40:12). (24) Isaiah 40:21. (25) Knowing, hearing, and tradition which is transmitted from generation to generation.

nothing is subject to chance. For example, you see that fire and water are opposites and are arranged one above the other. [Fire is in the heaven,[23] and water is below it upon the earth.] The air between them is powerless to stop the fire and the water from colliding with each other. Who then has imposed a border upon the fire which prevents it from descending from its place, and who prevents the water from ascending? Can anyone say that this arrangement occurred merely as a matter of chance without the direction of a Ruler? Something which occurs by chance does not continue steadily. Therefore, those who maintain that the world came into existence by chance without an act of the Creator can be refuted. For example,[26] if a person would splash ink upon paper, it is impossible that it would form a well planned and properly lined composition like that written with a pen. Anyone presented with a proper composition allegedly done by splashing ink upon paper would immediately challenge the allegation. Now, if this is true in the case of a mere composition, it certainly applies to a far more delicate work, the composition and order of which is so profound and immeasurably far incomprehensible.

To whom then will ye liken Me, that I should be equal?[27] "You can liken Me to many powers, but I cannot be equated with any of them, for I am One, the Holy One, and far above your thoughts."

Lift up your eyes on high, and see: who hath created these?[28] After saying that people should contemplate the four elements and the heavens that are stretched out like a tent,[29] G-d said that people should look upon the stars, which are mighty bodies, and seek to understand *who hath created these.* Through the ways of wisdom, you should realize that the world has been created. Since it has been created, it must have a Creator, Who can be but One. Thus, the countless stars themselves are the product of Creation and do not possess any creative power.

(26) The example is found in Rabbeinu Bachya ibn Pekuda's *Chovoth Halevavoth* (Duties of the Hearts), *Shaar Hayichud* (Gate of the Unity), end of Chapter 6. (27) Isaiah 40:25. (28) *Ibid.*, Verse 26. (29) See *ibid.*, Verse 22.

He that bringeth out their host by number, He called them all by name.[28] Man is incapable of determining the number of the stars, yet G-d has assigned a specific function to each of the luminaries, as our Rabbis said,[30] "There is not a single blade of grass below that does not have a constellation in heaven which smites it and says to it, 'Grow' It is said, *Knowest thou the ordinances of the heavens? Canst thou establish 'mishtaro' (the dominion thereof) in the earth?*[31] The name of each of these stars is in accordance with its power and dominion. Each one is *strong in power*[28] and not subject to change as the lower creatures are. None of the higher created beings ever fails[28] in whole or in part. They contain no deficiency; they are perfect in their creation.

Because Israel accepted the Ten Commandments, which begin with *Anochi* (I), they will merit that G-d will comfort them with the same word, as it says, *I, even I, am He that comforteth you.*[32] G-d commanded the prophets to comfort them, as it says, *Comfort ye, comfort ye, My people, saith your G-d.*[2] Therefore, when Isaiah uttered this consoling prophecy concerning the ingathering of the exiles, he began by speaking of Creation, saying, *Who hath measured the waters in the hollow of His hand?*[21] Isaiah concluded with the subject of the stars, saying, *Lift up your eyes on high and see: Who hath created these?*[28] His intent was to say that G-d, Who has the power to create heaven and earth out of absolute nothingness and Who has the power to bring out the stars, is certainly capable of bringing forth the people of Israel from the exile, out of the hands of their enemies.

Isaiah's reference to the stars—*He called them all by name*[28]—alludes to the people of Israel, who are likened to the stars. In the future, each one of the people of Israel will ascend to Jerusalem as if each one was called by name. The prophet's statement, *Not one*

---

(30) Bereshith Rabbah 10:7. (31) Job 38:33. The Midrash adds: "[*Mishtaro* is derived from the word] *shoteir* (executive officer)." See also Ramban, Commentary on the Torah, Genesis, p. 71. (32) Isaiah 51:12. This section is read on the fourth Sabbath of "the seven weeks of consolation" (see Note 1).

faileth,[28] also intimates that not one of the people of Israel living at that time will fail to ascend to Jerusalem. It is thus written in the Book of Ezekiel, *And I shall have gathered them unto their own Land, and I will leave none of them any more there.*[33] At that time, the rejoicing will be great and the comfort complete. The earth will be filled with knowledge and wisdom. *And the light of the moon shall be as the light of the sun, and the light of the sun shall be sevenfold, as the light of the seven days, in the day that the Eternal bindeth up the bruise of His people, and healeth the stroke of their wound.*[34] It is further written, *For the Eternal comforted Zion, He hath comforted all her waste places, and hath made her wilderness like Eden, and her desert like the garden of the Eternal; joy and gladness shall be found therein, thanksgiving, and the voice of melody.*[35] Again it is written, *As one whom his mother comforteth, so will I comfort you, and ye shall be comforted in Jerusalem.*[36]

(33) Ezekiel 39:28.   (34) Isaiah 30:26.   (35) *Ibid.*, 51:3.   (36) *Ibid.*, 66:13. The prophet mentions *whom his 'mother' comforteth,* because a mother is more affectionate to a child (R'dak).

נר חנוכה
The Chanukah Light

The Scriptural usage of the word 'light' refers to all benefits, while 'darkness' is referred to as evils and troubles / Various interpretations of the verse, 'Light is sown for the righteous, and gladness for those upright in heart' / The Torah is the greatest of all luminaries / The kindling of lights in the Sanctuary was a matter of great honor to Israel and to the Sanctuary / The great miracle of the westernmost lamp of the Candelabrum / The miracle of Chanukah / Various allusions that Chanukah is to be celebrated for eight days / The future Redemption will be similar to the Exodus from Egypt, but there will be more wonders performed in the presence of the nations of the world.

The Chanukah Light

LIGHT IS SOWN FOR THE RIGHTEOUS, AND GLADNESS
FOR THOSE UPRIGHT IN HEART.[1]

The Scriptural usage of the word "light" refers to all benefits in the world. This does not mean actual light, but rather peace, tranquility, honor, and health. It is thus similar to these expressions: *The Jews had light and gladness;*[2] *Arise, shine, for thy light is come;*[3] *For Thou art my light.*[4] You will also find that Scripture refers to all evils of the world as "darkness," as in the verse, *And the fool walketh in darkness.*[5] Scripture terms the days of a melancholy and complaining person as "darkness," as Job said, *Let that day be darkness.*[6] One who gives bad advice is called a "darkener," as in the verse, *Who is this that darkeneth counsel by words?*[7] It is evident from this that good counsel is light and improper counsel is darkness. This is also the purport of the verse, *I form the light, and create darkness, I make peace and create evil.*[8] Peace is thus placed in the category of light, and evil in the

---

(1) Psalms 97:11. The expression *Light is 'sown'* suggests that just as a single seed when sown can produce an abundant crop, so is the light of the righteous. By teaching and practicing the laws of righteousness, their following may at first be minute, but in the end they are assured of acceptance by all (Ibn Ezra). The text of this theme will contain other significant interpretations of this verse by our author. The connection between the subject of light and that of Chanukah is obvious. (2) Esther 8:16. (3) Isaiah 60:1. Light being the symbol of joy and beneficence, the prophet is thus saying to Jerusalem that her greater glory has come, and that she will be restored to her place of honor. (4) II Samuel 22:29. (5) Ecclesiastes 2:14. (6) Job 3:4. (7) *Ibid.,* 38:2. (8) Isaiah 45:7.

category of darkness. This thought is expressed in the verse here. *Light is sown for the righteous.*[1] That is to say, all good things and peace are reserved by G-d for the righteous; it is man himself who incurs most of the troubles which befall him. Although man is sinful and G-d consequently causes many afflictions to befall him, He nevertheless does not desire to do so. He prefers that man not sin so that he would not have to be afflicted with troubles.

The thoroughly righteous person who has never sinned is under G-d's absolute protection and providence and is worthy of all the benefits of the world, as the verse states, *Light is sown for the righteous.*[1] As the righteous man cleaves to G-d, so does G-d's providence cleave to him. The Talmud relates[9] that the goats of one thoroughly righteous person[10] would kill marauding wolves. This person was so completely protected by G-d that his animals were not subject to natural laws. Thus, not only were his goats unafraid of the predators, but they even killed them, as the Sages said,[9] "In the evening, each of the goats brought a bear on its horns."

The term *latzadik (for the righteous)*[1] is stated in the singular, serving as an allusion for the Sages' statement,[11] "For the sake of one righteous person, the world exists, as it is said, *And the righteous man is the support of the world.*"[12]

And gladness for those upright in heart.[1] After the psalmist stated that the righteous man is protected from hazards on account of his great distinction and merit, he mentioned *the upright in heart.* These are people who merely speak of righteousness and think of it in their hearts. Thy are thus not in the same category as the righteous and are

---

(9) Taanith 25 a.   (10) His name was Rabbi Chanina ben Dosa. A measure of his saintliness may be gathered from the following saying of Rav as quoted by Rabbi Yehudah in Taanith 24 b: "Every day, a Heavenly Voice comes forth and says, 'The entire world is fed only on account of my son Chanina, while Chanina is satisfied with a small measure of carobs from one Sabbath eve to the other.' "   (11) Yoma 38 b.   (12) Proverbs 10:25.

not protected from hazards. When afflictions befall them, however, they do not rebel against them but joyfully accept the Divine judgment upon them, knowing that their afflictions constitute an altar of forgiveness for them.

It is possible to interpret the verse, *Light is sown for the righteous,*[1] as a reference to real light. It is thus an allusion to the light called into being on the first day of Creation, concerning which the Sages commented:[13] *"And G-d saw the light, that it was good.*[14] He saw that the world was not worthy of using it, so He hid it for the righteous in the World to Come." Accordingly, the expression *for the righteous*[1] means "for the soul of the righteous," since the souls were created on the first day together with the light. In the Book of Job, G-d asks, *Where is the way to the dwelling of light?*[15] and He immediately states, *Thou knowest it, for thou wast then born, and the number of thy days is great.*[16] G-d is saying to Job: "If you know and understand how light came into existence, then you surely know it,[17] *for thou wast then born.* You were born with the light at that time, and from the first day of Creation, you could tell all that transpired, for you were there together with it." The expression, *and the number of thy days is great,*[16] thus intimates to Job that the souls were created together with the light on the first day of Creation. This is the thought conveyed by the poet Rabbi Yehudah Halevi,[18] when he wrote: "He ordained the existence of the souls together with the first light, that being the beginning of the word of G-d."[19] Because light and souls were created on the first day, they exist forever, as indicated by Scripture's use of an ex-

---

(13) Bereshith Rabbah 11:2.   (14) Genesis 1:4.   (15) Job 38:19.   (16) *Ibid.,* Verse 21.   (17) That is to say, "If you had knowledge of how light came into existence, you would surely know something of momentous significance, *for thou wast then born,* i.e., your soul came into existence at that time."   (18) He was the great Hebrew poet and philosopher of the Spanish Golden Era (1085-1142 C.E.). The quotation is part of a poem entitled *Borchi Nafshi* (O My Soul, Bless the Eternal), an introductory hymn to the Closing Prayer on the Day of Atonement.   (19) This entire paragraph is based upon Ramban's Commentary on the Book of Job. Its theme is also mentioned in Ramban's "Writings and Discourses," p. 87.

pression unique to them. Regarding the light it is said, *And there was light*,[20] and regarding the souls, it is said, *And man was a living soul.*[21] Scripture thus alludes that the soul of the righteous man exists forever as does the light itself.

The expression *sown* indicates the abundance of the reward and the overflowing sense of the increasingly wondrous joy of the soul of the righteous man. In the process of sowing, the small quantity which is put into the earth yields much. Similarly, the soul of the righteous man will merit boundless joy in the World to Come for the fulfillment of each commandment. Additionally, the term *sown* here signifies that the righteousness sown is not subject to any hazardousness, unlike the sowing of seeds in the earth which is exposed to risk, such as drought, blasting and hail. Solomon stated this thought elsewhere: *And he that soweth righteousness has a sure reward.*[22] That is to say, the outcome of all planting is unknown, for it is possible that the crop will be blighted. However, the reward of one who sows righteousness is not doubtful; it is assured in the World to Come. This is the sense of *sure reward*,[22] for it is the reward which certainly exists.

The term *latzadik (for the righteous)*[1] is stated in the singular although Scripture should have used the plural *latzadikim*, which would have parallelled the phrase, *and for those upright in heart*. However, the use of the singular intimates that not all people attain this high position, as the Sages said,[23] "Those enjoying the Divine Presence in the hereafter are few."[24]

And gladness for those upright in heart.[1] *Gladness* is associated with *those upright in heart* and *light* is associated with *the righteous* in order to imply that the gradation of gladness is inferior to that of light, just as the gradation of those upright in heart is inferior to that of the righteous. Throughout Scripture, you will always find that the

---

(20) Genesis 1:3. (21) *Ibid.*, 2:7. (22) Proverbs 11:18. (23) Succah 45 b. (24) In the Talmud *ibid.*, this statement is explained as referring to those righteous who enter the heavenly court without any restrictions. But of those who enter with certain qualifications, there are indeed many.

category of the righteous precedes that of the upright in heart. Moses said, *Righteous and upright is He.*[25] David said, *Surely the righteous shall give thanks unto Thy Name, the upright shall dwell in Thy presence.*[26] In the Rosh Hashanah prayers, the Sages ordained the statement, "Then shall the righteous see and be glad, and the upright shall exult." The verse[1] thus informs us that light is the principal joy. It is the righteous who merit light, and they will certainly attain gladness. Those upright in heart, however, merit gladness but not light. Therefore, our Sages said:[27] "Rav Nachman bar Yitzchak said, 'Not all will share in light and not all in gladness; the righteous will have light, and the upright will have gladness.' "[28]

In the Midrash, it is stated:[29] *"Light is sown for the righteous.*[1] This verse refers to Moses. When he was born, his entire house was filled with light, as it is said, *And she* [his mother] *saw him that he was 'tov' (good).*[30] The term *tov (good)* refers only to a righteous man, as it states, *Say ye of the righteous, that it shall be 'tov' with him.*[31] When Moses descended from Mount Sinai after receiving the Torah, it is written, *The skin of his face sent forth beams.*[32] This is the purport of the statement, *Light is sown for the righteous.*"[1] The Midrash utilized this verse to affirm that from the time of his birth, Moses our teacher was fit to enlighten the entire world through the Torah which he received on Mount Sinai. At first, he enlightened the world by making the Tabernacle, which was like the Sanctuary, the light of the world, as it is said, *And nations shall walk at thy light.*[33] Afterwards, he illuminated the world by making the Ark containing the Tablets of the

(25) Deuteronomy 32:4. (26) Psalms 140:4. (27) Taanith 15 a. (28) That not all will share in gladness obviously contradicts our author's statement that the righteous merit light *and* gladness. This problem is discussed more fully in my commentary to the Hebrew edition, p. 266, where our author's position is substantiated by a variant reading of Rabbeinu Chananel, which states: "the righteous and the upright share in gladness." (29) I have been unable to locate this Midrash. See Torah Shleimah, Exodus, 2, Note 16, where closely related texts are quoted. (30) Exodus 2:2. (31) Isaiah 3:10. (32) Exodus 34:29. (33) Isaiah 60:3. See above *Chillul Hashem* (Profaning G-d's Name), Note 34.

Covenant, the Torah and the commandment,[34] which are the light of the world, as it says, *For the commandment is a light, and the Torah is a flame.*[35]

Scripture compares the Torah to the flame of the sun,[35] for the sun is one of the most significant celestial creations visible to the naked eye and [thus serves to indicate G-d's majesty], as David said, *The heavens declare the glory of G-d.*[36] Afterwards, David stated, *The law of the Eternal is perfect,*[37] thereby informing us that there is a light greater than even the sun, and that light is the Torah, which *enlightens the eyes*[38] more than the sun does. The sun rules by day and not by night, but the light of the Torah prevails by both day and night. The light of the sun can be eclipsed during the day, but the light of the Torah shines forever. This is the meaning of the verse which states that the Torah endures forever.[39] In accordance with the arrangement of concepts in this psalm, the Sages ordained that in the Morning Service, after the benediction "Who Creates the Luminaries," we should say, "Enlighten Thou our eyes in Thy Torah" for this very reason.[40]

David compared the Torah to both a light and a flame, as it is said, *Thy word is a light unto my feet, and a flame unto my path.*[41] He compared the Torah to the flame of the sun, which is the largest visible light. At the same time, he compared it to a light, for the benefit of a light is sometimes more direct than that of the sun. With a light, for example, one can search in holes and cracks, but one can not do so with the flame of the sun. He stated *to my feet*[41] because the foot is prone to stumble and the Torah spares one from stumbling. This is similar to a person who walks at night with a light in his hand to assure that he will not fall. Thus, we may conclude that the Torah is the greatest luminary of all and that Moses our teacher enlightened the

---

(34) See above *Emunah* (Faith), Note 2. (35) Proverbs 6:23. (36) Psalms 19:2. (37) *Ibid.*, Verse 8. (38) *Ibid.*, Verse 9. See Ramban, Writings and Discourses, pp. 30-32. (39) See Psalms 19:10. (40) I.e., to inform us that there is a greater luminary than the sun. See *Eivel* (Mourning), Note 43. (41) Psalms 119:105.

world first with the Torah and afterwards by making the Candelabrum, [as will be explained below].

It is known that the making of the Candelabrum and the other vessels of the Tabernacle were all symbols and descriptions of rational matters, just as the Garden of Eden, in which Adam lived, and its rivers and trees all alluded to truths.[42] You will thus find that Scripture writes of the vessels of the Tabernacle, *And see that thou make them after their pattern, which is being shown thee in the mount.*[43] This teaches us that on Mount Sinai, Moses saw the example of their form and discerned the matters of knowledge and wisdom alluded to therein.

It is also known that the kindling of the Candelabrum lights is inconsequential to the Divine Presence. It is written of G-d, *And the light dwelleth with Him,*[44] and it is further written, *And the earth did shine with His glory.*[45] Why then should He need the lights of mortal beings? Rather the Candelabrum lights were intended to honor and distinguish the Sanctuary. They caused us to affirm in our hearts the greatness of the Temple and served to heighten its standing in the eyes of all who saw it. In Tanchuma,[46] the Sages expounded the verse, *to cause a light to burn continually,*[47] as follows: "G-d said, 'Do I need your light? A mortal king kindles a light from one that is already burning, but can he kindle a light from darkness? I, however, brought forth light out of darkness, as it is written, *And darkness was upon the face of the deep,*[48] immediately after which it says, *And G-d said: Let there be light. And there was light.*[20] Hence, you must realize that I have said, *to cause a light to burn continually,*[47] only to increase your esteem before all the nations.' " From this Midrash, we learn that the kindling of lights in the Sanctuary was a great honor to Israel and to the Sanctuary, so that the Sanctuary thereby be held in awe and sanctified.

(42) See Ramban, Commentary on the Torah, Genesis, pp. 85-86.   (43) Exodus 25:40.   (44) Daniel 2:22.   (45) Ezekiel 43:2.   (46) Tanchuma, *Beha'alothcha,* 8.   (47) Exodus 27:20.   (48) Genesis 1:2.

We can thus understand the custom of all the people of Israel to kindle lights in synagogues, for it is a means of honoring and beautifying a house of prayer. All who heed this practice bestow honor upon G-d. Accordingly, the prophet said, *Therefore glorify you the Eternal 'ba'urim,'*[49] which the Sages interpreted[50] as "with these lanterns."

You are already familiar with the great miracle which occurred to the Candelabrum in the Sanctuary. The western lamp[51] contained no more oil than the other lamps, yet while the other lamps burnt only until the morning,[52] the western lamp burned through the night and the entire day until the next evening. During the Service at dusk, the priest would then kindle the other lamps from it. This miracle attested that the Divine Glory rests among the people of Israel, as it is written, *Outside the Veil which is before the testimony, Aaron and his sons shall set it in order.*[53] The Sages commented:[54] "It is a *testimony* to the entire world that the Divine Glory rests among the people of Israel. What was *the testimony?* Rava said, 'This refers to the western lamp[51] into which the priest put as much oil as he did in the others, yet he concluded the kindling of the lamps[55] with the western lamp."

---

(49) Isaiah 24:15. The *ba'urim* is generally translated "in the valleys." (50) P'sikta d'Rav Kahana, 21. See above, *Beth Haknesseth* (The Synagogue), Note 23. (51) In the Sanctuary, the Candelabrum stood in an east-west direction. The first or easternmost of its seven lamps could not be considered as the one *before the Eternal* (Exodus 17:21) for that expression implies that there is at least one lamp farther away from the Holy of Holies where the Divine Glory abides. Hence, the first lamp which may be considered *before the Eternal* is the second from the east and that is the one called "the western lamp." See more on this theme in Ramban's Commentary on the Torah, Exodus, p. 474, Note 23. (52) The Candelabrum was kindled daily during the Service at dusk, at which time each of the seven lamps was filled with the same amount of oil. When the priest entered the Sanctuary for the following Morning Service, he would find all or some of the lamps extinguished with the exception of the western lamp, which he always found burning. — Forty years before the destruction of the Second Temple the western lamp was always found extinguished as a sign of the impending catastrophe (Yoma 39 b). (53) Exodus 27:21. (54) Shabbath 22 b. (55) At dusk, the priest would kindle the six lamps, which had already been extinguished, with the flame of the western lamp miraculously still burning since the previous day. After kindling the other six lamps, he would then extinguish the western one, set it in order,

We find in the Talmud[56] that there were righteous men who lived during the era of the [Second] Sanctuary that the western lamp was never extinguished during their lifetime. This is akin to the great miracle which occurred with the lamps at that time in the days of Matithyahu son of Yochanan, the High Priest, through whom a great deliverance was effected for Israel.[57] Matithyahu and his sons, who were mighty men of valor, slew thousands of Greek troops, and their prowess became so well known that all nations feared them. Israel regained its autonomy, and the power of Greece in the Land of Israel was vanquished by the Hasmoneans. On the twenty-fifth day of Kislev, the victorious Jews entered the Sanctuary [for the first time since the oppression had begun]. They found only one cruse of pure oil, the contents of which would suffice to keep the Candelabrum burning just one night.[58] However, a miracle occurred, and they used that small quantity of oil to kindle the Candelabrum for eight nights.

Why did this miracle extend over a period of exactly eight days? Some scholars[59] explain that the place from which the olive oil was brought was a distance of four days' travel from Jerusalem. The return trip took another four days, making eight in all. Furthermore, contemplation will reveal that most things in the Sanctuary hinged on the number eight. The High Priest wore eight garments—the breastplate,

and relight it with the flame of one of the other lamps. Thus the ceremony of kindling the Candelabrum concluded with the lighting of the western lamp. When the priest upon entering the Sanctuary found this not to be the case—such as during the final forty years of the Temple when all lights were extinguished—he would first relight the western lamp from the fire which burned on the altar outsidse the Court (Yoma 39 a). (56) *Ibid.*   (57) This occurred in the Grecian period when Antiochus Epiphanes of Syria banned the practice of the Jewish religion, aiming at Hellenizing all Jews. In the city of Modin, Matithyahu the Hasmonean raised the banner of revolt against the Syrian Greeks. Ultimately the revolt ended with the complete restoration of Israel's power as an independent nation for almost two hundred years.   (58) In Mishneh Torah, beginning of *Hilchoth Chanukah*, Maimonides specifies that the oil was sufficient for "one day." This is in accord with his opinion that the Candelabrum was lit every morning as well as at dusk. Our author, however, follows the opinion of most Sages that the Candelabrum was kindled only at dusk.   (59) So explained in Meiri, Shabbath 21 b.

the ephod, the robe, the checkered tunic, the miter, the belt, the breeches, and the plate. The Levites sang to the accompaniment of eight instruments—a stringed instrument,[60] *machalath*,[61] *alamoth*,[62] *masa*,[63] *shoshanim*,[64] pipes, *gittith*,[65] and *sh'minith*.[66] There are eight fragrant substances in the oil of anointment and the incense. Four were in the oil of anointment—myrrh, cinnamon, calamus, and cassia—[67] and four were in the incense—stacte, onycha, galbanum, and frankincense.[68] There were eight staves—two for the Ark,[69] two for the Table,[70] two for the golden altar,[71] and two for the altar of the burnt-offering.[72] Sacrificial offerings could be brought only when they were at least eight days old, as it is written, *And from the eighth day and thenceforth it may be accepted for an offering.*[73] [The number "eight" is also significant in other areas of religious observance. For example], on the eighth day [following the birth of a male child], circumcision takes place. There are also eight threads in the *tzitzith*, and there are eight prerequisites to prophecy.[74]

There is yet one other reason for the eight days of Chanukah. This world is distinguished by seven gradations of wisdom,[75] which were

(60) See Psalms 4:1.   (61) See *ibid.*, 53:1. The nature of this and some of the following instruments is unknown to us.   (62) See *ibid.*, 46:1.   (63) See I Chronicles 15:22. The *masa* produced a strong high pitched sound.   (64) See Psalms 45:1. Literally, *shoshanim* are "lilies," which suggests that this instrument was shaped in the form of a lily.   (65) See Psalms 8:1.   (66) See *ibid.*, 6:1. Literally, *sh'minith* means "eighth," suggesting that this was an eight-stringed instrument.   (67) See Exodus 30:23-24.   (68) See *ibid.*, Verse 34.   (69) See *ibid.*, 25:12.   (70) See *ibid.*, Verse 28.   (71) See *ibid.*, 30:5.   (72) See *ibid.*, 27:6.   (73) Leviticus 22:27.   (74) The thought suggested is that before a person can achieve a degree of prophecy he must first break down certain barriers which interfere with his achieving such status. They are: insufficient understanding, difficulty of discernment, passion, conceit, excitement, anger, fierceness, and love of money.—See my commentary in the Hebrew edition, p. 268.   (75) They are: "the wisdom of the constellations, the wisdom of measurements, the wisdom of the soul, the wisdom of nature, the wisdom of expression, the wisdom of mathematics, and the wisdom of values" (Abraham ibn Ezra, Yesod Morah, 1). Expressed in modern terms, the gradations of wisdom are equivalent to astronomy, geometry, psychology, natural science, language, mathematics, and liberal arts. See Rabbeinu Bachya's commentary on Exodus 25:31 (in my edition, p. 282).

symbolized by the seven lamps of the Candelabrum in the Tabernacle
and the Sanctuary. Accordingly, wisdom dictates that in the era of the
Messiah, there will be the additional gradation of knowledge of G-d, as
it is written, *For they shall know Me, from the least of them unto the
greatest of them.*[76] Our Sages expanded the explanation of this matter
and said in Tractate Arakhin:[77] "Rabbi Yehudah says that the harp of
the Sanctuary was a seven-stringed instrument, as it is said, *'Sova'
(fullness of) joy is in Thy presence.*[78] Do not read the word as *sova*, but
as *sheva* (seven).[79] In the era of the Messiah, the Sanctuary harp will
have eight strings, as it is said, *For the leader* [of the musicians] *on the
sh'minith' (eighth),* [i.e., on the eight-stringed instrument].[66] The
harp of the World to Come will have ten strings, as it is said, *Sing
praises to Him with the psaltery of ten strings.*"[80] These matters should
be contemplated on the eight days of Chanukah.[81] The word
"Chanukah" itself is derived from the expression, *'Chanoch' (Educate)
a child,*[82] and is related to the expression *'chanukath' (dedication) of
the House.*[83] It alludes to the era of the Messiah when we shall dedicate
the Sanctuary.

We have a tradition[84] that the future Redemption will be like the
one from Egypt. For example, just as the sea was parted after the Exodus, there will occur a similar parting of the sea during the future
Redemption. Just as Moses, the first deliverer was raised by Pharaoh's
daughter Bathyah in the king's own palace, whence he came forth and
destroyed it—as it is said, *I shall bring forth a fire from the midst of
thee, which shall devour thee*[85]—so will that final deliverer [destroy
Israel's enemies]. May he be revealed speedily in our days. Since we are

---

(76) Jeremiah 31:33.   (77) Arakhin 13 b. See Ramban, Writings and Discourses,
pp. 528-529, for a discussion of this subject.   (78) Psalms 16:11.   (79) With this
reading, the verse would then indicate that each of the seven strings in the harp constitutes a new source of happiness for the person entering the Sanctuary.   (80) Psalms
33:2.   (81) The eight days of Chanukah are suggesting, as explained, the era of the
Messiah, and are thus a source of solace and strength in our belief in the coming
Redemption.   (82) Proverbs 22:6.   (83) Psalms 30:1.   (84) See further in *Pesach*
(Passover), and *Succah* (Tabernacle), where Bachya elaborates on this
theme.   (85) Ezekiel 28:18.

now in exile, it is therefore proper for us to bear the troubles which
come upon us and to pray to G-d for the strength to endure them. We
must trust that it is all for our good, as the Sages said,[86] "Righteous
men suffer in the beginning but enjoy tranquility at the end." We
should realize that although G-d sent us into exile, He nevertheless has
not despised us, for the Torah testifies, *And yet for all that, when they
are in the land of their enemies, I will not reject them, neither will I
abhor them, to destroy them.*[87] Even at the time of the destruction of
the Temple, Jeremiah said, *How is she become as a widow!*[88] He did
not say that Jerusalem had become a real widow; she is only like a
woman whose husband has left for overseas but intends to return to
her.

You will find that all of the experiences of Jacob, the third of our
patriarchs, constitute an allusion to the present third exile.[89] Jacob
prevailed over all his adversaries and was saved from all of his troubles.
Scripture says of him, *And Jacob came* [back to the land of his fathers]
in peace.[90]

We find this very assurance was delivered by Daniel, who brought
tidings to the people of Israel regarding this long exile. He assured
them that they would retain their faith despite the troubles and afflictions which would befall them, as it is said, *And they shall stumble by
the sword, and by flame, by captivity and by spoil, many days.*[91] Yet,
the people of Israel would suffer no permanent harm from these afflictions, just as the heavens [suffer no damage from the darkness of the
night]. The firmament remains bright and clear, and darkness does
not cleave to it. [So too, the people of Israel will emerge from the
darkness of the exile unharmed], as it is written, *And they who are wise
shall shine as the brightness of the firmament, and they that turn the
many to righteousness as the stars forever and ever.*[92]

(86) Bereshith Rabbah 66:5. (87) Leviticus 26:44. (88) Lamentations
1:1. (89) The other two exiles were those in Egypt and Babylon. (90) Genesis
33:18. (91) Daniel 11:33. (92) *Ibid*, 12:3.

שמחה
Joy as a Mode of Divine Worship

Joy in this world is appropriate only in the service of
G-d / Such joy is required by the Torah and one is rewarded
for it as if he had performed a religious duty / The opposite is
true for one who rejoices over evil / The three stages in a person's life / The saying of the Sages regarding the limiting of joy
in this world / Joy in the performance of a commandment.

Joy as a Mode of Divine Worship

SERVE THE ETERNAL WITH JOY, COME BEFORE HIS
PRESENCE WITH SINGING.[1] KNOW YE THAT THE ETER-
NAL IS G-D INDEED: IT IS HE THAT HATH MADE US, AND
HIS WE ARE, HIS PEOPLE, AND THE FLOCK OF HIS
PASTURE.[2]

Joy in this world is appropriate only in the service of G-d.
Throughout the sacred Scriptures, joy is considered a virtue only if it is
related to the worship and contemplation of G-d. It is thus written: *Rejoice in the Eternal, O ye righteous;*[3] *Be glad in the Eternal, and rejoice, ye righteous, and shout for joy, all ye that are upright in heart.*[4]
It is also written, *I rejoice at Thy word, as one that findeth abundant
spoil,*[5] for the righteous, who are G-d's messengers, eagerly serve G-d
with joy. We find, too, that the sun, the great luminary eagerly courses
through its orbit and joyfully performs its task, as it is written, *And he
is as a bridegroom coming out of his chamber, and rejoiceth as a strong
man to run his course.*[6] In the first of the two benedictions before the
reading of the *Sh'ma* in the morning, we say that the luminaries "rejoice in their going forth and are glad in their returning."

---

(1) Psalms 100:2. Serving G-d is not a burden just to be carried out. Instead, it is to
be performed out of joy wherever we are, even outside of the Temple. Only when we
serve G-d with joy can we come before His Presence with singing (Hirsch). (2) *Ibid.*,
Verse 3. By coming into His Sanctuary we recognize His sovereignty and accept His
Law as our guide in life (Hirsch). (3) *Ibid.*, 33:1. (4) *Ibid.*, 32:11. (5) *Ibid.*,
119:162. (6) *Ibid.*, 19:6.

Solomon stated, *So I commended joy, that a man hath no better thing under the sun, than to eat, and to drink, and to be merry, and that this should accompany him in his labor all the days of his life which G-d hath given him under the sun.*[7] Now, eating, drinking, and merriment in this world do not accompany one in the World to Come. Hence, the verse must be referring to the joy in G-d's service. The Sages so stated in Midrash Koheleth:[8] *"To eat, and to drink, and to be merry.*[7] Does eating and drinking accompany a person in the World to Come? Rather, the verse refers to Torah, repentance, and good deeds."* Moses our teacher similarly stated, *Because thou didst not serve the Eternal thy G-d with joyfulness.*[9] G-d punished them since they did not serve Him with joy.

This joy is required by the Torah, and constitutes a great act of Divine worship, being more significant than the performance of the commandment itself. However, joy over physical pleasures, and the like, which result from a violation of a commandment, is forbidden. Thus, it is written, *And he that is glad at calamity shall not be unpunished.*[10]

Accordingly, joy can entail punishment or reward depending on whether its cause is a meritorious deed or a sin. If one rejoices over the performance of a good deed, *behold, his reward is with Him, and his recompense before Him,*[11] for the joy in serving G-d, which is rooted in the individual's heart reveals itself inwardly and is manifested outwardly [by the individual's disposition]. Therefore, he is rewarded for this joy just as if he had performed a good deed. Similarly, if one rejoices over the perpetration of some evil, he is punished for his joy just as if he had actually sinned. Therefore, a person should be heedful regarding

(7) Ecclesiastes 8:15. In his search to escape the insoluble problems of life, Solomon is commending the joy in the normal activities of life. Our author, assisted by the Midrash, interprets it as reference to the pleasure and satisfaction that come with the performance of one's duties. (8) Koheleth Rabbah 8:16. (9) Deuteronomy 28:47. (10) Proverbs 17:5. Reference is to rejoicing at another's misfortune. (11) Isaiah 40:10.

his feelings in performing a commandment or when [perforce] doing some sinful act.

It was to this kind of [commendable] joy that Solomon referred when he said, *Rejoice, O young man, in thy youth, and let thy heart cheer thee in the days of the adolescence.*[12] A person's life is divided into three stages: childhood, adolescence, and old age. Childhood and adolescence constitute the periods of joy and cheer, as it is said, *Rejoice, O young man, in thy youth.*[12] Scripture thus teaches you that childhood is the time of joy, for just as the sun begins to shine in the morning and steadily increases its light, so does the youth's body continue to grow during childhood. Adolescence is the time of cheer, for one is then at the height of his strength, just as the sun reaches its apex at midday. Old age is called *the days of darkness*[13] or *the evil days,*[14] as it is written, *And remember the days of darkness, for they shall be many; all that cometh is vanity.*[13] The verse[12] thus teaches you that a person will be judged for his joy in this world.

The Sages said in the Midrash:[15] *"I have said 'lahol'lim' (unto the boasters), Do not 'taholu' (boast).*[16] 'I have said *lachol'lim* (to the dancers), Do not *tacholu* (dance),' for joy does not tarry with a person in this world. Not everyone who rejoices today will do so tomorrow, and not everyone who is distressed today will be so tomorrow. This is the purport of Solomon's statement, *I said of laughter: It is mad; and of mirth: what doth it accomplish?*[17] You have proof that this is so. At the time of Creation, there was great joy before the Creator, as it is said, *May the glory of the Eternal endure forever, let the Eternal rejoice in His works.*[18] It is further written, *And G-d saw every thing that He had*

---

(12) Ecclesiastes 11:9. The verse concludes: *But know thou, that for all these things G-d will bring thee into judgment.* (13) *Ibid.,* Verse 8. (14) *Ibid.,* 12:1. (15) Tanchuma, *Shemini,* 2. (16) Psalms 75:5. — The Midrash explains the word *lahol'lim* (to the boasters) as *lachol'lim* (to the dancers), since the letters *hei* and *cheth* often interchange. The verse is thus a sobering reminder to those who dance with joy at earthly pleasures to curb their indulgence. (17) Ecclesiastes 2:2. (18) Psalms 104:31.

made, and behold, it was very good.[19] However, it is finally written, *And it grieved Him at His heart.*[20] Therefore, it is said, *I have said 'lahol'lim' (unto the boasters), Do not 'taholu' (boast),* which means 'I have said *lachol'lim* (to the dancers), Do not *tacholu* (dance).' If G-d's joy did not last, how much more fleeting is the joy of mortal man! Consider also these examples: Abraham rejoiced greatly. He was powerful, he had vanquished a number of kings, and he had begotten a son in his old age. Yet, in the end he was told, *Take now thy son, thine only son, whom thou lovest, even Isaac.*[21] Abraham returned from Mount Moriah to bury his wife Sarah. He searched for a burial place for her, but could not find one until he purchased a site for four hundred shekels of silver. Isaac rejoiced greatly when the Philistine lords told him, *We saw plainly that the Eternal was with thee.*[22] He was also saved from the sword and from the men of Gerar, but at the end it is written, *And his eyes were dim, so that he could not see.*[23] If the joy of Isaac, who was G-d's offering, did not endure, how much more fleeting is the joy of ordinary man! Jacob rejoiced greatly. He saw a ladder with *the angels of G-d ascending and descending on it,*[24] *and behold, the Eternal stood beside Him.*[25] Yet, in the end, many troubles befell him! He experienced the affliction of Laban and Esau and the grief of Joseph, Dinah, and Rachel! If Jacob did not tarry in his joy, other people certainly will not tarry in theirs! Joshua rejoiced greatly. He caused Israel to inherit the Land, he vanquished thirty-one kings, and all Israel honored him, as it is said, *Whosoever he be that shall rebel against thy command, and shall not hearken unto thy words,* etc., *he shall be put to death.*[26] Nevertheless, Joshua died without having had sons born to him. If this is the fate of the righteous, how much more grievous will the lot of the wicked be! Eli the priest rejoiced greatly. He was supreme ruler, priest, and chief justice, as it is said, *And Eli the priest sat upon his seat by the doorpost of the Temple of the Eternal.*[27]

(19) Genesis 1:31. (20) *Ibid.*, 6:6. (21) *Ibid.*, 22:2. (22) *Ibid.*, 26:28. (23) *Ibid.*, 27:1. (24) *Ibid.*, 28:12. (25) *Ibid.*, Verse 13. (26) Joshua 1:18. (27) I Samuel 1:9.

Yet, see what is written there: *And it came to pass, when he* [a messenger] *made mention of the Ark of G-d* [i.e., that it was captured by the Philistines], *that he* [Eli] *fell from off his seat backward by the side of the gate, and his neck broke, and he died.*[28] Furthermore, his two sons Chophni and Phinehas died! If this happened to the righteous Eli, how much more so will it happen to the wicked! There was no one happier than Elisheba the daughter of Amminadab.[29] Her husband Aaron was High Priest and a prophet. Moses, her brother-in-law, was ruler and prophet. Two of her sons were the High Priest's assistants, and her brother Nachshon the son of Amminadab was the foremost of all princes of Israel.[30] Yet, her joy did not last. When two of her sons — Nadab and Abihu — entered the Tabernacle to offer incense,[31] the fire devoured them.[32] Therefore, it is said, *I have said unto the boasters, Do not boast.*"[16] Thus far the Midrash.[15]

Because a person is obligated to limit joy in this world, the Sages ordained the recitation of a special benediction, "Who art good and dispensest good," when wine is changed at a meal. Since this is only done at an occasion of abundant joy, they ordained this benediction which is actually connected with mourning, in order to limit the joy of the moment. The blessing was originally formulated in Jabneh to commemorate those fallen in Bethar.[33] We also find that Rabbeinu Hakadosh,[34] one of the greatest men in Israel, in whose person were combined both erudition and high office,[35] hired Bar Kappara and paid him a great sum of money so that the latter would not do anything which might cause Rabbeinu Hakadosh joy and merriment.[36] Apparently, Bar Kappara frequently gladdened him with conversation.

(28) *Ibid.*, 4:18. (29) See Exodus 6:23. (30) Numbers 7:12. Nachshon was the prince of the tribe of Judah, the foremost of all tribes. (31) See Leviticus 10:1. (32) *Ibid.*, Verse 2. Regarding the particular offense committed by Nadab and Abihu, see Rashi, *ibid.*, and Ramban, Commentary on the Torah, Leviticus. p. 111. (33) See above in *B'rachah* (Blessing), Note 15. (34) See above in *Ahavah* (Love of G-d), Note 42. (35) See Gittin 59 a. (36) Nedarim 50b-51a.

Bar Kappara intended to honor G-d's Name thereby, for Rabbeinu Hakadosh would rejoice and thus continue to pursue the study of Torah joyfully. This is similar to the effect of the playing of musical instruments in the case of the prophets.[37] However, at the time of his death, Rabbeinu Hakadosh testified about himself that he "did not derive any benefit from the world either with his ten fingers or even with his smallest finger."[38] By this he meant to say that he was disciplined in all qualities of character, even in the traits of joy and merriment. All his actions resulted from his rational proficiency and were weighed on the scales of wisdom.

One is therefore obligated to limit joy in this world and to concern himself with Divine service. His essential joy should be confined to the worship of G-d and the performance of the commandments, as it is said, *Serve the Eternal with joy.*[1] Yet, even in the joy over the fulfillment of a commandment, it is said, *And rejoice with trembling,*[39] which means that "where there is joy, there should be trembling."[40]

It is possible to suggest that this was the intention of the Torah's directive in the case of the Festival of Tabernacles, *And thou shalt be 'ach' (only) rejoiced*[41] which utilizes the diminutive expression *ach.* [Earlier in the year], on the Festival of Weeks, the individual had had occasion to rejoice because it was *the feast of harvest.*[42] Now, on the Festival of Tabernacles, the person's joy is much greater, for it is the season of the ingathering of his produce, oil, wine, and his other fruits. Therefore, at the time of his great joy, the Torah returns him to the path of moderation. This is the sense of the expression, *and thou shalt be 'ach' (only) rejoiced.*[41]

Thus, when performing a commandment, it is proper to experience physical joy in moderation, hence David stated, *Serve the Eternal with*

(37) See I Kings 3:15. (38) Kethuboth 104a. (39) Psalms 2:11. (40) Berachoth 30b. (41) Deuteronomy 16:15. (42) Exodus 23:16. With the Festival of Weeks begins the season of bringing the first-fruits to the Sanctuary, which lasts until the end of summer.

joy.[1] He thus explained that joy is the perfection of Divine service. Accordingly, there was singing and instrumental music in the Tabernacle and Sanctuary because these induce joy. It is stated [with reference to the duties of the Levites] to do *'avodath avodah'* [literally: *'the service of service,'* or as rendered: *to do the work of service*],[43] which the Sages interpreted as follows:[44] "What is *the service of service?* I must conclude that it is song." The Levites were thus directed and commanded to sing and to arouse joy when the sacrifices were offered. In that way the commandment would be joyfully performed.

We find the following in the P'sikta:[45] *"This is the day which the Eternal hath made, we will rejoice and be glad 'bo.'*[46] Rabbi[34] said, 'I would not know whether *'bo'* refers to *the day* or to G-d, but Solomon explained it: *We will be glad and rejoice in Thee.*[47] *In Thee* means in Thy Torah; *in Thee* means in Thy deliverance.'"

It is impossible for a person to experience the joy of the soul until he subdues the power of the body. It is known that the soul within the body is like a light placed in an urn. The light cannot radiate fully until the urn is broken. Similarly, a person must first control his physical desires and weaken them, and only then will his soul ascend to the sacred mountain of G-d. Thus, Solomon said, *And the dust returneth to the earth as it was, and the spirit returneth unto G-d Who gave it,*[48] which means that when the material of the body is bent and lowly as the earth then the spirit inherits the true life, the true goodness, and the everlasting joy. This is the purport of the prophet Isaiah's assurance, *The humble shall increase their joy in the Eternal, and the neediest among men shall exult in the Holy One of Israel.*[49]

---

(43) Numbers 4:47.   (44) Arakhin 11a. The public offerings were accompanied by the singing of the Levites. Hence, the meaning of the verse, that the Levites are *to do the service of service*, that is, the service of song which accompanied the service of a public offering.   (45) P'sikta d'Rav Kahana, *Atzereth.*   (46) Psalms 118:24. The word *bo* means either "in it," thus referring to *the day,* or "in Him," referring to G-d. The text of the P'sikta gives us the correct interpretation.   (47) Song of Songs 1:4.   (48) Ecclesiastes 12:7.   (49) Isaiah 29:19.

סוכה

The Succah

All commandments of the Torah contain an overt and a concealed aspect, and this is also true of the words of the prophets and Sages / This concept also applies to the commandment of the Succah. Its overt aspect is that it was ordained to commemorate the booths that Israel erected in the wilderness / In order to ensure this very commemoration, the Torah has prolonged the account of the forty-two journeys of Israel in the wilderness / The concealed aspect of the Succah / There is an obligation to actually dwell in a Succah as well as to contemplate its theme, for human perfection can be achieved only through a combination of deed and thought / The Torah is the epitome of all wisdom and is therefore called 'the perfect one.'

The Succah

YE SHALL DWELL IN BOOTHS SEVEN DAYS; ALL THAT
ARE HOME-BORN IN ISRAEL SHALL DWELL IN BOOTHS.[1]

It is known that all of the commandments of the Torah contain an overt and a concealed aspect. The overt or outward aspect of the precept aims at benefiting the body or one's faith in G-d and fear of Him or some ethical principle which is advantageous to society. The concealed or inner aspect of the commandment is designed to benefit the soul by rewarding it and magnifying the portion of its recompense in the World of Reward [after death].

Solomon said, *Like apples of gold in settings of silver is a word fitly spoken.*[2] He thus informed us that the Torah is *fitly spoken*[3] i.e., that it contain a twofold aspect of inner and outward features. He compared the inner aspect to gold and the outward to silver, as he stated, *Like apples of gold 'b'maskioth' (in settings of) silver.*[2] *Settings of silver* are silver vessels of filigree work. No one can discern their contents. The

---

(1) Leviticus 23:42. The commandment of the Succah has had wide discussions in Jewish literature. The laws concerning its construction, its historic associations, religious significance, etc., all have contributed to the wealth of thought pertaining to this commandment. Our author will touch upon various aspects of the commandment. (2) Proverbs 25:11. (3) In Hebrew, the double expression *davar davur (a word . . . spoken)* suggests that there are two aspects to the Torah, as the text elaborates. See the introduction to Maimonides' Guide of the Perplexed, where this thought is elaborated.

word *maskioth* connotes "looking" — Onkelos translates the word *vayashkeif (and he looked)*[4] with the word *v'istechi* — for a vessel of filigree work deserves to be looked at on account of its importance. When examining it closely, one finds in it something more valuable than silver, and that is the *apples of gold.*

Solomon stated that the Torah *is fitly spoken*[2] for it has a twofold significance — outward and inner — just like the golden apples which are obscured by the silver filigree. Thus, Solomon compared the overt aspect of the commandments to the distinguished and excellent metal silver, and the concealed aspect to gold, which is still of higher value, for the esoteric meaning possesses an added advantage, even as gold is superior to silver. Considering this view, David said, *Open Thou mine eyes, that I may behold wondrous things of Thy Torah.*[5]

Although Solomon should have properly stated *d'varim d'vurim* (words . . . spoken) in the plural, he used the singular form *davar davur (a word . . . spoken)*[2] in order to intimate that the entire Torah is one band and one subject. For this reason it is necessary to count the letters of the Torah and to take particular care with regard to words written fully [i.e. with all the vowels] or diminutively, for these are matters upon which the entire world depends.

This twofold significance is also the way of the prophets, who speak metaphorically. They conceal their true subject with the metaphor, just as the golden apples lie hidden within the silver filigree. Thus, the prophet said, *Put forth a riddle, and speak a parable;*[6] *They say of me, Is he not a maker of parables?*[7] At the beginning of his book King Solomon declared, *The proverbs of Solomon,* etc.[8] *to know wisdom and instruction.*[9] He thus explained that the purpose of the proverb is to impart wisdom and instruction. Similarly, he said, . . . *to understand proverb and parable.*[10] The *proverb* is the overt wisdom, and the

---

(4) Genesis 19:28.   (5) Psalms 119:18.   (6) Ezekiel 17:2.   (7) *Ibid.,* 21:5.   (8) Proverbs 1:1.   (9) *Ibid.,* Verse 2.   (10) *Ibid.,* Verse 6.

object of the *parable* is the hidden truth. The Sages devised the following illustration:[11] "The parable is analogous to one who lost a diamond in the dark. He knows that the diamond is there, but he cannot locate it until he lights a candle." In itself, the parable, too, is insignificant, but through it, one is able to extract great and illustrious wisdom. The Talmud, too, utilizes the metaphor in its homilies and Midrashim, and in this respect, most of the words of the Talmud are overt and concealed in nature. Thus, the Talmud often states, "This can be compared to a mortal king," or "This can be compared to a lady."

Among the precepts of the Torah, the aspects of which are both overt and concealed is the commandment of the Succah. Its overt aspect is simple. It requires the erection of the Succah, which symbolizes the time when Israel wandered in the wilderness, a land of drought and waste, *no place of seed, or of figs, or of vine, or of pomegranates.*[12] In order to ensure that the coming generations would commemorate this journey of an entire nation—including men, women, and children—in a wilderness which in a natural way could not have sustained them, the Torah established this commandment. Therefore it says here, *Ye shall dwell in booths*, etc.,[1] *that your generations may know*, etc.[13] The Sages commented,[14] "They made for themselves booths in the literal sense." Thus through this commandment, the greatness of Israel's status in the wilderness [that in such circumstances they received Divine protection] would be made known to all.

In order to ensure that this very commemoration of the miracles which transpired in the wilderness would be firmly established in the hearts of the coming generations, the Torah in the section of *Eileh Mas'ei (These are the journeys)*,[15] has prolonged the account of these stages in the wilderness, for later generations might doubt or even completely deny these matters inasmuch as miracles do not last forever.

(11) Shir Hashirim Rabbah 1:8. (12) Numbers 20:8. (13) Leviticus 23:43. (14) Succah 11 b. This is the opinion of Rabbi Akiba. See Note 27 below. (15) Numbers 33:1-49.

Now, among the greatest wonders related in the Torah is Israel's survival in the wilderness for forty years and the daily finding of the manna. As in the case of other historical events, however, it is possible that certain critics will dispute [Israel's ability to have lived in the wilderness forty years]. They will suppose that Israel sojourned in the wilderness near the cultivated settlements. It is entirely possible for people to live in such areas, as the desert that the Arabs live in today. Perhaps the doubters will maintain Israel stayed in arable, crop-yielding areas or where there were grasses and plants suitable for human consumption. They may also contend that Israel sojourned in those places where manna naturally descended or where there were wells of water. To remove all such thoughts and to firmly establish the truth of all these miracles, G-d recorded Israel's journeys so that the future generataions would read of them and acknowledge the great wonders entailed in sustaining an entire nation in such places for forty years. Similarly, Joshua issued an imprecation against anyone who would rebuild Jericho.[16] [Leaving the conquered city in its state of ruin] would ensure the propagation of the effect of the miracle forever, for one who would see the wall sunk into the ground would understand that no ordinary demolition caused this condition but that the wall was sunk through a miracle. This is Maimonides'[17] explanation for the Scriptural enumeration of all these journeys.[15]

There is yet another reason[18] for the recording of these journeys: to make known the lovingkindness of G-d. Although He had decreed that the people of Israel had to move about and wander in the wilderness, you should not suppose that they wandered and moved unceasingly throughout the forty years. They journeyed only forty-two times. There were fourteen marches in the first year after the Exodus and

(16) See Joshua 6:26. Jericho was the first city captured by Joshua as he led the Hebrews into the Promised Land. After the miraculous collapse of the city wall, Joshua imprecated anyone who would rebuild it. The reason for it is stated in the text.   (17) Guide of the Perplexed, III, Chapter 50, and quoted by Ramban, Commentary on the Torah, Numbers, p. 383.   (18) Mentioned by Rashi on Numbers 33:1.

eight in the fortieth year, a total of twenty-two. Thus, during the intervening thirty-eight years, they wandered on only twenty occasions. During nineteen of those thirty-eight years, they stayed in Kadesh.[19] In the remaining nineteen years, they wandered through the balance of journeys. These movements were irregular. They stayed in one place for nineteen years and in other places only a day or a night.[20] However, all their marches were Divinely measured and in accordance with the ascent of the cloud.[21]

In order to let it be known that the people of Israel did not wander in the wilderness like those who have gone astray and who have become entangled in the land, but that they had even more to satisfy their needs than those who dwell in inhabited regions, the Sages devised the following parable concerning the prolonged Scriptural account of these journeys:[22] "This may be compared to a king whose son was ill and whom the king took to a distant place to cure him. When they returned home, the father began to enumerate all the stages, 'Here we stayed, here we caught cold, here you had a headache.' "

The account of the journeys in the wilderness also alludes to the future, for all prophets agree that the future Redemption will be like the first, [i.e., the Exodus from Egypt]. The prophet said, *As in the days of thy coming forth out of the land of Egypt, will I show unto him marvelous things.*[23] Just as Israel went out from Egypt into the wilderness, so in the final Redemption will many Israelites pass these places in the wilderness. G-d will lead them and sustain them there as He did lead and sustain ancient Israel, as the prophet foretold, *And I will bring you into the wilderness of the peoples.*[24]

We have thus explained various reasons for the account of the journeys in the wilderness. Generally, the account firmly establishes in our hearts the commemoration of Israel's stay in the desert. Their sojourn in the wilderness, was only temporary since they were destined to

---

(19) See Deuteronomy 1:46.   (20) See Numbers 9:21.   (21) See *ibid.*, Verse 17.   (22) Tanchuma, *Mas'ei,* 3, and mentioned by Rashi on Numbers 33:1.   (23) Micah 7:15.   (24) Ezekiel 20:35.

enter into permanent residence in the Land of Israel, which would contain the Holy Temple or "the Eternal House."[25] Accordingly, the Torah commanded us to leave our homes, our permanent dwelling, and live in a Succah which is a temporary dwelling. This is the purport of the Sages' statement,[26] "Go forth from a permanent dwelling into a temporary one." That is to say, "remember that you lived in the wilderness in a temporary dwelling and that G-d took you from there and settled you in a permanent dwelling in the choicest of places." This is the overt aspect of this commandment.

The concealed aspect of this commandment is as follows: The verse states, *Ye shall dwell in booths seven days,*[1] upon which the Sages commented,[27] "These were the clouds of glory," for in the wilderness, Israel was surrounded by seven clouds.[28] This was a great distinction for Israel, for our Sages expounded[29] that the Throne of Glory itself is surrounded by seven clouds. Therefore, we were commanded to erect a booth to correspond to those cloud-booths that surrounded us in the wilderness. Because there were seven clouds, we have been charged to perform this commandment for seven days in the seventh month. It is known and established that these clouds which are spread over the Throne of Glory stand open, ready to receive repentance and prayer, for "repentance reaches the Throne of Glory."[30] However, when Israel sins, these clouds close up and become like a booth. Thus, it is written, *Sakotha (Thou hast covered Thyself) with a cloud, so that no prayer can pass through.*[31] Because the source of pure souls lies in the Throne

---

(25) This is a synonym for the Temple in Jerusalem. It is called "the Eternal House" because even after it was destroyed, its site has remained holy, unlike other places in the Land of Israel where the House of G-d was temporarily established, such as Gilgal, Shiloh, *et al.* See Ramban, Commentary on the Torah, Leviticus, p. 123, Note 122. (26) Succah 2 a. (27) *Ibid.*, 11 b. This is the opinion of Rabbi Eliezer. See above, Note 14. (28) "Four clouds at their four sides, one below, one above, and one preceeding before them" (Tanchuma, *Beshalach,* 3). The clouds are referred to as booths, see Isaiah 4:5. (29) Pirkei d'Rabbi Eliezer, 4. (30) Yoma 86 a. (31) Lamentations 3:44. The Hebrew word *sakotah (Thou hast covered Thyself)* suggests the word Succah, thus intimating that the cloud becomes like a booth. — The verse was stated by Jeremiah with respect to the time of the destruction of the First Temple.

of Glory,[32] which is the essence of purity, we are commanded not to cover the booth with anything which can contract impurity. The required measurements of the booth likewise contain a profound secret, as the Sages mentioned[33] with regard to the verse, *And the depth of 'Succoth' (booths) I shall measure off.*[34] However, we should not prolong our discussion of this theme.

Rationally, we can explain this commandment as follows: The world was created in the month of Tishri, and we are commanded to erect a Succah on the fifteenth day of that month, for the building of a Succah alludes to and commemorates both this world and the World to Come. The allusion to this world lies in the fact that the Succah must have at least three walls just as the world is enclosed on three sides — east, west, and south. The north is not enclosed as Scripture states, *He stretches out the north over empty space.*[35] The Sages, too, said,[36] "The northern end is not enclosed." By law, the Succah must contain the form of a doorway.[37] [It would thus have an opening with] "a reed on each side and a reed on top." This form resembles the letter *hei*, with which, the Sages tell us, this world was created.[38] The Succah must be at least ten handbreadths, alluding to the World to Come which was created with the letter *yod*.[39]

Thus, the two worlds are alluded to in the commandment of the Succah. When a person is engaged in building it and enters it in fulfillment of the precept, he is made aware of the fact that one cannot inherit the World to Come unless he strives for it in this world. The Sages

(32) Chagigah 12 b. (33) I have been unable to locate this Midrash. (34) Psalms 60:8. The translation here is in accord with the Midrashic interpretation referred to by Rabbeinu Bachya. However, the verse is generally translated: "And the valley of Succoth I will measure off." (35) Job 26:7. (36) Baba Bathra 25 b. (37) Succah 7 a. (38) Menachoth 29b. With its three "walls" and one completely open side, the letter *hei* suggests the freedom of choice. In essence, "anyone who wishes to leave the enclosures of the Torah and go out on his own evil way has the freedom to do so." Note that the left side of the *hei* is broken. This indicates that if the sinner wishes to repent, he may reenter. (39) *Ibid.*, The *yod*, which is numerically equivalent to ten, is the smallest of the Hebrew letters, thus suggesting that the righteous who deserve the World to Come are few in number.

said,[40] "If one has made preparations on Friday, he will have food for the Sabbath, but if one has not made preparations, whence shall he eat?" Thus, when one fulfills the commandment of the Succah, and when he enters it with his eyes turned upward to its covering made for shade and concludes that G-d is the shade of the people of Israel—i.e. that He protects them as shade protects against the sun, as it is written, *The Eternal is thy guardian, the Eternal is thy shade upon thy right hand,*[41] and it is further written, *Under His shade I delighted to sit*[42]—[that person will inherit eternal life]. Accordingly, the Sages said,[26] "If the sun which penetrates through the covering is more predominant than its shade, the Succah is invalid."

The Succah also alludes to the Torah, for it must have a minimum of three walls, and the Torah contains three parts—the Five Books of Moses, Prophets, and Writings—which sustain the world, as it is said, *If it were not for My covenant, I would not have appointed day and night, the ordinances of heaven and earth.*[43] In order to be valid, the Succah must be at least ten handbreadths high, thus alluding to the Ten Commandments, and seven handbreadths wide, thus alluding to the seven wisdoms[44] included in the Torah. Consequently, a valid Succah requires a minimum of seventy square handbreadths, alluding to the "seventy countenances of the Torah."[45] Dwelling in a Succah is obligatory by day and night, thus alluding to the Torah, of which it is written, *And thou shalt meditate therein day and night.*[46] Women are excused from dwelling in a Succah just as they are not obligated to study Torah, for it is said, *And thou shalt teach them diligently unto thy sons,*[47] which excludes "thy daughters."[48]

(40) Abodah Zarah 3 a. (41) Psalms 121:5. (42) Song of Songs 2:3. (43) Jeremiah 33:25. In other words, if it were not for G-d's covenant with Israel at Mount Sinai by giving them the Torah, the entire world would not have been sustained. (44) See above, *Neir Chanukah* (The Chanukah Light), Note 75. (45) Bamidbar Rabbah 13:15. The Torah can be explained in seventy different ways. (46) Joshua 1:8. (47) Deuteronomy 6:7. (48) Kiddushin 29 b. This is generally understood to mean that women are not obligated to ponder the derivation of the law. However, they are obligated to know the law itself.

[From the above discussion, we can understand] Scripture's statement, *Is not My word like fire? saith the Eternal, and like a hammer that breaketh the rock into pieces?*[49] "Just as a sledgehammer shatters rock into many pieces, so the words of the Torah have many connotations,"[50] for one commandment contains many themes and meanings through its overt and concealed aspects. It is known that the Voice heard at the Giving of the Torah reached all human beings, and each person comprehended it according to his or her own power. Thus, the Sages said in the Midrash:[51] *"The Voice of the Eternal is with power.*[52] The verse does not say 'with His power,' but *with power,* i.e., with the power of each and every person. The Voice descended to each person according to his capacity. Sucklings received it according to their comprehension, pregnant women according to their understanding, adults to their capacity, and even Moses received it according to his perception. If you are surprised at this, you may derive its veracity from the manna which descended for Israel according to each individual's need. To sucklings it was as mother's milk, to adults it was as bread, to elders it was as honey, to the sick it was a fine flour mixed with honey and oil, while to non-Israelites it was bitter. If the manna could transform itself into different substances [to suit the tastes of different people], certainly the Divine Voice could certainly be adapted to each person's comprehension. In that manner, the people would not be harmed, as it is said, *And all the people perceived the voices.*[53] It does not say 'the Voice,' but the *voices.* It is thus written, *G-d thundered marvelously with His Voice.*[54] When G-d gave the Torah to Israel, He demonstrated wonders upon wonders with His Voice." Thus far the Midrash.[51]

A person is obligated to erect an actual Succah and to rationally contemplate its meaning, for the performance of a commandment is considered complete only when one attains an understanding thereof,

---

(49) Jeremiah 23:29. (50) Shabbath 88 b. (51) Tanchuma, *Shemoth,* 25. (52) Psalms 29:4. (53) Exodus 20:15. (54) Job 37:5.

not merely when it is physically performed. On the other hand, a person who knows the concealed meaning of the commandment, is not excused from its actual fulfillment. Regarding this principle, Scripture states, *The secret things belong to the Eternal our G-d, but the things that are revealed belong unto us and our children.*[55] Scripture is saying that the full knowledge concealed in the commandments belongs to G-d. Although we may succeed in attaining some part of that knowledge, we are still not freed from performing the commandments, for *the things that are revealed belong unto us and our children forever to do.*[55] I have heard this in the name of Rabbi Moshe[56] of blessed memory, who wrote it in his Commentary on the Torah, but we have not merited that it should reach our countries.

Although we have been charged to overtly fulfill the commandment of Succah in deed, its essential significance nevertheless lies in its hidden meaning. In fact, all forms of wisdom are undoubtedly alluded to in the Torah. For this reason, King David called the Torah "the perfect one," as it is said, *The Law of the Eternal is perfect,*[57] and if it were missing just one form of wisdom, David could not have called it *perfect.* King David himself always acted in accordance with the perfect Torah, and all his deeds were thus perfect. Whatever he did, he took counsel with the Torah, as he said, *Yea, Thy testimonies are my delight, they are my counsellors.*[58]

---

(55) Deuteronomy 29:28. (56) The Rome manuscript attributes this to Maimonides, and printed editions of Kad Hakemach, however, attribute the passage to "Ramban." This is obviously an error, for if Ramban were the author of this passage, Rabbeinu Bachya could not have written that his commentary did not "reach our countries." Concerning Maimonides' Commentary on the Torah, see B. Bacher's Hebrew work, Maimonides as Biblical Commentator, p. 22, Note 6. (57) Psalms 19:8. (58) *Ibid.*, 119:8. It should be noted how the author ends the theme of the Succah abruptly with a brief statement on the Torah being the source of all knowledge. The reason for this conclusion is undoubtedly the fact that having stressed the esoteric element in the commandment of the Succah, the author felt obliged to remind his audience that the extent of Torah is exceedingly broad, and not confined to any one aspect.

שִׂנְאַת חִנָּם
Baseless Hatred

Love is either natural, like that of a parent for a child, or social, like that of two neighbors. On the basis of both of these types of love, the people of Israel have been called 'brothers and friends' / Israel, more than any other nation, should shun hatred, for our G-d is One / The sickness of hatred and the extent to which a person should shun this repulsive characteristic / The commandment to rebuke / The responsibility for the fault of the generation lies with the leaders who have the power of correction / The blessings which accompany chastisement.

Baseless Hatred

THOU SHALT NOT HATE THY BROTHER IN THY HEART;
THOU SHALT SURELY REBUKE THY NEIGHBOR, AND
NOT BEAR SIN BECAUSE OF HIM.[1]

This verse warns man against hating his fellow without cause instead of loving him. Now, love is either natural — like the love of brothers, that of a father for his child, or a man's love for his wife — or it may be social. For example, by virtue of the fact that two absolute strangers are together a whole day, there develops between them an identical feeling and determination in all matters.

On the basis of both of these types of love, the people of Israel have been called "brothers and friends." This expression teaches us that one should love his fellow man like a brother, and socially, he should be on good terms with him like a friend. It is thus written, *For the sakes of my brethren and companions, I will now say: Peace be within thee.*[2]

Israel, more than any nation should have love implanted among its people and should shun hatred, for our G-d, the G-d of the world, is One, as it is written, *Have we not all one Father? Hath not one G-d created us?*[3] We are one people, as it is said, *And who is like Thy people, like Israel, a nation one in the earth?*[4] We have *one law and one*

---

(1) Leviticus 19:17. "Because it is the way of those who hate a person to cover up their hatred in their hearts, therefore Scripture speaks of the usual events, but the law forbids all hating, even if expressed openly" (Ramban, Commentary on the Torah, *ibid.*, pp. 291-292). (2) Psalms 122:8. (3) Malachi 2:10. (4) II Samuel 7:23.

448

ordinance.[5] Therefore, it is proper that we, more than other nations, be united in heart and will.

Causeless hatred is a grave sickness, and it is the cause of all the sins mentioned in the Torah. It causes the hater to utter falsehoods about his colleague, and one who habitually utters falsehoods cannot receive the Divine Presence, as it is said, *He that speaketh falsehood shall not be established before Mine eyes.*[6] In turn, prevarification will lead the hater to concoct a false charge against his fellow and to testify falsely against him. Thus, Solomon said, *A false witness shall perish,*[7] and he further stated, *A false witness breatheth out lies.*[8] Due to hatred, one will feel depressed over his colleague's success and will rejoice over his failure.

One who develops this loathsome characteristic demonstrates that he is not a descendant of Abraham, for all of Abraham's offspring follow in his ways, as it is written, *For I have known him* [Abraham], *to the end that he may command his children and his household after him,* etc.[9]

Causeless hatred brings about a division of hearts and makes a person differ with his fellow without any regard for the latter's greater esteem. Instead, all wish to be leaders, and thus their opinions and hearts are divided. The Divine Presence does not dwell among a people with a divided heart, for the Sages commented:[10] *"And there was a King in Jeshurun, when the heads of the people were gathered,*[11] i.e., when they comprised one brotherhood." The prophet further said, *Their heart is divided, now shall they bear their guilt*[12] of the divided heart. On the other hand, unity of heart is beneficial not only in Divine worship, but even in idolatry. This is the purport of the statement, *Ephraim is joined to the idols, let him alone,*[13] meaning: "They deserve

(5) Numbers 15:16. (6) Psalms 101:7. (7) Proverbs 21:28. (8) *Ibid.*, 6:19. (9) Genesis 18:19. The verse continues: *that they may keep the way of the Eternal, to do righteousness and justice.* (10) Bamidbar Rabbah 15:14. (11) Deuteronomy 33:5. *Jeshurun* is another name for Israel. The verse is thus stating: when Israel's leader are gathered together in harmony G-d's sovereignty is acknowledged by all. (12) Hosea 10:2. (13) *Ibid.*, 4:17.

to be destroyed because of their idolatry, but since they comprise one band and share one opinion, I will be patient with them."

Unity is the essential cause of peace, and dissension and change are the roots of quarrel. Thus, on the first day of Creation, which alludes to G-d's Unity, you will find no discord, variance, or dissension. However, on the second day, when the initiation of change is marked by the division between *the waters which were under the firmament from the waters which were above the firmament,*[14] discord, contention, and change began. Accordingly, on that day, G-d did not say "that it was good," for the good was lacking because of the dissension. Such dissension manifested itself on the following days of Creation, too, and on the sixth day, Adam and Eve sinned and were driven from the Garden of Eden. Thus, you see that division of hearts, which is the characteristic of causeless hatred, stems from the second day of Creation, which does not contain the expression "that it was good."

It is known that the Second Temple was destroyed because of this sin. The Sages declared:[15] "Why was the First Temple destroyed? It was destroyed because of idolatry.[16] However, we know that during the era of the Second Temple there were pious people and men of good deeds. Why then was that Temple destroyed? It was destroyed due to causeless hatred." The Sages further said in Midrash Eichah:[17] "Moreover, [during the Second Temple era], the people rejoiced over the downfall of one another, as it is said, *When thou doest evil, then thou rejoicest.*[18] It is further stated, *And he that is glad at calamity shall not be unpunished.*"[19]

A person is obligated to shun this characteristic of hatred. There are many people who feign friendship for their colleagues while hiding hatred in their hearts. They make a pretense of being their friends so that they will not be on guard against them. Regarding this type of person, Solomon stated, *He that hateth disguiseth with his lips,*[20] and

---

(14) Genesis 1:7. (15) Yoma 9 b. (16) See above, *Eivel* (Mourning), Note 120. (17) Eichah Rabbathi 1:21. (18) Jeremiah 11:15. (19) Proverbs 17:5. (20) *Ibid.,* 26:24.

he further mentioned, *Burning lips and a wicked heart are like an earthen vessel overlaid with silver dross.*[21] Instead of saying "overlaid with silver," he specified, *overlaid with silver dross,* in order to indicate that just as there is no benefit derived from the dross, so is [there no benefit derived from] division of heart. Such a person deceives others by making them think that he is sincere, but his words are of no benefit even as silver dross is of no value. For example, Ishmael the son of Nethaniah [acted in this deceitful manner] towards Gedaliah the son of Achikam until he killed him.[22] Whoever habitually conducts himself in this way towards his fellow man will ultimately do so towards G-d, as it is written, *And they beguiled Him with their mouth, and lied unto Him with their tongue.*[23] The Sages wise in ethics[24] said, "One who has planted hatred reaps regret."

Because of the severity of this sin, Scripture has applied a negative commandment against it, *Thou shalt not hate thy brother in thy heart,*[1] for whenever there is causeless hatred and division of hearts among the people of Israel, the Divine Presence does not dwell among them. The Torah, moreover, was given to Israel only when the entire nation was of one heart, as it is said, *And there* [at Mount Sinai] *Israel encamped,*[25] i.e., in complete unanimity. Hence, *vayichan (and he encamped),* the singular form of the verb, is used in that verse. Similarly, Scripture states, *All the signs which I have wrought 'b'kirbo' (among him).*[26] It does not say "*b'kirbam* (among them)," but *b'kirbo (among*

(21) *Ibid.,* Verse 23. (22) After the destruction of the First Temple by the Babylonians, Gedaliah gathered the remnants of the people who had not been exiled to Babylon and attempted to reorganize life. However, Ishmael, a scion of the royal family (see Jeremiah 41:1) planned to kill Gedaliah because he considered him an usurper, and he came to him with cunning. Gedaliah was warned of Ishmael's true intention (see *ibid.,* 40:15), but he refused to believe it. Ishmael finally killed Gedaliah, and the people were scattered. Some, including the prophet Jeremiah, went down to Egypt. Thus, because of Ishmael's treachery which concealed the hatred in his heart, Gedaliah was lulled into a sense of security. Upon his death, the destruction of the national entity was completed. The tragedy of that day is still commemorated on the Fast of Gedaliah, which is observed on the third day of Tishri. (23) Psalms 78:36. (24) Evidently, Rabbeinu Bachya is referring to Rabbi Solomon ibn Gabirol, who, in his *Mivchar Ha'pninim* (Choice of Pearls), similarly stated this principle. (25) Exodus 19:2. (26) Numbers 14:11.

him), which means when Israel was of one heart. Had that not been the case, they would not have deserved the signs [which G-d performed for them].

Thou shalt surely rebuke thy neighbor.[1] This constitutes a positive commandment[27] to rebuke one's friend who is sinning. Scripture has stressed the verb "rebuke" — *hochei'ach tochiach (thou shalt surely rebuke)* — in order to teach us that it is not sufficient to rebuke someone only once. One must rebuke his friend again and again.[28] Similarly, the Sages commented:[28] "*Thou shalt surely bring them back,*[29] i.e., even a hundred times." Similar thoughts are found wherever the Torah uses the double verb, such as: *Thou shalt surely open thy hand unto him;*[30] *Thou shalt surely furnish him;*[31] *Thou shalt surely lend him sufficient for his need.*[32]

Rebuke brings a person back to the Torah way of life. Thus it is written, *Reproofs of instruction are the way of life.*[33] Love of rebuke leads to fulfillment of the Torah, while the hatred thereof causes its nullification and leads one to the brink of denying the principle of faith, the result of which is banishment from this world and the World to Come. Solomon said, *There is a grievous instruction for him that forsaketh the way, but he that hateth reproof shall die.*[34] He is saying that one who temporarily *forsaketh the way* of the Torah will be punished with afflictions for his grievous sin. However, *he that hateth reproof* is in an even graver situation, for only death, not mere afflictions, will suffice for him.

The chief object in accepting rebuke is the rectification of one's character. If this is not achieved, the rebuke will have been in vain, for if one plows but never plants seeds, his plowing is futile. It is known that three things — plowing, planting, and watering — are necessary in farming. Similarly, the human soul requires three things: rebuke, acceptance of the rebuke, and correction of the character traits. For this

(27) The Commandments, Vol. I, pp. 219-220. (28) Baba Metzia 33 a. (29) Deuteronomy 22:1. (30) *Ibid.*, 15:8. You must help the needy again and again, until he is self-sustaining. (31) *Ibid.*, Verse 14. (32) *Ibid.*, Verse 8. (33) Proverb 6:23. (34) *Ibid.*, 15:10.

reason, Scripture compares rebuke to plowing, for in case of plowing the hard ground is crushed and restored, and in the case of rebuking, the heart becomes broken and contrite. Scripture compares the acceptance of rebuke to planting, for the main purpose of plowing is the seeding, and the chief motivation of the rebuker is that his words be accepted. Finally, Scripture likens the rectification of one's characteristics to watering, for the planting can succeed only with watering, and a person's acceptance of rebuke can succeed only if he corrects himself thereby.

In Tractate Arakhin, the Sages said:[35] "Whence do we know that when one observes some reproachful behavior on the part of his friend, he is obligated to rebuke him? We know it from Scripture, which states, *Thou shalt rebuke.*[1] If one rebuked his fellow but the latter did not accept it, whence do we know that one must rebuke him again? Scripture states, *Thou shalt surely rebuke.*[1] One might presume that rebuke is necessary even if it publicly[36] embarrasses the fellow. However Scripture states, . . . *and not bear sin because of him.*[1] From the verse, *Thou shalt surely rebuke*[1] we derive only that it is the duty of the master to rebuke his disciple. Whence do we know that it is likewise the duty of the disciple to rebuke his master? Scripture says, *Thou shalt surely rebuke,*[1] i.e., under all circumstances."

One who fails to protest against sin will be blamed for that sin, for it has been said:[37] "One who has the power to protest against reproachful matters in his household and does not do so, will be blamed [for the sins of everyone in the house. If he has the power to protest in his city and does not do so, he will be blamed] for the sins of the people in his city. [If his protest would be heeded] in the entire world and he remains silent, he will be blamed for the sins of the entire world. Rabbi Chanina said, 'What is the meaning of the verse, *The Eternal will enter into judgment with the elders of His people and the princes thereof?*[38]

---

(35) Arakhin 15 b.   (36) So in Rashi, *ibid.*, 16 a.   (37) Shabbath 54 b-55 a.   (38) Isaiah 3:14. The elders of the people are understood to be the leaders of the Sanhedrin, who as a rule are righteous people.

What fault is it of the elders of the Sanhedrin, if the princes have sinned? The elders are at fault only because they did not protest against the princes.' " Likewise, it states, *And I will cut off from thee the righteous and the wicked,*[39] for the righteous man will be punished for not having protested against the wicked. You also find that King Josiah [a most righteous monarch] was blamed for the sins of his generation, [and he was therefore killed in battle with Pharaoh-necoh, King of Egypt]. Scripture writes of Josiah, *And like unto him there was no king before him that turned to the Eternal with all his heart.*[40] Similarly Scripture states, *It is the sin-offering of the assembly,*[41] and the very next verse reads, *When a ruler sinneth.*[42] Scripture thus teaches you that the sin of the community is considered the sin of the ruler. Since he had the power to avert it [and did not do so], he is blamed for the sin of all. It is thus written, *And thou* [the prophet] *givest him no warning, nor speakest to warn the wicked from his wicked way, to save his life; the same wicked man shall die in his iniquity, but his blood will I require at thy hand.*[43] With reference to G-d, Job too said, *With Him is strength and sound wisdom; the deceived and the deceiver are His.*[44] He is saying that G-d, in His might, will punish the deceived and the deceiver, that is, the one who is led astray and the one who leads astray.

We were taught:[45] "Rabbi[46] says, Which is the correct course that a man should choose for himself? I must conclude that it is rebuke and the love thereof, for as long as there is reproof in the world, there is also gratification and blessing and evil is removed from the world,[47] for it is said, *And to those that reprove shall be delight, and a good blessing shall come upon them.* "[48]

---

(39) Ezekiel 21:8. (40) II Kings 23:25. (41) Leviticus 4:21. (42) *Ibid.*, Verse 22. (43) Ezekiel 3:18. (44) Job 12:16. (45) Tamid 28 a. (46) See above, *Ahavah* (Love of G-d), Note 42. (47) This answer should be compared to that found in Aboth 2:1: "That which one feels to be honorable to himself and which also brings him honor from mankind, etc." Apparently, since reproof is a matter of concern for society as a whole, the text before us is addressed to the community as well as to the individual. On the other hand, the answer in Aboth is addressed primarily to the individual. (48) Proverbs 24:25.

עֲרָבָה

The Aravah

Explanation of the verse, "He that rideth upon the 'Aravoth'
(Heavens)"/ Affirmation that G-d's dominion extends to the
highest of the seven heavenly spheres, called 'Aravoth' / The
Sages ordained the commandment of the 'aravah' (the willow
branch) for the seventh day of the Festival of Tabernacles / The significance of that day, which is called 'Hoshana
Rabbah,' and the reason for the seven circuits we make on that
day / The circuits we make nowadays are a sign that in the
future the wall of Edom will fall and Zion and Jerusalem will
rejoice.

The Aravah[1]

SING UNTO G-D, SING PRAISES TO HIS NAME; EXTOL HIM
THAT RIDETH UPON THE 'ARAVOTH' (HEAVENS),
WHOSE NAME IS THE ETERNAL, AND EXULT YE BEFORE
HIM.[2]

King David composed this psalm on the Exodus from Egypt and the
Giving of the Torah. Therefore, he said, *G-d maketh the solitary to
dwell in a house; He bringeth out the prisoners into prosperity.*[3] He
subsequently mentioned, *O G-d, when Thou wentest forth before Thy
people, when Thou didst march in the wilderness, Selah;*[4] *the earth
trembled, the heavens also dropped at the presence of G-d, even you
Sinai.*[5] He is saying: *"Sing unto G-d, sing praises to His Name*[2] *for the
redemption from Egypt. Extol Him that rideth upon the 'Aravoth'*

---

(1) The *aravah* (willow branch) is one of the Four Species taken on the Festival of
Tabernacles. The other three are the *ethrog*, the palm branch and the myrtle. On
Hoshana Rabbah, the seventh day of *Succoth*, an extra willow branch in addition to
the Four Species is taken, as the text will explain. It is now customary to take a band of
five willows. — It should be noted that the word *aravah* (willow branch) bears a
resemblance to the word *Aravoth*, which in Rabbinical tradition is the name of the
seventh heaven (Chagigah 12 b). The symbolic allusion of the willow to the heavenly
abode will be made clear in the text. (2) Psalms 68:5. The word *Aravoth*, translated
as "Heavens," here signifies the specific name for the highest abode of the heavens,
from which extends G-d's dominion over the universe. (3) *Ibid.*, Verse 7. In the
original Hebrew, the word *kosharoth* (prosperity) is interpreted by Rashi as "suitable."
Israel was taken out from Egypt in a month when the weather was most suitable for
journeying. (4) *Ibid.*, Verse 8. (5) *Ibid.*, Verse 9.

(Heavens), *Whose Name is the Eternal, and exult ye before Him*[2] for the Giving of the Torah." Note that with reference to the redemption from Egypt, which was accomplished with great power and a strong hand, David said, *Sing unto G-d, sing praises to His* Proper *Name.* Similarly, with reference to the Giving of the Torah, concerning which it is written, *I am the Eternal thy G-d,*[6] David said, *Extol Him that rideth upon the 'Aravoth' (Heavens), Whose Name is the Eternal,*[2] for the Proper Name of *Him that rideth upon the 'Aravoth'* is "the Eternal," as it is written, *For the Eternal is G-d, an everlasting Rock.*[7]

The expression, *Him that rideth upon the 'Aravoth'* refers to the fact that the highest of all heavenly spheres is *Aravoth.*[8] G-d is above them all and rules over them, for the Name "Eternal" signifies dominion and power. He created the spheres out of absolute nothingness, and their great and mighty strength is derived only from Him. All of them are His servants and ministers. When did G-d demonstrate His power over the high and the low? It was only at the sacred Revelation[9] at the Giving of the Torah, as is written, *Unto thee it was shown, that thou mightest know that the Eternal, He is G-d.*[10]

David said, *Exult ye before Him,*[2] for the Torah gladdens the heart, as it is written, *The precepts of the Eternal are right, rejoicing the heart.*[11] Furthermore, [David used this expression] because of the dancing and rejoicing which took place between the two camps, that of the 600,000 Israelites and that of the angels, of whom it is written, *The chariots of G-d are myriads, even thousands upon thousands.*[12] The

---

(6) Exodus 20 : 2.   (7) Isaiah 26:4. The thought suggested is that both in the Exodus and the Giving of the Torah the full power and glory of G-d was revealed, as is indicated by the Proper Divine Name, the Tetragrammaton.   (8) "There are seven heavenly spheres: *Vilon,* et al." The highest is *Aravoth* (Chagigah 12 b). The text below enumerates the specific names of each of the seven spheres.   (9) The Hebrew expression for the Revelation is *Ma'amad Har Sinai* (The Stand at Mount Sinai). It is based on Deuteronomy 4:10: *the day that thou stoodest before the Eternal thy G-d in Horeb.* The expression is prevalent in the works of Maimonides and Ramban. See the latter's Commentary on the Torah, Exodus p. 251, Note 17.   (10) Deuteronomy 4:35.   (11) Psalms 19:9.   (12) *Ibid.,* 68:18.

two camps went forth to meet one another, as it is said, *And Moses brought forth the people out of the camp to meet G-d*,[13] which means "to meet the camp of G-d." Thus, Solomon said, *As it were a dance of two companies*,[14] alluding to those two camps [of Israel and the angels]. The expression *solu (sing praises)*[2] is equivalent to "make a *m'silah* (path) and prepare the way for the Supreme Master, Who has come to give you the Torah." In Tractate Chagigah, the Sages commented:[15] "There are seven heavenly spheres: *Vilon* (Curtain), *Rakia* (Firmament), *Sh'chakim* (Skies), *Z'vul* (Residence), *Ma'on* (Dwelling Place), *Machon* (The Place), and *Aravoth* (Heavens)." Hence, *Aravoth* is the seventh, and with regard to *Aravoth*, Moses our teacher said, *He Who rideth upon the heaven is thy help*.[16]

To affirm that G-d's dominion extends over *Aravoth*, the seventh sphere, our Rabbis, the Sages of the Truth, ordained the commandment of the *aravah* (willow branch) for the seventh day of the Festival of Tabernacles. Each Israelite is obligated to take one willow branch in his hand. This is in addition to the willow branches bound to the palm branch, which allude to this very topic. The commandment of the palm branch entails the use of four different species, of which there are a total of seven individual items: one palm branch, one *ethrog*, three branches of the myrtle, and two of the willow. The seventh day of Tabernacles on which the *aravah* is used is the twenty-first day of Tishri, which is the twenty-sixth day after the anniversary of the Creation of the world on the twenty-fifth day of Ellul.[17] The seventh day of the Festival of Tabernacles is called "the day of the great seal," which

---

(13) Exodus 19:17.   (14) Song of Songs 7:1. See above, *Emunah* (Faith), text at Note 22, for fuller discussion of this topic. Here our author refers to it only briefly, since it is but part of the verse.   (15) Chagigah 12 b.   (16) Deuteronomy 33:26. The thought suggested is evidently based upon the similarity of the expressions: '*He Who rideth upon*' the heaven . . . and '*He that rideth upon*' the '*Aravoth.*' In both verses the reference is to Him in the highest abode of the heavens, Who is the Creator and Protector of Israel.   (17) Rosh Hashanah, the first day of Tishri, thus commemorates the sixth day of Creation, when the first man was created.

corresponds to the Great Name with which the world was created.[18] Therefore, this day is known as *Hoshana Rabbah*.

It is known that this day marks the end of the Festival of Tabernacles[19] and the end of the circuits [as will be explained]. It also marks the completion of the offering of seventy bullocks,[20] which correspond to the seventy nations whose gradually decreasing numbers betoken their waning power. The circuit is an intimation of [the Scriptural account of the fall of] Jericho, following the one circuit thereof by the Israelites on each of six days and seven times on the seventh day when *the wall fell down flat.*[21]

While the Sanctuary existed, [the priests] encircled the altar [on the first six days of the Tabernacles] once daily, and on the seventh day [*Hoshana Rabbah*] seven times.[22] Therefore, it is customary among all people of Israel, on the first six days of the Tabernacles to make one circuit daily in the synagogue, [with the Four Species in their hand], around the platform, while a person holds a Scroll of the Law. On the seventh day, *Hoshana Rabbah*, seven circuits are made. It is customary

---

(18) Thus, the significance of the seventh day of the Festival of Tabernacles occurring on the twenty-sixth day after the anniversary of the Creation of the world is that it alludes to the Hebrew letters of the Tetragrammaton which are numerically, equivalent to twenty-six. On the seventh day of Tabernacles the Heavenly seal is placed upon the judgment of each individual, which was decided on Rosh Hashanah and closed up on the Day of Atonement. The fate of each person is then finalized for the coming year. See Ramban, Commentary on the Torah, Numbers, p. 136, where he speaks of "the night of the seal," which is the night of *Hoshana Rabbah*. See also Note 103 there. (19) The eighth day, which is called *Sh'mini Atzereth*, a festival in itself, is independent of the preceding seven days of the Festival of Tabernacles. The theme on *Atzereth* (Solemn Assembly) explains in what respects it constitutes an independent festival. See text there. (20) On each of the seven days of the Festival of Tabernacles an additional offering was required by the Torah, thirteen bullocks on the first day (Numbers 29:13), twelve on the second day (*ibid.*, Verse 17), eleven on the third day (*ibid.*, Verse 20), etc. The offering of seven bullocks on the seventh day brought the total to seventy. This number corresponds to the seventy nations. On *Sh'mini Atzereth*, only one bullock was required (*ibid.*, Verse 36), thus signifying the exclusive rejoicing of G-d with Israel. (21) Joshua 6:20. (22) Succah 45 a.

to make the circuit by turning counterclockwise, for all circular movements around the altar and the sprinklings [of the blood of offerings upon the altar's corners] were made in that manner. This is based upon what is said, *And the steps thereof shall look toward the east,*[23] and the ascent to the altar was upon its south side.[24] Based on this the Rabbis derived the rule,[25] "Whenever you turn you should do so towards the right or eastward." They so commented in Tractates Yoma[25] and Zebachim.[26] Such is the custom in all Israel to make the circuit by turning counterclockwise.

One should contemplate the great significance of the day of *Hoshana Rabbah,* which is the twenty-first day of Tishri and the twenty-sixth day [after the anniversary of the Creation of the world].[18] It is also the day which marks the completion of the offering of the seventy bullocks,[20] which correspond to the seventy nations. Furthermore, *Hoshana Rabbah* is the day of the great seal,[18] which is in addition to the first sealing of fate on the Day of Atonement. All of these matters contain secrets and entail great principles and mighty fundamentals which are beyond human comprehension. A person can obtain knowledge thereof not by his own effort, but only by receiving it from another individual to whom the tradition of this wisdom was transmitted.

Thus[27] the circuits which Israel made at Jericho once each day for six days and seven times on the seventh day were all allusions to [the Emanations of] the Divine Presence. That is why the attribute of justice descended upon Jericho, and as a result, *the wall fell down flat.*[21] Similarly, in the Sanctuary, Israel atoned for its sins by means of

(23) Ezekiel 43:17. The ascent or ramp to the altar was on its south side. Thus, as the priest walked up the ascent to the altar, his right hand was toward the east and his left toward the west. When he arrived at the top of the altar and had to walk around it, he was to *look toward the east,* meaning he was to follow the direction to the right. Walking counterclockwise, he thus first reached the southeast corner, and in succession the northeast, the northwest, and the southwest corners. (24) Succah 48 b. (25) Yoma 58 b. (26) Zebachim 62 b. (27) Based upon these "secrets and great principles" mentioned above, it is apparent that the circuits which Israel made etc.

the altar, and the attribute of justice descended upon Israel's enemies and denied them access to go against Israel. Likewise, in the future, the Divine Presence will return to the Holy of Holies, and the attribute of justice will descend upon the enemies who have oppressed and enslaved Israel.

The circuit we make nowadays is thus a sign and an allusion that in the future the wall of Edom will fall and will be completely obliterated from the world. In his vision, Daniel prophesied about the fourth beast, [which symbolized Rome]:[28] *I beheld even till the beast was slain, and its body destroyed, and it was given to be burned with fire.*[29] Although Mount Zion and Jerusalem were called a wilderness and a parched land—as it says, *Zion is become a wilderness, Jerusalem a desolation*[30]—they will rejoice over the punishment of Edom at that time, as Isaiah said, *The wilderness and the parched land shall be glad, and the desert shall rejoice, and blossom as the rose.*[31]

---

(28) See Ramban, Writings and Discourses, pp. 609-627, for a full discussion on this topic.   (29) Daniel 7:11.   (30) *Ibid.*, Isaiah 64:9.   (31) *Ibid.*, 35:1.

עצרת
The Meaning of Atzereth

Intent of heart is the essential element in the worship of G-d. Therefore, a person can perform all natural functions in such a way that they will be a part of his worship of G-d. He will thus serve G-d with a pure dedicated heart / In prayer and in offerings, too, the principal requirement is intent of heart / The meaning of the seventy bullocks offered during the Festival of Tabernacles and the single bullock offered on the eighth day of the festival / 'Sh'mini Atzereth,' the eighth day of the festival, is as important as the day of the Giving of the Torah / The rejoicing at the Drawing of the Water / Hillel's adage concerning that occasion.

The Meaning of Atzereth

I WILL GIVE HEED UNTO THE WAY OF THE PERFECT;
OH, WHEN WILT THOU COME UNTO ME? I WILL WALK
WITHIN MY HOUSE IN THE INTEGRITY OF MY HEART.[1]

In this verse, King David informed us that the essential element in the worship of G-d is intent of heart, for the heart is the seat of the soul. It is known that all human activities are ultimately for the sake of the soul, not the body, for the body was created to serve the soul and to assist it in all of its rational activities. Similarly, woman was created to assist man, as it is written, *I will make him a help suitable for him.*[2] Our Sages interpreted this verse to mean that "if man is worthy, the woman will be a help; if not, she will contend against him."[3]

When the body assists the soul, both are united in the worship of G-d. Certainly, that is a great merit. However, if the body is not helpful to the soul but instead of following it, the body opposes it, there is no merit in that at all. Thus, the Sages said,[3] " . . . if not, she will contend against him." Hence, the soul is analogous to the male and the body to the female. Solomon therefore said, *To deliver thee from the*

---

(1) Psalms 101:2. The psalmist is expressing the highest goal of the Torah way of life, namely, that the Divine Presence dwell with him in his private life, when he is withdrawn from the scrutinizing eye of the public. This way of integrity will be his assurance of being worthy to come to rejoice before Him in His Sanctuary. — This theme is introduced here in connection with the special joyous celebration that took place in the Sanctuary on the occasion of the *Atzereth* festival. (2) Genesis 2:18. (3) Yebamoth 63a and Pirkei d'Rabbi Eliezer, 12.

strange woman,[4] and *The lips of a strange woman drop honey,*[5] for these are references to the worldly pleasures which the physical body seeks.

It is known that all human activities which are in accordance with G-d's command are rational in nature. On the other hand, all natural activities, which stem from physical instincts, can mislead a person and drive him into despair, as the Sages said:[6] "Satan, the evil inclination [that tempts a person to sin], and the angel of death are all one and the same." However, it is possible for a person to perform all natural functions in such a way that they will be a part of his worship of G-d. For example, one should eat and drink to have a healthy body, so that he can worship G-d, which would be impossible if he were sick. Even when engaging in sexual activity, one's intent should be to have children, who will worship G-d and whom he will lead in the right way. He should hope to have a child who may become a scholar and teacher among the people of Israel. The same motivation should apply to his business activity, the purpose of which should not be merely for amassing wealth, but to satisfy his needs so that he may worship G-d undisturbed by deprivation. With the proper intent, even sleeping can be transformed into an act of worshipping G-d.

Regarding this principle of devoting all actions to G-d, the Sages said,[7] "Let all your deeds be for the sake of Heaven." Scripture too states, *Commit thy works unto the Eternal, and thy thoughts shall be established.*[8] We thus learn from all this that the essence of worship of G-d rests on the intention of the heart. If one's heart is wholly devoted to G-d, every aspect of the person will be devoted to Him, and if one's heart is deficient in its devotions, everything will be deficient, as the Sages said:[9] "The Merciful One requires the heart." Therefore, David said, *I will give heed unto the way of the perfect,*[1] the meaning of

(4) Proverbs 2:16. (5) *Ibid.,* 5:3. (6) Baba Bathra 16 a. (7) Aboth 2:17. (8) Proverbs 16:3. (9) Sanhedrin 106 b.

which is that "I will regally invest myself with the faculty of the intellect, and I shall cause to radiate the Holy Spirit upon myself. I shall accomplish this by *the way of the perfect,* that is, when all of my powers and qualities will be perfectly attuned to G-d. I wait the whole day; *when wilt Thou come unto me?*"[1] David thus offered to become a Chariot of G-d like the patriarchs.[10] He said, "When will I be worthy of having the Holy Spirit come upon me? *I will walk within my house in the integrity of my heart,*[1] that is, I will remain constant in my heart's devotion and in the purity of my intent." Thus, David explained to us that the heart is the most essential element in the service of G-d, as it is written, *Thou will direct their heart, Thou wilt cause Thine ear to attend.*[11]

We also find that David cautioned his son Solomon regarding intent of heart, as he said, *And thou, Solomon my son, know thou the G-d of thy father, and serve Him with a whole heart and with a willing mind, for the Eternal searcheth all hearts.*[12] He mentioned the knowledge of G-d first, saying, *Know thou the G-d of thy father.*[12] This knowledge is the subject of the highest request which will be asked of man in the World to Come:[13] "Have you engaged in the study of Torah? Have you searched for wisdom?" This wisdom, which is the knowledge of G-d, is the ultimate perfection, as the prophet said, *But let him glory in this, that he understandeth, and knoweth Me.*[14] It is known that all fields of wisdom in the world are merely an introduction to this knowledge. This is true not only of the fields of wisdom, but it also applies to those commandments requiring action. Such knowledge is obligated by the Torah, as it is said, *Know this day, and lay it to thy heart, that the Eternal He is G-d in heaven above and upon the earth beneath; there is none else.*[15] It is appropriate that this knowledge of G-d precede the worship of Him, for if we do not know Him, how can we serve Him

---

(10) This phrase is based upon Bereshith Rabbah 47:8: "The patriarchs were indeed the Chariot of G-d." The thought is rich with meaning. The patriarchs disseminated a knowledge of the Divine Being and His role in the affairs of man. David aspired to accomplish similar goals. (11) Psalms 10:17. (12) I Chronicles 28:9. (13) Shabbath 31 a. (14) Jeremiah 9:23. (15) Deuteronomy 4:39.

through prayer and offerings? The Sages said in Torath Kohanim:[16] "The service of any priest who does not know to Whom he is bringing the offering or burning the incense is considered invalid." Therefore, David told Solomon, *Serve Him with a whole heart,*[12] for Solomon was destined to build the Sanctuary, the place for the offerings, and David thus conveyed to him that both prayer and offerings require intent of heart.

We know that prayer requircs intent of heart because it is written, *Thou wilt direct their heart, Thou wilt cause Thine ear to attend.*[11] The verse is explaining that the prayer which is accepted is the one uttered with sincere intent of heart. That the offerings require intent of heart is derived from the Sages' statement in Tractate Succah:[17] "Why were seventy bullocks[18] [brought as the Additional Offerings on the seven days of the Festival of Tabernacles]? They alluded to the seventy nations of the world. Why was only a single bullock [offered on the eighth day]? It alluded to Israel, the unique nation." The explanation of this statement is that [in the prayer for peace and welfare of the world] Israel offered these seventy bullocks to G-d as an atonement for the nations. This is the purport of the Sages' statement[17] "Woe unto the nations of the world! They have incurred a great loss and are unaware of their loss! While the Sanctuary existed, the offerings brought upon the altar by Israel atoned for them, but now that the Sanctuary is destroyed, what will bring them atonement?" Scripture thus states, *In return for my love they are my adversaries, but I am all prayer,*[19] upon which the Sages expounded:[20] "You find that on the

(16) Ordinarily, the name Torath Kohanim refers to the Sifra, the Tannaitic commentary on the Book of Leviticus, which contains the laws of the offerings and related priestly service. The quotation in the text is not found in Torath Kohanim. However, the term may be used by our author merely to indicate that in discussing "the law of the priests" the Sages required each priest to know "to Whom he is bringing the offering or burning the incense." The quotation is probably based on a similar statement in the Zohar, *Beshalach* 57:1. See my commentary in the Hebrew edition of Kad Hakemach, p. 292. (17) Succah 55 b. (18) See above in *Aravah* (The Willow Branch), Note 20. On the number of fourteen lambs of the seven days of the Festival of Tabernacles, see Numbers 29:13-32. (19) Psalms 109:4. (20) Bamidbar Rabbah 21:22.

Festival of Tabernacles, Israel offered seventy bullocks for the nations of the world, who should have loved us for our action. Instead of loving us, however, they hate us. This is the purport of the verse, *In return for my love they are my adversaries, but I am all prayer,*[19] for I continue to pray and bring an offering for them."

On each of these seven days of Tabernacles, two libations—one of wine and the other of water—were made. The libation of wine was made twice daily throughout the year, once with the morning burnt-offering and once with the evening burnt-offering. On the seven days of the Festival of Tabernacles, however, a libation of water [at the morning burnt-offering] was also made, for it was the season of judgment upon water [for the coming year, whether the supply of rains will be abundant or deficient]. Like the two offerings themselves, these two libations also required intent of heart.

The gradual decrease in the number of the bullocks offered each day[18] alluded to the [ultimate] gradual decrease of the nations, while the set number of fourteen lambs offered on each of the seven days, a total of ninety-eight, alluded to Israel, which is called a *scattered sheep,*[21] and served to nullify the ninety-eight imprecations in the Book of Deuteronomy.[22]

On the eighth day of the festival, only one bullock was brought as the Additional Offering to allude that the one nation of Israel has not been handed over to the power of any constellation, star, or angel. Scripture therefore states, *On the eighth day ye shall have 'Atzereth' (a solemn assembly),*[23] meaning: "*Atzarti* (I have detained) you before Me." "This is analogous to a king who made a banquet for his children for a number of days. When the time arrived for them to leave, he said, 'I beg you to stay with me for one more day, since your departure is hard for me to bear.'"[24] That is why this eighth day is called *Atzereth* (Detaining), for the Divine Glory detained Israel, the one nation, by commanding them to bring before Him a special offering.

(21) Jeremiah 50:17. (22) See Deuteronomy 28:15-68. (23) Numbers 29:35. (24) Rashi, *ibid.,* Verse 36.

Therefore, this day is set apart from the seven days of the Festival of Tabernacles, just as the Sages commented:[25] "On each of the seven days of Tabernacles many bullocks are brought as the Additional Offering, but on the eighth day, only one bullock is offered.[26] Regarding each of the days [beginning with the second] it is written, *'And' on the* [second, third, etc.] *day*[27] but on the eighth day, it is written simply, *On the eighth day.*"[23] This explains the saying of the Sages:[28] The eighth day [is not merely a continuation of the seven days of Tabernacles] but a festival in itself with regard to matters pertaining to *p'zar k'shab.*[29] It entails *payeis* (lot) for itself,[30] *z'man* (time) for itself,[31] *regel* (festival) for itself,[32] *korban* (offering) for itself,[33] *shir* (song) for itself,[34] and *b'rachah* (blessing) for itself.[35]

(25) Succah 47 a.   (26) See Numbers 29:36.   (27) *Ibid.*, Verse 17. The conjunctive *and* thus shows that all of the seven days are the continuation of one festival. The absence of the conjunction in the verse concerning the eighth day, as the text shows, however, underscores the separate and unique quality of that day.   (28) Succah 48 a.   (29) An acrostic of six words, each of which indicates a different aspect of the festival, as explained in the text.   (30) On the Festival of Tabernacles, all twenty-four Divisions of priests came to perform the Service. On the first seven days, no lot was cast to determine which Division would sacrifice the bullocks of the Additional Offerings; the Divisions of priest took their regular turns. On the eighth day, however, since it was an independent festival, a lot was cast for that purpose.   (31) At the beginning of every festival, we recite a special benediction praising G-d for having kept us alive so that we could reach this point in time. This benediction is recited at the beginning of the eighth day.   (32) On that day, one is not obligated to dwell in a Succah. Thus, the eighth day constitutes an independent festival during which the special requirements of the Festival of Tabernacles do not apply.   (33) The one bullock offered on that day is not related to the offerings of the other days. Had that been the case, six bullocks would have been offered on the eighth day in accordance with the gradually decreasing progression established during the preceding seven days.   (34) During the first seven days, the Levites recited psalms pertaining to the various tithes that had to be set aside from the new produce which had been harvested from the fields. On the eighth day, however, the recited psalm bore no connection to that theme. The psalm recited was Psalm 6, which begins: *For the leader, with string music, on the Sh'minith,* literally: "on the eighth" stringed instrument (Tosafoth, Succah 47 a).   (35) Throughout the liturgy, the eighth day is not referred to as "the Festival of Tabernacles," but as "the Eighth-day Feast of Solemn Assembly."

The seven days of the Festival of Tabernacles followed by the eighth day are like the seven days of Passover followed by the Festival of *Shavuoth*. We count seven weeks from Passover until *Shavuoth*, the festival of the Giving of the Torah. The days between Passover and *Shavuoth* are thus like the intermediate days between the first and eighth day of the Festival of Tabernacles. Therefore, our Sages call the Festival of *Shavuoth*, *Atzereth*, [17] just as Scripture designates the eighth day of Tabernacles as *Atzereth*. [23] You may conclude from this that the eighth day of Tabernacles is equivalent to the day when the Torah was given. The eighth day is called *Atzereth* because G-d detained the people of Israel for one more day so that they would bring another bullock as an offering before Him, and the day of the Giving of the Torah is called *Atzereth* because on that day the Divine Glory was revealed on Mount Sinai. Israel, who received the Torah, was retained as G-d's portion and accepted His G-dliness and His decrees.

That the *Atzereth* of the Giving of the Torah is so long after the seven days of Passover while the *Atzereth* of the eighth day is so close to the Festival of Tabernacles has been beautifully explained in a parable:[36] "A king had married daughters, some of whom lived nearby while others lived far away. To those who could come to visit him and return home in one day, he said, 'You and I will rejoice some other day.' The same is true with regard to Passover, which marks the transition from winter to summer. Due to the improved weather, Israel could go to the Sanctuary in Jerusalem and return home in one day. Therefore, the *Atzereth* of *Shavuoth* was postponed fifty days. However, since the seasons change from summer to winter at the time of the Festival of Tabernacles, travel becomes more difficult [and requires more time]. Therefore, the *Atzereth* of the eighth day was not postponed, since travel to and from Jerusalem in one day was impossible."

One is obligated to rejoice on the eighth day of this festival as much as on the preceding seven days. This is true even though Scripture

(36) Shir Hashirim Rabbah 7:4.

clearly states regarding the first seven days, *And ye shall rejoice before the Eternal your G-d seven days,*[37] while it mentions no such requirement in connection with the eighth day. This rejoicing on the festival does not mean that one should lock the doors of his house and privately eat and drink all kinds of delicacies with his wife and children. Such conduct is not included within the concept of rejoicing over a commandment; it is merely the satisfaction of one's selfish desire for pleasure of which it has been said, *And I will spread dung upon your faces, even the dung of your feasts.*[38] Rather, the essential aspect of joy in this regard is that one should eat and drink and provide the unfortunate poor with meals at his table. Those who disregard this matter and devote their efforts to satisfying themselves without sharing with the poor, of them Scripture states, *Their sacrifices shall be unto them as the bread of mourners, all that eat thereof shall be polluted, for their bread shall be for their appetite.*[39] This is not joy but frivolity, for joy should be primarily by worshipping G-d, [through sharing with the poor].

We have been taught in Tractate Succah:[28] "*Hallel* and the rejoicing[40] continue eight days." The following is a description of the Rejoicing of the Drawing of the Water, in which the Sages of Israel participated. Men of piety and good deeds and the heads of the academies danced with burning torches and sang praises, and the Levites played on harps and all other musical instruments. With regard to this rejoicing, the Sages said:[41] "One who has never seen Jerusalem in its glory has never seen a beautiful city. One who has never seen the Sanctuary in its finished state has never seen a glorious structure in his life. To

---

(37) Leviticus 23:40. (38) Malachi 2:3. (39) Hosea 9:4. (40) *Hallel* refers to the Psalms 113-118, which are recited on all eighth days of the festival. The collection of psalms derives its name from the first verse of the leading psalm: *Praise, O ye servants of the Eternal* (Psalms 113:1). The rejoicing mentioned here is to be distinguished from the "Rejoicing of the Drawing of the Water" which occurred only on a weekday night in the Sanctuary Court, as the text below will explain. The ordinary rejoicing of the festival, however, continued all eight days. (41) Succah 51 b.

which Sanctuary does this refer?[42] It refers to the building of Herod. Of what materials did he build it? Rava said, 'He built it of alabaster and white marble.' Some say, 'Of alabaster, blue and white marble.' Herod made one line of stone projecting outward and one line inside. He intended to cover them with gold, but the Rabbis said to him, 'Leave it as it is, for this is more beautiful; it gives the appearance of the waves of the ocean.' Rabbi Yehudah says, 'One who has never seen the Great Synagogue of Alexandria in Egypt, has never seen the glory of Israel.' The synagogue was in the shape of a large basilica, with a colonnade within a colonnade, and its congregation numbered 1,200,000, twice as many as those who went out of Egypt. It had seventy-one golden armchairs for the seventy-one elders,[43] and each of those chairs was made from a minimum of 25,000 golden *dinars*. In the middle of the synagogue, there was a golden[44] elevated stand[45] upon which the sexton stood with a flag in his hand. When the time came for the people to respond Amen, the sexton would raise the flag and the people would answer Amen. The congregants sat in groups according to trade: goldsmiths separately, coppersmiths separately, weavers separately, silversmiths separately, blacksmiths separately, etc. A poor man seeking help could thus recognize his fellow tradesmen and turn to them for support." They said[46] that "when Rabban[47] Shimon ben Gamaliel

---

(42) The First Sanctuary was built by Solomon. The Second Sanctuary was built by those who returned from the Babylonian captivity. It stood for over three hundred years when it was renovated by King Herod. It existed approximately for another one hundred years, for a total existence of 420 years.   (43) These elders comprised the Sanhedrin of the Jews of Egypt (Rashi, Succah 51 b).   (44) Manuscripts of the Talmud also describe the stand as golden, but printed editions specify that it was wooden. According to the latter reading, the elevated stand was wooden apparently because the people wished to follow the example of the Sanctuary, where the stand from which the king read the Torah was made of wood (Sotah 41 a). — It should be noted that the theme of the Alexandrian synagogue has no connection with the central discussion of the Rejoicing of the Drawing of the Water which took place in the Sanctuary. Our author though in his love to dwell upon the ancient glory of the Jews followed the text of the Talmud without any omissions.   (45) This is the earliest mention of a *bimah* (elevated stand) in a synagogue.   (46) Succah 53 a.   (47) Regarding the title Rabban, see above in *Ahavah* (Love of G-d), Note 14.

participated in the Rejoicing of the Drawing of the Water,[48] he would take eight burning torches in his hand, throw them into the air, and no torch ever touched another. When he used to prostrate himself, he supported his body by pressing his thumbs against the floor. He then kissed the floor and raised himself, a feat which no other person could do. Throughout Scripture, this form of prostration is called *kidah* (falling on the face). They said that when Hillel the Elder participated in the Rejoicing of the Drawing of the Water,[48] he would say: 'If I am here, all are here, but if I am not here, who is here?' "[49] Hillel the Elder was a man of great wisdom, as the Sages said:[50] "Hillel the Elder had eighty disciples. Thirty of them were worthy of having the Divine Presence rest upon them as it did upon Moses our teacher. Thirty of them were worthy of having the sun stand still for their sake as it did for the sake of Joshua the son of Nun. The remaining twenty of Hillel's disciples were average. The greatest[51] among all his disciples was Yonathan ben Uziel, and the least[51] among them was Rabban Yochanan ben Zaccai. It was said that in his studies, Rabban Yochanan ben Zaccai omitted not even one part of Scripture, Mishnah, Talmud, laws and homilies, special Rabbinical enactments, laws based on similar Scriptural expressions, astronomy and calculations, speech of the spirits, the trees, and the angels, the Divine

(48) On each of the seven days of the Festival of Tabernacles, there was a second libation of water in addition to the daily libation of wine. These libations of water were performed in the morning only during the Service of the burnt-offering. On each of the weekday nights preceding these libations, there was great rejoicing on the Sanctuary grounds. At daybreak, the entire assembly would proceed to the Fountain of Shiloach to draw a container of water for the libation upon the altar. (49) According to Rashi, Hillel was urging the assembly not to sin, saying in the name of G-d: "If I the Eternal will reside in this Sanctuary, all will come here, but if I will not be here because of your sins, who will come?" Rabbeinu Bachya will explain Hillel's saying somewhat differently. See Note 55 below. (50) Succah 28 a. (51) In the opinion of many scholars the Hebrew words for "greatest" and "least"—*gadol* and *katan* respectively—are here to be understood as meaning "old" and "young." Rabban Yochanan ben Zaccai, for example, who was active at the time of the destruction of the Second Temple about a hundred years after the era of Hillel, was the youngest of Hillel's disciples.

Chariot, and the discussions of Abaye and Rava.[52] This confirms the statement, *That I may cause those that love Me to inherit substance, and that I may fill their treasuries.*"[53]

Just as Hillel was great in wisdom, so was he outstanding in piety and humility. He made his soul a Chariot of G-d even as we have said of King David, who stated, *I will give heed unto the way of the perfect.*[1] Therefore, Hillel said, "If I am here, all are here."[49] He was not actually referring to himself, but only to the perfect person, as he said elsewhere,[54] "If I am not for myself, who will be for me?" The intent of this expression is that the Divine Presence rests upon the perfect person. Thus, Hillel's statement that "All are here" referred to the Divine Presence.[55] G-d then says to Israel, "If you will come to My house, I will come to yours, and if you will not come to My house, I will not come to yours."[46] The meaning of this is as follows: "If you will come to My house," that is, if you have the knowledge to declare the Unity of G-d's Name, then you will be associated with His Name and He will distinguish you. "I will come to your house," that is to say, G-d will draw near you and cleave to you. This was the object of David's question, *Oh, when wilt Thou come unto me?*[1] Just as David said here, *Oh, when wilt Thou come unto me?* so does G-d say to Hillel, "If you will come to My house, I will come to your house." Hillel derived this from the verse which states, *In every place where I cause My Name to be mentioned will I come unto thee and bless thee.*[56]

---

(52) Abaye and Rava were Babylonian Amoraim who lived some 300 years after Rabban Yochanan ben Zaccai. The point here is that the various legal discussions that were ascribed to the later generations had already been discussed in the era of Rabban Yochanan ben Zaccai. (53) Proverbs 8:21. (54) Aboth 1:14. (55) Rabbeinu Bachya's interpretation of Hillel's saying is thus the opposite of Rashi's understanding of it, as explained in Note 49 above. According to Rashi the pronoun "I" refers to G-d, but according to Rabbeinu Bachya the word "All" refers to G-d and "I" refers to the perfect person in whose name Hillel is speaking. (56) Exodus 20:21.

עֲנָוָה

Humility

The praiseworthiness of humility and the qualities connected with it / Scriptural proof that even G-d possesses this quality / One who practices humility is assured of life in the World to Come / The three characteristics that distinguish the disciples of our patriarch Abraham from the disciples of the wicked Balaam / Humility and timidity over committing a sin are signs of the seed of Abraham / The fear of G-d, which entails fear in the heart and 'fear upon the face,' constitutes a fundamental principle of the Torah.

Humility

THE REWARD OF HUMILITY IS THE FEAR OF THE ETER-
NAL, EVEN RICHES, AND HONOR, AND LIFE.[1]

This verse informs us of the praiseworthiness of the trait of humility,
for there are many good qualities connected with it. The literal meaning of the verse is that a person derives a fourfold benefit in this world
from humility: fear of the Eternal, wealth, honor, and life.

It is known that from a social standpoint, humility has practical connotations. Thus, one should be bashful and patient, and he should
honor others and speak of their good qualities. He should listen to his
own humiliation and remain quiet. From this practical aspect of
humility, a person will advance to the fear of G-d, which is a rational
trait. He will also attain wealth, for one who is humble rejoices over his
lot. Arrogance diminishes his satisfaction with his wealth, [for an arrogant person is never satisfied with what he has]. On the other hand,
one who is humble is satisfied with little, and is indeed wealthy, as the
Sages commented,[2] "Who is rich? It is the one who rejoices over his
lot." A humble person likewise will derive honor, for when one avoids
the pursuit of pleasures, he is satisfied with his status. This itself is a

(1) Proverbs 22:4. Humility is thus the key to the rich rewards of life both spiritually
and materially. Spiritually it leads to the attainment of the fear of G-d and avoidance
of sin. Materially it brings riches, honor, and long life, as will be
explained.   (2) Aboth 4:1. In every human desire there is a limit to one's satisfaction,
except in the quest for amassing wealth which is unquenchable. There is, therefore, no
rich man in the absolute sense, since he always desires to have more. The only truly
rich man is "the one who rejoices over his lot." (Midrash Shmuel).

source of honor to him, as it is written, *And he that is of a lowly spirit shall attain to honor,*[3] and it is further stated, *Before honor goeth humility.*[4] Humility will also bring him life. One who pursues after excesses lives a life of distress, for he cannot always attain his desire. His constant worry shortens his life as he concerns himself with a material world which is not his. However, one who rejoices over his lot will not fret over what he did not acquire, and he will thus live a life of peace. In the Midrash, the Sages said:[5] " *'Eikev' (The heel) of humility is the fear of the Eternal.*[1] What wisdom has made as a crown for its head—as it is said, *The head of wisdom is the fear of the Eternal*[6] — humility has made as a sole for its shoe." From this we may learn that the trait of humility is greater than that of wisdom, for the fear of the Eternal, which is at the head of wisdom, is only the sole of humility.

It is known, that every human characteristic has two extremes in addition to its point of moderation. Humility is the intermediate quality between arrogance on one hand and self-effacement on the other. Generally, the moderate course is the correct one which a person should choose for himself, as Solomon said, *Weigh the path of thy feet.*[7] The intent of this advice is that one should proceed between the two extremes just as the indicator of a balance stands precisely between the two plates. [If one so chooses the course of moderation], all his traits will be proper. Thus, Solomon subsequently added, *Turn not to the right hand nor to the left*[8] that is, proceed upon an intermediate course. However, regarding the trait of humility, we are instructed to bend towards the extreme trait of self-effacement, as the Sages said in their ethical instructions in Tractate Aboth:[9] "Be *m'od m'od* (ex-

(3) Proverbs 29:23. (4) *Ibid.*, 18:12. (5) Shir Hashirim Rabbah 1:9. (6) Psalms 111:10. (7) Proverbs 4:26. (8) *Ibid.*, Verse 27. See above, *Ga'avah* (Haughtiness), p. 135 where the author discusses the same topic. (9) Aboth 4:4. The concluding phrase, "since the hope of man etc." suggests the following thought. One should never lose himself to desist from his sense of humility even in the face of derision or insult, for one should give thought to the fact that the final end of those who attack him are but dust and worms, and therefore their attacks are insignificant. Why then should he forego his steady composure and humility? (Midrash Shmuel).

ceedingly) lowly of spirit, since the hope of man is the worm." They doubled the word *m'od* to teach people that one should bend towards the extreme trait of self-effacement.

Because humility is so praiseworthy and has mighty consequences which are visible to all, David said that he himself has *a broken and contrite heart.*[10] Although he was a great king, a prophet, and the leader of the seventy elders of the Sanhedrin, he nevertheless went as far as to describe himself as having *a broken and contrite heart.*[10] Similarly, we find that Moses our teacher, the foremost among all the prophets, was praised by Scripture only for his trait of humility rather than any of his other superior qualities, as it says, *Now the man Moses was very meek.*[11] Scripture used the word *very* in order to indicate that Moses did not desire to remain in the intermediate position of being merely humble; he bent away from the moderate course and leaned towards self-effacement. Therefore, Scripture mentioned that he was *very meek.*

In Bereshith Rabbah, the Sages said:[12] "Rabbi Shimon ben Nezira said, 'Who is as humble as G-d? A disciple says to his teacher, Teach me one chapter, and the teacher answers, Go and wait for me in that place. However, it is different with G-d. He said to Ezekiel, *Arise, go forth into the plain, and I will there speak with thee.*[13] When Ezekiel went forth, he found that G-d had preceded him, as it is said, *Then I arose, and went forth into the plain, and, behold, the Glory of the Eternal stood there.*[14] I must conclude, as the psalmist said, that *'Thy condescension hath made me great.'*[15] Rabbi Abba bar Kahana said, 'See G-d's humility! It is said, *And the Eternal said unto me* [Ezekiel]: *This gate shall be shut, it shall not be opened, neither shall any man enter in by it, for the Eternal, the G-d of Israel, hath entered in by it; therefore it shall be shut.*[16] For the sake of his honor, a mortal king

---

(10) Psalms 51:19.   (11) Numbers 12:13.   (12) I have been unable to locate this quotation in Bereshith Rabbah, but it is found in Tanchuma, *Ki Thisa* 15, with some variations.   (13) Ezekiel 3:22.   (14) *Ibid.*, Verse 23.   (15) Psalms 18:36.   (16) Ezekiel 44:2. The verse is interpreted by the Sages as follows. The "Great Gate" of the Sanctuary proper was not opened by the priests from the outside to enter

must enter through a great gate and not through a small one, but G-d's Glory came in through the small gate.[16] I must conclude, [as the psalmist has said], *Thy condescension hath made me great.*[15] Rabbi Simon said, 'See G-d's humility! A mortal king first mentions his name and then cites his praiseworthy accomplishments, but G-d first mentions His deeds—as it said, *Bereshith bara* (literally: *In the beginning He created*)[17]—and only afterward does He mention the Name *Elokim (G-d)*' "[17] Thus far the Midrash.[12]

In order to show the extreme importance of humiity and its far-reaching ramifications, the Sages said that one who practices this trait is assured of life in the World to Come. They stated in Tractate Sanhedrin:[18] "They sent the following text from the Land of Israel [to the Sages of Babylon]: 'Who has a share in the World to Come? It is the one who is humble, polite, and meek of spirit, who bends his head when entering and leaving a house, who constantly toils in the study of Torah, and who does not ascribe credit to himself.' The Rabbis ascribed all these qualities to Rav Ulla bar Ahavah." They first mentioned the supreme trait of humility and then noted its practical and spiritual applications. By "polite," they meant that one should gently conduct his affairs with other people. This is the practical aspect of humility. By "meek of spirit," they meant that one should be humble rather than arrogant. This is the spiritual aspect.

In Tractate Aboth, the Sages said:[19] "Whoever has the following three attributes is a disciple of our patriarch Abraham, and whoever

---

the inside, but instead was opened from the inside into the outside. This was accomplished through two wickets, one to the north and another to the south which were located in the Entrance Hall leading to the Sanctuary. The verse then tells us that the priest entered by the northern door leading into a cell and from the cell into the Sanctuary until he reached the Great Gate and opened it. He was not to use the southern wicket, *for the Eternal, the G-d of Israel hath entered in it.* (Tamid 3:7). This, then, is the meaning of "the small gate" mentioned in the text . (17) Genesis 1:1. The English translation—*In the beginning G-d created . . .* —does not convey this thought properly, due to the nature of English syntax. (18) Sanhedrin 88 b. See above, *Eivel* (Mourning), Part One, at Note 28, where this text is also quoted. (19) Aboth 5:23.

has the following three faults is a disciple of wicked Balaam. The signs of the disciples of our patriarch Abraham are a 'good eye,' [which will be explained below], a humble soul, and a low spirit. However, the signs of the disciples of wicked Balaam are [an evil eye, a haughty soul, and a proud spirit]. What is the distinction between the disciples of our patriarch Abraham and those of wicked Balaam?[20] The disciples of wicked Balaam inherit Gehenna, as it is said, *And Thou, O G-d, wilt bring them down into the pit of destruction,* etc.[21] However, the disciples of our patriarch Abraham enjoy this world and inherit the World to Come, as it is said, *That I may cause those that love Me to inherit substance,* etc."[22]

The explanation of this is as follows: A "good eye" means that one is not jealous of his friend and is as considerate of his friend's honor as he is of his own. A "humble soul" is one who lowers himself before all and who is sympathetic towards people. A "low spirit" refers to the attribute of humility.

Maimonides explained the Mishnah as follows:[23] "A 'good eye' means that a person should be satisfied with what he has, and not pursue excesses. A 'humble soul' refers to restraint, and a 'low spirit' means the extra degree of humility [beyond the course of moderation]. The three faults corresponding to these attributes all involve the obsession for acquiring money. Thus, an 'evil eye' is the opposite of a 'good eye,' a 'haughty soul' is an insatiable desire for pleasures, and a 'proud spirit'

---

(20) It has been asked: Why does the question of the Mishnah address itself to the distinction between the disciples of Abraham and Balaam, rather than to the differences between the men themselves? The answer, which is of great significance, is that a new movement cannot be judged by its founders, for the good and bad consequences of their theories cannot be ascertained so soon. The truth emerges with time in the behavior of their disciples. In the case of Abraham and Balaam their differences were not immediately perceptible, for Balaam himself spoke very convincingly. However, you can recognize the difference between light and darkness, between our patriarch Abraham and the wicked Balaam, by analyzing the differences between their disciples. (21) Psalms 55:24. (22) Proverbs 8:21. (23) Maimonides' commentary on Aboth 5:23.

is arrogance. The three desirable characteristics described above were publicized as having been the qualities of our patriarch Abraham. Therefore, anyone who lacks these traits is the disciple of wicked Balaam, since such a person obviously adopted Balaam's faults. The trait of restraint in Abraham is evidenced by his statement to Sarah, *Behold now, I know that thou art a fair woman to look upon,* [24] upon which the Sages commented, [25] 'He had never looked at her until now.' This is perfection in restraint. The trait of satisfaction was manifested when Abraham abandoned all the wealth of Sodom and refused to have any benefit from it, as he said, *That I will not take a thread nor a shoe-latchet.* [26] His humility is apparent in his statement, *I am but dust and ashes.* [27] Balaam, on the other hand, was known for his obsession for acquiring money, as it is said, *Because they hired against thee Balaam the son of Beor.* [28] He was a man who pursued pleasures, as evidenced by his counsel to Balak to have the Moabite women entice the Israelites into lewdness. Undoubtedly, a man's advice follows his nature. Balaam's arrogance is expressed in his self-praising statement, *The saying of him who heareth the words of G-d."* [29]

In Tractate Aboth, the Sages said, [30] "The insolent are destined for Gehenna, and the shamefaced for the Garden of Eden." It is known that humility and shamefacedness in a person indicate that he is of the seed of Abraham, for the nature of children follows that of their father. Thus, Scripture states, *For I have known him* [Abraham], *to the end that he may command his children and his household after him.* [31]

The attribute of humility is one of the ways of G-d, as mentioned above, and we who have received the Torah are commanded to walk in

---

(24) Genesis 12:11.   (25) Baba Bathra 16 a. Now, however, approaching Egypt, a land of dark-skinned people, Abraham tells Sarah, he must be concerned about her beauty, since it is now a source of danger to her.   (26) Genesis 14:23.   (27) *Ibid.*, 18:27.   (28) Deuteronomy 23:5.   (29) Numbers 24:4. Thus far is the language of Maimonides in his commentary on Aboth 5:23.   (30) Aboth 5:25.   (31) Genesis 18:19.

His ways, as it is said, *And thou shalt walk in His ways.*[32] Our patriarch Abraham held fast to this trait. Until his descendants, the people of Israel, acquired it, the Torah was not given to them, as it is written of the Revelation[33] at Sinai, *For G-d is come to prove you, and that His fear may be upon your faces, that ye sin not.*[34] Scripture should have said "that His fear may be in your hearts" [rather than *upon your faces*]. However, the Sages commented,[35] "The verse, *His fear upon your faces,* refers to the shamefacedness to sin." The fear of G-d, which entails both the fear in the heart and the "fear upon the face," constitutes the essential principle of the entire Torah, as Solomon stated, *The end of the matter, all having been heard: fear G-d, and keep His commandments, for this is the whole [duty of] man.*[36]

(32) Deuteronomy 28:9. (33) See above, *Aravah,* Note 9. (34) Exodus 20:17. (35) Mechilta, *ibid.* (36) Ecclesiastes 12:13.

עושר

The Challenge of Wealth

> *Being wealthy is neither a physical nor a spiritual quality. It is an external factor and may therefore come to a person without any effort on his part / The advantages and perils of wealth / Only those who are empty-hearted and devoid of wisdom pursue boundless riches / Wealth comes to Israel only as directed by Divine Providence. It is not dependent upon an individual's efforts or reasoning power. Therefore, one should not weary himself by attempting to attain it / Riches that endure and those that do not.*

The Challenge of Wealth

WEARY NOT THYSELF TO BE RICH; CEASE FROM THINE OWN WISDOM.[1] WILT THOU SET THINE EYES UPON IT? IT IS GONE, FOR RICHES CERTAINLY MAKE THEMSELVES WINGS, LIKE AN EAGLE THAT FLIETH TOWARD HEAVEN.[2]

Being wealthy is neither a physical quality like strength nor a spiritual quality like wisdom. It is an external factor and may therefore come to a person, without any toil on his part, through constant changes of conditions under the guidance of G-d, Who is supreme above all and Who does all.

Solomon said, *The rich and the poor meet together—the Eternal is the Maker of them all.*[3] The explanation of this verse is that rich and poor meet on the common ground of changing fortunes which make one man rich and the other poor. Yet, *the Eternal is the Maker of them all.*[3] That is to say, you should not assume that the matter of poverty and wealth is subject merely to the changes of fortune, for everything is done in accordance with the principles of reward and punishment as effectuated by the providence of the Creator, Who is supreme above all.

---

(1) Proverbs 23:4. It should be noted that the expression *Weary not thyself* etc. does not negate totally one's efforts to acquire wealth. Rather, it discourages the making of such acquisition the wherewithal of one's activity. A moderate effort of acquiring possessions is indeed commendable, as the text will show. (2) *Ibid.*, Verse 5. (3) *Ibid.*, 22:2.

Since wealth is different from the qualities of strength and wisdom, as explained above, the prophet therefore mentioned it last, as he said, *Let not the wise man glory in his wisdom, neither let the mighty man glory in his riches.*[4] He mentioned wisdom first because being spiritual, it is the most excellent of all qualities. He next mentioned strength, which is physical, and finally he mentioned riches, which are neither spiritual nor physical. Scripture thus teaches you that riches, which people esteem more highly than wisdom and strength, are the lowest quality from an intellectual standpoint. Consequently, the prophet mentioned them last.

Like every quality, wealth too, has its advantages and perils. The advantage is that wealth lends weight to one's words so that his opinion will be heard. As a result, the rich man will have many friends, as it is written, *And the rich hath many friends.*[5] Riches enable one to perform suitable and desirable deeds through which he will find *grace and good favor in the sight of G-d and man.*[6] E.g., he will do charitable deeds and disbursements for all types of precious objects.[7] In fact, riches were created only so that one could fulfill the commandments. Similarly, the Sages said in the Midrash:[8] "Gold was created only for the work in the Tabernacle, as it is said, *All the gold was for the work which was used in the work of the Sanctuary.*"[9]

It is known that one cannot attain perfection of wisdom without wealth, as it is said, *To be in the shade of wisdom is to be in the shade of wealth.*[10] Wisdom alone is incomplete; people hold an ignorant rich man in greater esteem than a wise man. Therefore, the perfection of wisdom requires riches, which are an honor and crown for the wise man, for he will use them for whatever the Torah has commanded and for whatever his reason dictates. Regarding this idea, Solomon said, *The crown of the wise is their riches, but the folly of fools remaineth*

---

(4) Jeremiah 9:22.   (5) Proverbs 14:20.   (6) *Ibid.*, 3:4.   (7) An example of such a disbursement would be the purchase of an *ethrog*. Rabban Gamaliel spent a thousand dinars for an *ethrog*, thus showing his great love of fulfilling commandments (Succah 41 b).   (8) Bereshith Rabbah 16:3.   (9) Exodus 38:24.   (10) Ecclesiastes 7:12.

folly.[11] Scripture is thus explaining that riches are a crown and an honor for the wise man, for he will use them in a way which will bring honor to himself and gratify the public. This is the exact opposite of the fool, who, upon becoming rich, uses his wealth for foolish things and ultimately becomes demented. In order to indicate that the foolishness brought by the riches is true folly, Solomon repeated the expression *folly: But the folly of fools remaineth folly.*[11]

Wealth entails many possible perils, for it might cause arrogance and impertinence, as it is written, *And the rich answereth impudently.*[12] The rich man's many friends will support him in all matters of sin, and he will sway them to emulate his deeds and activities as alien as they may be. Because of his wealth, he will want to prevail over other people, and if he supported some false notion, he will seek to verify it rather than retract it. Scripture states of riches, *And when thy herds and thy flocks multiply, and thy silver and thy gold is multiplied, and all that thou hast is multiplied;*[13] *then thy heart be lifted up, and thou forget the Eternal thy G-d.*[14] Scripture thus teaches you that abundant riches bring arrogance, which will cause one to forget G-d. Solomon prayed to G-d regarding this pitfall, saying, *Give me neither poverty nor riches, feed me with mine allotted bread.*[15] To explain his request, he added, *Lest I be full, and deny, and say: Who is the Eternal? Or lest I be poor, and steal, and profane the Name of my G-d.*[16]

Because of the dangers inherent in wealth and the many evils resulting therefrom, the Sages praised the opposite quality of poverty. They commented in Tractate Chagigah:[17] "Elijah said to Bar Kappara, or as some maintain to Rabbi Eleazar: 'What is the meaning of the verse, *Behold I have refined thee, but not as silver, I have tried thee in the furnace of affliction?*[18] It teaches us that G-d examined all of the good attributes and found that the one most suited to prevent

---

(11) Proverbs 14:24.   (12) *Ibid.*, 18:23.   (13) Deuteronomy 8:13.   (14) *Ibid.*, Verse 14.   (15) Proverbs 30:8.   (16) *Ibid.*, Verse 9.   (17) Chagigah 9 b.   (18) Isaiah 48:10.

Israel from sinning was poverty.' Shmuel said, 'Therefore people say that poverty becomes Israel as a red line befits a white horse.' "[19]

It is characteristic of wealth that when one has little he desires more, and when he attains more, he desires double, and so on *ad infinitum*. Thus, the Sages said:[20] "No person leaves this world with even half of his desire attained. If he has a hundred, he desires to make it into four hundred,[21] as it is said, *He that loveth silver shall not be satisfied with silver.*"[22] Wealth is thus like fire: the more wood you add, the more the flames increase and the fire blazes.

A person should understand that were it not that riches are indeed necessary for his sustenance, the perfection of wisdom, the giving of charity, and other causes, they would have absolutely no importance. They would be considered so insignificant that even if he were to find precious stones and pearls, he would not take them but would deem them ordinary river pebbles.

No one pursues boundless riches unless his heart is devoid of any wisdom, for one who has had a taste of wisdom perforce knows that all material objects are inconsequential to him, as Scripture says, *And lay thy treasure in the dust.*[23] Scripture is thus saying that Job should categorize all his riches and possessions along with dust, *and the gold of Ophir among the stones of the brooks.*[23] He should not place his trust in them, but should rely only upon G-d, as it says, *And the Almighty be thy treasure, and precious silver unto thee.*[24] for G-d is the true treasure that exists forever. Riches are not dependent upon man's

---

(19) Just as the red line accentuates the white color of the horse, so does poverty bring out the best features in the character of Israel (Iyun Yaakov).   (20) Koheleth Rabbathi 1:34.   (21) In Koheleth Rabbathi *ibid.*: "two hundred. If he has two hundred, he desires to make it four hundred." The text here is shortened correctly, for if "when one has a hundred he desires to make it into two hundred," then he does have half of his desire. Why then does it say, "no person leaves his world with even half of his desire attained?" It must therefore appear that the text as cited by our author is the correct one: "If one has a hundred, he desires to make it into four hundred." In that case he does not have even half of his desire.   (22) Ecclesiastes 5:9.   (23) Job 22:24.   (24) *Ibid.*, Verse 25.

strength or his reasoning power; there are many learned and hard-working people who have not obtained them, while others achieve wealth with no effort. Riches must therefore be dependent upon the Will of the Creator, as Scripture states, *And thou say in thy heart: My power and the might of my hand hath gotten me the wealth.*[25] *But thou shalt remember the Eternal thy G-d, for it is He that giveth thee power to get wealth.*[26] Scripture thus teaches you that wealth does not come to Israel because of the power of the constellations, but only through G-d, Who is our Portion and our Rock.

Since wealth is not dependent upon man's effort or reasoning and understanding, Solomon advised, *Weary not thyself to be rich.*[1] Do not seek to weary yourself in order to amass wealth like those who travel through deserts and dangerous places or those who sail the seas, for the accumulation of wealth is not dependent upon man's effort or reasoning. This is the purport of the statement, *Cease from thine own wisdom.*[1] This matter contains two improbable factors. First, your efforts notwithstanding, you may never attain wealth, and second, even if you do attain it, it is unknown whether you will retain it. This is the sense of the verse that follows: *Wilt thou set thine eyes upon it? It is gone.*[2] The eagle is known as the king of the birds[27] because of its ability to fly highest. Therefore, Solomon compared the rich man's loss of wealth to the flight of the eagle upon the firmament of heaven: [. . . *for riches certainly make themselves wings, like an eagle that flieth toward heaven*].[2]

The Sages commented in the Midrash:[28] "*Weary not thyself to be rich; cease from thine own wisdom.*[1] Riches that are Divinely sent endure, and those that are not Divinely sent do not endure. There have been two extremely wealthy men in the world, one from Israel, Korach, and one from the nations of the world, Haman. Both of these men lost their lives because their wealth was not assigned to them by

---

(25) Deuteronomy 8:17. (26) *Ibid.*, Verse 18. (27) Chagigah 13 b. (28) Bamidbar Rabbah 22:6-8.

Heaven. Similarly, the Gadites and Reubenites[29] had much wealth and cattle. Because of their possessions they chose to settle outside the Land of Israel, and separated themselves from their brethren. Therefore, of all the tribes, they were exiled first, as it is said, *And he* [the King of Assyria] *carried them away, even the Reubenites, and the Gadites, and the half-tribe of Menasheh.*[30] Thus, Scripture states, *A wise man's understanding is at his right hand, but a fool's understanding is at his left.*[31] *A wise man's understanding is at his right hand,* refers to Moses. *But a fool's understanding is at his left,* refers to the Reubenites and the Gadites, who relegated a primary concern[32] to a position of secondary importance and elevated a secondary concern to a position of primary importance. They did this because they loved their possessions more than their children, as they said to Moses, *We will build sheepfolds here for our cattle, and cities for our little ones.*[33] Moses, however, said to them, 'Do not do it this way. Instead, give precedence to primary matters. *Build you cities for your little ones, and* afterwards, *folds for your sheep.'*[34] I must therefore conclude that *a wise man's understanding is at his right hand.*[31] G-d said to them: 'You have shown more concern for your possessions than for humans. I swear that this venture will not prove to be a blessing, for it is said, *An estate may be gotten hastily at the beginning, but the end thereof shall not be blessed.*[35] It is therefore said, *Weary not thyself to be rich; cease from thine own wisdom.*[1] Who then is rich? It is the one who rejoices over his lot, as it is said, *When thou eatest the labor of thy hands, happy shalt thou be, and it shall be well with thee.'*[36]

(29) When Israel was about to enter the Holy Land, the tribes of Gad and Reuben approached Moses requesting permission to settle in the land east of the Jordan, apart from the other tribes, because of their numerous herds. Moses granted their request. During the entire Biblical period, Gad, Reuben, and half of the tribe of Menasheh, dwelled in the land across the Jordan and were later part of the Kingdom of Israel. (30) I Chronicles 5:26. (31) Ecclesiastes 10:2. (32) The primary concern should have been the welfare of their children, and the secondary concern the safety of their property. They instead, mentioned their cattle before their children. (33) Numbers 32:16. (34) *Ibid.*, Verse 24. (35) Proverbs 20:21. (36) Psalms 128:2.

פרנסה

Sustenance

Sustenance is an attestation of G-d's abundant mercies / The four categories of existence—inorganic matter, vegetation, living things, and humans—and how each is sustained / The necessity of relying upon G-d for one's sustenance / Rabbeinu Bachya ibn Pekuda's explanation for the withholding of sustenance from the righteous / Even without praying, one who is anguishly involved can usually nullify the ill effects of natural forces. In three areas, however—children, life, and sustenance—one must pray to supersede natural law.

Sustenance

CAST THY BURDEN UPON THE ETERNAL, AND HE WILL SUSTAIN THEE; HE WILL NEVER SUFFER THE RIGHTEOUS TO BE MOVED.[1]

It is well known that sustenance is an attestation of the wonders of G-d and His abundant mercies in giving food to all flesh and apportioning sustenance to all creatures. The Sages stated:[2] "Psalm 136 is called *Hallel Hagadol* (the Great Praise)[3] because G-d dwells at the height of the universe and apportions sustenance to all His creatures." It is G-d Who gives each one *sufficient for his need in that which he wanteth.*[4] He similarly sustains each of the seventy nations of the world, as well as all the moving creatures who have no rational power or knowledge, as it is written, *He giveth to the beast his food*, etc.[5] All are fed and sustained by His constant great and unfaltering mercy. Thus, David said that G-d *giveth food to all flesh, for His mercy endureth forever*,[6] upon which the Sages commented:[7] "The Holy One,

(1) Psalms 55:23. The constant burden of providing the necessities of life can be crushing to any individual. The psalmist urges one to remember that the Creator of life is also the Sustainer, and that He will not suffer the righteous to be moved forever. Therefore, one should never leave the path of righteousness, for ultimately he will be worthy of G-d's help. (2) Pesachim 118 a. (3) The name *Hallel Hagadol* (the Great Praise) distinguishes Psalm 136 from the collection of psalms known as *Hallel* which are recited on various festivals. See above, *Atzereth,* Note 40. The latter *Hallel* is also called *Hallel Hamitzri* (Praise of the Egyptian Miracle) because it contains the psalm *When Israel came forth out of Egypt* etc. (114:1). (4) Deuteronomy 15:8. (5) Psalms 147:9. (6) *Ibid.,* 136:25. (7) Abodah Zarah 3 b.

blessed be He, feeds the entire world, from the horns of the wild ox to the lice-nits," i.e., from the largest to the smallest of living creatures that lack the power of speech. The principle of Divine sustenance is certainly true in the case of man, a living creature who has the power of speech.[8] Because G-d maintains the world, He is called "Shepherd," as it is said, *Give ear, O Shepherd of Israel.*[9] In Midrash Tehillim, the Sages said:[10] *"Give ear, O Shepherd of Israel.*[9] Just as Divine redemption is wondrous, so is sustenance. Rabbi Shmuel bar Nachman said, 'Sustenance is even greater than Divine redemption, for the latter is accomplished by means of an angel, as it is said, *The angel who hath redeemed me from all evil,*[11] while sustenance is accomplished by G-d Himself, as it is said, *The G-d Who hath been my Shepherd.*[12] It is further written, *Give ear, O Shepherd of Israel.' "*[9]

Consider the great power of sustenance, for there are four categories of existence that are in need thereof—inorganic matter, vegetation, living things, and humans—and G-d designed the proper nourishment for each. The inorganic mountains, valleys, rocks, and metals are maintained by their very existence. When they crumble or rot, their sustenance ceases. Vegetation is superior to inorganic matter in that it has a "life force." Vegetation derives its sustenance from the elements nearby in the moist earth. Living things are superior to vegetation because they are mobile and can seek their food from afar. Man, with the power of speech, is superior to all by virtue of his rational soul. Because of his superiority, his sustenance is not made so easily available that he can find it ready for consumption just by moving from place to place. Instead, man must take the trouble to prepare his food by baking, cooking, etc. That man's sustenance is not as easily available to him as it is for the other three categories, is due to man's possession of a

---

(8) Man's greatest distinguishing quality above all creatures is his power of speech. The verse, *And man became a living soul* (Genesis 2:7) is rendered by Onkelos: "and man became a speaking soul." Since G-d provides the necessities of those living creatures that lack the power of speech, He will surely provide the needs of man. (9) Psalms 80:2. (10) Midrash Tehillim 80:2. (11) Genesis 48:16. (12) *Ibid.,* Verse 15.

reasoning faculty, which provides him with the ability to find suitable sustenance in all places as prepared for him by G-d's mercy.

For each raindrop, G-d prepares an individual path, without which the entire world would be flooded.[13] G-d prepares a naturally suitable area for each plant, otherwise, there would be no distinction among various kinds of vegetation. For each hair in a person's head, G-d creates a separate root from which it draws its strength to grow. G-d, Who does all these things, is the One Who prepares the sustenance for each person. Therefore, David stated, *Cast thy burden upon the Eternal, and He will sustain thee.*[1] The reason that *He will never suffer the righteous to be moved*[1] is as follows: One who depends upon G-d for sustenance will be sustained by Him. Occasionally, one's level of sustenance may decline because of his sin. However, the thoroughly righteous man will never suffer such decline, as it is written, *I have been young, and now am old, yet I have not seen the righteous forsaken,* etc.[14] This means: "I have never seen an opulent righteous person permanently forsaken or even impoverished." However, one who was never opulent, like Rabbi Chanina ben Dosa[15] and his companions, cannot be called "forsaken" and are not at all included in this category.

There are several reasons for the withholdings of sustenance from certain righteous people [like Rabbi Chanina ben Dosa]. The great scholar Rabbi Bachya ibn Pekuda[16] wrote in his book, *Chovoth Halevavoth* (Duties of the Heart), as follows:[17] "A righteous person may possibly have difficulty in obtaining his sustenance due to some

(13) This is derived by the Sages from the verse *Who hath cleft a channel for the waterflood?* (Job 38:25). When the rains come down from heaven, each drop reaches the earth through an appointed path, for without it it would make the soil muddy so that it should not yield any fruit (Baba Bathra 16 a).   (14) Psalms 37:25. (15) It was said of the saintly Rabbi Chanina ben Dosa that "every day a Heavenly Voice comes forth and says, 'The entire world is fed only on account of my son Chanina, while Chanina is satisfied with a small measure of carobs from one Sabbath eve to the other' " (Taanith 24 b).   (16) See above in *Yichud Hashem* (the Unity of G-d), Note 11.   (17) Chovoth Halevavoth, *Sha'ar Habitachon,* 3.

earlier sin which must perforce be accounted for, as it says, *Behold, the righteous shall be requited on the earth.* [18] Alternatively, such difficulty may be a kind of exchange for the World to Come, as it says, *To do thee good at the latter end.* [19] It may also serve to demonstrate to his generation his patience and good conduct so that people may learn from his example, as was the case with Job. It may be due to the righteous person's lack of zeal in asking for justice in his generation, as in the familiar case of Eli and his sons, of whom it is written, *And it shall come to pass, that every one that is left in thy house shall come and bow down to him for a piece of silver and a loaf of bread, and shall say: Put me, I pray thee, into one of the priests' offices, that I may eat a morsel of bread.* [20] On the other hand, G-d's beneficence toward the wicked may be due to some previous good deed the wicked one had done. G-d recompenses him in this world, as He said, *And He repays them that hate Him to their face, to destroy them,* [21] which the Targum renders: 'He rewards those that hate Him in their lifetime. They will thus be deprived of life in the hereafter.' It may be that G-d's goodness is entrusted to the wicked man for the sake of a righteous son that will be born to him, as Scripture states, *He* [the wicked] *may prepare it, but the just shall put it on.* [22] Solomon too said, *But to the sinner He giveth the task to gather and to heap up, that he may leave to him that is good in the sight of G-d.* [23] Possibly, the riches granted to the wicked by G-d may be the principal reason for his death and his evil fate, as Solomon said, *Riches kept by the owner thereof to his own hurt.* [24] The reason may also be that the Creator is waiting for the time when the wicked one will be worthy of his riches, as in the case of Menasheh. [25] Some good deed done by an ancestor may also be the reason for which

---

(18) Proverbs 11:31.   (19) Deuteronomy 8:16. The reward for their meritorious deeds will be complete in the World to Come.   (20) I Samuel 2:36. Eli was the High Priest at Shiloh. His sons — Chophni and Phinehas — *dealt disrespectfully with the offering of the Eternal (ibid.,* Verse 17). Their father, however, did not chastise them sufficiently for it, and therefore he was told by the prophet as the text explains.   (21) Deuteronomy 7:10.   (22) Job 27:17.   (23) Ecclesiastes 2:26.   (24) *Ibid.,* 5:12.   (25) See in *Kippurim* (Atonement), text beginning at Note 36.

the wicked offspring is being repaid, as it was said to Jehu,[26] *Thy sons of the fourth generation shall sit on the throne of Israel.*[27] It is further stated, *He that walketh in his integrity, as a just man, happy are his children after him.*[28] It is also written, *I have been young, and now am old, yet I have not seen the righteous forsaken.*[14] Finally, G-d's beneficence towards the wicked may serve to test deceitful people and their evil plans. When such people see the prosperity of a wicked man, they will hasten to turn away from the worship of G-d and will seek to find favor in the eyes of the wicked man and to adopt his ways. The wholehearted person in a similar situation, however, will become even more prominent by his truthful worship of G-d. As the object of persecution and ignominious treatment by the wicked, he will have his reward increased, as you know from the case of Elijah and Jezebel and that of Jeremiah and his contemporaries." Thus far from Chovoth Halevavoth.

A person's eyes should always look to G-d to supply him with his allotted bread, as King Solomon asked, *Feed me with mine allotted bread.*[29] Although the extent of Solomon's riches was vast indeed, he nevertheless asked for his allotted bread just as any lowly person would do. Moreover, [one should always depend on G-d for sustenance because] poverty is an existing feature of human society, as it is written, *For the poor shall never cease out of the land.*[30] The Sages commented:[31] "A person should always pray for protection against this evil of poverty, for if it does not come upon him, it may come upon his son, and if not upon his son, it may come upon his grandson, for it is said, *Because 'biglal' (on account of) this thing,*[32] which means that poverty is *galgal* (a wheel) that rotates in this world."[33] Accordingly, a person is

---

(26) Jehu abolished the worship of Baal, which had been introduced into the Kingdom of Israel by Ahab. For this good deed, Jehu was assured that his dynasty would continue for four generations. (27) II Kings 10:30. (28) Proverbs 20:7. Thus, the merit of the good father is transmitted to his children. (29) *Ibid.,* 30:5. (30) Deuteronomy 15:11. (31) Shabbath 151 b. (32) Deuteronomy 15:10. (33) In other words, changes of fortune take place constantly, and since

obligated to put his trust in G-d in the matter of sustenance. Even when his home is bare of everything, he should trust in G-d more strongly than if his home were so full of goods that they would be sufficient to supply him throughout his lifetime. It is always possible for some misfortune to befall that material abundance, but no such chance can affect his trust. When Israel was in the wilderness, the manna did not come down once or twice a month; it came down daily so that the people would learn to look to G-d each day for their sustenance and would thus become accustomed to trust in G-d. We have already mentioned this in the theme of *Bitachon* (Trust in G-d). Our Sages commented:[34] "One who has enough to eat today and says, 'What shall I eat tomorrow?' is a man of insufficient faith." He should trust that G-d, Who will bring forth the following day and Who will take the sun out of its sheath, will prepare his sustenance for him and will provide him his food in the proper time. Similarly, the Sages said in Tractate Kethuboth:[35] *"The eyes of all wait for Thee, and Thou givest them their food in his time.*[36] It does not state 'in their time,' but *in his time,* thus teaching you that each individual receives his sustenance from G-d in the proper time."

With this thought in mind, David said here, *Cast thy burden upon the Eternal, and He will sustain thee,*[1] i.e., He will sustain you with comfort and not with pain, with honor and not with shame. Although one's sustenance is limited and is attained with difficulty, it is still far better coming in this manner from G-d's hand than if one were to live more comfortably by being supported with gifts from other people. The Sages expounded:[37] *"And lo, in her mouth was an olive leaf torn off.*[38] The dove said to G-d, 'I wish that my food would be bitter as an

---

poverty is an unavoidable evil of society, one's trust in G-d must never falter that He will under all circumstances provide him with his necessities. (34) Sotah 48 b. (35) Kethuboth 67 b.   (36) Psalms 145:15.   (37) Eirubin 18 b.   (38) Genesis 8:11. This was the case when the dove came back to Noah with the olive leaf in her mouth, from which Noah knew *that the waters were abated from off the earth (ibid.).* The Sages in their explanation emphasize the meaning of the expression *in her mouth.*

olive and from the hand of G-d than that it be as sweet as honey and from the hand of mortal man.' "

The Sages said:[39] "Children, longevity, and sustenance are not dependent upon merit, but upon fortune." Now, this statement does not mean that prayer is of no avail in these matters. On the contrary, this adage informs us of the great power of prayer, for G-d can nullify the ill effects of natural forces. There are certain things which man can nullify through his merit without any prayer or supplication; he need only show concern and grief, as it is written, *He will fulfill the desire of them that fear Him.*[40] G-d will fulfill the mere desire [of those who fear Him] without their having to expressly request it. However, [regarding children, longevity, and sustenance], prayer is necessary, for these matters can be attained through prayer, notwithstanding natural forces. Children were given to Rachel, as it is said, *And G-d hearkened to her, and opened her womb.*[41] Life was given to Hezekiah, as it is said, *I have heard thy prayer, I have seen thy tears; behold, I will add unto thy days fifteen years.*[42] Food was given to Elijah[43] and to Elisha,[44] for we find that their food was blessed and they were saved from hunger. Since these prophets were provided with food through a miracle, the Sages therefore compared the granting of sustenance to the parting of the Red Sea. However, because the parting of the Red Sea was an overt miracle while the miraculous aspect of providing sustenance is hidden, the Sages deliberately stated the comparison in terms of a simile, " 'as' the parting":[45] "Man's sustenance is as difficult 'as' the parting of the Red Sea, for it is written, *To Him Who divided the Red Sea asunder, for His mercy endureth forever,*[46] and it is further written, *Who giveth food to all flesh, for His mercy endureth forever.*"[47]

---

(39) Moed Katan 28 b. (40) Psalms 145:19. (41) Genesis 30:22. (42) Isaiah 38:5. (43) See I Kings 17:6. (44) See II Kings 4:43. (45) Pesachim 118 a. (46) Psalms 136:13. (47) *Ibid.*, Verse 25.

פסח

Passover

Part One

The unique greatness of Solomon / A person should not engage oneself exclusively in the study of philosophy or the other sciences. He should rather study the wisdom of Torah and its commandments / The intent of the commandments of the Torah is to purify our knowledge and refine our minds. This is the goal of the Passover commandments and the prohibition of eating leavened bread / Various allusions contained in the laws of the renouncing of the possession of 'chameitz' (leavened bread).

Passover

THE WORD OF AGUR, THE SON OF JAKEH; THE BURDEN. THE MAN SAITH UNTO ITHIEL, UNTO ITHIEL AND UCAL.[1]

The expression *the words of* is usually found in regard to the study of philosophy and matters of natural law. Indeed, this chapter discusses the four elements, as it states: *Who hath ascended up into heaven, and descended? Who hath gathered the wind in his fists? Who hath bound the waters in the garment? Who hath established all the ends of the earth?*[2] Similarly, the Book of Ecclesiastes, a philosophical work, begins with the same expression: *'The words of' Koheleth, the son of David.*[3] The Book of Jeremiah also opens in the same way — *'The words of Jeremiah, the son of Hilkiah*[4] — and proceeds to mention a subject of natural law, saying, *Before I formed thee in thy mother's body I knew thee,*[5] for a seer must be made ready for prophecy from the outset of his formation.

(1) Proverbs 30:1. According to Ibn Ezra, Agur the son of Jakeh was a great sage in the days of Solomon, and Ithiel and Ucal were Agur's friends or disciples. Out of respect for Agur's wisdom, Solomon incorporated his sayings in the Book of Proverbs. As opposed to Ibn Ezra, Rabbeinu Bachya follows the Midrash which teaches that the name Agur alludes to Solomon himself. However, our author adopts the interpretation that Ithiel and Ucal were two independent sages in Solomon's generation, while the Midrash explains these names too as surnames for Solomon. The connection of this verse to Passover will become clear as Rabbeinu Bachya develops the theme of Solomon's unique wisdom. (2) Proverbs 30:4. *The heaven* is synonimous with fire, as explained further. Thus, the four elements — fire, wind, water, and earth — are mentioned in this verse. (3) Ecclesiastes 1:1. (4) Jeremiah 1:1. (5) *Ibid.*, Verse 5.

Solomon was called *Agur*[1] because he *agar* (stored up) knowledge. *The son of Jakeh*[1] also refers to Solomon, who *hikki* (discharged) wisdom to the people of the world. *The burden*[1] mentioned in the verse means that he was also great in prophecy, for *burden* is a metaphor for prophecy because the prophet must *masie* (lift himself up) above physical considerations.

The man saith unto Ithiel, unto Ithiel and Ucal.[1] These men were two sages in Solomon's generation. Ithiel was superior to Ucal in wisdom, and therefore Solomon repeated his name. We find this repetition elsewhere: *Noah, Noah*[6] and *Abraham, Abraham.*[7] The repetition of the name is an indication of the person's great importance.

I am more brutish than any man.[8] Solomon gave this description of himself but it is the opposite of Scripture's testimony about him: *And he was wiser than all men.*[9] Solomon continued, "*And I have not the understanding of a common man.*[8] I have not the understanding credited to man, which is the basis of his prerogative over the other living creatures." Solomon humbled himself to this extent because it is the way of those who are perfect in wisdom to speak modestly and humbly. It is the way of a person who is in search of wisdom for its own sake and not for self-glory. Thus, Scripture has said, *In the heart of him that hath understanding wisdom resteth, but in the inward path of fools it makes itself known.*[10] Our Sages expressed the same thought by means of a parable regarding the Tigris and Euphrates rivers:[11] "[The other rivers of the world] say to the Tigris, 'Why is your voice heard' [in the course of your flowing waters]? The Tigris answered, 'I do this in order that my voice be heard among the rivers!' The other rivers then asked the Euphrates, 'Why is your voice not heard?' That river answered, 'My deeds speak for me. When a person sows fields close to me, vegetables come forth in three days and a sapling brings

---

(6) Genesis 6:9. (7) *Ibid.*, 22:11. (8) Proverbs 30:2. (9) I Kings 5:11. (10) Proverbs 14:33. (11) Bereshith Rabbah 16:6.

forth shoots in three days.' " The explanation of this saying is that the
Tigris, a small river, rumbles loudly, while the Euphrates, a large
river, has a voice which is inaudible. In this regard, the Sages also
stated,[12] "A small coin in a bottle clatters."[13] A coin does not belong in
a bottle and therefore it clatters, but if it were placed in a purse, its
proper place, it would not be audible.

Who hath ascended up into heaven[14] *and descended? Who hath
gathered the wind in his fists? Who hath bound the waters in the garment? Who hath established all the ends of the earth? What is his
name, and what is his son's name, if thou knowest?*[2] *Every word of G-d
is refined, He is a shield unto them that take refuge in Him.*[15] *Add
thou not unto His words, lest He reprove thee, and thou be found a
liar.*[16] Solomon's intent in these verses is to restrain one from engaging
in the study of wisdoms other than the Torah, which embraces all
wisdoms within itself. Therefore, in the first verse, Solomon mentioned
the four elements, as follows: the Hebrew word for heaven (*shamayim*)
is a composite of *eish u'mayim* (fire and water). The verse thus means,
"Who understands the element of fire, and who will tell us its essence
and nature?" He then mentioned the wind, water, and earth, asking:
"What is the name of the wise man who knows the secret of all these
natural phenomena? In case he has left someone after him, what is his
son's name, for the branches of a tree attest to its healthy roots?"
However, after searching and not finding [a satisfactory answer to
these inquiries], Solomon declared, *Every word of G-d is refined.*[15]
That is to say, "One should not engage exclusively in the study of
philosophy or the other sciences. He should study only the Torah and
its commandments. The former wisdom without a knowledge of the
Torah will lead one to inquire into things which the Torah has forbid-

(12) Baba Metzia 85 b.   (13) In other words, an ignorant man boasts of what little
knowledge he has, while the learned person is humble and quiet.   (14) The Hebrew
word for *heaven* is *shamayim* — a composite of two words: *eish* (fire) and
mayim(water). Together with earth and wind mentioned in the verse, the four
elements are thus referred to. The connection of this topic to Passover will be made
clear in the text that follows.   (15) Proverbs 30:5.   (16) *Ibid.*, Verse 6.

den us, such as: 'What is above, and what is below? What has been before the world came into existence, and what will be after its existence?' "[17] Therefore, our Torah has been compared to *refined silver*[18] which has no dross. In other words, the other wisdoms are not considered refined silver because of their "dross," their impurity which leads to the formation of opinions damaging to the faith. This verse, [*Every word of G-d is refined,* etc.],[15] thus explains that G-d's intent in giving us the Torah and the commandments is to refine our knowledge and to enable us to understand rational principles.

The commandment of the Passover offering is designed to bestir our souls with an affirmation of the basis of the Jewish faith and the Divine service. Accordingly, G-d commanded our enslaved ancestors to slaughter the sheep before the very eyes of their Egyptian oppressors, who worshipped that animal as a deity.[19]

Kings would declare themselves deities because of their great power and dominion, as well as their superior ability to have people executed or to bestow favor upon them. Nimrod[20] and Pharaoh,[21] for example, both declared themselves gods. To counteract such dangerous opinion, David said, *Know ye that the Eternal He is G-d, it is He that hath made us,* etc.[22] Throughout the Torah, you will not find that any ordinary person declared himself a deity; this happened only in the cases of certain kings, for they had more power than other people. Out of consideration for this, the prophet warned Israel against worshipping any heavenly power or people from whom they derived certain benefits, saying, *For she* [Israel] *said: I will go after my lovers, that give me my bread and my water.*[23] These are the heavenly powers or the people that bestowed favors upon Israel. This, then, was the nature of the Egyptian faith.

The distinction which the Torah has made between permissible and forbidden foods also serves to refine our rational power, for the commandments are beneficial to the life of both body and soul, as Solomon

(17) Chagigah 11 b.   (18) Psalms 12:7.   (19) See Exodus 8:22.   (20) See Genesis 10:9.   (21) See Ezekiel 29:3.   (22) Psalms 100:3.   (23) Hosea 2:7.

said, *For they are life unto those that find them, and health to all their flesh.*[24] *For they are life unto those that find them* — this refers to the life of the soul; *and health to all their flesh* — this refers to the life of the body. The foods prohibited by the Torah are harmful to the body. They give rise to cruelty and evil characteristics because of their coarseness and abundance of liquids. Physicians know this to be so. It is thus proper that those who have accepted the Torah and practice it should refine their rational faculty through the ingestion of permissible foods and that they should be on guard against cruelty. This concept prompted the Sages to say:[25] "What difference does it make to the Holy One, blessed be He, whether an animal is slaughtered at the throat or the neck? Surely you must say that the commandments have been given to man only as a means of refinement, as it is said, *Every word of G-d is refined.*"[15] The commandments, in other words, serve to refine the rational soul so that man should not form cruel habits. Man should be merciful, e.g., he should slaughter, not stab, at the throat rather than the neck.

The prohibition of *chameitz*[26] on Passover also serves to refine the rational soul and to affirm in our hearts the belief in G-d, blessed be He, by commemorating the miracle entailed in the Exodus from Egypt. *Chameitz*[26] has also been prohibited as a reminder of our ancestors' dough, which did not have enough time to rise before they were redeemed, as it is written, *And they baked unleavened cakes of the dough which they brought forth out of Egypt,* etc.[27]

It is known that *chameitz*[26] alludes to the evil inclination,[28] and man is obligated to make the good inclination prevail over the evil one. This goal is the motivating force of the Torah in its directives to man to fast, pray, and give charity. This also provides the basic meaning of the

(24) Proverbs 4:22.   (25) Bereshith Rabbah 44:1. See Ramban, Commentary on the Torah, Deuteronomy p 266-270 for a full discussion of this text.   (26) The term *chameitz* includes leavened bread made from any of the five species of grain — wheat, barley, spelt, goat-grass, and oats. Other forms of leaven are called *s'or*.   (27) Exodus 12:39.   (28) I have been unable to find a clear source of this allusion. See though below in the text the Sages' statement, "What prevents me from doing so is the leaven in the dough."

verse, *A righteous man 'yodei'a' (knoweth) the life of his beast;*[29] The righteous man *yodei'a* (breaks and humbles) his beastly nature. This explanation of the word *yodei'a* is based on the expression, *Vayoda (And he broke) with them the men of Succoth.*[30] The word *chameitz*[26] is etymologically related to the expression, *My heart 'yithchameitz' (was in a ferment).*[31] In the language of the Sages, a heart which is inclined towards wickedness is said to have *hechmitz* (changed for the worse), as they said of King Cyrus of Persia:[32] "Here it speaks of Cyrus before *hechmitz* (he changed for the worse), and there it speaks of him after *hechmitz* (he changed for the worse." Similarly, the Sages clearly said:[33] "It is obvious and well known to You that I desire to do Your Will. What prevents me from doing so is the leaven in the dough," i.e., the evil inclination. Thus, you see that the Sages compared the evil inclination to leaven. They further stated in the Midrash:[34] *"For He knoweth our frame.*[35] Woe to the dough that is declared bad by the baker's testimony." Therefore, *chameitz*[26] was banned from the altar, and the Torah warned us not to offer it at all, as it is written, *For ye shall make neither leaven nor any honey cause to ascend in fumes as an offering by fire unto the Eternal.*[36] *As an offering of first fruits ye may bring them unto the Eternal, but they shall not come up for a sweet savor on the altar.*[37] The altar was especially designated as a place for atonement and for the acceptance of an offering, and *chameitz*[26] was not acceptable. Even the *chameitz*[26] in a thanks-offering[38] was not

---

(29) Proverbs 12:10. (30) Judges 8:16. The men of Succoth had refused to give food to Gideon's men when they were on the way to fight Israel's enemy. After he was victorious over the enemy, Gideon *took the elders of the city, and thorns of the wilderness and biers, 'vayoda' with them the men of Succoth.* The word *vayoda* generally translated "and he taught" is here understood as "and he broke" the resistance of the men of Succoth. (31) Psalms 73:21. (32) Rosh Hashanah 3 b. Reference is to Cyrus' original permission to rebuild the Sanctuary and on which he later reneged (Ezra, Chapters 5-6). (33) Berachoth 17 a. (34) Bereshith Rabbah 34:12. (35) Psalms 103:14. (36) Leviticus 2:11. (37) *Ibid.,* Verse 12. On Shavuoth, *the day of the first fruits* (Numbers 28:26), two loaves made from the new crop of wheat were brought into the Sanctuary Court as a wave-offering. These loaves were baked with leaven (Leviticus 23:17) and were eaten by the priests, but it was forbidden to offer them upon the altar. (38) See Leviticus 7:13. The Torah required

brought upon the altar; it was only used as a wave-offering. For this reason, the Torah has said, *There shall be no leavened bread seen with thee*,[39] and *no leaven shall be found in your homes*.[40] This means that *it shall not be seen* in actuality, and *it shall not be found* in thought. Rather, one should disown it in his heart.

There are three types of commandments. Some require verbal fulfillment, others require mental or rational fulfillment, and still others necessitate the performance of some deed, as it is written, *. . . in thy mouth, and in thy heart, that thou mayest do it*.[41] Accordingly, the Torah ordained that the *chameitz* be mentally renounced in the heart, and tradition has required that it be removed from the house or burnt and that we proclaim the *'Kol Chamira'* (All leaven, etc.,) a statement of renunciation. In this way, all three manners of observing a commandment are fulfilled with regard to the prohibition of *chameitz*.[26] Since *chameitz*[26] alludes to the evil inclination, we have here an intimation that just as we must renounce *chameitz*, so are we obligated to avoid the evil inclination from our heart and not allow it to rule over us, for it is written, *The inclination of man's heart is evil from his youth*.[42] Just as tradition has required us to remove *chameitz* from our homes and to search for it in the holes and cracks of our houses, so are we obligated to search and examine our innermost thoughts for any vestige of evil. Just as the search for *chameitz* cannot be accomplished by the light of the sun or the moon or a torch, but only by the light of a candle, so is the search for the evil inclination accomplished only by means of the light of the soul, which is called "lamp," as it is said, *The soul of man is the lamp of the Eternal, searching all the inward parts*.[43]

that forty loaves, ten of which were leavened and thirty unleavened, were to be brought together with the thanks-offering. These loaves were not brought upon the altar, but they were eaten by their owner after he had presented the priest with one loaf out of every ten. (39) Exodus 13:7. (40) *Ibid.*, 12:19. (41) Deuteronomy 30:14. (42) Genesis 8:21. (43) Proverbs 20:27.

Solomon stated that G-d *is a shield unto them that take refuge in Him.*[15] This means[44] that the Torah protects one against trouble and sickness. Absolute adherence to the Torah obviates the need for physicians, as Scripture clearly assures, *He will bless thy bread and thy water.*[45] Solomon further stated, *Add thou not unto His words, lest He reprove thee, and thou be found a liar,*[16] thus warning you against presumptiously applying our wisdom to the commandments and altering them, by adding to them. For example, one should not add a fifth species to the prescribed Four Species included in the precept of the palm branch, nor should one add a fifth section to the four prescribed for the phylacteries. Adding to the Torah constitutes a violation of a precept, as it is said, *Thou shalt not add thereto, nor diminish from it.*[46] The Torah is perfect, as it is said, *The Law of the Eternal is perfect, restoring the soul,*[47] and whatever is perfect does not need any addition or diminution. All the words of the Torah are pure and without dross, as David said, *The words of the Eternal are pure words, as silver refined in a crucible on the earth, purified seven times.*[48]

(44) Until this point, Rabbeinu Bachya was explaining the first half of Proverbs 30:5 — *Every word of G-d is refined* — by showing how the verse applies to the prohibition of *chameitz* on Passover. He now proceeds with the interpretation of the conclusion of the verse that G-d *is a shield* etc.   (45) Exodus 23:25.   (46) Deuteronomy 13:1.   (47) Psalms 19:8.   (48) *Ibid.*, 12:7.

Part Two

> *The existence of G-d was never made known by overt miracles to the nations of the world prior to the Exodus from Egypt / Pharaoh denied three things: G-d's providence over human affairs, His power, and Moses' prophecy / The nature and warnings of the ten plagues / Why Moses said to Pharaoh, 'About midnight, etc.' rather than 'At midnight, etc.' as G-d had stated it / The final Redemption will be similar to the first redemption, the Exodus from Egypt / The prophecies of Isaiah which, notwithstanding the opinion of our adversaries, have not yet been fulfilled.*

AS IN THE DAYS OF THY COMING FORTH OUT OF THE LAND OF EGYPT WILL I SHOW HIM MARVELOUS THINGS.[49]

This verse includes two redemptions: the Exodus from Egypt, and the final Redemption, which will occur in the future and concerning which Isaiah prophesied, *Arise, shine, for thy light is come.*[50]

It is known that there are seventy nations in the world, all of which are descended from the seventy offspring of the family of Noah, for it is written, *And of these were the nations divided on the earth after the Flood.*[51] Moses our teacher said of them, *When He separated the children of men, He set the borders of the peoples,* which number seventy, corresponding *to the number of the children of Israel,*[52] who

(49) Micah 7:15. The verse, as will be explained by our author, assures us that the future Redemption will be accomplished by miracles of like stature as was the redemption from Egypt. (50) Isaiah 60:1. (51) Genesis 10:32. (52) Deuteronomy 32:8. This follows the interpretation of Rashi *(ibid)* that the division of the seventy nations corresponds to the seventy souls in the family of Jacob that went down to Egypt.

numbered seventy.[53] All the people of the world worshipped idols except Noah and his sons. Just as Adam was the progenitor of all mankind and attested to G-d's creation of the world, so was Noah the progenitor of all generations after the Flood, which in a sense was like Creation.[54] Adam had three sons: Cain, Abel, and Sheth. Cain became corrupt, and Sheth was the precursor of all righteous men.[55] Noah too had three sons: Shem, Ham, and Japheth. Ham became corrupt, and Shem was the precursor of all righteous men after the Flood. It is also known that Lamech, Noah's father, saw Adam,[56] and Abraham saw Noah, for Abraham was fifty-eight years old[57] when Noah died. Thus, Noah and his son Shem heard from an eyewitness about the creation of the world.

Thus, you can see how the faith was handed down on an individual level from generation to generation. The deeds and activities of all of these individuals were guided by hidden miracles. However, the existence of G-d was never made known to the nations through the medium of overt miracles until Israel's Exodus from Egypt, at which time the nations witnessed the great signs and wonders of the changes in nature and came to recognize and admit that *there is a G-d that judgeth on the earth,*[58] Who changes nature in accordance with His will and Who prevails over the power of the stars. It is so written, *But I*

---

(53) See Genesis 46:27.   (54) "The Flood [and its aftermath] were like the creation of the world. Thus he who acknowledges the Flood necessarily admits the creation of the world" (Ramban, Writing and Discourses, p. 41).   (55) Abel is not mentioned, for he was killed by Cain, neither is Japheth, for his offspring separated to live in the isles. See Ramban, Commentary on the Torah, Genesis, p. 98.   (56) There were 1,056 years from Adam until the Flood (Seder Olam, 1). Lamech was born when Adam was 874 years old (see the commentary of the Gaon of Wilna on Seder Olam, which is quoted in my Hebrew edition of Kad Hakemach, pp. 314-315). Since Adam lived 930 years in all, Lamech had fifty-six years during which he was a contemporary of the first man.   (57) "Noah lived ten years after the dispersion of the nations, at which time our patriarch Abraham was forty-eight years old" (Seder Olam, 1). Thus, Abraham was a contemporary of Noah for fifty-eight years.   (58) Psalms 58:12. See Ramban's Commentary on the Torah, Exodus, pp. 65-66, and Leviticus, pp. 461-463, on overt and hidden miracles.

am the Eternal thy G-d from the land of Egypt,[59] which means that in
the land of Egypt, He became known throughout the world by means
of overt miracles. Therefore, the prophet used the expression, *the Eternal thy G-d,* which is also stated concerning Creation: *These are the
generations of the heaven and of the earth when they were created, in
the day that the Eternal thy G-d made earth and heaven.*[60] It is also expressed at the Giving of the Torah: *I am the Eternal thy G-d.*[61]

At first, the nations did not believe in Divine Providence. They
thought that the world was eternal and that there is no difference *between the righteous and the wicked, between him that serveth G-d and
him that serveth him not.*[62] They maintained that there was no reward
for one who saves lives and no punishment for one who kills, that there
was no judgment and no Judge. Although some nations did believe so
out of their ignorance, the Egyptians maintained this opinion because
of their extensive knowledge of the heavenly powers. Therefore, they
said, "Since this lower world has been given over to the influence of the
heavenly powers, which are the servants of the King, therefore one who
honors them, honors the King." For this reason, they worshipped these
celestial powers and denied the Essential Power, the Proper Divine
Name.

In particular, Pharaoh and the Egyptians denied three things: G-d's
Providence,[63] His power,[64] and Moses' prophecy.[65] Concerning Divine
Providence, scholars devised the following parable: In its totality, the
world is like a well structured house in which a table is set and candles
are burning. The heaven is like a ceiling over the house, the stars in the
heaven are like the candles, and the vegetation of the earth is like the
set table in the house. Man has been appointed over this house, but he
has never seen the Master Who built it. However, he was told that his
father had previously been appointed over the house and that he would

---

(59) Hosea 12:10.   (60) Genesis 2:4.   (61) Exodus 20:2. Thus, the Exodus from
Egypt and the Giving of the Torah were of equal importance to the Creation of the
world.   (62) Malachi 3:18.   (63) See Exodus 8:18.   (64) See *ibid.*, 9:14.   (65) See
ibid., Verse 29.

continue in that position after his father. In light of this information, a rational person would seek to determine Who this Master is so that he would be worthy of coming before Him. Knowing that sooner or later he must give the Master an accounting of himself, he will exercise care in all his activities. The fool, however, spends his time eating, drinking, and satisfying his desires, and says, "Who has told me that this house has a Master at all?" Regarding such a person David stated, *Who have said, 'Our tongue will we make mighty; our lips are with us: who is lord over us?'*[66] Thus did the Egyptians deny the Master of the world, His Providence and power, and the prophecy of Moses. Israel, however, merited being the medium through which G-d's existence—as manifested in the great wonders of the Exodus—was made to be known among the nations.

This thought was expressed here by the prophet: *As in the days of thy coming forth out of the land of Egypt will I show unto him marvelous things.*[49] This verse includes two redemptions: the first and the last. In the first, the redemption from Egypt, the wonders shown in the ten plagues were derived from the four elements. Blood and frogs came from the element of water; gnats and the mixture of noxious animals came from the element of earth; murrain, boils, hail, and locusts came from the element of fire; darkness, and the slaying of the firstborn came from the element of wind,[67] for *any* firstborn *in whose nostrils was the breath of the spirit of life*[68] was destroyed.

Most of the ten plagues were preceded by a warning, for G-d does not punish unless He has first issued a warning.[69] The Sages commented:[70] "Blood and frogs were preceded by a warning; gnats came

---

(66) Psalms 12:5.   (67) The gnats came from the earth, as stated in Exodus 8:12, and the noxious animals were already active upon the earth. The plagues that attacked the cattle, the boils, and the locusts are considered as coming from the devouring fire. Darkness and the slaying of the firstborn are the result of the element of wind, as the verse indicates, for *any* firstborn etc.   (68) Genesis 7:22.   (69) Yoma 81 a. The reason why the third (gnats), sixth (boils) and ninth plagues (darkness) came without warning was that these did not involve loss of life (see Ramban, Commentary on the Torah, Exodus, pp. 89-90).   (70) P'sikta Zutratha, Exodus 7:26.

without a warning; the mixture of noxious animals and murrain were preceded by a warning; boils came without a warning; and so forth." Close examination of Scripture will reveal that in each set of two warnings, one was given at the Nile River and the other in Pharaoh's palace. In my opinion, the reason for this is that wicked Pharaoh exalted himself over the river[71] and the palace.[72] Therefore, Pharaoh's downfall originated where the warnings took place and whence the plagues came upon him.

The final plague was the slaying of the firstborn, as Moses said, *Thus saith the Eternal: About midnight will I go out,* etc.[73] G-d had specified to Moses, "at midnight," as the Torah testifies, *And it came to pass, that at midnight the Eternal smote all the firstborn.*[74] However, Moses said, . . . *about midnight,*[73] and the Rabbis explained[75] that "it was because Pharaoh's astrologers might make a mistake [regarding the precise time of the slaying of the firstborn. They might err in their calculations and conclude that the slaying occurred a little earlier or later than midnight]. They would then declare Moses a liar."

One may wonder about [this explanation of the Sages]. Since the third plague, the astrologers and magicians had unwillingly admitted that *this is the finger of G-d.*[76] Therefore, they did not show themselves before Moses from that time on, nor did they come into the royal palace. How then could they now ascribe an error to Moses at the tenth plague? Moreover, why should Moses be so concerned with what they might say that he altered the words said to him by G-d? It appears, therefore, that until the third plague, the magicians and astrologers were firm in their opinion that Moses' deeds were not from G-d but were accomplished only through Moses' personal wisdom and cunning. From the third plague onward, they admitted the truth of Moses' prophecy. With each additional plague, the Name of G-d became more known and sanctified in the world through Moses. Consequently,

---

(71) See Ezekiel 29:3. *My river is mine own,* etc. (72) See Exodus 7:23. (73) Exodus 11:4. (74) *Ibid.,* 12:29. (75) Berachoth 4 a. (76) Exodus 8:15.

at this final plague, Moses feared lest the astrologers and magicians find a reason to doubt his words. If they would, they might deny all the previous wonders, and the Name of G-d would then be profaned. It was therefore necessary for Moses to say, . . . *about midnight,*[73] since the verification of all the preceding signs were dependent on this one.

As a result of this tenth plague, Israel was sent forth from Egypt. The Egyptians even found it necessary to send the Israelites out against their will, as it says, *And the Egyptians were urgent upon the people, to send them out of the land.*[77] It was indeed extremely wondrous and an indication of Divine intercession that after being stricken with ten plagues and suffering economic losses, the Egyptians still felt the urgent need to send the Hebrews out of the land. The Sages said in the Midrash:[78] *"Iron sharpeneth iron, so a man sharpeneth the countenance of his friend.*[79] The verse, *iron sharpeneth iron,* refers to the case of righteous Moses and wicked Pharaoh, who were striking at each other with words. When Moses entered Pharaoh's presence, the latter asked him, 'Who sent you?' Moses replied, 'The G-d of the Hebrews sent me to you.' Pharaoh said, 'What did He tell you?' Moses answered, 'Let My people go that they may serve Me.' Pharaoh rejoined, 'Is there a deity in the world that I do not know? I swear by your life that all the deities of the world have sent me missives, but this G-d you mention has never sent me any communication.' [He then searched his records for a reference to the G-d of the Hebrews.] Not finding the Name of G-d, Pharaoh said to Moses, 'I have told you that *I know not the Eternal.*[80] Thereupon, he summoned all the wise men in Egypt and asked them, 'Have you heard the Name of their G-d?' They replied, 'We have heard that He is a son of the wise, the son of ancient kings.' At that point, G-d declared, 'You fools! You call yourselves wise men, yet you call Me only a son of the wise. I swear that I will cause your wisdom to be eliminated from the world, as it is said, *And the*

---

(77) *Ibid.,* 12:33.   (78) Midrash Mishlei, 27. Rabbeinu Bachya broadened the theme by citing the conversation between Moses and Pharaoh as described in Tanchuma, *Va'eira,* 5.   (79) Proverbs 27:17.   (80) Exodus 5:2.

wisdom of their prudent men shall perish.[81] You, Pharaoh, have said, *I know not the Eternal,*[80] but ultimately, you will know of Me. You have said, *Moreover I will not let Israel go,*[80] but ultimately, you will of necessity urge them to go." This is the subject of the first redemption, of which the prophet said, *As in the days of thy coming forth out of the land of Egypt.*[49]

The concluding part of that verse, *I will show unto him marvelous things,*[49] refers to the final Redemption, which will be similar to the redemption from Egypt. Isaiah said, *When the report cometh to Egypt, they shall be sorely pained at the report of 'Tzor.'*[82] The Sages commented:[83] "Every *Tzor* in Scripture which is written diminutively without a *vav* refers not to Tyre, but to the wicked kingdom.[84] G-d, Who requited the first enemies, the Egyptians, will requite the last ones."

Isaiah similarly explained this concept in the chapter beginning, *Arise, shine, for thy light is come.*[50] Notwithstanding, the opinion of our adversaries,[85] this chapter refers to the future. They have no basis for saying that this prophecy has already been fulfilled.[86] All of the verses in that chapter clearly demontrate that it is a prophecy of the future. Thus, he said, *Lift up thine eyes round about, and see; they all are gathered together, and come to thee, thy sons come from far,* etc.[87] However, it is known that during the era of the Second Temple, only

(81) Isaiah 29:14.   (82) *Ibid.*, 23:5. The Hebrew word *Tzor*, which usually means Tyre, is here spelled *tzadi-reish*, without the usual *vav* between these letters. The Midrashic exposition of this variant spelling is cited in the text which follows.   (83) Tanchuma *Bo, 4.*   (84) The Midrash, *ibid.*, specifies the "kingdom of Edom," another name for Rome. This interpretation is based on the fact that *Tzor* without a *vav* can be read as *tzar* (adversary).   (85) The struggle against Israel was carried on at all fronts—political, spiritual, etc. The Jew was not only denied political rights, but attempts were made at all levels of State and Church to rob him of his hope for the future Redemption, claiming that all prophecies have already been fulfilled. It is to counteract these opinions that the author emphasizes this point: "Notwithstanding the opinion of our adversaries etc."   (86) See Ramban, Writings and Discourses, pp. 595-608, where it is proved that this prophecy and other cogent utterances of Isaiah perforce refer only to the future Redemption.   (87) Isaiah 60:4.

forty thousand returned from the captivity of Babylon.[88] Similarly, his statement, *And aliens shall build up thy walls*[89] has never yet been fulfilled. Not only did aliens refrain from participating in the construction of the Second Temple, but they even hindered and fought against the Israelites who were building it, as it is written, *They that built the walls, and they that bore the burdens, with those that loaded, every one with one of his hands wrought in the work, and with the other held his weapon.*[90] Likewise, the prophecy, *Thy gates also shall be open constantly,*[91] was not fulfilled during the Second Temple era. On the contrary, the gates were closed before sundown and not opened until well into the morning of the following day, as it is said, *Let not the gates of Jerusalem be opened until the sun be hot.*[92] Furthermore, the assurance that the *nation and the kingdom that will not serve thee shall perish*[93] was certainly not fulfilled during the Second Temple era. Instead, our ancestors at that time were subject to the various ruling kingdoms. It is well known through the Talmud that Rabbeinu Hakadosh,[94] the foremost man and leader of his generation, paid tax to the Imperial Roman government. When, then, was this prophecy fulfilled? Undoubtedly, it is an assurance of the future, notwithstanding the opinion of our adversaries.[85]

The Sages said in the Midrash:[95] "The First and Second Temples were built by mortal men, Solomon and Cyrus.[96] Because they ended in destruction, they were called by the name of mortal men, as it is said, *Zion is the city of David.*[97] It is further written, *the city where David encamped.*[98] The Third Temple, however, which will be Divinely built and which will exist forever, will be called by the Name of G-d, Who lives forever, as it is said, *And they shall call thee the City of the*

---

(88) See Ezra 2:64. (89) Isaiah 60:10. (90) Nehemiah 4:11. (91) Isaiah 60:11. (92) Nehemiah 7:3. (93) Isaiah 60:12. (94) See above *Ahavah* (Love of G-d), Note 42. (95) I have been unable to locate the source of the text here, but a somewhat similar thought is found in P'sikta Rabbathi, 29:1. (96) Cyrus, King of Persia, gave permission for the rebuilding of the Second Temple (II Chronicles 36:23). (97) I Chronicles 11:5. Although Solomon built the Temple, David had laid its foundations. (98) Isaiah 29:1. The prophet is speaking of the altar of G-d, which is in Jerusalem, *the city where David encamped.*

Eternal, the Zion of the Holy One of Israel.[99] The prophet Isaiah also said in that chapter, *For brass I will bring gold, and for iron I will bring silver, and for wood brass, and for stones iron.*[100] This refers to the taxes which they imposed upon us, and for the burdensome levy which they placed upon the wealth of Israel. They will be repaid in the time of the Messiah [for all their acts of oppression].

It is subsequently written there, *Violence shall no more be heard in thy Land.*[101] Now, if that chapter in Isaiah had already been fulfilled, how can one account for the violence and desolation which are still prevalent within the borders of the Land?[102] It is further written there, *The sun shall no more be thy light by day,* etc.[103] When was this fulfilled? How is G-d the *everlasting light*[103] and glory of the Holy Land, which is still despised, laid waste, and desolate without her children? Again, it is written there, *Thy sun shall no more go down . . . and the days of thy mourning shall be ended.*[104] How did the days of our mourning end during the era of the Second Temple if we are still anticipating the end of this long and terrible exile? We are still in captivity, the days of our mourning have not yet ended, [and so we will continue] *until the spirit be poured upon us from on high.*[105] The prophet has assured us that after the days of our mourning will have ended, the Land will become Israel's eternal and uninterrupted inheritance. This is the thought conveyed by the prophet's conclusion of this chapter, *Thy people also shall be righteous, they shall inherit the Land forever.*[106]

---

(99) *Ibid.,* 60:14. (100) *Ibid.,* Verse 17. (101) *Ibid.,* Verse 18. (102) This is a strong allusion to the various wars which ravaged the Land of Israel in the times of the author. In the face of so much devastation, how could it be said that the prophecy was already fulfilled? Isaiah's message must perforce be an utterance of the future when the Messiah will usher in the perfect Redemption of Israel. (103) Isaiah 60:19. (104) *Ibid.,* Verse 20. (105) *Ibid.,* 32:15. (106) *Ibid.,* 60:21.

Part Three

> *The wonders of G-d can be discerned from the creation of the human body / The three divisions of the body correspond to the three divisions in nature / Man's thankfulness for the mercy he constantly receives from G-d / The explanation of Psalm 136, 'Hallel Hagadol' (the Great Praise) / At the time of the Resurrection, the soul will rejoice together with the body / The allusion thereto in the Song of Songs.*

I WILL GIVE THANKS UNTO THEE, FOR I AM FEARFULLY AND WONDERFULLY MADE; WONDERFUL ARE THY WORKS AND THAT MY SOUL KNOWETH RIGHT WELL.[107] MY FRAME WAS NOT HIDDEN FROM THEE, WHEN I WAS MADE IN SECRET, AND CURIOUSLY WROUGHT IN THE LOWEST PART OF THE EARTH.[108] THINE EYES DID SEE MINE UNFORMED SUBSTANCE, AND IN THY BOOK THEY WERE ALL WRITTEN—EVEN THE DAYS THAT WERE FASHIONED, WHEN AS YET THERE WAS NONE OF THEM.[109]

With these words, King David intended to state that although the creation of other living things manifests the marvelous nature of G-d's deeds, there is none besides man who is aware of it. Man, reflecting upon the marvels of the organs of the body is inspired with awe and wonder. Therefore, David said, *I will give thanks unto Thee, for I am fearfully and wonderfully made.*[107] That is to say, "From the marvels of the creation of my body, I recognize that Your deeds are wondrous, and my rational soul knows this." This is similar to Scripture's statement, *And from my flesh shall I see G-d,*[110] i.e., from the structure of

---

(107) Psalms 139:14. (108) *Ibid.*, Verse 15. (109) *Ibid.*, Verse 16. (110) Job 19:26.

517

my body and from the wisdom apparent in my faculties, I see the work of G-d.

David's praise, *Wonderful are Thy works,*[107] referred to G-d's works both above and below. The expression, *Thy works* includes the three divisions of existence: the angels, the spheres, and this lower world. All of these divisions are reflected in the parts of the body, which correspond to these three divisions. For this reason, man is called a microcosm; he mirrors the world. Thus, the head with its reasoning power corresponds to the world of the angels, who are the Separate Intelligences.[111] The torso, from the neck down to the loins, contains the heart, which is the source of the body's movement. It corresponds to the world of the moving spheres, by which movement the world exists. The area from the loins down is the cause of existence and destruction. It corresponds to this lower world, the scene of birth and death.

In each part of his body, then, David became aware of the wonders of the three divisions of existence. Therefore, he said, *I will give thanks,*[107] for "thanks" is an expression used for recognition of the mercy that man receives from G-d. It is thus written, *O give thanks unto the Eternal, for He is good, for His mercy endureth forever.*[112] This refers to the lower world. The psalmist mentioned it first because only afterwards does one merit life in the World to Come. The verse, *O give thanks unto the G-d of gods,*[113] refers to the world of angels, who are called *elohim* (gods or powers). It is they who move the spheres, [while G-d is Master of them all]. The verse, *O give thanks unto the Lord of lords,*[114] refers to the world of the spheres, controlling this lower world. In each of this three verses, the psalmist mentioned *His mercy*, for all created things receive the mercy of G-d, blessed be He.

Psalm 136 proceeds to mention the wonders of G-d among His creatures. It speaks chiefly of Creation, the Exodus from Egypt, the

---

(111) "The angels are not material bodies but only forms distinguished from each other. . . . All these forms live and acknowledge the Creator, and their knowledge of Him is exceedingly great" (Maimonides, Mishneh Torah, *Hilchoth Yesodei Hatorah* 2:3-8). (112) Psalms 136:1. (113) *Ibid.*, Verse 2. (114) *Ibid.*, Verse 3.

parting of the Red Sea, the wonders in the wilderness and in the Land of Israel, and the exile and the redemption therefrom. The psalm consists of twenty-six verses, each of which concludes with the phrase, *for His mercy endureth forever*. The number of verses coincides with the numerical value of the letters in the Divine Tetragrammaton, and it also corresponds to the twenty-six generations from Creation to the Giving of the Torah.[115] The psalm thus intimates that these generations without Torah were sustained and supported by G-d in His great compassion.

After tracing the various mercies G-d has shown to the physical universe in general and to Israel in particular, the psalmist stated, *Who remembered us in our low estate*.[116] In other words, during our exile and state of humiliation He has remembered the covenant He made with the patriarchs to preserve us among the nations. This applies to both the Babylonian exile and our present Edomite or Roman exile, regarding which He has assured us, *And yet for all that, when they are in the land of their enemies, I will not reject them, neither will I abhor them, to destroy them utterly, and to break My covenant with them, for I am the Eternal their G-d*.[117] *And He hath delivered us from our adversaries*,[118] for His great mercy remains with us in our exile and keeps us alive among the nations. Finally, the verse, *Who giveth food to all flesh*,[119] expresses the great principle of G-d's kindness in giving food to all His creatures.

The Sages called this psalm *Hallel Hagadol* (the Great Praise),[120] and they explained it as follows:[121] "Rabbi Yochanan said, 'It is called *Hallel Hagadol* because it relates that G-d, Who dwells at the height of the universe, apportions food to all His creatures.' " They further said there:[121] "Since we have *Hallel Hagadol*, why then do we recite *Hallel*

---

(115) There were ten generations from Adam to Noah, and ten from Noah to Abraham. These twenty plus the generations of the three patriarchs, and those of Levi, Kehoth, and Amram, the father of Moses, complete the twenty-six generations from the Creation to the Revelation at Sinai. (116) Psalms 136:23. (117) Leviticus 26:44. (118) Psalms 136:24. (119) *Ibid.*, Verse 25. (120) See above, *Parnassah* Note 3. (121) Pesachim 118 a.

Hamitzri on festivals?[122] Rabbi Yochanan said, 'It is because there are five themes in it: the Exodus from Egypt, the parting of the Red Sea, the Giving of the Torah, the subjugation by the kingdoms, and the Resurrection of the dead. The Exodus from Egypt is mentioned in the verse, *When Israel came out of Egypt;*[123] the parting of the Red Sea is referred to in the verse, *The sea saw it, and fled;*[124] the Giving of the Torah in the verse, *The mountains skipped like rams;*[125] the subjugation by the kingdoms in the verse, *Not unto us, O Eternal, not unto us;*[126] and the Resurrection of the dead in the verse, *I shall walk before the Eternal in the lands of the living.*' "[127]

It is known that the principle of Resurrection is the foundation of the entire Torah and the root of the commandments. At the time of the Resurrection the soul will rejoice together with the body, for the body was the instrument of the soul. Hence, whatever the soul achieved in fulfilling the commandments, it did together with the body. If the body were denied a share in the reward for observance of the commandments, it would be an injustice, "and the Eternal does not withhold the reward of any creature."[121] Therefore, it is proper that the body and soul be rewarded together, just as they fulfilled the words of the Torah and commandments together. Thus, David said, *I shall walk before the Eternal in the lands of the living.*[127]

This great and wonderful distinction which is the soul's destiny was lauded by Solomon in his wisdom. He called it *love, above all other pleasures,* as he said, *How fair and how pleasant art thou, O love, above all other pleasures.*[128]

---

(122) The Hallel we recite on festivals (Psalms 113-118) is called *Hallel Hamitzri* (Praise of the Egyptian Miracle), because of reference in Psalm 114 to the Exodus from Egypt. (123) Psalms 114:1. (124) *Ibid.,* Verse 3. (125) *Ibid.,* Verse 4. The mountains shook when the Torah was given at Sinai. (126) *Ibid.,* 115:1. As the psalm continues: *Wherefore should the nations say, 'Where is now their G-d?'* etc. (Verse 2). (127) *Ibid.,* 116:9. (128) Song of Songs 7:7. See in *Ahavah* (Love of G-d), text at Note 38, beginning "The Song of Songs is devoted to . . . "

פורים

The Miracle of Purim

G-d's mercies are manifested in the conduct of His world / Even the sufferings which come upon a person are brought in a merciful manner and one should always be cognizant of that fact / G-d's mercies include the Exodus from Egypt, in which Israel was taken from slavery to freedom, and the salvation in the days of Mordecai and Esther, in which the Jews were spared death / Interpretations of the Book of Esther / Allusions in the Book of Esther regarding the future Redemption / David's prophecy in Psalm 124 on the duration of the present exile and the Redemption therefrom.

The Miracle of Purim

THE EARTH, O ETERNAL, IS FULL OF THY MERCY;
TEACH ME THY STATUTES.[1]

The word *earth* mentioned by David in this verse, includes this lower world and the three encompassing spheres of the elements [fire, wind, and water, which together with the earth, constitute the four elements in Creation]. Through the order and movements of these four elements, the discerning scholar knows and recognizes the wisdom of G-d and His great mercy as manifested in the conduct of His world. Therefore, in this verse, David entreats G-d to show him mercy by teaching him His statutes [regulating the universe], and that he may discern from His Torah how G-d, blessed be He, conducts His world with the attribute of mercy.

It is known that the mercy of G-d preceded the entire Creation. Before coming into existence, the creatures had no merit to speak of which would entitle them to existence. Hence, the entire world was created with mercy. Thus, David stated, *I have said: The world was built in mercy.*[2]

---

(1) Psalms 119:64. Since the earth is full of G-d's mercies, the psalmist is praying that He teach him a full knowledge of His will (Ibn Ezra). To gain a knowledge of Torah is thus a manifestation of G-d's mercy to man. (2) *Ibid.*, 89:3. According to tradition, G-d had at first created the world with the attribute of justice. But seeing that the world could not exist thereon, he combined it with the attribute of mercy (see Rashi to Genesis 1:1). It is in this sense that the verse of the psalmist — *The world was built in mercy* — should be understood.

Having created the world with mercy, G-d conducts Himself mercifully towards His creatures, as it is written, *He showeth mercy unto the thousandth generation.*[3] It is further written, *Thou hast granted me life and mercy.*[4] Based upon these verses, the Sages expressed the following thought in the liturgy:[5] "He guideth His world with lovingkindness." He commanded His creatures to practice mercy — as the prophet said, *Sow to yourselves according to righteousness, reap according to mercy*[6] — and to love mercy, as He said, *And what doth the Eternal require of thee: only to do justly, and to love mercy.*[7] This Heavenly mercy emanates constantly throughout the entire universe, and nothing can exist without it.

David further said, *All the paths of the Eternal are mercy and truth.*[8] The verse thus teaches you that if G-d brings sufferings upon a person as the result of some previously committed sin, then those sufferings are in the category of *truth*. On the other hand, if sufferings are G-d's means of testing the person in order to increase his reward for being able to withstand the trial, then they are in the category of *mercy*. Regarding this [kind of testing of one's character], David said, *For Thy mercy is better than life*[9] He meant that sufferings, even if not imposed because of sin, are more precious than life in this world, for through suffering, one achieves the true life in the World to Come. For example, a person who has to do some heavy work will endure anguish in order to accomplish his task. Nevertheless, he does not feel that he has harmed himself thereby, for he knows that through his toil, he is able to physically support himself.

When G-d brings afflictions upon a person, He does so in a merciful way, as David said, *And unto Thee, O G-d, belongeth mercy, for Thou renderest to every man according to his work.*[10] Note that David men-

---

(3) Exodus 20:6.   (4) Job 10:12.   (5) In the prayer entitled *Nishmath kol chai* (The breath of every living being), part of the Morning Service on Sabbaths and festivals.   (6) Hosea 10:12.   (7) Micah 6:8.   (8) Psalms 25:10.   (9) *Ibid.,* 63:4.   (10) *Ibid.,* 62:13.

tioned the Divine Name of *Aleph-Dalet-Nun-Yod,* which is indicative of the attribute of justice. David thus explained that even when afflictions are brought upon a person by the attribute of justice, *unto Thee, O G-d, belongeth mercy,*[10] that is, the attribute of mercy supersedes that of justice. Similarly, David said, *Thy righteousness is like the mighty mountains, Thy judgments are like the great deep,*[11] the explanation of which is: "*Thy righteousness* supersedes *Thy judgments,* even as *the mighty mountains* are higher than *the great deep.*"

Great is the power of the attribute of mercy, for Scripture connects it directly to G-d Himself. In this respect, it is like the Higher Light[12] — of which it is written, *And the Light dwelleth with Him*[13] — for regarding the attribute of mercy, it is similarly stated, *For with the Eternal there is mercy.*[14] No other nation can testify to G-d's mercy like Israel, as it is said, *For His mercy is great toward us.*[15] Since the attribute of mercy is so eminent and mighty, influencing the conduct of the entire universe, high and low, one is therefore obligated to contemplate the essence thereof and to be ever mindful of G-d's mercies, even as Isaiah said, *I will make mention of the mercies of the Eternal, and the praises of the Eternal.*[16]

The mercies that G-d bestowed upon the people of Israel include having taken them out of Egypt and saved them from the pursuit of Pharaoh, a mighty king. Suddenly they emerged from darkness into light, and from slavery into freedom. It was also a redemption of the soul, freeing them from the darkness of Egyptian idolatry. Ahaseurus, however, was even greater than Pharaoh, who was only King of Egypt, but Ahaseurus ruled over the entire world [then known], from India to Ethiopia,[17] which were at opposite ends of the [settled] world.[18] The redemption in Ahaseurus' days was from death to life, all as told in the Book of Esther.

---

(11) *Ibid.,* 36:7. (12) See above, *Orchim,* Note 51. (13) Daniel 2:22. (14) Psalms 130:7. (15) *Ibid.,* 117:2. (16) Isaiah 63:7. (17) See Esther 1:1. (18) This is in accordance with the opinion of one of the Amoraim (Megillah 11 a).

That the Divine Name is not explicitly mentioned anywhere in the Book of Esther was explained by Rabbi Abraham Ibn Ezra as follows:[19] "Mordecai composed the Book of Esther, as the verse states, *And he* [Mordecai] *sent letters,*[20] each of which was a copy of his writing. The Persians, in turn, transcribed Mordecai's work and included it in the chronicles of their kings. However, [had Mordecai mentioned G-d's Name in the Book], the Persians, being idolators, would have substituted the name of their abomination, in place of the Honored Name, just as the Cutheans wrote 'Ashima[21] created' in place of *In the beginning G-d created.*[22] Therefore, for the honor of G-d, Mordecai did not mention His Name." Thus far Ibn Ezra's language.

It is known that Ahaseurus and Haman were in accord in their desire to destroy and uproot the people of our faith. Therefore, to counteract them, both Mordecai and Esther were needed to help and protect Israel. G-d bestirred Esther to make a party for Haman and to ask leave to do so from Ahaseurus by alluding to the Name of the Supreme King.[23] In this way, the fall of Haman would be agreed by both the Heavenly and earthly powers.

Now, wicked Haman was well informed in Jewish matters. In his heart, he guarded an account of the first war, which Israel fought with his ancestor Amalek, of which it is written, *And Joshua discomfited Amalek.*[24] Although Haman knew that Israel's strength lay in the Cause of causes and the Foremost of all powers, he disregarded this completely and even scorned the idea. Hardening his heart, he said, *Yet all this availeth me nothing.*[25]

---

(19) This quotation is taken from Ibn Ezra's introduction to his commentary on the Book of Esther. (20) Esther 9:20. (21) This was the name of their idol. See II Kings 17:30. (22) Genesis 1:1. (23) The first letters in the expression, *Yavo hamelech v'Haman hayom (let the king and Haman come this day* — Esther 5:4), spell out the Tetragrammaton in its regular sequence. (24) Exodus 17:13. (25) Esther 5:13. The final letters of the expression, *Zeh einenu shoveh li (this availeth me nothing)*, spell out the Divine Tetragrammaton in reverse order. In regular sequence the Divine Name is indicative of the attribute of mercy; in reverse, the attribute of justice. By mentioning the Divine Name in reverse, Haman brought about his own

According to the literal meaning of Scripture, Haman was saying:
"All this honor accorded me by the king and the queen is of no avail
and completely worthless to me when I consider the feeling of deficiency and shame *so long as I see Mordecai the Jew sitting at the king's
gate.*"[25] However, according to the interpretation we have mentioned
[i.e., that Haman was defying the Cause of all causes] it is possible to
explain that when Haman said, *Yet all this availeth me nothing*[25] his
evil intent was to deny the Divine Being, for the word *'zeh'* is to be
understood in the light of the following expressions: *Behold, 'zeh' (this)
is our G-d,*[26] *'Zeh' (This) is my G-d, and I will glorify Him.*[27] *It is
because of 'zeh' (this) which G-d did for me.*[28] Thus, Haman con-
ceitedly and scornfully alluded to the Specific Divine Name here in the
word *Zeh,* since he was extremely arrogant, and *pride goeth before
destruction.*[29] He further *deeply rebelled*[30] by mentioning the Divine
Name in reverse.[25] Therefore, the Divine attribute of justice caused his
ruination.

Notwithstanding all this, Haman paid no attention to his situation
and gave no heed to the power of the Specific Divine Name. At the
commencement of his decline when he had to bring the royal apparel
and the king's horse for Mordecai, he began to realize that he was being undone. *The wise men and Zeresh his wife said unto him: If
Mordecai, before whom thou hast begun to fall, be of the seed of the
Jews, thou shalt not prevail against him, but shalt surely fall before
him.*[31] When Esther pleaded before the king, *Let my life be given me
at my petition, and my people at my request,*[32] the king asked, *Who is
he, and where is he, that darest presume in his heart to do so?*[33] Esther
replied, *An adversary and an enemy, even this wicked Haman.*[34] At
that point, Haman fully realized that his downfall occurred through
the power of the Specific Divine Name, as it is written, *For he [Haman]
saw that there was evil determined against him by the King.*[35] [In this

downfall.   (26) Isaiah 25:9.   (27) Exodus 15:2.   (28) *Ibid.,* 13:8.   (29) Proverbs
16:18.   (30) Isaiah 31:6.   (31) Esther 6:13.   (32) *Ibid.,* 7:3.   (33) *Ibid.,* Verse
5.   (34) *Ibid.,* Verse 6.   (35) *Ibid.,* Verse 7.

verse, the word *King* refers to G-d], the Supreme King, since it does not say "Ahaseurus."

After Haman was hanged, the king removed the royal ring from Haman's hand and gave it to Mordecai.[36] The ring, which is round, symbolizes the rotating wheel of fortune, for the power which had previously belonged to Haman was now given to Mordecai. This is an intimation of the future, when destiny will change. Those who are in a higher place will be lowered, and those who are now in a low place will be elevated. Thus, David said of the future Redemption, *Let the heavens be glad, and let the earth rejoice.*[37] This indicates that the government of the wicked Edom will be destroyed and that power and dominion will return to Israel. The widespread proselytism of many of the nations in the days of Mordecai and Esther—as it is written, *And many from among the peoples of the land became Jews, for the fear of the Jews was fallen upon them*[38]—alludes to the future when the nations will become proselytes and will enter into the covenant of G-d. They will serve Him with unanimous consent, as it is said, *For then will I turn to the peoples a pure language, that they may all call upon the Name of the Eternal, to serve Him with one accord.*[39]

David previously foretold this exile when he said. *If it had not been the Eternal Who was for us,* etc.[40] After seeing the length of this exile through which we have persevered, and the subsequent Redemption therefrom, he gave thanks to G-d, saying, *Blessed be the Eternal, Who hath not given us as a prey to their teeth.*[41] *Our soul is escaped 'k'tzipor' (as a bird) out of the snare of fowlers,* etc.[42] He compared Israel to a *tzipor,* which is representative of the ritually pure birds. The *tzipor* also calls to mind the speed of a bird in flight and thus additionally

(36) See *ibid.,* 8:2.   (37) Psalms 96:11. The first letters of the Hebrew words, *Yismechu hashamayim v'thagel ha'aretz (Let the heavens be glad, and the earth rejoice),* spell the Divine Tetragrammaton in its order of sequence. This indicates etc.   (38) Esther 8:17.   (39) Zephaniah 3:9.   (40) Psalms 124:1. As the Psalm continues: *Then they would have swallowed us up alive,* etc., (Verse 3).   (41) *Ibid.,* Verse 6.

alludes to the swiftness of the Redemption. *The snare is broken*[42] is a reference to the kingdoms of Edom and of Elam[43] which will be destroyed. Notwithstanding the wish of these powers, *we are escaped.*[42] *Our help is in the Name of the Eternal, Who made heaven and earth.*[44]

David mentioned *heaven and earth* in connection with the subject of the Redemption in order to teach us that the Redemption will be as wondrous and novel as Creation out of nothingness. It will then be made clear to all the nations that G-d's mercy is upon us and that He has neither forgotten us, nor abandoned us in exile. It is so written in the Book of Ezra: *For we are bondmen; yet our G-d hath not forsaken us in our bondage, but hath extended mercy unto us in the sight of the kings of Persia.*[45] Then they will realize that G-d's mercy is permanently with us even as the existence of the everlasting mountains. In fact, G-d's mercy upon us goes beyond the existence of the mountains, for with the passage of time, the mountains will disappear in the distant future. However, G-d's mercy upon Israel will never be shaken, and will never be removed. Thus the prophet assured us: *For the mountains may depart, and the hills be removed, but My kindness shall not depart from thee, neither shall My covenant of peace be removed, saith the Eternal that has compassion for thee.*[46]

---

(42) *Ibid.*, Verse 7.   (43) An ancient name for Persia. Here, Elam represents the Islamic kingdoms.   (44) Psalms 124:8.   (45) Ezra 9:9.   (46) Isaiah 54:10.

צְדָקָה
Charity

Who is entitled to charity? / The reward for giving charity / All nations must practice charity and mercy for they exist because of these practices and are punished for neglecting them / The manifold aspects of the greatness of charity / The wealthy donor derives more benefit from his act of giving charity than the poor recipients / Charity must be given in accordance with the donor's means and the goodness of his heart / Charity includes sharing the poor man's grief / One who causes others to do good is more meritorious than one who merely does good himself / Charity annuls many punitive decrees and brings the Redemption closer.

Charity

HE HATH SCATTERED ABROAD; HE HATH GIVEN TO THE
NEEDY. 'TZIDKATHO' (HIS CHARITY) ENDURETH
FOREVER.[1]

David stated this verse with reference to the practice of charity. He informed us that there is a great and mighty reward for this practice in this world and in the World to Come. He used the term *scattered*, which indicates that the donor dispenses his money freely and magnanimously. David also specified *needy*, which denotes one who requires help most of the time, even for small things. Therefore, David said that the commandment of charity is essentially intended for such people. The assistance given them should not be merely limited: it should rather be *scattered* freely.

If one practices charity in this manner, G-d will give him two assurances: a material one for this world, and a spiritual one for the World to Come, [as will be explained below]. If one extends help to the poor at times liberally, then, even if at other times he does it with a limit, *'tzidkatho' (his charity) endureth forever.*[1] G-d will bless him

---

(1) Psalms 112:9. The perfect form of giving charity is not to embarrass the recipient. This is the deeper meaning of the expression, *He hath scattered abroad,* without awareness of who is the poor recipient of his help. A further realization is that the recipient does more for the donor than the donor does for him. In this sense the verse states, *he hath given to the needy,* making him the true owner, and it is the donor who is now rewarded with the full blessings thereof. The spiritual benefit of such form of charity indeed endures forever.

with permanent wealth so that he will be able to give charity forever, just as David's son Solomon mentioned, *There is a man that scattereth and groweth still richer.*² Moses our teacher also mentioned, *'Nathon titein' (Thou shalt surely give) him.*³ That is to say, "if you have given charity to the poor, G-d will give you the means to be able to continue to do so."

Moses designated a material blessing, for the observance of this commandment, as it is said, *Because for this thing, the Eternal thy G-d will bless thee in all thy work,*³ giving you additional benefit and increased success in this world. Since Moses assured us only of a material reward in this world, David revealed to us [that the reward for fulfilling this precept entailed] the two assurances mentioned above. *His charity endureth forever,*¹ which David said, is a material assurance that the donor will continue to possess his wealth and will be forever able to give charity. David also stated, . . . *and his horn shall be exalted in honor,*¹ which is a spiritual assurance that the soul will live in the World to Come. In the verse, the word *honor* refers to the soul, which will merit to return to its source, the Throne of Glory. Solomon, David's son, often referred to this concept, as he said, *'Tzedakah' (Charity) exalteth a nation.*⁴ That is to say, any nation that practices charity *is exalted, but mercy to any people is sin*⁴ if it fails to practice it. All nations must practice charity and mercy, for they exist because of these practices and are punished for their neglect.

The power of charity is great indeed, as our Rabbis commented:⁵ "If you bring a gift to a mortal king, it is unknown whether he will accept it or not. Even if the king will accept it, it is unknown whether the donor will actually see the king or not. However, this is not the case with G-d. When a person gives a *p'rutah* (coin of lowest denomination) to a poor man, he becomes worthy of receiving the Divine Presence, as it is said, *As for me, 'b'tzedek' (in charity) I shall behold Thy*

---

(2) Proverbs 11:24.   (3) Deuteronomy 15:10.   (4) Proverbs 14:34. See Ramban, Commentary on the Torah, Leviticus, pp. 324-325.   (5) Baba Bathra 10 a.

Presence.'[6] In Midrash Tanchuma,[7] we find: "Charity is great indeed, for it will be used to praise G-d Himself when He comes to bring salvation to Israel, as it is said, *I that speak in charity, mighty to save.*[8] Charity is great indeed, for it bestows honor and life upon those who practice it, as it is said, *He that followeth after charity and mercy, findeth life, prosperity, and honor,*[9] i.e., he finds them on the day of judgment. Charity is great indeed, for our patriarch Abraham was praised with it,[10] as were David[11] and Israel.[12] Charity is great indeed, for G-d Himself will be lauded with it on the day of judgment, as it is said, *And the Eternal of hosts will be exalted through justice, and G-d the Holy One will be sanctified through charity.'*[13]

We find that the practice of charity gives a person life and longevity, as it is said, *The hoary head is a crown of glory, it is found in the way of charity.*[14] It is further written, *Treasures of wickedness profit nothing, but charity delivereth from death.*[15] This means that the wealth obtained through robbery and other illegal means will be of no avail. One would fare better through the money he spends on charity, for that will save him from death. Thus, the diminution of one's wealth by dispensing charity yields life to the donor, while the increase of one's wealth through illegal means brings death.

Solomon's statement that *charity delivereth from death*[15] means not only from a painful death, but from death itself. It happened that "during a year of famine, a woman came to Benjamin the Righteous, the treasurer of a charity fund, and asked him to support her. He said to her, 'I swear by the Service in the Sanctuary that the charity fund has been depleted.' She persisted, 'If you will not support me, a woman with her seven children will be dead.' He then supported her from his personal funds. Some time later, Benjamin became sick and was about to die. The ministering angels then said before G-d, 'Master of the

---

(6) Psalms 17:15.   (7) This passage is actually in Midrash Mishlei, 14.   (8) Isaiah 63:1.   (9) Proverbs 21:21.   (10) See Genesis 18:19.   (11) See II Samuel 8:15.   (12) See Deuteronomy 6:28.   (13) Isaiah 5:16.   (14) Proverbs 16:31.   (15) *Ibid.,* 10:2.

universe! You have said that one who saves a single life[16] is considered as if he saved an entire world. Should Benjamin the Righteous, who saved a woman and her seven children, die in his prime?' It was taught in the Beraitha that [as a result of the angels' plea], Benjamin's life was prolonged by twenty-one years."[17] It is of this kind of blessing that Solomon said, *I will walk in the path of charity.* [18]

The benefit derived by the donor of charity is greater than that derived by the poor recipient. The benefit derived by the poor is only transitory; it exists only in this world. However, through his act, the donor merits life in the World to Come. Thus, [after having gleaned in the field of Boaz], Ruth said to Naomi, *The man's name with whom I wrought today is Boaz.* [19] The Sages commented,[20] "It does not say 'who wrought with me,' but rather *with whom I wrought.* Scripture thus teaches you that it is she who did many favors to him [bringing him more blessings than she received from him]."

The poor are called the people of G-d, as the Sages expounded:[21] "*If thou lend money to any of My people.* [22] Who are *My people?* They are the poor, as it is said, *For the Eternal hath comforted His people, and hath compassion upon his poor.* [23] It is further written, *And in her* [Zion] *shall the poor of His people take refuge.* [24] A mortal man who is rich and who has poor relatives usually does not acknowledge them, as it is said, *All the brethren of the poor do hate him.* [25] It is further written, *The poor is hated even of his own neighbor.* [26] However, this is not

---

(16) Our editions of the Talmud read: "the life of one Jew." (17) Baba Bathra 11a. Some Talmudic manuscripts and other early writings agree with the reading of "twenty-one years" as specified here by our author. See Dikdukei Sofrim, *ibid.,* Note 7. Our editions of the Talmud specify "twenty-two years." — The reading of "twenty-two years" has been explained on the basis of the fact that since Benjamin the Righteous saved the life of the mother and her seven children he thereby "fulfilled the whole Torah which is written with the twenty-two letters of the Hebrew alphabet," for each letter of which he was added one year of life. (18) Proverbs 8:20. (19) Ruth 2:19. (20) Ruth Rabbah 5:9. (21) Shemoth Rabbah 31:5. (22) Exodus 22:24. (23) Isaiah 49:13. (24) *Ibid.,* 14:32. (25) Proverbs 19:7. (26) *Ibid.,* 14:20.

true of G-d. Although He is rich—as it is said, *Both riches and hon-
or come of Thee*[27] — He cares only for the poor, as it is said, *For the
Eternal hath founded Zion, and in her shall the poor of His people take
refuge.*[24] Therefore it is said,[28] *If thou lend money.*"[22]

It is known that here the conjunction *if—If thou lend money* does
not suggest an option, but a mandate. The verse means: "You are
obligated to lend money *to any of My people.*[22] If you must choose between lending money on interest to a non-Israelite friend or gratuitous-
ly to a poor Israelite, the poor Israelite takes precedence, as it is said,
even to the poor;[22] if you must choose between the poor of your city
and the poor of another city, the poor of your city comes first, as it is
said, *with thee,*[22] meaning who are physically with you; if between the
poor of your city and your poor relatives, your poor relatives come first,
as it is said, *even to the poor with thee.*[22] You are obligated to lend
money to the poor. If you do not, know that poverty may be with you,[29]
as it is said, *the poor with thee.*"[22]

Let no one say, "Since the poor are called 'G-d's people'[23] and He
loves them, why then does He Himself not support them?" The answer
is that G-d arranged His world in this way [with the rich supporting the
poor] only so that other people can earn merit and be rewarded
through the poor. The Sages explained:[5] "Rabbi Meir said, 'An oppo-
nent could raise the question: If your G-d loves the poor, why does He
not support them? You, in turn, should tell him that charity is for the
purpose of saving the donor from the judgment of Gehenna.' Turnus
Rufus [the Roman governor of Judea] asked this question of Rabbi
Akiba, who gave him the answer mentioned above. Turnus Rufus rejoined: 'On the contrary, You deserve the punishment of Gehenna
because of charity. I will illustrate my view with a parable, A king

(27) I Chronicles 29:12.   (28) The thought suggested is that since the poor are the
concern of G-d, we must walk in His ways and lend money to the poor in order to
enable them to gain their economic self-sufficiency.   (29) Although you may deem
yourself protected by your wealth, know that at the slightest turn of fortune poverty is
close to you.

became angry at his slave and imprisoned him. The king further decreed that no one should feed the slave. One individual, however, went and fed him. Now, when the king will have become aware of it, should he not be angry at that individual? Since you Israelites are called slaves—as it is said, *For unto Me are the children of Israel servants*[30]—[it follows that no one should support your poor]!' Rabbi Akiba answered: 'I will give you another parable. A king became angry at his son and imprisoned him. The king further decreed that no one should feed him. One individual, however, went and fed him. When the king will have become aware of it, should he not send that individual a gift for his act? Since we Israelites are called G-d's children—as it is said, *Ye are the children of the Eternal your G-d*[31]—[it is thus fitting to support our poor].' Turnus Rufus, however, replied, 'When you do the will of G-d you are called His children, but now that you are not doing His will [as evidenced by the destruction of the Temple], you are called slaves.' Rabbi Akiba answered: 'Scripture says, *Is it not to deal thy bread to the hungry, and that thou bring the poor that are cast out to thy house?*[32] When do we find *the poor that are cast out?* We find them now, in our present circumstances, and yet Scripture nonetheless states, *Is it not to deal thy bread to the hungry?*' "[32]

One should be heedful concerning the practice of charity, for it is equal in importance to all the commandments, as it is said, *Also we made ordinances for us, to charge ourselves yearly with the third part of a shekel for the service of the House of our G-d.*[33] When one disburses his money for charity, he is storing away eternal treasures for his soul in heaven, as Solomon said, *He that soweth charity hath a sure*

(30) Leviticus 25:55.   (31) Deuteronomy 14:1.   (32) Isaiah 58:7. (33) Nehemiah 10:33. "Scripture does not state 'ordinance,' but *ordinances*. Hence, you derive the principle that charity is of equal importance to all the commandments." (Baba Bathra 9a)—"The levy was *the third part of a shekel* [instead of the half a *shekel*] because in the days of Ezra [and Nehemiah] they added to the value of a *shekel*, so that the third of a *shekel* was then ten *gerahs* [the equivalent of half a *shekel* in the days of Moses]" (Ramban, Commentary on the Torah, Exodus, p. 512).

reward.[34] All other sowings are subject to blight, hail, and other external occurrences, but the sowings of charity always succeed and are the treasures in heaven. The Sages expounded:[17] "It happened that King Monbaz[35] distributed his own treasures and those of his father in the years of famine. The entire household joined together and said to him, 'Your ancestors saved treasures and added to those of the former generations, while you squander your treasures and those of your father.' He replied, 'My ancestors stored up treasures below, while I am storing them in heaven, as it is said, *And charity hath looked down from heaven.*[36] My ancestors stored away their treasures in a place which can be reached by human hands, while I am storing them away in a place that cannot be reached by human hands, as it is said, *Charity and justice are the foundation of Thy Throne.*[37] My ancestors stored them away in a place where they do not bear fruit, while I am storing them away in a place which does bear fruit, as it is said, *Say ye of the righteous, that it shall be well with him, for they shall eat the fruit of their doings.*[38] My ancestors stored away treasures of money, while I am storing away treasures of souls, as it is said, *The fruit of the righteous is a tree of life.*[39] My ancestors stored away for others, while I am storing for myself, as it is said, *And it shall be charity unto thee.*'"[40]

A person is obligated to give charity according to his means and the goodness of his heart. He should give it secretly. If he does not do so, his merit is incomplete, and this is especially so if he gives charity with an unhappy countenance and reproaches the recipient. One who does so commits a sin and forfeits the merit of his charity. Therefore, it is forbidden to reproach a poor man, for his grief over his dependence upon others is enough of a reproach in itself. On the contrary, one is

(34) Proverbs 11:18.   (35) Monbaz was a son of Queen Helena, ruler of Adiabena, a district of Assyria. In the days of the Second Temple, Helena and her entire family converted to Judaism. They became proficient in the study of Torah, and their names are often mentioned in the Talmud.   (36) Psalms 85:12.   (37) *Ibid.*, 89:15.   (38) Isaiah 3:10.   (39) Proverbs 11:30.   (40) Deuteronomy 24:13.

obligated to share in the poor man's grief, for this is part of charity. Job, for example, who was a non-Israelite, claimed that he fed, clothed, and shared in the sorrow of the poor, saying, *If I have not wept for him that was in trouble.*[41]

One who causes others to give charity is more meritorious than one who merely gives charity himself. The Sages explained:[42] "Rabbi Eleazar said, 'One who causes others to do good is more meritorious than one who merely does good himself, for it is said, *And the work of charity shall be peace.*'[43] Rava said to the inhabitants of Mechuza,[44] 'Take care of one another so that you will have peace in the affairs of the city.' "

The redemption of captives is a commandment related to giving charity, and it is even greater than the latter.[45] "It is a great commandment." It is possible to say that because of the greatness of this commandment, G-d lauded Himself with it in the first of the Ten Commandments, when He said, *I am the Eternal thy G-d Who brought thee out of the land of Egypt.*[46] He did not describe Himself as the One "Who created heaven and earth" because He wanted to mention the commandment of redeeming captives—600,000 of them in this case—which is greater than the mighty wonder of Creation. Indeed, G-d has commanded us, *And thou shalt walk in His ways.*[47]

Charity annuls many punitive decrees, as it is said, *A gift in secret pacifieth anger,*[48] We find in the Talmud,[5] "Rabbi Yehudah says, 'Charity is great, for it brings the Redemption nearer, as it is said, *Thus saith the Eternal: Keep ye justice, and do charity, for My salvation is near to come, and My favor to be revealed.*' "[49]

---

(41) Job 30:28.   (42) Baba Bathra 9 a.   (43) Isaiah 32:17. *"The work of charity* is the work involved in bringing others to give" (Rashi, Baba Bathra 9 a).   (44) A Babylonian city in which Rava resided.   (45) Baba Bathra 8 b.   (46) Exodus 20:2.   (47) Deuteronomy 28:9.   (48) Proverbs 21:14.   (49) Isaiah 56:1.

צִיצִית
The Precept of Tzitzith

The traditional commandments are the mainstay of Israel's sanctity / Among the traditional commandments, that regarding 'Tzitzith' is equal in importance to all the commandments / The simple and Midrashic explanations for this commandment / Careful observance of the commandments of 'Tzitzith, Mezuzah,' and the declaration of the sanctity of the Sabbaths and festivals affords compensation in this world. However, the principal reward for one who observes these precepts is stored away in the World to Come / Similarly, we find that G-d requited Joseph in this world with the fruits of his reward and saved the principal for the World to Come / The future Redemption will be in the merit of Jacob and Joseph.

The Precept of Tzitzith

SHE [THE WOMAN OF VALOR] SEEKETH WOOL AND
FLAX, AND WORKETH WILLINGLY WITH HER HANDS.[1]

It is known that Israel's sanctity is dependent upon the commandments, as the Sages said in the Sifre:[2] "The verse, *Sanctify yourselves,*[3]
refers to the sanctity of the commandments." These are the traditional
commandments[4] which are the mainstay of Israel's sanctity. Our Rabbis, the Sages of the Truth, ordained that before we fulfill these
precepts, we should recite the benediction, " . . . Who has sanctified
us with His commandments and commanded us etc."[5] Because of these
traditional commandments, Israel at Sinai was called *a holy nation,* as
it is said, *And ye shall be unto Me a kingdom of priests and a holy nation.*[6] No people would be called *a holy nation* by fulfilling the rational
commandments; the nations that are *void of counsel, and there is no
understanding in them,*[7] are also engaged in some of the rational com-

---

(1) Proverbs 31:13. The toil of the ideal wife is one of pleasure. Working the
material of wool and flax into garments for her household, she bestows her individuali-
ty upon her family. — The connection of this verse to the theme of *Tzitzith* will be made
clear in the text which follows. (2) Sifre, *Shelach,* 115. (3) Leviticus
11:44. (4) "These are the commandments which no person would have conceived by
himself, nor would anyone have founded them based upon his reason. Instead, they require a foundation of tradition, like the commandments of the Shofar, the Succah,
etc." (Rabbeinu Bachya's introduction to the Book of Genesis). (5) Thus, no
benediction is recited before the fulfillment of any of the rational commandments, for
their fulfillment is not a specific expression of sanctity, as the author explains
further. (6) Exodus 19:6. (7) Deuteronomy 32:28.

mandments [but are by no means considered holy]. Likewise, the Sages did not ordain the recitation of a benediction over the fulfillment of the rational commandments since the main blessing and holiness [of the commandments] are found only in the traditional precepts.[8]

Among the traditional commandments is that of *Tzitzith* (Fringes). In order to emphasize its importance, our Sages hyperbolized that it is equal in significance to all of the commandments. They achieved this by *gimatria* (the use of letters for their numerical value) as follows:[9] "The word *tzitzith* is numerically equivalent to six hundred.[10] With the eight threads and five knots,[11] the total is thus 613." Every person learned in the mysteries of the Torah will see that the commandment of *Tzitzith* is indeed equal in importance to all the commandments [which total 613], and that it contains the root of all of the precepts. The Sages merely adjoined their tradition regarding *Tzitzith* and their knowledge thereof to the *gimatria* so that the latter would serve as proof and attestation of their tradition. Tradition, after all, is the main principle, "and the *gimatrioth* are merely the ancillaries of wisdom."[12]

(8) The thought suggested is that in fulfilling the traditional commandments no other element enters into it except the belief in His existence and sovereignty. Hence, the spiritual benefit and holiness that the observance confers upon the individual is complete. In the fulfillment of the rational commandments, however, the human factor may enter, causing the person to believe that it is of his own mind that he is duty bound to perform that act, and therefore, the blessing and holiness of the commandment cannot be complete. (9) Rashi, Menachoth 43 b.(10) *Tzitzith* is spelled *tzadi-yod-tzadi-yod-tav*. Respectively, the letters are numerically equal to ninety, ten, ninety, ten, and four hundred. Their sum is thus six hundred. (11) Four sets of four threads are especially woven for their use as *Tzitzith*. Half the length of each set is then passed through openings in the four corners of a squared garment. With four half-threads on each side of each opening, there are thus a total of eight threads suspended from every corner of the garment. The full length generally measures over two feet. However, each set of four has one thread, called the *shamash* (beadle), which is longer than the others in the set. The *shamash* is wound around the seven half-threads of each group in four series of windings. The first series from the top has seven windings, the second eight windings, the third eleven, and the fourth thirteen. Each series terminates in a knot made by tying four of the half-threads with the other four. Together with the first upper knot which precedes the first series of windings, there are thus five knots to each group of threads. (12) Aboth 3:23.

The simple explanation for this commandment is that it constitutes a reminder of all the commandments. The requirement of white and blue threads mentioned in the Scriptural passage[13] is not two separate commandments but rather a single precept. Thus, if one dons a garment which has only white fringes or white and blue fringes together, he fulfills only one commandment in either case, for it is said, *And they shall put with the fringe of each corner a thread of blue.*[13] *And it shall be unto you for a fringe.*[14] The verse thus teaches us that the two [kinds of thread, white and blue], comprise one commandment.

The law requires seven white threads and one blue,[15] for it states, *a thread of blue,*[13] i.e., one thread of blue. The blue color was imparted to the wool thread by dying it in the blood of the *chalazon,* a fish found in the *Yam Hamelach.*[16] Some authorities say that there must be two blue treads and six white.[17] It is known that the white threads are the main part of *Tzitzith.* In making the windings,[11] one must begin and end with the white thread,[18] for Scripture states, *And they shall put with the fringe of each corner a thread of blue.*[13] *And it shall be unto you for a fringe.*[14] Scripture thus begins and ends with the white fringe and mentions the blue in their midst.

Although at present we do not have the blue thread,[19] we are nevertheless obligated to observe the precept of *Tzitzith* for even when the

(13) See Numbers 15:38. (14) *Ibid.,* Verse 39. (15) This is the opinion of Maimonides in his Mishneh Torah, *Hilchoth Tzitzith* 1:6. (16) *Ibid.,* 2:2. Generally, *Yam Hamelach* (Salt Sea) is the Hebrew name for the Dead Sea in the Land of Israel. However, since nothing lives in the waters of the Dead Sea, we must understand the term *Yam Hamelach* as a reference to the Mediterranean Sea, which is also salty, although to a far lesser degree. (17) This is the opinion of Rabbi Abraham ben David, known as the Rabad, as expressed in his notes on Maimonides, *ibid.,* 1:6. (18) He must begin the winding with the white thread in order to adjoin the whiteness of the thread to the corner of the garment which is white. He must conclude the winding with the white thread because of the general principle "we may promote a thing to a higher degree of sanctity, but not degrade it." Since the windings were started with the white thread, we must also conclude the windings with it (*ibid.,* 1:7). (19) The blue thread can be dyed only with the blood of the *chalazon,* which

blue thread was available, the white threads were the main component of the *Tzitzith*. Our Sages said:[20] "We have been taught in a Beraitha that Rabbi Meir used to say, 'Failure to don *Tzitzith* comprised solely of the white threads is more serious than failure to don those containing blue threads. This can be understood through a parable: A king said to his servants, Bring me two seals. He specified a gold seal to one servant, and a clay seal, which is more readily available, to the other.' " [Which of these servants will incur greater wrath of the king for failing to obey his request? Surely, the king will be angrier at the one to whom he specified a seal of clay], for that type of seal is commonly found and there can be no excuse for not fulfilling the royal command. [Regarding *Tzitzith,* too, the white threads are more readily available than the blue. Hence, failure to don *Tzitzith* of all white threads is a more serious offense than failing to don one containing the blue.]

In the Midrashic interpretation, the word *Tzitzith* denotes "seeing," as in the expression, *'Meitzitz' (Looking) from the lattice.*[21] The person who dons *Tzitzith* should be wary of sin for G-d sits on the Throne of Glory, which resembles the blue thread, and sees him.

In the language of the Sages, the garment which bears *Tzitzith* is called a *Talith,* which is an expression of height and elevation, as in the verse, *'U'ntilath' (And it was lifted up) from the earth.*[22] It is an allusion to Him Who is exalted and eminent above all. We are commanded to enwrap ourselves in the fringed garment on the basis of the Sages' explanation:[23] *"And the Eternal passed by before him.*[24] The verse teaches us that the Holy One, blessed be He, enwrapped Himself on Sinai like a reader of a congregation and showed Moses the order of prayer. He said to Moses, 'Whenever Israel will sin, let them perform

---

we cannot identify. In modern times, one spiritual leader of the Chasidic Radziner dynasty did identify the *chalazon,* and his followers wear *Tzitzith* comprised of white and blue threads. (20) Menachoth 43 b. (21) Song of Songs 2:9. (22) Daniel 7:4. (23) Rosh Hashanah 17 b. (24) Exodus 34:6.

this service before Me. I will then forgive them all their sins.' " The intent of this text is to teach us the order of prayer and supplication and to instruct us to enwrap ourselves in a fringed garment and devotedly recite the Thirteen Attributes[25] before Him. Because of these acts, G-d will forgive our sins.

In the above passage, when the Sages said G-d "enwrapped Himself," they meant with a white garment, for Scripture says, *Who coverest Thyself with light as with a garment.*[26] It is further stated, *His raiment was as white snow,*[27] and we have been commanded, *And thou shalt walk in His ways.*[28] We are therefore obligated to enwrap ourselves in a white garment, for white is a sign of forgiveness and atonement just as red is a sign of sin. Thus, the prophet Isaiah said, *Though your sins be as scarlet, they shall be as white as snow.*[29] The donning of the fringed garment is also an allusion to G-d, Who clothes His creatures, as it is said, *And the Eternal G-d made for Adam and for his wife garments of skin, and clothed them.*[30] It further serves as an allusion to G-d because He will revive the dead and raise them in their garments, as it is written, *It is changed as clay under a seal, and they stand as a garment.*[31]

The Sages said:[32] "One who regularly observes[33] the commandment of *Tzitzith* will merit a beautiful garment. One who regularly observes[33] the commandment of the *Mezuzah*[34] will merit a beautiful dwelling. One who regularly declares the sanctity of Sabbaths and festivals will merit jars filled with wine." Of course these rewards are not the principal recompense for the observance of these commandments. Heaven forbid! Instead, these are only the by-products thereof which one receives in this world. The principal reward for the faithful observer, is stored away in the World to Come. The earthly reward is

(25) See above at end of *Kippurim* (Atonement) for an explanation of the Thirteen Attributes of G-d. (26) Psalms 104:2. (27) Daniel 7:9. (28) Deuteronomy 28:9. (29) Isaiah 1:18. (30) Genesis 3:21. (31) Job 38:14. (32) Shabbath 23 b. (33) In our editions of the Talmud, *ibid.*, the reading is: "One who strictly observes, etc." (34) See above in *Mezuzah*, Note 13.

.

given him measure for measure. One who regularly observes the commandment of *Tzitzith* will be privileged to have beautiful clothes which will bring him honor in this world. Similarly, if one regularly observes the commandment of *Mezuzah*,[34] he will merit a beautiful home. Likewise, if he goes to the trouble of obtaining wine in order to declare the sanctity of the Sabbath or festival, rather than exempting himself by reciting the *Kiddush* (Sanctification) over bread, he will merit treasures of wine. However, the principal reward for fulfilling these and other commandments lies in the World to Come.

We find in the case of Joseph that G-d recompensed him in this world with the by-products of his reward while the principal reward remained for him in the World to Come, as the Sages said in the Midrash:[35] "G-d recompensed Joseph for whatever he did. It is written of Joseph, *And he fled, and went outdoors.*[36] Therefore, when the sea saw his coffin, it fled, as it is said, *The sea saw it, and fled.*[37] What did it see? It saw the coffin of Joseph. Moreover, Joseph's coffin preceded[38] the Ark of the Eternal. The nations of the world said to the Israelites: 'What is the nature of this chest that is carried together with the Ark of the Torah?' The Israelites answered, 'It is the coffin of Joseph.' " Joseph deserved this honor because he observed whatever is written in the Torah. G-d said to Joseph,[39] "I have only partly paid you your reward; the principal thereof is stored away for you in the World to Come. Israel's permanent Redemption will be in the merit of your father Jacob and in your merit, as it is said, *Thou hast with Thine arm redeemed Thy people the sons of Jacob and Joseph, Selah.*"[40]

(35) Mechilta, *Beshalach, P'sichta.* (36) Genesis 39:12. (37) Psalms 114:3. (38) In our editions of the Mechilta, the reading is: "proceeded alongside." However, the Tanchuma, end of *Naso,* also states "preceded." (39) Tanchuma, *loc. cit.* (40) Psalms 77:16.

קדושה
Essentials of Holiness

The essential elements of holiness / Israel was sanctified at Sinai with two qualities: purity and holiness. Holiness is divided into nine parts, all of which emanate from the Sanctuary / The ministering angels, G-d's host on high, likewise derive their holiness from the Sanctuary. Israel, G-d's host on earth, are thus akin to the ministering angels / Why the word 'Holy' is repeated thrice by the angels in their praise of G-d / G-d loves Israel more than He does the ministering angels.

Essentials of Holiness

A G-D DREADED IN THE GREAT COUNCIL OF THE HOLY
ONES, AND FEARED BY ALL OF THEM THAT ARE ROUND
ABOUT HIM.[1]

A person attains the mighty and wonderful quality of holiness
through purity. That is the sequence of the attributes, as the Sages explained:[2] "Purity leads one to holiness." This is proven in the
Yerushalmi,[3] for it says, *And he shall purify it, and hallow it.*[4]
Concerning the quality of holiness, we have been commanded in the
Torah, *And ye shall sanctify yourselves, and be ye holy.*[5] It is likewise
stated, *Ye shall be holy, for I the Eternal your G-d am Holy.*[6]

The nature of this holiness[7] concerning which we have been commanded is that a person should practice self-restraint and even avoid
indulging in those pleasures which are permissible, as the Sages said,[8]
"Sanctify yourself even in permissible matters." For example, one
should eat and drink permissible things only to sustain his body and he
should engage in sexual intercourse only for the purpose of procre-

(1) Psalms 89:8. G-d's holiness is reflected throughout His abode in the heavens,
and in His relations to Israel. Whatever change takes place in the whole world it is He
Who has decreed it, since He is the undisputed Ruler over all. (2) Abodah Zarah
20 b. (3) Yerushalmi Shekalim, end of Chapter 3. (4) Leviticus 16:19. The High
Priest shall purify the altar of incense of its past defilement, and sanctify it for future
use. (5) *Ibid.*, 11:44. (6) *Ibid.*, 19:2. (7) The explanation which follows in the
text is based upon Ramban's interpretation of the concept of holiness. See his Commentary on the Torah, Leviticus, pp. 282-284. (8) Yebamoth 20 a.

ation, fulfilling the commandment concerning conjugal rights,[9] or evading sinful thoughts. All other motivations are forbidden by law of the Torah.[10] Similarly, one should discipline himself to speak sparingly. He should strive to be even more concise than necessary except in those matters which involve his spiritual welfare, such as conversation pertaining Torah matters, or those which involve physical welfare, i.e., livelihood and sustenance. One should also avoid touching his body, especially below his belt, with his bare hands. On account of self-restraint in this regard, Rabbi Yehudah the Prince was called Rabbeinu Hakadosh, as the Sages said:[11] "Why do they call him Rabbeinu Hakadosh? It is because he never lowered his hands below his belt." All of these matters are part of holiness and self-restraint.

The Sages explained in Torath Kohanim:[12] "*And ye shall sanctify yourselves, and be ye holy.*[5] Just as I [G-d] am Holy, so should you be holy. Just as I abstain, so should you abstain." Thus far the Torath Kohanim. There is a great purpose and benefit contained in this commandment. Had it not been written, a person would easily become addicted to filling himself with permissible food and uttering any thoughts that come to his mind. He would ultimately make himself abominable with evil habits, all of which would be within the legal limitations of the Torah! Therefore, after listing the prohibited foods, the Torah directed, *And ye shall sanctify yourselves, and be ye holy,*[5] thus warning people to be abstemious even with permissible foods just as one abstains altogether from forbidden foods. If one who abstains from a forbidden food is called "holy," *a fortiori* one who abstains from permissible things is certainly worthy of being called "holy," for he has

---

(9) See Exodus 21:10. (10) "By law of the Torah." This phrase is not found in the Rome Manuscript of Kad Hakemach. (11) Shabbath 118 b. Regarding the name *Rabbeinu Hakadosh,* see above, *Ahavah* (Love), Note 42. (12) Sifra, end of *Shemini.* Torah Kohanim (The Law of the Priests) is the name of the book containing the Tannaitic interpretations of the Book of Leviticus. It is also known as Sifra, which is to be distinguished from Sifre, the corresponding work on the Books of Numbers and Deuteronomy. — It should be noted that while G-d's abstention is absolute, man's abstention can only be relative, within the confines of human nature.

humbled and broken his desire in the mortar of his reason in honor of his Creator, blessed be He.

Israel was sanctified at Sinai with two qualities: purity and holiness. When a non-Jew comes to find shelter under the wings of the Divine Presence [i.e., to become a proselyte], he must undergo circumcision and immersion and he must bring an offering.[13] The essential goal of these three requirements is purity. One must undergo circumcision because the foreskin is called "impurity."[14] Therefore, he must be circumcised to become pure. He must undergo immersion because purity is principally attained through water. He must also bring an offering because sin is called "impurity"; one who atones for his sin through an offering is pure. At Sinai, Israel was also sanctified with holiness, as it is written, *And ye shall be unto Me a kingdom of priests and a holy nation.*[15]

It is a known fact that all forms of holiness emanate from the Sanctuary [i.e., from G-d Who abides in the Sanctuary], just as a river flows from its stream, and the stream from its source. Now, at Sinai, at the Giving of the Torah, Israel was divided into three categories: priests,[16] Levites, and Israelites. All together they were sanctified with a total of nine degrees of holiness. Thus: the priest was sanctified in his own right, as a Levite [for he was indeed a member of the tribe of Levi] and as an Israelite, for he was also part of the people of Israel. The Levite was sanctified in his own right and was also hallowed through the priests who were part of his tribe and through the sanctity of Israel. Thus, there are six forms of holiness. The Israelite was sanctified in his

---

(13) Kerithoth 9 a. See above in *Geir* and *Kippurim* where this topic is also mentioned.   (14) Isaiah 52:1: *The uncircumcised and the unclean* shall no more come into Jerusalem. — The prophet thus mentioned together the uncircumcised and the unclean, implying that the one is equally rejectionable as the other.   (15) Exodus 19:6.   (16) Strictly speaking, the priests and Levites did not replace the priestly functions of the firstborn until after the firstborn were disqualified on account of having worshipped the golden calf — an event which took place forty days after the Giving of the Torah. We must then say that the author's use of the phrase "at Sinai, at the Giving of the Torah" is to be understood "at the season of the Giving of the Torah," which was somewhat later than the Revelation at Sinai.

own right and was also hallowed with the sanctity of the king, [who must be an Israelite].[17] Finally, the priest, Levite, and Israelite each derived his sanctity from [Him Who abides in] the Sanctuary. Hence, you have nine degrees of holiness.

Scripture has compared Israel to the ministering angels, whose holiness also emanates from the Sanctuary, as it is written, *And He came* [to Sinai] *from the holy myriads.*[18] Israel is G-d's host on earth even as the ministering angels are His host above. All laud Him in unison and honor His Name. The angels in their sanctity and Israel in its hallowed state praise the Name of the Holy One with the expression "Holy." Isaiah the prophet testified that he heard groups of ministering angels praising G-d, as it is written, *And one called unto another, and said: Holy, Holy, Holy is the Eternal of hosts; the whole earth is full of His Glory.*[19] With reference to this, David said here, *A G-d dreaded in the great council of the holy ones, and feared by all of them that are round about Him.*[1] That is to say, He is even more awesome than indicated by all the praise with which He is lauded, as it is written, *He is exalted above all blessing and praise.*[20]

According to the plain meaning of Scripture, the word *Holy* is repeated three times because the first two are a form of address; one angel calls another, "Holy, holy." This repetition is similar to *Moses, Moses*[21] and *Samuel, Samuel.*[22] [The first angel then continues "Let us sanctify G-d in unison and say],[23] *Holy is the Eternal of hosts; the whole earth is full of His Glory.*"[19] It may be that all three words are a reference to G-d, Who founded the world and created it in three parts: the realm of the angels, the spheres, and the lower world. The explanation of the verse would then be that G-d is "*Holy* in the lower world, *Holy* in the spheres, *Holy* in the realm of the angels." The devotion and thought would thus proceed upwards from below, declaring that "G-d is Holy and One in all the worlds with all their hosts."

(17) Deuteronomy 17:15. (18) *Ibid.,* 33:2. (19) Isaiah 6:3. (20) Nehemiah 9:5. (21) Exodus 3:4. (22) I Samuel 3:10. (23) This interpretation is found in Rabbi David Kimchi's commentary on Isaiah 6:3.

Blessing and holiness are equivalent, for blessing emanates from holiness, as it is written, *Lift up your hands to the Sanctuary, and bless ye the Eternal.*[24] Therefore, a person should not pause between the recitation of *Holy, Holy,* etc., and *Blessed be the Glory of the Eternal from His place.*[25] There are many people who are not careful in this matter. Yet, this was included in the statement of the Sages:[26] "*When vileness is exalted among the sons of men.*[27] This refers to the things which stand at the height of the universe and which are treated lightly by man." I am almost inclined to say that one who speaks and interrupts between the two verses of the *Kedushah* is like one who mutilates the shoots of faith.

You should know that the expression "mutilating the shoots of faith" is applied by our Rabbis to two types of people: one who completely ceases his own study of Torah or causes others to cease or annul it, and one who strays from the path of the true faith to believe in the existence of two supreme powers or to entertain any thoughts about their possible existence. Either one of these types is termed "one who mutilates the shoots of faith." Elisha ben Abuyah, known as Acheir,[28] was such a person. The Sages related in Midrash Shir Hashirim Rabbah:[29] "Elisha ben Abuyah mutilated the shoots of faith. He would enter synagogues and houses of learning, and seeing children succeeding in the study of Torah, he would utter words of perversion to them, causing them to stop learning." This clearly explains that the Sages called the interruption of learning Torah an act of mutilating the shoots of faith, and the same applies to an interruption in the *Kedushah* prayer between the verses '*Holy*' and '*Blessed.*'[25] However, one who prays with proper devotion and who does not interrupt his

(24) Psalms 134:2.   (25) Ezekiel 3:12. This verse together with the verse (*Holy, Holy,* etc.) are part of the *Kedushah* (Sanctification) recited by the individual before the reading of the *Sh'ma* at the Morning Service, and also in the public Service during the repetition of the *Shemoneh Esreih.*   (26) Berachoth 6 b.   (27) Psalms 12:9.   (28) See above, *Kibbud Av V'eim* (Honoring Father and Mother), Note 34.   (29) Shir Hashirim Rabbah 1:28.

prayer by speaking will have his prayer fulfilled, as it is said, *Thou wilt direct their heart, Thou wilt cause Thine ear to attend.*[30]

In Tractate Chullin, the Sages expounded:[31] "G-d loves Israel more than He does the ministering angels, for Israel may recite songs to G-d at all times and hours whenever they so desire, but the ministering angels may recite such praise only once a day, or as others contend, once a week, or once a month, or once a year, or once a Sabbathical cycle, or once a Jubilee, or as some contend only once for all time. Moreover, Israel mentions the Name of G-d after two words, as it says, *Hear O Israel, the Eternal our G-d,*[32] while the ministering angels mention G-d's Name after three words, as it says, *Holy, Holy, Holy is the Eternal of hosts.*[19] Furthermore, the ministering angels above do not recite songs to G-d until Israel does so below, for it is said, *When the morning stars sang together, and all the angels of G-d shouted for joy.*[33]

(30) Psalms 10:17. (31) Chullin 91 b. (32) Deuteronomy 6:4. In Hebrew, the Divine Name is mentioned here right after the two words: *Sh'ma Yisrael (Hear, O Israel).* (33) Job 38:7. *The morning stars* is a reference to Israel, which is like the stars (Rashi, Chullin 91 b). Thus, after *the morning stars*, the people of Israel, sing together, the angels of G-d then shout for joy.

קנאה

Jealousy

Jealousy is an incurable sickness / The sin of jealousy has brought many ruinations upon the world / The opposite of jealousy is 'a gentle heart' / The repulsiveness of jealousy exists only in worldly matters. In the study of Torah and the performance of good deeds, jealousy is a worthwhile quality.

Jealousy

A GENTLE HEART IS THE LIFE OF THE FLESH, BUT ENVY
IS THE DECAY OF THE BONES.[1]

Throughout the entire Book of Proverbs, Solomon consistently de-
nounced repulsive characteristics and praised desirable ones. In most
of the verses, various traits are presented as antitheses.

In the verse before us,[1] the *gentle heart* is a healthy heart, for it is a
good heart that is jealous of no one. On the other hand, one who envies
the wealth of his fellow man will always be subject to a feeling of
discontent until his acquisitions equal those possessed by another.
However, even if he attains this goal, he will then seek to acquire honor
and power in worldly matters. From an obsession with power, he will
proceed to worship idols. If, in the first instance, he will not obtain the
wealth he seeks, he will be miserable throughout his life. Ultimately, he
will cause either his own undoing or that of his friend. He will cause his
own undoing, as the Sages said,[2] "Jealousy, desire, and ambition take a
man from the world." Eliphaz too said, *And envy slayeth the silly one.*[3]
That is to say, by allowing himself to be enticed by envy, he brings
death upon himself or his friend. Envy will lead him to hatred, and

---

(1) Proverbs 14:30. The contrast between the life of tranquility and gentleness,
which give health to body and mind, and the life of envy with its corroding effect, are
here clearly indicated. The text will elaborate on this theme. (2) Aboth
4:28. (3) Job 5:2. Eliphaz the Temanite was one of Job's friends who had come to
console Job on his misfortunes.

556

hatred to murder, for it is written, *And if any man hate his neighbor, and lie in wait for him, and rise up against him, and smite him mortally that he die.*[4]

However, one who is wholehearted possesses what the Sages call "a good heart." He is not envious of his friends, as they explained in Tractate Aboth:[5] "What is a good demeanor to which a man should cleave? Rabbi Eleazar [ben Arach] said, 'It is a good heart.' " Rabban Yochanan ben Zaccai concludes the Mishnah, "I approve of the words of Rabbi Eleazar, for his words include yours."[6] Similarly, Solomon called [the "good heart"] *a gentle heart,*[1] for envy is the opposite of gentleness, even as *the decay of the bones*[1] is the antithesis of *the life of the flesh.*[1] The intention thereof is to state that one will live with the quality of a gentle heart, and that one will die on account of envy. The expression *decay of the bones* bespeaks an incurable sickness. When the flesh decays, it can be renewed, but the bones cannot. Envy, too, is an incurable disease. The wise man expressed it thus in his ethical epigrams:[7] "All forms of hatred have a remedy except envy."

It is known that Korach did not seriously contend against Moses until he became completely arrogant, and it was this quality which drove him out of the world. Korach believed that Moses our teacher was making appointments and bestowing honors on his own volition, not at the command of G-d. From Moses' response to Korach's supporters, *. . . I have not done them of mine own mind,*[8] you can deduce Korach's evil intention, i.e., he accused Moses of doing these things on his own authority. Korach claimed that the purpose of the substitution of the Levites [for the firstborn Israelites to perform the Divine Service

---

(4) Deuteronomy 19:11. The teaching is clear: hatred leads to bloodshed. (5) Aboth 2:9. (6) Various opinions were expressed, *ibid.*, by Rabban Yochanan ben Zaccai's other disciples. Thus: "Rabbi Eliezer said, 'A good eye.' Rabbi Yehoshua said, 'A good friend.' Rabbi Yosei said, 'A good neighbor.' Rabbi Shimon said, 'One who foresees the fruit of an action.' " (7) Found in Solomon ibn Gabirol's *Mivchar Ha'pninim* (Choice of Pearls), quoted in Israel Davidson's Otzar Hameshalim V'hapithgamim, p. 28. (8) Numbers 16:28.

in the Tabernacle] was only to give prominence and glory to the children of Levi, Moses' family. Korach was also provoked over the appointment of Elizaphan the son of Uzziel as prince of the Kohathite families;[9] Uzziel was the youngest of Moses' uncles on his father's side, [while Korach's father Itzhar was an older uncle].[10] The Sages expounded:[11] "What induced Korach to quarrel with Moses? He envied the princehood of Elizaphan the son of Uzziel. Korach claimed, 'My father and his brothers were four: Amram, Itzhar, Hebron, and Uzziel.[10] Moses and Aaron, the sons of Amram, the eldest, assumed high positions. Moses, [as leader of the nation], became a veritable king, and Aaron became High Priest. Who is entitled to assume the next highest position? Is it not I, the son of Itzhar, who was closest in age to Amram? Yet Moses has appointed the son of Amram's youngest brother Uzziel as prince over the Kohathites. I will therefore take issue with him and annul his decision." What did Korach do? He assembled four hundred men who were heads of judicial courts. Most of them were from the tribe of Reuben.[12] He then had all of them dress in robes of blue wool." The Sages explained this in the Midrash:[11] "*And Korach took.*[13] What did he take? He took his robe and came before Moses. All of his men did the same. They said to Moses, 'Is a garment entirely of blue wool subject to the law of *Tzitzith* (Fringes)?' Moses answered, 'It is subject to that law.' Thereupon, they began to jest: 'Is this possible? Just one thread of blue fulfills the requirement for a garment of any other color, yet a robe that is entirely blue does not exempt itself! [They further asked,] Is a house full of holy Scrolls of the Torah subject to the law of *Mezuzah*?' Moses answered, 'It is subject to the law.' They rejoined: 'The entire Torah, which contains 275 sections does not ex-

(9) See *ibid.*, 3:30.   (10) Exodus 6:18. *The sons of Kohath* [listed in their order of birth, beginning with the eldest]: *Amram, and Itzhar, and Hebron, and Uzziel.*   (11) Bamidbar Rabbah 18:1-2, and Tanchuma, *Korach*, 1-2. The quotation here follows that of Rashi at the beginning of *Korach*.   (12) The Reubenites were the neighbors of Korach, for both encamped on the south side of the Tabernacle. See Numbers 2:10 and 3:9.   (13) *Ibid.*, 16:1.

empt the house from a *Mezuzah,* yet a single *Mezuzah* fulfills the requirement! Apparently, G-d has not commanded these laws, but you are proclaiming them on your own.' "

In his wisdom Solomon mentioned the general categories in which jealousy is prevalent. He stated, *Again, I considered all labor and all excelling in work that it is from jealousy of one toward the other.* [14] *All labor* refers to material acquisitions such as riches, properties, honors, and other manifestations of power. The phrase, *all excelling in work* connotes Torah, repentance, and good deeds. *It is from jealousy of one toward the other* in matters of both wealth and wisdom, that the desire to surpass one's fellow is ever present. *This is also 'hevel' (vanity).* [14] That is to say, *Hevel* (Abel) stumbled over *this* sin for he envied his brother Cain, who brought an offering of fruits to G-d. Prompted by his envy, Hevel arose and like his father, [15] brought an offering of animals. [16] This jealousy gave rise to hatred, and then to a quarrel over the inheritance of the earth until Abel was killed. Thus, jealousy was the cause of this tragedy. Jealousy was also responsible for the division of the united Kingdom of Israel [17] and the exile of the ten tribes, who were envious of the royalty which was bestowed upon the tribe of Judah. Thus, [in speaking of the future] the prophet said, *Ephraim shall not envy Judah.* [18]

Because this abominable and repulsive trait brings much harm and many ruinations upon man, Solomon called one who is devoid of jealousy *a gentle heart.* [1] The latter brings a healing to the body and soul and tranquility to the bones, as the Sages said: [19] "If one has no jealousy in his heart, his bones will not decay [in the grave]." However, if one has jealousy in his heart, his bones will decay, as it is said, *but envy is the decay of the bones.* [1]

---

(14) Ecclesiastes 4:4.   (15) Adam was the first to bring a living animal as an offering (Chullin 60 a).   (16) See Genesis 4:4.   (17) See I Kings 12:26-27.   (18) Isaiah 11:13. Ephraim is synonymous with the Kingdom of Israel, which consisted of ten tribes. It was founded by Jeroboam, who was of the tribe of Ephraim.   (19) Shabbath 152 b.

This jealousy of which we have been speaking is only with reference
to the vanities of the world—power, wealth, honor, and the perpetration of evil deeds. However, in regard to the Torah,[20] the commandments, and the performance of good deeds, envy is commendable. The
Sages stated,[21] "Envy among scholars increases wisdom." Solomon
likewise warned us to invest ourselves with envy only in matters affecting the fear of G-d, as he said, *Let not thy heart envy sinners, but
be in the fear of the Eternal all day.*[22]

(20) Thus, it is permissible to be envious of his friend's wider knowledge of the
Torah, for the result of this kind of envy will be the motive to increase his own
knowledge. The same reasoning applies to envy in the other matters
mentioned. (21) Baba Bathra 21 a. (22) Proverbs 23:17.

רשות

Deference to the Congregation
One Addresses

Part One

The four stages in the development of a righteous per-
son / The ultimate goal of the human soul is the study of
Torah and fulfillment of the commandments / The Congrega-
tion of Israel is equal in importance to the ministering
angels / The need for a speaker to be in reverential fear of his
audience.

Deference to the Congregation
One Addresses [1]

WHO IS SHE THAT LOOKETH FORTH AS THE DAWN,
FAIR AS THE MOON, CLEAR AS THE SUN, AS AWE-
INSPIRING AS AN ARMY WITH BANNERS? [2]

This verse speaks of the soul of the righteous man. As long as the soul is engaged in the study of Torah, the fulfillment of commandments, and the performance of good deeds, it progresses through the four stages of its development. The first stage is childhood, when the child is steeped in physical desires and his power of conception is weak. It is therefore necessary to *train a child in the way he should go.* [3] The second stage is adolescence, when the youth reaches the age at which he becomes obligated to fulfill the commandments. At that time, the

(1) Customarily, a speaker asks the permission of his audience before beginning his address. This practice is based upon the teaching of the Mishnah: "The wise man does not speak before one who is greater than he in wisdom" (Aboth 5:9). Out of respect to his audience, therefore, a speaker first requests permission to make his address. He will thus not be suspected of presuming to instruct his superiors. A perfect example thereof is found in Ramban's "Discourse on a Wedding," wherein he states: "Therefore I may not speak before you except by your leave, and I will furthermore speak only of those matters that you taught me" (Writings and Discourses, p. 6). Rabbeinu Bachya has here included ten of such requests which he uttered on various occasions. (2) Song of Songs 6:10. The four ways of describing the beauty of his beloved — *she looketh forth as the dawn, fair as the moon,* etc. — suggest the four ways of arousing the soul to higher achievements, as the text will explain. A congregation of worshippers is likened to these four overpowering elements. Therefore, the speaker must be in full cognizance of the merits of his audience. (3) Proverbs 22:6.

power of conception is strengthened in the soul, and the individual begins to engage in commandments and the performance of good deeds. The third stage is reached at forty years of age, when one's reasoning power reaches its peak. The fourth stage comes with old age, which is called *the evil days*.[4] The powers of the body are waning at that time, and one is completely engaged in the spiritual matters of service to G-d and prayer; it is the time when the individual desires G-d, to Whom he will cleave at the end.

Therefore, the verse with which we opened our remarks mentions four degrees of light—each higher than the other—alluding to the soul, which progresses from stage to stage until it attains its goal. Thus, Solomon first mentioned the light of *the dawn*,[2] the morning star, for just as its emanation of light is weak because of the darkness of the still surrounding night, so is the soul weak during childhood. Solomon continued with the phrase, *fair as the moon*.[2] The moon, which sheds more light than the morning star, symbolizes the soul which increases its light and power of conception as it gains a knowledge of the commandments and the study of Torah. However, the light of the moon tends towards darkness. Moreover, its light is borrowed from the sun. Therefore, Solomon added the description, *clear as the sun*,[2] which indicates that just as the light of the sun is clear and is not borrowed from elsewhere, so does the light of the soul proceed from itself. Yet, the sun is imperfect in itself and in its activity. It is imperfect in itself for it is sometimes eclipsed, as are the moon and stars. It is also imperfect in its activity since the heat of its rays can bring harm. Hence, Solomon finally said that the soul is *as awe-inspiring as an army with banners*,[2] a reference to groups of ministering angels that are comprised of the light of reason similar to the light of the soul. This is in contrast to the light of the sun, which is physical. This form of light is higher than that of the sun, as the Sages commented:[5] *"And there is no advantage*

---

(4) Ecclesiastes 12:1.   (5) Koheleth Rabbathi 1:4.

under the sun.[6] There is no advantage under the sun, but there is an advantage above the sun."

Accordingly, Solomon in his wisdom mentioned in this verse the four kinds of light, each higher than the other: the light of the morning star, the light of the moon, the light of the sun, and the light of the ministering angels. These correspond to the four stages in the development of the soul. Until the soul reaches its peak of development, its progress through the various stages is only a result of the study of Torah and the commandments.[7] Thus, the Sages said:[8] "G-d desired to make Israel worthy. Therefore, He increased their obligations through the Torah and the commandments."

In the Midrash, the Sages said:[9] *"Who is she that looketh forth as the dawn?*[2] Rabbi Chiya and Rabbi Shimon ben Chalafta were walking in the Valley of Arbel [in Galilee near Tzipori] and saw the first rays of the morning dawn. Rabbi Shimon said to Rabbi Chiya: 'Thus will the Redemption of Israel burst forth, as it is written, *Though I sit in darkness, the Eternal is a light to me.*[10] At first, only a little light comes forth, but then it bursts forth, increases and grows brighter and brighter. So will it be with the Redemption. At first, *In those days, Mordecai sat in the king's gate;*[11] afterwards, *And Mordecai went forth from the presence of the king in royal apparel;*[12] and finally, *The Jews had light and gladness.*"[13]

---

(6) Ecclesiastes 2:11. The thought suggested is that in all turns of fortune in the earthly scene of man's activities, there is little of abiding worth to the true meaning of man's existence. Only in that which is "above the sun," transcending the vicissitudes of time — in other words, in the life of Torah — is there true and abiding advantage to man. (7) See above, *Emunah* (Faith), Note 2, for an explanation of the phrase "Torah and the commandments." (8) Makkoth 23 b. (9) Shir Hashirim Rabbah 6:16. (10) Micah 7:8. (11) Esther 2:21. Mordecai's sitting in the king's gate was thus the beginning of the final relief of the Jews from the threat of Haman. In this way he came to know of the conspiracy of the king's chamberlains against the monarch's life. The record of this information, credited to Mordecai, played a vital role in the deliverance of the Jews. (12) *Ibid.*, 8:15. (13) *Ibid.*, Verse 16.

Solomon termed the Congregation of Israel *awe-inspiring as an army with banners*,[2] and the Midrash[9] teaches that in this respect Israel is like the ministering angels. Thus, whoever wishes to address the people of Israel must show fear before them. Even the priests, the seed of Aaron, who administer the Priestly Blessing, must be submissive to the people of Israel and stand in fear of them. The Sages commented:[14] "The fear of the public should always be before you, for even when the priests lift their hands [to recite the Priestly Blessings], they face the people[15] and have their backs towards the Sanctuary." Moreover, once an Israelite directs the priests to commence their Blessing, they must not refrain from doing so. A priest who does so refrain violates the positive commandment, *Ye shall say unto them*,[16] which is rendered by the Targum, "When ye [the Israelites] shall direct them [the priests]."[17] Now, if one who is a descendant of Aaron and who bears the crown of the priesthood must be submissive to the public, surely one who is not a priest, and certainly an Israelite such as I, must today show respect and fear of the public by speaking before them only with their permission.

(14) Sotah 40 a. See further in Part Three, where the author quotes this text again and offers additional explanation.   (15) The Priestly Blessing must be recited face to face.   (16) Numbers 6:23.   (17) In other words, when an Israelite calls upon the priests at a certain point in the public service to recite the Priestly Blessing, the priest who is present in the congregation and does not go up to the platform to recite it thereby violates a positive commandment of the Torah.

Part Two

David's complete reliance upon G-d and his fearlessness of any human being / The fear of G-d as an antidote to the fear of man / Although man in general is not to be feared, scholars, including the audience that one is to address, are to be reverently feared.

A PSALM OF DAVID, THE ETERNAL IS MY LIGHT AND MY SALVATION; WHOM SHALL I FEAR? THE ETERNAL IS THE STRONGHOLD OF MY LIFE; OF WHOM SHALL I BE AFRAID?[18]

David wrote this psalm with reference to his personal enemies, as he mentioned, *When evil-doers come upon me.*[19] He further stated, *Deliver me not over unto the will of mine adversaries.*[20] Some scholars[21] maintain that David was referring to the enemies of Israel and that he was acting as Israel's spokesman, as he did in many psalms.

According to either interpretation, the psalm demonstrates the great degree of perfection in David's character, for he utterly relied on the Holy One blessed be He, to guard his soul and body. He trusted that G-d would guard his body from his enemies in this world and that He would bind his soul with the bond of eternal life[22] in the World to Come. Hence, he said, *The Eternal is my light and my salvation,*[18] i.e., "He is *my light* in matters of the soul, which is the light of the body, and He is *my salvation* in matters of the body." The body is troubled by the perils and dangers of this world, which David overcame with the help of G-d. Therefore, David continued: Since G-d *is the stronghold of my life, of whom shall I be afraid?*[18] This is an essential aspect in the fear of G-d; as long as a person fears the power of a mortal man, his fear of G-d is incomplete, since the individual divides his fear between G-d and a mortal creature. Thus, David said, *In G-d do I trust, I will not be afraid; what can man do unto me?*[23] He further stated, *The Eternal is for me, I will not fear; what can man do unto me?*[24] Similarly

(18) Psalms 27:1. In a spirit of steadfast faith in G-d, the psalmist expresses the thought that his mind is no longer beset by the fear of man. However, as the text will show, the good man inevitably feels the fear of G-d, of the learned scholars of the Torah, and of the audience he is about to address. (19) *Ibid.*, Verse 2. (20) *Ibid.*, Verse 12. (21) Ibn Ezra, in his commentary (*ibid.*), mentions the first interpretation in the name of "Rabbi Moshe." The second interpretation is evidently that of Ibn Ezra himself. (22) See I Samuel 25:29. (23) Psalms 56:12. (24) *Ibid.*, 118:6.

566

the Torah removed the fear of man from our consideration and warned us not to fear the nations, as Scripture states, *When thou goest forth to battle against thine enemies, and seest horses and chariots and a people more* [numerous] *than thou, thou shalt not be afraid of them.*[25] It is further written, *If thou shalt say in thy heart, These nations are more* [numerous] *than I, etc.,*[26] *thou shalt not be afraid of them, thou shalt well remember what the Eternal thy G-d did unto Pharaoh and unto all Egypt.*[27]

For this reason, the Torah commanded that the fainthearted should return home before battle.[28] Since a fainthearted person has not made the fear of G-d his supreme concern, his merit is incomplete. It is known that Israel's victories were not accomplished through the numerical superiority of troops nor through superiority of armaments; the sword is the inheritance of Esau.[29] The secret of Israel's victories was its merit. It is so stated: *For not by their own sword did they get the Land in possession, neither did their own arm save them; but Thy right hand, and Thine arm, and the light of Thy countenance, because Thou wast favorable unto them.*[30] If you ask: "Since merit was the cause of their victory, why did they go out to battle with many people when only a few would have sufficed? Why indeed did they go out armed at all?" The answer to these questions is that even when the people of Israel are worthy of victory, they should conduct themselves in a natural manner in warfare. A person should always try to do whatever lies within his power and leave the rest in the hands of Heaven. Were this not the case, Noah would not have made the ark. Similarly, the Red Sea would not have divided itself, for it was possible for G-d to save Israel in other ways.

David repeated himself by stating, *Whom shall I fear? of whom shall I be afraid?*[18] to correspond to the two aspects of the fear of G-d; the fear of punishment in this world and in the World to Come, and the fear that issues from a profound realization of the Greatness of G-d and

(25) Deuteronomy 20:1.   (26) *Ibid.*, 7:17.   (27) *Ibid.*, Verse 18.   (28) See *ibid.*, 20:8.   (29) Genesis 27:40.   (30) Psalms 44:4.

His mighty deeds and wonders. These two aspects of the fear of G-d are alluded to in a verse which was said by Job: *For calamity from G-d was a terror to me, and by reason of His loftiness I could do nothing.*[31] The verse, *For the calamity of G-d was a terror to me,* expresses the fear of His punishment, and the verse, . . . *by reason of His loftiness I could do nothing,* indicates the soul's acceptance of His majesty and the remembrance of His wonders at every season and at every moment.

Although we have said that only G-d is to be feared and not man, we are nevertheless commanded to fear Torah scholars. Rabbi Akiba expounded,[32] *"Thou shalt fear 'eth' the Eternal thy G-d.*[33] The word *eth* includes Torah scholars."* One who fears the Sages attests thereby to his fear of G-d, for he would not have attained this quality of fearing the Sages if he were not mindful of the fear of G-d. This was the concept which Rabbi Akiba, the foremost of the Sages, proved from the verse which cautions us about the fear of G-d.

This fear of the Sages entails fear of the public, for wherever there is an assembly of people, there rests the Divine Presence. The merits of the many ascend heavenward, and their reward is great. Thus, the fear of the Sages and the fear of the public are all included in the fear of G-d, and one aspect of the fear of the Sages and the public is not to speak in their presence without their permission.

(31) Job 31:23.   (32) Pesachim 22 b.   (33) Deuteronomy 6:13.

Part Three

<table>
<tr><td>

The commandment to appoint a king over Israel, and why we are to fear him / The Sages' warning to fear the public.

</td></tr>
</table>

THOU SHALT BY ALL MEANS SET A KING OVER THEE.[34]

This verse constitutes a positive commandment of the Torah to appoint a king over Israel immediately upon entering the Land. This commandment is pursuant to Israel's subsequent request for a ruler, as it is written, *And thou shalt say: I will set a king over me.*[35] This request was not G-d's wish, for why should Israel, G-d's special people over whom He reigns, want a mortal king? Since the people of Israel were elevated above other nations, their request for a king in order to be like the other nations was considered a sin, as the prophet Samuel said, *And ye shall know and see that your wickedness is great.*[36]

Scripture explains here[34] that whenever the people of Israel will appoint a king, he must be an Israelite, as the Sages explained:[37] "Both his father and mother must be of Israelite stock," as it is said, *. . . from among thy brethren.*[34] The reason for this is that [if the king were other than a pure Israelite], he might be drawn to his origins and corrupt the true faith. The Sages commented in Tractate Sanhedrin:[38] "*Thou shalt by all means set a king over thee*[34] so that his fear will be upon you.[39] No one may sit on his throne, no one may ride on his horse, and no one may make use of his sceptre or his crown."[40] This fear will

---

(34) Deuteronomy 17:15. (35) *Ibid.,* Verse 14. (36) I Samuel 12:17. (37) Sotah 41 b. (38) Sanhedrin 20 b. (39) The explanation is based upon the double use of the verb: *Som tasim (Thou shalt by all means set . . .).* (40) The restriction against utilizing the royal crown is not found in Sanhedrin 20 b, but it is mentioned by Maimonides, *Hilchoth Melachim* 2:1.

prompt people to desist from violence, robbery, and murder as the
Sages remarked,[41] "If not for the fear of the government, men would
swallow each other alive."

Just as the Sages warned us to fear the king, they similarly commanded us to fear the public, as they said:[14] "The fear of the public
should always be before you, for even when the priests lift their hands
[to recite the Priestly Blessing], they face the people[15] and have their
backs toward the Sanctuary." That they should turn their backs to the
Sanctuary is surprising. However, the explanation thereof is that when
the priest lifts up his hands for the Blessing, the Divine Presence rests
upon his hands, as the Sages commented:[42] "The verse, *He looketh in
through the windows,*[43] refers to the hands of the priests." Since the
Divine Presence rests between the priest's two hands as it did between
the two cherubim [on the Ark of the Covenant in the Holy of Holies],
we are not concerned about the priests turning their backs to the Sanctuary, for the sanctity of the innermost part of the Sanctuary stems only from the holiness of the Divine Presence. A clear indication of this is
the prophet's statement, *And when ye spread forth your hands, I will
hide Mine eyes from you.*[44] This was said in a time of wrath. In a time
of acceptance, though, the Divine Presence does dwell upon their
hands.

Thus, the fear of the public has been likened to the fear of the
Divine Presence, and it is known that the fear of the public entails not
speaking in their presence without obtaining their permission.

(41) Aboth 3:2. (42) Shir Hashirim Rabbah 2:21. (43) Song of Songs
2:9. (44) Isaiah 1:15.

Part Four

The importance of curbing speech / Even words of Torah should be uttered with careful deliberation out of reverential fear of the public.

BE NOT RASH WITH THY MOUTH, AND LET NOT THY HEART BE HASTY TO UTTER A WORD BEFORE G-D, FOR G-D IS IN HEAVEN, AND THOU UPON EARTH; THEREFORE LET THY WORDS BE FEW.[45]

This verse warns man not to speak hastily but to exercise caution and deliberation in his speech. Even then, his words should be few. He should be especially careful when uttering *a word before G-d,* i.e., G-d's camp or the people of Israel, who are called *G-d's camp*[46] and *children of the Most High*[47] and among any ten of whom the Divine Presence rests. A wise man said,[48] "It is highly beneficial to address the public, for if you succeed in teaching them, they will praise you, and if not, they will teach you." Notwithstanding that advice, Solomon warned us to minimize our words to the public out of fear of them.

The Sages said in the Midrash:[49] "*Be not rash with thy mouth,* etc.[45] This is the purport of Scripture's statement, *He loveth transgression that loveth strife; he that raiseth his gate seeketh destruction.*[50] What is the meaning of the phrase, *he that raiseth his gate?* It refers to one who presumptiously utters inappropriate words. G-d destroys such a person." Thus far the Midrash. The literal and Midrashic meanings of Scripture thus agree that the verse above[45] is a warning that a person's

(45) Ecclesiastes 5:1. (46) Genesis 32:3. (47) Psalms 82:6. (48) The source of this quotation is unknown to me. See, though, Israel Davidson's Otzar Hameshalim V'hapithgamim, p. 87, No. 1368. (49) Tanchuma, *Bereshith*, 7. (50) Proverbs 17:19.

571

words before G-d should be few. Needless to say, this naturally applies
to rebellious speech before G-d, as in the cases of Pharaoh[51] and
Hiram,[52] who considered themselves deities and spoke irreverently
before Him. This rule, however, also applies even when uttering words
of Torah before the public, who comprise the children of G-d.[53] One
should not address them hastily but should speak with caution and
conciseness. This is because of the fear of the public. It is known, too,
that a person should not address the public without first obtaining
their permission.

(51) See Exodus 5:2. (52) See Ezekiel 28:2. (53) See Deuteronomy
14:1.

Part Five

> A public speaker should first consider the theme on which he
> wishes to speak and set the goal he wishes to accomplish / Hav-
> ing prepared himself, he should then rely upon G-d to bring his
> desired goal to fruition / The importance of thoughtful
> preparation even by a learned person and certainly by the
> unlearned.

HE THAT GIVETH HEED UNTO THE WORD SHALL FIND
GOOD, AND WHOSO TRUSTETH IN THE ETERNAL, HAP-
PY IS HE.[54]

This verse warns a person to first contemplate the theme upon which
he wishes to speak or the goal he wishes to accomplish and to consider
the ways by which he will succeed. If he does these things, *he shall find*

(54) Proverbs 16:20.

good.[54] Similarly, Solomon said, *He that spareth his words hath knowledge.*[55] Man's deeds, which fall into the categories of thought, speech and action, are subject to the influence of the evil inclination. Thus, they are always prone to follow the course of materialism. Therefore, Solomon warned here that a person should first carefully consider the theme upon which he wishes to speak and to bring his thoughts to bear upon his speech and deed. Yet, all the preparation notwithstanding, he should not rely upon himself, but only upon G-d, to bring his desired goal to complete success, as it is said, *And whoso trusteth in the Eternal, happy is he.*[54] Thus, Scripture states, *Trust in the Eternal with all thy heart.*[56]

With reference to this thought, Solomon said, *Counsel in the heart of man is like deep water.*[57] The verse intends to make man desist performing any action or uttering any word until he first patiently considers it in his heart. Proper counsel comes only with thought. The lovers of wisdom said that the tongue is the spokesman of thought. It is therefore written, *Counsel in the heart of man is like deep water,*[57] for just as it is impossible to draw deep water without a vessel, so it is impossible to accomplish anything without proper thought.

Since Solomon warned even intelligent and learned people to first consider what they are about to say, surely I, an unlearned man, should have considered what I wish to say. Had I considered it, I would not be speaking, for I would have realized my lack of wisdom and knowledge, which is all the more pronounced in the presence of men who are greater and wiser than I. Yet, by asking their forgiveness, it is possible to speak, for our Sages said,[58] "If a teacher permits his disciple to omit an act of reverence, his honor is set aside [i.e., the disciple may avail himself of the permission]." Thus, after obtaining permission . . .[59]

(55) *Ibid.*, 17:27.   (56) *Ibid.*, 3:5.   (57) *Ibid.*, 20:5.   (58) Kiddushin 32 a. (59) " . . . I will interpret one verse." See end of Part Six.

Part Six

> David's primary concern as compared to that of other kings / The advantages in discussing matters of Torah / David's reticence before his superiors.

I WILL SPEAK OF THY TESTIMONIES BEFORE KINGS AND WILL NOT BE ASHAMED.[60]

King David said: "When I hear kings and lords recounting their valor, I feel ashamed. Why? They should have been speaking of the miracles and wonders that G-d does with them, but instead, they waste their time in foolishness. They pride themselves for having conquered a certain country through their own might, but the power is only Yours, as it is said, *Thine, O Eternal, is the greatness, and the power.*[61] They glorify themselves in victories which are not theirs, as it is said, *. . . and the glory, and the victory, and the majesty.*[61] They boast of armies which are not theirs but Yours, as it is said, *A king is not saved by the multitude of a host.*[62] With whom, then, does salvation rest? It rests with G-d, as it is said, *Salvation belongeth unto the Eternal.*"[63]

David continued: "When the kings and lords are engaged in such conversation, I speak words of Torah and inform everyone of Your mighty acts. I am not ashamed to speak of Your testimonies, as it is said, *I will speak of Thy testimonies before kings and will not be ashamed.*"[60] It should be understood why David uses the expression

(60) Psalms 119:46. (61) I Chronicles 29:11. (62) Psalms 33:16. (63) *Ibid.*, 3:9.

Thy testimonies rather than "Thy commandments" or "Thy Law." When a person testifies, he takes special note of every word in order to avoid embarrassment. Therefore, David is saying, "I will speak of Your testimonies even before kings and will not be ashamed, for Your testimonies are trustworthy and teach man wisdom. This is true even of the simple man—as it is said, *The testimony of the Eternal is sure, making wise the simple*[64] — and certainly of the wise man, as it is said, *Give to a wise man, and he will be yet wiser.*"[65]

David further said, *Thy testimonies are my conversation,*[66] for they are designed to yield a true discernment of the Torah. If an uninstructed person speaks before a learned man and makes an error, the learned man will correct him. If an uninstructed person speaks before his equal, they will discuss the matter until they bring forth the truth. If he speaks before one who is less informed than he, the other will derive instruction. Therefore, David said, *"I will speak of Thy testimonies before kings and those more learned than I, and will not be ashamed."*[60]

Since King David, who also excelled in all qualities, hesitated to speak in the presence of those greater than he without such extensive preliminary remarks, how much more should a person lacking such qualities desist from speaking before those more learned than he. However, he may do so after obtaining permission, for the Sages have said:[58] "If a teacher permits his disciple to omit an act of reverence, his honor is set aside [i.e., the disciple may avail himself of the permission]." Thus, with your permission I will explain one verse.

(64) *Ibid.,* 19:8.   (65) Proverbs 9:9.   (66) Psalms 119:99.

Part Seven

Controlled speech is a sign of knowledge, for once uttered, a word is like a stone which, after being thrown, cannot be recalled / The significance of speech / The duty of speaking in matters of Torah.

HE THAT RESTRAINETH HIS WORDS HATH KNOWLEDGE, AND HE WHO IS SELF-CONTROLLED IS A MAN OF DISCERNMENT.[67]

This verse teaches man to restrain his words, for the control of speech betokens possession of knowledge. Before uttering a word, man has that word in his control, but after he has spoken it, it is like a stone which, when cast, cannot be brought back. Therefore, the Sages praised the quality of silence, as they said in Tractate Aboth:[68] "Rabbi Shimon the son of Rabban Gamaliel the Elder says, 'All my life, I have grown up amongst the wise, and I have found nothing better for a man than silence.' " The Sages further said:[69] "Silence is good for the wise and *a fortiori* for the simple." To express the great importance of silence, Solomon said, *Even a fool, when he holdeth his peace, is counted wise,*[70] and the teachers of ethics said,[71] "If speech is silver, silence is gold." Therefore, Solomon said here, *He that restraineth his words hath knowledge.*[67] Similarly, *he who is self-controlled* and speaks not hurriedly but with self-imposed restraint *is a man of discernment.*[67]

---

(67) Proverbs 17:27. (68) Aboth 1:17. The thought suggested is as follows: "In my contacts with the wise I have not been stationary, but instead I have grown up and steadily progressed from rank to rank. This distinction I have accomplished only through silence, that is, by observing the ways of the wise and imbibing their words of wisdom." (69) Pesachim 99 a. (70) Proverbs 17:28. (71) See in Israel Davidson's Otzar Hameshalim V'hapithgamim, p. 86. No. 1349. The source of this adage is Megillah 18 a: "A word is worth a *sela*; silence is worth two."

The reason for this admonition is that speech stems from the soul, through which man is superior to the other creatures. Therefore, man should utilize measured speech and only when it is of great necessity for the benefit of body or soul. As an indication of the significance of speech, we find it attributed to the Creator, blessed be He, as it is said, *He createth the utterance of the lips.*[72] G-d is lauded thereby as He is through the creation of the heavens, of which it is said, *He that created the heavens.*[73]

Silence must be observed even in matters of Torah when one is in the presence of those who are greater than he in wisdom, as Solomon said, *Glory not thyself in the presence of the king, and stand not in the place of great men.*[74] Since he restrained us from merely standing in the presence of great men, we may conclude that speaking in their presence is certainly to be avoided. Thus, it would be appropriate for us to remain silent, but we must nevertheless contend with the Sages' statement:[75] *"Do ye indeed in silence speak righteousness?"*[76] What should man's occupation be in this world? He should make himself dumb. I might think that this also refers to matters of Torah. Therefore, Scripture states, *Speak righteousness."* The wise man thus said:[48] "Be diligent to speak in the presence of great men, for if you will succeed in teaching them, they will praise you, and if not they will teach you." Hence, with the pardon and permission of the great men and learned people here, we shall explain one verse.

(72) Isaiah 57:19.   (73) *Ibid.,* 42:5.   (74) Proverbs 25:6.   (75) Chullin 89 a.   (76) Psalms 58:2.

Part Eight

The commandment to honor the priest in every respect and 'a fortiori' the wise men, who are greater than priests / The respect due wise men includes not speaking in their presence without their permission.

THOU SHALT SANCTIFY HIM [THE PRIEST], FOR HE OF-
FERETH THE BREAD OF THY G-D: HE SHALL BE HOLY UN-
TO THEE.[77]

This verse refers to the priests, upon whom the Torah has devolved more commandments than upon Israelites. Thus, unlike Israelites, priests are commanded to shun the impurity of the dead and are enjoined from marrying certain women. The Sages similarly said:[78] *"Thou shalt sanctify him"[77]* even against his will.[79] *He shall be holy unto thee[77]* to be the first in all matters of honor,[80] the first to recite the benediction at a meal, and the first to receive a seemly portion." All these matters are aspects of the deference due the priests.

This is the order of distinction: priest, Levite, and Israelite. The priest is more distinguished and sanctified than the Levite, and the Levite more than the Israelite. Therefore, the Torah has obligated us to take a fiftieth part of our produce as *terumah* (heave-offering), which is called *holy,*[81] and give it to the priest, whom Scripture called *holy*, as it says, *And Aaron was separated, that he should be sanctified as most holy.*[82] [The Torah also directed that we give] the Levite the

---

(77) Leviticus 21:8.   (78) Yebamoth 88 b.   (79) "That is to say, this commandment is upon us Israelites; it does not depend on the priest's wishes"(Maimonides, The Commandments, Vol. I, p. 41).   (80) "E.g., [he shall be the first called to] the reading of the Torah, and when in conference, he should be the first to speak" (Rashi, Gittin 59 b).   (81) Leviticus 22:14.   (82) I Chronicles 23:13.

first tithe, a tenth of which must be given by the Levite to the priest. Thus, just as the Israelite is indebted to the Levite, so is the latter indebted to the priest.

Since we have been commanded to sanctify the priests and to honor them in all matters, *a fortiori* we must do so to the wise men, who are superior to the priests. The Sages commented:[83] "*She* [Wisdom] *is more precious 'mi'pninim' (than rubies),*[84] Wisdom is more precious than the High Priest who enters the innermost part of the Sanctuary." In the order of superiority the Sages taught:[83] "A wise man takes precedence over a king, and a king over the High Priest." They further stated:[85] "There are three crowns: the crown of Torah, the crown of priesthood, and the crown of royalty. The crown of priesthood was merited by Aaron, and the crown of royalty was merited by David. The crown of Torah, however, is available to anyone who desires it. You may suppose that the crown of Torah is inferior to the others. Scripture therefore informs us that it is greater than they, for it includes them, as it is said, *By me* [Wisdom] *kings reign.*"[86] The Sages further stated there:[87] "Honor is only for the wise,[88] as it is said, *The wise shall inherit honor.*"[89] Part of the honor due the wise is not to speak in their presence without their permission.

(83) Horayoth 13 a.   (84) Proverbs 3:15. The word *mi'pninim* (than rubies) suggests the meaning "the innermost parts of a structure." The thought then follows that the Torah scholar is more precious than the High Priests who alone is privileged to enter the Holy of Holies on the Day of Atonement.   (85) Aboth 4:13. The second half of this quotation is from Yoma 72 b.   (86) Proverbs 8:15.   (87) Aboth, *Kinyan Torah*, 3.   (88) In our versions of this Mishnah, the reading is: "Honor is only for the Torah."   (89) Proverbs 3:35.

Part Nine

The function of the High Priest in the Sanctuary / His right to enter the Holy of Holies on the Day of Atonement depended upon his merits / The speaker must be worthy of addressing the congregation / Hearing words of Torah from anyone is like hearing them from the mouth of Moses our teacher.

'B'ZOTH' (WITH THIS) SHALL AARON COME INTO THE HOLY PLACE; WITH A YOUNG BULLOCK FOR A SIN-OFFERING, AND A RAM FOR A BURNT-OFFERING.[90]

The Sages commented:[91] "The [building of the] Tabernacle was equal in importance to the creation of the world." The intent thereof is that just as man, the foremost of all species, was placed upon the earth to recognize his Creator and to serve Him, so was the priest designated for the Divine Service, which he performed at first in the Tabernacle and later in the Sanctuary of Jerusalem. The priest was specifically appointed for the Service in the Sanctuary, and through him, the Divine Glory rested there.

Although the High Priest served in the Sanctuary and was designated for the worship of the Great G-d, he could not enter [the innermost part of] the Sanctuary without making great preparations, i.e., he first had to bring the offerings, as it is said, *With this shall Aaron come into the holy place,* etc.[90] He required the many merits that entered with him, for so the Sages said in the Midrash:[92] "When

---

(90) Leviticus 16:3. The verse begins the passage which sets forth the special Divine Service on the Day of Atonement, which was performed only by the High Priest. During the course of that Service, the High Priest entered the Holy of Holies four times. (91) Tanchuma, *Pekudei,* 2. (92) Vayikra Rabbah 21:8.

the High Priest entered the Holy of Holies, he took along the merits of the performance of many commandments, as it is said, *'B'zoth' (With this) shall Aaron come into the holy place.*[90] He took the merit of the Torah, as it is said, *And 'zoth' (this) is the Torah.*[93] He took the merit of circumcision, as it is said, *'Zoth' (This) is My covenant, which ye shall keep.*[94] He took the merit of the Sabbath, as it is said, *Happy is the man that doeth 'zoth' (this), etc., that keepeth the Sabbath from profaning it.*[95] He took the merit of Jerusalem, as it is said, *'Zoth' (This) is Jerusalem.*[96] He took the merit of the tribes, as it is said, *And 'zoth' (this) is what their father* [Jacob] *spoke unto them.*[97] He took the merit of Judah, as it is said, *And 'zoth' (this) for Judah.*[98] He took the merit of the Congregation of Israel, as it is said, *'Zoth' (This) thy stature is like to a palm tree.*[99] He took the merit of the *terumah* [the voluntary offering for the building of the Sanctuary], as it is said, *And 'zoth' (this) is 'haterumah' (the offering),*[100] He took the merit of the tithes, as it is said, *And try Me now with 'zoth' (this).*[101] Finally, he took the merit of the offerings, as it is said, *'B'zoth' (With this) shall Aaron come."*[90] Thus far in the Midrash.[92]

The High Priest was the one upon whom depended the entire Sanctuary Service on the Day of Atonement and through whom all Israel was expiated. One may conclude *a fortiori* that if the High Priest was not permitted to enter the innermost part of the Sanctuary unless he had all these merits with him, how much more does this principle apply to the common people devoid of wisdom, knowledge, and merit as they are, who desire to speak before a large assembly. The latter constitutes *G-d's camp,*[102] which is equal in importance and significance to the ministering angels themselves! However, we shall rely upon the protection of the merits of the assembly when I speak a few words of

(93) Deuteronomy 4:44. (94) Genesis 17:10. (95) Isaiah 56:2. (96) Ezekiel 5:5. (97) Genesis 49:28. (98) Deuteronomy 33:7. (99) Song of Songs 7:8. See above, *Emunah* (Faith), Note 22. (100) Exodus 25:3. (101) Malachi 3:10: *Bring ye the whole tithe into the storehouse, that there may be food in My House, and try Me now with 'zoth' (this) . . . If I will not open you the windows of heaven, etc.* (102) Genesis 32:3.

Torah. Although the speaker is most insignificant, our Rabbis already said:[103] "One who hears words of Torah from an inferior person in Israel is considered as if he heard them from the mouth of Moses." For this reason, Malachi, the last prophet, sealed [his prophecies with the words], *Remember ye the law of Moses, My servant,*[104] thus ascribing the Torah [with G-d's consent] not to Him but to Moses. Since we have shown that one who hears words of Torah from an inferior person in Israel is considered as if he heard them from the mouth of Moses, and since the Torah has been ascribed only to Moses, it is therefore necessary for everyone to listen to such words, for the audience is not to be concerned with the speaker's knowledge but rather with the awareness of G-d.

The Sages commented:[105] "*Incline thine ear, and hear the words of the wise, and apply thy heart unto My knowledge.*[106] The verse does not say 'unto their knowledge,' but *unto My knowledge,* for they are speaking through the Holy Spirit." From here we learn not to lightly regard one who teaches Torah and who preaches in public, for our concern should be the knowledge of G-d. Thus, with the permission of G-d, and with the permission of the wise men and those assembled here, we shall explain one verse.

---

(103) Sifre, *Eikev,* 41, and Bamidbar Rabbah 14:14. (104) Malachi 3:22. (105) Chagigah 15 b. (106) Proverbs 22:17.

Part Ten

> *Wise lips are a storehouse of wealth / The secret of wise lips / One of the aspects of wisdom is not to speak in the presence of people superior in knowledge unless one is speaking words of Torah with the permission of his audience.*

THERE IS GOLD, AND A MULTITUDE OF RUBIES, BUT THE LIPS OF KNOWLEDGE ARE A PRECIOUS JEWEL.[107]

In this verse Solomon taught us that a person can achieve all precious things through wise lips. Solomon further said, *Through wisdom is a house builded.*[108] He is saying that gold and rubies are found with the rich, but an uncommonly *precious jewel* is *lips of knowledge,* of which there are but few. He called *lips of knowledge* a *kli yakar,* [which literally means "a precious vessel"]. Just as a vessel is a receptacle, so do the lips [act as a receptacle] by receiving instruction from the person's thoughts. The lips draw their power therefrom, for it is improper for one to speak before his words have been readied in thought. Similarly, the wise man said,[109] "Speech is the vessel of the heart!"

It is known that when one has wise lips, he speaks appropriate words that are accepted and listened to by all. Regarding this, Solomon said, *He kisseth the lips that giveth a right answer,*[110] meaning that one who gives a *right answer* is considered as if he kisses the lips of his listeners, for they listen attentively to his words and refrain from conversation while he speaks.

---

(107) Proverbs 20:15. (108) *Ibid.*, 24:3. (109) I have been unable to identify the source of this quotation. (110) Proverbs 24:26.

583

An aspect of *wise lips* is not speaking in the presence of people more learned than the speaker, for the fear of the wise has been compared to the fear of G-d.[111] The Sages commented:[112] "One who respects scholars will have sons-in-law who are scholars. One who loves scholars will have children who are scholars. One who fears scholars will himself be a learned person."[113] Nevertheless, it is possible to speak [in the presence of one's superiors] with their leave, for the Sages said:[58] "If a teacher permits his disciple to omit an act of reverence, his honor is set aside [i.e., the disciple may avail himself of the permission]." Furthermore, a wise man said:[48] "Be diligent to speak in the presence of great men, for if you will succeed in teaching them, they will praise you, and if not, they will teach you." The Sages commented in Midrash Koheleth:[114] "*He who loveth abundance* has *increase.*[115] One who loves to speak words of Torah in public will have abundant increase." Since there is so much benefit entailed in speaking [words of Torah in public], with the forgiveness and permission of the great and wise men here, we shall explain one verse.

(111) Pesachim 22 b.   (112) Shabbath 23 b.   (113) Of the three characteristics described here, the fear of G-d is clearly the most commendable.   (114) I have not located this text in Midrash Koheleth. However, it is found in Makkoth 10 a.   (115) Ecclesiastes 5:9. The verse actually reads, *has no increase.* However, since the Hebrew words *lo* (no), spelled *lamed-aleph,* and *lo* ("to him" or "has") are homonyms, the Sages interpreted the verse to suggest an ethical lesson relative to the study of Torah.

ראש השנה

The New Year

Part One

G-d assigned repentance before He created the world / The gradations and conditions of repentance / The Ten Days of Penitence / The positive aspects of existence are more numerous than its negative features / The attributes of justice and mercy in judgment.

The New Year

THE BALANCE AND SCALES OF JUSTICE ARE THE
ETERNAL'S; ALL THE WEIGHTS OF THE BAG ARE HIS
CONCERN.[1]

Among the mercies which G-d bestows on His creatures is repentance, which He assigned [i.e., established the right to] before He
created the world. G-d did so because He knew that man's nature is
steeped in evil inclinations and that man was destined to sin before his
mind could mature and enable him to overcome those inclinations.
Therefore, G-d in His mercy created the cure before the ill and
established man's right to repent.

Seven things were created prior to the creation of the world: Torah,
repentance, the Garden of Eden, Gehenna, the Throne of Glory, the
Sanctuary, and the name of the Messiah.[2] This is the correct order of
their creation based upon the mystical inference among them, as
known to those initiated into the mysteries of the Torah. These seven
things are linked as follows: The Torah, which Israel observes,
necessitates repentance, as well as the Garden of Eden as a reward for
those who repent and Gehenna as a punishment for those who do not.
The fulfillment of Torah requires a lower world, which exists through
the movement of the heavens, i.e., the Throne of Glory. The world in

---

(1) Proverbs 16:11. Justice is of Divine origin. Established by G-d, the balance and
scales of justice cannot be shifted to one's convenience. Instead, *all the weights of the
bag* must be used justly, as they are all His concern and under His watchfulness. The
connotation of the verse to the Day of Judgment on the New Year will be explained in
the text. (2) Pesachim 54 a.

586

general is in need of a particular [sacred] place, the Sanctuary, and therefore the concept of the Sanctuary was a necessary prerequisite [to the creation of the world]. Because G-d foresaw the destruction of the Sanctuary, the coming of the Messiah was necessitated, too. The creation of these [seven things prior to the creation of the world] thus made possible the attainment of a knowledge of G-d and the granting of reward for the observance of the commandments. It was unnecessasry, though, for the Sages to include Israel among these seven things, for Israel's preeminence in this regard is well known, and our Rabbis, in fact said elsewhere,[3] "The thought of Israel [preceded the creation of the world]."

The Sages commented:[4] "Great is the power of repentance, for it reaches the Throne of Glory, as it is said, *Return, O Israel, unto the Eternal thy G-d.*"[5] They further stated,[6] "The place where penitents stand cannot be attained by even the thoroughly righteous."

There are many gradations of repentance which bring man nearer to his Creator. The degree to which one subdues his inclinations, the shame for the sins he committed against G-d, the degree of chastisement he suffered and the fasts he has accepted upon himself — all these factors determine one's nearness to G-d. Every penitent should carefully weigh his deeds with a scale and balance, and he should be ready to bear pain and vexation equal in degree to the benefit he derived from his sins. David said, *Mine eyes run down with rivers of water, because they have not observed Thy law.*[7] He should have said, "because I have not observed Thy law," but his intent was to state that since *they* [i.e., the eyes] were the agents of sin, it is proper that *they* be overcome with sorrow and shed tears.

Repentance is a cure, as it is written, *Return, and be healed.*[8] It is called a cure because sin is the sickness of the soul. Just as the physical

(3) Bereshith Rabbah 1:5.   (4) Yoma 86 a.   (5) Hosea 14:2. The thought implied is that repentance reaches His very Self.   (6) Berachoth 34 b.   (7) Psalms 119:136.   (8) Isaiah 6:10.

body is subject to health and sickness, so is the soul. The health of the soul is indicated by its good deeds, and its sickness by its sins. Just as a physical sickness is cured only by its antithesis, so is the sick, sinful soul restored to health by its antithesis. It is thus said, *By mercy and truth iniquity is atoned for.*[9] That is to say, the iniquity of wickedness and falsehood are forgiven through the qualities of mercy and truth.

Repentance requires four conditions. First, one must abandon the sin in deed and in thought, as the prophet proclaimed, *Let the wicked forsake his way* of action, *and the man of iniquity his thoughts.*[10] Because there are certain people who believe that there is harm only in speech and in action but not in thought, Scripture informs us, *A glad heart maketh a cheerful countenance.*[11] The heart is the root, and the thoughts spread forth from the heart like branches spread forth from the root of a tree. Hence, we may derive that the heart that rejoices in sin incurs punishment, for the [heart's sinful] thought crystallizes in deed just as joy is manifested in the body. The righteous, however, rejoice in the Torah and the commandments, and the essence of their joy lies in the worship of G-d, as Scripture states, *I rejoice at Thy word.*[12] *Be glad in the Eternal, and rejoice, ye righteous.*[13] The wicked, on the other hand, rejoice in sin and wickedness, as it is written, *Folly is joy to him that lacketh understanding.*[14] The Sages further stated:[15] "Sinful imaginations are more injurious than the sin itself." That is to say, they are more injurious to the soul because the thought of the sin becomes affixed to the soul forever, whereas the perpetration of the sinful deed requires only a fixed amount of time.

The second condition of repentance is regret for the sins of the past, as the prophet said, *Surely after that I was turned, I regretted.*[16] The third condition is that one resolve in his heart never to commit that sin again, as it is said, *Neither will we call any more the work of our hands*

---

(9) Proverbs 16:6. Thus, the punishment of sin is averted by the practice of mercy and truth. (10) Isaiah 55:7. (11) Proverbs 15:13. (12) Psalms 119:162. (13) *Ibid.*, 32:11. (14) Proverbs 15:21. (15) Yoma 29 a. See also above at end of *Taharath Heleiv* (Purity of Heart). (16) Jeremiah 31:18.

our gods.[17] He should abide by this resolution and never again perpetrate that deed. This is the essence of confession. The fourth condition is that he should orally confess, "I have sinned, I have committed iniquity, I have transgressed against You." It was to this confession that the prophet referred when he said, *Take with you words, and return unto the Eternal.*[18] This is the subject of [oral] confession. You are aware that oral confession constitutes a positive commandment of the Torah, as it is said, *When a man or woman shall commit any sin,* etc.,[19] *then they shall confess their sin.*[20]

The penitent must have a submissive, broken, and contrite heart for having rebelled against G-d's command, as David said in his penitential psalm, *The offerings of G-d are a broken spirit.*[21] The Sages explained this concept by analogy: The law concerning impure vessels states that if the vessels are broken, they cease to convey impurity.[22] Submissiveness is one of the essential elements of repentance, as Isaiah said, *But on this man will I look, even on him that is poor and of a contrite spirit.*[23] Similarly, regarding the subject of repentance, the Torah clearly states, *If then perchance their uncircumcised heart be humbled,*[24] thus teaching us that the principal element in repentance is submissiveness. It is said of King Ahab, *Seest thou* [Elijah] *how Ahab humbled himself before Me?*[25] It is also written of him, *And he went softly,*[26] unlike other kings who noisily move about with arrogance.

The penitent must also have a sense of shame before G-d. He must feel like a lowly servant who has rebelled against the command of the Great King, Who knows his thoughts and Who tests hearts and consciences. This is expressly stated in Scripture: *I was ashamed, yea, even confounded, because I did bear the reproach of my youth.*[27] Elsewhere it says, *Confusion hath covered my face.*[28] When a sinner realizes that

---

(17) Hosea 14:4. (18) *Ibid.*, Verse 3. (19) Numbers 5:6. (20) *Ibid.*, Verse 7. (21) Psalms 51:19. (22) Keilim 2:1. One of the ways an impure vessel ceases to convey impurity is if it becomes broken. The analogy to a human being who has become impure because of sin is thus clear. A broken heart and contrite spirit will restore his state of purity. (23) Isaiah 66:2. (24) Leviticus 26:41. (25) I Kings 21:19. (26) *Ibid.*, Verse 27. (27) Jeremiah 31:18. (28) Psalms 69:8.

G-d forgives his sin and does not punish him commensurately, he should feel an even greater sense of shame, for if a mortal king had forgiven him, he would certainly be susceptible to this feeling. [Regarding the feeling of shame], the Sages said:[29] "One who commits a sin and subsequently feels ashamed because of it is forgiven for all his sins."

Repentance atones for sins at all times and in all seasons. It is especially effective in the first ten days of Tishri, the awesome days of law and judgment, which all the people of Israel call "the Ten Days of Penitence." These days have always been designated for prayer and supplication at the heavenly Gates of Repentance. There are Jewish communities where the people fast on these days. The Sages said that during these ten days, G-d is accessible to each and every individual, as they expounded:[30] "*Seek ye the Eternal while He may be found.*[31] This refers to the Ten Days of Penitence between New Year and the Day of Atonement." For this reason, the Torah has established that the first day of the month of Tishri shall be a Day of Judgment for all creatures, and that the sealing of their judgement shall be on the tenth day of the month. Thus, the Torah has allowed ten intervening days to give the sinner an opportunity to repent of his sin before the sealing of his judgment. Because the creation of the world was completed on the New Year with the attribute of justice, Divine Wisdom therefore prescribed that the annual Day of Judgment shall occur on New Year so that all the deeds of man, meritorious and sinful, will be weighed thereon. With this thought in mind, Solomon said, *The balance and scales of justice are the Eternal's.*[1] With them He weighs the deeds of the world, good deeds and sinful ones, inconsequential deeds and serious ones. *And the weights of the bag are His concern;*[1] He determines the exact weight of even the smallest amount.

You should know that the word *peles* (balance) denotes a single-pan weighing instrument, and *moznayim* (scales) denotes a two-pan instru-

_____

(29) Berachoth 12 b.   (30) Rosh Hashanah 18 a.   (31) Isaiah 55:6.

ment, as its plural form indicates. There are other words like the latter. The plural form of *Yerushalayim* (Jerusalem) points to a Jerusalem
on high and a Jerusalem below. Another example is *shamayim*
(heaven), as known to the scholars of the mysteries of the Torah. Thus,
the word *moznayim*, the two-pan weighing instrument, signifies the
two attributes with which G-d conducts the world, the attribute of *din*
(justice) and the attribute of *rachamim* (mercy). *Rachamim* itself is in
the plural, while *din* is in the singular. This indicates that the measure
of Divine mercy exceeds that of justice, and the reason for this is that
existence is more positive than non-existence, [i.e., there is more good
than evil in the world]. At the founding of the world, the Master of
Creation so established that [the positive aspects of] existence should
outnumber its negative aspects. This is true in the universe as a whole,
in the lower world in general, and particularly in the case of each individual person.

The world is generally divided into three parts: the realm of the
angels, the realm of the spheres, and the lower world. With this in
mind, you will surely realize that the good things in existance are more
numerous than the evil things. The first two realms, for example, are
permanent in their existence; they are not subject to destruction. Only
one of the three parts of the world is subject to destruction. Therefore,
you will find the word *rachamim* (mercy) in the plural, for the world
requires a greater amount of mercy. Similarly, the word *chayim* (life) is
in the plural. [When speaking of the physical and spiritual needs of
man], you will only find the word *chayim* in that form. It is known that
the very existence of life is an aspect of the Divine attribute of mercy as
we say in the *Amidah* [during the Ten Days of Penitence], "Who in
mercy remembereth Thy creatures *l'chayim* (to life)."

You will also find that man is composed of three parts: the intellect,
the soul, and the body. The first two parts exist forever; [for the rational powers he attained during his lifetime become part of the active
intellect of the world, and the soul returns to its Divine origin], only the
body is subject to change and decay. Thus, within the individual

himself, we can discern aspects of both attributes of justice and mercy, with that of mercy predominating. Because the need for mercy is so great in the world, we say in the *Amidah* of New Year and the Day of Atonement, "Thy word is truth and endureth forever." The Midrash relates:[32] "The Attribute of Mercy said to G-d, 'Since You have created the world with the attribute of justice, as it is said, *In the beginning 'Elokim' (G-d) created*[33] — indeed, it is impossible to conduct the world without it — why then did You create me?' G-d replied, 'I swear that I will not conduct My world without you.' " This is the "word" which we ask G-d to fulfill [when we pray, "Thy word is truth"], and it is this thought which is conveyed here in the verse, *The balance and scales of justice are the Eternal's.*[1] The verse refers to the two pans in the scales, that of merit and that of guilt, which represent the attributes of justice and of mercy.

The Sages expanded this concept by saying that G-d judges the world with a scale, i.e., He knows how to evaluate sins in relationship to merits. For example, if Reuben gave a *perutah* (coin of the lowest denomination) to a poor man, he has gained one meritorious deed. If he robbed someone of two *perutoth,* he has committed two sins. These two actions are then weighed in the Heavenly tribunal, as follows: When Reuben gave the *perutah* to the poor man, the latter and his family were dying of hunger. Thus, Reuben's act saved many lives. On the other hand, when Reuben robbed someone of two *perutoth,* he himself was poor. He robbed in order to save his life; the robbery he committed was not prompted by greed. Thus, Reuben's single meritorious deed outweighs the two sins he committed. As a further example, let us examine the case of two people who are studying Torah; one of them is elderly and the other young. The elderly person must expend much more effort to achieve his goal. Hence, his reward is greater than that of the youth even though both of them are engaged in the same meritorious deed.

(32) I have been unable to locate this passage.   (33) Genesis 1:1. The Divine Name *Elokim* signifies the attribute of justice.

the messenger [Moses], and He commanded us to rely upon Moses "even if he tells us that the right hand is the left and the left is the right."[42] He further called the Written Law "Torah" because it "teaches" man the way of life through the observance of the commandments. He compared *the Torah* to *light* and *the commandment* to *a lamp* because the light of the Torah is self-illuminating, while a lamp is kindled from another source. By the same token, the Oral Law emanates from the Written Law.

The commandments of the Written Law cannot be explained without the Oral Law, for Scripture does not explain the details of the observance of many commandments. Those are known only through tradition. For example, the true tradition enlightens our eyes as to our obligation in the commandment of *Tzitzith*—there must be eight threads and five knots[43]—which is not mentioned in the Torah. Similarly, the observance of the commandment of the *Tefillin* is based entirely upon the tradition and laws declared to Moses on Sinai.

The commandment of the Shofar, which we are to observe on the day of New Year, also falls under the above category. Scripture states, *And in the seventh month, on the first day of the month*, etc., *is a day of blowing 't'ruah' to you.*[44] The instructions are vague; Scripture does not specify whether the blowing is to be done with a horn or with trumpets or with any other instrument. Also unexplained is the reason G-d commanded such blowing, nor does Scripture set forth that it is the Day of Judgment. If you will examine the pertinent passages, you will find that Scripture speaks at length about the other festivals,[45] but here [concerning New Year], it shortens the subject and conceals the theme. Yet, it is clear that the theme is significant, for such is the way of Scripture: the more esoteric the subject, the shorter the account thereof. For example, in the chapter on Creation, G-d abbreviated the account of how the Higher Light was formed, merely including it in

---

(42) Sifre, *Shoftim*, 154. (43) See above, *Tzitzith* (Fringes), Note 11. (44) Numbers 29:1. (45) See Ramban, "Writings and Discourses," Discourse on Rosh Hashanah, pp. 240 ff., where this entire subject is discussed at great length.

the statement, *Let there be light. And there was light.*[46] This serves to
prevent the simple-minded from being misled [into thinking that the
Higher Light is some deity], while the true knowledge thereof is reserved for individuals [of sufficient erudition].

Because the details of this commandment of blowing the Shofar
have not been specified in the Torah, tradition, the lighted lamp
which illumines our eyes, has explained that it is to be done with a
horn, deriving it from the rule of similar expressions, as follows:[47]
"Here [in the case of the New Year], it is written, *in the seventh
month,*[44] and there in connection with the Jubilee, it is said, *Then
shalt thou make proclamation with the blast of the horn on the tenth
day of the seventh month.*[48] Just as the blowing on the Jubilee is to be
done with a horn, so is it to be done with a horn on the New Year."
Tradition also requires the blowing of a *t'kiah* (a sustained sound)
before and after a *t'ruah* the precise nature of which was discussed by
the Sages of the Talmud. The Tanna of the Mishnah maintained that
a *t'ruah* is a wailing sound. Thus, the mnemonic device [for the blowing of the Shofar] is *t'rat,* [which stands for *t'kiah—t'ruah—t'kiah*].
The Sages of the Beraitha, on the other hand, contended that the
t'ruah is a groaning sound. Thus, the mnemonic device is *t'shat
[t'kiah—sh'varim—t'kiah].* Afterwards, Rabbi Abahu, an Amora,[49]
apprehended that the word *t'ruah* might include both a groaning and
wailing sound. Therefore, he ordained [the blowing indicated by the
mnemonic device] *tashrat [t'kiah—sh'varim—t'ruah—t'kiah].* He
believed that only by blowing these sounds could we fulfill our duty
because these sounds satisfy the requirements of both the Tanna in the
Mishnah and the Sage of the Beraitha. However, because of the

---

(46) Genesis 1:3. (47) Rosh Hashanah 34 a. (48) Leviticus 25:9. (49) The
Sages of the Talmud who lived after the redaction of the Mishnah by Rabbi Yehudah
Hanasi (the Prince) were known as *Amoraim* (Interpreters). The Sages mentioned in
the Mishnah are known as *Tannaim* (Teachers). Rabbi Abahu, who flourished about
the year 250 C.E., lived in Caeserea, the seat of the Roman government, in the Land
of Israel. He was a disciple of Rabbi Yochanan, who in turn was a disciple of Rabbi
Yehudah Hanasi.

questions posed in the Gemara[47] — "Perhaps it is a kind of groaning?"
"Perhaps it is a kind of wailing?" — the later scholars agreed that
all these sounds should be blown together: *tashrat*
[t'kiah—sh'varim—t'ruah—t'kiah], *t'shat [t'kiah—sh'varim—t'kiah]*,
and *t'rat [t'kiah—t'ruah—t'kiah]*.

The reason for this commandment is to bestir the heart. Sound
arouses the heart to various emotions. Certain sounds evoke joy, others
evoke grief. The sounds of joy are such as those produced by violins,
harps, and other musical instruments. The prophets played upon these
instruments in order to renew their spirit of joy, as the Sages commented:[50] "The Divine Presence does not rest on a person who is in a
state of idleness or grief, but only on someone who is in a joyous mood,
for it is said, *And it came to pass, when the minstrel played, that the
hand of the Eternal came upon him* [Elisha]."[51] The Levites, the
ministers in the Sanctuary, likewise played upon musical instruments
in order that the offerings be accepted favorably, and to make the worship itself joyous. For the same reason, our patriarch Isaac asked for
savory food[52] [before blessing his son] so that the Holy Spirit would rest
upon him in a mood of joy; his request was not intended to merely
gratify his physical appetite.

The sound which evokes grief and trembling is the sound of the
Shofar, as Scripture states, *Shall the horn be blown in a city, and the
people not tremble?*[53] Thus, we have been commanded to blow the
Shofar so that we can sound therewith the *t'ruah* to bewail our sins. We
will then awaken ourselves and tremble because of the fear of the
Divine judgment, for the *t'ruah* is an allusion to the attribute of justice,
as it is said, *G-d is gone up amidst the 't'ruah,' the Eternal amidst the
sound of the horn.*[54] Upon hearing the sound of *t'ruah* [during their

(50) Pesachim 117 a.   (51) II Kings 3:15.   (52) See Genesis 27:4. The explanation offered by Rabbeinu Bachya follows that of Ramban (see his Commentary on the
Torah, Genesis, p. 323).   (53) Amos 3:6. The sound of the Shofar signaled the approaching danger to the city. Would it be possible then — asks the prophet — for the
citizenry not to be stirred by the disaster that might overwhelm the city? The implication to the blowing of the Shofar on the New Year is obvious.   (54) Psalms 47:6. See
Ramban, Commentary on the Torah, Numbers, pp. 89-90.

war against Israel], the Philistines knew that the Ark of G-d had come, and they immediately said, *G-d is come into the camp.*[55] This is the intent of the verse, *And when the Philistines heard the noise of the 't'ruah,' they said, What meaneth the noise of this 't'ruah'?*[56]

There is another reason for this commandment of blowing the Shofar. The day of New Year marks the completion of the creation of the world and the establishment of G-d's Kingdom over it, for there can be no king if there are no people [for him to rule]. It is customary among mortal kings to have the horn blown at the beginning of their reign, as it is said, *And they blew the ram's horn, and all the people said, Long live King Solomon.*[57] Royal majesty on earth is akin to that of heaven.[58] Therefore, G-d has commanded us to blow the Shofar on this day which marks the beginning of His Kingdom, thus teaching us that *G-d reigneth over the nations, G-d sitteth upon His holy Throne.*[59] It is this thought that David expressed [in the verse mentioned above], *Say among the nations: The Eternal reigneth.*[39]

The blowing of the Shofar also alludes to the destruction of the Sanctuary, which took place amidst shouts and blasts of the horn, as it is stated, *Thou hast heard, O my soul, the sound of the Shofar, the alarm of war.*[60] [Upon hearing the Shofar], then, we should experience consternation and cry and pray for the Temple's restoration. Additionally, the blowing of the Shofar alludes to the coming Redemption, as the prophet assured us, *And it shall come to pass in that day, that a great Shofar shall be blown.*[61] There is also an intimation of the Resurrection of the dead, which will occur by means of blowing the Shofar, as it is written, *All ye inhabitants of the world, and ye dwellers on the earth,* etc., *when the Shofar is blown, hear ye.*[62] *All ye inhabitants of the world* refers to the living; *ye dwellers on the earth,* refers to the dead, as it is said, *Awake and sing, ye that dwell in the dust.*[63] The blowing of the

---

(55) I Samuel 4:7.   (56) *Ibid.,* Verse 6.   (57) I Kings 1:39.   (58) Berachoth 58 a.   (59) Psalms 47:9.   (60) Jeremiah 4:19.   (61) Isaiah 27:13.   (62) *Ibid.,* 18:3.   (63) *Ibid.,* 26:19.

Shofar, moreover, alludes to the Binding of Isaac, for although the Sages said,[64] "All horns are valid [for the blowing of the Shofar]," it is nonetheless known that a ram's horn is the most preferred means of performing the commandment, [for a ram has been sacrificed in Isaac's stead].[65]

We have been commanded to blow the Shofar on this day [of the New Year], the Day of Judgment, when the sustenance for each individual and his family is decreed. Hence, we say [in the prayers of that day]: "Thereon sentence is pronounced upon countries — which of them is destined for the sword and which to peace, which to famine and which to plenty — and each individual creature is visited thereon to be recorded for life or for death." On this day, all creatures pass individually before G-d, and all secret and overt things are clarified before Him. This is "the day the world was called into being." We do not recite the *Hallel*[66] on this day, for the Sages explained:[67] "Rabbi Abahu[49] said, 'The ministering angels asked G-d, Why does Israel not recite the song of *Hallel* before You on the New Year and the Day of Atonement? G-d replied, when the King sits on the Throne of Judgment with the books of the living and the books of the dead open before Him, is it possible that Israel should be expected to recite the song of *Hallel*?' "

Therefore, His Wisdom ordained that these Ten Days of Penitence [from the New Year to the Day of Atonement inclusive] shall be the time for the sinner to repent his sin. That there are ten days is a matter of necessity for the preservation of the world, for the Sages said,[68] "The world was created with ten Sayings." After Adam sinned, the world became steeped in idolatry and was marked for destruction, but Noah — the tenth generation after Adam — rectified the world through his merit. So it was with Abraham, the tenth generation after Noah.

---

(64) Rosh Hashanah 26 a.   (65) See Genesis 22:13.   (66) See above in *Atzereth* (Solemn Assembly), Note 40.   (67) Arakhin 10 b.   (68) Aboth 5:1. Actually Scripture mentions only nine times the expression *And G-d said* in the chapter on Creation. The tenth one is considered to be the verse, *In the beginning G-d created the heaven and the earth* (Genesis 1:1), for it is said, *By 'word of the Eternal' were the heavens made* (Psalm 33:6, Rosh Hashanah 32 a).

Because of Abraham, his seed merited the opportunity to accept the Torah, which is comprised of the Ten Commandments, the means of the world's preservation. Therefore, in the prayer of Rosh Hashanah, the Sages ordained the recitation of ten verses pertaining to the Sovereignty of G-d, ten verses pertaining to Remembrance, and ten verses in which the role of the Shofar is mentioned.

This day, being holy to the Eternal,[69] is distinctly dedicated to the [forementioned] purpose. Tishri, the seventh month, is likewise set apart for the observance of many commandments. The Sages called Tishri "the mighty month of commandments" because of the many precepts which apply therein: the New Year, the Shofar, the Day of Atonement, the Succah, the palm branch, the willow, and the libation of water. Additionally, there is a great inspiration to be derived in this month from its constellation, the zodiacal sign of the Balance, which intimates that the deeds of all creatures are weighed at this time, *to give every one according to his ways, and according to the fruit of his doings,*[70] or as we say in the liturgy, "On this day, the world was called into being. On this day, You cause all creatures of the universe to stand in judgment either as children or as servants, etc." That is to say, we do not know whether You will judge us in our capacity as Your children—as it is said, *Ye are the children of the Eternal your G-d*[71]—or as Your servants, for it is said, *For unto Me the children of Israel are servants.*[72] If as children, have pity upon us as a father has pity upon his children.   It is usual that a father will chastise his son and at times be delighted by him, as it says, *For whom the Eternal loveth He correcteth, even as a father the son in whom he delighted.*[73] If we have not merited to be treated as children but only as servants, there are many masters who have pity upon their servants, as Scripture states, *Behold, as the eyes of the servants unto the hand of their master, as the eyes of a maiden unto the hand of her mistress, so our eyes look unto the Eternal our G-d, until He be gracious unto us.*[74]

(69) See Isaiah 58:13. (70) Jeremiah 32:19. (71) Deuteronomy 14:1. (72) Leviticus 25:55. (73) Proverbs 3:12. (74) Psalms 123:2.

שבועה
Inviolability of an Oath

One should first fear the King on high and then a mortal king / One should be extremely careful about mentioning the Divine Name / The great sin of uttering G-d's Name in vain and the punishment thereof / The violation of an oath to a non-Jew constitutes a profanation of G-d's Name in the extreme.

Inviolability of an Oath

I [COUNSEL THEE]: KEEP THE KING'S COMMAND, AND
[ABOVE ALL] THAT IN REGARD OF THE OATH OF G-D.[1]

Solomon warned us to fulfill and observe all of the commands of the king, whom we have been charged to fear, as the Sages expounded:[2] *"Thou mayest indeed set him king over thee[3]* so that his fear will be upon you." Similarly, Solomon said, *Fear thou the Eternal, my son, and the king,*[4] by which he meant that we should first fear the King on high, and afterwards fear the king on earth. Solomon equated the fear of both [G-d and the mortal king] to teach us that just as one fears G-d although he does not see Him so should one fear the mortal king even when not in his presence.

Solomon continued, *Meddle not with them that are given to change.*[4] That is to say, do not fear the mortal king first at the cost of violating the will of G-d. Hence, the phrase *my son* occurs between *the Eternal* and *king* in contradistinction with the usual style found in other sections of the Book of Proverbs[5] [where the author begins the

---

(1) Ecclesiastes 8:2. The supreme authority of the king is superseded by the loyalty one owes to G-d, Who is the King of kings. It is the oath given to Him at Sinai by all the generations that takes precedence to the command of the earthly monarch. The fear of the king of the land though is a necessary factor in the preserving of peace in society, as will be explained. (2) Kiddushin 32 b. (3) Deuteronomy 17:15. (4) Proverbs 24:21. "Fear the king, provided he does not turn you aside from the fear of G-d, for the Divine will must always be above the will of any human being" (Rashi, *ibid.*). (5) E.g., *ibid.*, 5:1: *My son, attend to my wisdom,* and elsewhere.

verse with the expression "my son"]. This indicates that although Solomon equated the fear of G-d and the mortal king, they are nevertheless not equal in status nor are they to be associated together; there is a vast difference between them *as far as light excelleth darkness.*[6]

Thus, the purport of the verse[1] is that the fear of the king on earth is necessary for the preservation of the country and is highly beneficial to the people, but the paramount and mighty basis of it all is the fear of the Supreme King, in Whose power lies the life of all kings and their dominions. Accordingly, Solomon said here, "*I* [counsel thee]: *keep the king's command* and do whatever he charges you to do. Above all else, however, you should keep *that in regard of the oath of G-d.*[1] That is to say, if the king wishes you to transgress any of G-d's commandments, do not heed him. Rather, you should first remember the fear of G-d and the oath you gave at Sinai to accept upon yourself the Torah and the commandments." The Sages similarly explained in the Midrash:[7] "*I keep the king's command.* I am ready to obey the command of the kings of the nations with regard to tributes and poll-taxes. However, *that in regard of the oath of G-d,*[1] I will not obey their command. We find that Hananiah, Mishael, and Azariah[8] said to King Nebuchadnezzar, [who attempted to force them to worship an idol]: '*O Nebuchadnezzar, we have no need to answer thee in this matter.*[9] You are our king for tribute and poll-tax, but when you tell us to worship idols, you are only Nebuchadnezzar and not a king.' " That is to say, "We are not permitted to violate the oath we have taken at Sinai."

One should be extremely careful about mentioning the Divine Name, for this is part of the fear of G-d. The Sages said in Temurah:[10] "The admonition against uttering the Name of G-d in vain is derived from the verse, *Thou shalt fear the Eternal thy G-d.*"[11] It is also based on the statement, *Thou shalt not take the Name of the Eternal thy G-d*

---

(6) Ecclesiastes 2:13.   (7) Bamidbar Rabbah 15:11.   (8) They were three captive Judean princes who were serving in the palace of King Nebuchadnezzar of Babylon. Risking their lives for the observance of the laws of the Torah, they ultimately rose to great power in the Babylonian royal court.   (9) Daniel 3:16.   (10) Temurah 4 a.   (11) Deuteronomy 6:13.

in vain. [12] Consider this latter verse, which is the third of the Ten Commandments. It occurs after the admonition against idolatry, thus teaching us that just as one must be heedful in mentioning G-d's Name and not to attribute His Glory to any other thing, so is one obligated to honor His Name. Thus, one who uses G-d's Name in vain is guilty of profanation, as it is written, *And ye shall not swear by My Name falsely, and thou thereby profane the Name of thy G-d.* [13]

This verse, *[Thou shalt not take the Name of the Eternal thy G-d in vain],* [12] prohibits swearing in G-d's Name in vain. Thus, it is forbidden to swear to something that is contrary to well known facts or to the truth of a self-evident fact. For example, one should neither swear that a pillar of gold is of marble, nor should he swear that it is of gold. The Sages commented: [14] "[When dedicating a beast for a sacrificial offering], a man should not say, 'Unto the Eternal, this is a whole burnt-offering' or 'Unto the Eternal, this is a sin-offering.' [Instead, he should say, 'This is a whole burnt-offering unto the Eternal' or 'This is a sin-offering unto the Eternal.'] We know this because Scripture says, . . . *an offering unto the Eternal.* [15] Surely, we should apply the method of *kal vachomer!* [16] If the Torah has said about one who is about to dedicate [something to Heaven], 'Let not My Name be pronounced until you have first mentioned the offering, is it not logical that we certainly must not pronounce the Name of G-d to no purpose whatsoever!"

If a person took an oath, whether he did so while holding a sacred object [e.g., a Scroll of the Torah or *Tefillin*] in his hand or not, the violation of any part of that oath is as grave a matter as denying the Torah itself. The renowned scholar Rabbi Abraham ibn Ezra wrote: [17]

---

(12) Exodus 20:7.   (13) Leviticus 19:12.   (14) Nedarim 10 b.   (15) Leviticus 1:2. The word *korban (an offering)* thus precedes the word *Lashem (unto the Eternal).* The reason for the prohibition of mentioning the Name of G-d first is that perhaps after having uttered the Divine Name he will change his mind and decide not to bring the beast as an offering. He will thus have pronounced the Divine Name to no purpose.   (16) See above, *Emunah* (Faith), Note 106.   (17) Ibn Ezra in his commentary on Exodus 20:7.

"One who violates an oath is considered as if he has disavowed and denied G-d, for the intent of the oath is as follows: 'Just as G-d is true, so are my words true.' Hence, if he does not fulfill his words, it is as if he has disavowed G-d. In the Ten Commandments, we find a distinct reward only for honoring one's father and mother, and we find an express punishment only for the sin of idolatry and an oath taken in vain. Many people think that taking the Name of G-d in vain is not a great sin. However, I [Abraham ibn Ezra] will demonstrate that it is the most severe of all sins. When one commits murder and adultery, which are very grave sins, he cannot continue to commit these sins at all times because of fear of punishment. On the other hand, one who is in the habit of swearing in vain will do so countless times each day. He will even precede any statement he makes with an oath, for such a person considers swearing an elegant style of speech. If Israel were guilty of this sin alone, that would suffice as a reason to prolong the exile and to add a blow to the beatings we endure. I will further demonstrate to those people the senseless folly of such action: One who commits murder, adultery, or theft or one who bears false witness gains some pleasure or benefit from his act, but one who swears falsely[18] profanes G-d's Name in public without deriving any benefit." Thus far Ibn Ezra.

The Sages said in the Midrash:[19] "One who violates an oath is considered as if he has violated a ban, for the two are identical in severity."

Because of the sin of swearing falsely, the world is ruined, society wavers, and even the fruits of the earth spoil, for Isaiah said, *Therefore swearing devoureth the earth*, etc., *and men are left few.*[20] *The new*

---

(18) At this point, Ibn Ezra's commentary, *ibid.*, adds these words: " . . . at a time when he is not under obligation to swear."   (19) Pirkei d'Rabbi Eliezer, 38. A ban carries with it severe forms of ostracism, which affect the religious, social, and economic status of the person to whom it applies. The thought of the Midrash is that the same consequences apply to whoever takes the Name of G-d in vain or in falsehood.   (20) Isaiah 24:6. The thought is clear. For other sins the transgressor alone is punished, except for swearing by the Name of G-d falsely which implicates the whole world.

wine faileth, the vine fadeth, etc.[21] *The mirth of tabrets ceaseth, the noise of them that rejoice endeth.*[22]

Headfulness regarding an oath entails being careful with sacred objects as well as with vows and freewill offerings. One who commits trespass and derives any benefit from sacred objects is guilty of a heinous sin. Similarly, one who vows to bring a freewill offering on the occasion of his wedding or because of sickness or any other event that befell him and does not redeem his pledge has indeed stumbled and is guilty of a heinous sin. One who says, "I will study this chapter or this tractate," has made a great vow to the G-d of Israel.[23] This applies to any commandment, for mere utterance of intent to do a meritorious deed is equal to a real vow. Certainly, then, when one publicly pledges a contribution to some meritorious cause, he must fulfill his promise. If not, it is a false claim of a meritorious deed, concerning which it is written, *As vapors and wind without rain, so is he that boasteth himself of an unredeemed gift.*[24] Moreover, his unpaid pledge is like a stolen article in his possession, for he deprives the sacred cause of his promised donation. However, one who abides by his words and fulfills his promise of a gift he helps bring rain to the world in time of need, for the Sages commented:[25] "*I will be that which I will be.*[26] G-d said, 'As you are with Me, so am I with you. If you open your hand and give charity, as it says, *Thou shalt surely open thy hand,*[27] I also will open My hand, as it says, *The Eternal will open unto thee His good treasure the heaven to give the rain.*"[28] Thus, it is clearly mentioned here that the rains increase through the merit of giving charity.

(21) *Ibid.*, Verse 7. (22) *Ibid.*, Verse 8. (23) Nedarim 8 a. Although he has not expressed his wish to "study this chapter or this tractate" in the precise language of a vow, his mere expressed wish to do a meritorious deed is deemed to be like a vow. A similar instance is if one expresses a wish to contribute charity, although he has not done so in the form of a vow (Rabbeinu Asher). (24) Proverbs 25:14. (25) Ramban, in his Commentary on the Torah, Exodus, p. 36, also quoted this passage in the name of "a Midrash Agadah." (26) Exodus 3:14. (27) Deuteronomy 15:8. (28) *Ibid.*, 28:12.

One who swears to a non-Jew and violates his oath profanes G-d's Name. We derive this from the case of Zedekiah, [the last King of Judah prior to the destruction of the First Temple]. Zedekiah had sworn loyalty to King Nebuchadnezzar of Babylon and violated his oath, for which he was punished, as Ezekiel said, *And he* [Nebuchadnezzar] *took of the royal seed* — a reference to Zedekiah, a scion of the royal family — *and made a covenant with him*[29] and *made him swear by G-d.*[30] In addition to the imprecation and oath which Zedekiah took upon himself, he left a number of princes and prominent men with Nebuchadnezzar as guaranties that he would not rebel but would remain submissive to him. However, as soon as Zedekiah violated his oath, the prophet said of him, *Shall he prosper? Shall he escape that doeth such things?*[31] The prophet continued to state[32] that G-d swore that Zedekiah would die in Babylon, the city of Nebuchadnezzar. The verse, *And I will spread My net upon him,*[33] refers to the chain of events mentioned in the Midrash:[34] "There was a cave that extended from the house of Zedekiah to the plains of Jericho. Zedekiah attempted to flee [from the Babylonians] through this cave, but G-d designated a deer [to run along the surface above the cave]. When the Babylonians saw the deer and pursued it, they spied Zedekiah emerging from the cave and caught him."

All this punishment befell Zedekiah for the sin of violating the oath he had tendered to the King of Babylon. From this, you may learn the severity of the sin involved in violating an oath made to a non-Jew. It is thus stated in Scripture, *And ye shall not swear by My Name falsely, and thou thereby profane the Name of thy G-d; I am the Eternal.*[13] That is to say, "I, G-d, will punish you if you will in any way swear falsely, even to a non-Jew, because you will have profaned the Divine

---

(29) Ezekiel 17:13. (30) II Chronicles 36:13. (31) Ezekiel 17:15. (32) See *ibid.*, Verse 16. (33) *Ibid.*, Verse 20. (34) Cited by Rashi and R'dak in their commentaries on Ezekiel 17:20. The source of this Midrash, however, is unknown.

Name." Similarly, wherever the expression *I am the Eternal* is written,
the purport thereof is, "I am the Eternal Who rewards for the fulfillment [of this precept] and Who punishes for the violation thereof."
Therefore, Solomon warned people to be heedful of any commandment concerning which Scripture relates the utterance of the King: *I
am the Eternal,* as Solomon said, *I* [counsel thee]: *keep the king's command, and* [above all] *that in regard of the oath of G-d.*[1]

שבת

The Sabbath

The observance of the Sabbath is the first commandment with which Israel was charged after the Exodus prior to the Giving of the Torah / The explanation of Isaiah's prophecy concerning the Sabbath / Scripture attributes the destruction of the First Sanctuary to the desecration of the Sabbath although the people were guilty of other sins, too / The preservation of the Sanctuary was dependent upon the observance of the Sabbath / The greatness of the Sabbath and the secret contained in its observance / The reward for one who rejoices on the Sabbath / One should be grieved by the public desecration of the Sabbath, and the courts must rectify the situation / The Sabbath is a sample of the World to Come.

The Sabbath

IF, BECAUSE OF THE SABBATH, THOU TURN AWAY THY FOOT FROM PURSUING THY BUSINESS ON MY HOLY DAY, AND CALL THE SABBATH A DELIGHT, AND THE HOLY OF THE ETERNAL HONORABLE, AND SHALT HONOR IT, NOT DOING THY WANTED WAYS, NOR PURSUING THY BUSINESS, NOR SPEAKING THEREOF;[1] THEN SHALT THOU DELIGHT THYSELF IN THE ETERNAL, AND I WILL MAKE THEE TO RIDE UPON THE HIGH PLACES OF THE EARTH, AND I WILL FEED THEE WITH THE HERITAGE OF JACOB THY FATHER; FOR THE MOUTH OF THE ETERNAL HATH SPOKEN IT.[2]

It is known that the observance of the Sabbath is the first commandment with which Israel was charged in Marah[3] prior to the Giving of the Torah on Sinai, as the Sages said:[4] "At Marah, they were commanded concerning the Sabbath and the laws of justice, as it says, *There He made for them a statute and an ordinance.*"[5]

---

(1) Isaiah 58:13. The centrality of the thought and law of the Sabbath is a cardinal principle of Judaism. Here the prophet speaks of the physical and spiritual blessings entailed in the observance of the Sabbath, when it is honored and made into a day of delight. (2) *Ibid.*, Verse 14. Why *the inheritance of Jacob* is singled out more than that of the other patriarchs, will be made clear in the text. (3) See Exodus 15:23. Marah was the site of the people of Israel's first encampment after they left the shores of the Red Sea, on the way from Egypt to Sinai. The precept of the Sabbath was later included in the Ten Commandments proclaimed at Sinai. (4) Sanhedrin 56 b. See Ramban, Commentary on the Torah, Exodus, pp. 208-210. (5) Exodus 15:25. *A statute* refers to the Sabbath, and *an ordinance* to the laws of justice.

The commandment of the Sabbath alludes to Creation out of absolute nothingness. Therefore, we are charged to remember the Sabbath every day, as it says, *Remember the Sabbath-day, to keep it holy.*[6] According to the simple meaning of Scripture, this remembrance requires that we call the days of the week "one day after the Sabbath," "two days after the Sabbath," etc. We should not designate them by any particular name [of the celestial ministers, e.g., Sunday for the "sun's day," Monday for the "moon's day," etc.]. Thus, the verse, *Remember the Sabbath-day, to keep it holy,*[6] means "remember it every day." This is the case with the Exodus, concerning which the same expression is used: *Remember this day in which ye came out from Egypt.*[7] The commandment is that we should remember the Exodus daily, as it is written, *That thou mayest remember the day when thou camest forth out of the land of Egypt all the days of thy life.*[8]

It is further known that the commandment *Remember the Sabbath-day, to keep it holy*[6] was stated on the day of the Sabbath, for the Torah was given on the Sabbath-day as explained in Tractate Shabbath.[9] It is therefore fitting that the Sabbath be considered as important as the entire Torah, for the Sabbath-day was designated as the one on which the Torah would be given.

The observance of the Sabbath is comprised of both a negative commandment, *In it thou shalt not do any manner of work,*[10] and a positive commandment, *And on the seventh day thou shalt rest.*[11] Isaiah likewise mentioned both the negative and positive commandments. He stated, *If thou turn away thy foot,*[1] which means that even if you are already on the road and you remind yourself that it is the Sabbath, you should turn back. All the more so should you refrain *from pursuing thy business.*[1] If it is prohibited to journey beyond the Sabbath limits,[12] the transgression of which entails a simple prohibition,

(6) *Ibid.,* 20:8. (7) *Ibid.,* 13:3. (8) Deuteronomy 16:3. (9) Shabbath 86 b. (10) Exodus 20:10. (11) *Ibid.,* 23:12. (12) By law of the Torah, we may go twelve miles in any direction beyond the boundaries of the town we are in. By Rabbinic

one is so much more answerable for performing work on the Sabbath, for one who wantonly works on the Sabbath in the presence of witnesses who have warned him incurs the death penalty; in the absence of witnesses, he incurs extirpation.

Isaiah stated, *on My holy day,*[1] meaning the day which G-d sanctified and distinguished from the other days. He further stated, *And call the Sabbath a delight,*[1] meaning that you should delight on the Sabbath by eating and drinking more than you normally do on other days. You will then remember the Creation and give thanks to G-d for having created the world *ex nihilo.* In this way, both body and soul will be delighted: the body through food and drink, and the soul through remembering the deeds of G-d and His wonders.

The Sabbath is to be welcomed just as one welcomes a king to join him at his meal. The expression, *And call the Sabbath a delight,*[1] is thus as if Isaiah said, "And you shall welcome the Sabbath, in reward for which you will merit delight, the true reward of life in the World to Come." Isaiah added, *and the holy of the Eternal honorable.*[1] That is to say, the Glory of G-d will cover you and you will be honored by Him, adorned and crowned with glory.

And thou shalt honor it, not doing thy wanted ways, nor pursuing thy business, nor speaking thereof.[1] The prophet explained here that one should distinguish the Sabbath from the other days of the week in three ways: dress, cessation of the pursuit of business, and speech. The Sages commented:[13] "It is forbidden to pursue *thy business* but it is permissible to engage in heavenly [i.e., religious] affairs," e.g., stipulating the betrothal of girls and make arrangements for teaching a boy to read or contemplate to teach him some trade. The consequence of the latter is considered a religious affair, since a trade will provide him with a livelihood and keep him away from theft and robbery. One's manner of speech on the Sabbath should also be different. He

ordinance, however, a Sabbath journey is limited to two thousand cubits (Mishneh Torah, *Hilchoth Shabbath* 27:1). A cubit is 21.85 inches long. (13) Shabbath 113 a.

should speak quietly and limit his conversation. The Sages also commented:[13] "*Nor speaking thereof.*[1] This indicates that discussing business [on the Sabbath] is forbidden, but thinking about it is permitted." Throughout the generations, however, pious people have avoided thinking about secular affairs. Rather, their thoughts and speech have been devoted only to sacred matters, which are their delight.

During the era of the First Temple, Israel was guilty of many sins, yet Scripture ascribes the destruction of the Temple to the lack of observance of the Sabbath, as the prophet Jeremiah said, *And if ye will not hearken unto Me to hallow the Sabbath-day, and not to bear a burden and enter in at the gates of Jerusalem on the Sabbath-day; then will I kindle a fire in the gates thereof, and it shall devour the palaces of Jerusalem, and it shall not be quenched.*[14] This teaches you that the Sabbath is equal in importance to all the commandments; it is an attestation of the creation of the world.

The people of Israel were exiled from the Holy Land, the center of the world, only when they desecrated the Sabbath, which is midway between the three days preceding it and the three days following it. In Sefer Yetzirah (Book of Creation),[15] it is said: "The Holy Temple is situated exactly at the center of the world." Therefore, it was proper for the existence of the Temple to depend upon the observance of the Sabbath. Furthermore, the Sabbath is called "rest," as it is written, *And He rested on the seventh day,*[16] and the Land of Israel is also termed *the rest*, as it is written, *. . . to the rest and to the inheritance.*[17] Scripture thus assures us that if we observe the rest on the Sabbath, G-d will protect the Land, and if not, He will order its destruction.

A person should heed the observance of the Sabbath. He should make it a day of delight and a day of rest, for that day is so sacred and

(14) Jeremiah 17:27. (15) Sefer Yetzirah 4:4. — This work is one of the oldest books of Jewish mysticism. Its theme, the creation of the world, has challenged the greatest Jewish mystics throughout the generations to fathom the profoundness of its texts. (16) Exodus 20:11. (17) Deuteronomy 12:9.

distinguished that even the wicked ones in Gehenna[18] find rest thereon.
It is said in the Midrash:[19] The wicked Turnus Rufus[20] met Rabbi
Akiba on the Sabbath and asked him, 'Why is this day different from
others?' Rabbi Akiba rejoined, 'What makes one person more
distinguished than another?' Turnus Rufus answered, 'My master [the
emperor] desired it so,' Rabbi Akiba replied, 'The same is true of the
Sabbath; the Master desired it to be holy. Moreover, the people that
ate the manna testified that it descended on all days of the week but
not on the Sabbath. Furthermore, the river Sabbatyon[21] flows on the
six weekdays and rests on the Sabbath.' Turnus Rufus argued, 'Do not
discuss the manna, for it is not of our times. As for the Sabbatyon, I do
not believe you.' " Rabbi Akiba then told him to verify the matter at
his father's grave in order to be convinced that the Sabbath is different
from the other days of the week. The Roman did so and found that his
father's day of rest in Gehenna is the Sabbath, since a smoke did not
arise from his grave on that day as it did on other days of the week.
Turnus Rufus then communicated with his father through sorcery and
asked him, " 'You did never observe the Sabbath in your life, yet you
do so in your death! When did you become a Jew?' His father explained, 'My son, if one does not observe the Sabbath while he is alive, he
will be forced to observe it when he comes here. All during the week we
are punished, but on the Sabbath we rest. At the conclusion of the
Sabbath, after the regular evening prayers are completed, the an-
nouncement to return to Gehenna is heard.' " Thus far in the
Midrash.[19] This is why it is customary among all the people of Israel to
recite the evening prayers slowly at the conclusion of the Sabbath.

The subject of the Sabbath contains esoteric matters which the
Supreme One commanded Moses to reveal to individuals in Israel.
Thus, Scripture begins [the subject of the Sabbath], *And thou* [Moses],

(18) See above, *Orchim* (Hospitality), Note 12.   (19) Tanchuma, *Ki Thisa*,
33.   (20) Turnus Rufus was the Roman governor of Judea in the time of Emperor
Hadrian, who, in his infamy, had decreed against the observance of the commandments of the Torah.   (21) See Ramban, Commentary on the Torah, Deuteronomy,
pp. 362-363.

speak unto the children of Israel,[22] i.e., inform them of the overt and mystical aspects of the Sabbath. However, Moses made no mention of the mystical higher allusions of the Sabbath, for he spoke to all the men and women of the entire congregation of Israel. Therefore, he concealed the esoteric aspects of the Sabbath and spoke only briefly of its overt matters. From here we have clear proof that one should not reveal and expound mystical matters in public.

Then shalt thou delight thyself in the Eternal.[2] If you will *call the Sabbath a delight,*[1] *then* you yourself will *delight in the Eternal*[2] measure for measure. That is to say, He will give you physical delight in such abundance to the extent that you will thank Him for His beneficence and your soul will delight in remembering Him. Rabbeinu Saadia Gaon,[23] however, explained this as a reference to physical delight. That is to say your physical delight will reflect your belief in G-d. Your delight will not be like that of the fools, of whom it is said, *Delight is not befitting a fool.*[24] Rather, you will enjoy it in its measured and weighed amounts, for it is the way of the intelligent person not to indulge excessively in pleasures but to partake of them only moderately. In this manner, his intellect improves and his threefold strength — discernment, thinking, and memory — increases.

And I will make thee to ride upon the high places of the earth.[2] G-d thus assured us [that we will possess] the Land. The Sages commented:[25] *"And I will feed thee with the heritage of Jacob thy father.*[2] One who delights in the Sabbath is rewarded with an unlimited inheritance, as it says, *and I will feed thee with the heritage of Jacob thy father.* The verse does not mention Abraham, to whom it was said, *Arise, walk through the land,*[26] nor Isaac, to whom it was said, *And I will give unto thy seed all these lands.*[27] Rather, Scripture

---

(22) Exodus 31:13. (23) See above, *Hashgachah* (Divine Providence), Note 52. (24) Proverbs 19:10. Abundance of wealth does not befit a fool, for his ostentatious display of his possessions and his selfish use thereof, merely confirm his folly and lack of proper understanding. (25) Shabbath 118 a-b. (26) Genesis 13:17. *"The land* denotes only this land and not others" (Rashi, Shabbath 118 b). (27) Genesis 26:4.

mentions Jacob, to whom it was said, *And thou shalt spread abroad to the west, and to the east, and to the north, and to the south.*[28] It is so written, *And He established it unto Jacob for a statute, to Israel for an everlasting covenant;*[29] *saying: Unto thee will I give the land of Canaan.*[30] Although the Land was given to all the patriarchs, it was nonetheless designated as an inheritance only to the sons of Jacob.

Since we have demonstrated the great power of the commandment of the Sabbath, the overt and mystical aspects of which indicate *the wondrous works of Him Who is perfect in knowledge,*[31] it behooves us now to bestir ourselves to share in the sorrow and concern over the scandalous condition in the land,[32] for there are Jews who desecrate the Sabbath while judges and officers avert their eyes and fail to discipline the rebellious ones. We experience a full measure of shame—as well as contempt and wrath—when we realize that Israelites publicly profane the Sabbath. The nations of the world do observe their festival days, but Israel does not observe the Sabbaths and festivals, which are called *the appointed seasons of the Eternal.*[33] Thus, the desecration of the Sabbath entails a sin in itself as well as a profanation of G-d's Name. Therefore, it is proper for the courts to exercise their power, and their efforts at correction will not be futile. May G-d in His mercies cleanse us of iniquity and prepare our hearts to fear Him. May He reward us together with those who observe the Sabbath in accordance with the law and with those who worship Him, for the Sabbath is a sample of the World to Come. It is stated in the Midrash:[34] "The Sabbath was given to Israel only as a sample of the World to Come, for it is said, *And ye shall eat in plenty and be satisfied,* etc.[35] *And My people shall never be ashamed.*"[36]

---

(28) *Ibid.*, 28:14. (29) Psalms 105:10. (30) *Ibid.*, Verse 11. (31) Job 37:16. (32) Reference is undoubtedly to cities in his own country of Spain. "Judges and officers" refer to the Rabbis and leaders of the communities. (33) Leviticus 23:4. (34) Zohar, *Bereshith,* p. 48 a. The Scriptural support for this statement, however, is not mentioned in the Zohar passage. (35) Joel 2:26. (36) *Ibid.*, Verse 27. The word *never (never be ashamed)* suggests the World to Come, wherein Israel will never again be ashamed.

שלום
Peace

> *Peace is the foundation and principle of the entire Torah / Peace is the essential element in the creation and preservation of the world / The greatness of the power of peace / Peace within a city and the management thereof is dependent upon its leaders / The importance of greeting a fellow man / The significance of avoiding dissension and the enemies of peace / The return of the exiles to Jerusalem will be through the merit of peace.*

Peace

HER WAYS [THE WAYS OF TORAH] ARE WAYS OF
PLEASANTNESS, AND ALL HER PATHS ARE PEACE.[1]

This verse teaches us that peace is the foundation and principle of
the entire Torah and the essential element in the creation of the world.
Thus, the Sages commented,[2] "At the time of Creation all beings came
into existence with their acquiescence and with pleasure in their form,
for it says, and all *'tz'va'am' (the host of them)*."[3]

It is known that the heavens were created first. [The Hebrew term
for heavens is] *shamayim,* for the heavens are composed of *eish* (fire)
and *mayim* (water). These two opposites are held together only
through peace. It is thus written, *He maketh peace in His high places.*[4]
The expression *in His high places* denotes two things. First, it refers to
the very heavens, which consist of essential substances [fire and water]
that could not continue to exist together without making peace among
themselves. Second, it refers to G-d's angels in the high places, for He

(1) Proverbs 3:17. The Torah does not impose upon man any burdensome tasks,
such as endangering his life or health. On the contrary, all commands of the Torah
contribute to the complete wholesome pleasantness of life, and all its paths are designed to bring peace between man and G-d, and between man and man. (2) Chullin
60 a. (3) Genesis 2:10. The Sages in Tractate Chullin 60 a, expounded, "Read not
the word as *tz'va'am* (their host), but as *tzivyonam* (their pleasure)," which Rashi,
ibid., interprets, all beings came into existence "according to the shape of their own
choice." Thus, peace and harmony reigned at the Creation. (4) Job 25:2.

makes peace among them, as the Sages commented,[5] *"Dominion and fear are with Him; He maketh peace in His high places.[4] Dominion* is a reference to the angel Michael; *and fear* is a reference to the angel Gabriel." Michael consists of water, Gabriel consists of fire, and G-d makes peace between them. In Midrash Shir Hashirim Rabbah, we find:[6] "Rabbi Abin said, 'Not only does G-d make peace between one angel and another, but He does so even within one angel, half of whom is snow and half fire.' Rabbi Yochanan said, *'He maketh peace in His high places.[4]* The heavens are made of water and the stars of fire, yet they do not damage each other. The sun never faces the concave of the moon's crescent.' "[7]

Consider the greatness of the power of peace! Even if Israel would worship idols, the attribute of justice would not be brought to bear against them [immediately] if they were united, as it is said, *Ephraim is joined to idols; let him alone.[8]* The power of peace is great indeed, for the Priestly Blessing concludes with peace, as it is said, . . . *and give thee peace.[9]* Great is the power of peace, for the sake of which the Torah contains accounts such as [Joseph being told by his brothers], *Thy father did command before he died, saying: So shall ye say unto Joseph: Forgive, I pray thee now, the transgression of thy brethren,* etc.[10] Actually, Jacob had never issued such a command; the brothers said it on their own volition.[11]

G-d Himself is called *Shalom* (Peace), as it is said, *And he* [Gideon] *called it* [the altar], *The Eternal is Peace.[12]* It is further written, *The*

(5) Bereshith 12:7. (6) Shir Hashirim 3:20. (7) The concave side of the crescent is always away from the sun so that the moon should not feel humiliated by the sun whose light is whole while hers is incomplete. In this way, G-d keeps peace between the sun and moon (Rosh Hashanah 23 b). (8) Hosea 4:17. Ephraim is a surname for the Kingdom of Israel, consisting of ten tribes, and founded by Jeroboam who was of the tribe of Ephraim. (9) Numbers 6:26. (10) Genesis 50:16-17. (11) Rashi, *ibid.*, explained that Jacob never suspected Joseph of desiring to punish his brothers. Hence, enjoining Joseph from doing so would have been unnecessary. (12) Judges 6:24.

Song of Songs, which is Solomon's.[13] G-d chose the people of Israel from among seventy nations and called them Shulamith, as the Sages commented:[14] *"Return, return, O Shulamith,*[15] a nation in the midst of which the Perfect One of the universe dwells."* G-d gave Israel the Torah, which is entirely peace, as it is said, *Her ways are ways of pleasantness, and all her paths are peace.*[1] All of the precepts of the Torah bring peace to the body and soul. It brings peace to the body, as it is said, *If thou wilt diligently hearken to the voice of the Eternal thy G-d, and wilt do that which is right in His eyes, and wilt give ear to His commandments, and keep all His statutes, I will put none of the diseases upon thee,* etc., *for I am the Eternal thy Healer.*[16] It brings peace to the soul because through the fulfillment of the commandments, the soul will return in a state of perfection and purity to its source—as it is said, *The law of the Eternal is perfect, restoring the soul,*[17] that is, to its original Divine source. This is the basis of the Sages' comment:[18] "When the righteous leave this world, the ministering angels come forth to meet them, saying, *He entereth into peace.*[19] On the other hand, when the wicked leave the world, angels of wrath come out to meet them, saying, *There is no peace, saith the Eternal concerning the wicked."*[20]

Great is the dimension of peace. Our Sages, therefore, sealed the prayer [of the *Amidah*] with a blessing for peace:[21] "[Blessed art Thou . . .] Who blessest Thy people Israel with peace." Thus, the Sages said in Tractate Megillah:[22] The blessing of G-d is peace, as it is said, *The Eternal will give strength unto His people; the Eternal will bless His people with peace."*[23] Solomon likewise concluded the Song of Songs with peace, saying, *Then was I in his eyes as one that found*

(13) Song of Songs 1:1. "[The Hebrew word] *lishlomoh* (generally translated, *which is Solomon's*) is here understood as 'to the King Whose essence is peace' " (Shir Hashirim Rabbah 1:12). (14) Shir Hashirim Rabbah 7:1. (15) Song of Songs 7:1. (16) Exodus 15:26. (17) Psalms 19:8. (18) Kethuboth 104 a. (19) Isaiah 57:2. (20) *Ibid.,* 48:22. (21) The *Amidah* is the prayer recited three times daily on weekdays, four times on the Sabbath and festivals, and five times on the Day of Atonement. (22) Megillah 18 a. (23) Psalms 29:11.

peace.[24] Thus you learn that the preservation of the world depends upon peace.[25]

In Vayikra Rabbah, the Sages said:[26] "Chizkiyah said two things [about the greatness of peace]; Bar Kappara said three. Chizkiyah said, 'Great is peace, for concerning all other commandments, it is written, *If thou see,*[27] *If thou meet,*[28] *If a bird's nest chance to be before thee.*[29] That is to say, if the occasion occurs, you must fulfill the commandment. Here in the case of peace, however, it is written, *Seek peace, and pursue it;*[30] seek it in your place, and pursue it in other places as well. Peace is great indeed. Regarding all of the journeys in the wilderness, it is written, *And they journeyed, and they pitched.*[31] [The plural forms of the verbs in these verses intimate] that the people of Israel journeyed in dissension and pitched their camps in dissension. However, when they came to Mount Sinai, they were in complete unanimity, for it is written, *and Israel encamped there.*[32] [The Hebrew verb *vayichan* (and he—Israel—encamped) is in the singular form, which indicates unity.] G-d said, This is the moment that I will give them My Torah.' Bar Kappara said: 'Great is peace, for Scripture attributes certain words to a person in order to maintain peace between people. Thus, it is written that Sarah had said, *And my lord* [Abraham] *is old,*[33] yet when G-d related her words to Abraham, it is written [that she said], *And I am old.*[34] Peace is great indeed, for the prophets made such a change in order to make peace between Manoah [Samson's father] and his wife. It is written [that the angel said to Manoah's wife], *Behold now, thou art barren, and hast not borne,*[35]

---

(24) Song of Songs 8:10. (25) This is obvious from the fact that the concluding prayer in the *Amidah* asks for peace, thus suggesting that all previous requests depend upon fulfillment of this final prayer. (26) Vayikra Rabbah 9:9. (27) Exodus 23:5. (28) *Ibid.*, Verse 4. (29) Deuteronomy 22:6. (30) Psalms 34:15. Not only must you *seek peace,* but you are also to *pursue it,* meaning you are to persist in your endeavor until you achieve such goal. (31) Numbers 33:5. (32) Exodus 19:2. (33) Genesis 18:12. (34) *Ibid.*, Verse 13. A change was made in the words of Sarah so that Abraham would not be offended by her remark. This was done for the sake of maintaining peace. (35) Judges 13:3.

but to Manoah he said, *Of all that I said unto the woman let her beware.* [36] That is to say, she needs only medicine [to restore her fertility, but she is really not barren]. Peace is great indeed. If the higher beings, among whom there is no jealousy, hatred, dissension, or malevolence, require peace—as it says, *He maketh peace in His high places* [4]—the lower creatures that are subject to all these evils—all the more—require peace.' In the academy of Rabbi Yishmael, it was taught: 'Great is peace, for the Divine Name, which is written in sanctity, is erased into the water of bitterness [37] in order to make peace between a man and his wife [whom he suspected of adultery].' Rabbi Shimon ben Chalafta said, 'Great is peace, for when G-d created the world, He made peace between the higher and the lower worlds. Thus, on the first day, G-d's creation applied to both worlds, as it says, *In the beginning G-d created the heaven and the earth.* [38] On the second day, He created things for the higher world, as it is written, *Let there be a firmament in the midst of the waters.* [39] On the third day, He created things for the lower world, as it says, *Let the waters be gathered together.* [40] On the fourth day, He created things for the higher world, as it says, *Let there be lights in the firmament.* [41] On the fifth day, He created things for the lower world, as it says, *Let the waters swarm.* [42] On the sixth day, when G-d was about to create man, He said, If I make man for the higher world, the latter will have the advantage over the lower world. If I make man for the lower world, it will have the advantage over the higher world. What did G-d do? He created man for the higher and the lower worlds. [The soul of man is for the higher world, and his body is for the lower world.] It is thus written, *Then the Eternal G-d formed man of the dust of the ground, and breathed into His nostrils the breath of life.'* [43] Thus far in Midrash Vayikra. [26]

In Bamidmar Sinai Rabbah, the Sages said: [44] "Great is peace, for it has been given to the humble ones, as it is said, *And the humble shall*

---

(36) *Ibid.*, Verse 13. (37) See Numbers 5:23. (38) Genesis 1:1. (39) *Ibid.*, Verse 6. (40) *Ibid.*, Verse 9. (41) *Ibid.*, Verse 14. (42) *Ibid.*, Verse 20. (43) *Ibid.*, 2:7. (44) Bamidbar Rabbah 2:12.

inherit the land and delight themselves in the abundance of peace.[45]
Peace is great indeed, for it has been given to lovers of Torah, as it is
said, *Abundant peace have they that love Thy law.*[46] Great is peace,
for it has been given to students of Torah, as it is said, *And all thy
children shall be taught of the Eternal, and great shall be the peace of
thy children.*[47] Peace is great, for it has been given to those who
distribute charity, as it is said, *And the work of charity shall be
peace.*"[48] Thus far in Bamidbar Sinai Rabbah.[44]

It is known that the peace within a city and the management thereof
is dependent upon the city leaders. The Sages commented:[49]
"Everything depends upon the leader. Moses was righteous and made
the multitude righteous. Jeroboam the son of Nebat[50] sinned and made
the multitude sin." When the leaders of a city do not conduct
themselves properly, dissension increases among their people, who
become like scattered sheep without a shepherd, as Jeremiah said, *For
the shepherds are become brutish and have not inquired of the Eternal; therefore they have not prospered, and all their flocks are scattered.*[51] *The shepherds* are Yehoyakim and Zedekiah, kings who were
unsuccessful in their administration of government because they did
not inquire of the Eternal as [the righteous] King Josiah did.[52]
Therefore, Israel was exiled because of the failure of its leaders.

In order to further the cause of peace, the Sages commanded that a
person should be sure to greet his fellow man, for greetings induce cor-
dial relations and increase love among men. A Sage[53] of the Talmud
praised himself by saying, "No man, even a non-Israelite, saluted me
first." The Sages have further said:[54] "If one who usually greets his
friend fails to do so one day, he is guilty of [the prophet's accusation],

(45) Psalms 37:11. (46) *Ibid.*, 119:165. (47) Isaiah 54:13. (48) *Ibid.*,
32:17. (49) Zohar, *Beshalach* 47 a. See p. 404, Note 72, in my Hebrew edition of
Kad Hakemach for the verbatim quotation. (50) See above, *Orchim* (Hospitality),
Note 40. (51) Jeremiah 10:21. (52) II Chronicles 34:26. (53) This was Rabban
Yochanan ben Zaccai (Berachoth 17 a). See above, *Matar* (Rain), Note
22. (54) Berachoth 6 b.

That which is stolen of 'he'ani' (the poor) is in your houses,"[55] i.e.,
"that which is stolen of *ha'aniyah* (answering) [the other person's
greeting]."

Consider the great power of greeting, for our Rabbis permitted mentioning G-d's Name in salutations.[56] It is written of Boaz, *And he said
unto the reapers, The Eternal be with you.*[57] Similarly, the angel said
to Gideon, *The Eternal is with thee, thou mighty man of valor.*[58] All
this is ethical instruction and good conduct commanded by the Torah
in order to increase love and social relations among the people of
Israel.

One should avoid dissension and people who are the enemies of
peace, for it is known that whole kingdoms and communities have been
destroyed because of controversy. We find in the case of the revolt of
Korach, for example, that the punishment [of the rebels] included
even *their wives, and their sons, and their little ones.*[59] The Sages commented:[60] "Four people are called wicked. First, there is the one who
lifts his hand to smite his fellow man even though he does not actually
strike him, for it is said, *And he* [Moses] *said to the wicked one, Why
wilt thou smite thy fellow?*[61] It does not say, 'Why did you smite?' but
Why wilt thou smite? Second, there is the one who borrows money and
does not repay it, as it is said, *The wicked borroweth and payeth not.*[62]
Third, there is the arrogant person, as it says, *A wicked man
hardeneth his face.*[63] Finally, there is the quarrelsome person, as it is

---

(55) Isaiah 3:14.   (56) Berachoth 54 a.   (57) Ruth 2:4. Boaz thus used the Divine
Name in greeting the workers in his field.   (58) Judges 6:12. This verse is mentioned
to show that the custom of greeting a person with G-d's Name was used not just by
Boaz but also by the angel when greeting Gideon.   (59) Numbers 16:27.   (60) Tanchuma, *Korach,* 8.   (61) Exodus 2:13.   (62) Psalms 37:21. This verse has been
broadened to embrace the following thought: The growth and development of any individual is accomplished through "borrowing" the benefits and blessings of one's society. The righteous man, as the verse concludes, *dealeth graciously, and giveth back*
manifoldly but the *wicked borroweth, and payeth not* back. The longer he lives the
greater his unpaid debt becomes (Hirsch).   (63) Proverbs 21:29.

said, *Depart, I pray you, from the tents of these wicked men,* [who joined the revolt of Korach against Moses]."[64]

In Midrash Tanchuma, we find:[65] "In the future, when G-d will return the exiles to Jerusalem, He will do so with peace, as it is said, *Pray for the peace of Jerusalem.*[66] It is further stated, *Behold, I will extend peace to her like a river.*"[67] In Tractate Megillah,[21] it is written: "The blessing of G-d is peace, for it is written, *The Eternal will give strength unto His people; the Eternal will bless His people with peace.*"[22]

---

(64) See Numbers 16:26. (65) Tanchuma, *Tzav,* 7.   (66) Psalms 122:6. (67) Isaiah 66:12.

שבועות

Shavuoth

---

*All the commandments in the Torah are divided into three
categories: those that relate to speech, those that relate to the
heart, and those that pertain to action / The heart is the most
vital organ and therefore it is located in the middle of the
body / The meaning of David's prayer for a 'pure
heart' / Why the Ten Commandments begin with the precept
that relate to the heart / The order of the positive commandments of the Torah as intimated in the positive precepts among
the Ten Commandments.*

מִצְוֹת עֲשֵׂה

The Positive Commandments

CREATE ME A CLEAN HEART, O G-D, AND RENEW A
STEADFAST SPIRIT WITHIN ME.[1]

All the commandments in the Torah are divided into three
categories. First, there are those that relate to speech, such as studying
the Torah, proclaiming the sanctity of the Sabbaths and festivals, by
reciting the *Kiddush* when they commence, and their distinction from
the other days of the week, by reciting the *Havdalah* when they conclude, and also the reading of the Scroll of Esther on Purim. Second,
there are those that relate to the heart, such as believing in G-d's Existence and Unity and loving G-d. Third, there are those that relate to
actions, such as the commandments of *Tzitzith, Tefillin, Mezuzah,
Lulav, Succah,* Circumcision, Charity, etc. These three categories are
alluded to in one verse: *But the thing is very nigh unto thee, in thy
mouth, and in thy heart, that thou mayest do it.*[2] Scripture thus sets

(1) Psalms 51:12. This verse already served as the main source for Rabbeinu
Bachya's theme in *Taharath Haleiv* (Purity of Heart). There, the author's emphasis
was on the word *clean* since his discussion dealt with the heart's purity. Here, however,
the keynote is *heart,* for the author explains the function of that organ in the observance of the commandments, which constitute the theme of the Festival of *Shavuoth,*
the day of the Giving of the Torah. The author has divided the theme into two main
divisions: the positive commandments, and the negative commandments. — It should
be noted that the presentation here does not exhaust the entire list of the commandments. In general, in listing the commandments our author was influenced by the
"Commentary on the Song of Songs attributed to Ramban." See Notes in my Hebrew
edition of Kad Hakemach, pp. 403-420.   (2) Deuteronomy 30:14.

forth that the categories of the commandments are those that are connected with the mouth, the heart, and action.

It is known that all the commandments of the Torah serve only to mend the heart, which is the essential concern. That is why Scripture mentions *thy heart* in the midth of the three categories, for the essential power of anything concentrates in the center. Thus the heart of man is in the center of his body, because the heart is the body's principal organ. Similarly, the Land of Israel is in the middle of the world, Jerusalem is in the middle of the Land, the Temple Mount is in the middle of Jerusalem, and the Temple itself is in the center of the Mount. Therefore, when King David prayed for a steadfast spirit to be created within him, he asked G-d to help him by creating a pure heart within him, so that he might repel debased desires. Solomon expressed a similar thought when he said, *He that loveth pureness of heart*[3] that is, he that is innocent of any evil thought—*hath grace in his lips.*[3] He will find grace in the eyes of everyone, and he will be worthy to *have a king for his friend.*[3] It says *a king,* not "the king," in order to teach you that a person who possesses a pure heart is more important than "the king."[4]

This concept was the reason for beginning the Ten Commandments with a precept relating to the heart, the commandment of belief [in the Existence of G-d], as it is said, *I am the Eternal thy G-d.*[5] Scripture thus warns man to strengthen himself in the belief that the world has a Creator, a Being Who brought everything into existence and Whose Existence is always absolute. Therefore, Scripture began with the word *Anochi, (I am),*[5] which indicates the Existence of G-d, blessed be He. This is the positive commandment expressed by the verse, *Know this*

(3) Proverbs 22:11. (4) Had the verse said that he is fit to be the friend of "the king," it would be referring to a specific king, who might be a debased individual. Therefore, it would be no credit to the pure-hearted person to say that he merits having "the king" for his friend. However, since the verse speaks of *a king,* it is referring to one who deserves to be a king, thus teaching you that *he that loveth pureness of heart* is worthy to be held as a friend of a monarch, since he is superior to the ruler. (5) Exodus 20:2.

*day, and lay it to thy heart, that the Eternal, He is G-d in heaven above
and upon the earth beneath.*[6]

The next expression [in the first commandment] is *the Eternal,*[5] The
Divine Tetragrammaton. The intent is to declare the Unity of the Being Who is the Creator. Thus, He mentioned the Tetragrammaton,
which denotes His Unity, as known to students of the mystic teachings
of the Torah. This is the positive commandment, *Hear, O Israel: the
Eternal our G-d, the Eternal is One.*[7] Next is the expression *thy G-d,*[5]
and the intent thereof is to direct us to love the One Being, blessed be
He, as it is said, *And thou shalt love the Eternal thy G-d.*[8] Thus you
learn that these three words, *'Anochi Hashem Elokecha' (I am the
Eternal thy G-d),*[5] allude to the first three positive commandments
which precede all others: to believe in His Existence, to declare His
Unity, and to love Him. All three are indicated in the verses of the
reading of the *Sh'ma: the Eternal our G-d*[7] refers to His Existence; *the
Eternal is One*[7] establishes His Unity; *And thou shalt love the Eternal
thy G-d*[8] commands us to love Him.

[The commandment to] love G-d includes the positive precepts of
Tefillin and *Tzitzith.*[9] A lover always remembers his beloved, and it is

---

(6) Deuteronomy 4:39. This is in consonance with the opinion of Rabbeinu Bachya
ibn Pekuda, who in his Chovoth Halevavoth, *Sha'ar Hayichud* 3, used this verse as the
basis of the commandment to believe in G-d's Existence. This opinion is also found in
the Commentary on Shir Hashirim, attributed to Ramban (Kithvei Haramban, Vol.
II, p. 521). Most scholars, however, derive the commandment directly from Exodus
20:2. (7) Deuteronomy 6:4. (8) *Ibid.*, Verse 5. (9) This is obvious from
Maimonides' arrangement of the commandments in his Mishneh Torah, for in the section entitled "The Book of Love" he includes the laws of *Tefillin* and *Tzitzith*. It should
be noted at this point that Rabbeinu Bachya's intent was to demonstrate that all of the
613 commandments are included in the Ten Commandments. This concept had been
expressed by Saadia Gaon, but our author undoubtedly had even earlier authority to
substantiate his position. Having established the commandment to love G-d from the
word *Elokecha (thy G-d)*, Rabbeinu Bachya now proceeds to list all precepts which are
included within this category. This will be his line of reasoning in the following sections
on both the positive and negative commandments.

written of the *Tefillin, And they shall be . . . for a memorial between your eyes.* [10] Of the *Tzitzith* it is also written, *And ye shall remember all the commandments of the Eternal.* [11] The love of G-d entails the love of a fellow man, as it is said, *Thou shalt love thy neighbor as thyself.* [12] The latter precept in turn, embraces the following:

Damages for inflicting injury; [13] laws of injuries caused by animals, [14] and injuries caused by an open pit. [15] The law of slaying a thief in self-defense, or exacting restitution from a convicted thief. [16] The law of damage caused by a fire. [17] The laws of an unpaid bailee, [18] a paid bailee, [19] a hirer, [20] and a borrower. [21] The laws of buying and selling, [22] and of litigants. [23] There is thus a total of eleven positive commandments.

The commandment to love one's neighbor further embraces the commandments of rebuking the sinner, [24] — which in turn includes the commandment to impose the penalty of stripes [25] — and loving the stranger. [26]

The fear of G-d emanates from the love of Him, for one who loves his master also fears him lest he transgress his will. On the other hand, it is possible that one who only fears his master may not love him. Therefore, love is not included in fear, while fear is included in love. Because we are commanded to love G-d, we are by the fact itself commanded to fear Him, as it is written, *Thou shalt fear the Eternal thy G-d.* [27] Fear of G-d includes the following commandments:

---

(10) Exodus 13:9.   (11) Numbers 15:39.   (12) Leviticus 19:18.   (13) Exodus 21:18.   (14) *Ibid.*, Verse 35.   (15) *Ibid.*, Verse 33.   (16) *Ibid.*, 22:1, 3.   (17) *Ibid.*, Verse 4.   (18) *Ibid.*, Verse 8.   (19) *Ibid.*, Verses 9-12.   (20) *Ibid.*, Verse 14.   (21) *Ibid.*, Verse 13.   (22) Leviticus 25:14.   (23) Exodus 22:8. (24) Leviticus 19:17.   The reproof, however, should not be in such a manner as to shame the transgressor in public. In this way the observance of the commandment bespeaks an attitude of love to a fellow being who strayed from the right path.   (25) Deuteronomy 25:3. The punishment must in no way be administered to cause bodily harm, or out of revenge. Instead, it is to be carried out in order to fulfill the obligation placed upon the court by the Torah. (26) *Ibid.*, 10:19. (27) *Ibid.*, 6:13.

Building the Sanctuary, which is designated for prayer[28] and offer-ings;[29] revering the Sanctuary;[30] guarding the Sanctuary;[31] dedicating the tribe of Levi for services in the Sanctuary;[32] honoring the priests;[33] attiring the priests in their sacred garments;[34] anointing the priests with the sacred Oil of Anointment;[35] and giving the priests the *terumah* (heave-offering).[36] [Also included within the fear of G-d are these commandments which devolve upon] the priests: kindling the lamps in the Sanctuary;[37] blessing the Israelites;[38] arranging the Showbread and incense upon the Showtable;[39] burning the incense, which indicates only joy;[40] arranging the perpetual fire on the altar;[41] removing the ashes from the altar daily;[42] ministering in divisions;[43] [the priests] washing [their hands and feet] before performing the Ser-vice,[44] and [the High Priest] marrying only a virgin.[45] All these precepts comprise the fear of G-d.

Yet another group of positive commandments falls under the category of the fear of G-d: The Assembly during the Festival of Tabernacles at the end of every seventh year;[46] eating the second tithe in Jerusalem;[47] writing a Scroll of the Torah, one for each individual and two for the king, one to deposit in his treasury and the other to be

(28) As clearly expressed by Solomon when he dedicated the Sanctuary. See I Kings 8:29-30. (29) Exodus 24:8. (30) Leviticus 19:30. (31) Numbers 18:2-3. (32) *Ibid.*, Verse 23. (33) Leviticus 21:8. (34) Exodus 28:2. See above, *Ga'avah* (Haughtiness), Note 29. (35) Exodus 30:31. At the initiation of Aaron and his sons into the priesthood, both he and his sons were anointed by Moses (Leviticus 8:30). Their whole lineage thus became sanctified for all time to come. The High Priests after Aaron, however — the office not being of an hereditary nature — had to be anointed at their induction. See "The Commandments," Vol. I, p. 43. (36) Deuteronomy 18:4. (37) Exodus 27:21. (38) Numbers 6:23. (39) Exodus 25:30. (40) *Ibid.*, 30:7. The burning of incense was not for the purpose of atoning for some sinful deed or thought. Instead, it was an indication of joy in the Divine Service, as it says, *Oil and incense rejoice the heart* (Proverbs 27:9). (41) Leviticus 6:6. (42) *Ibid.*, Verse 3. (43) Deuteronomy 18:6. (44) Exodus 30:19-21. (45) Leviticus 21:13. See in Sefer Hachinuch, Positive Commandment 272. (46) Deuteronomy 31:12. The verse continues, *that they may hear, and that they may learn, and fear the Eternal your G-d.* (47) *Ibid.*, 14:23: . . . *that thou mayest learn to fear the Eternal thy G-d.*

with him always;[48] fearing father and mother;[49] and the commandment of circumcision.[50]

The love and fear of G-d also encompass the following commandments: Praying before Him;[51] cleaving to Him;[52] taking an oath by His Name;[53] sanctifying His Name;[54] studying Torah and teaching it to others,[55] since it is impossible to achieve the love of G-d without the study of Torah; reciting the Grace after meals;[56] emulating the Creator [as far as it is in our power] and walking in His holy ways;[57] and avoiding impurity, such as:

Defilement through contact with the carcass of animals[58] and certain creeping creatures.[59] Defilement of food and drink.[60] The impurity of menstruants,[61] women after childbirth,[62] lepers,[63] the *zav* and *zavah*,[64] and the impurity of a corpse.[65] [Also encompassed within the love and fear of G-d are] the laws of the water of sprinkling,[66] the Nazirite,[67] marrying a woman only by a binding ceremony.[68] The laws of divorce,[69] and the suspected adulteress.[70] It is thus written, *Sanctify yourselves, therefore, and be ye holy,*[71] upon which the Sages expounded in the Sifre:[72] "*Sanctify yourselves, therefore,* by observing the commandments, *and be ye holy,* for the very observance of the commandments is sanctity."

Asher (Who).[73] This alludes to all the positive commandments which utilize the word *asher,* such as: using correct weights and

(48) *Ibid.,* Verse 19: . . . *that he* [the king] *may learn to fear the Eternal his G-d.* (49) Leviticus 19:3. (50) Genesis 17:10. (51) Deuteronomy 10:12. (52) *Ibid.,* Verse 20. (53) *Ibid.* See Maimonides, "The Commandments," Vol. I, pp. 10-11. (54) Leviticus 22:32. (55) Deuteronomy 6:7. (56) *Ibid.,* 8:10. (57) *Ibid.,* 28:9. (58) Leviticus 11:19. (59) *Ibid.,* Verse 29. (60) *Ibid.,* Verse 34. (61) *Ibid.,* 15:19. (62) *Ibid.,* 12:2. (63) *Ibid.,* Chapter 13. (64) *Ibid.,* 15:2, 25. A *zav* is a man suffering a flux. A *zavah* is a woman suffering a flux outside her menstrual period. (65) Numbers 19:11-17. (66) *Ibid.,* Verses 18-21. (67) *Ibid.,* Chapter 6. (68) Deuteronomy 24:1. (69) *Ibid.,* Verse 3. (70) Numbers 5:12. (71) Leviticus 11:44. (72) Sifre, *Shelach,* 115. (73) Exodus 20:2.—Having completed the list of commandments which stem from the first three words of the first commandment, the author now turns to each of the following words and lists the commandments relative thereto. This arrangement is,

measures, as it says, *Just balances, just weights,* etc., *I am the Eternal your G-d 'asher' (Who) brought you out of the land of Egypt;*[74] a robber restoring the actual article he took by force;[75] slaughtering animals in the prescribed manner before eating the flesh;[76] covering the blood of slain birds and animals.[77] Searching for prescribed characteristics in cattles and animals,[78] fish,[79] grasshoppers,[80] and birds.[81] The laws of breaking the neck of the heifer;[82] penalizing false witnesses with the penalty they sought to bring upon others;[83] appointing judges and officers of the court,[84] and honoring father and mother.[85]

Hotzeithicha (Brought you out).[73] The actual release from bondage occurred at night, as it says, *The Eternal thy G-d brought thee forth out of Egypt by night.*[86] Although the Exodus itself took place during the day,[87] the permission to go was given at night.[88] Thus, the word *hotzeithicha* alludes to the following commandments which apply at night: eating unleavened bread on the eve of the fifteenth day of Nisan;[89] eating the Passover-offering;[90] recounting the departure from Egypt,[91] and counting the Omer.[92]

Mei'eretz (Out of the land).[73] This embraces all commandments which pertain to the earth, such as the laws of: *orlah;*[93] the fruits of fourth-year plantings;[94] allowing the land to remain fallow during the

---

to my knowledge, not mentioned by any other source. The author follows the same procedure with the other words of the Ten Commandments, as will be seen below. (74) Leviticus 19:36. (75) *Ibid.,* 5:23. Here too the expression is, *'asher' (that) which he took by robbery.* Similar expressions are found in each of the other commandments mentioned in this category. (76) Deuteronomy 12:21. (77) Leviticus 17:13. (78) *Ibid.,* 11:2. (79) *Ibid.,* Verse 9. (80) *Ibid.,* Verse 21. (81) Deuteronomy 14:11-12. (82) *Ibid.,* 21:4. (83) *Ibid.,* 19:19. (84) *Ibid.,* 16:18. (85) Exodus 20:12. (86) Deuteronomy 16:1. (87) Numbers 33:3. (88) Exodus 12:31. (89) *Ibid.,* Verse 18. (90) *Ibid.,* Verse 8. (91) *Ibid.,* 13:8. (92) Leviticus 23:15. The counting of the forty-nine days of the Omer begins on the second night of Passover and continues every night until *Shavuoth.* (93) The fruit yielded by young trees during the first three years, *ibid.,* 19:23. (94) *Ibid.,* Verse 24.

Sabbatical year,[95] and all positive commandments concerning the offerings which can be brought only in the place chosen by G-d.[96]

Mitzrayim (Egypt).[73] This includes all positive commandments connected with the Exodus from Egypt, as follows: sanctifying the firstling of a ritually clean beast and bringing it as an offering [when the Sanctuary existed];[97] redeeming firstborn children;[98] redeeming the firstling of an ass;[99] breaking the neck of the firstling of an ass;[100] bringing the Additional Offerings on the various festivals;[101] observing the three festivals;[102] appearing in the Sanctuary during the festivals;[103] rejoicing on the festivals;[104] removing leaven on the fourteenth day of Nisan;[105] slaughtering the Passover-offering;[106] eating the Passover-offering;[107] bringing the Second Passover-offering;[108] eating the Passover-offering together with unleavened bread and bitter herbs,[108] and dwelling in a Succah on the Festival of Tabernacles.[109]

Mibeith (Out of the house of).[73] This includes two positive commandments [pertaining to houses]: affixing a *Mezuzah,*[110] and building parapets around roofs.[111]

---

(95) Exodus 34:21. (96) Deuteronomy 12:11. (97) *Ibid.*, 15:19. When the Sanctuary is not in existence, the firstling of a clean beast is to be given to a priest, who may slaughter it for food only after it has of itself received a blemish which would have invalidated it for an offering if the Sanctuary were in existence. (98) Numbers 18:16. (99) Exodus 34:20. (100) *Ibid.*, 13:13. (101) Numbers 28:9-29:38. (102) Exodus 23:14. The three festivals are: Passover, Weeks, and Tabernacles. (103) *Ibid.*, Verse 17. (104) Deuteronomy 16:14. (105) Exodus 12:15. (106) *Ibid.*, Verse 6. It should be noted that the slaughtering of the Passover-offering itself, is an independent commandment distinct from the commandment to eat thereof. In all other offerings the act of slaughtering is part of the overall commandment of that particular offering. For the unique significance why the slaughtering of the Passover-offering should be counted as a separate commandment, see above in Passover, Part One. (107) *Ibid.*, Verse 8. (108) Numbers 9:11. (109) Leviticus 23:42. (110) Deuteronomy 6:9. (111) *Ibid.*, 22:8. This commandment includes removing all obstacles and sources of danger from the place in which we live. See Maimonides, "The Commandments," Vol. I, p. 197.

Avadim (Bondage).[73] This includes lavishing gifts on a Hebrew bondman or bondmaid on the occasion of their liberation,[112] the law of a Hebrew bondman,[113] espousing a Hebrew bondmaid,[114] and the law of a Canaanite bondman.[115]

E-il kana (A jealous G-d).[116] This includes the commandments pertaining to the administration of the death penalty by the court, as well as the blowing of the Shofar on the New Year,[117] which serves to remove the anger and wrath from upon the world on the Day of Judgment.

V'oseh chesed (And He showeth mercy).[118] This embraces all positive commandments that call for acts of lovingkindness: giving charity to the poor;[119] lending money to the poor;[120] giving gleanings to the poor,[121] the forgotten sheaf,[122] the corner of the field, defective grape clusters, and grape-gleanings;[121] giving poorman's tithe;[123] returning a pledge to a needy owner;[124] paying wages on time;[125] allowing an employee to eat some of the produce on which he is working;[126] unloading a burden from a fellow man or a tired animal;[127] assisting the owner in lifting a burden onto his beast;[128] restoring lost property to its owner;[129] and the law of the levirate marriage,[130] which is also an act of mercy to the childless decedent.

Ul'shomrei mitzvothai (And to those who keep My commandments).[118] This includes the positive commandment of *Chalitzah* [where a childless widow "takes off" the shoe of her late husband's brother, if he will not marry her], as it is said, *and shall remove his shoe from off his foot,*[131] the expression *ul'shomrei* [which literally means: and those who "watch"] intimates the case of this widow who

(112) Deuteronomy 15:14. (113) Exodus 21:2. (114) *Ibid.*, Verse 8. (115) Leviticus 25:46. (116) Exodus 20:5. See above Note 73. (117) Numbers 29:1. (118) Exodus 20:6. See above Note 73. (119) Deuteronomy 15:11. (120) Exodus 22:24. (121) Leviticus 19:9-10. (122) Deuteronomy 24:19. (123) *Ibid.*, 14:28-29. (124) *Ibid.*, 24:13. (125) *Ibid.*, Verse 15. (126) *Ibid.*, 23:25. (127) Exodus 23:5. (128) Deuteronomy 22:4. (129) *Ibid.*, Verse 1. (130) *Ibid.*, 25:5. (131) Deuteronomy 25:9.

"watches" whether her brother-in-law will marry her or whether she will have to perform *Chalitzah* on him.

Remember the Sabbath-day. [132] Remembering the Sabbath includes the positive commandment of resting on the Sabbath as well as on the various festivals; sanctifying the New Moon and determining the years and months by the court, [133] for all the festivals are dependent upon such reckoning, and the counting of the Sabbatical years and the Jubilee. [134]

But the seventh day is a Sabbath unto the Eternal thy G-d. [135] This includes renouncing ownership of the land on the Sabbatical year, [96] resting the land on the Jubilee, [136] and granting the right of redemption to the seller of land. [137]

Honor thy father and thy mother. [138] This includes honoring G-d, Who is the First Cause, the Supreme Father of all. Honoring G-d in turn encompasses the law of burying the condemned man on the same day as his execution, because delaying his burial exposes the body to unnecessary shame, and in case of hanging it is a reproach to G-d in Whose image man is made. [139]

There are other positive precepts, such as that of the palm branch and the commandment to be fruitful and multiply, which are also contained in the word *Anochi (I am).* [5] The palm branch alludes to G-d, as explained in the Midrash, [140] and so does the commandment to be fruitful and multiply, for the Rabbis said [141] that "One who fails in this duty is like one who sheds blood and diminishes the Image of G-d."

---

(132) Exodus 20:8. The commandment to rest on the Sabbath is found *ibid.*, 23:12. (133) *Ibid.*, 12:2. (134) Leviticus 25:8. (135) Exodus 20:10. (136) Leviticus 25:10. (137) *Ibid.*, Verse 24. (138) Exodus 20:12. (139) Deuteronomy 21:23. The same law—of burial on the day of death—is binding as regards all other dead. Delaying the burial for the sake of honoring the deceased—such as bringing a coffin and shroud, or the arrival of relatives, or informing the public—is permissible (Yoreh Deiah 357:1). (140) Vayikra Rabbah 30:9. See above, *Lulav* (The Palm branch), p. 363. (141) Yebamoth 63 b.

This commandment also includes a bridegroom rejoicing with his wife for a full year.[142]

The 248 positive commandments correspond to the 248 organs of the body. The Rabbis commented:[143] "There are 248 words in [the three sections of] the *Sh'ma*,[144] and one should take care in uttering them, for G-d said, 'If you guard what is Mine, I will guard what is yours.' " That is to say, "If you will be heedful with the 248 words in the *Sh'ma* or the 248 positive commandments of the Torah, I will guard the 248 organs of your body." When David said, *Keep me as the apple of the eye*,[145] G-d answered him, *Keep My commandments, and live.*[146] Thus, David said, *I cleave unto Thy testimonies, O Eternal, put me not to shame.*[147] *I will run the way of Thy commandments, for Thou doest charge my heart.*[148]

---

(142) Deuteronomy 24:5. (143) Tanchuma, *Kedoshim,* 6. (144) There are actually 245 words in the three passages of the *Sh'ma*. The three missing words necessary to complete the total of 248 are provided either by reciting *E-il Melech Ne'eman* (G-d the Faithful King) before the *Sh'ma* when praying privately, or by the congregational Reader repeating *Hashem Elokeichem Emeth* (The Eternal your G-d is True) at the conclusion of the *Sh'ma* in public prayer. (145) Psalms 17:8. (146) Proverbs 4:4. The verse, although recorded by Solomon, is attributed here to his father David, who was so told by G-d. (147) Psalms 119:31. (148) *Ibid.,* Verse 32.

מִצְוֹת לֹא תַעֲשֶׂה
The Negative Commandments

The seven righteous people who rectified the world until the generations were worthy to receive the Torah / From Jacob on, only a lack of a multitude of people deterred the Giving of the Torah. That deficiency was eliminated when Israel in Egypt reached a population of 600,000. Then, when G-d's power was visibly manifested through the miracles of the Exodus, the Torah was revealed / The order of the negative commandments as they emanate from the prohibitions in the Ten Commandments / The basis for the doctrine that the Ten Commandments embrace all the precepts / Proofs that the 613 commandments are eternal.

I SAID: I WILL CLIMB INTO THE PALM TREE, I WILL
TAKE HOLD OF THE BRANCHES THEREOF.[149]

Israel is here compared to the palm tree, as it is said, *The righteous shall flourish like the palm tree.*[150] "Just as the palm tree has only one heart [i.e., its sap cells are only in its stem, not in its branches], so the people of Israel have one heart which is directed towards their Father in heaven."[151]

I will take hold of the branches thereof.[149] That is to say, G-d will select [from among the generations] those righteous people who bore

---

(149) Song of Songs 7:9. The verse serves our author in a symbolic way, alluding to the fact that just as by climbing on a palm tree one can take hold of its branches, so when mankind achieved a certain high moral stature the time was ready for G-d to reveal His Torah to Israel in order to reach all branches of mankind.   (150) Psalms 92:13.   (151) Succah 48 b.

fruit for life eternal and through whom the world was purified. These
are the seven righteous men, from Adam to Jacob, who cleared the way
for the pure generation to receive the Torah: Adam, Seth, Noah,
Shem, Abraham, Isaac, and Jacob. There was impurity among some
of the children of each of these men. For example, Adam fathered
Cain, who killed his brother Abel. Enosh and his entire generation, the
descendants of Seth, began worshipping idols. These impure elements
were finally purged by Jacob, whose twelve sons were all wise and
righteous and devoid of any undesirable or debased element. Thus, the
conditions necessary for the acceptance of the Torah were met; a great
multitude of people was the only missing factor. This was eliminated in
Egypt, where the people of Israel were blessed with abundant increase
until they reached the number of 600,000.[152] This figure represents the
sum total of all divergent minds and opinions;[153] it was not proper that
the Torah should be given to any smaller group. After the performance of the signs and wonders in Egypt which proclaimed G-d's
Existence and Unity to the nations, the matter culminated in the Giving of the Torah at Sinai, where He showed Israel *His glory and His
greatness*[154] and where He made known to the world His Existence and
power.

The Midrash comments:[155] "*I said: I will climb into the palm tree. I
will take hold of the branches thereof.*[149] This refers to Hananiah,
Mishael, and Azariah, [the captive Judean princes who served in the
palace of Nebuchadnezzar, King of Babylon]. In their upright car-
riage, they refused to bow to the golden idol [erected by the king].
What did the king do? He said to them, 'Do you not see what the idol is
doing? Observe it, and on your own volition, you will bow down to it.'
What did the wicked Nebuchadnezzar do? He took the High Priest's
breastplate, [upon which was inscribed the Divine Tetragrammaton],·
and placed it in the mouth of the idol. He then brought musicians to

---

(152) See Exodus 12:37.   (153) This thought is mentioned by Ramban in "The
Law of the Eternal is Perfect" Writings and Discourses, p. 94.   (154) Deuteronomy
8:21.   (155) Shir Hashirim Rabbah 7:13.

play before it, and it uttered the words, *Anochi Hashem Elokecha (I am the Eternal thy G-d).*[5] Seeing this, Daniel obtained the king's permission to kiss the breastplate. He then adjured it, 'I am but a mortal human being who is the messenger of G-d. Take care that G-d's Name not be profaned through you. I enjoin you [the Divine Tetragrammaton] to leave the plate.' He then kissed it and swallowed the writing with his mouth. When he came down, the musicians played again, but no further utterance came out of the idol. Then the statue fell, as it is written, *Bel bowed down, Nebo stoopeth.*[156] When the nations of the world saw the miracles and the mighty deeds that G-d had performed for Hananiah and his companions, they smashed their idols and made bells out of them. They hung these bells on the necks of their dogs and asses, as it is stated, *Their idols are upon the beasts and upon the cattle.*[156] Israel then said to the idolaters, 'See what you were worshipping!' " Thus far the Midrash.[155] What prompted Hananiah and his companions to surrender themselves to be thrown into the burning furnace?[157] It was their desire not to transgress the precept, *Thou shalt have no other gods before Me.*[158]

Thou shalt have no other gods before Me.[158] This negative commandment prohibits us from deifying anything other than G-d, in our thoughts. It includes the prohibition against appointing a king who is not a born Israelite[159] so that no such a ruler would [ever be in a position to] harm the true faith [by enticing the people to worship idols]. The king himself is enjoined from taking many wives,[160] owning many horses,[161] and amassing great personal wealth.[160]

Thou shalt not make unto thee a graven image nor any manner of likeness,[162] for making the image leads to worshipping it. We are also prohibited from making idols for others to worship.[163] This prohibition of idolatry includes all related subjects.[164]

---

(156) Isaiah 46:1. (157) See Daniel 3:21. (158) Exodus 20:3. (159) Deuteronomy 17:15. (160) *Ibid.*, Verse 17. (161) *Ibid.*, Verse 16. (162) Exodus 20:4. (163) Leviticus 19:4. (164) See Maimonides, The Commandments, Vol. II, pp. 1-56.

And to those who keep My commandments.[165] This alludes to the prohibitions entailed in acts of lovingkindness, such as: taking a pledge from a widow;[166] demanding payment from a debtor known to be unable to pay;[167] excluding the proselytized descendant of Esau, beyond the second generation, from marrying into the Jewish community, the same applying to the Egyptian proselytes;[168] lending money on interest;[169] participating in a loan on interest, whether as surety, witness, or notary;[170] employing a Hebrew bondman in degrading tasks;[171] selling a Hebrew bondman by public auction;[172] employing a Hebrew bondman for rigorous work;[173] allowing the maltreatment of a Hebrew bondman;[174] selling a Hebrew bondmaid;[175] afflicting one's espoused Hebrew bondmaid;[176] selling a captive woman;[177] enslaving a captive woman;[177] and delaying payment of an employee's wages.[178]

Thou shalt not take the Name of the Eternal thy G-d in vain.[179] This [is one of the Ten Commandments, and] includes the following prohibitions: violating an oath by which we swear to do some act or not to do some act which religion neither requires nor forbids;[180] profaning the Name of G-d;[181] blaspheming the Name of G-d;[182] testing His promises and warnings;[183] and failing to fulfill any oral obligation, even if undertaken without an oath.[184]

Thou shalt not do any manner of work [on the Sabbath].[185] This prohibition includes: journeying on the Sabbath beyond the two

(165) Exodus 20:6. (166) Deuteronomy 24:17. (167) Exodus 22:24. (168) Deuteronomy 23:8. (169) Leviticus 25:37. (170) Exodus 22:24. (171) Leviticus 25:39. (172) *Ibid.*, Verse 42. (173) *Ibid.*, Verse 43. Unnecessary work is called "rigorous work" ("The Commandments," Vol. II, p. 246). (174) Leviticus 25:53. (175) Exodus 21:8. (176) *Ibid.*, Verse 10. This applies to diminishing her food, raiment, or conjugal rights, in such manner as to cause her pain and suffering ("The Commandments," Vol. II, p. 248). (177) Deuteronomy 21:14. (178) Leviticus 19:13. (179) Exodus 20:7. (180) Leviticus 19:12. E.g., "I swear that I will eat this loaf" or "I swear that I will not eat this loaf." (181) *Ibid.*, 22:32. (182) *Ibid.*, 24:16. (183) Deuteronomy 6:16. (184) Numbers 30:3. (185) Exodus 20:10.

thousand-cubit limit outside the town;[186] carrying out punishments on
the Sabbath,[187] and working an ox and an ass together.[188] For this
reason, it says here [in the Ten Commandments], . . . *Nor thine ox,
nor thine ass.*[189]

Thou shalt not murder.[190] This prohibition against killing an innocent person includes: a court convicting in a capital case by a majority
of one;[191] a judge arguing in favor of conviction in a capital case after
he had declared himself in favor of acquittal;[191] appointing a judge not
proficient in the wisdom of the Torah on the basis of his other good
qualities;[192] carrying out a sentence in a capital case on the basis of a
strong and nearly conclusive presumption;[193] acting as a judge in a
capital case in which he has also served as witness;[194] executing a
murderer without a trial;[195] sparing the life of one who pursues another
with intent to kill him;[196] punishing someone for committing a sin
under duress;[197] accepting ransom from one who has willfully committed murder;[198] accepting ransom from one who has unwittingly committed murder, thus absolving him from exile to a city of refuge;[199]
neglecting to save the life of one who is in danger;[200] leaving obstacles
in a public domain;[201] putting a stumbling-block before the blind;[202]
inflicting severe corporal punishment on a wrong-doer, thus causing
him injury;[203] an evil tongue;[200] hating one another;[204] shaming someone;[204] taking food utensils as a pledge,[205] and taking vengeance on one
another or bearing a grudge,[206] for whoever takes vengeance or bears a

(186) *Ibid.*, 16:29. See above, *Shabbath* (The Sabbath), Note 12. (187) Exodus
35:3. (188) Deuteronomy 22:10. (189) *Ibid.*, 5:14. (190) Exodus
20:13. (191) *Ibid.*, 23:2. (192) Deuteronomy 1:17. (193) Exodus
23:7. (194) Numbers 35:30. (195) *Ibid.*, Verse 12. (196) Deuteronomy 25:12.
See Maimonides, "The Commandments," Vol. II, p. 272. (197) Deuteronomy
22:27. (198) Numbers 35:31. (199) *Ibid.*, Verse 32. A person who unwittingly
commits murder is exiled to one of the cities of refuge and stays there until the death of
the High Priest. If the victim's next of kin kills him there during that time he is to be
held accountable for his death. (200) Leviticus 19:16. (201) Deuteronomy
22:8. (202) Leviticus 19:14. This is to be understood as to mislead any person who
seeks our advice. (203) Deuteronomy 25:3. (204) Leviticus 19:17.
(205) Deuteronomy 24:6. (206) Leviticus 19:18.

grudge does not walk in the paths of G-d, as it is said, *For I am merciful, saith the Eternal, I will not bear a grudge forever.*[207]

Thou shalt not commit adultery.[190] This prohibition includes the forbidden degrees of marriage and related subjects.[208]

Thou shalt not steal.[190] This prohibition against abducting an Israelite also includes the following: stealing money;[209] wronging one another in business;[210] cheating in measurements and weights;[211] keeping false weights and measures;[212] returning a fugitive bondman;[213] and dealing harshly with orphans and widows.[214]

Thou shalt not bear false witness.[190] This includes the prohibition against planning to divorce a wife while still living with her. This is akin to the statement, *Devise not evil against thy neighbor, [seeing he dwelleth securely by thee],*[215] and the prophet Malachi said, *For He hates* [the husband] *that sends away* [a wife].[216] [The prohibition of bearing false witness] also includes: divorcing a woman whom one had been compelled to marry after raping her;[217] accepting a wicked man's testimony,[218] and receiving testimony from a litigant's relative.[219]

---

(207) Jeremiah 3:12. (208) See Maimonides, "The Commandments" Vol. II, Commandments 330-361. (209) Leviticus 19:11. (210) *Ibid.*, 25:17. (211) *Ibid.*, 19:35. (212) Deuteronomy 25:14. The prohibition pertains to keeping false weights and measures in the house, even without the intention of ever using them. (213) *Ibid.*, 23:16. The commandment prohibits to surrender to his master an escaped bondman who has fled for refuge into the Land of Israel, "seeing that he has come to dwell in the clean Land, which has been chosen for the exalted people" ("The Commandments," Vol. II, pp. 241-242). See also Ramban, Commentary on the Torah, Deuteronomy, pp. 287-288. (214) Exodus 22:21. (215) Proverbs 3:29. Divorce itself is of course permitted by the Torah—see Deuteronomy 24:1—if for various reasons the husband and wife are incompatible. However, it is altogether improper for a husband to continue living with his wife whom he secretly plans to divorce (Gittin 90 a). (216) Malachi 2:16. While divorce is permissible, nevertheless, whoever divorces his first wife is in disgrace before G-d, for as the prophet says, *Because the Eternal hath been witness between thee and the wife of thy youth, against whom thou hast dealt treacherously, though she is thy companion, the wife of thy covenant (ibid.,* Verse 14, Gittin 90 b). (217) Deuteronomy 22:29. (218) Exodus 23:1. (219) Deuteronomy 24:16.

Thou shalt not covet.[220] This prohibition enjoins us from directing our thoughts to covet another's possessions. Thus, [the Ten Commandments] conclude with a percept pertaining to the heart even as they began with a precept pertaining to the heart [i.e., the belief in the Existence of G-d]. This proves that all [of the Ten commandments] are united; the end is connected to the beginning just as the flowing waters from a stream are connected to their source, and just as many sparks come forth from a single live coal. The prohibition against coveting includes the following: committing robbery;[221] fraudulently altering land boundaries;[222] usurping debts;[223] repudiating debts;[224] coveting another's property;[225] a hired laborer eating from the still growing crops among which he is working,[226] and a hired laborer consuming more of the crops than he needs for his meal.[227]

We have thus shown that the concept of 613 commandments is included within the Ten Commandments. These two divisions of positive and negative commandments aim to lead man in paths of goodness so that he can emulate the Creator. They also serve to help him avoid evil and indecency, thus causing his body and soul to be united in the worship of the Creator, blessed be He, as it says, *Depart from evil, and do good.*[228]

These 613 commandments apply forever; they are not dependent upon a specific time, as Scripture states, [*Moses commanded us a Torah*], *'an inheritance' of the congregation of Israel,*[229] the same expression as is used in connection with the Land of Israel, *and I will give it to you for 'an inheritance,'*[230] of which it is written, *as the days of the heavens above the earth.*[231] Another proof for this may be found in the

---

(220) Exodus 20:14. This is the tenth commandment. (221) Leviticus 19:13. (222) Deuteronomy 19:14. (223) Leviticus 19:13. E.g., withholding the wages of an employee. (224) *Ibid.*, Verse 11. (225) Deuteronomy 5:18. (226) *Ibid.*, 23:26. He is permitted to eat only from the crops he is cutting which have already fully ripened. (227) *Ibid.*, Verse 25. (228) Psalms 34:15. (229) Deuteronomy 33:4. (230) Exodus 6:8. (231) Deuteronomy 11:21. Similarly, the Torah which is also called *an inheritance* is forever.

Sages' statement:[232] "The 248 positive commandments correspond to the number of organs in the human body. It is thus as if each and every organ says to the person, 'Perform a commandment with me.' The 365 negative commandments correspond to the number of days in a solar year. It is thus as if each and every day says to the person, 'Do not commit a transgression on this day.' " Maimonides wrote:[233] "This is proof that the sum of 613 will never be diminished. If their number would decrease when a particular commandment would be completely fulfilled by the attainment of its object,[234] the statement [that the sum of 613 is immutable] would then prove to have been correct only at a particular time." Therefore, we must believe that the 613 commandments apply at all times. It is well known that all who observe them have great merit, as David said, *In keeping them there is great reward.*[235] It is further written, *Oh how abundant is Thy goodness, which Thou hast laid up for them that fear Thee, which Thou hast wrought for them that take their refuge in Thee, in the sight of the sons of men!*[236]

(232) Makkoth 23 b and Tanchuma, *Ki Theitzei*, 2.   (233) See Maimonides, "The Commandments," pp. 377-378.   (234) Maimonides fully explains this thought. See "The Commandments," Vol. I, Positive Commandment 187, pp. 200-201. (235) Psalms 19:12.   (236) *Ibid.*, 31:20.

תורה

The Torah: A Guide for Life

Part One

> *The benefits derived from the study of Torah are greater than those received from the sun / The magnitude of Torah necessitates the Oral Law, without which the Written Law could not be understood / Man was created primarily to study Torah, and one should be concerned about his neglect thereof / The greatness of the powers of the Torah / Man should search for ways to study Torah / The great punishment for neglecting to study Torah and the great extent of the reward for engaging therein.*

The Torah: A Guide for Life

> THE LAW OF THE ETERNAL IS PERFECT, RESTORING THE SOUL; THE TESTIMONY OF THE ETERNAL IS FAITHFUL, TEACHING WISDOM TO THE SIMPLE.[1] THE PRECEPTS OF THE ETERNAL ARE RIGHT, REJOICING THE HEART; THE COMMANDMENT OF THE ETERNAL IS PURE, ENLIGHTENING THE EYES.[2] THE FEAR OF THE ETERNAL IS PURE, ENDURING FOREVER; THE ORDINANCES OF THE ETERNAL ARE TRUE, THEY ARE RIGHTEOUS ALTOGETHER.[3]

These three verses were uttered by David in praise of the Torah. They follow those verses in which David spoke of the great luminaries that sustain the world and he described some of their many activities and benefits. At that point, however, David abruptly deviated [from his discussion of the luminaries] and declared that there is a still greater luminary than the sun, and that is the Torah. While it is true that the sun attests to and proclaims the grandeur, power, and majesty of G-d, the Torah does so far more extensively. For one who sits too long in the warm sun can be hurt, as was the case with the prophet Jonah, of whom it is said, *And the sun beat upon the head of Jonah,*

---

(1) Psalms 19:8. See Ramban, Writings and Discourses, pp. 30-32, where this theme is discussed. Our author was undoubtedly influenced by Ramban's work. (2) Psalms 19:9. The Divine wisdom revealed in the Torah brings to man both instruction and discipline. It brings him instruction, for it enlightens his eyes when he is in search of truth. It disciplines his desires and further restores his spirit when he is in distress. (3) *Ibid.*, Verse 10.

that he fainted.[4] However, one who engages steadily in Torah is *restoring the soul.*[1] Furthermore, if one looks directly at the sun, his eyes will become dim, but the Torah *enlightens the eyes.*[2] The sun is occasionally covered by clouds, which obscure its clarity. Moreover, it is even the object of idolatrous worship, which makes it a source of impurity. The Torah, however, is always pure, as the verse says, *The fear of the Eternal is pure, enduring forever*[3] without any interruption. The sun shines only during the day, not at night, but the light of the Torah serves incessantly. Furthermore, even during the day, the light of the sun diminishes after midday, but regarding the Torah it is said, *The ordinances of the Eternal are true, they are righteous altogether.*[3] Thus we learn that there are greater benefits flowing from the Torah than from the sun. Our Sages also ordained the wording in our prayers, "Enlighten our eyes in Thy Law and in Thy commandments." This is stated just after the benediction "Creator of the luminaries,"[5] intimating that man's only means of escape from the oppressive darkness of material things under the sun is through the fulfillment of the Torah and the commandments, which are higher than the sun.

David mentions here six expressions which describe the Torah as follows: law, testimony, precepts, commandment, fear and ordinance. These six key words corrspond to the six Orders of the Mishnah, as the Sages have commented in Midrash Tehillim:[6] "*The law of the Eternal is perfect*[1] corresponds to the Order of *Nashim* (Women).[7] *The testimony of the Eternal is faithful*[1] corresponds to the Order of *Zeraim* (Seeds), for the farmer who plants his seeds demonstrates his faith in the life of this world. *The precepts of the Eternal are right, rejoicing the heart*[2] corresponds to the Order of *Mo'eid* (Festival). This section is comprised of the laws of prayer, the Succah, the palm branch, and the

---

(4) Jonah 4:8.   (5) See above, *Eivel* (Mourning), Note 43, on the significance of this point.   (6) Midrash Tehillim 19:7.   (7) This section in the Mishnah deals with family laws, thus teaching man to be heedful of forbidden relations, and thereby be saved from mortal punishment. The Torah is thus the perfect guide safeguarding one's life.

festivals, concerning which it is written, *And thou shalt rejoice in thy feast.*[8] *The commandment of the Eternal is pure, enlightening the eyes*[2] corresponds to the Order of *Kodashim* (Consecrated Things), which provides enlightenment in distinguishing between the non-sacred and the sacred. *The fear of the Eternal is pure*[3] corresponds to the Order of *Taharoth* (Purities). *The ordinances of the Eternal are true*[3] corresponds to the Order of *Nezikin* (Damages), which deals with all civil laws." These six Orders of the Mishnah correspond to the six periods in the order of the world: *cold and heat, summer and winter, and day and night.*[9] The six Orders of the Mishnah embody the Oral Law, for on account of the magnitude of the Torah, the Oral Law is indispensible, since without it the Written Law could not be explained, as the Sages commented;[10] "G-d made a covenant with Israel only for the sake of the Oral Law, as it is said, *According to these words have I made a covenant with thee and with Israel.*"[11]

Man was created primarily to study Torah. Therefore, one should be disconcerted by the sinful neglect of the study of the Torah by the majority of people. Most people concentrate all their efforts upon vanity and totally forget their duty to set aside regular hours for study on the Sabbaths and festivals and to study occasionally on weekdays and even nights. One should consider that if he received a written communication from a mortal king and he was unsure about its meaning, he would certainly endeavor with all his might to understand it. If this is true with respect to the writing of a mortal king, who is alive today and dead tomorrow, it is so much more true of the Torah, the writing of the King of kings, for the Torah is man's life and deliverance, as it is

(8) Deuteronomy 16:4. (9) Genesis 8:22. (10) Gittin 60 b. (11) Exodus 34:28. During the entire period of ancient Jewish history, ending about 125 years after the destruction of the Second Temple, the Oral Torah was not written down. It was handed down from master to disciple by word of mouth. In the era of Rabbeinu Hakadosh, due to the forced exodus of Jews from the Land of Israel, and the fear that in the lands of exile the Oral Torah might be forgotten, the Mishnah, comprising the essentials of the Oral Torah, was written down. Thus, *According to these words* spoken by G-d to Moses, as contained in the Oral Law, has G-d made His covenant with Israel.

written, *For that is thy life and the length of thy days!*[12] Our Sages commented:[13] "Every day, a Heavenly Voice bursts forth from Mount Horeb [Sinai] and proclaims, 'Woe to men for their contempt of the Torah.' " Thus you learn that man was primarily created to engage in the study of Torah.

The world exists only for the sake of Torah, as it is said, *Were it not for My covenant* [i.e., the Torah], *I would not have appointed day and night, the ordinances of heaven and earth.*[14] We also find that Malachi, the last of the prophets, warned us concerning [the neglect of the study of] Torah and concluded his prophecy with that subject. He said, *Remember ye the law of Moses My servant,* etc.[15] *Lest I come and smite the land with utter destruction.*[16] It is thus as if he said, "*Remember the law of Moses My servant,* and I will bless the entire world; if not, I will destroy the entire world." From here you derive that the entire world depends upon Torah. The Sages commented,[17] "The Holy One, blessed be He, has only the four cubits of law in His world." That is to say, He has no desire or craving in His world except for the kind of human being who engages in the study of the law and who occupies but four square cubits. How sinful then is the person who has the time for studying Torah and fails to use it, for the Sages expounded:[18] "*Because he hath despised the word of the Eternal.*[19] This refers to one who could have engaged in the study of Torah but failed to do so."

The power of Torah is great indeed, for the Sages completely prohibited selling a Scroll of the Torah even in the face of hunger. The only exception [to this restriction is when the Scroll is sold to raise funds] for the purpose of studying Torah, as they said:[20] "They may only sell a Scroll of the Torah if the money will be used for the purpose of study-

---

(12) Deuteronomy 30:20. (13) Aboth, *Kinyan Torah,* 2. The "contempt of Torah" spoken of in this text is the neglect of studying Torah. Failing to study Torah is the source of all evils that come upon man. (14) Jeremiah 33:25. (15) Malachi 3:22. (16) *Ibid.,* Verse 24. (17) Berachoth 8 a. (18) Sanhedrin 99 a. (19) Numbers 15:31. (20) Megillah 27 a.

ing Torah or for entering into marriage." The reason for these exceptions are that marriage sustains the human species and that the study
of Torah is more important than the Scroll itself since the study leads
to fulfillment of the commandments.

One must review his Torah studies, as the Sages commented:[18] "One
who studies Torah but does not review it is like a person who sows but
does not reap." A person can avoid forgetting his studies by constantly
reviewing them and by repeatedly uttering his learning. We find that
the Sages of Israel carefully observed such habits, and even in their dying moments they did not cease learning, as in the cases of Rabbah bar
Nachmani[21] and Rav Chisda.[22] Similarly, we find that on the day King
David was to die, "he did not cease studying Torah. [Hence, the
angel of death could not take his life. What did the angel do? He went
to an orchard behind David's palace and shook the trees. David, hearing the noise, went out to see the cause and as he climbed the ladder to
the tree] the angel slipped the ladder away from him."[23] [Since David
had stopped studying, the angel took his life, which he was unable to
do while David was studying Torah] because G-d made a covenant at
Sinai with those who received the Torah that the angel of death would
not have power over them while studying, for the Torah is a *tree of
life*,[24] and where there is life, there is no death.

Should you ask, "Do we not find that many prophets and righteous
men have died without interrupting their studies?" The answer undoubtedly is that they momentarily forgot their Torah, and in that moment death overpowered them. Thus, in the case of Moses our teacher,

---

(21) Baba Metzia 86 a. Rabbah bar Nachmani was the leading Sage in the third
generation of Babylonian Amoraim. He was known for his great acumen of reasoning
power.   (22) Makkoth 10 a. Rav Chisda was of the second generation of Babylonian
Amoraim. He was a pupil of Rav Yehudah, who was a pupil of Rav, the first Babylonian Amora. With Rav begins the glory of Babylonian Jewry in the field of Torah. Rav
was a pupil of Rabbeinu Hakadosh, the redactor of the Mishnah in the year 200 Common Era.   (23) Shabbath 30 b. The love of Torah was also conspicuous in the lives of
Jehoshaphat (Pesachim 92 a) and Hezekiah (Sanhedrin 94 b), Kings of
Judah.   (24) Proverbs 3:18.

the master of all the prophets, the Sages were forced to say that [before his death], "the wellsprings of wisdom were stopped up for him."[25] Of course, his demise was not — Heaven forbid! — caused by the power of death; it was brought about by "the Divine Kiss."[26] Thus you learn how much the Sages and kings[23] of Israel loved the Torah.

We also find that the Sages of the Talmud studied Torah despite personal distress and poverty, as told of Rabbi Shimon ben Yochai[27] and his son Rabbi Eleazar, who "hid themselves in a cave for thirteen years and sat in the sand up to their necks the entire day [in order to save their clothes] and studied. A miracle occurred for them and a carob tree and a fountain of water were created for them."[28] Concerning the generation of Rabbi Yehudah the son of Rabbi Ilai,[29] it is told "that six pupils would cover themselves with one garment and still be absorbed in study."[30]

A person is obligated to teach Torah to his fellow man, for all Israelites are responsible for one another with respect to all commandments. Concerning one who teaches Torah to others, he is assured that *his reward is with Him, and his recompense is before Him.*[31] The Sages commented:[32] "Scripture considers one who teaches Torah to his neighbor's son[33] as if he [the student] received it from Mount Sinai, for it is said, *And make them known unto thy children and thy children's children.*[34] Immediately after that, it says, . . . *the day that thou stoodest before the Eternal thy G-d at Horeb.*"[35]

---

(25) Sotah 13 b.   (26) Baba Bathra 17 a.   (27) Rabbi Shimon ben Yochai, a disciple of Rabbi Akiba, was a severe critic of the Romans, who were notorious at that time for their persecution of the Jews. Merely for remarking that the Romans provided certain benefits — e.g., bridges and marketplaces — to their conquered countries solely for their own benefit, the rabbi and his son had to flee for their lives, and for more than a decade, they hid in a cave.   (28) Shabbath 33 b.   (29) Rabbi Yehudah, a collegue of Rabbi Shimon ben Yochai, was also a disciple of Rabbi Akiba. The extent of the poverty of his generation may well be surmised from the episode mentioned in the text. Nevertheless, that generation's love of Torah was in no way diminished.   (30) Sanhedrin 20 a.   (31) Isaiah 40:10.   (32) Kiddushin 30 a.   (33) Our texts of the Gemara read "his grandson."   (34) Deuteronomy 4:9.   (35) *Ibid.*, Verse 10.

The study of Torah requires solitude, as Solomon said, *He that separateth himself seeketh his own desire.*[36] The meaning of this verse seems to be that one who desires a knowledge of Torah should seek separation and seclusion, for study requires that one occasionally stay apart from friends and withdraw into solitude so that he can concentrate on his studies. If he does so, *he breaketh out in all sound wisdom.*[36] That is to say, he will become known as an expert and comprehensive scholar in all fields of wisdom.

Exile came upon Israel for the sin of neglecting the study of Torah, as it is said, *Her king and her princes are among the nations, instruction is no more,*[37] i.e., because the study of Torah is no more, [Israel's leaders went into exile]. It is further written, *Israel hath cast off that which is good, the enemy shall pursue him.*[38] That is to say, because Israel *cast off that which is good* — the only *good* is Torah, as it is said, *For I give you good doctrine, forsake ye not My teaching*[39] — the enemy will pursue Israel.

The concerns of the world are insignificant; only Torah is essential, for David said, *I considered my ways and turned my feet unto Thine testimonies.*[40] He was saying, "When I think of all the world's affairs and contemplate their purpose, I find in them nothing of any consequence. Only the Torah is essential, and therefore *I turned my feet unto Thine testimonies.*"

The study of Torah is greater than bringing all the offerings, for the Sages commented:[41] *"The iniquity of Eli's house shall not be expiated with sacrifice nor offering.*[42] It will not be expiated through sacrifices and offerings, but it will be atoned for with Torah."

---

(36) Proverbs 18:1. (37) Lamentations 2:9. (38) Hosea 8:3. (39) Proverbs 4:2. (40) Psalms 119:59. (41) Rosh Hashanah 18 a. (42) I Samuel 3:14. The sons of Eli had shown disrespect to the offerings brought in the Tabernacle at Shiloh. As a punishment thereof, Eli their father — who knew of their misconduct but did not reprove them sufficiently — was told by a prophet, *The iniquity of Eli's house* etc. Upon this the Sages commented, that their sin will not be forgiven with sacrifice and offering, but it will be forgiven by study of Torah.

Although the reward for the study of Torah is reserved for the World to Come, one nevertheless enjoys the fruits thereof in this world.

It is known that if one merely reads the words of Torah, even if he does not understand what he is reading, it is a great and virtuous deed. One's reward is especially great if he concentrates upon the meaning of the words. Thus, when reading the Sh'ma,[43] one should direct his thoughts to three things: the reading itself, the meaning of the words, and the fulfillment of his obligation to read them. If one reads the Sh'ma with the intention of fulfilling his obligation to do so, his reward is greater than one who merely reads words of the Torah [without such intention].

In Tractate Aboth,[44] the Sages commented:[45] "Honor is only Torah, as it is said, *The wise shall inherit honor.*[46] Seek not greatness more than you seek learning. Crave not for the table of kings, for your table in the World to Come[47] will be greater than theirs in this world,[47] and your crown will be greater than theirs. Royalty requires thirty qualifications[48] and the priesthood twenty-four,[49] but the acquisition of Torah requires forty-eight qualifications."[50]

It is stated:[51] "One who studies Torah in this world merits teaching it in the World to Come, as Scripture assures us, *And he that satisfieth abundantly shall be satisfied also himself.*"[52]

---

(43) See above, *Eivel* (Mourning) Note 42.   (44) See above, *Emunah* (Faith in G-d), Note 10.   (45) Aboth, *Kinyan Torah,* 3.   (46) Proverbs 3:35.   (47) Our texts of Aboth contain no references to the World to Come or to this world.   (48) These are listed in the Mishnah Sanhedrin 2:2 ff.   (49) Mentioned in Numbers 18:8-32.   (50) These are enumerated in Aboth, *Kinyan Torah,* 4: "By audible study, by distinct pronunciation, by understanding and discernment of the heart, etc."   (51) Sanhedrin 92 a.   (52) Proverbs 11:25. "One who satisfied his disciples in matters of learning will also teach them in the World to Come" (Rashi, Sanhedrin 92 a).

Part Two

> The study of Torah engenders two great benefits: one for the body in this world and one for the soul in the World to Come / As long as the people of Israel engaged in the study of Torah, they vanquished their enemies / The dual legacy of David / The need for encouraging the study of Torah, especially among children / The greatness of the study of Torah by children.

THOUGH A HOST SHOULD ENCAMP AGAINST ME, MY HEART SHALL NOT FEAR; THOUGH WAR SHOULD RISE UP AGAINST ME, IN THIS WILL I BE CONFIDENT.[53] ONE THING HAVE I ASKED OF THE ETERNAL, THAT WILL I SEEK AFTER; THAT I MAY DWELL IN THE HOUSE OF THE ETERNAL ALL THE DAYS OF MY LIFE, TO BEHOLD THE GRACIOUSNESS OF THE ETERNAL, AND TO VISIT EARLY IN HIS TEMPLE.[54]

It is known that a righteous person fears no one but G-d, since fear of a mortal disparages the soul. However, the fear that one shows for a king is comprised of two parts, one of which is permissible and the other of which is not. The permissible part, which conforms with the precept of the Torah,[55] has a qualification: one may fear a king provided that he does not thereby transgress the Will of G-d, the Supreme King Who gave sovereignty to the mortal ruler. The prohibited part of

---

(53) Psalms 27:3. The good life has never been free of its external enemies or of the inner promptings to sin. At times it would appear as if *a host* of enemies encompassed against the individual. But the psalmist in his implicit faith in G-d assures one of the ultimate triumph of the good. (54) *Ibid.*, Verse 4. (55) Deuteronomy 17:15. See above *Yir'ah* (Fear of G-d), p. 283, where this topic is fully discussed.

fearing a king concerns royal commands which require the violation of G-d's will, for ultimately, that will lead to forgetting G-d completely.

This thought was expressed here by David: *Though a host should encamp against me, my heart shall not fear; though war should rise up against me, in this will I be confident.*[53] He is thus saying that his trust in G-d is so strong and his fear of Him so great that he no longer fears the multitudinous enemy host and the perilous conditions of war. Therefore, he said, *In this will I be confident,*[53] i.e., *in this* which I mentioned above, namely, that *the Eternal is my light and my salvation.*[56] The Midrashic interpretation is:[57] "*In this will I be confident*[53] is a reference to the Torah, as it is said, *And 'this' is the Torah.*"[58]

David thus taught us the two great benefits which are engendered by the study of Torah. One is overt and consists of the physical benefits in this world; the other is hidden and consists of the spiritual beneficence reserved for the soul in the World to Come. The physical benefits in this world are that one's enemies will fall before him and that he will not fear them, as David said, *Though a host should encamp against me, my heart shall not fear.*[53] Indeed, as long as the people of Israel engaged in the study of Torah, they were not harmed by their enemies. On the contrary, they subdued them. However, when they neglected the Torah or were careless in their observance thereof, the attribute of judgment was aimed against them. Thus, we find that an angel appeared to Joshua in the form of a man *with his sword drawn in his hand, and Joshua went unto him, and said unto him, Art thou for us, or for our adversaries.*[59] The angel answered, *Nay, but I am captain of the host of the Eternal, I am now come.*[60] The Sages commented on this:[61] "[The angel said to Joshua], 'You have neglected to bring this

(56) Psalms 27:1. (57) Midrash Tehillim 27:1. (58) Deuteronomy 4:44. (59) Joshua 5:13. This episode of Joshua's conversation with the angel took place near Jericho, the first city assaulted by the Israelites after entering the Land. The problem before Joshua was the capture of Jericho, but the angel turned his attention to the immediate problem of neglecting the study of Torah. (60) *Ibid.*, Verse 14. (61) Megillah 3 a.

evening's offering,[62] and now you are neglecting the study of Torah.' Joshua replied, 'For which sin have you come?' The angel answered, '*I am now come*'[60] [i.e., for the sin of neglecting the study of Torah, which applies day and night]. Thereupon,[63] Joshua lodged *that night in the midst of the vale,*[64] i.e., in the depth of the Law." Because the Israelites were engaged in the study of the Torah, they succeeded in vanquishing their enemies, for it is known that the Israelites' success or failure in battle depended upon their merit or their punishable guilt, as the Sages said,[65] "It is not the wild ass that kills, but it is sin which deprives one of the right to life."

The hidden benefit of the study of Torah affects the soul in the World to Come. This is expressed in the second verse [mentioned above]: *that I may dwell in the House of the Eternal all the days of my life.*[54] The intent thereof is that by means of the Torah, a person will merit life in the World to Come. Such merit is achieved only by worshipping G-d, knowing Him, and studying Torah, for how can a servant find grace in the eyes of his Master without serving Him; how can he serve Him without knowing Him, and how can he know Him without the study of Torah? Thus David said, *Open Thou mine eyes, that I may behold wondrous things out of Thy Torah.*[66]

These two benefits—the destruction of one's enemies in this world and the beholding of G-d's graciousness in the World to Come—were thus the legacy of David, for the Sages said in Midrash Tehillim:[67] "David bequeathed to the throne [of Israel] a dual legacy in this world and in the World to Come. He stated, 'I sing for both legacies,' as it is said, *For the leader; upon the Nechiloth,*[68] *a psalm of David.*"[69] It is

---

(62) Two whole-offerings were brought daily, one in the morning and one at dusk (Numbers 28:4, 8). (63) That is, when Joshua was engaged at the city of Ai in his next battle, he took the angel's counsel into consideration and spent the night studying Torah. (64) Joshua 8:13. (65) Berachoth 33 a. (66) Psalms 119 a. (67) Midrash Tehillim, 5. (68) *Nechiloth* are wind instruments or flutes, The word is written in the plural and suggests the word *nachalah* (inheritance). Thus the Midrash sees in this particular psalm David's song for his dual legacies, as explained in the text. (69) Psalms 5:1.

stated in Midrash Tehillim:[70] *"One thing have I asked of the Eternal, etc.*[54] G-d said to David: 'David, first you say, *One thing have I asked of the Eternal, that will I seek after; that I may dwell in the House of the Eternal all the days of my life,*[54] but then you add, *to behold the graciousness of the Eternal,* etc.!'[54] David answered, 'Should not the servant imitate his Master? Have You not approached us with one request, as it is said, *And now, Israel, what doth the Eternal thy G-d require of thee, but to fear the Eternal thy G-d,*[71] after which You gave us many commandments, as it is said, *to walk in all His ways, and to love Him?*[71] It is sufficient for the servant to be like his Master.' "[72]

In Tractate Berachoth, the Sages said:[73] "What is the meaning of the verse, *The Eternal loveth the gates of Zion more than all the dwelling places of Jacob?*[74] G-d said, 'I love the gates that are distinguished with [an impressive gathering of the public to hear words of] law more than I love all the synagogues and houses of study.' This agrees with Rabbi Chiya bar Ami's statement in the name of Ulla, 'Since the destruction of the Temple, the Holy One, blessed be He, has nothing but the four cubits of the law.' "

Since we have been informed of the superiorioty of the Torah, the essence of all existence, it is incumbent upon the public to strengthen itself in the study thereof and to ensure that children attend school, for children are the main concern of the study of Torah. Thus, the Sages said,[75] "One who learns when a child, is like ink written on clean paper. One who learns when an old man, is like ink written on blotted paper." Hence, the leaders of the community are obligated to engage in this virtuous deed, and if they are neglectful in the matter, they will incur punishment.

---

(70) Midrash Tehillim, 27:4. (71) Deuteronomy 10:12. (72) The Midrash is conveying the thought that David's two requests are really one, for the purpose of his request to *dwell in the House of the Eternal* is *to behold the graciousness of the Eternal.* Similarly, the fear of G-d, a principal requirement of the Torah, is only for the purpose of walking in all His ways. Hence, it was from the Torah that David learned to formulate his singular request. (73) Berachoth 8 a. (74) Psalms 87:2. (75) Aboth 4:25.

Consider the great power of the study of Torah by children, for the Sages said in Tractate Shabbath:[76] "Rabbi Shimon ben Lakish said in the name of Rabbi Yehudah Nasiah (the Prince): The entire world exists only for the breath of study by school children.' Rav Papa said to Abaye, 'What about my study and yours?' He answered, 'The breath of study which comes forth from one who has sinned is not equivalent to the breath of study of one who has not sinned.' Rabbi Shimon ben Lakish further said in the name of Rabbi Yehudah Nasiah, 'School children should not be stopped from studying even for the rebuilding of the Temple.' Rabbi Shimon ben Lakish said to Rabbi Yehudah Nasiah, 'I have the following tradition from my ancestors or, according to others, from your ancestors: A city which has no school for children will ultimately be destroyed.' Ravina said, 'Such a city shall be placed under a ban [until the community provides for a school].' " From these words of the Sages, we learn the greatness of the study of Torah.[77]

Similarly, we find that Malachi, last of all the prophets, warned Israel exceedingly about the Torah, as it is said, *Remember ye the law of Moses My servant, which I commanded unto him at Horeb for all Israel, even statutes and ordinances.*[78] Malachi thus informed the people of Israel: "Henceforth, until the Messiah will come, there will not be any prophet. Therefore, engage in the study of the Torah and its commandments, for thereby you will merit the coming of the redeemer." Hence, Malachi said afterwards, *Behold, I will send you Elijah the prophet before the coming of the great and fearful day of the Eternal.*[79] And may it so be His gracious will. Amen.

---

(76) Shabbath 119 b. Rabbi Yehudah Nasiah was a Palestinian Amora, a great-grandson of Rabbi Yehudah Hanasi.   (77) After quoting this entire paragraph of our author, Menachem di Lunzano (an Italian rabbi of the eighteenth century) makes the following remark: "These words of Rabbeinu Bachya are certainly correct with reference to community leaders' responsibility regarding the education of young children. How much more so should attention be given to those young people who have had a proper Torah foundation in their youth, but who neglect it afterwards when pursuing wordly affairs" (Derech Chayim, pp. 14-15, Lemberg 5691).   (78) Malachi 3:22.   (79) *Ibid.*, Verse 23.

תפילה

The Power of Prayer

Through prayer, man comes nearer to his Creator / David established the order of prayer for all mankind / The miraculous power of prayer / The methodical arrangement of the prayers in the 'Shemoneh Esreih' (The Eighteen Blessings or 'Amidah') / The great power of prayer and the importance of praying in a synagogue / The requirement of prayer.

The Power of Prayer

O ETERNAL, G-D OF HOSTS, HEAR MY PRAYER: GIVE EAR, O G-D OF JACOB, SELAH.[1]

David uttered this verse, entreating G-d to hear his prayer, for it is through prayer that man comes nearer to his Creator. Thus, David established the order of prayer for all mankind, strengthening its foundations, guiding people therein, and teaching them how to approach the Master of the universe through prayer and supplication.

The power of prayer is so great that it can even change the course of nature, save one from danger, and nullify a Heavenly decree. That prayer can change the course of nature may be gathered from the case of Rebekah, whose barrenness was removed by prayer.[2] Prayer can also save one from danger, as it is written, *They that go down to the sea in ships, that do business in great waters*[3]—*These saw the works of the Eternal, and His wonders in the deep.*[4] *For He commanded and raised the stormy wind, which lifted up the waves thereof.*[5] *They mounted up to the heaven, they went down to the deeps; their souls melted away*

---

(1) Psalms 84:9. Selah, in the Book of Psalms, indicates a musical direction, perhaps a pause, during the Levites' rendition of the psalms. — The concept of prayer, basic to Torah life, is that G-d is near to all that call upon Him in truth. Though His dominion extends to the remotest corners of the universe, in which sense it is said that He is *G-d of hosts*, He is yet distinguished in that He is the *G-d of Jacob* and of every individual that offers prayer to Him. (2) See Genesis 25:21. (3) Psalms 107:23. (4) *Ibid.*, Verse 24. (5) *Ibid.*, Verse 25.

because of trouble.[6] *They cried unto the Eternal in their trouble,*[7] immediately after which it is written, *He made the storm a calm, so that the waves thereof were still.*[8] Thus, prayer protects in a moment of danger. Similarly, it is within the power of prayer to nullify a Heavenly decree against a person, as was the case with Hezekiah, King of Judah. G-d gave him an additional fifteen years of life because of his prayer, as it is said, *Behold, I will add unto thy days fifteen years.*[9] The word *add* indicates that his time had been set and that it had been decreed that he should not live longer, but the power of prayer abrogated that decree. The Sages commented in Tractate Berachoth:[10] "Isaiah said to Hezekiah, 'I say to you, *Set thy house in order, [for thou shalt die, and not live],*[11] and you tell me, Give me your daughter![12] The decree has already gone forth!' Hezekiah answered, 'Son of Amoz, conclude your prophecy and leave! I have the following tradition from my ancestors: Even if the sword already lies upon a person's neck, he should not refrain from praying for mercy, as it is said, *Though He slay me, yet will I trust in Him.'* "[13] The Sages of the Truth[14] have pointed out that this episode shows that prayer is superior to prophecy, that is, stronger than the source of prophecy.

You should know that from the days of Moses our teacher until the period of the Men of the Great Assembly,[15] prayer in Israel was not arranged in a definite order for everyone alike. Each individual prayed for himself according to his knowledge, wisdom, and clarity of expression. This was the general practice until the Men of the Great

---

(6) *Ibid.*, Verse 26. (7) *Ibid.*, Verse 28. (8) *Ibid.*, Verse 29. (9) Isaiah 38:5. (10) Berachoth 10 a. (11) Isaiah 38:1. (12) As related in Berachoth 10 a, Isaiah had told Hezekiah, that because the latter had not married, his early death had been decreed by Heaven. Hezekiah justified his celibacy by explaining that through the Divine Spirit, he had foreseen that evil children would issue from him. Isaiah rejoined, "What have you to do with the secrets of G-d? You must fulfill your obligations, and let G-d do whatever pleases Him! "If so," said Hezekiah, "give me your daughter for my wife." Isaiah replied, "I say to you, *Set your house in order,* and you tell me, Give me your daughter!" (13) Job 13:15. (14) This is a reference to the wisdom of Cabala, which deals with the mysteries of the Torah. (15) See above, *Yeitzer Hara* (The Evil Inclination), Note 32.

Assembly ordained the Eighteen Blessings, so that there would be a set prayer for all the people of Israel alike. Accordingly, they composed it in a very simple and understandable language so that one's thoughts would not be distracted by having to grasp complex phraseology. Thus the people of Israel, learned and unlearned, would be equals therein. However, the Men of the Great Assembly ordained the Eighteen Blessings with great devotion and extreme caution. They arranged three blessings of praises of G-d to precede the petitions which follow. These three blessings are *Avoth* (Fathers),[16] *G'vuroth* (Powers),[17] and *Kedushath Hashem* (Sanctity of G-d).[18] For the last three blessings they composed *Avodah* (Service),[19] *Hoda'ah* (Thanksgiving),[20] and the Priestly Blessing or *Shalom* (Peace).

Between these two groups of blessings, [the Men of the Great Assembly] ordained twelve blessings [i.e., petitions]. Later in Jabneh,[21] the Sages added the petition against the sectarians, making a total of thirteen middle blessings, which encompass all the needs of man. Contemplate these thirteen blessings and you will find that the first six relate to man's needs and the final six pertain to the restoration of the crown of [Israel's glory] to its former state of preeminence and the Kingdom of the House of David to its position of authority. Together with the petition against the sectarians, they total thirteen, thus in-

(16) Abraham, Isaac, and Jacob, the three patriarchs, are named in this blessing, and G-d is praised as the G-d of our fathers. The blessing unites all generations of Jewish history into one family bond. (17) This blessing proclaims that G-d sustains the living by providing them with food, healing the sick, etc., and that He resurrects the dead. It thus expresses the powers of the Omnipotent G-d. (18) In public prayer, the *Kedushah* (Declaration of G-d's Holiness) is interjected here. (19) The Service in the Temple is mentioned herein, and the blessing is extended to the general worship of G-d. (20) Here we give thanks to G-d for keeping us alive and preserving us and for His constant miracles which are with us daily. (21) Jabneh was established as the seat of the Sanhedrin shortly before the destruction of the Second Temple, at the initiative of Rabban Yochanan ben Zaccai. About six hundred years after the Men of the Great Assembly, an additional petition, which is described in the text here, was introduced in Jabneh and incorporated into the *Shemoneh Esreih*.

timating that the entire world and its goodness, whether affecting the individual man or the establishment of the Kingdom of G-d in the world, all emanate from the Thirteen Divine Attributes. One should therefore pray to the Cause of causes, praised be He, through Whose power the attributes emanate, as it is said, *For what great nation is there, that hath G-d so near unto them, as the Eternal our G-d is whensoever we call upon Him?*[22]

The power of prayer is great indeed, for the Sages said,[23] "Supplication is appropriate both before and after the final decree has been pronounced." In Midrash Tanchuma, the Sages commented:[24] "Moses taught all generations that a person should not say, 'Since I am fatally ill and have made my testament and distributed all my belongings, I will not pray any longer.' Rather, he should pray, for G-d does not reject the prayer of any creature. Indeed, Moses himself made his testament and still prayed, as it is said, *And the cities thereof, I gave unto the Reubenites and to the Gadites*[25] close to which it says, *And I besought the Eternal.*"[26]

When the people of Israel pray, G-d is accessible to them, as it says, *And from thence ye will seek the Eternal thy G-d, and thou shalt find Him.*[27] Israel's main strength lies only in prayer, as it says, *The voice is the voice of Jacob.*[28] In the first chapter of Tractate Berachoth, the Sages commented:[29] "If one attends synagogue services daily and misses one day, G-d inquires about him, as it is said, *Who is among you that feareth the Eternal, that obeyeth the voice of His servant? Though he walketh in darkness, and hath no light.*[30] If [he missed the services because] he went to perform a meritorious deed, there will be *splendor* for him, but if his absence was caused by business matter, it will be devoid of it for him." This is because G-d is strict with righteous people. This person, who practices the great and meritorious deed of at-

(22) Deuteronomy 4:7. (23) Rosh Hashanah 18 a. (24) Tanchuma, *Vaethchanan*, 4. (25) Deuteronomy 3:12. (26) *Ibid.*, Verse 23. (27) *Ibid.*, 4:28. (28) Genesis 27:22. (29) Berachoth 6 b. (30) Isaiah 50:10.

tending synagogue services daily and allows himself to be absent one day because of his personal affairs, demonstrated thereby that his trust in G-d is not complete. Had his trust been perfect, he would not have forsaken public prayer in order to attend to his own business.

The Eighteen Blessings ordained by the Men of the Great Assembly correspond to the eighteen times the names of all three patriarchs are mentioned together in the Torah, as explained in the Midrash.[31] "Why did the Sages ordain twenty-four blessings[32] on fast days? They correspond to the twenty-four expressions for prayer which Solomon used[33] when he brought the Ark of the Covenant into the Holy of Holies on his fast day.[34] Why did the Sages ordain nine blessings[35] for Rosh Hashanah? These correspond to the nine Divine invocations mentioned by Hannah in her prayer.[36] Why did the Sages ordain seven blessings for the Sabbath? It is because of the verse which states, *Seven times a day do I praise Thee.*[37] Which day is unique and without equal? I must say it is the Sabbath," for the Sabbath has been given for the purpose of endowing Israel with rest, and delight. Therefore, the Sages ordained that the first three blessings consist of praise, and the last three of thanksgiving, and the one in the middle pertain to rest.

"G-d said to Israel: 'Be heedful of prayer, for there is no superior mode of Divine worship,' since it is greater than all the offerings, for it is said, *To what purpose is the multitude of your sacrifices unto Me?*[38] *Yea, when ye make many prayers, I will not hear.*[39] This proves by implication that prayer is greater than all offerings."[31]

(31) Tanchuma, *Vayeira*, 1.   (32) Six blessings are added to the original Eighteen Blessings (Taanith 15 a). At present this is not the prevailing custom.   (33) See I Kings 8:23-53.   (34)   For the reason that Solomon fasted on that day, see above, *Vidui* (Confession of Sin),   p.217.   (35)   Three blessings —Sovereignty, Remembrances, and *Shofroth*— are added to the regular seven blessings in the festival prayer. Since the blessing of Sovereignty is joined to the blessing for the festival day itself, there are actually only a total of nine blessings.   (36) See I Samuel 2:1-10.   (37) Psalms 119:164.   (38) Isaiah 1:11.   (39) *Ibid.*, Verse 15.

Prayer requires tears, for David said, *Hear my prayer, O Eternal, and give ear to my cry; keep not silence to my tears.*[40] Similarly, we find that when Hezekiah prayed, he wept profusely,[41] and G-d said to him, *I have heard thy prayer, I have seen thy tears.*[42] Finally, it is also said of Hannah, *And she prayed unto the Eternal and wept profusely.*[43]

(40) Psalms 39:13.   (41) II Kings 20:3.   (42) *Ibid.*, Verse 5.   (43) I Samuel 1:10.

תשובה

Repentance: The Way to Atonement

Ways leading to repentance / The great power of repen-
tance / The Midrash Tanchuma on the verse, 'Seek ye the
Eternal while He may be found' (Isaiah 55:6) / David's repen-
tance / Repentance leads to redemption.

Repentance: The Way to Atonement

SEEK YE THE ETERNAL WHILE HE MAY BE FOUND, CALL
YE UPON HIM WHILE HE IS NEAR.[1] LET THE WICKED
FORSAKE HIS WAY, AND THE MAN OF INIQUITY HIS
THOUGHTS; AND LET HIM RETURN UNTO THE ETER-
NAL, AND HE WILL HAVE COMPASSION UPON HIM, AND
UNTO OUR G-D, FOR HE WILL ABUNDANTLY PARDON.[2]

It is known that repentance is one of the seven things created before
the world came into existence. The seven things are: Torah, repentance, the Garden of Eden, Gehenna, the Throne of Glory, the
Sanctuary, and the name of the Messiah.[3] I have already explained
these topics in the theme on *Rosh Hashanah* (The New Year). It was
due to G-d's mercy upon His creatures that He created repentance
before the world came into existence, for He knew that man would sin.
Therefore, He created the means of healing man before He incurs the
wound. There [in the theme on *Rosh Hashanah*], I explained that
these seven things are all interconnected and that each one requires the
other.

You should know that repentance requires that man should realize
his lowliness and insignificance, for he is dust and ashes in his life and

---

(1) Isaiah 55:6. According to R'dak (Rabbi David Kimchi), one of the great Biblical
commentators, the prophet Isaiah is here calling upon Israel to seek G-d in ways where
He can truly be found, and through such deeds and thoughts that will be acceptable
before Him. In other words, repentance should consist of spiritual anguish for the sins
committed, and of a profound resolve to amend one's way of life in the future. Rabbeinu Bachya will further develop this thought. (2) *Ibid.*, Verse 7. (3) Pesachim 54 a.

worms and maggots in his death. By bearing this in mind, his effort to repent will be successful and he will achieve perfect contrition with proper and pure intent. Similarly, we find that Job negated and belittled man because of the nature of his birth and his subjection to accidents, as he said, *Man that is born of a woman is of few days and full of trouble.*[4] *He cometh forth like a flower, and withereth,* etc.[5] It is possible to say that in these verses, Job mentioned five of man's disparaging characteristics. First, his foundation is the earth, and that which is founded upon an inanity cannot long sustain itself. This is the intent of the verse, *Man is like a vapor.*[6] Second, man is *born of a woman,* and all his affairs are affected by it. Third, he *is of few days.* Fourth, he is *full of trouble,* for he may live a short life and have many troubles and worries. Fifth, as soon as he dies, his luster departs immediately. This is the purport of the verse, *He cometh forth like a flower, and withereth,*[5] for as soon as he leaves this world he is at once cut off therefrom.

In the P'sikta, the Sages commented:[7] "The power of repentance is great indeed, for it annuls a Divine oath and decree. It voids a Divine oath, for it is said, *As I live, saith the Eternal, though Coniah the son of Yehoyakim, King of Judah, were the signet upon My right hand, yet would I pluck thee thence;*[8] and it is further written, *In that day, saith the Eternal of hosts, will I take thee, O Zerubbabel, My servant, the son of Shealtiel, saith the Eternal, and will make thee as a signet.*[9] Repentance abrogated the decree, for it is written, *Thus saith the Eternal: Write ye this man* [Coniah] *childless,*[10] and it is written, *And the sons of Jeconiah: Assir, Shealtiel his son.*"[11]

---

(4) Job 14:1. (5) *Ibid.*, Verse 2. (6) Psalms 144:4. The Hebrew word for *vapor* can also be translated as "vanity." Hence, the verse declares that physical man is devoid of any everlasting substance. (7) P'sikta d'Rav Kahana, *Shuvah,* pp. 163 a-b, in Buber's edition. (8) Jeremiah 22:24. (9) Haggai 2:23. Shealtiel was a grandson of Coniah (I Chronicles 3:17), the exiled king. Because of Coniah's repentance, the Divine oath against him was annulled. Zerubbabel, his descendant, became the favored one of G-d, for he was the leader in the building of the Second Temple. (10) Jeremiah 22:30. (11) I Chronicles 3:17. It was thus clear that the

With this concept of repentance in mind, the prophet Hosea said here, *Seek ye the Eternal while He may be found, call upon Him while He is near.*[1] He is saying: "Seek G-d by those means that He can be found. *Call upon Him while He is near* in ways through which He will be accessible to you. These ways are repentance, contriteness of heart, and lowliness of spirit, the latter two being components of repentance."

Our Sages commented:[12] "*Seek ye the Eternal while He may be found.*[1] This refers to the ten days between the New Year and the Day of Atonement." G-d is more accessible to the individual during these ten days than throughout the rest of the year. *Let the wicked forsake his way.*[2] This refers to one who denies G-d. Let him forsake his evil way, and G-d will have compassion and forgive him. Because man sins in thought and in deed, the prophet therefore speaks of *his way* and *his thoughts.*[2] He states *and to our G-d,* [using the Divine Name which indicates the attribute of judgment], for even by applying the attribute of judgment, G-d will abundantly pardon him. This is the sense of the expression, . . . *and unto our G-d, for He will abundantly pardon.*[2]

In the Midrash Shir Hashirim Rabbah, the Sages commented:[13] "*His mouth is most sweet, yea, he is altogether lovely, this is my beloved, and this is my friend.*[14] Scripture therefore states, *For thus saith the Eternal unto the House of Israel: Seek ye Me, and live.*[15] Is there anything more persuasive than this? *And when the wicked man turneth away from his wickedness that he hath committed, and doeth that which is lawful and right, he shall save his soul alive.*[16] Is there anything more persuasive than this? Reish Lakish said, 'This applies when the wicked person regrets his deeds of the past. Moreover, G-d considers all the sins he committed as merits, as it is written, *Myrrh,*

decree for Coniah to be childless was voided, as the verse indicates that he did leave offspring. (12) Rosh Hashanah 18 a. Prayer throughout the year is always acceptable. But on the Ten Days of Penitence it is more readily accepted, for the reason that one's deeds and thoughts at that time of the year bespeak the type of a person who is more worthy to approach the Divine Throne. In other words, G-d is then more easily found. (13) Shir Hashirim Rabbah 6:1. (14) Song of Songs 5:16. (15) Amos 5:4. (16) Ezekiel 18:27.

and aloes, and cassia are all 'bigdothecha' (thy garments).'[17] That is to say, 'All *b'gidothecha* (your sinful acts) which you committed are like myrrh and aloes to Me.' "

The Sages further commented in the Midrash:[18] "*Seek ye the Eternal while He may be found.*[1] From this we learn that G-d is sometimes seen and sometimes not. He is sometimes seen, as it is said in the case of Moses, *And the Eternal spoke to Moses face to face.*[19] He is not seen, as it is said, *Take ye therefore good heed unto yourselves, for ye saw no manner of similitude on the day that the Eternal spoke unto you at Horeb.*[20] He is sometimes near — as it is said, *The Eternal is nigh unto all them that call upon Him*[21] — and sometimes He is not near, as it is said, *The Eternal is far from the wicked.*[22] *Seek ye the Eternal while He may be found.*[1] This can be compared to a king who said to his servants, 'Go and proclaim throughout my country that whoever has any civil dispute with his fellow man should come to my court. I will adjudicate it favorably before I begin to judge criminal cases.' Similarly, G-d said to Israel, 'My children! There are four seasons in the year, when I judge the entire world. At Passover, I judge the world with regard to produce, at Shavuoth with respect to the fruits of the trees, at Tabernacles with respect to rain, and on the New Year with respect to man. In the first three sessions, the judgment pertains to earthly matters. [The decision is rendered] to make people rich or poor and to make food supplies plentiful or scarce. However, the judgment on the New Year pertains to capital cases, i.e., the decision is made whether to grant life or death. If you repent before Me, I will accept you favorably and judge you on the scale of merit, for the gates of heaven are open and I will hear your prayer. I look in *through the window and*

(17) Psalms 45:9. Repentance generally comes either out of fear of punishment, or out of a sense of true regret for having wasted one's life in sin instead of having lived a life of merit. It is in the case of this latter conviction that the sinful acts one has committed are sublimated to be counted as merits. (18) Tanchuma, *Ha'azinu,* 4. The appeal of the prudent man is of a more urgent nature, reminding his listeners that while the king was with them they failed to take advantage of his presence, and now before he leaves them they should not fail to appear before him. (19) Exodus 33:11. (20) Deuteronomy 4:15. (21) Psalms 145:18. (22) Proverbs 15:29.

peer through the lattice[23] before I pronounce the decree on the Day of Atonement, [for I wish to see whether the wicked have repented].' *Seek ye the Eternal while He may be found,*[1] Rabbi Shmuel bar Nachmani said in the name of Rabbi Yonathan that this can be compared to a king who was very angry at his countrymen. Therefore, he traveled about ten miles outside his city and stayed there. Someone who saw him, arrived in the city and said to the townspeople, 'The king is angry at you and is about to send his legions to destroy the city. Go forth and appease him before he gets too far from you.' Thereupon, a prudent man observed to them, 'Fools! While the king was with you, you did not seek him. Now, before he leaves, you go forth to him, hoping that he will accept you.' It is thus said, *Seek ye the Eternal while He may be found,*[1] i.e., during the ten days between the New Year and the Day of Atonement."[18]

With regard to David, the Sages commented:[24] "*The saying of David the son of Jesse, and the saying of the man raised 'ol' (on high).*[25] [He was so called] because he was the man who raised an *olah* (a whole-offering) of repentance." This saying refers to David's relationship with Bath-sheba. When the prophet Nathan came to David and told him the parable of the ewe lamb,[26] which alluded to Bath-sheba, David confessed and was not ashamed to say, *I have sinned.*[27] Moses our teacher, master of all prophets, assured the people of Israel that when being in exile, through the merit of their repentance, G-d would redeem them and gather them from the four corners of the world, as he said, *And it shall come to pass, when all these things are come upon thee,* etc.,[28] *and thou shalt return unto the Eternal thy G-d, and hearken to His voice.*[29] It is subsequently written, *Then the Eternal thy G-d will turn thy captivity, and have compassion upon thee, and will return and gather thee from all peoples.*[30]

---

(23) Song of Songs 2:9. (24) Moed Katan 16 b. (25) II Samuel 23:1. (26) *Ibid.,* 12:1-6. (27) *Ibid.,* Verse 13. (28) Deuteronomy 30:1. (29) *Ibid.,* Verse 2. (30) *Ibid.,* Verse 3.

The Torah's conception of the human soul is that it is one entity which consists of three forces: the animalistic, the organic, and the rational. The superiority of the righteous over the wicked is the manifestation of the righteous man's subjugation of the animalistic force and the strengthening of the rational faculty / An important factor in the subjugation of the animalistic force is fasting. Thus the Torah has ordained fasting on the Day of Atonement / The essentials of fasting / Prayer is heard when combined with tears.

Fast Days

> A RIGHTEOUS MAN KNOWETH THE SOUL OF HIS BEAST, BUT THE TENDER MERCIES OF THE WICKED ARE CRUEL.[1]

The ancient scholars, who discussed the soul and its mystery, and who have written countless books on that subject, are divided into two groups. One group maintains that man's soul is one entity which consists of three forces: the animalistic, the organic, and the rational. The other group of scholars contends that there are three separate souls in man. Through his animalistic soul, man joins the other moving creatures, i.e., cattle, beasts, and birds. Like them, man desires to eat, to procreate, to dominate, to have honor and other physical pleasures. The center of that soul is the liver. This soul is called *nefesh* (the vital one) and *ruach* (spirit). In his organic soul, man joins the trees and plants by growing and expanding. This soul is not centered in any particular part of the body. In his rational soul, man partakes of the nature of those *angels whose dwelling is not with flesh*.[2] These are the higher Separate Intelligences.[3] The center of that soul lies in the brain, and it is called *n'shamah* (soul). It knows its Creator and praises Him constantly.

(1) Proverbs 12:10. The contrast between the righteous man and the wicked is here clearly expressed. The righteous man has regard even for his animals. But the mercy of the wicked is cruelty, for it is only an outward display of feelings which do not correspond to the reality of his true self. The connection of this verse with the subject of fasting will be made clear in the text. (2) Daniel 2:11. (3) See above in Passover, Note 111.

Among the sayings of our sacred Rabbis, the Sages of the Talmud, we find one dictum which inclines towards the opinion that there are separate souls in man, as follows:[4] "Rava brought into existence a man and sent him to Rabbi Zeira. The latter spoke to the man, who did not answer [for the power of speech is given only to man created by G-d]. Rabbi Zeira said to him, 'You were created by one of the rabbinical colleagues; return to your dust.' " The Sages thus explained to us that in his great wisdom, Rava created this man with the knowledge found in the Book of Creation. He was able to bestow upon him the animalistic soul of movement, but he could not invest him with the rational soul, one of the functions of which is speech. However, it appears[5] that the Torah's conception of the human soul is that it is one entity which consists of three forces, each of which is termed *nefesh*.

It is further known that the superiority of the righteous over the wicked is the manifestation of the righteous man's subjugation of the animalistic drives within him and the strengthening of his rational faculty. The main intent and basis of the Torah are that man subjugate his physical desires and bring them to such a degree of contrition that they will be subject to his rational faculty. A person who achieves this is called "righteous," and Solomon said of him, *A righteous man knoweth the soul of his beast,*[1] thus teaching us that "a righteous man" is one who subjugates his animalistic soul.

The great factor which assists one in subduing his physical desires is fasting, for the nature of man is such that as soon as he lacks his necessary food, his physical strength wanes. Upon fasting, therefore, the animalistic drives weaken and man's material substance diminishes. At that time, the light of reason shines upon him, and he is able to aim at the truth. His worship of G-d will then be welcome, and his prayer will be accepted. For this reason, the Torah has ordained

---

(4) Sanhedrin 65 b. See Ramban, Commentary on the Torah, Genesis, p. 68, where he discusses the same topic.   (5) Rabbeinu Bachya in his commentary on Genesis, (p. 63 in my Hebrew edition) corroborates his opinion on the basis of Scriptural authority. See also Ramban, Commentary on the Torah, Genesis, pp. 67-68 for a full discussion of this theme.

fasting on the Day of Atonement on which human beings are judged, for eating and drinking induce coarseness and arrogance, as it is said, *When they were fed, they became full, they were filled and their heart was exalted, therefore have they forgotten Me.*[6] Since that day has been designated for the atonement of sins and for capital judgment, we have therefore been commanded to fast on that sacred day, as Scripture states, *And ye shall afflict your souls.*[7] Tradition affirms that this "affliction" is accomplished through fasting, as it is said, *And He afflicted thee and suffered thee to hunger.*[8] Tradition is thus the lamp which directs its light [to the true meaning of the Torah]. Without it, I might have said that this "affliction" can be accomplished by great physical effort and heavy toil, e.g., by carrying beams and other heavy things. However, since it says, *And ye shall afflict your souls,*[7] it obviously includes both the affliction of the body with hunger, as affirmed by tradition, and the affliction of the soul by purging it of evil thoughts and impure fancies, which are more deleterious to the rational faculty than the sin itself.[9]

It is also known that affliction of the soul is essential, for merely afflicting the body by fasting without afflicting the soul places such a person in the category of a sinner, and he has no merit gained from fasting alone. Isaiah similarly expressed it when he said, *Behold, ye fast for strife and contention, and to smite with the fist of wickedness; ye fast not this day so as to make your voice to be heard on high.*[10] *Is such the fast that I have chosen?*[11] He explained here that afflicting the body without afflicting the soul is not at all the principal aim of acceptance by G-d. Bodily affliction must be accompanied by purging the soul of its evil thoughts and deeds of wickedness. The prophet expressed this thought, as he continued, *Is not this the fast that I have chosen?*[12] *Is it not to deal thy bread to the hungry?*[13] He is thus saying

---

(6) Hosea 13:6. It is for this reason that saying Grace after a meal is obligatory by law of the Torah, for satiety could easily be the cause of forgetting the Creator Who provided us with food. (7) Leviticus 23:27.—Yoma 74b. (8) Deuteronomy 8:3. (9) See above in *Taharath Haleiv* (Purity of the Heart), where the author discusses the broad implications of this statement. (10) Isaiah 58:4. (11) *Ibid.*, Verse 5. (12) *Ibid.*, Verse 6. (13) *Ibid.*, Verse 7.

that the intent of fasting is not merely to subject your body to hunger, but to feed the hungry. Thus, the prophet said, *And hide not thyself from thine own flesh,*[13] for it is forbidden to constantly afflict your flesh alone. The principal intent in the fasting is the affliction of the soul. You may gather that it is so from the fact that in the matter of afflicting the body, a dangerously ill person may be given even forbidden things [on ordinary fast days] or he may be fed on the Day of Atonement,[14] as the Sages said:[15] "Desecrate one Sabbath for him, so that he will be able to observe many other Sabbaths." However, the matter of afflicting the soul — e.g., where one has an overwhelming desire for forbidden sexual relations to the extent that his very life is endangered — the law is not relaxed at all even if the individual may die because of its enforcement.[16] Thus you see that the main intent in fasting is the affliction of the soul, not the affliction of the body alone. However, the affliction of both body and soul is considered a desirable fast. It is reckoned as an offering, and the reward for it is greater than that of bringing an offering, for an offering comes only from one's money, while fasting, which diminishes his fat and blood, is accomplished with his body.

On a fast day, it is appropriate to grieve over one's sins and to shed tears thereon, for tears attest to a broken and contrite heart. Tears with fasting are like the libation of water with an offering.[17] When a person strengthens himself with prayer and tears on a fast day, he is assured that his prayer will be heard on high provided that he does not have against him one of the twenty-four obstacles to repentance.[18] Thus, the prophet said, *Ye fast not this day so as to make your voice be heard on high.*[10] From this we learn that a proper fast causes one's prayer to be heard on high, and this is the main intent of the fast. We find that because of fasting, the prayers of the people of Israel were heard and they were redeemed from death in the days of Ahaseurus, as

---

(14) Yoma 83 a.   (15) *Ibid.*, 85 b.   (16) Sanhedrin 75a.   (17) See above in *Atzereth*, p. 467.   (18) See Maimonides, Mishneh Torah, *Hilchoth Teshuvah*, Chapter 6.

Esther commanded, *And fast ye for me, and neither eat nor drink three days, day and night.* [19]

The principal goal of the Torah, whether through the medium of praying, fasting, or giving charity, is for man to subjugate his animalistic desires and to be drawn after the rational faculty in worshipping G-d. Thus, Solomon said, *A righteous man knoweth the soul of his beast.* [1] The wicked person is the opposite. Not only does he fail to subjugate his animalistic desires but he even has compassion for them and satisfies all its lusts. A person of this kind is cruel to his rational faculty, as Scripture states, *But the tender mercies of the wicked are cruel.* [1] Showing mercy to the lustful animal soul is cruel to the rational soul, for physical desires are the veil which prevents one from perceiving rational concepts. The Sages commented:[20] "Moses fasted on Mount Sinai, and he left no fence and wall unpierced." Of course, the "fence and wall" in heaven cannot be understood in a literal sense, but the purport is that his rational faculty superseded the physical matter of his body, and he was fit to receive rational truths.

[When Israel's Redemption will be complete] in the future, all fast days [commemorating the destruction of the Temple and Jerusalem] will be converted to days of feast, for the prophet assured us: *The fast of the fourth month,* [21] *and the fast of the fifth,* [22] and the fast of the seventh, [23] *and the fast of the tenth,* [24] *shall be to the House of Judah joy and gladness and cheerful seasons; therefore love ye truth and peace.* [25]

(19) Esther 4:16.   (20) I have been unable to find the source of this quotation.   (21) This is the fast of the Seventeenth of Tamuz, which commemorates the breaching of the wall of Jerusalem. Preceding the destruction of the First Temple, the breaching of the wall of Jerusalem occurred on the ninth day of Tamuz (Jeremiah 52:6-7). At the Second Temple, it occurred on the seventeenth day of Tamuz (Taanith 26b).   (22) This is the fast of the Ninth of Ab, commemorating the destruction of the First and Second Temples.   (23) This is the fast of Gedaliah, held on the third day of Tishri. After the destruction of the First Temple, Gedaliah made an effort to save the remnant of the people and reestablish the government of Judah. His assassination signaled the destruction of all organized authority.   (24) This is the fast of the Tenth of Tebeth, which marks the day Nebuchadnezzar began his siege of Jerusalem.   (25) Zechariah 8:19.

תפילין

Tefillin

True opinions remain incomplete unless accompanied by some physical action. Therefore, the idea that the Divine Presence cleaves to Israel finds its physical expression in the commandment of the 'Tefillin' / Those who fail to observe this commandment, because they think themselves unworthy, commit a great sin / The greatness of various laws relative to this commandment.

Tefillin

THY HEAD UPON THEE IS LIKE CARMEL, AND THE HAIR
OF THY HEAD LIKE PURPLE, A KING HELD CAPTIVE IN
THE TRESSES THEREOF.[1]

It is known that true opinions—e.g., the belief in the creation of the world, the idea of G-d's providential care of individual members of the human species, the concept of the Divine Presence cleaving to Israel, and similar teachings—remain incomplete unless accompanied by some physical action. When a person performs the action, the opinion becomes firmly established in his heart. Thus, the idea of the creation of the world has been permanently strengthened through the observance of the Sabbath, and the doctrine of G-d's providence over individuals has been unalterably fixed by means of the *Mezuzah,* through which G-d's watchfulness and individual care of man are apparent. The opinion of the Sages that the Divine Presence cleaves to Israel likewise requires some act, and that is the commandment of *Tefillin,* the sign that the Divine Presence has been attached to us and has surrounded us on all sides.

In order for this opinion to be engraved upon our hearts, we have been commanded to place the *Tefillin* upon designated limbs—i.e.,

---

(1) Song of Songs 7:6. While the verse, literally speaking, describes the outward beauty of the head which is the crown of the human personality, our author sees in it an expression of the moral beauty of true thoughts that reside in the head and thus influence the whole behavior of that person. The *Tefillin* which a person dons, with the manifold teachings it represents as will be explained, gives the wearer the assurance that his thoughts will always be guarded to follow in the path of truth.

682

the head and the arm—which comprise the roots of our thought and deeds. The bands of the *Tefillin* encompass the head. This is why Scripture calls the *Tefillin*, *'totafoth*,*[2]* a word which connotes an adornment or ornament. It thus signifies that we, the people who received the Torah, glory in the Divine Presence, Who is our splendor, as it is written, *For Thou art the glory of their strength*.[3] Likewise, the Divine Presence glorifies in us, as it is said, *Israel, in whom I will be glorified*.[4]

In order to indicate the great extent to which G-d cleaves to Israel, the Sages of the Truth [i.e., of the Talmud] found it necessary to say[5] that the Holy One Himself, blessed be He, dons *Tefillin*. They thus taught people that just as we are *His people and the sheep of His pasture*[6] who exult in His Unity and His marvelous works and wonders, so does He glory in us by proclaiming our unique quality of being the one nation upon the earth designated as His portion. Hence, the act of donning the *Tefillin* serves to engrave [upon our hearts] this truth that the Divine Presence cleaves to Israel. Accordingly, you will find an allusion to the Divine Presence in the *Tefillin*. This allusion consists of the *shin*, [which is embossed on the outside faces of the two outer compartments of the phylactery of the head. The *shin* is the first letter of the word *Sha-dai* (Almighty), and its presence on the phylactery of the head is] mentioned by the Sages of the Truth:[7] "That the *shin* must be embossed upon the phylactery of the head is a law handed down to Moses on Mount Sinai."

There are some people who are indolent about donning *Tefillin* because they think that *Tefillin* require an extra degree of sanctity and purity of which they are unworthy. Such thinking is erroneous, and these people unintentionally commit a grievous sin albeit with integrity of heart. A Scroll of the Torah has more sanctity than *Tefillin*, yet all Israelites ascend [the synagogue platform] to read in the Torah and are indeed worthy to do so; no one is inclined to avoid doing so because of

(2) Deuteronomy 6:8. (3) Psalms 89:18. (4) Isaiah 49:3. (5) Berachoth 6 a. (6) Psalms 100:3. (7) Shabbath 28 b.

the sanctity of the Torah. If such is the case with regard to the Torah, it is needless to say that it should be so with *Tefillin,* which contain only four sections of the Torah. Therefore, as long as an individual exercises the proper caution with regard to *Tefillin,*[8] he is obligated to don them. If he does not, he transgresses the commandment. Since he has no reason for being excused from his obligation, either he must be guilty of neglecting this precept or he must be avoiding it rebelliously.   The Sages enumerated[9] "the head which does not don the phylactery among the wrongdoers of Israel who sin with their body," thus teaching us that if a person's iniquities are more numerous than his good deeds, and if his iniquities include not putting on *Tefillin* because of rebellion, it is impossible for such a person to escape the punishment of Gehenna.

Accordingly, anyone whom G-d has graced with knowledge, understanding, and discernment should contemplate the greatness of the commandment of *Tefillin* and should hold fast to it. So it was in all times: everyone reverently heeded the commandments of *Tefillin* and *Tzitzith* and all the other precepts. However, on account of the rise of oppression and the lassitude of the generations, [this strict observance began to decline]. When the Romans [in their effort to accomplish] wholesale apostasy, decreed that they would split the head of anyone wearing *Tefillin,* it brought about the remiss of the observance of this commandment, unlike that of circumcision for which they were ready to give their lives. To this day, the observance of the commandment of *Tefillin* has been slack in the hands of the people. However, now that man has the ability to fulfill this commandment unimpeded, no one should treat it with laxity. This is true not only of adults, who are obligated therein, but even minors,[10] so that they may be trained in the

---

(8) I.e., while wearing *Tefillin,* one should neither sleep, nor pass wind, nor enter a privy.   (9) Rosh Hashanah 17 a. The expression that by not donning the *Tefillin* one is counted among those "who sin with their 'body' " suggests the thought that failure to observe this commandment ultimately affects one's physical nature, making him prone to unbridled desires and appetites.   (10) It is now customary to buy *Tefillin* for a minor two or three months before he reaches his Bar Mitzvah at the age of thirteen years (Orach Chayim 37,3, Magen Abraham).

observance of the commandments. Thus, the Sages said in Tractate
Succah,[11] "If a minor knows how to care for *Tefillin,* his father should
buy them for him."

We must now explain various aspects and laws of the *Tefillin.* The
obligation of this commandment is great indeed, for it is equal to all
the precepts of the Torah. The Sages commented:[12] "Ulla said:
'Whoever reads the *Sh'ma* without wearing *Tefillin* is like one who
testifies falsely against himself." The word "himself" may be taken as a
euphemism for G-d, meaning that it is as if He never commanded this
precept,[13] or it may really refer to the person himself since he does not
fulfill the words he utters.[14] "Rabbi Yochanan said, 'It is as if he had
brought a burnt-offering without the accompanying meal-offering or
an offering without the libation of wine.'[15] Rabbi Yochanan further
said: 'One who desires to completely accept upon himself the yoke of
the Kingdom of Heaven must first ease himself, wash his hands, don
Tefillin, read the *Sh'ma,* and recite the Prayer [the Eighteen
Blessings].' Moreover, Rabbi Yochanan said: 'Scripture considers
whoever performs all of the above as if he had built an altar and
brought an offering thereon, for it is said, *I will wash my hands in innocence, and I will compass Thine altar, O Eternal.'* "[16] The explanation of this is that when one does these things, he draws upon himself
[the blessings of] the Divine attributes as one who actually brings an offering.

The commandment of *Tefillin* contains the three letters
[shin—dalet—yod] which spell the Divine Name *Sha-dai* (Almighty).
The *shin* is embossed on the outside of the two outer compartments of
the phylactery of the head. The *dalet* is formed by the knot at the back
of the band which encircles the head, and the *yod* is formed by the

(11) Succah 42 a.   (12) Berachoth 14 b.   (13) This is the explanation of Rashi,
ibid.   (14) The commandment of *Tefillin* is mentioned in the *Sh'ma.* Since the person recites the *Sh'ma* without wearing *Tefillin,* he is "like one who testifies falsely
against himself."   (15) "So, too, by reciting the *Sh'ma* and not heeding the precepts
mentioned therein, he has not completely fulfilled the commandment of the *Sh'ma*
itself" (Berachoth 14 b).   (16) Psalms 26:6.

knot of the loop of the band which secures the phylactery of the arm opposite the heart. There are wonderful and fundamental reasons for all this, which Solomon expressed when he said, *Thy head upon thee is like Carmel, and the hair of thy head like purple, a king held captive in the tresses thereof.*[1] *Thy head upon thee is like Carmel* alludes to the *shin* which is embossed upon the phylactery of the head; *and the hair of thy head like purple* alludes the *dalet; a king held captive in the tresses thereof* alludes to the *yod.* Scripture thus revealed to you in this verse that by virtue of the commandment of *Tefillin,* the Divine Presence is connected with us and cleaves to us. The *Tefillin* thus adorn the one who wears them and are a sign of lordship. Based upon this, the Sages said[17] that if a Canaanite servant dons *Tefillin* in the presence of his master,[18] he gains his freedom, for *Tefillin* are a sign of lordship and royalty. This is why the phylactery of the head should be set upon the high part of the skull, the place where the kings of Israel were anointed with the Oil of Anointment.[19]

The laws of donning the *Tefillin* require that the phylactery of the arm be put on first, followed by the phylactery of the head, for Scripture states, *And thou shalt bind them for a sign upon thy hand, and they shall be for frontlets between thine eyes.*[2] The Sages received the tradition[20] that *hand* in the verse means the left or weaker hand, as intimated in the verse, *And it shall be for a sign upon 'yadchah' (thy hand),*[21] [which is here spelled: *yod—dalet—kaph—hei,* suggesting *yad keihah* (the weak hand)]. Additionally, the right hand is called *yamin* in Scripture while the left is termed *yad,* as it is written, *Yea, 'yadi' (My hand) hath laid the foundation of the earth, and 'yemini' (My right hand) hath spread out the heavens.*[22] It is further written, *'Yadah' (Her hand) she put to the tent-pin, and 'yeminah' (her right hand) to the workmen's hammer.*[23]

---

(17) Gittin 40 a. (18) I.e., if the master assists the servant in putting on the *Tefillin (ibid.)* (19) Horayoth 12 a. (20) Menachoth 36 b-37 a. (21) Exodus 13:16. (22) Isaiah 48:14. (23) Judges 5:26. Hence, since the word *hand* means "the left hand," when Scripture says that the phylactery of the arm shall be for a sign upon thy *hand,* it must also mean the left hand.

The reason for donning the phylactery of the arm before that of the head is that the former is called *a sign*[2] while the latter is called *a memorial*.[24] A "sign" always precedes a "memorial," for if there is no sign, there is nothing to remember. Therefore, the Sages said[25] that when one dons the *Tefillin*, he first puts on the phylactery of the arm and afterwards that of the head. When he removes the *Tefillin*, he should first remove the phylactery of the head and then that of the arm, for it is written, *And thou shalt bind them for a sign upon thy hand, and they shall be for frontlets between thine eyes.*[2] The Sages commented upon this[25] "As long as *they* are between your eyes, there shall be two phylacteries upon you."

The phylactery of the arm consists of one compartment [containing a single parchment on which the following four sections of the Torah are inscribed: Exodus 13:1-10 and 11-16, and Deuteronomy 6:4-9 and 11:13-21]. It is written, *And it shall be for a sign unto thee,*[24] which indicates a single sign. On the other hand, the phylactery of the head consists of four compartments — each of which holds a scroll containing one of the four Scriptural passages referred to above — as it is written, *and for frontlets between thine eyes.*[21] The phylactery of the arm is fastened on the left upper arm [directly opposite the heart], and the phylactery of the head is fastened directly above the center of the forehead. The expression *between thine eyes*[21] is thus not to be understood literally. This is evident from a similar expression, *And ye shall not make any baldness between your eyes*[26] for one cannot be made bald between the eyes, but only on the forehead above the eyes.

Tefillin must be worn during the day and not at night, for Scripture states, *And thou shalt keep this ordinance in its season from day to day.*[27] They are worn on weekdays but not on Sabbaths and festivals because *Tefillin* are termed *a sign*,[2] thus excluding Sabbaths and festivals which are themselves "signs."[28] Likewise, the *Tefillin* are not worn on the intermediate days of Passover and Tabernacles.[29]

(24) Exodus 13:9. (25) Menachoth 36 a. (26) Deuteronomy 14:1. (27) Exodus 13:10. (28) See *ibid.*, 31:13, and Orach Chayim, 31:1. (29) In this matter, Rabbeinu Bachya follows the opinion of his master Rashba, as mentioned in Beth

One who wears *Tefillin* daily has two witnesses testifying that he
fulfills the commandments. How so? There are three commandments
with which Israel has been charged that are called a "sign." These are
the commandments of *Tefillin*,[2] the Sabbath,[28] and circumcision.[30]
Therefore, one who is heedful concerning donning *Tefillin* daily has
two witnesses—circumcision and *Tefillin*—testifying for him every
day. On Sabbaths and festivals, when he is not wearing *Tefillin*, the
other two witnesses—circumcision and the Sabbath or festival—are
still with him. Thus, whoever fulfills the commandment of *Tefillin* is
always accompanied by two witnesses, whether on weekdays or on Sabbaths.

One who wears *Tefillin* is assured that he will not sin, for the Sages
commented:[31] "Whoever wears the phylactery of the head and the
phylactery of the arm and has *Tzitzith* on his garment is presumed not
to sin, as it is said, *And a threefold cord is not quickly broken.*"[32] We
find that some of the Sages of the Talmud gloried in wearing *Tefillin*,
such as the great Rav Sheisheth, who said,[33] "May I be credited with
having fulfilled the commandment of *Tefillin*." Other Sages rejoiced
greatly on the day they wore *Tefillin*, as it is said:[34] "Rabbi Yirmiyah,
who was sitting before Rabbi Zeira, was very cheerful. Rabbi Zeira
remarked to him, 'Does not the master agree with what is written, *In
all labor there is profit, [but the talk of the lips tendeth only to destitu-
tion]?*'[35] Rabbi Yirmiyah answered, 'I have *Tefillin* on.'"[36] Other
Sages prayed to G-d that their portion in the World to Come be among

Yoseif, Orach Chayim, 31. See further in Shulchan Aruch, *ibid.* (30) See Genesis
17:11. (31) Menachoth 43 b. (32) Ecclesiastes 4:12. (33) Shabbath 118 b. I.e.,
"in not walking a distance of four cubits without wearing the *Tefillin*" (Rashi,
ibid.). (34) Berachoth 30 b.—"On the day they wore *Tefillin*," is interpreted by
Ravad as follows: When, "after a period of sickness which incapacitated them to wear
Tefillin, they finally recovered" and were able to fulfill the commandment. So quoted
in Sefer Hamichtam, p. 49. (35) Proverbs 14:23.—"Why then is the master so cheerful, which can tend to your being deprived of your self-restraint."
(Maharsha). (36) "The *Tefillin* I wear testify that I am aware of G-d's dominion and
His authority over me" (Rashi, Berachoth 30 b).

those who don *Tefillin,* as it is stated:[37] "Rabbi Yosei said, 'May my portion [in the World to Come] be among those who fasten *Tefillin* upon themselves, enwrap themselves in a fringed garment, and recite the *Sh'ma* in reverence.' " The Sages further commented:[38] "Whoever regularly wears *Tefillin* lives a prolonged life, as it is said, *The Eternal is upon them, they shall live, and altogether therein is the life of my spirit, wherefore recover Thou me, and cause me to live.*"[39]

(37) I have been unable to find the source of this quotation.   (38) Menachoth 44 a-b.   (39) Isaiah 38:16. In other words, "those who bear upon themselves the Name of G-d contained in the *Tefillin* shall live" (Rashi, Menachoth 44 b).

שירי חתימה

Closing Verses

Closing Verses

THE AUTHOR DECLARES:

Here is the collection of sermons
which I have composed
following my search into the Sages' homilies,
which are mostly my finding [1]
With them, I have set a table
before all disciples;
I have cleared the path for all who wander about
in the forest of Midrashim.
For the upright in heart and the pure in soul,
I have made a path in the sea of homilies,
for there is a time to speak
and a time to keep silence. [2]
I shall put my trust in the Rock
Who took me out of the womb. [3]
May He hold me worthy to be among those
who find favor in His eyes,

(1) The search into Rabbinic sources of Talmud and Midrash for appropriate texts in which one is interested is no easy task even nowadays when books are printed. This was all the more true in the days of our author when books were all handwritten and there was no pagination of any sort. In this sense Rabbeinu Bachya's expression, that the texts he quotes are "mostly of my findings," takes on a real personal meaning.   (2) Ecclesiastes 3:7: *A time to keep silence, and a time to speak.*   (3) See Psalms 22:10.

Who delight in the rivers of pleasure,[4]
who walk before Him in the lands of the living
in keeping with the statement,
> *I shall walk before the Eternal*
> *in the lands of the living.*[5]

These are the strophes[6] containing the names of all the discourses in this book:

Remember FAITH, LOVE, and HOSPITALITY,
as well as MOURNING, in the world of trial. [7]

TRUST in G-d. Acquire an [understanding] heart
by reciting His BLESSINGS,
and give exultation in THE SYNAGOGUE.

Despise ROBBERY and HAUGHTINESS
and love THE PROSELYTE;
remember that REDEMPTION
is a root and basis of the faith.

Study THE LAW given on Mount Sinai,
emanating from the Glory of Him Who dwells on high.

Practice SUBMISSIVENESS.
To believe in DIVINE PROVIDENCE is important;
to SHAME another person is indecent.

Contemplate when CONFESSING SINS
and take up weeping, wailing, and lamenting for them.

LUST OF HEART AND EYE
is like prostrating to the sun or moon.

---

(4) See *ibid.*, 36:9.   (5) *Ibid.*, 116:8.   (6) These were referred to by the author in his Introductory Verses.   (7) I.e., in this world where death and mourning are integral parts of man's destiny, in contrast to the World of Reward, the World to Come, in which there will be neither death nor mourning.

Avoid FLATTERY of men,
PROFANING OF G-D'S NAME, and COVETING.
Give song to the BRIDEGROOM.

Attain PURITY OF HEART and thought;
like precious gold, they are fitting traits.

Have FEAR OF G-D and conceive His UNITY;
keep THE EVIL INCLINATION
far from yourself and despise it.

For your own good, be mindful
of HONORING FATHER AND MOTHER;
on the Day of ATONEMENT, let your soul be afflicted.

Reject THE EVIL TONGUE,
and apprehend the hidden and mystical wisdom
of THE PALM BRANCH and its related species.

Perceive THE EXISTENCE OF G-D,
and emplace the MEZUZAH upon your doorpost;
remember the secret of CIRCUMCISION
and the season of RAIN.

Recall and examine THE COMFORTING OF ISRAEL;
the commandment of THE CHANUKAH LIGHT
bears a hidden secret.

Worship G-d in JOY,
and make yourself a SUCCAH;
uproot BASELESS HATRED from your heart.

Remember THE ARAVAH,
ATZERETH,
and HUMILITY;
WEALTH flies away as a dove.

Perceive the Divine wonders
of SUSTENANCE AND PASSOVER;

celebrate the miracle of PURIM
in the time of noon. [8]

Give CHARITY and wear TZITZITH,
which are as scented as myrrh and spices.

Respond to the declaration of G-D'S HOLINESS,
and realize that JEALOUSY
is like decay in the bones and a testing of the soul.

Pay DEFERENCE TO THE CONGREGATION
you are to address,
and remember the NEW YEAR annually.

Observe THE SOLEMN OATH given to G-d,
as well as THE SABBATH, PEACE, and SHAVUOTH,
on which the religion was declared to the people.

Be diligent in TORAH, PRAYERS, REPENTANCE,
and FAST DAYS, as well as TEFILLIN,
which contain the mystery of the faith.

---

(8) "If he held the festive Purim meal at night-time, he has not fulfilled his religious duty" (Mishneh Torah, *Hilchoth Megillah* 2:14).

Index

OF NAMES, PLACES, BOOKS AND SUBJECTS

Index

A

Abaye and Rava, 474 (Note 52).

Abraham,
- — his great love for G-d, 31.
- — was first to teach the virtue of hospitality to the world, 42-43.
- — personified compassion, 42-43.
- — his intervention at time of the destruction of Temple, 77-78.
- — his choice of exile rather than destruction if Israel will sin, 148-149.
- — contained the merits of many generations, 209-210.
- — deemed worthy to enter into covenant with G-d, 387.
- — the disciples of —, 479-481.

Abraham ibn Ezra, 251, 525.

Adam,
- — if not for —'s sin, man would have lived forever, 53.
- — seven commandments with which — was charged, 114 (Note 2).

Acheir: see Elisha ben Abuyah.

Adorning a religious duty, 33.

Agrippa, King, 233.

Ahab, King, 174, 250, 326.

Amen,
- — importance of answering — at public prayers, 25-27.

Amidah, 101 (Note 23), 591, 664.

Aravah, 456 (Note 1)-461.

Asaph, the psalmist,
- — on providence, 183-185.

Atonement, 320-347.
- — degrees in —, 241.
- — see also: Day of —.

Atzereth, meaning of, 464-474.

B

Bachya ben Asher, ix-xiii.
- — activity and writings, xi-xii.

Bachya ibn Pekudah, 292 (Note 11)-293, 494-496.

Balaam,
- — the disciples of —, 480-481.

Bethar, 99 (Note 15), 432.

Blessings we recite daily, 94-103.
- — why G-d desires to hear the —, 95-96.
- — the wording of —, 96.
- — the hundred —, 96-101.
- — the eight — we recite at the table, 97-100.
- — when deriving benefit from utilizing the human senses, 224-225.
- — only for the sensory activities in which one's intellect participates, 225.

J

Jabneh, 432, 664 (Note 21).

Jealousy, 556-560.
— exceptions, when envy is commendable, 560.

Jeremiah,
— on providence, 11.
— on the offerings, 23.
— on faith, 23.
— on general and specific providence, 185, 187.
— on flattery, 234-235.
— on future Redemption, 425.

Jeroboam
— his haughtiness which drove him out of World, 132-133 (Note 21).

Jerusalem,
— mourning over destruction of —, 75-82.
— sins which caused destruction of First and Second Temples, 77-78.
— center of the Land of Israel, 359, 629.
— on high, and below, 591.

Job,
— his erroneous opinion, 11.
— extremely pious and thoroughly righteous person, 142.
— example of —'s kindness for all Jews, 143.
— Book of —, 188-204.
— his friends, 189, 194-198.
— the two responses of G-d to —, 201-203.

Jonah,
— why — fled to Tarshish, 80, 329.
— the role of submissiveness in story of —, 180.
— Book of —, 328-337.

Jonathan,
— his friendship for David, 63.

Joy,
— the true — at a wedding, 263.
— as a mode of Divine worship, 428-434.
— to limit — in this world, 432.
— on Festival of Tabernacles, 433.
— on the eighth day of Festival of Tabernacles, 470-471.
— the essential aspect of —, 471.

Justice, see: Law, rule of.

K

Kad Hakemach, ix (Note 1), xii-xiv, 3, 4-5.

Kal vachomer, 27 (Note 106).

Kingdom of House of David, 61, 664.

Knowledge of G-d,
— the ultimate perfection, 466-467.

L

Law, rule of, 164-170.
— very creation of world founded upon justice, 164.
— where there is no justice, there is no peace, 166.
— power of justice, 166-167.

Libations, 468, 473 (Note 48).

Light,
— usage of the word —, 414-418.
— comparison of Torah to both a — and a flame, 419-420.
— four degrees of —, 563-564.
— see also: Higher Light.

S

Alphabetical Listing

Alphabetical Listing